Adjustment in Africa

Lessons from Country Case Studies

WORLD BANK

REGIONAL AND

SECTORAL STUDIES

Adjustment in Africa

Lessons from Country Case Studies

EDITED BY

ISHRAT HUSAIN

AND

RASHID FARUQEE

The World Bank
Washington, D.C.

Manufactured in the United States of America
First printing March 1994
Second printing June 1994

The World Bank Regional and Sectoral Studies series provides an outlet for work that is relatively limited in its subject matter or geographical coverage but that contributes to the intellectual foundations of development operations and policy formulation. Some sources cited in this paper may be informal documents that are not readily available.

The findings, interpretations, and conclusions expressed in this publication are those of the authors and should not be attributed in any manner to the World Bank, to its affiliated organizations, or to the members of its Board of Executive Directors or the countries they represent.

The complete backlist of publications from the World Bank is shown in the annual *Index of Publications*, which contains an alphabetical title list and indexes of subjects, authors, and countries and regions. The latest edition is available free of charge from Distribution Unit, Office of the Publisher, The World Bank, 1818 H Street, N.W., Washington, D.C. 20433, U.S.A., or from Publications, The World Bank, 66, avenue d'Iéna, 75116 Paris, France.

Cover design by Sam Ferro and The Magazine Group

Library of Congress Cataloging-in-Publication Data

Available directly from the Library of Congress.

ISBN 0-8213-2787-9

Contents

Foreword

This report, *Adjustment in Africa: Lessons from Country Case Studies,* provides an assessment of structural adjustment policies undertaken by seven African countries in the mid-1980s. The report is a companion volume to the main study, *Adjustment in Africa: Reforms, Results, and the Road Ahead,* produced by the Policy Research Department.

This report is distinct from other studies on this subject. First, it emphasizes the specific economic and social circumstances of each country that led to the adoption of an adjustment program. Second, it measures and analyzes the extent to which the adjustment policies were, in fact, implemented in each case. Finally, the report attempts to assess economic performance in relation to the strength of the implementation of policy reforms. This research was initiated to supplement the main study, which is more aggregated and covers a cross-section of twenty-nine countries. The motivation behind the research was to capture the diversity of experiences in implementing reforms.

The period covered by these case studies ends, for most countries, in 1991. Since these studies were completed, there have been significant developments in each of the case study countries. A large devaluation of the CFA franc took place in January 1994, removing one of the principal obstacles to the full interplay of policy instruments required for adjustment in the CFA zone countries. It is hoped that Côte d'Ivoire and Senegal, which have been adversely affected by the overvaluation of the CFA franc since 1985, will enter a new period of adjustment. Nigeria, which has a new military government, has announced the abandonment of its adjustment policies and reverted to its pre-1986 regime. Burundi has witnessed a bloody coup d'état and the assassination of its elected president. Ghana and Kenya held multiparty elections, but the incumbents were returned to power. And Tanzania is preparing for multiparty elections in 1995.

These drastic changes in the political and economic environment have created uncertainty about the future direction of economic policies. As the report notes, economic recovery was still fragile in most of these countries, and the ensuing uncertainty has made the situation even more difficult. The path to economic progress and revival is now much better understood in Africa than at any time before, but managing this change has proved difficult. It is hoped that the process of political transition, when completed, will reinforce economic reforms in most countries and set high standards of probity, accountability, and governance.

The findings of this report reinforce those of the main study and other studies of successful developing countries. Progress has been mixed, but the countries that have established and maintained macroeconomic stability, eliminated discrimination against agriculture, and taken measures to remove antiexport bias experienced the biggest turnarounds in their economies. Despite these gains, per capita growth rates remain fairly low; even if sustained, they would be insufficient to make a dent in the rising incidence of poverty.

Economic reforms should thus be seen as the foundation upon which sustainable and equitable development can be built in Africa. Human capital investment, infrastructure improvements, better governance and, most important, indigenous capacity building are the other key ingredients that, together with economic policy reforms, will accelerate growth, alleviate poverty, and protect the environment in Africa.

The World Bank's long-term perspective agenda remains valid and, with suitable modification to respond to changing circumstances, will guide the Bank's assistance to its member countries in Africa. This report confirms the critical importance of good macroeconomic policies and management in the implementation of this agenda.

Edward V. K. Jaycox
Vice President
Africa Region

Acknowledgments

This report has benefited from the review, comments, and suggestions of many people in the World Bank. Regional vice president Edward V. K. Jaycox and the Africa Region Country Department directors Francisco Aguirre-Sacasa, Kevin Cleaver, Francis Colaço, Stephen Denning, Olivier Lafourcade, Edwin Lim, and Katherine Marshall were the prime movers behind this report, and they broached the original suggestion for carrying out country case studies. Ajay Chhibber, Lawrence Hinkle, François Laporte, Peter Miovic, Ulrich Thumm, and Gene Tidrick steered the study and provided extensive comments at various stages of the report. Christine Jones and Miguel Kiguel were most helpful in the design and early stages of the study. Pierre Landell-Mills and Michael Walton were the main discussants at the Bankwide review of the report.

The report has also benefited from the comments and contributions of Mark Baird, Deepak Bhattasali, Carlos Primo Braga, Michael Carter, Simon Commander, Luc de Wulf, Bill Easterly, Brendan Horton, Ravi Kanbur, Will Martin, Vikram Nehru, Brian Ngo, Steve O'Brien, Paul Popiel, Sanjay Pradhan, Raed Safadi, Bill Shaw, Bension Varon, and Richard Westebbe. The assistance of the country teams of Burundi, Côte d'Ivoire, Ghana, Kenya, Nigeria, Senegal, and Tanzania is gratefully acknowledged.

The editorial production team for the report consisted of Nandita Tannan, Susan Chase, and Andi Carlson.

1

Adjustment in seven African countries

Rashid Faruqee and Ishrat Husain

The World Bank report *Adjustment in Africa: Reforms, Results, and the Road Ahead* (New York: Oxford University Press, 1994) concludes that there has been some improvement in the overall policy environment in the twenty-nine countries that embarked on adjustment programs in the mid-1980s, but that the improvements have been far from uniform across countries and sectors. The biggest improvements have been in the macroeconomic sphere (except in countries with fixed exchange rates in the CFA franc zone) and in agricultural policies. There has also been some (mixed) progress in deregulating and liberalizing markets. But in other areas, reform has been more difficult, with public enterprises and the financial system the most resistant to change. The report also finds that the reform programs work: In countries and policy areas where policy performance has been reasonably good, the outcomes have been reasonably good; conversely, poor policy progress has been reflected in poor performance.

Conditions and adjustment in the case study countries

The analyses of the seven countries examined in this collection of case studies—Burundi, Côte d'Ivoire, Ghana, Kenya, Nigeria, Senegal, and Tanzania—reinforce these findings. The case studies are intended to supplement the cross-country study with in-depth analysis of a few country experiences. The studies shed further light on the processes and outcomes of reform programs in different African contexts. The selection of countries was guided by the desire to include as much variety as possible with regard to "initial conditions" and adjustment processes and programs. In Ghana and Tanzania economic conditions hit rock bottom before the adjustment program started. In Burundi, Côte d'Ivoire, and Nigeria there were serious distortions and pronounced declines in economic performance, with Côte d'Ivoire and Nigeria suffering from the "Dutch disease" after the commodity boom of the late 1970s. In Kenya and Senegal distortions have been serious, but no period can be identified as most critical; the two countries have also had—on again, off again—reforms that mitigated the impact of these distortions.

Along with initial conditions, different motivation and processes of adjustment in the seven case study countries influenced the progress of reforms and the results achieved. Improvement in domestic economic performance—increased domestic savings, higher export earnings, greater domestic production, and so on—is the key motivation for decisions to initiate an adjustment program. Another common element in the calculus is the expectation of external resources from international financial institutions and bilateral donors and the prospects for rescheduling debt. The conditions in the seven countries varied as follows:

- In Nigeria a new government found the country in the midst of an economic decline, with a large debt burden exacerbated by a precipitous decline in oil prices—the main source of the country's foreign exchange earnings. The motivation for reform seems to have stemmed primarily from the desire to find a solution to the external debt problems faced by the country and the implicit expectation that the cash flow relief would free foreign exchange for domestic users.
- In Ghana the economic free-fall was almost complete when the Rawlings government assumed power in 1982. The driving force for reform appears to have been the conviction that policy reforms would improve the economy by eliminating corruption.
- In Tanzania as in Ghana, economic conditions had deteriorated dramatically before a reform program was launched. The fundamental policy changes that were instituted may have been precipitated by an upsurge in popular resentment. The change in the top political leadership came with an open admission that the previous economic policies had not worked and that alternative solutions needed to be found for arresting the economic collapse. Tanzania has always received exceptionally high amounts of gross aid flows; the availability of the foreign aid flows was, therefore, not the motivating factor behind that country's decision to follow the path of adjustment.
- In Kenya the economic decline was not as pronounced or perceptible as in other countries. In 1979 a sharp fall in the price of coffee and a doubling of the price of imported oil forced Kenya to adopt a stabilization program to reduce the ensuing macroeconomic imbalances. Kenya decided to undertake structural adjustment to obtain quick-disbursing funds from the World Bank at a time when the country was faced with serious foreign exchange shortages and payment pressures.

- Senegal was confronted with a financial crisis in the late 1970s, when a combination of poor financial and investment policies, worsened terms of trade, and successive droughts made adjustment unavoidable. The decision to initiate structural adjustment was apparently made in the belief that the country's financial and economic imbalances could be resolved with financial support from the International Monetary Fund and the World Bank.
- In Côte d'Ivoire the interplay between external and internal factors led to macroeconomic destabilization, but the government's own diagnosis was that the crisis was a result of temporary terms of trade deterioration and that external financing could tide them over the crisis.
- Donors financed 80 percent of Burundi's investment program, and the influence of Bretton Woods institutions on the design of adjustment was most visible. Aid seemed to be a key factor in the decision to embark on an adjustment program.

Four of the seven countries began their adjustment program in the same year, 1986. Ghana and Kenya started their adjustment program earlier: Ghana in 1983 and Kenya in 1985 (although a half-hearted stabilization program was initiated earlier in Kenya). In Côte d'Ivoire the adjustment program actually started in 1987, although some attempts at stabilization were made before that date.

The adjustment programs in all seven countries attempted to eliminate distortions—distortions sometimes created or exacerbated by external or internal shocks—which often prevent an efficient allocation of resources in the economy. The programs also aimed at mobilizing resources to stimulate the resumption of growth. Broadly speaking, the adjustment programs in all seven cases addressed distortions such as an overvalued exchange rate, high current account and fiscal deficits, low factor mobility, restrictions on domestic and foreign trade, distorted pricing for tradables, and inefficient public services. Adjustment programs generally included reforms to:

- Establish a market-determined exchange rate.
- Bring fiscal deficits under control and rationalize public investment.
- Liberalize trade (for example, by abolishing licenses and quantitative restrictions) and tariff policy (by moving toward low and uniform tariff rates), liberalize agricultural prices and marketing, deregulate internal prices, and similar measures.
- Improve financial sector policy (to achieve competitive returns on financial assets, increase the marginal productivity of capital, and boost the saving rate).
- Improve the efficiency of public enterprises and labor markets (to enhance the mobility of goods and labor and to make prices and wages more flexible).
- Improve the coverage and quality of social services.

Most of the seven countries have successfully implemented many of the policy reforms outlined above—devaluing the exchange rate, decontrolling prices, and liberalizing agricultural marketing. There has also been some progress in liberalizing imports, but export incentives other than the devalued exchange rate (namely, duty drawbacks and institutional support for export promotion and insurance guarantees) still lack bite. Monetary and fiscal reforms are another area in which progress has been mixed. The greatest difficulties, however, have been in reforming public enterprises, the financial sector, and the civil service. Social spending, although seriously low to begin with, has been largely protected, and labor market reforms are just beginning. Ghana and Tanzania have a fairly good track record in sustaining their programs, but the other five countries have had difficulty maintaining the initial momentum and, for them, the implementation of reforms has been erratic.

Results of adjustment

The questions that have been raised most frequently about the results of structural adjustment programs in Africa are:

- Has growth performance been adequate?
- Has supply response been strong?
- Do investment-to-GDP ratios show improvement?
- Have external flows been excessive?
- Have adjustment policies hurt the poor?

Increase in growth

Except for Côte d'Ivoire, the case study countries had positive per capita GDP growth during the adjustment period 1986–91—growth higher than before the crisis (before 1981) and, for most countries, much higher than during the crisis (1981–86). The average growth rate of six countries in this sample over the adjustment period has been 4.5 percent a year—not bad considering that average growth in the preceding period was barely 1 percent. Burundi and Kenya had fairly good initial conditions and maintained their previous growth. The biggest turnarounds were in Ghana (8.8 percentage points), Nigeria (8 percentage points), and Tanzania (4 percentage points). Nigeria achieved this growth despite the fact that the quality of its economic management faltered. Even Senegal registered a growth turnaround, though a small one, despite the handicap of an overvalued exchange rate. Côte d'Ivoire, which once had an impressive growth rate, cannot return to its precrisis rate unless it resolves its exchange rate problems.

The supply response

The most significant contributor to domestic supply and output in the region is agriculture, and closely related to it is the export sector, which relies heavily on agricultural commodities, mining, and petroleum. Although the data on agricultural production and value added do not always seem to tell the same story, all seven countries showed improvement in this sector—a trend corroborated by evidence on prices, food imports, and food aid.[1] Food prices in real terms declined in Nigeria. Average food imports declined by 30 to 60 percent in Nigeria, Kenya, Tanzania, and Burundi and remained the same in Côte d'Ivoire, Senegal, and Ghana. The index of food production per capita has risen in all countries except Tanzania, where it declined slightly.[2] In Burundi food production per capita seems to have stagnated, but food production at least kept pace with the population growth rate for the 1980s.

The volume of cash crop exports grew rapidly in Ghana, Tanzania, Senegal, Burundi, and Nigeria—but declined in Côte d'Ivoire. New nontraditional agricultural exports have emerged in almost every country in this group, although the amounts are still modest. This indicates that African farmers do respond to price incentives and allocate labor to activities yielding better returns. In Nigeria there was a reverse migration of labor to rural areas after 1986 as the relative returns to farming improved dramatically. The combination of the availability of land, erosion of urban employment opportunities, and improved producer incentives for agricultural production have facilitated a supply response in agriculture.

The growth in agricultural production cannot be sustained by good incentives alone. Complementary investments in rural infrastructure and small-scale irrigation; adequate availability of credit, fertilizers, and other inputs; and dissemination of new technology through research and extension are also needed to maintain this momentum. There is evidence, however, that the aggregate agricultural supply response has been positive in countries that implemented policies to reverse the discrimination against agriculture. Another good indicator of the supply response is the behavior of total exports. The most consistent finding that emerges from this study (and which is corroborated by other studies) is that export growth has been remarkably high despite declines in the terms of trade, with exports not only recovering from the crisis period but also surpassing their precrisis level.

The country case studies also investigated whether there was any diversification from the main traditional commodities. Oil dominates Nigerian exports so heavily, and the anecdotal evidence on Nigerian unofficial exports of manufactured goods to neighboring countries is so fragmentary, that it is difficult to arrive at any definite conclusion. But unlike the case in the early

1980s, Nigerian goods are now competing with other imports in the West African markets. Ghana has more than doubled its exports in the past seven years despite a sharp fall in cocoa prices in the world market, but gold exports have now replaced cocoa as the number one export. At least 20 percent of Ghana's export earnings today come from products other than cocoa, gold, and timber, compared with 8 percent a decade ago. Tanzania shows the biggest documented rise in nontraditional exports, and its unrecorded exports are also large—according to some estimates, $400 million to $500 million a year, although the composition of these exports is not known. Côte d'Ivoire, Kenya, and Senegal have export bases that are among the most diversified in Africa, but the changes during their adjustment have been minor and show no persistent trend. Burundi is the only country among the seven to show heavy continuing reliance on coffee; its diversification efforts, though started, have been negligible.

Investment response

The response of investment to adjustment policies has been generally slow in the seven countries studied. Despite increased inflows of foreign savings to supplement the limited domestic savings, investment has recovered to precrisis levels only in Tanzania.

The precrisis investment ratios may not have been sustainable in the first place, and the investments may not have been efficient or productive. In all seven countries much of the investment was of dubious worth, its efficiency and productivity low. "White elephant" projects, inflated contracts, flight capital, and other associated ills became rampant before—and eventually contributed to—the crisis in each case. A major aim of adjustment programs has been to weed out these undesirable investments (particularly in the public sector) and to improve overall efficiency.

In the short run, a slowdown in public investment (in an attempt to reduce budget deficits and cut uneconomic projects) is bound to depress overall investment ratios. In almost all of the case study countries, public investment has fallen in relation to GDP. But the efficiency of investment has improved: roughly similar investment ratios generated one percentage point of annual growth in the crisis period but close to five percentage points in the adjustment period.

A crucial issue is whether private investment will take up the slack created by this slowdown in public investment. The evidence so far is hardly reassuring, and this investment gap remains the daunting challenge for African countries. The case studies confirm the vital importance of the stability, continuity, and credibility of policies for providing signals to domestic and foreign economic actors. Of the seven countries, Ghana and (until recently) Kenya came closest to meeting this objective, but both could have achieved more. If the Ghanaian authorities' general attitude toward the private sector had been less ambiguous, Ghana no doubt would have seen a greater revival of private investment. In Kenya the lack of transparent policies and the general perception of capricious governance discouraged potential investors, even though Kenya had a more stable economic environment than other countries in this sample.

Adjustment programs in the seven countries are aiming to reform the financial sector, end public enterprise monopolies, and promote competitive policies. But progress has not been impressive in these areas. The unfinished agenda of reforms will, therefore, have to focus more deeply on this set of policy and institutional changes. Unless the *domestic* private sector takes off and shows that it can do business without undue government interference, the prospects for *foreign* investment are likely to remain unattractive.

External flows

The flow of external resources has risen for four of the seven countries—Tanzania, Ghana, Kenya, and Burundi, in that order—during the adjustment period. Côte d'Ivoire and Senegal have experienced declines in the ratio of net external transfers to GDP. Only Nigeria has had negative net flows of external resources. But even where external flows were rising, they were unable to compensate for terms of trade losses: allowing for terms of trade losses, six of the seven countries had declines in net external resource inflows, with Tanzania the lone exception.

The central question is how much of the renewed growth of the adjusting countries can be ascribed to external factors (aid and terms of trade changes) and how much to policy reform. The case studies reached the following conclusions:

- Nigeria has done much better than terms of trade changes and increased external flows would have suggested. And because Nigeria transfers an amount equal to 5 percent of its GDP to its external creditors every year, its growth could have been even higher were it not so heavily burdened with debt.
- Côte d'Ivoire has been hurt by terms of trade losses and a relative decline in external flows—and by poor policies. Côte d'Ivoire is also severely indebted, but it has avoided a cash flow crunch by not paying (most of) its creditors and by accumulating arrears.
- Kenya (until recently), Ghana, Burundi, and Senegal are among a select group of African countries that are fully servicing their debt—all four have been hurt by terms of trade losses. The gross flows appear large in each of these cases, but when they are adjusted for the debt service paid and terms of trade losses, the "net external resource availability" indicator does not appear large. Kenya's growth record reflects some

positive impact of adjustment. Clearly, Ghana's growth turnaround was due far more to better policies than to the other changes.

- Tanzania's growth can be ascribed to factors other than aid. Generally perceived as highly dependent on external donors, Tanzania has received very large sums of aid historically. But once debt servicing and terms of trade losses are accounted for, the real external resource flows to Tanzania during its adjustment are no different in absolute terms than those during its crisis. Whether even this level of external assistance is sustainable is hard to say. It is relevant to note that in successful developing countries generally, domestic savings are the foundation for their development activities. External resources can only fill the gaps temporarily—and to a limited extent.

A straightforward comparison of policy progress and turnaround in per capita GDP growth shows that Nigeria (despite recording net negative transfers), Tanzania, Ghana, and Kenya had positive turnarounds along with policy progress. Burundi and Senegal had moderate policy progress, with a small turnaround in per capita growth. Côte d'Ivoire clearly had negative per capita growth with little policy progress, but also had a decline in external flows.

To sum up, the aid dependency syndrome is a complex phenomenon that makes generalization difficult. Although net external resource transfers to Sub-Saharan Africa have almost doubled as a proportion of the region's GDP, national incomes have been lower across the region because of terms of trade shocks. A full accounting of these various measures shows a picture that is highly mixed. Although increasing domestic saving is the preferred course to pursue, doing so is not easy. Domestic saving ratios improved marginally in Nigeria, Kenya, and Ghana during the adjustment period, while they declined in Côte d'Ivoire and Burundi. There has been significant improvement in Senegal and Tanzania, but the levels are still abysmally low. The scope for improvement is substantial. In Tanzania the auditor general estimated that the combined financial losses of the state enterprise sector amounted to almost 10 percent of GDP. The story is similar in most of the other case study countries. If action is taken to reduce these losses, the domestic saving rate could almost double. Fiscal deficits are the main reason for low saving rates, and any vigorous attempt to reduce fiscal deficits will also raise the saving ratios. Making solid progress in reducing fiscal deficits is crucial not only for macroeconomic stability but also because the future viability of Sub-Saharan Africa will depend on how quickly it turns domestic saving rates around.

Adjustment and the poor

An important finding of the World Bank's Policy Research Report *Adjustment in Africa* is that adjustment has generally improved the welfare of the poor, but that not all the poor have benefited, with the urban poor who produce nontradables and consume tradables (a small group relative to the rural poor) likely to have been hurt. That report also notes that the growth attained thus far is still not enough to reduce poverty and that public expenditure programs still do not pay adequate attention to the basic services essential to improving the welfare of the poor.

Two key measures of the effects of adjustment on the poor are income changes and public spending on social services. But precise quantitative data on these two measures are available for only one of the countries in this study (Côte d'Ivoire). The case studies have nevertheless assembled the best available evidence from diverse sources (not always consistent).

The most vehement criticism of adjustment programs has been their neglect of social sectors. While the early generation of these programs might not have explicitly addressed the consequences of reforms on the social sectors, the subsequent awareness and sensitization of these issues have changed the scene. Evidence presented in these case studies shows that cuts in social expenditures were more pronounced during the periods of crisis than during those of adjustment. In none of the seven countries is there any indication of significant declines in total real spending on education and health. In Ghana and Tanzania the increase from the precrisis levels of social expenditure has been impressive, although much needs to be done to improve the quality and delivery of services.

In all seven countries the majority of the poor live in rural areas, are smallholders and self-employed, and derive their incomes from producing and marketing food and export crops. Because the rural terms of trade improved in six of the countries (Côte d'Ivoire in the second half of the 1980s is an exception)—as a result of devaluation, liberalized marketing, higher producer prices, and lower taxes—the rural poor appear to have benefited from real income gains over an extended period. Some analysts would emphasize that the increased availability of consumer goods has been part of the reason for the supply response, particularly in Ghana and Tanzania. Export crop producers, particularly nontraditional export crop producers, have gained more than other agricultural producers. Real food prices to farmers have declined in many countries, but the marketed output has increased, replacing food imports in many cases. The real income gains to food producers have varied according to the incremental proportion they sold to the market after adjustment and the kind of foodcrops they produced. Food producers in Nigeria, Tanzania, and Ghana seem to have benefited the most. Burundi and Kenya have been self-sufficient in food and, therefore, the foodcrop farmers there have not gained much. The situation in Côte d'Ivoire and Senegal is unclear, because both these countries have increased their reliance on food imports.

The impact on the urban poor does not appear to have been unambiguously unfavorable. In Ghana and Tanzania the urban poor are better off after adjustment, as consumer goods have become available, real food prices have declined, and informal sector activities have expanded. To the extent that the urban poor were buying their essential goods (including food) in the black market before adjustment, there has been no change in the welfare of this group. In Côte d'Ivoire and Senegal the urban poor are worse off. This would also seem to be the case for the unemployed, fixed-income earners, and minimum wage earners in Nigeria. Because there are no data on Burundi and Kenya, it is unclear whether the real incomes of the urban poor worsened or improved.

What the case studies tell us

To sum up, the seven case studies show that whenever adjustment programs have been pursued vigorously, results have been clearly positive with respect to both growth and alleviation of poverty—an outcome that is independent of external flows. A consistent and successful adjustment program has been the most important factor, and one of the key elements of successful adjustment programs was the motivation and strong commitment by the leadership of the countries to launch and sustain the programs in the face of harsh external circumstances and internal pressures. Other studies also show that too frequent, abrupt, and unpredictable changes and reversals of policies erode the credibility of the programs, intensify uncertainties, and weaken investor confidence. The stability, continuity, and predictability of policies play an important role in the success of reforms.

Notes

1. The evidence on agriculture and exports is based on the comparison of data for the adjustment period with data for the precrisis and crisis periods. Because weather conditions are the most important determinant of agricultural production, we use five-year to seven-year averages to smooth the fluctuations from droughts or exceptionally good weather.

2. The result for Tanzania is surprising, and the Food and Agriculture Organization data used for Tanzanian food production do not appear to be consistent with the import and retail price data. Food imports in Tanzania were about 300,000 tons on average during 1981–85. Real consumer prices of maize, beans, and rice in the major urban centers declined, and food aid for Tanzania fell by nearly 70 percent. This suggests that per capita food production has risen, and the data in the case study support this finding.

2

Burundi: learning the lessons

Pierre Englebert and Richard Hoffman

Burundi's development problems run deep. The country has a large and undiversified subsistence sector with a fast-growing population and weak institutional structures and capacities. Burundi also suffers from relatively inflexible and oligopolistic markets, and from a public sector that controls the majority of productive enterprises. Not only is agriculture's contribution to GDP superior to that of industry and services, but it depends highly on a single crop, coffee. As a result, Burundi is excessively exposed to the fluctuations of a single market, making diversification policies typically recommended by an adjustment program difficult to implement.

In retrospect, the government's reform effort, initiated in 1986, was too optimistic about how quickly the economy could be transformed given the initial limited commitment to the program, the extent of structural distortions in the economy, and the sensitive sociopolitical environment. Other significant factors that limited effectiveness included instability in Rwanda and Zaire, declining terms of trade, and periods of drought.

Despite the initial difficulties, Burundi's adjustment program has been path-breaking and should be deemed successful if only in the sense that for the first time it introduced the notions and practice of more effective macroeconomic management. Indeed, fundamental change is under way in Burundi. Taken as a whole, the business climate in Burundi has improved markedly in recent years. Most of the cumbersome procedures of the past have been either eliminated or simplified. The system is considerably more transparent, thus promoting the competitive advantages of private firms in Burundi. And, in the social sector, access to health, education, and potable water shows signs of improvement despite continued high population growth.

While support for the adjustment process may have been in doubt in 1987–88, Burundi has since reexamined its commitment to reform and come away with a renewed sense of the program's importance for economic development. One of the more important lessons that has been learned is that the adjustment program, while generously supported by the international community, is an undertaking whose success requires increased ownership by the government. Further progress will also depend on the continued liberalization of the economy and the institution of appropriate incentives to encourage economic diversification. Perhaps as a further indication that change is both beneficial and inevitable, in the summer of 1993 the country held its first democratic elections and the outcome surprised almost everyone—the incumbent presidential candidate, and his ethnic group's traditional hold on important government positions and the military, lost to a relatively unknown banker. Burundi's new government now has Sub-Saharan Africa's first female prime minister.

The setting before the adjustment program

Burundi has been a poor country with little natural endowment and an undiversified economy since its independence from Belgium in 1962. Its per capita GNP was $210 in 1990, making it one of the poorest countries in the world. It is also one of the smallest countries, and its landlocked situation and hilly terrain have contributed to its traditional isolation and difficult economic situation. There are only a limited number of travel routes and transport costs are high. Burundi is at a stage of development where agriculture is still the predominant engine of growth and source of income (more than 50 percent of GDP). The secondary sector is limited to 14 percent of GDP and 6 percent of exports. Burundi is, however, one of the few Sub-Saharan African countries that is self-sufficient in staple foods. It is also wrestling with a population growth rate of 3 percent and the second highest population density in Sub-Saharan Africa after Rwanda. Life expectancy at birth is 49 years. Only 34 percent of the adult population is literate. In rural areas, only 35 percent of the population has access to safe water. In addition to a low per capita income, Burundi suffers from an agitated political and social history. The country has witnessed several coups and major outbreaks of ethnic violence between the majority Hutu and the minority Tutsi, the latter of which controlled most levels of the government and the productive sectors of the economy. After ethnic fighting in 1988, then-president Pierre Buyoya appointed a new government with equal Hutu and Tutsi representation and, for the first time, a Hutu prime minister. A new constitution was adopted in a referendum in March 1992, paving the way for national elections in June 1993, in which Mr. Ndadaye, a Hutu, became the first democratically elected president since Independence.

Economic performance in the late 1970s was largely positive, stemming from high coffee prices, increased foreign aid, and political stability. Government activity in the productive sectors expanded, both through direct increases in public spending and through a pronounced increase in the size of the public enterprise sector.[1] By the late 1970s, however, the situation began to change. There was an abrupt fall in coffee prices and a doubling of import prices (including higher oil prices), which brought a drop in domestic income and pressure on the balance of payments and fiscal accounts. To compound the situation, adverse weather conditions contributed to low agricultural output. The government responded by relying on discretionary administrative measures to ration credit and foreign exchange and resorting to external borrowing and increased taxation of both domestic activity and international trade. The government also imposed administrative controls to contain the external deficit and protect domestic industry. From 1981 to 1984 the economic situation went from bad to worse due to a further deterioration in the terms of trade, the continuation of expansionary fiscal and monetary policies, and a prolongation of the drought.

Real GDP growth, which had averaged 5 percent a year during 1978–81, grew by less than 1 percent during 1982–84. In 1983 the external current account deficit (excluding official transfers) reached 16.5 percent of GDP, and the overall fiscal deficit (on a commitment basis and excluding grants) reached 18.7 percent of GDP (up from 13 percent the previous year and 2 percent in 1978). Inflation reached 8.3 percent in 1983, and increased to 14.4 percent the following year. The real effective exchange rate of the Burundi franc (FBu) appreciated by 8 percent in 1983, penalizing agricultural exports and encouraging consumption of imported goods. External borrowing, especially on nonconcessional terms, accelerated: total debt as a percentage of GDP doubled between 1982 and 1984, and the debt service ratio, which had averaged 4.2 percent of exports of goods and nonfactor services in the late 1970s, increased to 23 percent in 1985. The distortions introduced through these measures reinforced the role of the state in the economy and aggravated disincentives to private sector development. These measures, however, only served to highlight Burundi's major structural constraints: excessive dependence on coffee exports, the excessive and inefficient role of the public sector, and inadequate incentives for sustained growth in agriculture and industry. The need for stabilization and adjustment had become evident. The failure of the government's interventionist policies and the deteriorating economic situation prompted the government to approach the World Bank and the International Monetary Fund (IMF) for assistance.

It was not the first time that Burundi received balance of payments support from one of the Bretton Woods institutions. The country has been a member of the IMF since September 1967, and over the years has concluded several stand-by arrangements and benefited from technical assistance in the areas of foreign exchange, fiscal reform, and bank supervision. The first IMF adjustment operation was approved in 1986 in conjunction with the World

Bank's first adjustment credit. The International Development Association's (IDA) second adjustment operation, equivalent to $90 million, followed in July 1988, and cofinancing from Japan, Germany, and Saudi Arabia increased the total envelope to $117 million. The two structural adjustment credits had three principal objectives: (1) improve the incentives for production by removing constraints to growth and by redirecting the economy toward more reliance on market forces and a greater outward orientation, (2) promote private sector development and investment, and (3) increase the efficiency of public resource utilization, especially through public enterprise reform and improved public expenditure management. In addition to the World Bank's structural adjustment credits, the IMF supported stabilization measures that aimed to correct the overvalued exchange rate and pursue a policy of adjustable exchange rates; strengthen the balance of payments and increase foreign reserves; reduce the debt service; decrease domestic financing of the budget deficit to avoid crowding out the private sector's access to investment credit sources; and increase budgetary revenues and public savings.

Lessons learned

Ownership: improving internalization and implementation

From the start, the government did not assume sufficient ownership of its own program. It failed to sensitize critical economic and political actors to the merits and requirements of the program and to sufficiently delegate authority throughout the administration for its implementation. Much of the limited internalization was also due to the delicate political climate, one that rendered administrative performance and technical assistance ineffective. By 1987 the political climate had so deteriorated that a quasi-rupture ensued among the major sociopolitical groups, the churches, and donors. As a consequence, the government's commitment to implementing the first phase of the program cooled considerably.

Despite Burundi's initial experience with adjustment, the government was still only partially involved in the preparation of the second phase of the program. The second phase was designed soon after a new government was installed after a coup in September 1987, so the new team was introduced to the program without having the opportunity to analyze the current economic situation or the impact of the initial effort. Negotiations occurred before the government had completed its analysis of sectoral policies and the appropriateness of the latest five-year plan. The design of the second phase suffered not only from a lack of substantive participation by the administration, but also from the limited number of experienced personnel—under the former regime only a small number of civil servants had been privy to the contents of and authorized with implementing the first reform package. The lack of awareness among the public and civil servants created a climate of uncertainty and distrust in the country as to the likely implications of the program.[2] The result of limited ownership and frequent turnover in government personnel placed a premium on the pedagogical role of World Bank and IMF supervision missions.

Early on, the World Bank and the IMF played a major role in introducing the reform program to the country and effectively drafted the first three Policy Framework Papers—in 1986, 1988, and 1989. With this significant expertise came elements that worked against government ownership of the program. As Laïdi (1989) points out, governments of developing countries are unable to compete with the World Bank's and the IMF's capacity to collect data and analyze their economies. Thus, they sometimes abdicate their responsibility in this domain, and because they consider themselves less than full participants during the conceptualization stage, proper internalization is not achieved. The government's commitment to the program was also undermined because the World Bank's aide-mémoires predominantly reflected the position of mission staff, rather than the outcome of discussions with the government. Only in November 1990 did the World Bank accept the principle of cosigned aide-mémoires with the government (although this principle had already been applied to government missions visiting Washington). Further, consistent management of World Bank programs was denied due to turnover of World Bank experts and their varying recommendations.

Another reason for poor ownership was the government's eagerness to move ahead with the program in order to receive balance of payments financing. Without considering the full policy implications of such a program, the government's desire for quick-disbursing support overshadowed other contentious policy issues, in particular, the reform of the public enterprise sector. When the time came to implement certain measures, the authorities were unprepared to internalize and move ahead with reforms that it felt were imposed from the outside and which elicited internal resistance.

Another important reason for the government's limited internalization was the circumscribed participation that it imposed on key economic sectors—those that could have played an important role in promoting the overall goals of the program in the country. For example, the government did not involve the private sector fully, whose response to the adjustment measures could have been increased investment. Furthermore, the involvement of other groups—the army and the church—was sought only after 1989 (and their support proved to be quite valuable, as indicated in box 2.1). Moreover, economic agents were not always informed of relevant measures. For example, importers were not alerted to the automatic granting of import licenses, and changes in the transactions tax and price liberalization were not announced, although most of the proposed prices had been officially accepted. In Burundi this lack of awareness among the general public, business leaders, and civil servants about the objectives and likely implications of the adjustment program created a climate of uncertainty and cast doubts on the sustainability of the program.

The strained political climate also manifested itself in the poor use of technical assistance resources by the government. In some cases, experts were either not qualified or simply not used effectively. For example, experts hired to reinforce the agency restructuring the private enterprise sector could not apply their expertise effectively because strong government leadership was

Box 2.1 Adjustment and popular participation in Burkina Faso and Burundi

It took the government of Burkina Faso two years to decide to adopt a structural adjustment policy. Once it did, it took more than two years to finalize a program. One of the reasons for such protracted negotiations was the government's desire to have complete control over its adjustment policies, to assess their full impact, and to ensure the support of the population. It was mostly with the latter point in mind that the government convened the "Assises Nationales sur le Programme d'Ajustement Structurel" in May 1990. Some 2,000 delegates from political parties, trade unions, and other social and professional groups (including agricultural producers and traditional groupings, such as churches and ethnic authorities) came together to answer the question: "Does Burkina need a structural adjustment program?"

Delegates voted in favor of a structural adjustment program that would not reduce the overall wage bill, and the conference gave the government a mandate to continue negotiations with the World Bank and the IMF "while preserving the major gains of the people." The program eventually reflected the conference's recommendation, and employment in the civil service was not reduced. There has been little opposition to the program since, and the government has not blamed the World Bank or the IMF for the policies that had been endorsed by the people.

In 1989, after embarking on the second phase of adjustment, the government of Burundi became aware of the need to generate more widespread support for its own program. In an effort to increase general understanding, it expanded the monitoring committee of the structural adjustment program to include the ministries of labor and civil service, organized seminars for the private sector, civil servants, university students and faculty, and donors. Finally a countrywide information campaign was launched to explain the program to provincial administrators, high-ranking civil servants, the army, economic agents, and labor unions. The World Bank organized a seminar on the adjustment program in September 1989 with participants from the public and private sectors, the army, and the church. As a result, the government's participation in the design of the third phase was more active and included a much wider group of people than previous phases.

lacking and because privatization policy was not well defined. And technical assistance was often supply-driven by donors and not tailored to support the government's work program. The poor use of technical assistance also prevented the further development of institution-building capabilities.

Effective ownership was also constrained by the late establishment of key ministerial and technical committees. It was not until the second operation that a permanent secretariat was established to monitor the program. The technical committee never became fully operational, reflecting the lack of personnel and a breakdown in communication between the permanent secretariat and sectoral ministries. The secretariat attempted to duplicate tasks that fell within the competence of the planning ministry's macroeconomics unit, causing confusion on policy issues as diverging data analyses were generated. Coordination between the secretariat and the World Bank's resident mission was also inadequate; meetings were held irregularly. Although supervision by the World Bank was probably adequate and sought to bring areas of difficulty to the attention of the authorities, government decisionmaking and follow-through was slow.

Hard lessons about the consequences of limited internalization were learned. In large part, these were the result of vacillating commitment to and insufficient management of the government's own reform effort.

Overcoming resistance to the redistribution of economic opportunities

The adjustment program, particularly its attempts to reduce policy rents and rent-seeking behavior and encourage a more equitable redistribution of wealth, faced strong resistance in Burundi. This was especially true in the area of public enterprise reform, where entrenched interests had developed primarily along ethnic lines. Public enterprises were sometimes used as platforms for acquiring wealth and power, and their reform implied that these privileges would be relinquished. The slow pace of reform reflects the strengths of vested interests, which feared loss of employment and the emergence of a small elite group of private owners or a return to the dominance by foreign investors that prevailed before Independence. In fact, the transition from a strong, state-controlled system toward more indirect macroeconomic management based on market signals required a profound change of attitude. As Manguelle (1991) asks in his book on cultural adjustment in Africa, "Why would all powerful civil servants accept the emergence and accumulation of fortunes other than theirs when they have the means to prevent it?" Indeed, until 1991, some key ministers and senior civil servants were purposefully undermining the reform process.

In Africa the fluidity of the concepts of governance and accountability—of the interaction between the individual and authority (or state)—has seemingly lowered the quality of governance and has been a potential impediment to development. The government may have underestimated the importance of such cultural variables to the pace and direction of public enterprise reform and to efforts to create a more vibrant private sector. In many African countries, government accountability has historically been limited, due primarily to states' limited legitimacy of power.[3] The dichotomy between traditional civil society and the nascent rise of modern African states has been a primary determinant of this situation. The new state apparatus responded to questions of its legitimacy by avoiding civil control—that is, by reducing its accountability to traditional elements of society. This stance further weakened the notion of a benevolent state and opportunities for civil accountability and allowed personal interests to develop, using the state as a source of wealth and power (Migdal 1988). At times, public enterprises provided the means for obtaining such ends. Personal interests that developed within state sectors are understandably wary of efforts that call for an end to their privileges and a more accountable redistribution of society's wealth, all in the name of productive efficiency. Brautigam (1991) highlights this point in a World Bank review: "One result of this state-society struggle is the fear by government officials of independent economic power. When the state is the primary route to accumulation, rent-seeking becomes an important basis for wealth, keeping control of financial resources ultimately with the state, but hamstringing efficient production" (p. 31).

The political climate of Burundi also had an impact on the success of reform efforts. During the early reform phase of the program, both fiscal and public enterprise reforms suffered from destabilization in the country when, under President Bagaza, restrictive policies toward individual freedoms clashed with the views of the Catholic church, major sociopolitical groups, and donors. Consequently, the government's commitment to implementing the reform program waned. The Third Republic, instated in September 1987 under President Buyoya, had to contend with the tensions inherited from the previous regime. The ethnic violence that erupted in August 1988 had a further destabilizing effect on the country, relegating economic policy considerations to the back burner of national concerns and leading to a reevaluation of the entire adjustment program by all actors—the government, the World Bank, the IMF, and donors.

The lesson here is that in attempting to restructure an economy—which implies a redistribution of income and, along with it, power—a government must recognize not only the economic but also the social and political bonds that hold a society together. Ignoring these dimensions may limit the effectiveness of an otherwise well-planned reform program. Policymakers should not lose sight of the idiosyncratic nature of African states, since this can hold clues to the reasons for their sometimes excessive involvement in productive activities and their reluctance to abandon them.

Resource transfers and conditionalities: part of the solution or part of the problem?

Adjustment support in the form of external financial aid can help alleviate the transitional costs associated with an economy undergoing structural reforms. But besides the beneficial aspects, several drawbacks with balance of payments supports should be noted. First, it artificially boosts economic performance—a sizable chunk of GDP growth being supported by foreign donor financing—giving a false sense of external financial equilibrium. Second, it can prevent adjustment in the level and composition of the import sector. Third, financial aid can discourage governments from implementing reform policies aggressively, particularly if aid appears generous and forthcoming.

So after six years of adjustment support, what conclusions can be drawn about the benefits and drawbacks of adjustment lending in Burundi? The findings suggest that overall resource transfers provided much-needed support for improving the country's financial equilibrium given the limits of Burundi's economic potential, the extent of its structural distortions, and the inopportune decline in world coffee prices. In retrospect, foreign aid to Burundi has been generous. Total adjustment support (grants and loans) to Burundi represented 13.8 percent of all official development assistance from 1986 to 1991.[4] In 1990 alone it was equivalent to as much as 22 percent of foreign aid and constituted nearly 63 percent of foreign exchange receipts from exports of all goods and services. From 1986 to 1991, adjustment support averaged 11 percent of imports of all goods and services, with a peak of almost 18 percent in 1990. During the first two phases of the program, the fact that Burundi notably increased its gross foreign reserves indicates that during some periods it probably received more aid than necessary to maintain a minimum reserve level.[5] Table 2.1 provides a summary of foreign aid flows to Burundi during the adjustment period.

How does one measure the amount of external resources required to offset balance of payments disequilibrium? One method is to consider terms of trade indicators. The impact of a country's declining terms of trade can be observed in a deteriorating external position. Depending on the methodology, the derived financing requirement can reflect commodity price changes and therefore suggest levels of compensating external assistance. That Burundi's export-to-import-price ratio had deteriorated during the adjustment period is clear: the terms of trade index in 1986 was 148 but registered only 70 in 1991. The effects of the drop in world coffee prices is largely to blame. A simple calculation can help highlight the extent of the change. Assuming that coffee prices had remained at their 1986 prices, the loss of foreign exchange revenue (the difference between actual and assumed revenue) comes to $316 million, or 27.5 percent of total official development assistance.

Counterpart funds. Foreign exchange received in the form of adjustment financing is made available to the economy for purchases of imported goods, which in turn generates local currency, or counterpart funds, for government use. One of the problems that arise from allocating counterpart funds through the public sector is that scarce domestic resources can be freed up for purposes contrary to the overall thrust of an adjustment program. One of the main goals of the program in Burundi was to reduce the role of government in the economy while promoting private sector development. Yet counter-

Table 2.1 Indicators of external financing, 1980–91

Indicator	*1986*	*1987*	*1988*	*1989*	*1990*	*1991*	*1980–85*	*1986–91*	*1980–91*
Net official development assistance (US$ millions)	160.1	214.6	157.2	179.1	212.2	228.4	135.2	191.9	163.6
Percentage of exports (gnfs)	121.5	128.4	161.9	148.5	210.9	271.6	145.3	173.8	159.6
Percentage of GDP	13.3	19.0	14.5	16.4	19.1	19.4	13.2	16.9	15.1
Per capita ($)	33.1	43.3	30.6	33.5	38.5	40.4	30.4	36.6	33.5
Structural adjustment program[a] (percentage)									
Of development assistance	8.1	15.1	11.0	13.4	22.2	13.3	—	13.8	—
Of exports (gnfs)	8.7	35.9	16.4	28.3	62.8	30.2	—	30.4	—
Of imports (gnfs)	5.9	13.6	8.0	12.0	17.8	10.6	—	11.3	—
Of GDP	1.3	3.5	2.1	2.8	5.0	3.0	—	3.0	—
Current account/GDP, excl. grants	-8.6	-17.9	-14.5	-14.3	-20.8	-18.1	-13.8	15.7	-14.7
Current account/GDP, incl. grants	0.1	-8.6	-6.5	-2.2	-6.0	-2.7	-5.5	-4.3	-4.9
Fiscal deficit/GDP, excl. grants	-8.5	-16.8	-11.2	-9.7	-12.9	-9.2	-12.6	-11.4	-12.0
Fiscal deficit/GDP, incl. grants	-5.1	-12.9	-8.8	-2.7	-4.7	-0.9	-8.6	-5.9	-7.2
Terms of trade (1980=100)	147.8	92.2	97.4	80.8	64.5	70.2	102.4	92.1	97.3
Net reserves[b]	2.3	1.7	1.6	3.1	2.1	3.2	1.7	2.3	2.0
Gross reserves[b]	3.4	2.3	2.9	5.2	3.9	5.5	2.4	3.9	3.1

— Not applicable.
a. Gross disbursements.
b. In months of imports (goods and nonfactor services—gnfs).
Source: Government of Burundi.

part funds replaced local financing for development projects and permitted the government to finance public enterprise subsidies and military expenditures (increasing nondevelopmental expenditures). Counterpart funds also encouraged additional investments by the government and crowded out private sector investment opportunities. Finally, tariffs for many public services were maintained below long-run marginal costs, due in part to the large amount of external resources available to finance the working capital of public enterprises and the budget deficit. It was not until late 1989 that some public service tariffs (for example, water, electricity, and transportation) were adjusted. Because they were subsidized by the government, private sector entry into these services was precluded. One possible solution is to attach conditionalities to using counterpart funds or introduce mechanisms for channeling the funds directly to the private sector. Without adequate attention to how counterpart funds are used, there is the risk of nullifying the potentially positive impact of other reform measures on economic growth and the quality of public services.

Conditionalities. Another potential problem with the official lending process pertains to the number and effectiveness of conditionalities. The experience in Burundi indicates that IDA structural adjustment credits probably contained an excessive number of conditions, that some were not monitorable, and that many were worded in such a way that their meaning was left to differing interpretations. Structural adjustment credit I contained 45 conditions and structural adjustment credit II contained 94.[6] Because the wording of the conditions was at times unclear, reform was difficult—as was made apparent in the case of public enterprise reform. Conditions were vague and centered almost exclusively on the initiation of the liquidation process and related studies. Few concrete actions or mechanisms were ever proposed on how the recommendations contained in the studies should be implemented. Furthermore, certain conditionalities are inherently more difficult to monitor and enforce than others.

The large number of conditionalities also led to problems for the World Bank at the supervisory stage. In structural adjustment credit II, the number of conditionalities and their dispersion across sectors required that missions be large enough to accommodate many experts. The lack of World Bank expertise in certain areas covered by conditionalities (particularly public enterprise, civil service reform, and the social action program) required managing a sizable number of consultants whose advice was sometimes contradictory. Experience has shown that conditions of adjustment loans should be limited and prioritized for effective implementation. The next phase of the government's adjustment program has attempted to apply these lessons by restricting the number and nature of its conditions.

Encouraging more effective coordination among donors

At the outset of the program, donor coordination was largely effective since much of the cofinancing was of a joint nature—financing from donors was managed by the World Bank. Some problems did arise from the absence of a link between adjustment objectives and those objectives pursued in the context of donor-financed project aid. Under the second phase, however, cofinancing was parallel and was organized under the special program of assistance for Africa. Here donors administered their own financing but respected the conditionality agreements and disbursement schedules of the World Bank. Furthermore, the reform agenda was significantly more ambitious than during the first phase, and more cofinanciers were involved. The increased scope of the program and the greater need for participation by the donor community was compounded by the government's lack of experience and ownership. For example, because the government did not discuss the public investment or public expenditure programs regularly with other donors until early 1991, project design and financing remained largely "supply-driven," and in some cases, were inconsistent with macroeconomic or sectoral objectives. The lack of coordination also led to a high level of foreign assistance to Burundi, financing imports and favoring increased demand at the expense of economic stabilization.

The donor community played an important role in financing nonviable investments in the industrial sector, lowering the technical efficiency of enterprises and increasing the capital intensity of investment. For example, in the case of the Moso Sugar Company, intense lobbying by overseas equipment producers to finance related investment clouded economic and financial judgment. While most of the donors have exerted their influence more carefully since the late 1980s, the problem resurfaces occasionally.

While it is probable that the problems associated with poor coordination among donors could have been alleviated had the government assumed greater ownership of the adjustment program, the government is not entirely guilty in this area—the IMF and the World Bank have also found it difficult to reach a consensus about the extent of the adjustment program. For instance, as structural adjustment credit II was being prepared, the macro-economic framework proposed by the World Bank was rejected by the IMF as being too optimistic. Midway through the program, the opposite was true. The two institutions did not always discuss the potential tradeoffs between the stabilization and structural adjustment measures adequately. The IMF's emphasis on revenue enhancement sometimes had an unintended impact on private sector development, and the reform of the transactions tax recommended by the IMF did not account fully for tariff reform initiated at the advice of the World Bank. IMF program monitoring ceased at the end of the three-year arrangement in December 1989, which also contributed to fiscal and exchange rate policy slippages.

The lesson here is that effective donor coordination, particularly in an aid-dependent country such as Burundi, is an essential element for the successful implementation of a reform program. With the third phase of the program, an attempt is being made to improve the coordination process among all donors to ensure that macroeconomic stabilization accounts sufficiently for the economy's supply-side and private sector requirements, and that project aid supports economic policy reforms. Several areas are targeted for greater coordination and greater transparency: phasing out tied balance of payments assistance to support the open generalized licensing system for imports, creating common management of counterpart funds and reaching agreement on their allocation each year, imposing a moratorium on the financing of new public investment in productive sectors and applying minimum economic rates of return systematically for all other public investments, implementing a harmonized approach to private sector development, and developing a coordinated strategy for dealing with the social aspects of development.

Improving program design: the importance of macro-micro linkages

Thus far, the supply response under the adjustment program has been less than anticipated—due largely to mixed signals from the government to the private sector and to the rigidities that still prevail in the large public enterprise sector. The core of the problem, however, is deficiencies in program design introduced at the start of the reform process.

A major limitation of the reforms was that they did not adequately address the linkage between the macro (broad) scope of policies and the micro (institutional) elements that were being targeted. Program policies spoke of ultimate goals that were to be achieved and offered broad instruments for attaining them, but they failed to account for second-generation (downstream) constraints that arose during implementation. For example, the deregulation of interest rates (a macroeconomic policy) sought to improve access to savings and credit but actually liberalized the financial sector because of the industry's high rate of concentration and limited competition (a microeconomic problem). Similarly, macroeconomic policies on exchange rates or price deregulation, which attempted to set the conditions for liberalizing several sectors, were partly defeated by the quasi-monopolistic position of public enterprises in these sectors (a microeconomic issue), creating market distortions and impeding the supply response.

In the area of private sector development, macroeconomic prescriptions (devaluation, and the removal of quantitative restrictions and official price controls) proved insufficient for generating the desired supply response. While these reforms could have improved the general business environment, the depth and extent of the reform and its long-term sustainability were questionable because supportive measures (such as improved training in vital business skills) were lacking. The importance of intersectoral linkages was ignored. In the agricultural sector this was particularly true where heavy public involvement and policy constraints remained. For example, little attention was given to organizational problems that impeded productivity, such as the poor quality of extension and the absence of improved agricultural inputs. Consequently, some viable opportunities for the private sector failed to materialize. This problem is beginning to be addressed, for example, in the coffee sector, through privatization efforts.

The lesson here is that supply response is a function of effective program design and an enabling macroeconomic environment. One possible solution for achieving a more coherent and effective program design, and establishing the link between policies and outcomes, is to introduce intermediate targets, improve the coverage of indicators (a more timely, detailed, and broad data base), and review implementation and performance more frequently.

The design and implementation of the adjustment program

The sociopolitical situation in Burundi during the late 1980s played an important role in determining the formulation and the subsequent implementation of the government's program. The sociopolitical climate during the initial phase of the program was marked by tension, and, for the most part, the reform agenda was prepared by World Bank and IMF staff with minimal participation from the government. The second phase of the reform program was negotiated with a new and inexperienced leadership, and adherence to the program was further undermined by ethnic fighting that erupted in 1988. The delicate sociopolitical situation contributed to the government's initial lack of ownership, hampering the effectiveness of reform design and implementation, and ultimately the success of the program.

Given the extent of the financial disequilibrium in Burundi prior to adjustment and the nature of the structural distortions in the economy, the program spelled out macroeconomic reforms in the areas of fiscal and monetary policy, exchange rate management, and price and external trade liberalization. Sectoral reforms were also designed for factor markets, financial sector liberalization, public enterprises, the regulatory framework, and social sector policies. For each area, this section presents the general setting prior to the introduction of the reforms, outlines their design, and describes the extent of their implementation.

Fiscal policy and management

Setting. At the onset of adjustment, the government was unable to contain expenditures in general and nondevelopmental expenditures in particular. Its institutional arrangements for budget preparation and public expenditure programming were weak, and the civil service and the number of administrative units within the ministries were bloated. The fiscal situation was exacerbated by unstable coffee prices—a sector of major importance to government revenue. On the expenditure side, recurrent costs were underfinanced, while spending on higher education (at the expense of primary and secondary levels) and on hospitals was excessive. Military expenditures were also high (about 3 to 4 percent of GDP), and external debt from capital expenditures on military items (generally outside the budget) represented another 3 to 4 percent. Direct and indirect subsidies to public enterprises further drained the budget, usually in the form of elevated debt service payments. And the inefficiency of investments in public projects generated operating deficits that had to be covered partially by the budget. Restoring sustainable economic growth and the viability of Burundi's financial equilibrium and external position thus necessitated reducing the budget deficit significantly and improving the composition and quality of public expenditures.

Reforms. The first phase of the program introduced three public expenditure policies. First, the government agreed to reduce the size of the public investment program, but also to maintain allocations to the major sectors (notably agriculture). It sought to conform to an investment plan compatible with the availability of resources and stabilization requirements, and to make foreign financing concessional or grant-based. Some measures sought to reduce the scope of the large Moso Sugar Company project and to improve its projected rate of return. Second, in the area of budgetary reform, the government agreed to merge its ordinary budget and its extraordinary budget into a unified budget system, clearly identifying and separating current revenue, current expenditures, and capital expenditures financed by both the budget and foreign aid. It also agreed to prepare a rolling three-year public expenditure program, which included recurrent and capital expenditures for each agency. Finally, to improve capacity building the government sought to strengthen the agencies responsible for preparing the annual budget at the ministry of finance, and to establish a system for monitoring project implementation.

The second phase continued to focus on the same three areas. Since several of the measures of structural adjustment credit I had not been implemented sufficiently, they were carried over into the next operation. Instruments for more effective and transparent budget execution and public expenditure programming were set in place, again including a rolling three-year public investment program for rationalizing public investment, satisfactory public expenditure programs for four major sectors (health, education, agriculture, and transport), the consolidation of a unified budget, and a project monitoring system. In June 1991 the government prepared an action plan to enhance the efficiency of the civil service while limiting the creation of new positions to the social sector. In the third phase, the government is seeking to increase the funding of investment-related recurrent costs and to promote quality basic services, thus improving the composition of public expenditures.

Implementation. The size and structure of the public investment program improved considerably under adjustment. The rolling three-year public investment program has now become an official implementation tool for investment programming and is adopted each year by the council of ministers. The public investment program process has helped scale down the size of projects and promote more realistic sectoral objectives that recognize resource and debt service constraints. The project selection process must still be strengthened, however, since the government does not consistently apply the minimum rate-of-return criterion in selecting projects.

About three-quarters of capital expenditures in the public investment programs go to economic infrastructure—30 percent to roads and between 30 and 40 percent to the rural sector. Social infrastructure receives between 10 and 13 percent of investments, primarily for health and education. Within current expenditures, maintenance costs are substantially underfinanced. In agriculture, which accounts for 60 percent of underfinancing, large neglected items include the maintenance of livestock infrastructure, and forestry and irrigation facilities. Shortfalls in the health sector represent about 14 percent of the total underfinancing, and include utilities, medicines, equipment, and vehicles. Underfinancing of road maintenance represents 16 percent, and the remaining 10 percent is spread across other sectors. Yet the overall sectoral composition of expenditures has improved. Relatively large public investment projects in the productive sectors have gradually shifted toward smaller investments targeted primarily at improving the quality of social services.

The rationalization of public expenditures was delayed by the absence of public expenditure programs. In 1989 and 1990 World Bank staff and resident technical advisers were obliged to prepare the public expenditure programs, indicating that appropriate technical assistance had not yet been identified. Only in 1991 was a harmonized methodology for preparing public expenditure programs adopted. Until recently government expenditures were insufficiently restructured, revealing a weak commitment to reducing public expenditures and the poor management of counterpart funds generated from the substantial amount of balance of payments support received from external donors. The wage bill was excessive in relation to expenditures on goods and services, compromising the quality of rapidly expanding public services. The accumulation of large counterpart funds by the public sector undermined one of the principal goals of the program—to reduce the role of the state in the economy. Counterpart funds replaced local financing for development projects, permitting the government to allocate freed-up local resources to finance public enterprise subsidies and military expenditures.

Recurrent costs were also not budgeted adequately. Thus, some existing assets have deteriorated rapidly and require expensive rehabilitation, a project that could have been avoided had maintenance costs been budgeted regularly. Donor policies that generally preclude aid financing of recurrent costs have encouraged rehabilitation over maintenance. Another reason for low recurrent budgets is that investments are sometimes selected without sufficient recognition of the capacity of the government or users to assume maintenance costs.

The management of public debt has also been an important part of public expenditure reform. Burundi's external debt policy since 1986 has been to contract loans exclusively on concessional terms. Nevertheless, because investments financed by previous borrowings did not generate the necessary receipts to cover the corresponding debt service, and because the world price for coffee sharply declined, servicing obligations are now more than 40 percent of foreign exchange earnings. The large number of public expenditures created in the late 1970s and early 1980s has now become a significant burden, impairing Burundi's future borrowing capacity. But improvement has been noted: average loan terms have fallen from 5.4 percent in 1982 to about 1.0 percent in 1990, while the grant element has increased from 35 to 75 percent for the same period. Despite the successive devaluations of the Burundi franc, which worsen the external debt burden, the government continues to service its foreign debt obligations on schedule.

The budget reform process progressed satisfactorily once an IMF adviser was named in July 1989. A unified budget was adopted in 1992, combining all central government expenditures, whether financed with domestic or external resources. However, previous efforts to tackle budget reform and to strengthen the capacity of the ministries of finance and planning met with little success. High staff turnover in the administration during 1986–89 negatively affected reform implementation as it did training for preparation of the public expenditure program component. Implementation was also delayed because reform called for substantial changes in the way sectoral ministries were to program their expenditures. Foreign technical assistance, which was to advise and facilitate the reform process, failed to adequately play its trainer role and often seemed to operate outside the context of the administration. The consolidation of all budgetary authority under the ministry of finance in 1992 (which was previously shared with the ministry of planning) has been a major institutional improvement, but in practice much needs to be done to improve budget preparation.

The government has been successful in revenue collection, leaving little room for further revenue increases without jeopardizing productive sectors. The volume of noncoffee receipts rose in real terms from FBu 9.3 billion in 1983–85 to FBu 11.4 billion in 1987–90. This growth is essentially due to the transaction tax reform, an increase in indirect taxes on beer and nonalcoholic beverages, and an expansion of the statistics tax base. Devaluations have also enhanced revenue from import taxes, despite tariff reductions. (For a discussion of taxation, see box 2.2.)

Under the third phase of the reform program, measures in public resource management have already been introduced, such as the consolidation of all budgetary authority under the ministry of finance. Satisfactory 1992–94 public expenditure programs covering agriculture, education, health, and transport, and representing about 80 percent of public expenditures, have now been completed. The public investment program is being revised to improve transparency in the breakdown of financing among loans, grants, and public savings. In May 1992 the government established an interministerial commission to supervise the public investment program process and to ensure that new criteria for project evaluation and selection are applied—that is, that projects provide a 10 percent internal rate of return, help alleviate poverty, and generate employment. Measures to curtail public expenditures are already under way, including plans to reduce subsidies to public enterprises, curtail nondevelopmental recurrent expenditure, and monitor civil service recruitment.

Monetary policy

Setting. Prior to adjustment, the monetary sector reflected the dirigiste approach adopted by the government—overregulation and interest rates that failed to reflect the supply and demand for money and provide the necessary incentives for private investment. Monetary and credit policies depended primarily on the evolution of the budget deficit and the coffee sector, which absorbed more than 30 percent of total credit and generated large oscillations in money supply. Since 1981 broad money increased in line with the trend in nominal GDP (about 10 percent annually). World Bank credit to parastatals rose significantly in the early 1980s; credit to the private sector (other than parastatals) declined by 25 percent in the same period. Despite an array of monetary and credit policy instruments in the early 1980s, government budgetary policies were expansive and the level of domestic liquidity high. Interest rates were finally changed in August 1986, after remaining the same in nominal terms since October 1981.

Reforms. Monetary reform sought to reduce inflation, strengthen the balance of payments, and promote resource mobilization through stable real

Box 2.2 Investment incentives and marginal effective tax rates

Taxation plays a dual role in the Burundi economy: it generates revenue needed to support government spending consistent with macroeconomic stability, and it influences production decisions by creating a wedge between social (economic) and private returns on investments. Tax exemptions affect competition and efficiency. Although tax collection is adequate, the system of direct taxation in Burundi has been found to distort investment decisions. The issue at hand is the impact of various taxes on incentives. On average during the adjustment period, receipts from corporate income tax and other taxes accounted for only about 14 percent of total tax revenue, implying that there is scope for reforming corporate taxation without creating significant fiscal losses.

What is the general tax situation in Burundi? First, implementation of the tax code is uneven. Exemptions are unevenly applied, and administration is weak. A pattern of tax evasion and uneven implementation of the fiscal provisions is evident. These distortions can affect decisions to invest in capital assets. The net impact of these taxes can be quantified in the marginal effective tax rate, which is defined as the difference between the gross of tax and the net of tax real returns to an investment, expressed as a percentage of the gross return. The higher the marginal effective tax rate, the higher the rate of effective taxation becomes. The primary goal of the marginal effective tax rate analysis is to describe the overall effects of a tax system on marginal investment incentives. In a recent study Zodrow (1990), using marginal effective tax rates, has shown that (i) debt financing is favored over equity financing, particularly where there is inflation and where assets appreciate slowly; (ii) trade taxes on capital goods significantly lower capital income and discourage investment; and (iii) taxation of realized nominal capital gains raises effective taxation on investments financed with retained earnings.

During a recent dialogue with the private sector, the government was made aware of the problems caused by the distorted and heavy tax burden and indicated its willingness to reform the tax system. The basic thrust of reforms should be the development of a tax regime that does not favor certain activities over others (tariffs and the investment code already serve that purpose). In fact, some reforms have already been implemented by the government following IMF recommendations. Among the anticipated reforms are (i) a lower rate of corporate income tax to help attract new investments; (ii) a revision of the turnover and dividend tax; (iii) a reduction in the capital gains tax; (iv) simplification of the rental income tax system; and (v) reversal of the tax-exempt status of government securities as it tends to distort the interest rate structure.

interest rates. The policy framework papers set monetary targets for credit to the economy and government. The intermediate objective of monetary policy was to control broad money (M2).[7] Total domestic credit was to decline by 16.9 percent in 1986 and 16.1 percent in 1987, grow by 1.4 percent in 1988, and fall again by 15 percent in 1989 (table 2.2). These figures essentially reflected a contraction in credit to the government (primarily to public enterprises), which was to fall by 20 percent on average from 1986 to 1988. The

Table 2.2 Program targets and actual performance, 1986–91

	1986		1987		1988		1989		1990		1991	
Indicator	*Prog.*	*Act.*	*Prog.*	*Act.*	*Prog.*	*Act.*	*Prog.*	*Act.*	*Prog.*	*Act.*	*Prog.*	*Act.*
Percentage growth												
GDP	4.0	3.3	4.0	5.5	4.0	4.9	4.5	1.5	4.5	3.5	4.6	4.9
Consumer prices	10.0	1.8	9.0	7.1	8.0	4.5	5.0	11.7	4.5	7.0	4.0	8.9
Domestic credit[a]	-16.9	-2.6	-16.1	4.9	1.4	8.7	-15.0	4.9	..	12.1	..	8.4
Government	-23.5	-6.2	-22.6	3.3	-14.3	-11.5	..	-12.7	..	-8.2	..	-4.9
Private sector	6.6	3.3	6.5	0.2	15.6	12.9	..	14.4	..	17.2	..	17.7
Export volume	5.0	10.7	5.3	-7.4	5.4	13.4	-0.1	-8.4	8.2	-5.8	4.8	16.7
Import volume	6.4	-5.7	5.7	0.8	4.0	-5.4	9.5	-7.2	7.3	20.3	4.1	9.3
As percentage of GDP (unless noted otherwise)												
Current account deficit[b]	-3.4	-8.6	-6.5	-17.9	-7.0	-14.5	-18.1	-14.3	-17.6	-20.8	-17.4	-18.2
Debt service ratio[c]	16.3	21.7	19.6	49.0	19.3	36.4	39.8	46.2	32.9	45.4	32.2	32.2
Government revenue[d]	19.2	15.3	17.6	13.5	16.0	15.4	21.4	18.1	19.2	15.7	19.2	16.8
Government expenditure[e]	23.4	23.8	24.0	30.4	22.8	26.6	30.5	27.8	26.2	29.1	24.2	29.2
Overall deficit[f]	-4.1	-8.5	-6.4	-16.8	-6.6	-11.2	-9.2	-9.6	-7.0	-13.4	-5.0	-12.4
Fixed investment	15.7	14.0	19.2	20.9	19.8	15.1	20.1	16.9	21.5	18.4	21.5	16.7
Private	2.9	2.6	5.7	4.5	6.9	1.7	4.1	1.9	4.8	2.8	5.1	2.5
Public	12.8	11.4	13.5	16.4	12.9	13.4	15.5	15.0	16.2	15.7	15.9	14.2
Domestic savings	7.2	1.1	7.1	6.9	7.4	1.6	3.5	3.3	5.0	-2.6	5.2	-2.1

.. Not available.
a. Expressed as percentage of beginning-of-period money stock.
b. Including grants.
c. Ratio of debt service to exports of goods and nonfactor services.
d. Excluding grants.
e. Total expenditure.
f. On a commitment basis and excluding grants.
Source: World Bank and IMF data; Government of Burundi.

aim was to make credit available to the private sector, with credit growth targeted to increase by 9.6 percent on average over the same period.[8]

Implementation. The government's monetary policy was passive and conservative under the adjustment program. Credit policies fell somewhat short of expectations, although the overall trend was in keeping with the objectives of the program. Overall credit to the economy fell in 1986 by 2.6 percent, then climbed by 7.8 percent between 1987 and 1991 (table 2.3). Despite the expansion, most of the increase reflected additional credit to the private sector, not to the government. Credit to the government fell by 6.7 percent; credit to the private sector increased by 10.9 percent. The supply of broad money (M2) maintained steady but slow growth over the period, increasing by 8.3 percent. In real terms, however, credit and money supply were stagnant from 1986 to 1990.

Overall, the real money supply was held in check and helped keep inflation low during the late 1980s. But the failure to further cut the level of credit to the government was due primarily to greater than expected fiscal deficits, and net credit to the government exceeded agreed upon targets, which in the initial phase of the adjustment program crowded out credit available to the private sector. But since 1988, credit to the private sector has picked up considerably.

Deposit and borrowing real interest rates generally remained positive. Restrictions on interest rates have progressively been removed, and most bank deposit rates and loans are now "proximately determined by market conditions" (IMF 1992a). The structure of the central bank's refinance rates has been simplified since May 1991, and a uniform rate of 10 percent has been applied. The monthly auctions of treasury certificates, introduced in 1988, provide a benchmark for the market-based determination of interest rates.

Table 2.3 Summary of monetary indicators, 1986–91

(annual percentage change, unless noted otherwise)

Indicator	*1986*	*1987*	*1988*	*1989*	*1990*	*1991*
Credit to[a]						
Economy	-2.6	4.9	8.7	4.9	12.1	8.4
Government	-6.2	3.3	-11.5	-12.7	-8.2	-4.9
Public enterprises	1.1	0.8	7.2	3.4	3.0	-4.4
Coffee sector	-0.4	1.4	5.0	2.0	4.1	3.1
Private sector	3.3	0.2	12.9	14.4	17.2	17.7
Money and quasi-money (M2)	4.6	5.4	1.5	12.1	13.3	12.9
Nominal GDP	-1.1	1.7	9.3	13.7	9.5	12.7
M2/GDP[b]	0.18	0.19	0.18	0.17	0.18	0.17

a. Annual change as percentage of beginning-of-period broad money.
b. Ratio of M2 to GDP.
Source: Government of Burundi.

Financial savings increased substantially during the program, albeit from an initially low base. Term deposits rose by 143 percent between 1986 and 1989, compared with 22 percent between 1982 and 1986. The best performance was registered by the rural savings cooperatives, whose deposits increased by nearly 600 percent between 1986 and 1988.

Government support for public enterprises is one reason that public sector credit continues unabated, with a relatively small share going to the private sector. Benefiting from large indirect subsidies, public enterprises have accumulated cash reserves that in turn give them much borrowing power with domestic banks. The fact that until early 1991 banks were able to lend to public enterprises virtually risk-free impeded private sector access to credit for productive investments. The third phase of the adjustment program calls for a more radical approach to public enterprise reform measures for privatizing public enterprises (or rehabilitating or liquidating them) and a subceiling on credit to public enterprises. These reforms should increase the availability of credit to the private sector and create a more growth-oriented credit policy.

Exchange rate management

Setting. At the onset of adjustment, Burundi faced an external financial disequilibrium and deteriorating international price competitiveness. From 1976 to April 1992, the country had a fixed exchange rate system, whereby the FBu was first pegged to the U.S. dollar and later to the special drawing right (SDR).[9] By 1986, despite continuous deterioration of its current account and an inflation level above those of its trading partners and SDR basket currencies, the government had not devalued the FBu since its initial peg to the SDR in 1983. Furthermore, by being linked to the SDR, Burundi's currency fluctuated with the U.S. dollar against other currencies as it appreciated to unprecedented levels in 1984 and 1985.[10] Between 1980 and June 1986, the real effective exchange rate of the FBu appreciated by 23.6 percent. Equally important was that the exchange rate had evolved independent of developments in Burundi's economy, but was tied instead to economic policies that were pursued in industrial states, primarily the United States. The central bank authorized all payments abroad and received all foreign exchange. Commercial banks were prohibited from trading in foreign currencies and were required to apply to the central bank to make external payments. In addition to the official exchange mechanism, foreign exchange was also traded substantially on the parallel (black) market, comprising border trade, smuggling, and gold exports and trading.[11]

Reforms. Reform sought to improve the competitiveness of nontraditional exports and import substitution activities by promoting a return to external equilibrium and an efficient allocation of resources. In the medium to long term, the exchange rate can compensate for a rising demand in foreign exchange when the current account is liberalized and lower tariffs are adopted. A country with large current account deficits and significant compensatory capital flows (which are not sustainable in the long run) can use devaluation to maintain equilibrium between supply and demand for foreign exchange.[12] Exchange rate adjustment (under the domain of the IMF) and successive devaluations were made throughout the reform period in conjunction with the World Bank-supported structural adjustment credits. While devaluations were triggered to promote overall competitiveness, they were necessary in the latter part of the 1980s to compensate for the fall in world coffee prices and the terms of trade loss. The coffee sector incurred losses because domestic production, processing, and transportation costs exceeded the international sales price. In the absence of measures to cut domestic costs directly (the government rejected a reduction in producer prices on political grounds), devaluation was required. Devaluation was also encouraged to facilitate the eventual move to convertibility. The move to an open general license for goods, transportation, and insurance was planned to liberalize service payments and to stimulate the development of nontraditional exports.[13]

Implementation. By 1987 the real effective exchange rate had returned to its 1980 level (table 2.4). Further devaluations followed, enhancing Burundi's competitiveness. By 1990 the real effective exchange rate had declined by another 28 percent (IMF 1992b). From 1986 to 1991, 25 exchange rate adjustments helped realign the overvalued FBu, leading to a nominal effective devaluation of 40 percent and a real effective devaluation of about 33 percent in relation to the SDR.

One method for gauging the effectiveness of the devaluations is an effectiveness index, defined as the cumulative ex post elasticity of the real effective exchange rate to the nominal effective exchange rate for different periods after the devaluation (Frenkel and Klein 1992). A ratio of "one" would

Table 2.4 Real effective exchange rates, 1980–91
(1980=100)

Item	*1980–85*	*1986*	*1987*	*1988*	*1989*	*1990*	*1991*
Real effective exchange rate	127.3	116.4	99.8	87.9	89.1	77.4	77.8
Terms of trade	102.4	147.8	92.2	97.4	80.8	64.5	70.2
Resource balance							
(percentage of GDP)							
Constant	-11.4	-11.4	-11.6	-9.6	-6.6	-9.6	-8.6
Current	-14.0	-10.5	-15.8	-13.4	-13.5	-20.3	-18.3

Source: Government of Burundi.

show that a nominal devaluation has translated fully into a real devaluation; an index of "zero" would indicate the total erosion of the nominal devaluation by inflation. Burundi's effectiveness index was 0.76 for the 12 months following July 1986, 0.49 for the 12 months following March 1988, and 0.75 for the 12 months following December 1989. Thus, one-half to three-fourths of the magnitude of the devaluation effectively translated into the real exchange rate. Devaluations did not trigger price rises sufficient to cancel out much of their effect.

The impact of the devaluations on bilateral exchange rates (a measure of Burundi's competitiveness with individual trade partners) varied considerably. From 1985 to late 1989, the FBu depreciated in real terms by 11.1 percent to the dollar, 40.1 percent to the deutsche mark, 46 percent to the yen, and 38.9 percent to the French franc (Frenkel and Klein 1992; IMF 1992b). Table 2.5 shows the proportion of trade with various countries. Yet the magnitude of the real depreciation compared to regional trading partners was less, essentially because such countries as Tanzania and Kenya also devalued their own currencies. However, Burundi's devaluations at least prevented what would have otherwise been an excessive appreciation of the FBu in relation to regional trading partners. The zaire and Rwandese franc depreciated in real terms.

Table 2.5 Direction of trade, 1984–90
(percentage of total trade)

Region or country	1984	1985	1986	1987	1988	1989	1990
Exports							
Africa	7.8	8.0	7.6	18.2	7.8	14.5	8.8
Zaire	1.6	1.3	1.5	2.9	3.1	4.7	3.2
Kenya	3.5	1.5	1.4	3.3	1.0	6.5	2.2
Rwanda	1.4	2.8	2.1	5.5	2.8	1.8	1.0
Asia	6.4	3.0	2.3	4.0	5.4	5.1	2.2
Europe	81.8	82.0	80.9	64.2	83.7	72.5	76.9
Germany	34.1	54.5	53.6	30.0	26.9	15.2	13.7
France	0.3	1.2	1.7	6.7	3.1	6.4	9.6
North America	1.6	6.1	6.7	7.5	0.6	7.3	11.7
Others	2.4	1.0	2.5	6.1	2.4	0.6	0.3
Imports							
Africa	2.6	12.7	10.7	10.5	13.2	13.3	12.0
Zambia	1.9	0.9	3.1	4.1	3.4	2.4	2.8
Kenya	3.4	26.8	2.7	2.6	2.8	3.0	2.5
Zimbabwe	1.8	1.2	57.8	0.9	1.6	2.2	2.5
Asia	29.9	27.1	22.8	26.8	27.3	25.7	27.3
Europe	49.7	53.8	60.0	57.8	54.8	54.8	53.7
Germany	8.8	11.7	11.8	13.1	9.7	13.6	12.9
France	14.0	12.3	9.8	8.3	12.3	10.2	9.9
Belgium/Luxembourg	14.7	18.7	19.1	18.9	16.8	15.5	14.5
North America	5.8	6.0	2.6	2.2	2.7	3.7	1.5
Others	2.0	2.4	2.2	2.6	2.0	2.4	5.6

Source: Government of Burundi.

Although these adjustments improved the competitiveness of some traditional exports (hides) and nontraditional exports (fruits and vegetables, garments, rice, and tobacco), they did not fully reflect the terms of trade loss incurred from the decline in world coffee prices at the end of the decade. Real depreciation was greater against currencies of industrial countries than against those of regional trading partners. Finally, exchange rate adjustment was linked more to pressure from the Bretton Woods institutions than to the government's own response to economic and financial constraints. The government recognized these shortcomings and requested IMF assistance to establish a new foreign exchange system that better reflected the pattern of the country's international trade. As a formal element of the extended structural adjustment facility program, a new scheme of more automatic exchange rate adjustments was put in place in April 1992. The FBu is now pegged to a trade-weighted basket of currencies. The peg is to be reviewed daily and adjusted flexibly based on movements in key financial and economic indicators (for example, the evolution of monetary and credit aggregates, foreign exchange reserves, trends in inflation, trends in nominal and real effective exchange rates, the parallel exchange rate, and international coffee prices). This system provides the same degree of flexibility as a floating arrangement, but does not require major changes in the organization of Burundi's foreign exchange market. The arrangement takes into account the imbalance in the payments and receipts of foreign exchange, and the oligopolistic structure of the commercial banking system, which precludes introducing an interbank market at this juncture.[14] The latest significant change took place from April to June 1992, when the FBu depreciated by about 11 percent (in foreign currency terms) compared to the basket.

The ultimate success of a devaluation depends on its impact on domestic inflation, and thus on the relative prices of Burundi and its major trading partners. In Burundi, monetary management was passive yet conservative, as domestic credit was generally kept under control and credit to the government declined between 1986 and 1991. Money supply was stable while quasi-money grew slowly. Fiscal deficits were not generally financed through money creation. The simultaneous deregulation of the import sector (by lowering barriers and increasing competition) helped control prices by reducing importers' profit margins and keep inflation down. Inflation fell from an average of 9.2 percent for the 1980–85 period to 6.9 percent for the 1986–91 period.

Trade liberalization

Setting. A study of the protection system prior to adjustment identified a wide spread in customs tariffs (68 to 336 percent), quantitative restrictions (quotas for most products and a ban on imports that competed with locally manufactured products), import regulations, foreign exchange controls, and compulsory advance deposits with the central bank. Imports were subjected to three different types of tax: customs duties, a statistics tax, and a transactions tax. These taxes, combined with an incoherent tariff structure that consisted of a wide range of rates, contributed to an excessive and inconsistent system of protection. Importers complained (until mid-1990) of administrative harassment and constraints. All commercial imports required licenses. Such distortions helped foster a public import-substitution industrial sector that was inefficient and absorbed a large part of national savings and loan resources. The introduction of the open general license in May 1992 addressed these problems.

Reforms. Sequenced with the first series of devaluations, structural adjustment credit I reforms sought to liberalize the trade regime. First, import licenses were to be granted automatically for most products (except for cotton textiles, glass, and pharmaceutical products). In addition, regulations on importers were to be eased to facilitate competition. A simplified tariff structure was also proposed to reduce the number of duties from 3 to 2, the number of duty rates from 57 to 5, and the spread from 50 to 15 percent in 1986 to 40 to 20 percent in 1989 (keeping luxury goods at 100 percent). A maximum surcharge of 30 percent for three years could be applied to protect infant industries.

The second phase of the program called for reforming the tariff structure further, liberalizing the import of locally manufactured products (eliminating the remaining quantitative restrictions), increasing the ceiling on import licenses granted by commercial banks, and requiring that the central bank pay interest on the FBu 10 million that foreign importers are obliged to deposit as a guarantee against illegal business practices. To promote exports, the program called for adopting simplified drawback procedures for import taxes, authorizing the deduction of marketing expenses incurred abroad, and simplifying administrative procedures for businessmen traveling abroad. An office for weights and measures was to be set up, and a study on potential exports was to be carried out.

Implementation. In retrospect, tariff reductions and the liberalization of import licensing were slower and less profound than anticipated. While quotas were abolished and the tariff structure simplified as planned, tariffs on luxury goods remained, and those on intermediate and equipment goods fell more slowly than programmed. Yet at the same time, the transactions tax rate, a tax applying to one of three stages—imports, production, or service—was increased as part of a revenue enhancement package of the stabilization program and canceled out some of the impact of lower tariffs. Capital goods, which had previously been exempt, became taxable in 1988. On the whole, the adjustment program reduced the effective protection primarily by eliminating nontariff barriers, but not by as much as had originally been projected.

Until mid-1990 importers continued to complain about administrative harassment and constraints. All commercial imports required licenses. Authority to grant import and export licenses has been delegated progressively to the commercial banks, particularly since 1990. An open general license was introduced in May 1992, delegating full authority to commercial banks to issue import licenses and provide necessary foreign exchange. The import profession is now considerably more open and the range of eligible products wider.[15] Substantial aid flows have now made foreign exchange amply available in Burundi. The effects of trade liberalization are clearly having an impact on import substitution firms. Requests for protection have increased since 1989, particularly from enterprises producing soap, matches, and shoes (box 2.3). Several distortions due to the improper classification of products have also been corrected. However, the impact of the reform has been somewhat limited because more than 50 percent of imports enter the country essentially duty-free because they are aid-financed. All quantitative restrictions on imports were abolished in August 1990.

Under the third phase, additional reforms in trade and tariffs are being introduced to improve tariff administration and further reduce effective protection and antiexport bias. The government plans to cut maximum tariff rates from 40 to 30 percent for nonluxury goods, and from 100 to 70 percent for luxury goods. To make the reform revenue-neutral, the government will substantially reduce exemptions and introduce an excise tax on such goods as alcohol and tobacco. Within broad sectors, tariff rates are also to be harmonized. When the reforms have taken hold, Burundi will have one of Sub-Saharan Africa's most liberal trade regimes.

Prices and market deregulation

Setting. Prior to the program, all prices of imported and locally manufactured goods were subject to controls exercised by the ministry of commerce and industry. Prices were set on a cost-plus basis, with the manufacturer receiving a net profit margin of 10 to 20 percent. Price controls sought to prevent producers and traders from reaping excessive profit in a monopolistic market, but they had serious drawbacks. The cost-plus formula discouraged importers from looking for the cheapest source of supply. Manufacturers, assured of a fixed profit margin, had little incentive to reduce costs and increase efficiency and quality. A unit of about 10 staff in the ministry of commerce and industry was responsible for reviewing all prices submitted for approval and for making periodic inspections.

The export crop subsector has traditionally been the most regulated sector of the economy. Prices for inputs and producer prices of export crops are fixed (except for rice). Government price policies tend to subsidize inputs while taxing output prices, which discourages output while promoting the inefficient use of inputs. Moreover, overregulation of the agriculture sector inhibits producers from responding adequately to world prices.

Reforms. Recognizing that price controls were not compatible with liberalization and a rational allocation of resources, the government decided to

Box 2.3 Enterprises and devaluations

In order to obtain information on the impact of the devaluation on economic activity in Burundi, an enterprise survey was conducted in 1990 under the guidance of the World Bank resident mission in Bujumbura. Covering about 50 enterprises, the survey looked for information on the evolution of economic activity in the private and parastatal sectors, the current business climate in the modern sector, and the prevailing view among entrepreneurs on exchange rate policy.

The overall impression that emerged from the responses is that there was a significant increase in economic activity. Nevertheless, 55 percent of entrepreneurs had a negative assessment of the effects of the devaluations, even though 60 percent of the enterprises had displayed a positive trend in sales between 1985 and 1990. In fact, the prevailing gloomy view of the devaluations suggests that exchange rate adjustments functioned as expected. New firms created after the beginning of the adjustment program have a significantly better opinion of the devaluation than older firms. Positive opinions increased from 10 percent of the firms created between 1980 and 1985 (the years of overvaluation), to 33 percent of the firms created before 1980, to 50 percent of the firms created since 1986. This observation suggests a relationship between a firm's creation date and its performance under adjustment: firms that had benefited from the strongest distortions suffered most from the devaluations.

SAVONOR, Burundi's leading soap producer, provides an example of the latter. Traditionally importing many of the company's inputs, the management claimed that the company had been severely hurt by the devaluations, which pushed its production costs upward, an increase that could not be offset by an increase in domestic sale prices. Domestic prices were even pushed down as a result of competition from small-scale manufacturers in the informal sector that did not pay taxes and relied solely on domestic inputs. The company faced direct competition from more efficient producers that used cheap local inputs, and consumers increasingly shifted from SAVONOR to domestically produced substitutes. Fortunately the company adjusted to its new environment. It replaced its imported components with domestically produced palm oil, reduced its production costs, regained some of its competitive edge, and contributed to the country's adjustment process.

deregulate prices at the outset of the program and address both producer and consumer prices. The government agreed to continue to let foodcrop producer prices be market-determined, and to establish prices for cash crops at levels sufficient to provide incentives for increasing production and quality, taking into account the evolution of international prices. The government agreed that its consumer price control system, which had previously set a fixed profit margin for manufacturers, hampered the process of relative price adjustment—and it thus chose to liberalize these prices along with those for imports. Products for which importation was liberalized would not be subject to controls, and only certain strategic products, such as flour, sugar, and powdered milk, would be submitted to a temporary price ceiling if acute shortages occurred.

Reforms supported under structural adjustment credit I sought to introduce an automatic system for adjusting producer prices for cash crops to spur improved quality of products and expanded production. Structural adjustment credit II included measures to improve efficiency in the coffee subsector, reduce subsidies on fertilizers, encourage higher producer prices in agriculture, liberalize the rice sector, reform the sugar sector, and undertake a study of the country's comparative advantages.

Implementation. An automatic system for adjusting producer prices was not implemented under structural adjustment credit I. Although measures to improve the quality of certain export crops and to increase their production were partially successful, progress toward improving international marketing arrangements and maintaining competitive producer prices has not been satisfactory. Measures to liberalize the rice sector and restructure the sugar complex were implemented. A long-term fertilizer policy was not formulated as planned, but is now being formulated as part of an agricultural services project.

Coffee prices, which were to be adjusted regularly after cost of living assessments were made for each region, remained below their 1980 level in real terms (by as much as 20 percent in 1989). Nominal producer prices increased from FBu 125/kg (in 1985) to FBu 160/kg (during 1986–88) to FBu 175/kg (during 1989–91). Decisions about production and producer prices continued to be made administratively. The government determined both producer prices and the amount of plants (freely distributed to peasants) that were to be produced in the nurseries. Concurrently, the compulsory controls on the plantations (for example, uprooting was forbidden) prevented farmers from shifting to crops with higher returns. Yet the decline in producer prices also reflected the larger collapse of world prices. Based on the total value and quantity of coffee exports, the world price for a kilo of Burundi's coffee fell from FBu 426 in 1986 to FBu 288 in 1990, a 32.4 percent decline.

The price paid to tea planters also declined in real terms (5 percent annually) during the adjustment period, precipitating a shortage of manpower for harvesting. This decline occurred while world prices for tea climbed from FBu 172/kg (1986) to FBu 382/kg (1990). Cotton suffered from similar policy-induced problems: real producer prices fell by 13 percent from 1986 to 1989, while world prices expressed in FBu rose by 44 percent. In addition, cotton was imposed upon farmers as a "compulsory crop" in certain regions. The impact of mandatory planting regulations was serious. Sanctions included the loss of access to publicly held land, a critical necessity since little acreage is available to expand production. Consequently, the overregulation of the agricultural sector prevented producer prices for export crops from moving with world prices and limited the supply response possible from a dynamic exchange rate policy.

Despite attempts at deregulation, the markets for most crops remained monopolistic or quasi-monopolistic as public enterprises continued to dominate these sectors. For example in the cotton sector, the Cotton Management Company markets all production, and the Cotton Textile Company of Burundi purchases 90 percent of the Cotton Management Company's output. The coffee sector also remains dominated by public enterprises, despite recent reforms. As of 1991 the coffee parastatal, Burundi Office of Industrial Cultures, had forsaken its operational activities and extended its regulatory functions by becoming the Office du Café, a mixed-capital company in which the shareholders represent groups from the industry and the government (34 percent). In addition, the Burundi Coffee Company no longer enjoys a monopoly over coffee exports. In 1991, 30 percent of the crop was sold to private exporters through public auction. Nevertheless, full-fledged liberalization and privatization are still a long way off, and the sector remains monopolistic. As for tea, there is no private marketing as yet. The high concentration in these markets, dominated by a few public enterprises, prevents real competition. Thus, effective deregulation remains elusive.

Virtually no policy change occurred at the farmgate level, and the few changes that did take place were sterilized partly by the monopolistic nature of these markets. However, the boom in nontraditional exports (rice and tobacco) offers an interesting contrast to the lack of success in the more visible areas of coffee, tea, and cotton. The liberalization of rice prices and the introduction of private rice hullers led to price increases of about 20 percent between 1989 and mid-1990, turning Burundi from a net importer to a net exporter of rice. Increases in the production of tobacco (which rose from nothing in 1987 to FBu 223 million in 1990) also reflect price incentives, as well as the technical and input support offered by the Burundi Tobacco Company to farmers under contract.

The successful liberalization of the agricultural sector is critical for long-term development in Burundi. In May 1992, based on the lessons of structural adjustment credits I and II, the upfront conditionality of structural adjustment credit III included several new measures to address market and price deregulation. The regulatory framework for smallholders was simplified, through, among other things, the elimination of government constraints on mandatory crops and the quantity and types of inputs to be applied; government-administered producer prices for traditional export crops and agricultural inputs were eliminated; and public enterprise monopoly rights for purchasing, marketing, and processing agricultural products were abolished. In addition, a moratorium was imposed on all new public sector investments in the tea, rice, and palm oil sectors, and transparent criteria for allocating available public lands and resolving land ownership disputes were established.

Factor market liberalization: labor and wages

Setting. The structure of Burundi's labor market reflects the country's low GDP, large rural population, and sizable government sector. The structure of the country's active labor force has changed little since 1979. About 94 percent are employed in the primary sector, 2 percent in the secondary, and 3 percent in the tertiary (table 2.6). Nonsalaried workers represent 94 percent of the active population (80 percent of those older than 10), while wage earners make up only 5 percent of the active population. The private sector provides 29 percent of all salaried employment.

During the first part of the 1980s, the cost per job created in the modern sector reached a high level—between $60,000 and $70,000 (1981 prices). This level reflects the high concentration of public investment in infrastructure and the bias of past policies against labor-intensive investment. In terms of wages, the nominal minimum wage in the two principal cities (Bujumbura and Gitega) grew at about 7.2 percent per year, which, because inflation grew faster, probably did not prevent some erosion in workers' purchasing power. In addition to wages, employers bear substantial social charges, ranging between 30 and 60 percent of the wage bill.

At the onset of adjustment, the expansion of wage labor in Burundi faced many constraints. Freedom of movement was restricted. Labor mobility was restrained, preventing rural labor from moving into urban centers. The

Table 2.6 Comparative structure of the active labor force, 1990
(percent)

Sector	*Burundi*	*Rwanda*	*Zaire*	*Low-income countries*[a]
Primary	94.0	93.0	80.0	79.0
Secondary	1.8	3.0	8.0	8.0
Tertiary	3.4	4.0	12.0	13.0

a. Low-income countries in Africa.
Source: International Labour Office-PECTA (1990).

ministry of labor had to approve all hiring, whether in the public or private sector. Social regulations were numerous, generating considerable red tape. Private employers were responsible for 100 percent of the cost of medical insurance of their employees, which made hiring labor expensive, and indirectly privileged capital-intensive investments (particularly in parastatals in which aid-financed capital goods were transferred frequently to the enterprises without payment). The government is the most important employer, accounting for nearly 40 percent of employment in the modern sector.

Reforms. Labor market deregulation was not the primary focus of either structural adjustment credit I or II. Although structural adjustment credit I did not contain specific employment measures, it did provide incentives for using labor extensively—one of Burundi's comparative advantages. For example, the investment code was amended to reduce incentives for large and highly capital-intensive projects, promoting small and medium-size enterprises instead. The program called for lifting tariff exemptions and removing import prohibitions, as well as measures favoring employment.

Structural adjustment credit II included direct measures for deregulating the labor market by revising labor legislation to allow entrepreneurs to recruit their personnel directly without approval by the labor department; reorienting the role of the placement commission toward supervising the technical staff of the labor department, and reviewing the effects of employment policy; and strengthening the labor department's capacity to assess the skill requirements of employers. Supplementary measures included the abolition of the flat-rate wage tax and of administrative constraints on the mobility of labor.

Implementation. Some employment reform measures under structural adjustment credits I and II were fully implemented (fiscally related measures), but many were implemented only partially (institutional strengthening of the ministry of labor). The ministry of labor preferred to control the labor market rather than promote and review employment policy, impeding the effective liberalization of the sector. Moreover, the measures included in the structural adjustment credits were undoubtedly not those of highest priority for the sector. Again, this was not a question of overall design of the program, since certain constraints not captured by the program appear to have hindered adjustment efforts, including the cost of labor and overregulation. The rigidities of the economy, resource immobility, and the small impact of devaluation on price restructuring harmed the employment market, a situation aggravated by constraints inherent in the employment sector itself. Recent trends suggest that the employment market has not yet adapted to the adjustment processes. Unemployment has risen fivefold since the beginning of the decade, affecting unskilled and semiskilled labor, due in part to a supply-demand mismatch caused by an inadequate skills mix.[16]

On a more positive note, the efforts under structural adjustment credits I and II helped relax conditions for foreign labor and eliminated some fiscal disincentives to employment. Feasibility studies for a private health insurance scheme were also completed. The government eliminated the obligation that private and mixed public-private enterprises obtain prior approval from the ministry of labor for recruitment, and it liberalized conditions for recruitment in public enterprises—they are required to establish a transparent mechanism for announcing vacancies and recruiting. Private and parastatal firms with private capital were authorized to recruit freely, provided that the persons whom they hired were registered with the ministry of labor and were Burundi nationals. Employees still cannot be dismissed without government approval. In January 1992 the government also authorized the establishment of private placement offices and approved the creation of a national confederation of labor unions, unattached to any political party.

Efforts to liberalize the labor market have been positive. For example, in 1990 the average salary in the private sector for managers, accountants, and computer specialists was somewhat higher than in the public sector—triggering resignations by civil servants to seek employment in the private sector. Within the private sector, salary growth in banking and insurance has been the most pronounced. While overall salaries in the modern sector increased by only 14 percent from 1989 to 1990, the nominal increase in banking and insurance was 54 percent. In 1990 and 1991, job offers in business grew at the most rapid rate.

Yet the bias toward capital-intensive investment persists, due to several factors. The cost of creating employment has remained high, preventing a substantial increase in private employment, due essentially to red tape in labor regulations and the comparatively high cost of labor. The bias also exists in the public enterprise sector because aid-financed capital investments tend to be either free or highly subsidized. And several enterprises seem to have taken advantage of the investment code without creating the promised additional jobs. Nonsalary costs (such as social security and medical insurance) represent 30 to 60 percent of base salaries, and formal sector labor compensation is still about four times that of the informal sector. The labor code has not yet been reformed completely, and many employers and employees are still unaware of the new and more liberal regulations. Private employers bear the entire burden of medical insurance. Excessive regulations are still pervasive, and taxes, particularly on foreign-owned private enterprises, are high.

Under the third phase of the program, the government is seeking further reforms to reduce the costs of employing labor, thus promoting production techniques in the modern sector that more accurately reflect

Burundi's comparative advantage in abundant and relatively inexpensive labor. To this end the government has proposed a new draft labor code and measures to deregulate the formal sector and reduce the disparity between it and the informal sector. It also delineates general principles that leave room for collective bargaining, and it eliminates many regulations that would discourage employment.

The labor code will be revised further to introduce flexibility into nondisciplinary layoffs and for temporary employment and apprenticeships. The new labor code is expected to be adopted in late 1993. The revised code calls for a cost-sharing arrangement to replace the requirement that private employers cover 100 percent of costs of medical care for employees; it will also ease regulations on dismissal, and eliminate mandatory wages for various professional groups (with the exception of the minimum wage for unskilled labor).

The financial sector

Setting. Burundi's financial sector is fairly diversified for a country its size. It consists of the central bank, 5 commercial banks, 3 other deposit-taking institutions, 2 well-managed and solvent development banks, 4 insurance companies, a network of 75 savings cooperatives and 3 credit cooperatives, several special funds primarily for home financing and guarantee operations, and 2 social security institutions. Government participation in the equity of financial institutions is pervasive and is either direct or through public sector entities. The government holds a 42 percent share in the capital of the two largest and oldest commercial banks (Credit Bank of Bujumbura and Commercial Bank of Burundi), with foreign parent banks (Société Générale de Belgique and Banque Bruxelles Lambert) holding 49 percent of the capital. Although Burundi has a relatively large number of financial institutions, financial intermediation remains very low, attributable to the low per capita income of the country, the low monetization of the economy, and the lack of competition among financial institutions.

The major constraints on Burundi's financial sector include insufficient orientation toward productive investments and a de facto discrimination against small private sector borrowers. The financial sector is plagued by a lack of financial depth, even in comparison with other Sub-Saharan countries: the central bank does not have full control over money and credit growth, and the legal and regulatory framework for nonbank financial intermediaries, insurance companies, and social security institutions is deficient. While efforts to mobilize domestic credit resources through various guarantee funds date back to 1976, they were eventually harmonized into a single National Guarantee Fund in 1986 because they proved inadequate. The credit system is burdened by an overly complex administrative and regulatory framework, insufficiently adapted to the increasing sophistication of domestic financial institutions. Prior to the adjustment period, the requirement that all credit requests of more than FBu 3 million (about $25,000) be approved in advance by the central bank frequently led to delays (and uncertainty) for potential borrowers. The capital market could not function efficiently because credits were to be classified as discountable or nondiscountable with different lending rates, and various regulations were imposed on each commercial bank, such as minimum liquidity amounts.

Reforms. The government sought to improve credit and monetary policies in the financial sector in order to make the financial intermediation process more efficient, raise the level of funding for productive purposes, and improve resource mobilization by banks and financial institutions.

The first phase of the adjustment program proposed raising the authorized credit ceiling of commercial banks by more than 300 percent to FBu 10 million and reinforcing the guarantee fund to promote small and medium-size enterprises. Furthermore, an ad hoc committee was to address discrimination implicit in the distinction between discountable and nondiscountable credits, the compulsory ratios, and the structure of interest rates.

In the second phase, the government sought to liberalize interest rates and replace credit rationing with a more indirect but efficient way to manage credit and liquidity: it would establish a simplified interest structure with only two rediscount rates—one preferential and the other nonpreferential. The central bank would periodically adjust the discount rate while other rates would be market-determined, and the government called for simplifying credit regulations. Moreover, public enterprises would be allowed to reduce their deposit requirements in the central bank and invest their excess liquidity in alternative financial assets that would yield greater profitability. The agenda also called for eliminating central bank approval for loans of less than FBu 10 million, as well as for the issue of treasury certificates and the establishment of reserve requirements.

Implementation. In general, the reforms have been slow and incomplete. Their design suffered from an inadequate analysis and understanding of the sector's financial structure, position, and performance, and they were formulated without sufficient recognition of monetary credit and regulatory policies.

As part of structural adjustment credit I, the guarantee fund was reactivated and interest rates were brought up to real positive levels. Yet overregulation and oligopolistic behavior (including informal rate-fixing among banks) continued to limit competition among financial institutions. Credit

Bank of Bujumbura's monopoly on obligatory savings, constraints on where public enterprises could deposit their funds, the strict regulation of interest rates, and discriminatory treasury certificate policies—all continued to prevent an efficient allocation of financial resources.

The government and the central bank progressively introduced a more flexible interest rate policy, linking interest rates to the rates obtained during the treasury certificate auctions. Denominations of these certificates were reduced to encourage more potential buyers, and the central bank refinanced them at rates more attractive than their rediscount rate. Interest rates on term and savings deposits were liberalized. More efficient and less discriminatory instruments to manage bank liquidity were introduced, and the monopoly of the parastatal savings institution, Savings Bank of Burundi, over the compulsory savings deposits of wage earners was eliminated. Interest rates, however, did not become fully market-determined.

The monopolistic nature of the financial system has prevented real competition and has hampered the effective liberalization of the financial market. Credit Bank of Bujumbura and Commercial Bank of Burundi alone account for about 80 percent of lending. This situation is compounded by the high concentration of credit recipients. For example, at one big commercial bank, the 5 largest users of credit account for 40 percent of loans outstanding, and the 20 largest account for 68 percent.

Burundi's economic development requires a more competitive, sound, diversified, and institutionally strong financial sector. Institutions must be run according to sound commercial principles, and the government should disengage itself from the equity capital of financial institutions. Institutions whose long-term viability is doubtful should be closed down; other institutions should be merged or restructured. The next phase of the government's reform agenda calls for strengthening the institutional capacity of the central bank to supervise the financial sector, and creating and implementing new credit policies. Institution-building efforts will target banks for strengthening, and weed out nonviable institutions. Additional measures call for reforming the taxation system to remove savings disincentives and the excessive taxation of investment in equity capital. Further reforms in the legal and regulatory environment seek to foster competition among financial institutions, ensure their solvency, and remove impediments to financial innovation.

Public enterprises

Setting. Economic management at the outset of the adjustment program, particularly industrial and commercial policy, was highly centralized and dirigiste. This was a time when command economies were prevalent in Africa. Many public enterprises were created between 1978 and 1981, to provide, among other things, public services, export sector management, and manufacturing goods (filling the gap created by a nonexistent private sector). Public enterprises accounted for 40 percent of gross fixed capital formation, 42 percent of foreign public debt, and 58 percent of debt service and contributed only 16 percent of the formal labor force and about 6 percent of GDP.[17] Directly or indirectly, they controlled all of Burundi's cash crops and 60 percent of its formal manufacturing. At the design level, the lack of feasibility studies led to unsuitable decisions about product types, technology, and production capacity. The situation was further aggravated by poor management, little attention to rate-of-return criteria, inadequate monitoring by the government, and an inappropriate pricing system.

Burundi's public enterprises create several distortions in the country's economy, specifically in resource allocation. Although labor is relatively abundant and inexpensive in Burundi, investments in public enterprises are highly capital-intensive. Yet returns to capital are disappointing, with the sector registering substantial losses. The sector also captures 25 percent of the government's total expenditure, whether through subsidies or forgone revenue. Its debt represents 28 percent of all public debt. However, public enterprises pay only a fraction of the service on their debt, the rest being serviced by the national budget. In addition, an excessive share of public enterprise investments are debt-financed, with equity financing marginalized. At least 75 percent of public enterprise assets have been financed by loans, 35 percent short-term. The government also routinely covers public enterprise losses and exempts them from custom duties and some of their tax burden.

Public enterprises also create significant subsectoral distortions. In the coffee subsector, for example, the administered pricing system allowed the coffee parastatals to receive large margins unrelated to costs or performance. Public enterprises in the coffee subsector also subsidized inputs up to 100 percent. By encouraging large-scale, agroindustrial projects in this and other subsectors, donors, who financed 83 percent of investments in the agricultural sector, supported these distortions. Distortions also exist in the transport and water subsectors in the form of unrealistically low prices for services. The public enterprise that provides passenger transport services relies on regular budgetary subsidies that allow it to set fares at levels that do not guarantee the company's sustainability. In the water and electricity subsectors, REGIDESCO cannot generate sufficient funds to finance, operate, and maintain its infrastructure. This excessive and inefficient presence in the productive subsectors obviously impedes long-run adjustment efforts.

Reforms. Structural adjustment credit I sought to increase the efficiency of public resource allocation by reforming the public enterprise sector. The World Bank wanted to reduce the number of public enterprises and improve the management of those that remained. The main objective of public enterprise reform was thus to limit government participation to only those enterprises that provide vital public services or operate in strategic sectors (box 2.4). Enterprises deemed beyond redemption would be liquidated. Others could be rehabilitated under the discipline of "program contracts," and under the overall supervision of the service in charge of monitoring public enterprise reform. Studies were also to be conducted to identify enterprises that could viably be privatized and to establish a privatization program at a later date. New public enterprises would be limited to economically viable activities for which private investment was not forthcoming. Specifically, structural adjustment credit I proposed closing four enterprises, reintegrating three in public administration, rehabilitating five through program contracts, designing and implementing program contracts for six, reviewing enterprises in the trade and tourism sectors for rehabilitation in a second phase, and preparing a

Box 2.4 The privatization process

Under the privatization legal framework, the government has to choose between three basic privatization approaches: (i) privatization of management through contracts in which private companies are paid to manage publicly owned assets; (ii) privatization of management through leasing arrangements or concessions in which a private company pays the government for the use of publicly owned assets; and (iii) privatization of ownership of the company.

The government is committed to withdraw progressively from the productive sectors to make room for private investors to improve profitability through more effective management. Public agroindustries, however, present a specific challenge as they provide income for tens of thousands of smallholder farmers. Therefore, the government favors a progressive and controlled transfer from public to private ownership consistent with ongoing development projects supporting the agroindustries. The government is convinced that hasty decisions on socially sensitive issues could stall or even derail the ongoing democratization of Burundi institutions. As a result, management or performance contracts are considered as a first (although transitional) step toward other forms of privatization. For the public agroindustries, performance or management contracts will be concluded in 1992. The Moso Sugar Company management contract with a private firm was approved in March 1992, the OTB performance contract is currently under review by the government, and COGERCO's current incentive system, which is based on actual performance, will be used as the basis for a formal performance contract.

In the coffee sector, leasing of public assets is currently under experimentation for the management of coffee-washing stations (SOGESTAL) and coffee-hulling factories (SODECO). Some of the management companies already have majority private ownership and it is expected that they will be fully privatized in the future. For the divestiture of ownership, the government favors a process that will promote ownership among domestic owners.

diagnostic report to assess the potential demand for public enterprises by the private sector. Because implementation progress under structural adjustment credit I was slow, the same measures were carried over to structural adjustment credit II—the four liquidations were to be completed, program contracts were to be signed for 13 enterprises, a privatization program was to be agreed upon, and performance monitoring was to be reinforced.

Implementation. Program contracts developed after detailed diagnostic studies and audits on a case-by-case basis were unsuccessful because of the time and cost required to undertake detailed studies on a systematic basis. From 1986 to 1991, only four enterprises signed program contracts with the government. Thus, in January 1991 the government adopted a more comprehensive approach, classifying public enterprises into categories according to whether they were to be rehabilitated, privatized, or liquidated, and formulating a specific timetable and action plan for each. Since then, 10 enterprises have been liquidated and 5 have been privatized; bids for privatizing the capital or management of another 4 have been issued, and subsidies have declined by 12 percent.

In the third phase, the government is seeking to enhance competition in key sectors by promoting private sector entry, thus increasing the probability of a stronger supply response, and reducing the financial burden of public enterprises on the government. Rehabilitation, privatization, and liquidation are expected to continue. A moratorium will be imposed on new investments in public enterprises targeted for privatization or liquidation. As part of the unified budget process, the public investment program will capture the investments of public enterprises that receive direct or indirect subsidies, and investments will require prior approval from the minister of finance. The government will no longer extend its guarantee of lending to the public enterprises; subsidies to commercial and industrial public enterprises will be eliminated. When structural adjustment credit III reforms are complete, at least 55 percent of the government's current public enterprise portfolio is expected to be under private management, an additional 30.5 percent will be entirely privatized, and 14.5 percent will have been liquidated or reintegrated into the administration. The service in charge of monitoring public enterprise reform will also be restructured.

The regulatory framework

Setting. After a period of emphasizing large public sector projects as an instrument for industrial growth, the government recognized that further industrial development appropriate to the country's scale and needs should largely involve privately owned, small and medium-size enterprises. In the past, private sector development was constrained in part by cultural values, but the major impediment to creating small and medium-size enterprises was the myriad regulations that discouraged entrepreneurial initiative.[18] Administrative regulations hindered businesses in many critical areas, including the length of time required for enterprise creation (see box 2.5 on incorporation) and initial operations (industrial and commercial licensing). The cumbersome regulatory framework reduced the supply response of the private sector to such measures as price deregulation and trade liberalization.

Commercial activities suffered not only from the difficulties associated with the creation of new firms, but also from business laws that were not conducive to profitable business ventures. Many laws are obsolete, dating from the colonial period. Corporate law suffers from a lack of clarity and coherence, and the hierarchy of texts is unclear. For example, two decrees govern bankruptcy laws, but neither one is applied, largely because they are too

Box 2.5 The hurdles of enterprise creation

The process of enterprise creation was a lengthy and complicated affair, and the hurdles for the aspiring entrepreneur were many. The typical process went as follows. First, prior authorization had to be obtained from the ministry of justice. Refusal was possible on many grounds, including the possibility that the company would run against the ill-defined concept of "general interest." Documentation that was required by the ministry included: proof of identity, three copies of the statutes, an extract of judicial and police records for all partners, a document delivered by a tribunal stating that none of the partners had experienced bankruptcy, certification from a bank that equity had been paid in, and an assessment of the value of contribution in kind delivered by appraisers. The minister of justice did not grant incorporation without a favorable written response from the technical ministries whose approval he had requested.

The statutes of the company had to be ratified and signed in the presence of a civil servant, the directeur du notariat, of which there was only one. Once the above conditions were satisfied, the minister's approval was delivered through an ordinance. The status of the company then had to be recorded at the department of judicial affairs of the ministry of justice, which in turn was responsible for publishing it in the Official Bulletin of Burundi. Finally, the company's existence had to be registered at the commercial registry. Relatively heavy fees were associated with this procedure.

Once these steps were completed, the company had legal status but still could not engage in business activities; a secondary process of accreditation was required that involved obtaining a trader card and accreditation as an importer or exporter. Without these, a firm could not legally engage in commerce, import raw materials, or export. Each permit required more paperwork, often duplicating information given at the time of incorporation.

complex. Bankrupt businesses usually close without formal notification, thus creditors cannot easily recuperate outstanding debts.

Reforms and implementation. Structural adjustment credits I and II did not impose specific conditionalities on the regulatory framework. Nevertheless, the government has recognized that the framework must be expanded and has identified various constraints that hinder its development. In May 1990 a World Bank mission made recommendations about the regulatory framework, and the government simplified its procedures in October of the same year. Since then, the regulatory system has been revised several times in an effort to liberalize business activities. A new law allows businesses to register their corporate statutes in one step, and the authorization of the minister of justice for incorporation is no longer required. A trader's card is still required, but its delivery is conditional solely upon registration at the commercial registry. Accreditation of importers and exporters was maintained, but the need for central bank approval was lifted. The ministry of commerce and industry can still deny or delay accreditation, however, and the paperwork remains complex.

Indications suggest that reform of the regulatory framework is progressing well. Thus, structural adjustment credit III will concentrate on revising business laws, specifically the commercial code. These measures call for eliminating inconsistencies and loopholes in existing legal texts, defining the legal status of various types of firms more clearly, and simplifying and extending bankruptcy laws to public enterprises to facilitate the exit of firms.

Social policies and the alleviation of poverty

Setting. In addition to economic and political measures, adjustment and development in Burundi must also account for social dimensions of reform. Among the more important are population pressures, rural poverty, inadequate health care, limited education, the role of women in the social and economic fabric of the country, and the environment. These issues not only have short- to medium-term implications for development (for example, per capita income growth and food security), but also long-term implications for sustainability (as demonstrated by education), as Burundi becomes increasingly active in a competitive international environment. Burundi's social indicators are about average for Sub-Saharan Africa (table 2.7).

Reforms. Social sector policies under the adjustment program were limited, focusing primarily on alleviating poverty. The focus is crucial, because with a per capita income of only $220, Burundi remains one of the poorest countries in the world. In Burundi, poverty is essentially a rural problem given that 94 percent of the population lives in nonurban areas. Everyday hurdles for the poor include distance from schools and health care centers, and lack of potable water.

Structural adjustment credit I did not contain specific policy recommendations with respect to the social sectors or poverty alleviation. Structural adjustment credit II included the preparation of a social action plan and a poverty alleviation program. In collaboration with UNICEF, the UNDP, and the World Bank, the government targeted child nutrition, the role of women in development, support for small productive projects, a food security strategy, and a monitoring system for social indicators.

Implementation. Although structural adjustment credit II measures did not encompass specific actions to cope with the direct social costs of the adjustment program (particularly employment and income redistribution), they were introduced at the same time as certain other reforms began, thus some potentially negative effects were counteracted. For example, when tariffs on electricity, water, and transportation were adjusted, "social," or low-cost, tariffs were instituted for the lowest income segments. The full benefits of structural adjustment credit II social policies were not realized because they could not be put in place easily, and coordination among public agencies, donors, and nongovernmental organizations was inadequate in the face of weak government leadership. In retrospect, the negative social impact of the program on vulnerable groups appears to have been fairly small in Burundi, in part because social sector spending was protected, and in part because 90 percent of the population operates in the subsistence sector.[19]

Unlike many countries pursuing adjustment, Burundi has maintained priorities for health and education. Prior to the adjustment program in 1985, social sector expenditures were about 28 percent of total expenditures. The ratio increased to 33 percent, or 4.4 percent of GDP, in 1991.

Table 2.7 Comparative social indicators, most recent estimates

Indicator	*Burundi*	*Low-income countries*[a]	*Sub-Saharan Africa*
Life expectancy in years	47	62	51
Population/physician	21,000	13,910	23,850
Population/nursing person	4,375	1,740	2,460
Daily caloric supply/capita	1,932	2,416	2,120
Access to safe water[b]	30	68	36
Primary school gross enrollment ratio	71	109	69

a. Same region and income group.
b. As percentage of total population.
Source: World Bank (1992).

The access of low-income groups to health, education, and potable water has improved: more than 60 percent of the population now live within 5 kilometers of a health facility, 70 percent are enrolled in primary education, and 34 percent of the rural population have access to drinking water (tripling from 10 percent).

Despite significant progress in the quality and coverage of public services during the 1980s, poverty remains a critical problem, particularly for the 94 percent of the population living in rural areas. While government expenditures on the social sectors are adequate, public expenditures must be reoriented toward basic services for the poor. Although much has improved, social services are still plagued by many problems in management, quality, urban bias, and insufficient resource allocation for the expansion of social infrastructure.

The third phase of the government's program seeks to improve essential services for the poor by effecting greater cost recovery from high-income users and increasing participation of private and nongovernmental organizations. The government intends to reorient expenditures toward basic services that benefit the poorest segment. Cost recovery in health and in tertiary education will finance improvements in quality. Private sector involvement in social services will be encouraged. Poverty will be attacked through income-generating activities, and actions targeted at the most vulnerable groups and at specific issues, such as AIDs. The continued stress on labor-intensive policies and deregulation of the labor market also seeks to promote the alleviation of poverty.

Outcomes of the adjustment program

Performance during the first two stages of Burundi's adjustment program was mixed. While the reason lies in part with the overly optimistic goals established at the outset, negative internal and exogenous factors also influenced outcomes. Among these were the limited scope of some reform measures, initial hesitancy by the government in implementing reform, the delicate sociopolitical climate, a decline in the terms of trade, periods of drought, and a minimal level of cooperation among donors at the outset.

Macroeconomic indicators

Targets. Performance targets in the first policy framework paper (1986–89) included an average growth rate of 4 percent, an annual inflation rate of less than 10 percent, a reduction in the external debt service ratio to 18.5 percent in 1989, and an increase in the level of official reserves to three months of imports. The external current account deficit (excluding grants) was targeted at an average 6 percent of GDP, and the overall budget deficit ratio (on a commitment basis and without grants) was targeted at an average 5.7 percent for 1986–88. The second and third policy framework papers took into account the weaker outlook for world coffee prices, the marked increase in debt service and aid dependency, and the expanding scope of the reforms. The main objectives were to accelerate annual average GDP growth to about 4.5 percent for 1988–91, reduce the inflation rate from 8 percent in 1988 to 4 percent in 1991, reduce the external debt service ratio from 44 percent in 1987 to about 32 percent in 1991, build up net foreign reserves to four months of imports starting in 1988, reduce the overall budget deficit to 5 percent of GDP in 1991, and increase government revenue and maintain the expansion of domestic credit in line with balance of payment objectives.

Outcomes. On the whole, the macroeconomic goals embodied in the policy framework papers were either not achieved or proved difficult to sustain. (Table 2.2 reveals the mixed results of the adjustment effort. Table 2.8 offers selected indicators of Burundi's actual economic performance.) On average, GDP growth under adjustment fell below that of the early 1980s—3.9 per-

Table 2.8 Selected macroeconomic indicators, 1980–91

Indicator	*1980–85*	*1986*	*1987*	*1988*	*1989*	*1990*	*1991*
Real growth rate (percent)							
GDP at market price	4.6	3.3	5.5	4.9	1.5	3.5	4.9
GDP/capita	1.5	5.8	-3.8	2.6	-5.0	-0.5	2.5
Exports (gnfs)	9.1	-13.1	6.8	10.5	-2.9	-6.0	15.9
Coffee volume	7.1	7.6	-16.1	13.9	-7.9	-0.2	20.6
Imports (gnfs)	1.9	8.1	6.9	-1.1	-15.1	14.7	5.5
Ratios (percent)							
Debt service/exports (gnfs)	14.6	21.7	49.0	36.4	46.2	45.4	32.2
DOD/GDP	24.7	49.7	61.4	79.6	89.0	77.0	83.9
Investment/GDP	16.7	11.6	22.7	15.0	16.8	17.7	16.2
Domestic savings/GDP	2.7	1.1	6.9	1.6	3.3	-2.6	-2.1
Coffee/exports	86.1	88.4	71.0	82.8	80.3	72.3	79.3
Current account/GDP[a]	-13.8	-8.6	-17.9	-14.5	-14.3	-20.8	-18.1
Overall deficit/GDP[a]	-12.6	-8.5	-16.7	-11.6	-9.6	-13.0	-9.7
Other							
Consumer price index (Bujumbura; percentage change)	9.2	1.8	7.1	4.5	11.7	7.0	8.9
Terms of trade (1980=100)	102.4	147.8	92.2	97.4	80.8	64.5	70.2
Unit export price of coffee (cts/lb)	125.6	184.8	102.9	133.3	105.2	73.9	84.8
Real effective exchange rate (1980=100)	127.3	116.4	99.8	87.9	89.1	77.4	77.8

a. Excluding grants.
Source: Government of Burundi.

cent compared with 4.6 percent. Real per capita growth registered an average of 1.5 percent in the early 1980s but only 0.3 percent during the adjustment period. Average growth in all three sectors also declined from the first part of the decade to the next. (The primary sector even experienced negative growth in 1989, but this was largely attributable to the cyclical nature of agricultural production and inclement weather, the repercussions of which were felt throughout the economy.) While the overall structure of output did not change, the modest shifts that did occur were in the direction that would be expected under an adjustment program. The share of agriculture in GDP (at factor cost) declined from an average of 60 percent in the preadjustment period to an average of 56 percent under adjustment. The secondary sector's share increased from 14 percent to 16 percent for the same period, and the tertiary sector increased from 26 percent to 29 percent. Real growth in all three sectors was disappointing, declining from the first part of the decade to the next.

In the *external area,* current account deficits were generally higher than those projected, as the average deficit-to-GDP ratio (excluding grants) rose from 13.8 percent in 1980–85 to 15.7 percent in 1986–91. Export merchandise volume grew by 4.4 percent, slightly less than the average of 6.7 percent in 1980–85. The average ratio for the export of goods and nonfactor services to GDP during the preadjustment period was 9.8 percent. After six years of adjustment, the average increased only to 10.4 percent. The actual volume of imports was lower than target levels in all years except 1990 and 1991, and average volume growth fell to 2 percent in the latter part of the decade.

The volume of coffee exports has followed an uneven pattern since the beginning of the adjustment program. (The recent evolution of coffee exports presented in table 2.9 documents a pattern that corresponds more to agricultural cycles than to changes in external prices and adjustment measures.) Efforts to revitalize Burundi's export sector have unfortunately coincided with a significant drop in world coffee prices, and in 1992 they were at their lowest level in a decade. At the domestic level, the incentives to coffee producers to increase production were marginal given that domestic prices for green coffee remained fixed at FBu 160/kg from 1986 to 1988, increasing only slightly to FBu 175/kg in 1989.

In a fully liberalized coffee sector, a fall in world prices would be expected to signal an exit from the sector or increased production to compensate for lost revenue or both. In practice, fixed producer prices and prohibited uprooting of plants have prevented coffee growers from reacting to price signals. The series of successive devaluations instituted during the adjustment period also permitted the government to refrain from reducing producer prices in the face of collapsing world prices. Devaluation allowed the government to maintain the nominal incomes of coffee planters at comparable

Table 2.9 Export performance, 1980–91

Indicator	Before adjustment						Under adjustment						1980–85 avg.	1986–91 avg.	1980–91 avg.
	1980	1981	1982	1983	1984	1985	1986	1987	1988	1989	1990	1991			
Percentage of total goods (fob)															
Coffee	87.7	87.1	88.5	86.0	82.9	84.3	88.4	71.0	82.8	80.3	72.3	79.3	86.1	79.0	82.5
Tea	2.3	3.1	3.2	3.0	7.2	5.3	2.7	5.3	4.5	6.0	11.5	9.7	4.0	6.6	5.3
Cotton	1.7	1.7	2.8	3.3	0.7	0.3	0.1	4.1	0.6	0.2	0.2	0.0	1.7	0.9	1.3
Hides	0.9	0.5	0.1	0.9	0.7	0.9	0.8	1.5	1.7	3.4	4.7	2.6	0.7	2.5	1.6
Other primary	4.1	3.8	1.1	2.8	2.8	3.7	2.4	3.3	2.4	4.0	4.7	3.5	3.1	3.4	3.2
Manufactures	1.7	2.6	3.3	2.6	4.5	5.3	5.6	13.1	5.8	4.5	5.7	3.8	3.3	6.4	4.9
Re-exports	1.6	1.2	0.9	1.5	1.3	0.1	0.1	1.8	2.1	1.6	0.9	1.1	1.1	1.3	1.2
Total	100.0	100.0	100.0	100.0	100.0	100.0	100.0	100.0	100.0	100.0	100.0	100.0	100.0	100.0	100.0
Growth rates[a]															
Coffee	-31.7	46.3	12.4	-18.5	16.8	17.6	7.6	-16.1	13.9	-7.9	-0.2	20.6	7.1	3.0	5.1
Tea	-18.0	76.6	-2.8	-3.4	46.3	32.3	-15.1	8.6	-5.5	-15.2	24.6	32.7	21.8	5.0	13.4
Cotton	-58.1	6.0	164.1	-6.8	-79.0	-45.3	-36.7	2,187.9	-84.1	-70.5	-33.3	-99.9	-3.2	310.6	153.7
Hides	-50.1	35.4	-21.6	238.0	-34.5	38.6	13.6	-0.4	17.6	29.0	2.7	-10.4	34.3	8.7	21.5
Other primary	-37.3	26.5	-68.7	47.4	-3.9	52.8	54.9	-4.3	248.6	31.3	-40.5	-30.1	2.8	43.3	23.1
Manufactures	42.1	-4.3	111.4	-25.4	95.0	-6.6	129.7	61.5	-19.4	-60.1	-25.8	51.5	35.3	22.9	29.1
Re-exports	0.0	0.0	24.9	25.0	-60.0	167.0	8.8	-32.9	69.5	-44.0	-61.0	2.2	26.1	-9.6	8.3
Total	-31.7	43.8	11.9	-15.2	13.0	18.7	10.7	-7.4	13.4	-8.4	-5.8	16.7	6.7	3.2	5.0

a. Change in the volume of exports.
Source: Government of Burundi.

production levels, sheltering them from the effects of low prices. Failure to adjust domestic producer prices and to introduce quality incentives, combined with large aid-financed sector investments, contributed to delayed reform in the coffee sector.

In terms of *foreign financing*, official development assistance was an important determinant of the country's external financial equilibrium. Net official development assistance averaged $135 million annually in the early 1980s, and increased to $192 million in 1986–91, with per capita equivalents amounting to $30 and $37, respectively. The amount of financing for the overall structural adjustment program (which includes World Bank, IMF, and related donor contributions) mirrors the increases observed in official development assistance. The share of the structural adjustment financing to GDP was 1.3 percent in 1986, and jumped to 3 percent in 1991 (with a high point in 1990 at 5 percent). The grant element throughout the program increased relative to loans: in 1986 it was only 7.3 percent, while in the 1986–91 period it was 24.4 percent.

Total *foreign public debt* soared from 25 percent of GDP in the first half of the 1980s to 74 percent in the second half, and the debt service ratio for the same period increased from 14 percent to 37 percent. This increase reflects the increased levels of borrowing and the nonconcessionality of the loans that were assumed. Both total debt stocks and debt service ratios have now reached levels that, if allowed to rise, could jeopardize the country's long-term adjustment efforts. Much to its credit, Burundi has maintained an excellent repayment record on its debt service, and has begun to address its debt exposure by accepting external assistance in the form of either grants or debt on a concessional basis. The donor community has also made initial efforts to alleviate the debt burden by canceling some outstanding debt, exemplified most recently by France and Belgium.

In the *budgetary* area, government revenue remained slightly below expectations, and expenditures generally rose above agreed-upon ceilings. Compared with the early 1980s, current expenditures increased by 2 percent under adjustment, while capital and net lending expenditures declined from 14.6 percent of GDP to 13.2 percent. Nonetheless, the overall situation has shown very modest improvement. The fiscal deficit as a ratio of GDP declined from an average of 12.6 percent in 1980–85 to 11.5 percent in 1986–91. And despite successive devaluations, the nonmonetary financing of the budget deficit helped bring down inflation from 9.2 percent in 1980–85 to 6.8 percent in 1986–91.

While efforts to increase *investment* bore minimal results, the observed trends were encouraging. Fixed investment rose from an average of 15.6 percent of GDP in the first period to more than 17 percent in the next (the share of private investment increased from 2 percent to almost 3 percent).

The public to private investment coefficient fell from 7.6 to 5.9. The sectoral composition of public investments was essentially unaffected by the adjustment program. While 74 percent of investments went to economic infrastructure in the 1983–88 period, this percentage remained basically unchanged at 76 percent in the 1989–90 period. Investment in social infrastructure declined from 17 percent in the first period to 11 percent in the second; its main components, however—education and health—moved only from 47 to 49 percent, and from 39 to 35 percent, respectively. This relative inertia in the structure of public investments reflects their dependence on aid financing, which shielded them from price incentives, as well as their administratively determined levels and the slow pace at which the government began favoring social and economic infrastructure over productive sectors.

The share of *consumption* in GDP remained largely the same, registering about 98 percent in both periods. Attempts to increase domestic savings were disappointing, as the savings-to-GDP ratio dropped from 2.7 to 1.7 percent.

Summary. There is no single explanation for Burundi's mediocre macroeconomic performance. Rather, several factors contributed to these outcomes. First, the mixed results reflect problems with the policy framework papers' projections. In fact, a World Bank paper covering policy framework papers for 21 different Sub-Saharan African countries acknowledged that "overall, the majority of projected values have turned out to be ambitious in the sense that they diverge from actual values by more than 10 percent" (Faruqee 1992), and the budget and current account deficit projections (as ratios to GDP) have deviated substantially across countries. More specifically, the study found that Burundi's policy framework papers were "overly optimistic" for budget deficits and domestic savings as a percentage of GDP and for the growth of exports of goods and nonfactor services. They were deemed "optimistic" for investment-to-GDP ratios and real GDP growth. In retrospect, it is clear that certain targets could have been met only in the best of circumstances.

Second, external and domestic variables account for some of the results. Deteriorating terms of trade, poor weather, and civil disturbance from years of ethnic rivalry are partly to blame. Third, flaws in the design and delays in the implementation of some adjustment measures are also responsible, the latter a function of the change in government in 1987 and the absence of government internalization.[20] Another important consideration is the mobilization of generous but untied financial assistance to the country by the donor community, and the minimal initial coordination among the donor community to reinforce adjustment reforms. Untied external investments that serve national commercial interests may have delayed restructuring and encouraged the status quo.

Sectoral outcomes

Primary sector and diversification. Because Burundi has one of the highest agriculture-to-GDP ratios in the world (close to 60 percent of GDP at factor cost prior to adjustment), restructuring its primary sector was of paramount importance. Throughout the program, the share of agriculture declined somewhat to 55 percent, but the shares of the food and export crop subsectors did not register any growth (remaining at 77 and 9 percent respectively, in the preadjustment and postadjustment periods). Food crops grew at an annual average of only 3.1 percent during the decade (just keeping pace with population growth), while cash crops grew by 16 percent. The markets for food crops are poorly developed, and the only incentive for increasing production is meeting population growth. Bananas, roots, and tubers account for the majority of food crop production, while cereals and beans contribute a much smaller share of total output. Overall, banana and root crop production expanded under the adjustment program. Despite significant increases in rice output (box 2.6), cereal production rose only slightly, reflecting the stagnation of maize and declining bean output after 1987.

Although there has been little evidence of a production shift from nontradables to tradables, there has been a discernible movement toward diversification within the tradables sector. There are also some indications

Box 2.6 Liberalization and supply response in the rice markets

Rice production increased significantly under the adjustment program due to government investments in irrigated and rain-fed rice, the introduction of high-yielding varieties, a growing urban demand, and the liberalization of rice marketing.

Large-scale rice growing was introduced in Burundi in the early 1970s. At that time, the country consumed more rice than it produced and imported the difference. At present, however, roughly 30,000 tons of rice a year are produced, leaving a surplus in excess of domestic consumption. Yet government investments in the Imbo plain, where most rice is grown, account for only part of the rice success story. It was the steps taken in 1989 to liberalize paddy marketing that led to an increase in exports of hulled rice by private companies. Until then, the parastatal SRD-Imbo had a monopoly for the purchase and marketing of rice.

In 1989 the company transferred its rice-purchasing functions to village associations, which have since freely competed with each other. The value of exports rose from FBu 53 million in 1988 to FBu 182.9 million in 1989. Although there is potential for exporting rice to neighboring Rwanda and Zaire, the complexity of distribution networks tends to preclude public involvement and leaves only private companies to exploit such opportunities. Output projections for the areas now under cultivation indicate the potential for rice exports to triple.

that producers have become more interested in producing tobacco and food, for which the relative price has increased over the past few years. However, few agricultural producers seem to have measurably changed the composition of their production. The explanation for this lies in some of the main causes of the general lack of a supply response in Burundi: farmers are unfamiliar with other crops, the government places pressure on them to remain in their subsectors, sufficient price signals are absent, and, in coffee, large-scale, aid-financed development projects promote production and export.

Administrative impediments and price rigidities aside, indications suggest that some level of export diversification did take place at the expense of coffee (table 2.9). Calculations show that the proportion of coffee in total exports declined steadily between 1979 and 1991 (from 92 percent to 80 percent).[21] This is an encouraging development given the preponderance of coffee among Burundi's export crops and the fluctuations of world prices, two factors that can have a significant impact on the financial health of Burundi's balance of payments and government budget. Tea exports, which rose in the 1980–85 period, have since stagnated, due to poorly managed tea factories, insufficient producer incentives (which discourage producers from harvesting), and inadequate fertilizer supply. Since 1986 the production of cotton fiber has declined, attributable to noncompetitive producer prices (which have remained constant since 1987), low and stagnating yields, and irregular input supplies from the managing parastatal Cotton Management Company. Hides have displayed the most regular and uninterrupted increase, from less than 0.5 percent in 1981 to more than 4 percent in 1990.[22] Again on the positive side, several nontraditional exports have developed in the past few years, representing a small proportion of total agroindustrial exports (4.6 percent), but increasing due to the government's more positive attitude toward the private sector. Though nontraditional exports contribute only a small share of total exports, their high average annual growth rate of 10.6 percent since 1985 underscores the dynamism of the emerging private sector and its ability to respond to incentives. The proportion of manufactures increased under the adjustment program, a sector that began exporting goods only relatively recently (figure 2.1).

The impact of exchange rate adjustments on the external trade sector has generally been favorable. Overall, exports grew and diversified in response to devaluations. However, for traditional exports, which are subject to fixed producer prices, the devaluations had limited impact on production but did increase the profitability of the subsectors as a whole, especially for coffee and tea. In contrast, since prices in tobacco are not controlled, these producers appear to have benefited the most. Among nontraditional exports, primary products appear to have grown significantly in response to exchange rate measures. (The main constraint on increasing nontraditional exports has been the unavailability of reliable, cheap, and frequent flights to Europe, and for horticultural products, it also has been poor project design.) Conversely, imports remained stagnant or declined. All categories of imports fell (except for capital goods), which can be explained in part by the increased competitiveness of local production relative to imports following the devaluations and increased aid flows.

During the second phase of adjustment, the government was committed to becoming more of a regulator and promoter than a producer and processor for the majority of productive activities. Commitment, however, did not translate into action. The government's dominant position, exercised through numerous public enterprises, restricted supply response in the agricultural sector. Increased export earnings from successive devaluations were absorbed almost entirely by agroindustrial public enterprises. To date, the government remains the only real economic agent for the principal export and import-substitution crops. Coffee marketing and agricultural inputs were not liberalized (although the rice sector was successfully reformed). Prior to April 1992, agricultural inputs had been subsidized, and the price of traditional export crops administered (and kept at low levels) by the government. This stance encouraged the inefficient use of inputs and discouraged increased and better-quality output. Other deterrents to supply response were capital constraints, inadequate access to land, the weak domestic demand for food crops (a function of the scarcity of urban centers and a tradition of subsistence agriculture), poor soil fertility due to erosion and overuse, and the reluctance of farmers to increase their dependency on a largely government-controlled market, given the country's political and

Figure 2.1 Burundi's coffee and merchandise exports, 1982–91

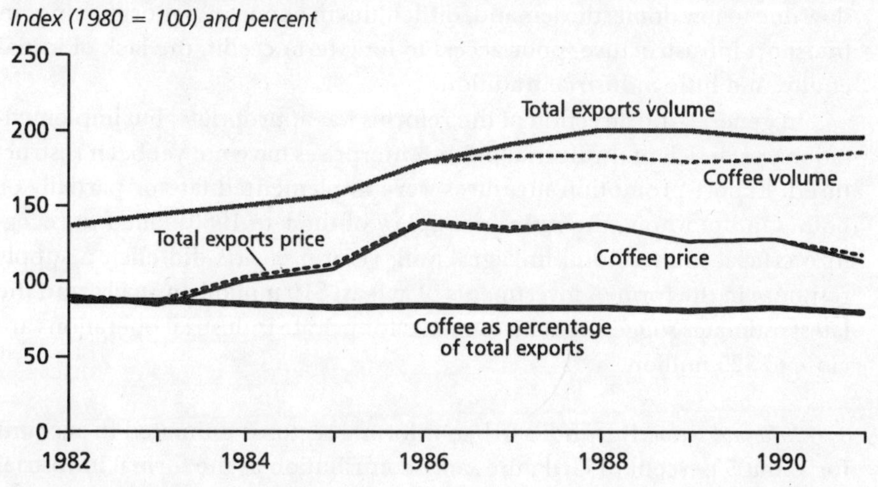

Source: World Bank data.

social history. Nonetheless, new export diversification initiatives, such as green beans, passion fruit, and flowers, have emerged.

Industrial sector. Burundi's industrial sector accounts for about 5 percent of GDP (about the same as in 1984 and about half the share in most other low-income countries), comprises some 200 firms engaged in manufacturing, and is dominated by public enterprises. The modern sector employs about one percent of the active population. Production and employment in the private manufacturing sector are dominated by two breweries. Foreign ownership has declined since the early 1980s.[23] Most of the manufacturing output goes to the local market, and production is concentrated in typical simple import-substitution activities. The import intensity of the sector is more than one-third of gross output.

Since the mid-1980s, industrial growth has been slow but positive. Real output increased by about 4.6 percent annually between 1986 and 1991. (Manufacturing output fell by 5.8 percent in 1989 due to a drop in demand—attributable to the drought, which increased food prices and reduced disposable income—and due to an increase in the transaction tax from 12 to 15 percent.) Investments picked up in absolute terms during the second half of the 1980s. This growth reflected a stimulated private sector under the adjustment measures: the share of the private sector in industrial investments rose from about 25 percent in 1978–82 to 85 percent in 1989.

Both the overwhelming presence of the government as a producer and the large share of aid-financed investment (which was inevitably channeled through the public sector) have been the primary determinants of the industrial sector's slow take-off and relative inability to respond to market signals. The progress of the industrial sector under adjustment has also been slow due to low domestic demand, difficulties in exporting, shortcomings in transport infrastructure, poor access to long-term credit, the lack of initial equity, and little industrial tradition.

In general, the direction of the reforms was appropriate, but implementation was deficient. Industrial public enterprises have not yet been restructured. Export promotion measures were implemented late or partially or both. On the whole, the industrial policy of the late 1980s failed to recognize crucial intersectoral linkages. Still, reform efforts did elicit a supply response in the form of investments of at least $10 million annually, and the latest estimates suggest that investments for private industrial operations are close to $25 million.

Informal sector. Burundi's urban informal sector is estimated to account for about 5 percent of GDP, the same contribution as the formal industrial sector. The main activities are food production, tailoring, wood and metal working, construction, and repairs. Half of the activities are concentrated in the garment subsector. Half of the businesses are conducted in private homes, and about 20 percent rent equipment from other entrepreneurs. Only 12 percent of the firms have access to electricity. Most informal workers are Burundi nationals (75 percent), while many of the foreigners are Zairians who emigrated in the 1960s. The level of education is relatively low—two-thirds did not finish the third grade, and only 14 percent have secondary education. The average monthly salary is the equivalent of $17, which is three to four times less than average compensation in the formal sector.

Concentrated primarily in Bujumbura, the informal sector doubled in size between 1986 and 1989, based on national accounts statistics. The sector's growth is due largely to the more liberal economic environment under the adjustment program, particularly the greater freedom of movement, which was tightly controlled until late 1988. Yet the sector remains relatively underdeveloped, constrained by poor access to credit, by regulatory and legal issues, and by local taxation. Despite recent growth, the sector remains relatively small—at about half the average size estimated for Sub-Saharan Africa—attributable to minimal trading and industrial traditions.

Public enterprises and private sector development. In general, outcomes were unsatisfactory. Public enterprise management remained inefficient, an employment policy based on productivity criteria was still absent, and the public sector was not opened to private investors. In fact, the government continued to acquire shares in public enterprises and their numbers actually increased from 74 in 1986 to 86 in 1991, despite seven liquidations. A proposed study on the potential for privatization was not completed until July 1991. And it was not until the same year that the government adopted a global approach to public enterprises, classifying them according to whether they would be liquidated, privatized, or rehabilitated. As of 1991 public enterprises still controlled directly or indirectly all of Burundi's cash crops and 60 percent of its formal manufacturing. The public sector's overall share in the economy has remained essentially unchanged, averaging 27 percent in 1983–85 and an estimated 28 percent in 1990. Furthermore, transfers and subsidies (primarily to public enterprises) increased from an average of 1.2 percent of GDP between 1983 and 1985 to an estimated 2.4 percent of GDP in 1990, primarily in the form of capital subsidies provided by Burundi's external donors.

Efforts to promote private sector development have been disappointing, particularly in terms of shifting productive activities from the public to the private sector, and promoting private sector growth. Legacy is one of the important factors in the slow transition. Years of isolation have limited the exposure of private enterprises to international business practices. Past restrictions on travel, limited participation in import-export trade, and tightly circumscribed foreign financial transactions all weakened outside experience and precluded contacts for local private entrepreneurs. More recently, private entrepreneurs suffer from poor information services and expensive telecommunications, airfares, and freight fares. Furthermore, management expertise is weak: most managers do not know their firm's production costs, nor the importance of using depreciation and replacement value in cost accounting (rather than nominal purchase values). Product quality is poor. Policy barriers, regulatory constraints, and low domestic demand have also hampered the sector. And poor access to long-term credit and the absence of initial equity have hindered private investment. But the foremost reason has been the overwhelming presence of the government and the almost total absence of any long-standing tradition in trade, handicrafts, or industry.

As for measures already taken, private investment has not yet responded to them, probably because the measures, while necessary, were insufficient by themselves. Burundi's heavy juridico-regulatory environment, the inadequacy of the banking sector and its credit rationing policies, the crowding out of the private sector by public sector borrowing, the difficulty of entering those sectors monopolized by public enterprises, and the high cost of the transactions tax and of labor all contributed to limiting private sector development. In addition, little has been done to encourage direct foreign investment, and the bias toward loan-financed, capital-intensive investment has persisted. Price-fixing agreements among banks also undermined sectoral reform. Although real term deposit rates fluctuated annually with the inflation rate, they were not adjusted systematically to remain positive. The cost of employment creation remained high, preventing a substantial increase in private sector employment. This constraint was due essentially to red tape in labor regulations and the comparatively high nonwage costs of labor. The discretionary way in which tax breaks under the investment code were granted encouraged uneven treatment of entrepreneurs and lowered predictability and accountability, essential variables for private sector development.

Despite the false starts, some progress has been made. Under the second phase of adjustment, several nonviable public enterprises were liquidated, program contracts for public companies scheduled for rehabilitation were established, the recovery of onlent funds to public enterprises and the collection of taxes and dividends were improved, and two enterprises made staff cuts. The performance of the sugar complex (Moso Sugar Company) improved significantly, allowing it to assume part of its debt service obligations, and private interests assumed the management of the company with an option to purchase it later. The efficiency of the public transit company also improved as fares were increased and cost-cutting measures introduced. The structural adjustment effort has clearly played an important role in establishing an environment that is conducive to private sector development, especially for nontraditional products not controlled by public enterprises. These sectors have shown a strong supply response, and farmers generally receive a better return to labor than for state-administered crops. Most recently, new exports have been developed by the private sector in hides, decorative plants, and fruits and vegetables.

The business climate in Burundi has improved markedly since 1990. Most of the cumbersome procedures of the past have been either eliminated or simplified. The system is considerably more transparent, improving the competitiveness of private firms. The authorities are increasingly recognizing that private sector development is in the interest of the economy as a whole, since private business could generate a significant share of tax revenue and employment. For example, in the urban areas, a recent USAID-financed study indicates that, while private firms accounted for only 7.3 percent of national GDP, they contributed 58 percent of the national total value-added tax, 55 percent of the tourist tax, 40 percent of import duties, 24 percent of corporate income, and 9 percent of export taxes.

Private sector development has been disappointing, particularly in the shift of productive activities from the public to the private sector and in overall private sector growth. Part of the reason is years of isolation, past restrictive policies, poor information services, and high transport costs. But the foremost reason has been the overwhelming presence of the government in the productive sectors. In the public sector, progress was disappointing in terms of improving the efficiency of public enterprise management, developing an employment policy based on productivity criteria, and opening the public sector to private investors. In short, the private sector was constrained from developing, and in the public sector the government was reluctant to encourage reform and reduce the number of public enterprises.

More time will be required so that past efforts and new reforms can be translated into concrete performance. Private sector development will continue to depend on macroeconomic approaches that seek to remove policy and regulatory impediments, to increase know-how, and to develop a skilled labor force. In the short term, the focus should be on improving and expanding vocational training facilities and management programs. In the long term, the objective should be to upgrade and expand primary and secondary education. Further political change may be necessary for long-term confidence to be restored. Investors, both domestic and foreign, need the assurance of long-term political and economic stability before they risk their assets in productive activities. All this takes time.

Social sectors and income distribution. The potentially adverse social effects of adjustment programs can take the form of a decline in real wages, poorer nutrition, reduced subsidies, higher interest and tax rates, and increased unemployment. Fortunately, the overall social impact of the adjustment program seems to have been fairly small in Burundi. In general, access to health, education, and potable water registered improvements under the adjustment program, despite a rapid population growth rate.

While GDP per capita improved only slightly during the adjustment period, the real monetary income of farm households rose by almost 1 percent. In the modern sector, civil service pay rose by an average of 5 percent annually in the late 1980s.[24] And the income of the export production sector apparently rose faster than that of local trade. Following devaluations, exporters enjoyed a greater increase in income than did producers of import substitutes and local market products.

In terms of nutrition, Burundi is practically self-sufficient in food, which accounts for less than 5 percent of imports. Per capita daily caloric intake, while having declined slightly, averages around 2,200 and is still above the FAO minimum of 2,100. However, the lipid intake is inadequate (44 percent of the FAO minimum), and regional disparities in caloric intake exist.

One area that appears to have placed a burden on economic groups is taxes. The overall tax burden (as measured by receipts over GDP) rose during the adjustment period—from about 14 percent in 1980–85 to about 17 percent in 1986–90. Caviezel and Fouga (1989) suggest that the tax burden on farmers rose from 34.1 to 39.5 percent. Conversely, the tax burden on town dwellers eased, from 65.9 percent to 60.5 percent. In another aspect of fiscal policy, capital expenditures in social sectors declined, but current expenditures increased. The reduction in social investment is due in part to greater financial responsibility at the local government level, and by municipalities and communities.

In education, the share of current expenditures (primarily salaries) allocated to this sector increased from 20.7 percent in 1980–85 to 26 percent in 1986–90. Expenditures on textbooks and small equipment were defrayed by external donations. However, the share of educational costs borne by families is high relative to the rest of Africa, amounting to about 30 percent in primary school, 2 percent in secondary, and 13 percent in higher education. While primary school enrollment has risen and benefited a greater number of the poor (by splitting sessions and increasing class sizes), the potential exists for negatively affecting the quality of education. Similarly, in the health sector, a considerable improvement in primary health care infrastructure was not accompanied by appropriate personnel assignments and recurrent cost allocations. In sum, public expenditures in the social sectors should be reoriented toward further quality improvements in basic services that benefit the poor.

The stabilization policy slowed the growth of employment in the public and semipublic sector. Thus far, it appears that laid-off workers have managed to find new jobs, although the small size and growth of the private sector continues to offer limited opportunities. It is assumed that poverty will rise in agriculture as it will be the first to absorb the growing population. Given the regulatory rigidities, incomplete implementation of reforms, and unsteady economic growth, it seems that the current employment situation is due more to lack of adjustment than to the process itself.

The prudent monetary policy followed by the government during adjustment has kept prices relatively low. Inflationary pressures have been due to fluctuations in food production, agricultural marketing problems, and poor weather. And while some public tariffs were raised in 1989–90, the lowest-income groups were spared the full impact by the imposition of special low-cost tariffs.

Income distribution was affected by devaluations of the FBu under the adjustment program, both directly through wages and indirectly through spinoffs from import substitution. A widespread perception now shared among government officials in Bujumbura is that wages and salaries in the private sector are substantially higher than those in the public sector given the same level of qualification. This gap is believed to have widened as private sector wages increased with inflation, while public sector wages remained frozen (aside from two isolated 10 percent raises in 1989 and 1992). The relative wage differential is beginning to encourage the better elements of the civil service to seek employment in the private sector, thereby laying the foundation for the further disengagement of the state from some economic activities, and boosting the development of the private sector.

The rise in the price of imported goods—due to devaluation—has affected persons with fixed incomes, such as government employees and those working for minimum wage. Yet, since fixed-income earners are still relatively well off relative to the entire population and make up a very small percentage of the total population, the devaluations have in fact hurt higher-income groups more than they have lower-income groups. This dimension of the adjustment program has tended to improve rural-to-urban terms of trade, since most of the higher-income group lives in Bujumbura. The devaluations have also affected consumption patterns, shifting purchases toward locally produced goods as opposed to imported items. The main beneficiaries of such spending are domestic producers, primarily in the informal sector.

In general, rural purchasing power has remained the same except for producers of coffee, tea, and cotton, who have suffered real declines in producer prices. The monetary income of rural households has increased annually by 0.9 percent during the adjustment period, compared with 0.3 percent in the preceding period. In the modern urban sector, the wages of civil servants increased by 5 percent annually between 1986 and 1989. Yet consumer prices in Bujumbura increased by 6.3 percent annually during the same period, eroding purchasing power by about 1.3 percent annually. Inflation was lower in rural areas, in which imports represent only about 10 percent of consumption and fewer exchanges are monetized, thus reducing the nominal income gap in favor of urban dwellers.

Final remarks

It is perhaps too early to judge the efforts of all who have contributed to Burundi's incipient adjustment effort. Economic adjustment is a medium- to long-term undertaking, not one that can be measured fully in the short term according to targets and indicators. Measuring the success of programs poses challenges, particularly during the initial stages. Depending on the methodology used for determining outcomes, performance may appear satisfactory or less so. What may at first appear a failure may instead be only an early prognosis as certain reforms simply require a longer sustained effort than had been originally anticipated. An appreciation of the difficulties in introducing structural change is essential to determining the performance of an adjustment program.

The nascent stages of Burundi's adjustment effort are now over. As the country continues to tackle its pressing development challenges and engage itself further in an increasingly competitive and international environment, the need to continue its reform program remains more necessary than ever. The effort will not be without its difficulties; as demonstrated, adjustment programs encompass a complex series of interdependent policy prescriptions that are often sensitive in nature and that can be difficult to implement. Structural reform, as a means of contributing to effective economic change and sustainable growth in developing countries, has proven to be a long-term undertaking. And though the experience has shown that the successful application of adjustment efforts may not yield immediate returns, the efforts ensure a foundation for sustainable and equitable growth.

Notes

1. The public enterprise (PE) sector greatly expanded during 1978–81, appropriating 40 percent of gross fixed capital formation (GFCF), 42 percent of outstanding foreign debt, and 58 percent of debt service, but accounting for only 16 percent of the formal sector labor force and almost 6 percent of GDP. The average for Sub-Saharan Africa is 20–25 percent of GFCF, 25–30 percent of modern sector employment, and 15 percent of GDP. By the mid-1980s, the government owned and operated 57 PEs, which were engaged in a wide variety of commercial and social activities.

2. It was apparently for the sake of prudence and with the objective of introducing the measures gradually that the government did not officially inform the public of any new measures.

3. Under the leadership of President Buyoya, this trend has begun to be reversed. Most notably, a referendum on a new pluralistic constitution was submitted to popular vote in March 1992 and approved by a majority of the voting population. National legislative and presidential elections took place in the summer of 1993.

4. Contributors to Burundi's structural adjustment program have included Germany, France, USAID, the European Community, Japan, Switzerland, IDA, and Saudi Arabia.

5. Gross foreign reserves amounted to 2.3 months of imports (goods and nonfactor services) in 1987 and jumped to 5.2 months of imports in 1989. Due partly to excessive foreign reserves, the World Bank proposed a smaller structural adjustment credit III operation in the amount of $30 million. (Structural adjustment credit I, in combination with a special facility for Africa of $16.2 million, amounted to $31.2 million; structural adjustment credit II was $90 million.)

6. The problem of conditionality overload is not unique to Burundi. The average number of World Bank conditions per structural adjustment credit increased almost threefold between 1980–82 and 1988–89.

7. Policy framework papers drafted jointly by the government, the IMF, and the World Bank outline the expected outcomes of policy reforms and key macroeconomic targets. As of May 1991, 87 policy framework papers had been prepared for 29 countries with structural adjustment facility and extended structural adjustment facility programs. Burundi's participation in drafting policy framework papers was minimal until the third policy framework paper in 1989. The fifth, and latest, policy framework paper covers 1992 to 1995.

8. Later policy framework papers did not mention specific credit targets.

9. From 1976 to November 1983, the Burundi franc was pegged to the U.S. dollar at $1 for FBu 90. This rate was implicitly devalued by 30 percent in November 1983 when Burundi adopted its peg to the SDR at a rate of FBu 122.7 per SDR.

10. The weight of the U.S. dollar in the SDR is about 42 percent.

11. According to the IMF (Johnston and Williams 1991), gold exports are exempt from the foreign exchange surrender requirement, and gold traders are permitted to import and hold foreign currency. The foreign currency is used by traders to purchase gold locally, which is bought primarily in hard currency. The sellers of gold hold or export the hard currency or convert it into Burundi francs (or the currencies of neighboring countries) through the black market to purchase goods and services locally. In some cases, gold is purchased with a transfer of hard currency to the gold seller's bank account held abroad.

12. Devaluations can also be used to moderate the gap between the official and parallel exchange rates. One measure of the effectiveness of nominal devaluations is the real effective exchange rate, which takes into account relative price developments. It is through changes in the real exchange rate that nominal devaluations can improve a country's international competitiveness. However, if devaluations lead to excessive inflation, their effectiveness is diminished.

13. The purpose of the open general license system is to liberalize exports and imports more fully. Only a limited number of goods are restricted, primarily for security reasons. An open general license was introduced in May 1992.

14. The public sector is the main beneficiary of foreign exchange receipts, while private sector importers constitute the lion's share of the demand for foreign exchange.

15. The number of importers grew from 145 in 1985 to more than 400 in 1991.

16. For a thorough discussion of employment issues, see *Politique de l'emploi au Burundi: bilan et perspectives*, ILO-PECTA, Addis Ababa, 1990.

17. The average for Sub-Saharan Africa is 25–30 percent of gross fixed capital formation, 25–30 percent of modern sector employment, and 15 percent of GDP.

18. Higher social status was given to administrative and military positions compared with those in trade and industrial activities.

19. The terms of trade of agriculture improved slightly in relation to the modern sector, owing essentially to the fall in real incomes in the urban (essentially public) sector. The stabilization program was reflected in a slowdown of employment in the public sector, while absorption of labor by the nonagricultural (informal and formal) sector was very low due to rigidities that persisted in the economy (regulations).

20. Yet, even if the adjustment measures had been implemented fully and the performance indicators had shown impressive improvements, it would be fallacious to suggest that the reform measures by themselves were solely responsible for successful adjustment.

21. A three-year running average method was used to smooth over odd values and to yield a better estimate of the overall trend. Calculations based on volume reveal that the coffee index fell noticeably relative to total merchandise exports beginning in 1987, the year when the world price of coffee began its downward spiral.

22. Hides have a small import component in their production and thus respond well to devaluations that do not affect their input prices.

23. This phenomenon is attributable to the "Burundization" efforts of the past, to foreigners selling their interests in nonviable activities (made temporarily profitable by protection and tax exemptions) when investment code benefits run out, and to the emergence of a small number of new Burundi entrepreneurs.

24. This increase was due to a general salary increase of 10 percent at the end of 1989 and regular annual increments.

References

Banque de la République du Burundi. 1988–92. *Bulletin Trimestriel.*

Brautigam, Deborah. 1991. "Governance and Economy: A Review." Policy Research Working Paper 815. World Bank, Policy and Review Department, Washington, D.C.

Burundi, Ministère du Travail. 1990. "Le secteur non-structuré urbain au Burundi: analyse des données d'une enquête réalisée dans quatre villes." Service de la Planification de l'Emploi et des Ressources Humaines.

Caviezel, L., and P. Fouga. 1989. "L'Ajustement structurel: l'emploi et la pauvreté au Burundi." University of Bujumbura, Faculty of Economic and Administrative Sciences, Bujumbura.

Corbo, Vittorio, and Stanley Fischer. 1991. "Adjustment Programs and Bank Support: Rationale and Main Results." Policy Research Working Paper 582. World Bank, Country Economics Department, Washington, D.C.

Faruqee, Rashid. 1993. "How Macroeconomic Projections in Policy Framework Papers for the Africa Region Compare with Outcomes." Policy Research Working Paper 1168. World Bank, Africa Regional Office, Washington, D.C.

Frenkel, Michael, and Martin Klein. 1992. "Burundi: The Exchange Rate and Its Role in the Adjustment Process." University of Mainz, Mainz, Germany, and University of Bonn, Bonn, Germany.

International Labour Office-PECTA. 1990. *Politique de l'emploi au Burundi: bilan et perspectives.* Addis Ababa.

International Monetary Fund. 1992a. "Burundi: Improving Central Bank Monetary and Foreign Exchange Operations." Exchange and Trade Relations Department, Washington, D.C.

International Monetary Fund. 1992b. *International Financial Statistics.* Washington, D.C.

Johnston, Barry, and J. Calvin Williams. 1991. "A Review of the Exchange Arrangement and Exchange System of Burundi." International Monetary Fund, Exchange and Trade Relations Department, Washington, D.C.

Laïdi, Zaki. 1989. *Enquête sur la Banque Mondiale.* Paris: Fayard.

Lonsdale, John. 1986. "Political Accountability in African History." In Patrick Chabal, ed., *Political Domination in Africa: Reflections on the Limits of Power.* New York: Cambridge University Press.

Manguelle, Daniel Etounga. 1991. *L'Afrique, a-t-elle besoin d'un programme d'ajustement culturel?* Paris: Editions Nouvelles du Sud.

Migdal, Joe S. 1988. *Strong Societies and Weak States: State-Society Relations and State Capabilities in the Third World.* Princeton, N.J.: Princeton University Press.

Montalti, Lydia, and Claude Pigariol. 1992. "Burundi: éléments pour l'élaboration d'une politique nationale de l'emploi" (Employment Study). World Bank, Africa South Central and Indian Ocean Department, Country Operations Division, Washington, D.C.

Phillips, Luci Colvin. 1991. *Burundi: Regulatory Framework for the Private Sector in Burundi.* United States Agency for International Development, Bujumbura.

World Bank. 1988. *Adjustment Lending: An Evaluation of Ten Years of Experience.* Policy and Research Series 1. Washington, D.C.: World Bank.

———. 1992. *Social Indicators of Development 1991–92.* Baltimore: Johns Hopkins University Press.

———. 1993. *Social Indicators of Development 1992–93.* Baltimore: Johns Hopkins University Press.

Younger, Stephen D. 1991. *Aid and the Dutch Disease: Macroeconomic Management When Everybody Loves You.* Cornell Food and Nutrition Policy Program Working Paper 17. Cornell University, Ithaca, N.Y.

Zodrow, G. 1990. "Capital Income Taxation in the Industrial Sector in Burundi." Rice University, Department of Economics, Houston, Texas.

3

Côte d'Ivoire: fettered adjustment

Lionel Demery

Economic adjustment has not been easy for Côte d'Ivoire, and the record shows that after ten years of "adjustment," little fundamental had changed by the end of the 1980s. The limited adjustment that was achieved was at considerable cost. Negative real GDP growth characterized the decade, and poverty has risen steeply as a result. Both adverse trends can be attributed in part to weaknesses in the adjustment effort. Despite its reliance on expenditure-reducing policies, the government has failed to solve its fiscal problems. And policy-induced distortions in trade and exchange rates have persisted. From these perspectives, the case illustrates some of the repercussions of not adjusting in any fundamental sense, and it offers insights into what the counterfactual to structural adjustment might entail. Adjustment operations by the World Bank and the International Monetary Fund have achieved some measure of policy reform, but this can be characterized as too little and too late. The fundamental problems remain unaddressed.

Early attempts at adjustment were made during 1981–86, and some progress was achieved, due in part to more favorable external circumstances. In the event, however, the adjustment impetus failed, and later efforts at adjustment during 1987–91 did not achieve the macroeconomic policy reforms that are needed. In short, we distinguish three periods in the adjustment experience of Côte d'Ivoire. The first, 1975–80, is the destabilizing period, when macroeconomic imbalances grew to crisis proportions. The second, 1981–86, can be termed a period of partial adjustment. The third, 1987–91, is a period of inadequate or fettered adjustment.[1]

Three major constraints fettered the adjustment effort:

- The severity and recurrence of economic shocks, as evidenced by the continued decline in the terms of trade over the decade. The decline is due in part to a concentration on coffee and cocoa in the country's foreign exchange earning sector.

- The persistence of rigidities and distortions, including the pegging of the CFA franc to the French franc, the movements of which have undermined the country's competitiveness; nominal rigidity in domestic wages; domestic price rigidity, due to the oligopolistic structure of the country's product markets; and the pervasive influence of the state in the domestic economy.
- The reluctance of the government to take the need for adjustment seriously and to identify itself with the adjustment programs supported by the World Bank. Political commitment to the reform process has suffered from this lack of ownership. And the government has been reluctant to revise its expectations sufficiently quickly in the face of rapidly changing external circumstances.

Given the fettered nature of adjustment in Côte d'Ivoire, what lessons can be learned? The following lessons are highlighted in this chapter:

- An appropriately determined real exchange rate is critical for an adjustment program. Failing to correct disequilibrium in the real exchange rate can undo the major part of the adjustment effort. For Côte d'Ivoire it is clear that the overvaluation of the real exchange rate has not only seriously fettered trade policy, but has also obliged the authorities to rely heavily on internal adjustment. It is also difficult to achieve other objectives of adjustment with such a serious underlying relative price distortion: trade liberalization and export diversification are difficult if not impossible to achieve when real exchange rates are misaligned. Internal adjustment could not correct the overvaluation in the real exchange rate for two main reasons. First, domestic product and labor markets lacked sufficient flexibility for the adjustment to occur. Internal adjustment requires that market rigidities should first be removed, and this was not achieved during the 1980s. Second, internal adjustment failed because world inflation rates were low, making it difficult for the real exchange rate to be corrected through low domestic inflation.
- A second lesson emerging from the Ivorian experience concerns the phasing of policy reforms. First, internal adjustment required that the distortions and inflexibilities in the domestic economy be addressed prior to (or at least concurrently with) the macroeconomic adjustment. In the case of Côte d'Ivoire, these measures were undertaken after almost a decade of internal adjustment. Second, it is clear that unless and until the real exchange rate issue is addressed, progress on other policy reforms will be mixed. Third, the reforms of the banking system cannot be expected to be effective unless policies are implemented to correct fundamental macroeconomic imbalances, to reform the public enterprise system, and to restore private confi-

dence, investment, and growth. Without such reforms, the financial sector is likely to continue to be troubled by bad debts, arrears, and capital flight.

- Côte d'Ivoire's experience emphasizes that fiscal adjustment is not confined simply to reducing the fiscal deficit, important though that is. The Ivorian authorities have gone some way toward reducing the primary deficit but have not addressed the fundamental issues of fiscal restructuring. Given the significant increase in the share of wages and salaries in total government expenditures, the effective delivery of public services is likely to have been adversely affected.
- Another major lesson from Côte d'Ivoire's experience concerns the difficulty in replicating in the real world the textbook symmetry between a nominal devaluation and an export tax plus import subsidy. The tariff plus subsidy policy failed to work in part because of breakdown of the textbook symmetry and in part because of policy implementation weaknesses.
- A number of lessons derive from the Ivorian debt experience. The 1980s showed just how difficult it can be for countries to extricate themselves from the longer-term effects of unsustainable investment programs. The debt overhang that emerged from a relatively short period of Ivorian history (basically just five years of easy spending) has dominated macroeconomic policy since 1980. But more fundamental lessons are to be derived from the debt experience. Given the constraints that it faced, the Ivorian government had little choice but to allow arrears to accumulate. While this is a short-term solution of a sort, it has deep-seated effects that extend throughout the economy. The effects of public sector arrears on the financial system and their effects on private investment activities are the two main areas highlighted in this chapter. Concerns also extend to the effects of debt nonpayment on the underlying fabric of trade and exchange. If economic agents consistently default on payments, the basic functioning of the economic system might be weakened in a more fundamental sense.
- The social costs of nonadjustment, especially poverty, can be considerable. Given the inability of the Ivorian government to adjust properly to the terms of trade shocks of the decade, the effects on poverty and other welfare indicators have been serious. In this sense the Ivorian case represents a counterfactual to the adjustment case. Whereas many criticize adjustment on the grounds of its social costs, the alternative represented by Côte d'Ivoire's experience suggests a much more dismal scenario for the poor.

The setting for the adjustment experience

Understanding the adjustment efforts of Côte d'Ivoire in the 1980s is impossible without an awareness of the country's institutional setting. Institutional characteristics have been in part responsible for macroeconomic destabilization and have seriously constrained the ability of the country to undertake effective adjustment with minimal social cost. To prepare the reader for what follows, this section describes the main economic institutions of Côte d'Ivoire, emphasizing the ways in which they circumscribe policy choice. Four main areas are reviewed: the fiscal system, the monetary setting, the labor market setting, and the product market.

The fiscal system

Fiscal policy in Côte d'Ivoire must be understood in the context of a fairly complex set of government financial arrangements. The financial operations of the government are carried out by six principal agencies of the central government, several centrally operated, special-purpose funds, and 137 local authorities. The following main agencies are responsible for the financial operations of the central government:

- The *direction général du budget* is in charge of the budget. Within this agency the *direction des budgets et comptes* is responsible primarily for the current budget (revenue and expenditures other than debt service) and for the component of the government investment program that is financed by earmarked tax revenue and domestic borrowing. The *direction des investissements publics* is responsible for the special government investment budget. The present aim of the government is to unify the budget process into a *"budget unique"* within two years.
- The autonomous amortization fund comprises two departments, dealing with public debt and banking.
- The agricultural price stabilization fund was set up to stabilize producer prices of important export crops—cocoa, coffee, and cotton. Whether the agricultural price stabilization fund generates revenue for the government depends on the relationship over the period between the (government-determined) producer price and the world price for the commodity. The fund generated large surpluses for the government up to 1986. These revenues (which amounted to as much as 15 percent of GDP in 1977) were either invested or transferred to other government departments. However, since 1986 the operations of the agricultural price stabilization fund have involved significantly lower contributions to the exchequer. This fundamental change in the flow of funds

between the government and the agricultural economy is a key to understanding macroeconomic destabilization during the decade. An important characteristic of the agricultural stabilization fund is that its activities were not part of the routine budget process of government.

- The price equalization fund for staple products was established to stabilize the consumer prices of imported rice and sugar.
- The social security sector comprises two components: the National Social Security Fund and the Pension Fund for government employees.

In addition to these central financial agencies, the central government includes several agencies dedicated to specific funds, including the National Sewerage Fund, the National Hydraulics Fund, the National Investment Fund, the National Office for Vocational Training, the Oil Palm Fund, and various petroleum funds. The allocation of revenues to these agencies is generally inflexible, with systematic earmarking of tax revenues preventing cross-agency transfers. The main source of financial flexibility lay in the agricultural price stabilization fund, which in the past was used to finance some major items of government expenditure. However, this more flexible source of financing is also the most variable, the least transparent, and the most unplanned. These funds have been an unstable source of revenue. Their share in total government revenue ranged from 40.7 percent in 1977 and 28.8 percent in 1985 (due to high world prices) to lows of 4.7 percent in 1981 and 1.2 percent in 1987. In more recent times world prices have remained low, keeping the contribution of the stabilization funds at modest levels.

Local government consists of 137 local authorities, which prepare their own budgets. In addition to local revenue and earmarked funds, these authorities receive transfers from the central government. Finally, there are as many as 250 nonfinancial public enterprises in Côte d'Ivoire, most of which are not monitored closely by the central government.

The tax base of the central government (which traditionally amounts to about 20 percent of GDP) is marked by a heavy reliance on indirect taxes, with about a third of revenue deriving from domestic indirect taxes, another third from taxes on imports, and just less than 10 percent from taxes on exports. The remaining 25 percent of tax revenue is derived from direct taxes.

The monetary setting

Côte d'Ivoire is a member of the West African Monetary Union, which was established in 1962.[2] The monetary affairs of the West African Monetary Union are governed by the West African Central Bank. The common currency is the CFA franc (*franc de la communauté financière d'Afrique*), which is pegged to the French franc (FF). Its parity (CFAF 50 = FF 1) has not changed for more than forty years (since 1948). The free convertibility between the CFAF and the French franc at this fixed parity is maintained through an operations account *(compte d'opérations)* of the West African Monetary Union with the French treasury, and an obligation by France to support the West African Monetary Union to maintain unlimited and full convertibility of the CFA franc (see chapter 7 on Senegal for the framework for monetary policy).

Although the operations account pools individual countries' external balances (or overdrafts) with the French treasury, the West African Central Bank maintains separate accounts for each country and credits or charges each country according to its contribution to the pooled accounts.[3] The guarantee of convertibility is subject to several rules that apply to the West African Central Bank and how it manages the operations account. Whenever the pooled external reserves of the West African Central Bank fall below 20 percent of its sight liabilities for three consecutive months, the board of administrators must meet in order to take appropriate monetary action. These decisions are reached through simple majority.

Within the constraints of the fixed parity of the CFA franc, the West African Central Bank decides on credit policy. The most important instrument operated by the central bank is an annual credit ceiling for each member country. Until 1989, two discount rates were applied: the regular rate (*taux d'escompte normal*) and a preferential rate (*taux d'escompte préférentiel*). The latter applied to crop credit, housing loans, and loans to small and medium-size enterprises. The margin between the two rates was usually 2.5 percentage points. In a package of reforms implemented in October 1989, the preferential discount rate was abolished and interest rates are to be used as a more flexible instrument of policy.

Credit to a member government in any given year is limited by statute to 20 percent of the country's total annual tax receipts collected two years previously. This limit on the amount of borrowing by a government in any year is an important feature of the fiscal and monetary scene in Côte d'Ivoire. It seriously restricts the opportunity for seignorage financing and has favorable effects on the rate of inflation. However, the government has three other major financing avenues. First, it can use the public enterprise sector, which is not included in the West African Central Bank restrictions (the central bank accounts treat public enterprise finances as part of the private sector category). By reducing its own direct financing to public enterprises and forcing them to borrow within the banking system, the government can increase total public sector borrowing and circumvent the 20 percent limit.

Second, the government can simply build up its arrears to the private sector. This source of finance can have serious effects on policy implementation (as, for example, with export subsidies) and on the private sector in general.[4] Third, the government (and public enterprises) can borrow externally without violating the guidelines of the West African Monetary Union.

Thus, the leverage that the West African Central Bank can exert on public sector financing in Côte d'Ivoire is greater when the government's access to borrowing is limited. This aspect explains why monetary control slipped somewhat during the late 1970s when external financing was available and was restored in the 1980s when access to external finance was more difficult (Lane 1989 provides more details on the effectiveness of monetary policy in Côte d'Ivoire).

The labor market

The labor force in Côte d'Ivoire is predominantly rural. Wage labor, however, is very uncommon in rural areas. The Côte d'Ivoire Living Standards Surveys, which cover the latter half of the 1980s, report that only about 5 percent of rural household income is derived from wage employment (Demery 1993). The rural labor market is generally unaffected directly by institutional and other rigidities.

The urban labor market, however, is influenced by three types of distortion. First, it is subject to labor legislation, much of which is inherited from the country's colonial past. Minimum wage levels are specified for all categories of workers in large and medium-size firms. Legislation also requires that employers provide fringe benefits and restricts their freedom to lay off workers. Because minimum wages are not index-linked, the government has some freedom to allow real values to fall. The urban real minimum wage fell throughout much of the 1980s (table 3.1).

The wage system is also influenced by *conventions collectives,* which are periodic negotiations among firms, unions, and the government to determine wage scales by skill and seniority. Average wages for unskilled workers have risen above the minimum wage as workers gain seniority, as table 3.1 illustrates. This seniority effect makes the evidence on urban wage trends difficult to interpret. Levy and Newman (1989) argue that the slight increase in real wages from 1980 to 1987, despite a sharp fall in minimum wages (by 25 percent), is to some extent a statistical illusion. During the recession a large number of firms in Côte d'Ivoire were liquidated. Those remaining in business have been obliged to cut their work forces, which has generally affected the lower half of the pay scale. The effect of this recession-induced increase in seniority has been to increase mean wages, despite the fall in real minimum wages.

The implications of these trends for the adjustment programs are difficult to establish. If the growth in seniority is reflected in higher productivity levels, then the wage cost per unit of output may have fallen, thus improving the country's competitiveness. But if limited or no productivity gains are to be obtained from the growth in seniority, the wage costs per unit of output may well have risen. It is also important to distinguish between the real *consumption* wage and the real *product* wage. According to Berthélemy and Bourguignon (forthcoming), "while wage-earners experienced a drop in their real purchasing power, the real product wage paid by employers *increased substantially*" (emphasis added). If this is the case, real wage rigidity is likely to have impaired the adjustment process.

Finally, the high public sector wages, which are more closely related to French civil service wage levels than to domestic conditions, influence wage setting in Côte d'Ivoire. Expatriate-level salaries and wages are also common in the private sector, especially at the executive level. Berthélemy and Bourguignon (forthcoming) conclude that "there is probably considerable room for reductions in wages and salaries throughout the modern labor market that would make wages and salaries more competitive." A similar conclusion is drawn by an internal World Bank document of 1991: "Overall the evidence is clear that unit wages per unit of output as well as wages per employee are comparatively high in Côte d'Ivoire." Little is understood of these wage interrelationships in Côte d'Ivoire, and this is a subject in need of further research.

Table 3.1 Selected data on real wages, 1970–85
(thousands of CFA francs per month)

Year	Minimum nonagricultural wage	Average wage for modern sector workers			Average wage for informal sector workers		Minimum agricultural wage
		Unskilled	Skilled	All	Industry	Services	
1970	40.7	68.0	132.7	118.2	..	..	24.2
1971	41.0	..	..	..	..	..	24.4
1972	40.9	..	..	..	..	..	24.3
1973	40.8	..	..	..	..	..	21.9
1974	47.5	63.6	119.6	110.6	..	..	23.9
1975	44.4	..	..	..	..	..	21.5
1976	49.5	..	..	..	..	..	23.9
1977	38.9	..	..	..	..	..	18.8
1978	43.0	..	..	..	..	..	..
1979	40.5	49.4	84.2	95.6	..	..	15.7
1980	38.9	..	..	..	..	..	13.7
1981	35.6	..	..	..	..	..	12.6
1982	36.8	..	..	..	..	..	12.9
1983	34.7	..	..	..	..	..	12.2
1984	33.3	49.5	76.2	95.8	..	..	11.7
1985	32.7	..	..	..	26.3	26.4	11.5

.. Not available.
Note: Monthly wages in 1984 CFA francs (thousands), deflated by the consumer price index for Abidjan.
Source: Berthélemy and Bourguignon (forthcoming).

The product market

Three characteristics of the product market are central to understanding the events of the 1980s. The first is the dominance of the agricultural sector, especially the importance of two key export crops—cocoa and coffee—and of forestry and timber products. The output of this sector is predominantly for export. With a large number of planters in cocoa and coffee production and of logging companies in the forestry sector, the product markets are potentially highly competitive. However, given the government's role in marketing these products, outcomes have not always reflected this competitiveness.

The second important characteristic of the product market is the public sector dominance, through two broad channels: the influence of the state in marketing and the role of public enterprises. The government has historically maintained the right to control both prices and margins at all stages of distribution. This control has been generally evaded in the industrial sector, although it has been suggested that, since it acts as a de facto barrier to entry, it encourages an oligopolistic market structure. These controls over marketing and price determination are more effectively applied in agriculture, especially export agriculture. Although export crops are marketed by private companies, their activities are subject to close control by the Agriculture Price Stabilization Fund. The companies are obliged to pay producers the price determined by the Agriculture Price Stabilization Fund and, having upon approval sold the produce in world markets, are also required to remit to the Agriculture Price Stabilization Fund the difference between the export price and the producer price plus the exporters' margin. Because the activities of the marketing companies must be monitored carefully, those that trade in cocoa and coffee must renew their permits annually.

The state exerts control over economic activity in Côte d'Ivoire partly through a network of public enterprises, which are either wholly or partly owned by the state. The rules governing these sectors vary according to the degree of state ownership. During the 1970s the number of public enterprises grew rapidly, with the result that the state became involved directly in nearly every area of economic activity. In 1977 there were 113 public enterprises wholly or partly owned by the state, constituting one-third of the country's total employment and contributing 27 percent of total value added. The activities of these enterprises covered a wide range of sectors, from basic infrastructural services, such as water and electricity supply, to major industrial undertakings, such as oil extraction and sugar processing. Compared with the private sector, the public enterprises have generally been inefficient. Although the government owns about 50 percent of the capital of the modern sector, the share of value added earned by public enterprises is only about

25 percent (Berthélemy and Bourguignon forthcoming). From 1982 to 1988 the government invested more than $500 million (net cumulative investment) in the sector, but the estimated return on this investment has been only 2 percent annually. These enterprises ran surpluses during the 1970s and deficits for much of the 1980s. In April 1983 President Houphouët-Boigny acknowledged publicly that mismanagement was largely responsible for public enterprise losses, which amounted to about 1.2 percent of GDP that year (Berthélemy and Bourguignon forthcoming).

The third key characteristic of the Ivorian product market is the highly oligopolistic nature of the modern sector. More than half of the manufacturing industrial sectors are dominated by one or two firms, in the sense that these firms produce more than 50 percent of the output of the industry (Berthélemy and Bourguignon forthcoming). Given the influence of the state and the highly protected nature of much of the manufacturing activity, the sector is highly oligopolistic. This structure leads to price rigidity, which constrains the extent to which internal adjustment can correct external imbalances (given a fixed nominal exchange rate). But it all clearly undermines competition and allocative efficiency.

The nature and causes of macroeconomic destabilization

Given these institutional characteristics of the Ivorian economy, what were the main factors that led to macroeconomic destabilization and the need for structural adjustment?

A false dawn: terms of trade instability

In many respects, the origins of macroeconomic instability in the 1980s can be traced to the success of the previous decade. Côte d'Ivoire had achieved a GDP growth rate of 8 percent annually between 1965 and 1975 and was considered a notable success story among African economies—as reflected in the title of a volume on the Côte d'Ivoire economy during this period, *The Challenge of Success* (Den Tuinder 1978). However, from the mid-1970s onward, events were to take a different course. Ironically, it was a favorable external shock that interrupted the stable growth.

A boom in cocoa and coffee prices in 1976 (generated by a frost-induced failure for the Brazilian coffee harvest) led to a dramatic increase in the country's terms of trade—from 77.9 in 1975 to 100.5 in 1976 and 140.2 in 1977. The Agriculture Price Stabilization Fund kept producer prices stable during this period and thus accumulated large surpluses for government revenue (amounting to 16 percent of GDP in 1977). The government used these resources to embark on an ambitious investment program, which was to have a significant adverse effect on macroeconomic balances in the following decade. Yet given the strong growth performance already achieved, and the expectation that commodity prices would enter an upward secular trend, the events in the mid-1970s were viewed as the dawn of self-sustained growth. Although not quite matching the earlier period, GDP grew by 6.5 percent annually between 1975 and 1979, with strong growth in agriculture at 4.2 percent and industry at 13.4 percent (table 3.2 and table 3B.1 in appendix 3B).

But the price boom was short-lived. Between 1977 and 1980 export prices fell by 30 percent, and the country's terms of trade declined from a peak of 140.2 to only 98.1. Taking the 1980s as a whole, the terms of trade declined by 38 percent. This single shock dominated all macroeconomic accounting in Côte d'Ivoire during the 1980s.

Côte d'Ivoire is particularly susceptible to terms of trade losses for two reasons. The first is its heavy dependence on two main export crops—cocoa

Table 3.2 National accounts, constant 1987 prices, 1975–91

Account	1975–79	1980–84	1985–89	1990–91	1975–79	1980–84	1985–89	1990–91
A. GDP	*(billions of CFA francs)*				*(average annual percentage change)*			
GDP at market prices	2,545.6	2,917.9	3,088.4	2,931.9	6.5	0.6	0.9	-2.2
Net indirect taxes	670.2	687.7	638.8	439.1	11.2	-1.1	3.8	-23.6
GDP at factor cost	1,875.5	2,230.2	2,449.6	2,492.8	6.1	1.1	1.1	3.5
B. GDP by sector of origin	*(as percentage of GDP factor cost)*							
Agriculture	44.3	42.8	32.1	36.5	4.2	1.5	0.1	1.2
Industry	22.0	25.2	21.3	18.6	13.4	2.3	-0.8	-8.4
Mining and quarrying	0.9	3.7	8.2	..	12.7	64.8	6.7	..
Manufacturing	..	..	..	..	..	..	..	..
Services, etc.	33.7	32.0	46.6	44.9	6.8	1.8	7.4	11.9
C. GDP by demand components	*(as percentage of GDP at market prices)*							
Resource balance	-7.9	-3.7	5.1	16.1	138.1	-97.6	168.7	28.2
Imports of GNFS	37.4	35.3	30.3	30.4	12.1	-5.8	2.7	-1.2
Exports of GNFS	29.5	31.6	35.3	46.5	1.6	4.7	4.9	6.0
Total expenditures	107.9	103.7	94.9	84.8	9.8	-2.7	-0.2	-4.5
Total consumption, etc.	74.3	77.3	86.8	90.1	8.1	1.5	0.0	-4.5
General government	24.2	27.6	21.0	10.3	12.6	-2.5	0.4	..
Private, etc.	75.8	72.4	79.0	89.7	6.8	4.0	0.3	8.6
Gross domestic investment	25.7	22.7	13.2	9.9	16.4	-15.5	2.0	-5.8
GDFI	97.0	96.2	93.0	99.7	19.0	-14.7	-3.2	-4.2
Public sector	44.1	45.9	34.4	28.5	29.0	-16.6	-3.5	-8.4
Private sector	55.9	54.1	65.6	71.5	13.1	-11.2	-1.4	-2.3
Changes in stocks	3.0	3.8	7.0	0.3	166.6	6.9	-93.9	..

.. Not available.
Source: World Bank data.

and coffee. This dependency increased rapidly over the past two decades. The second is that its exports constitute a significant share of total world trade in these commodities. At the end of the 1970s Ivorian exports of cocoa and coffee represented 16 percent and 8 percent of total world trade by volume.

Despite the fact that the favorable coffee price shock was temporary (due to the Brazilian frost), the government perceived the cocoa price increase as permanent. The cocoa price boom did indeed continue slightly longer than the coffee price boom, but this does not explain why the government made such a distinction between the cocoa and coffee price shocks. One possible explanation for the prevailing optimism was the view that the world economy was entering a phase of increases in commodity prices (an expectation that was also fueled by the oil price hikes of 1973 and 1979).

The government's expectation that prices would continue an upward trend prompted it to cast its expenditure plans (especially its investment plans) in this light. It is difficult to appreciate the grounds for this optimism. Chamley and Ghanem (1991) could find no evidence of any trend in the prices of either cocoa or coffee over the period between 1970 and 1987. Nor could they detect any evidence of an upward trend based on historical data up to 1979 (when these expectations were formed). The slump in cocoa and coffee prices in the latter half of the 1980s does not appear to be out of line with historical fluctuations. Yet the government did not perceive the price movements in this way. The increase in prices in the mid-1980s served only to encourage this misperception, and it appears that the government continued to believe that the fair prices of these commodities were higher than those operating or than those that applied before the 1970s' price boom. The failure of the government to adjust its expectations to emerging economic realities led to the continuation of its expenditure plans and to an accumulation of debt, which together precipitated the severe crises of the 1980s.

Unsustainable investment

The investment program underpinning many of the macroeconomic imbalances of the early 1980s originated in a report of the ministry of planning entitled *Côte d'Ivoire 2000.* Although the plan was prepared in 1974, final decisions on many of its aspects were made at the beginning of 1977, when the commodity price boom was under way. The *Côte d'Ivoire 2000* investment program was the government's attempt to reach a consensus about the country's economic strategy for the future. It was ambitious even by the favorable standards of the time. The original public sector investment projection that undergirded the plan amounted to CFAF 1,350 billion in 1975 prices. The World Bank considered this level of investment unsustainable and estimated that an investment of about CFAF 800 billion was consistent with available resources. The final figure adopted in the plan was CFAF 1,020 billion, lower than originally planned but noticeably higher than what the Bank considered to be sustainable. The plan assumed a GDP growth rate of 8.7 percent, which exceeded what had been achieved in the recent past (8.3 percent between 1965 and 1973).

Table 3.3 compares planned and actual levels of investment and finance under *Côte d'Ivoire 2000*. The table highlights the following main weaknesses in the implementation of the program:

- *Tendency toward overspending.* The investment targets were exceeded, indicating significant overspending—particularly in the transport, energy, and housing sectors (but also in education, agriculture, trade, and tourism). Investment in manufacturing was far below what was planned (a target of CFAF 59.5 billion, compared with CFAF 16.1 actually invested). The overspending was due to the absence of expenditure control in the public sector—primarily because many expenditures (especially by public enterprises) are not subject to normal budgetary approval and procedure. The discretionary use of the revenues generated by the Agriculture Price Stabilization Fund was another determinant of fiscal undiscipline. These difficulties in controlling public expenditures were to be a continuing problem in the following decade.

Table 3.3 Planned and actual investment expenditures and outcomes, 1976–80

Item	Planned	Realized
	(billions of 1975 CFAF)	
Total investment	1,591	1,670
Public	826	1,135
Private	765	535
Public financing of investment	1,020	1,433
External borrowing	534	555
Public	327	438
Private	207	117
	(percent)	
Debt-service-to-export ratio, 1980	7.5	25.0
Annual growth rates (1976–80)		
GDP	8.7	7.7
Agriculture	6	4.7
Manufacturing	14.1	11.0
Manufacturing exports	15.9	7.4
Cash crop exports	5.4	3.6
Total exports	7.3	4.2
Building and public works	9.3	11.1
Services	9.1	8.3

Source: Berthélemy and Bourguignon (forthcoming).

- *Underinvestment in tradables.* Much of the public investment was in the nontradables sector, and too little was directed toward activities that would diversify the tradables sector. Exacerbating this allocation was a weak private sector response to *Côte d'Ivoire 2000*, which can be attributed in part to the overvaluation of the real exchange rate. Export performance was significantly below target—particularly manufacturing exports, which were projected to grow at 15.9 percent annually but actually grew at only 7.4 percent.
- *Long gestation lags and inefficient investments.* Poorly selected projects yielded low income streams. The major cause was the emphasis on infrastructure investment, especially in the northern Savannah region, which had very long gestation lags. In some cases the gestation periods were longer than anticipated because implementation was incomplete (for example, a bridge was constructed in the Savannah region, but construction of its connecting roads was delayed). But the unproductive investment was also due simply to inefficiency. One example is the SODESUCRE program, which absorbed 37 percent of the plan's allocation to agricultural investment, yet yielded little in return. Production costs in SODESUCRE factories were high, and the incremental capital-output ratio for these investments was about 5.8. In some cases, investment projects were selected for their prestige value, such as the construction of a new capital city at Yamoussoukro. The emphasis on infrastructure and the selection of low-yielding (especially prestige) projects yielded an incremental capital-output ratio of about 4.1 for the investment program as a whole (Berthélemy and Bourguignon forthcoming). The planned ratio was close to 3 (which was more in keeping with recent experience).

Decline in savings

A major destabilizing event toward the end of the 1970s was a dramatic fall in national savings—from 25 percent of GDP in 1977 to only 10 percent in 1980 and 6.8 percent in 1981 (appendix table 3B.1). Both private and public savings were significantly lower than had been planned in *Côte d'Ivoire 2000*. The fall in private savings was probably due to an increase in remittances by foreign workers. But Berthélemy and Bourguignon (forthcoming) suggest also that an increase in food prices (due to the shock-induced boom) had an effect on aggregate savings, because most formal savings in Côte d'Ivoire are made by food-deficit (urban) households. However, there are other explanations. During the destabilizing period the temporarily favorable commodity price shock may have induced agents to increase consumption, because, although temporary, the shock would raise permanent income levels (Bevan,

Collier, and Gunning 1990). The terms of trade decline, the recession, and falling profits after the boom, combined with the emerging effect of debt service in the public sector, would then explain much of the downturn in national savings during the adjustment period.

This low level of savings, combined with the poor export performance, meant that a larger proportion of the investment program had to be financed through foreign borrowing, particularly by the public sector. While external borrowing scheduled under the program amounted to CFAF 327 billion, public sector external borrowing in fact amounted to CFAF 438 billion (an overprojection of 34 percent, see table 3.3). This accumulation of debt was to dominate macroeconomic policy for the foreseeable future. The role played by the expansion of private consumption in aggravating the external deficit is discussed below.

An increasing debt service burden

The increased external borrowing and a general increase in world interest rates caused a significant increase in debt service, creating a financial crisis in 1980. Whereas *Côte d'Ivoire 2000* projected a debt-service-to-export ratio of just 7.5 percent, the ratio was actually significantly higher (table 3.4). The debt service ratio increased from just under 7 percent of exports in 1975–77 to almost 18 percent in 1978–80. An important share of the debt was to commercial banks, which left the government vulnerable to the vicissitudes of world interest rates.

Real exchange rate appreciation

Both the favorable export price shock and the increased foreign borrowing to finance the investment program could be expected to lead to an appreciation of the real effective exchange rate, as explained in the "Dutch disease" literature (Devarajan and de Melo 1987). The mechanism involved in such models usually entails a fixed nominal exchange rate and appreciation of the real exchange rate due to an acceleration in domestic inflation relative to world inflation. For Côte d'Ivoire the movement of the real exchange rate is due to changes in both the nominal rate (from fluctuations in the value of the French franc) and the relative inflation index.

In the destabilizing period (1975–80) the real effective exchange rate appreciated. Since the nominal effective exchange rate was stable over the period (reflecting the stability of the French franc, to which the CFA franc was tied), the main reason for this appreciation in the real rate was the movement in the Ivorian price level relative to inflation among its competitors (second column of table 3.5). The relative price index based on the consumer price index rose from 103.7 in 1975 to 128.1 in 1980. Thus an acceleration in the rate of Ivorian inflation was the principal factor behind this loss of international competitiveness during the latter half of the 1970s. And there can be little doubt that the acceleration in the inflation rate was due to the commodity price boom and the concurrent investment boom. The investment boom was partly financed through internal borrowing (the money supply grew by 19 percent annually between 1975 and 1980), which inevitably increased domestic inflation.[5] Lane (1989) suggest two broad reasons for the relative slackness of domestic monetary policy in the late 1970s: the role of external finance, enabling the commercial banks to expand credit financed by borrowing from parent banks, and shifts in the proportions of financial assets toward less liquid assets, which enabled commercial banks to increase credit without relying on central bank financing.

Market distortions

The overvaluation of the real exchange rate is one of several market distortions during the destabilizing period. Two broad sources of market intervention distorted price signals and resource allocation: a system of import tar-

Table 3.4 External debt, 1975–91
(US$ millions)

Type of debt	*1975–77*	*1978–80*	*1981–83*	*1984–86*	*1987–89*	*1990–91*
Total external debt	1,632.3	4,807.4	7,444.2	9,646.0	14,410.7	18,463.3
Use of IMF credit	18.8	41.3	545.5	653.6	494.1	401.4
Short-term debt	159.3	881.7	1,052.5	725.3	2,011.1	3,198.2
Total long-term debt	1,454.2	3,884.4	5,846.2	8,267.1	11,905.5	14,863.6
Public/publicly guaranteed						
long-term debt	1,356.2	3,598.7	4,803.9	5,762.8	8,227.2	10,306.1
Official creditors	490.9	1,071.3	1,439.3	2,669.9	4,989.3	7,264.1
Multilateral	184.9	429.3	752.8	1,243.9	2,186.7	2,813.5
IDA	3.7	7.5	7.3	7.3	7.1	22.4
IBRD	92.7	236.4	533.3	995.6	1,740.2	1,949.6
Bilateral	306.0	642.1	686.5	1,426.0	2,802.6	4,450.6
Private creditors	865.3	2,527.5	3,364.6	3,092.9	3,238.0	3,042.0
Bonds	20.9	17.5	6.8	3.8	1.5	0.0
Commercial banks	450.3	1,358.5	2,106.7	2,194.1	2,606.6	2,694.2
Other private	394.0	1,151.4	1,251.1	894.9	629.9	347.8
Private nonguaranteed						
long-term	98.0	285.7	1,042.3	2,504.3	3,678.3	4,557.5
Debt service payments as percentage of exports						
of goods and nonfactor services (cash basis)						
Before rescheduling	6.7	17.7	33.4	38.8	53.3	27.4
After rescheduling	6.7	17.7	32.7	23.8	20.2	8.9

Source: World Bank and IMF data.

iffs and export taxes on international trade, which created distortions within the tradables category of commodities, thereby increasing the domestic prices of protected goods and penalizing others, and the state's pervasive role in marketing (especially agricultural) commodities, with a plethora of state-run marketing boards and public enterprises engaged directly in economic activity.

At the beginning of the 1980s Côte d'Ivoire relied on tariff and nontariff barriers to provide protection to domestic producers. (Table 3.6 reports the structure of nominal and effective tariffs in Côte d'Ivoire in 1971 and 1980.) The average tariff rate reported in the table (estimated at around 30 percent) is misleadingly high because of the numerous exemptions to the tariff code: Berthélemy and Bourguignon (forthcoming) report that less that half of all imports were subject to the full import tariff, generating an effective average tariff rate of about 25 percent (28 percent for manufactured products)—a figure that includes the value added tax.

However, tariffs were not the main mechanism for protecting domestic producers. Quantitative restrictions were also applied, and they influenced

Table 3.5 Nominal and real effective exchange rates, 1975–91

Year	*NEER*[a]	*Multilateral CPI/FWPI*[b]	*Multilateral REER(CPI)*[a]	*Bilateral REER*[c]	*Terms of trade*	*Resource balance*[d] *(% GDP)*
1975	105.1	103.7	108.9	83.1	77.9	0.1
1976	101.1	104.2	105.3	86.6	100.5	5.5
1977	98.3	119.3	117.3	104.6	140.2	6.3
1978	101.5	124.3	126.1	113.1	126.4	-0.9
1979	108.4	126.5	137.1	116.5	112.7	-3.1
1980	108.2	128.1	138.5	122.7	98.1	-6.1
1981	97.2	123.6	120.2	120.3	85.4	-7.1
1982	89.9	121.3	109.0	116.4	83.4	-2.9
1983	85.8	113.5	97.4	111.0	84.9	-1.7
1984	95.2	104.6	99.5	102.2	97.0	11.5
1985	100.0	100.0	100.0	100.0	100.0	13.2
1986	120.5	105.0	126.6	110.4	101.8	7.5
1987	139.1	101.0	140.5	110.7	83.8	4.4
1988	141.9	99.3	140.9	112.5	76.4	2.8
1989	146.4	92.0	134.7	107.8	65.4	3.0
1990	163.3	87.6	143.0	108.3	61.2	4.4
1991	166.3	86.1	143.2	111.4	62.6	4.8

a. The multilateral nominal effective exchange rate (NEER) is a trade-weighted index of the nominal exchange rates of Côte d'Ivoire's main trading partners. The multilateral real effective exchange rate (REER) is the NEER adjusted for price changes in the home country relative to the trading partner. The home price index used in this adjustment is the consumer price index (CPI), and the trading partner price index is the wholesale price index (WPI). (See text for details.)

b. The home country CPI divided by the trade-weighted WPI of trading partners.

c. The bilateral real exchange rate index is the CFAF/French franc rate multiplied by the relative CPIs of Côte d'Ivoire and France.

d. Resource balance is measured in current prices.

Source: World Bank data.

Table 3.6 Nominal and effective tariff structure, 1971 and 1980

Sector	Nominal tariff protection coefficient		Effective tariff protection coefficient	
	1971	*1980*	*1971*	*1980*
Food canning	1.3437	1.3099	2.518	2.123
Coffee processing	1.3167	1.2767	17.924	4.554
Cocoa processing	1.4375	1.4909	..	..
Edible oils and fats	1.3461	1.4052	1.006	1.829
Other food processing	1.3767	1.4932	0.638	1.829
Spinning, weaving, dyeing	1.4283	1.4276	1.277	2.26
Other textile products	1.3882	1.4158	1.597	2.649
Leather and shoe products	1.3029	1.3031	1.687	1.307
Wood processing I	1.25	1.2117	1.155	1.222
Wood processing II	1.2822	1.3046	1.232	1.33
Chemicals	1.2933	1.2322	1.504	1.384
Plastics	1.49	1.3867	1.376	1.289
Rubber products	1.49	1.3867	1.223	1.489
Cement, construction materials	1.2373	1.2097	0.662	1.198
Basic metals	1.2178	1.1587	1.087	1.136
Vehicles	1.3263	1.2449	0.925	1.245
Simple metal products	1.224	1.2615	0.993	1.365
Machinery	1.2038	1.2303	1.242	1.236
Other industrial products	1.2351	1.309	0.782	1.339

.. Not available.
Source: Berthélemy and Bourguignon (forthcoming).

the domestic price more than did the tariff structure. A list of 310 foreign products (drawn up in 1975) either could not be imported at all or were subject to import licensing. By 1982 the number of manufactured items on the list had increased to 426, accounting for 38 percent of total imports (Berthélemy and Bourguignon forthcoming). In addition, a system of prior authorization was introduced in 1984, requiring importers to obtain authorization from the external trade department. All imports had to be cleared by the external trade department, even those that could in principle be imported freely. In practice, the system of prior authorization proved to be a serious impediment to trade—all categories (except those that were totally unrestricted) were progressively administered through licenses by the external trade department.

Tariffs and import restrictions were not the only distortionary forces at work prior to structural adjustment in Côte d'Ivoire. The combination of tariffs, quantitative restrictions, real exchange rate overvaluation, and direct price-setting policies seriously distorted the domestic price and incentive structure in product markets. Estimates of the effects of these four policy-induced distortions on agricultural incentives during the destabilizing period have been reported by Schiff and Valdés (1992).[6]

Their results show that the price distortions in Côte d'Ivoire between 1960 and 1982 were due as much to the indirect effects of real exchange rate overvaluation as to the direct effects of tariffs and quantitative restrictions (table 3.7). Overall, agricultural producers were taxed at the rate of about 49 percent in nominal terms, 23.3 percent arising from exchange rate distortions and 25.7 percent from direct trade and other tax and price-setting distortions. Yet these nominal protection rates differed significantly across agricultural sectors. Importable commodities (particularly rice) received significant direct protection from external competition—approximately 26 percent from 1960 to 1982 (which is higher than the 14 percent average reported by Schiff and Valdés for all 16 developing countries covered). Although producers of importables (and all other tradables) were penalized by the overvalued exchange rate, their total protection rate was positive (just under 3 percent).

Trade policy interventions taxed the exportables sector, however. Between 1960 and 1982 these activities were taxed directly at a rate of 28.7 percent (table 3.7), and at a total rate of 52 percent (which captures the effects of the exchange rate distortion). The tendency of trade policy to tax exportables and protect importables led to serious distortions of prices and resource allocation in Côte d'Ivoire. The distortionary effects of trade policy were even higher during the destabilizing period. For 1976–82 Schiff and Valdés (1992) report a positive net protection of importables of just less than 7 percent and highly negative protection for exportables of 78 percent. These figures confirm that trade policy seriously distorted resource allocation in Côte d'Ivoire prior to the adjustment and that trade reform was required to improve resource allocation and efficiency.

Adjustment policies during the 1980s

In dealing with the problems arising from these destabilizing events, the government turned to both the IMF and the World Bank for assistance. An

Table 3.7 Direct, indirect, and total rates of nominal protection of agriculture, 1960–82

Period/category	*Indirect protection*	*Direct protection*	*Total protection*
1960–82			
All agricultural products	-23.3	-25.7	-49.0
Importables		26.2	2.9
Exportables		-28.7	-52.0
1960–72			
All agricultural products	-17.5	-32.2	-49.7
Importables		27.3	9.8
Exportables		-35.7	-53.2
1976–82			
All agricultural products	-34.5	-39.6	-74.1
Importables		41.4	6.9
Exportables		-43.5	-78.0

Source: Schiff and Valdés (1992).

extended arrangement covering a three-year period was agreed on with the IMF in February 1981, followed by five standby arrangements during the decade and another in 1991. In the ten-year period IMF support amounted to SDR 1 billion (table 3.8). The World Bank provided three structural adjustment loans between 1981 and 1986 (a total of $650 million) and six sectoral adjustment loans between 1989 and 1991 (a total of $780 million).

As each of these loans was provided, external circumstances changed. Movements in the terms of trade (particularly cocoa and coffee prices) and in the value of the U.S. dollar had important repercussions for the design of the adjustment programs. In most cases, the changes could not have been anticipated, so that program designs were often found wanting. These changes in external events are the basis for the two-part division of the 1980s—the period of partial adjustment in 1981–86 and the period of fettered adjustment in 1987–91. In the first period the real exchange rate depreciated and the terms of trade recovered somewhat (at least between 1984 and 1986). In the second period the real exchange rate appreciated and the terms of trade fell, thus fettering the adjustment effort.

Summary of progress during the decade

Fiscal policy was generally contractionary throughout the decade, aside from a brief respite in 1984–86, when revenue was generated from improved commodity prices (table 3.9 and appendix table 3B.2). But internal adjustment

Table 3.8 World Bank and IMF support for structural adjustment programs

Date	*World Bank loans*	*US$ millions*
1981	Structural adjustment loan I	150
1983	Structural adjustment loan II	250
1986	Structural adjustment loan III	250
1989	Agricultural sector adjustment loan	150
1989	Energy sector adjustment loan	100
1990	Water supply sector adjustment loan	80
1991	Financial sector adjustment loan	200
1991	Competitiveness adjustment loan	100
1991	Human resources adjustment loan	150
	IMF support	*SDR millions*
Feb. 1991	Extended arrangement (3 years)	484.50
May 1984	Standby arrangement (1 year)	82.75
June 1985	Standby arrangement (1 years)	66.20
June 1986	Standby arrangement (2 years)	100.00
Dec. 1987	Standby arrangement (16 months)	94.00
Nov. 1989	Standby arrangement (17 months)	175.80
Sept. 1991	Standby arrangement (1 year)	82.75

Source: Grootaert (1993).

in Côte d'Ivoire generally meant a dramatic cutback in investment expenditures in the first adjustment period, followed by some cuts in current expenditures later. Although tax rates increased somewhat, the increases were not enough to compensate for the loss in revenue from the stabilization funds. Moreover, raising taxes during recessionary times is difficult, because of the smaller tax base. The government generally followed a contractionary monetary policy successfully, bringing growth of broad money under control. However, with the persistence of the fiscal deficit and a growing stock of domestic public sector arrears, the Ivorian banking system faced serious financial and liquidity problems.

Given the continued decline in the price of the principal exports, the government had only limited opportunity to raise producer prices significantly. Thus, it directed policy reform largely at increasing marketing efficiency, lowering marketing costs, and providing incentives to maintain the coffee orchard stock and quality. The main constraint facing agricultural pricing policy was the real exchange rate overvaluation, which effectively constrained the real returns that can be offered to export producers. Trade policy reform sought to mimic an exchange rate depreciation, but the policies were not implemented effectively, primarily because fiscal constraints prevented the timely payment of export subsidies.

Progress with institutional reform, particularly export crop marketing and the public enterprise sector, has been noticeably slow. For much of the decade very little was achieved, although recent years have seen evidence of a momentum toward marketing liberalization and privatization. Since 1991 there has been improved progress in these areas.

Partial adjustment, 1981–86

Adjustment during this period was supported by the initial IMF extended arrangement, by two IMF standby arrangements, and by structural adjust-

Table 3.9 Trends in fiscal deficit, 1976–91
(percentage of GDP)

Item	Destabilizing period		Partial adjustment		Fettered adjustment
	1976–77	1978–80	1981–83	1984–86	1987–91
Total revenue	33.5	31.7	28.0	30.7	24.1
Tax revenue	20.8	20.5	21.4	19.3	19.9
Nontax revenue	12.7	11.1	6.6	11.4	4.2
Total expenditure	34.9	42.3	39.9	33.4	37.3
Current expenditure	16.4	21.1	25.7	26.5	33.9
Capital expenditure	18.5	21.1	14.2	6.8	3.5
Primary deficit	0.1	-8.0	-4.9	6.0	-3.6
Overall fiscal balance	-1.4	-10.6	-11.9	-2.7	-13.2

Source: See appendix table 3B.2.

ment loans I and II. Adjustment policies were partially successful, due in part to a depreciation of the French franc (and thus the CFA franc) against the U.S. dollar and in part to the recovery of commodity prices. However, both the structural adjustment loan documentation and the World Bank audits of the operations saw the structural adjustment process of Côte d'Ivoire as a medium-term task. While initial adjustment policies were focused on short-term objectives, such as fiscal and monetary restraint, more fundamental weaknesses in the Ivorian economy would be addressed only in the long term. They include institutional weaknesses in government and the public enterprise sector and distortions in trade and exchange rates.

Contractionary fiscal policy. The first priority of adjustment in Côte d'Ivoire was to control and reduce the fiscal deficit. The overall deficit had risen to 12 percent of GDP in 1980, averaging more than 10 percent of GDP from 1978 to 1980. Even the primary deficit was 9 percent of GDP in 1980. Policy response to the fiscal problem was twofold: a contractionary fiscal policy and more fundamental efforts to improve economic management.

Given the low levels of world cocoa and coffee prices, there was little room for policy maneuver on the revenue side, at least between 1981 and 1983. However, the taxation policy stance was contractionary—excise taxes were raised on petroleum products, alcoholic beverages, and tobacco. These changes had little effect on tax revenue, which increased from 20.5 percent of GDP in 1978–80 to just 21.4 percent in 1981–83, slipping back to 19.3 percent in 1984–86. Fluctuations on the revenue side were due primarily to changes in nontax revenue, especially revenue from cocoa and coffee. Revenue fell markedly in 1981–83 but recovered just as dramatically during 1984–86.

The government did not attempt to revise the tax system in order to broaden the tax base and reduce its dependency on trade taxes. It was thus obliged to focus on restricting expenditures, particularly investment expenditures, cutting them from their peak of 23 percent of GDP in 1978 to 13 percent in 1983 to less than 5 percent in 1986 (appendix table 3B.2).[7] Current expenditures were not cut as drastically under the fiscal contraction, hovering around 23 percent of GDP between 1979 and 1982, and 27 percent of GDP in 1983–87.

This policy closed the primary deficit to just 2.2 percent of GDP in 1983, and generated a surplus between 1984 and 1986. However, the poor revenue performance, combined with significant increases in interest rates and debt service, left an overall fiscal deficit between 1981 and 1983; only in 1986 was it reduced to manageable proportions (to just less than 3 percent of GDP), when the increase in commodity prices raised government revenue.

In short, contractionary fiscal policy during the partial adjustment period closed the fiscal deficit, which had mushroomed during the destabilizing period. The smaller deficit was due to more favorable revenue generation in 1984–86, but also to dramatic cutbacks in investment spending. Revenue did not improve as a result of the widening of the tax base, since revenue from standard taxes did not increase. The improvement came primarily from an increase in revenues from cocoa and coffee. On the expenditure side, government consumption was not reduced to any great extent, despite efforts to curtail the rapid growth in wages and salaries.

Investment planning procedures were also reformed in the early 1980s. One of the factors behind the destabilizing events of the late 1970s was the absence of control over investment decisions. To ensure proper control in the future, the government introduced the *schéma-directeur* in 1981—a three–year macroeconomic framework that determines the overall envelope for public investment, accounting for available financing among other things. The *schéma-directeur* also makes proposals for sectoral investment allocations in the context of the Five-Year Plan. Details of investment projects to be implemented during the three-year period are set out in the Loi-Programme, which covers the investment programs of both the central government and major public enterprises. In this way, the investment activities of public enterprises were brought within the discipline of the budgetary process. The Direction et Contrôle des Grands Travaux reinforced investment planning at the project level by monitoring all projects that cost more than CFAF 700 million.

Monetary and financial policy. The first half of the 1980s witnessed a significant return to monetary discipline from the adverse monetary effects of the fiscal expansion of the late 1970s. Under the extended fund facility–supported program, credit ceilings were set on net domestic assets of the banking system and on net claims on the public sector. These credit ceilings were met, in part because the demand for private sector credit was low—due to an extremely tight credit policy followed by the central bank, which crowded out the private sector at a time when the government increased its use of credit from the banking system (as opposed to external borrowing). But it was also due to low levels of demand for credit. Borrowers were cautious because they were uncertain about the debt issue and its rescheduling, and concerned about the drought and the general recession. With nonperforming assets increasing from 1.9 percent of total bank credit in 1985 to 8 percent in 1986,[8] and with total credit to the private sector growing only marginally, the absolute amount of credit to productive activities fell during the partial adjustment period.

The policy of monetary restraint reduced the growth of money supply dramatically in 1982–83, but monetary expansion returned during 1984–85, with M2 growth averaging 16.6 percent annually. This expansion was fueled primarily by the balance of payments surplus during these years. But it was also due to an increase in time deposits (partly a response to increased real interest rates), and to a decline in the velocity of circulation from historically high levels in 1981–84. With a return to an external deficit in 1986, monetary expansion continued to be constrained successfully.

In previous years the West African Central Bank relied primarily on credit ceilings as the instrument of monetary control, keeping interest rates low in order to encourage private investment. With the reforms introduced in 1981, the West African Central Bank adopted a more flexible interest rate policy in order to control credit and to prevent capital outflows. The basic rediscount rate was raised from 8 percent prior to April 1980 to 10.5 percent between April 1980 and April 1982 and 12.5 percent prior to April 1993 (and adjusted back to 10.5 percent in April 1983). The increases pushed real interest rates into double digits between 1982 and 1985 (see appendix table 3B.1). However, the two-rate system was continued—with a normal rate (the nominal discount rate) 2.5 percent higher than the preferential rate (the preferential discount rate). Monetary policy relied less on quantitative credit constraints with the associated sector-specific allocations, and increasingly on indirect methods of control.

At the beginning of the decade, the banking system in Côte d'Ivoire included 21 deposit money banks—15 commercial banks and 6 specialized credit institutions—set up primarily to finance specific sectors.[9] These institutions had serious difficulties in competing with the commercial banks, due mainly to their relatively extensive portfolios of bad debt, which resulted from their commitment to lend to inefficient public enterprises. To avoid bankruptcy, the development banks relied primarily on arrears "financing," and on high-interest overdraft facilities with the West African Central Bank.

Trade policy. Major reform was necessary to restore international competitiveness to the economy, and to lay the foundation for an expansion (and diversification) of exports. An export subsidy scheme and a revision of the customs tariff were features of the adjustment program. Duties were reduced on many products (while those on intermediate goods were increased), and quantitative restrictions were replaced with temporary surcharges to be reduced gradually to zero over a five-year period. The objective was to achieve a 40 percent effective protection rate. The export subsidy scheme called for a subsidy on value added on exports to countries outside the West African Economic Community. It was applied first to 52 percent of industrial value added, and was extended gradually to all industry. A further incentive to export was introduced by accelerating reimbursement of the value added tax paid on exports. Yet progress toward implementing this policy was slow. It was not completed under the structural adjustment loan II operation, and was effectively postponed to later operations (structural adjustment loan III).

Agricultural policy reform. The benefits of the boom in world cocoa and coffee prices during the destabilizing period were generally not passed on to the farmer. Producer prices were not increased significantly during the destabilizing period. Under structural adjustment loans I and II, several policy reforms were introduced to raise agricultural production incentives. First, prices for all major crops, including cocoa and coffee, were increased substantially in an effort to raise export production. Between 1981 and 1984, producer prices of major export crops were raised by 25 to 35 percent, bringing them closer to world prices.

Second, the consumer price of rice was also raised, in effect raising the producer prices of foodcrops (such as yams, plantain, cassava, and maize). These prices were increased under favorable external circumstances. Both the depreciation of the CFA franc against the U.S. dollar and the recovery in world commodity prices between 1984 and 1986 meant that the Agriculture Price Stabilization Fund was able to maintain large surpluses while also raising producer prices. Producer prices remained below world market prices, so that in effect producers continued to be taxed.

Third, a pruning premium was introduced to encourage the restoration of the coffee orchard. Fourth, several agriculture-based public enterprises were reformed, including SODESUCRE (sugar), extension services in the Savannah, PALMINDUSTRIE (oil palm, coconut, and copra), and Forest Area extension service.

The new structure of price incentives in agriculture had a strong impact on cocoa and cotton, whose increased production was due essentially to higher producer prices and to a rebound in output after two years of drought. The response for coffee was weaker, since price parity with cocoa had induced farmers to plant more cocoa while neglecting coffee.

Public enterprise reform. The sheer size and influence of the public enterprises, their generally low levels of efficiency, and the macroeconomic implications of their inefficiency made it inevitable that public enterprise reform would remain on the adjustment agenda for the entire decade. However, it has proved to be a difficult undertaking. The most important measures adopted under structural adjustment loans I and II were the establishment of a systematic and comprehensive financial and economic monitoring system *(tableau de bord)* in the Ministry of Finance, and a rehabilitation program for several enterprises. Public expenditure policy was targeted at improving the management of enterprises, rather than changing their ownership. Some public enterprises were merged with others, and some were liquidated. In general, the program lacked clearly defined policy objectives. Privatization (or divestiture) was not on the policy agenda in this period.

Fettered adjustment, 1987–91

The measure of success during the partial adjustment phase can be attributed to three major factors: the implementation of structural adjustment reforms, which began to improve economic management and restore production incentives; the depreciation of the French franc, which caused a real depreciation in the exchange rate, at least until 1983; and improved terms of trade. However, as the terms of trade took another sharp downward turn in 1987, crisis economic management returned, thus exposing the underlying weaknesses of the Ivorian economy, and calling for continued and intensified policy reform. Throughout the remainder of the 1980s, the terms of trade continued to decline. Adjustment was also fettered by another key external shock—the appreciation of the real exchange rate, brought about by a stronger French franc and by currency devaluations in several competitor countries, such as Nigeria and Ghana. The combination of these events forced the government to rely on internal adjustment, in which competitiveness was to be restored by reducing domestic absorption.

During this period, adjustment was supported by a third structural adjustment loan, which sought to intensify the policy initiatives of earlier years. But the government drew back from its commitment to adjustment, and essentially abandoned the program in 1987. This stance led to an interruption in World Bank lending to Côte d'Ivoire for a two-year period (1987–89). However, after an agreement was reached with the IMF in 1989 for a new standby arrangement, World Bank lending was resumed with the approval of six sectoral adjustment operations, mobilizing a total of $780 million (see table 3.8). The medium-term framework that undergirded the last three of these sectoral adjustment loans acknowledged that the competitiveness problem had to be addressed before second tranche releases. The sectoral adjustment loans should thus be viewed not so much as attempts to replace macroeconomic policy reforms (aimed at competitiveness), but rather as necessary complements to such reforms. Without the necessary adjustment in the real exchange rate, sectoral adjustment loans cannot be expected to restore sustainable growth.

Fiscal policy. The sharp decline in commodity prices in 1987 revealed the fragility of the favorable fiscal policy outcomes during the partial adjustment phase. Because producer prices remained unchanged as world prices fell, the Agriculture Price Stabilization Fund's operating surplus of 9 percent of GDP in 1985 fell dramatically in 1987 to just 0.3 percent. Given that expenditures had been trimmed to the bone earlier in the decade, fiscal policy required an even more austere taxation stance. Tax-raising measures were taken in 1987 and 1988 (primarily on indirect taxation), but the outcomes were disappointing, particularly for import taxes, which did not improve revenue as expected.[10] Three factors explain the disappointing outcomes. First, revenue was eliminated from the agricultural stabilization funds. Second, import tax increases generated poor revenue outcomes, due in part to evasion. Third, the tax base contracted, due primarily to the recession. Revenue from direct taxation fell from CFAF 161.5 billion in 1986 to CFAF 143.4 billion in 1990, primarily because tax revenue declined.

With little room for maneuver on the revenue and expenditure fronts, the government found it difficult to reduce the fiscal deficit. Having improved during 1984–86, the primary deficit rose to 7.6 percent of GDP in 1989 (appendix table 3B.2), while the overall deficit increased to 17.6 percent of GDP in the same year. Since then further expenditure cuts, notably on current expenditures other than wages and salaries, have reduced the deficit somewhat. With the government unable to close the fiscal deficit, and with external financing opportunities limited, it has had little alternative but to allow arrears to accumulate even further during the latter half of the decade. Again, the major limitation of fiscal policy was its failure to restructure the tax system, and reduce the reliance on trade taxes. Given this constraint, the government did remarkably well in containing the fiscal deficit.

Monetary and financial policy. Monetary and credit contraction continued during the second half of the decade, with credit ceilings being applied successfully. Broad money growth was negative from 1987 to 1991 (an average of –2.2 percent annually). Credit to the private sector was constrained, which had serious effects on the economy. The financial problems of the government and the sharp deterioration in commodity prices forced the Agriculture Price Stabilization Fund to finance its operating losses by accumulating arrears to exporters. This accumulation of crop credit crowded out noncrop or ordinary credit, thus aggravating the recession.

Interest rate policy was also changed during this period. The regular interest rate had been cut from a peak of 12.5 percent in 1983 to just 8.5 percent in 1986. However, several upward adjustments were then made, and the rate increased to 10 percent in 1989. The premium on the preferential interest rate was reduced in March 1989 and then abolished in October.

The banking system continued to have serious problems due to poor-quality bank portfolios, and a serious liquidity shortage due to the credit squeeze, payments arrears, and a low level of deposits.[11] The problems of the former development banks were particularly acute. In 1987 measures were taken to address them—to reform and restructure the BNDA (with foreign assistance), and to liquidate BICT and BNEC. The BIDI and CCI were to be merged. In 1989 the BIDI and CCI were also to be liquidated. But the program to restructure the BNDA was not effectively implemented, and its future is in serious doubt. The government is currently arranging for its liquidation, and is seeking to replace it with alternative arrangements for providing rural credit.

The government also sought to assist the commercial banks. In 1988 margins between deposit and lending rates were widened to ease pressures on banking profitability. Yet the problems of these banks continued, and the government is currently engaged in a rehabilitation program. Similar difficulties, stemming originally from the payments arrears problem, have confronted the insurance sector. In response, the government introduced measures to restructure the sector, including new regulatory arrangements.

Trade policy. Trade policy reform was a major unfinished task on the agenda of structural adjustment loans I and II. Consequently, structural adjustment loan III sought to maintain the impetus of this reform. The objective of tariff and export incentive system reform was twofold—to create a framework of incentives in which inefficient enterprises were induced to adjust in an environment favorable to exports, and to neutralize the depressing effect on the productive sectors of the difference between domestic and international prices. The reform sought to provide a uniform effective protection rate of 40 percent across activities, including a 20 percent subsidy payment for exports. In effect, the reforms were to mimic an exchange rate depreciation. The new tariff code was revised. The export subsidy scheme was to be funded in the 1987 budget. A World Bank loan of $30 million was made in fiscal 1986 to provide financing to help industry adjust to the new incentive environment.

Most of the basic legislative changes necessary for implementing trade reforms were enacted between 1985 and 1988. However, the negotiations between the World Bank and the government were difficult, and the legislation was much criticized by the national press and local industrialists. The fiscal deterioration experienced by the government explains these difficulties in part. The government increased import duties by 30 percent in 1987, raising the target level of effective protection to 52 percent. This increase partly compensated for the continuing deterioration in the terms of trade and the declining U.S. dollar. But increasing pressure on the exchequer led to reluctance to implement the export subsidy scheme, due to be paid at the rate of 20 percent of value added by June 1990. By that time, despite its intention of doing so, the government had not yet taken into account the 30 percent increase in import duties in calculating the export subsidy. This created a lack of symmetry between import taxation and the rate of export subsidy, which operated to the disadvantage of exports. The government did streamline the approval process, but government officials and the industrial community were not confident that the export subsidy was to be continued. The investment necessary to take advantage of export opportunities was thus uncommitted. Yet the export subsidy scheme did increase the profits of existing exporters, enabling them to remain in business despite the overvalued exchange rate.

The removal of import controls was very painful for Ivorian manufacturers, especially in the textile, footwear, electronic equipment, appliances, and vehicles industries. The press and some officials alleged that eliminating import controls made it easier to avoid customs inspection, or to engage in underinvoicing on an extensive scale. Studies by Direction Générale des Grands Travaux (DGGTx) estimated that CFAF 30 billion in tax receipts (or 13 percent of total 1987 tax receipts) may have been lost annually. Yet import tax collection figures and omissions recorded in the balance of payments did not reveal evidence of fraud. Nevertheless, in February 1988 the government reapplied reference prices and quantitative restrictions to some 300 products, including textiles and footwear, in response to these fears of fraud. Their reimposition was a setback to the program, but without a system equipped to value imports effectively and realistically the problem will remain.

The government did not fully appreciate the painful impact of the import reforms on the industrial sector. The effects of the reform became even more acute after 1986 as the CFA franc appreciated against the U.S. dollar, while other potentially competitive countries (Nigeria and Ghana) devalued their currencies as part of their adjustment process. Removing quantitative restrictions on imports at this time was particularly damaging to parts of the industrial sector, and, in any event, proved to be politically unsustainable.

Agricultural policy. The weaknesses of Ivorian agriculture again became evident as the international prices of cocoa and coffee fell sharply in 1987. Whereas value added in agriculture grew by 3.8 percent annually from 1965 to 1980 (with the export crop sector growing by 6.5 percent annually), value added declined by 1.5 percent annually from 1980 to 1987 (and the export crop sector declined by 0.5 percent annually). Thus adjustment policy reform in agriculture did not restore agricultural growth, and further reforms were to be on the policy reform agenda for the remainder of the decade.

The main policy issue facing the government was the continued weakness in world commodity prices, especially for cocoa and coffee. In an effort to reverse the decline in world cocoa prices, the authorities implemented a policy in 1988 whereby the cocoa crop was partially retained. This policy disrupted the agricultural marketing cycle. Exporters were not reimbursed by the Agriculture Price Stabilization Fund, and were unable to obtain export permits. Thus, they were unable to repay crop credit, which in turn aggravated the liquidity problems of the banking system. But the retention policy failed to influence the world price, simply because the markets anticipated that the Ivorian stocks would eventually have to make their way into the market. The policy cost Côte d'Ivoire some of its market share, notably to Ghana.

Although the initial policy thrust was to raise the producer prices of cocoa and coffee under structural adjustment loan III, the marked decline in world prices precluded implementing the policy. The reforms thus sought to achieve two main objectives. The first was to increase price incentives for coffee production relative to cocoa. In determining producer prices, the government had persisted in ignoring a world price differential in favor of coffee (amounting to 25 percent on average between 1987 and 1989). This was corrected by the introduction of a coffee quality premium of CFAF 33 per kilogram. The second was to reform marketing arrangements for both crops—restructuring the Agriculture Price Stabilization Fund, whose charter was amended in April 1991. Its operations were limited to cocoa and coffee, where domestic marketing arrangements have been liberalized. The Agriculture Price Stabilization Fund was also to cease undertaking direct exports on its own account. A new system of setting producer prices on the basis of the average realized export prices of forward sales was implemented in late 1991. The role of the Agriculture Price Stabilization Fund in quality control, which had been quite ineffective and did little to encourage farmers to produce good-quality produce, was abolished. These reforms sought to reduce the costs (margins) of export crop marketing, and thus create the potential for raising producer prices.

Export taxes on all export crops other than cocoa, coffee, and timber products were eliminated. In addition, trade policy reforms (which were initially framed under structural adjustment loan II and extended in structural adjustment loan III) were applied to the entire agricultural sector (except cocoa, coffee, and cotton). The reforms extended the export subsidy scheme, which sought to provide an effective protection rate of 20 percent for such products. These reforms sought to encourage agricultural diversification, and the production of high-value export crops, such as fruits, rubber, and vegetables. However, the granting of export subsidies was patchy—the policy was applied to some crops (notably palm oil, rubber, and coconut), but not to others (such as pineapples and bananas). Moreover, payments were often delayed.

Public enterprise reform. Public enterprise reform changed gear in the 1987–91 period, with greater emphasis placed on divestiture, and not simply on restructuring. Between 1987 and 1989 almost 30 public enterprises were privatized. Several divestiture techniques were used, usually involving direct negotiations with potential buyers. These privatizations were conducted with little transparency, and little strategic study was pursued prior to privatization. In short, the privatizations were not particularly well managed. The new government in 1990 adopted a more strategic approach to privatization, supported by the International Development Association (IDA). The government has already privatized 4 enterprises under this initiative, and is currently bringing another 20 enterprises to the market to complete a first phase of privatization (between 1991 and 1993). Another phase involving some 30 enterprises is scheduled for implementation in 1993. The privatization program has been subject to repeated delays in implementation, and progress to date has been patchy. At the same time, policies have been framed to strengthen the existing public enterprises by giving them greater financial and management autonomy, and requiring greater accountability from them.

Summary

Appendix 3A summarizes the main elements of the structural adjustment issues in Côte d'Ivoire and how they were addressed under the reform programs. Fiscal policy has been generally contractionary throughout the decade, apart from a brief respite in 1984–86, when revenues were generated from improved commodity prices. Apart from those years, internal adjustment in Côte d'Ivoire has meant a dramatic cutback in public investment expenditures in the first instance, followed by cuts in current expenditures. Although there was some increase in tax rates, this has been insufficient to compensate for the loss in revenues from the stabilization funds. The authorities were generally successful in following a contractionary monetary policy, with broad money growth being brought under control. However, with the persistence of the fiscal deficit and a growing stock of domestic public sector arrears, the Ivorian banking system has faced, and continues to face, serious financial and liquidity problems. This has tended to crowd out credit to the private sector.

Given the continued decline in the price of the principal exports (cocoa and coffee), there was only limited opportunity for the government to raise producer prices. Policy reforms have therefore been directed at increasing marketing efficiency, lowering marketing costs, and providing incentives to maintain the orchard stock and quality. The main constraint facing agricultural pricing policy is the real exchange rate overvaluation, which effectively constrained the real returns that could be offered to export producers. Trade policy reforms attempted to mimic an exchange rate depreciation, but were not effectively implemented, mainly because fiscal constraints prevented timely payment of export subsidies. Quantitative restrictions were reapplied, in part because of the weaknesses of the customs administration.

Finally, progress with institutional reforms, particularly reforms of export crop marketing and the public enterprise sector, has been noticeably slow. For much of the decade very little was achieved, though in 1990–91 there was some evidence of more rapid change, including moves toward marketing liberalization and privatization.

Principal economic outcomes

The previous section set out the content and limitations of the adjustment programs of the 1980s. But what of the main economic outcomes? Do these confirm these weaknesses? In what follows, we divide the economic objectives of macroeconomic policy reform into four main groups: stabilization, resource allocation, economic growth, and equity and poverty reduction.

Stabilization

How successful were the adjustment programs at restoring macroeconomic balance in the face of serious destabilizing events of the decade? The main macroeconomic aggregates are reviewed in turn.

Fiscal deficit. The effects of the investment boom in the late 1970s can be seen in an increase in capital expenditures—from 14.8 percent of GDP in 1976 to 23.3 percent in 1978, and to 22.0 percent in 1979 (table 3.9 and appendix table 3B.2). Consequently, the fiscal deficit rose to 10.8 percent of GDP in 1979, despite a relatively favorable revenue position (total revenue averaged 35 percent of GDP from 1977 to 1979).[12] Despite cutbacks in investment spending to 13.1 percent of GDP in 1983 (from an annual average of 18.6 percent from 1978 to 1982), the primary fiscal deficit persisted (averaging just less than 5 percent of GDP in 1981–83). This was because lower world commodity prices led to a deterioration in revenue. More favorable world prices and revenues in 1984–86, combined with further cuts in investment spending, enabled the government to achieve a primary surplus of 6 percent of GDP and to close the overall fiscal deficit (to only 2.7 percent of GDP). Yet the gains in the terms of trade were short-lived, and the downward trend in revenue continued for the remainder of the decade, reaching its lowest level in 1991—22.7 percent of GDP. Although the government restrained the primary deficit to only 3.6 percent of GDP between 1987 and 1991, two fiscal problems remain—the persistence of an overall deficit (more than 13 percent of GDP) and imbalances in the fiscal accounts.

Despite severe cutbacks in investment spending and an improvement in the primary deficit, a high overall fiscal deficit has persisted. The main reason for the large deficit during the latter half of the decade was the strain that interest payments on public debt placed on the governmental accounts. Debt increased from negligible levels in the early 1980s to 12.3 percent of GDP by 1991, most of which was external debt. The debt problem has not yet been resolved. Insofar as the debt service problem has been addressed by accumulating arrears, interest payments and the fiscal deficit are in effect self-financing.

The closure of the primary deficit to an approximate balance in 1991 should not be interpreted as the solution of the fiscal deficit problem. The process of restoring this macro balance in turn created imbalances in the structure of the fiscal accounts, whose effects are arguably as serious as a persisting deficit. The contractionary fiscal policy in the latter half of the 1980s has created two major imbalances—between investment and recurrent expenditures, and between wages and salaries and other recurrent expenditures.

During the fettered adjustment period, investment expenditures comprised only 9.4 percent of total expenditures, compared with a 50 percent share during the boom of 1978–80. Future generations will thus bear much of the burden of the current adjustment effort. Restoring growth and "crowding in" private investment calls urgently for major fiscal adjustment in Côte d'Ivoire to restore investment expenditures by the government.

But this is only one aspect of the fiscal problem. The overall fiscal constraints facing the government have seriously distorted the composition of government recurrent expenditures. The share of wages and salaries in noninterest expenditures increased from 49 percent in the destabilizing period to 54 percent in the partial adjustment period, and remained at this level up to 1991 (appendix table 3B.2). The ratio of wages to materials costs rose from 1.8 to 2.9 during the same period. Wage and salary levels in the government sector are significantly higher than those in other countries of the region. The average civil service wage was 9 to 10 times GDP per capita, calling for civil service reform and a reduction in the wage and salary component of public expenditures.

Interest payments on foreign debt were suspended in May 1987, and irregular payments to the official bilateral creditors were resumed only with the rescheduling arrangement of that year. Thus, despite the adjustment efforts that have been made, fiscal problems were as evident at the end of the 1980s as they were at the beginning, if not more so. Aside from the persistence of the debt problem, the adjustment in the primary deficit has led to low levels of public investment and high relative levels of wage and salary expenditures, making it more difficult for the government to pursue equitable growth in Côte d'Ivoire.

Arrears. Given the monetary discipline imposed on the government by the West African Monetary Union, the options available to the government to finance its fiscal deficits are limited. External borrowing has been reduced significantly, due in part to the debt overhang. Borrowing from nonbanking domestic sources is limited by the shallowness of the domestic financial sector. Thus, the one option left is to accumulate arrears.

External arrears have become a major problem. Whereas the stock of total arrears to external creditors amounted to only $36 million in 1986, it rose to $2.15 billion by 1991. These figures underscore the effects of the destabilization on Côte d'Ivoire's international creditworthiness. But another major problem from the persistent fiscal deficit and the absence of a long-term solution to its financial crises has been the accumulation of arrears due to *domestic* creditors. By the end of 1989, the central government had accumulated arrears of CFAF 556 billion (more than $4 billion), or about 18 percent of GDP. These arrears are due not only on repayments of interest and principal on loans from the private banking system, but also on bills from private sector suppliers and contractors. Ruenda-Sabater and Stone (1992) give a graphic account of the extent of defaulting; almost all firms supplying the government or receiving refunds or subsidies from the government have been affected. The government and its agencies have simply stopped paying many of their bills. Even small and medium-scale enterprises are affected. Domestic arrears therefore had pervasive economic effects, damaging the financial sector and private investment, and thereby affecting overall economic activity.

The external deficit. The investment boom of the late 1970s widened the external current account deficit to 16.5 percent of GDP by 1991 (table 3.10 and appendix table 3B.3). The deficit fell to a negligible level in 1984–86 (just 1.6 percent of GDP) primarily because commodity prices recovered. However, the continued deterioration in prices thereafter, combined with the growing burden of interest payments on external debt, have led to the reemergence of significant external deficits on the current account. As with the fiscal deficit, this macroeconomic imbalance changed little throughout the 1980s. At the end of the decade, the current account deficit was only marginally lower than it was at the beginning. The main difference in the external account is the increasing importance of interest payments on external debt. In 1991 interest payments accounted for more than 80 percent of gross factor payments, and gross factor payments rose from just $184 million in 1975 to $1,278 million in 1991. Thus, the current account deficit in 1991 can be explained almost entirely by interest payments (with the deficit amounting to $1,132 million). In contrast, the deficit that was recorded in 1980 was almost three times the gross factor payments.

Given the negative effect of net factor income and net current transfers on the current account of the balance of payments (including interest payments on external public debt), the resource balance must be sufficiently in surplus to contain the current account deficit. Unfortunately, no surplus was recorded for much of the decade.

Table 3.10, which reports growth rates of export and import volumes during the three periods, clearly shows the nature of constrained adjustment. For much of the 1980s export growth was sluggish, averaging only 3.9 percent annually in the partial adjustment period, and only 1.8 percent between 1982 and 1988. The recent improvement is encouraging, and is due to a significant increase in the export volumes of cocoa (in 1989) and coffee (in 1990). Yet import volumes declined throughout much of the decade, by 1 percent annually between 1981 and 1986, but by 8 percent annually in 1987–88. The destabilizing period showed a positive growth of more than 13.9 percent. These figures indicate that export growth has been insufficient to achieve an external balance under the structural adjustment programs, and that, insofar as some adjustment has been made in the external (resource) balance, it has been brought about by import compression. Given

Table 3.10 Balance of payments trends, 1975–91
(US$ millions)

Item	Destabilizing period 1975–80	Partial adjustment 1981–83	Partial adjustment 1984–86	Fettered adjustment 1987–91
Exports of GNFS	2,668.1	2,719.6	3,271.2	3,431.3
Imports of GNFS	2,773.4	2,949.1	2,478.6	3,161.6
Resource balance	-105.4	-229.6	792.6	269.6
(as percentage of GDP)	0.3	-3.9	10.7	3.9
Net factor income	-304.2	-511.2	-602.7	-1,019.2
Net current transfers	-428.1	-401.9	-332.5	-470.5
Current account				
Balance before official grants	-837.6	-1,142.6	-142.6	-1,220.1
(as percentage of GDP)	-10.7	-14.9	-1.60	-12.4
Official capital grants	28.8	23.9	41.7	80.4
Balance after official grants	-808.8	-1,118.7	-100.9	-1,139.8
Long-term capital inflows	617.4	784.4	247.1	267.6
Other items	155.1	110.4	-269.1	602.5
Changes in net reserves	16.6	14.7	213.0	-17.3

Memorandum items: Growth rates

Item	Destabilizing period 1976–80	Partial adjustment 1981–86	Fettered adjustment 1987–88	Fettered adjustment 1989–90
Exports of goods and nonfactor services	4.9	3.9	-0.2	12.1
Imports of goods and nonfactor services	13.9	-0.9	-8.0	-1.0
GDP growth	4.3	2.0	-1.4	-1.8

Source: World Bank data.

the decline in real GDP in 1983–84 and in 1987–91 (see table 3.2), it is clear that expenditure *reduction* has been more important to Ivorian adjustment than has expenditure *switching*.

The current account deteriorated in the 1980s in part because the debt service burden grew, thus placing greater pressure on the resource balance to show a surplus sufficient to contain the current account deficit. What factors have determined the movements in the resource balance during the period? To investigate the underlying real-economy sources of external adjustment in Côte d'Ivoire, we decomposed the changes in the resource balance based on its underlying identities in the national income and product accounts.[13] It is possible to decompose changes in the resource balance into changes in total output and changes in the various expenditure components (public and private consumption and investment). Such calculations establish the extent to which the adjustment in the external accounts was brought about through changes in output or expenditure—and if the latter, which of the components of expenditure have borne the brunt of the adjustment.

Table 3.11 reports the results of the decomposition for Côte d'Ivoire. It records how changes in the resource balance were related to GDP and aggregate expenditure changes. Three periods are distinguished based on changes in the resource balance over the period.[14] The first period is 1977–80, when the resource balance deteriorated, and when the seeds of macroeconomic destabilization were sown. During this destabilizing period, the current account deficit increased to about 17 percent of GDP, associated with a deterioration in the resource balance. The second period is 1980–85, the period of partial adjustment, during which both the current account and the resource balance improved. The third is 1985–91, when the external imbalance continued—with an increase in the current account deficit to 12 percent of GDP and a decline in the resource balance. These trends in the external account are clear from the memorandum items of table 3.11.

To what extent were these changes induced by changes in aggregate supply or aggregate demand? The memorandum items address this question. For the first period (1977–80), the increase in output was insufficient to prevent a deteriorating external situation in the face of the massive increase in aggregate expenditures. This scenario is not surprising, given the investment-led boom of the late 1970s. The growth in aggregate absorption dominated through this period. During the partial adjustment phase (1980–85), the improvement in the external balances was associated with an expansion in aggregate supply, rather than an adjustment in absorption. Total expenditures increased, but by significantly less than the growth in output, reducing the external deficit. Thus, insofar as an adjustment took place during this period, it was through an expansion in supply rather than a contraction in demand.[15] Finally, the deterioration in the external deficit in the second

Table 3.11 Trade and resource balances and their related identities, 1975–91

(CFAF billions)

Item	*1975*	*1976*	*1977*	*1978*	*1979*	*1980*	*1981*	*1982*	*1983*	*1984*	*1985*	*1986*	*1987*	*1988*	*1989*	*1990*	*1991*
Trade balance/ GDP (%)	-10.8	-6	-3.5	-11.1	-15.2	-17.5	-16.9	-13.8	-14.1	-1.5	0.6	-3.9	-10.7	-12.6	-13.5	-13.2	-11.9
Resource balance	1.2	61.2	96.9	-16.3	-59.5	-134.6	-162.8	-72.2	-43.2	330.2	414.3	242.3	137.7	86.6	88.9	119.6	128.4
GDP	834.5	1,114.0	1,539.2	1,782.8	1,944.9	2,221.6	2,291.5	2,486.5	2,581.9	2,869.3	3,137.8	3,244.3	3,117.8	3,067.2	2,947.5	2,705.4	2,690.0
Public consumption	141.8	180.3	209.7	290.4	353.8	395.9	398.0	427.8	435.0	438.0	483.0	476.4	501.3	635.7	546.2	491.5	470.8
Private consumption	504.2	616.4	811.9	978.1	106.7	1,333.6	1,462.0	1,553.9	1,658.5	1,787.8	1,783	2,129.9	2,114.0	1,880.6	2,007.7	1,829.0	1,809.2
Public investment	76.9	105.3	165.8	238.0	258.7	201.0	202.4	169.1	162.7	131.0	117.4	153.0	123.0	143.0	93.0	74.7	74.4
Private investment	110.4	150.8	254.9	292.6	285.2	425.7	391.9	407.9	368.9	182.3	340.1	242.7	241.8	321.3	211.7	190.6	207.2
Total expenditures	833.3	1,052.8	1,442.3	1,799.1	2,004.4	2,356.2	2,454.3	2,558.7	2,625.1	2,539.1	2,723.5	3,002.0	2,980.1	2,980.6	2,858.6	2,585.8	2,561.6

	Change in 1977 to 1980		*Change in 1980 to 1985*		*Change in 1985 to 1991*	
Memorandum items	*CFAF (billions)*	*Percent*[a]	*CFAF (billions)*	*Percent*[a]	*CFAF (billions)*	*Percent*[a]
Resource balance	-231.5	100.0	548.9	100.0	-285.9	100.0
GDP	682.4	-294.8	916.2	166.9	-447.8	156.6
Total expenditures	913.9	-394.8	367.3	66.9	-161.9	56.6
Public consumption	186.2	-80.4	87.1	15.9	-12.2	4.3
Private consumption	521.7	-225.4	449.4	81.9	26.2	-9.2
Public investment	35.2	-15.2	-83.6	-15.2	-43.0	15.0
Private investment	170.8	-73.8	-85.6	-15.6	-132.9	46.5

a. Components as a percentage of changes in the resource balance.
Source: World Bank data.

half of the decade appears to have been due to a contraction in aggregate output, rather than to changes in aggregate absorption. In fact, absorption declined during the period, which, all else equal, would have reduced the external deficit. However, these absorption cuts were simply insufficient to counteract the output shortfalls that increasingly characterized the Ivorian economy in the late 1980s.

To explore the role of the various expenditure components in movements in the external balances, table 3.11 disaggregates the four main components of absorption (private and public consumption and private and public investment). The surge in absorption during the destabilizing period (1977–80) was related not only to public investment, but also to increases in private and (to a lesser extent) public consumption. In fact, the peak in public investment appeared earlier than the emerging external deficit—reaching 13.3 percent of GDP in 1978, when the current account deficit was 11.1 percent of GDP, far below its peak of 17.5 percent in 1980 (table 3.11). While the boom in public investment triggered the destabilization, it was the related boom in private and public consumption that really fueled domestic absorption and led to the deterioration in the external balances. Private investment had no significant effect on the destabilization.

During the partial adjustment period, both consumption components continued to rise, thereby exerting upward pressure on the external deficit. However, GDP growth in this period dominated these absorption changes. (Note that both of the investment components of absorption declined between 1980 and 1985, reinforcing the beneficial effects on the external deficit.) Finally, the destabilization at the end of the decade saw cuts in public consumption and (especially) investment, as well as reductions in private investment. However, they were not sufficient to prevent a continued increase in the external deficit, due to declining GDP.[16]

Money supply growth and inflation. Price inflation is one of the aggregates that has been stabilized under the adjustment program, primarily because monetary discipline was restored during the decade (table 3.12). The expansionary monetary policies of the destabilizing period (which witnessed a growth in money supply of 19 percent annually) were corrected during both the partial and the fettered adjustment phases (with money supply growth falling to 9 percent annually in 1981–86 and to –2 percent annually in 1987–91).

This restoration of monetary discipline is reflected in recorded rates of price inflation. Table 3.12 reports two measures of domestic price inflation—one based on the consumer price index, and the other based on the implicit GDP deflator. The two measures are quite different—the GDP deflator records a significantly greater decline in inflation during the period (from

15.0 percent in 1976–80 to –2.8 percent in 1987–90). Aside from the 1981–86 period, the GDP deflator indicates a lower rate of price increase than the consumer price index–based inflation index. The consumer price index is sensitive to the expenditure weights that are selected. Table 3.12 compares consumer price index–based rates of inflation according to three alternative sets of weights (European, African, and low-income patterns of expenditures). The African weights generally yield higher inflation rates than the others, and these are usually the basis for the official consumer price index. The lower inflation rate indicated by the GDP deflator is due to the weight given in the deflator to export commodities, the prices of which fell during the latter half of the decade. The consumer price index does not reflect this. Both indices show that, compared with earlier in the decade, inflation has been significantly reduced. Given the monetary discipline imposed by the West African Monetary Union and the severity of the recession (due in part to contractionary adjustment policies), this outcome is not surprising.

Relative prices and resource allocation

Besides being a measure of international competitiveness, the real effective exchange rate reflects a key relative price that directs resource allocation in the economy. The real appreciations in the exchange rate during the late 1970s and the late 1980s would usually indicate resource allocations away from the tradables sector in general, toward nontradable activities. To what extent do direct indicators of the price of tradables relative to the price of nontradables confirm this change in the price structure of the Ivorian economy, and how responsive have resource allocations been to these changes?

Appendix table 3B.4 reports estimates of the relative price structure of the Ivorian economy based on the broad sectoral, implicit GDP deflators. It is clear that the relative price signal indicated by the real exchange rate is not

Table 3.12 Measures of price inflation, 1976–90

Inflation measure	*1976–80*	*1981–86*	*1987–90*
Annual inflation rate, CPI (percent)	16.7	5.8	4.3
African weights	16.7	5.8	4.3
European weights	..	..	2.1
Low-income weights	..	..	3.5
GDP deflator (annual percentage change)	15.0	7.1	-2.8
Consumer price index/wholesale price index	120.5	111.3	95.0
GDP deflator/wholesale price index	132.2	104.9	76.1
Money supply growth (M2)	20.8	9.0	-3.2

.. Not available.
Source: World Bank and IMF data.

reflected consistently in the GDP deflator series. Although the series indicates that the relative price of services increased during the destabilizing period (when the real exchange rate appreciated) and declined in 1984 (when the real rate depreciated), the story thereafter is confused. In particular, the prices of services fell noticeably after 1985, whereas tradable prices increased—this, during a period of significant real exchange rate appreciation. Certainly, the table does not provide evidence of a significant movement in the relative price series that favored the services sector in the latter half of the 1980s. One factor that has prevented the relative price of services from rising is the severe recession, as evidenced by declining GDP and resource underutilization. The tentative conclusion to be drawn from these data is that, while the reliance on internal adjustment has failed to restore the international competitiveness of tradables in Côte d'Ivoire, it has prevented perverse price signals that favor nontradables.[17] To what extent does resource allocation reflect the stable pricing of nontradables?

GDP growth rates by sector of origin (see table 3.3) are more consistent with the real exchange rate signals, with the services sector growing rapidly during periods of exchange rate appreciation (at 8.68 percent between 1985 and 1991), and less so when the real exchange rate was depreciating (at only 1.83 percent from 1980 to 1984). Similarly, the tradables sectors (agriculture and industry) have exhibited slow and even negative growth since 1985, and grew faster during the period of real exchange rate depreciation. Although these indicators are too aggregative to provide accurate measures of the effects of movements in the exchange rate or resource allocation, they are at least consistent with the real exchange rate movements identified in table 3.5.

Changes in trade distortions

To what extent have the adjustment programs removed the fundamental trade distortions of the Ivorian economy—exchange rate overvaluation, import restrictions, and price controls? The adjustment effort failed to reverse the real exchange rate appreciation that dominated the decade (especially its second half). But what of trade policy? How have the reforms changed this source of incentive distortion?

With the increasing overvaluation of the real exchange rate, any significant reduction in the level of protection granted through trade controls would be unlikely, given the penalty of an overvalued real exchange rate on export producers and import-substituting producers alike. As already noted, the major thrust of structural adjustment loans II and III was to increase protection to import-competing activities and allocate subsidies to exporters in order to mimic a real exchange rate depreciation. (The reason for the failure of this policy is reviewed in the next section.) Given that levels of protection must be maintained when the real exchange rate is overvalued, how can trade policy reforms be assessed from the standpoint of structural adjustment and its objectives? Reform could have reduced the distortionary effects of trade policy in Côte d'Ivoire in two ways, without obviating the objective of proxying a devaluation. First, trade liberalization could be achieved by substituting tariffs for quantitative import restrictions. Second, the tariff structure could be designed to minimize the distortion of the incentive structure and resource allocation.

Both of these objectives were part of the adjustment lending operations of the World Bank. The first was an essential part of the tariff plus subsidy scheme, since the replacement of quantitative restrictions by tariffs would generate revenue to the exchequer to help finance export subsidies. The second objective was set during structural adjustment loans II and III, which sought to achieve a uniform effective protection rate of 40 percent for all protected activities. Were these more limited trade liberalization measures achieved?

Quantitative restrictions were replaced by tariffs in 1985 as part of the structural adjustment program, with surcharges to be applied temporarily during the transition. But the continued appreciation of the CFA franc, devaluations in Nigeria and Ghana, the persistent decline in commodity prices, and well-based rumors of fraud, smuggling, and underinvoicing led to a progressive reversal of this policy after 1987. The World Bank reports that about one-third of imports were still subject to quantitative restrictions at the end of the decade. Consumer goods with mass-market potential (such as textiles, clothing, shoes, refined oil, rubber products, processed food, and electrical appliances) all continued to be subject to licensing. About half of food imports continued to be subject to either prior authorization or licensing. In other words, the limited liberalization objective of replacing quantitative restrictions with tariffs was not met.

Achieving a uniform level of effective protection in order to minimize the distortions of trade policy in resource allocation is not easy. These rates can change as input use responds to major changes in relative prices, thus derailing the policy. These difficulties, as events proved, also confounded the policy in Côte d'Ivoire. Table 3.13 reports the structure of nominal and effective protection in Côte d'Ivoire in 1990, as reported by the World Bank. Trade policy involved a combination of tariffs and export subsidies. The latter were not consistently paid to exporters, and so the protection they actually received was significantly less than the level to which they were notionally entitled. The first two columns of table 3.13 report nominal rates of protection for outputs and inputs. These are combined to generate estimates of effective rates, reported in the remaining columns. The third and fourth columns report effective protection rates for actual export subsidy payments and for the full (notional) payment. These data clearly show a wider dispersion in protection afforded by trade policy at the end of the decade, ranging from –40 percent in agroindustry to more than 40 percent in plastics and packaging. A comparison of the third and fourth columns readily shows the effect of the export subsidy arrears problem.

The final column in table 3.13 estimates the rate of effective protection when the real exchange rate overvaluation is considered (estimated to be 33 percent in the computations reported).[18] It suggests that, even had the export subsidy been paid in full, it would not have been sufficient to compensate for the exchange rate overvaluation. Despite some high rates of effective protection, most activities remain taxed due to the trade policy regime.

In sum, the limited attempts at trade liberalization were not implemented effectively during the partial and fettered adjustment periods. The role of the real exchange rate appreciation in limiting the government's room for maneuver is self-evident. Yet even within this constraint, it appears that little or no progress has been made toward removing import restrictions or making trade policy more evenhanded. Trade policy seemed to be as much a source of incentive distortion and resource misallocation at the close of the decade as it was at the beginning.

Economic growth

The growth record of Côte d'Ivoire in the 1980s was dismal. Between 1983 and 1991, real GDP growth averaged –0.4 percent annually, despite high growth in 1985 and 1986, when commodity prices were favorable. At the same time, population growth increased steadily—from 3.4 percent annually in the early 1980s to 3.9 percent in 1991 and 1992. The net result of these trends has been a devastating decline in per capita income.

Table 3.13 Structure of nominal and effective protection, 1990

Sector	*Nominal protection*		*Effective protection*		*Net effective protection; actual export subsidies*
	Outputs	*Inputs*	*Actual export subsidies*	*Full export subsidies*	
Textiles	19.1	18.4	29.7	44.2	-1.6
Agroindustry	0.1	15	-39.8	-39.4	-54.8
(excluding cocoa)	10.4	21.8	-16.9	16	-34.3
Wood	6.5	11.8	3.8	10.6	-22.2
Plastics/packaging	30.6	13.7	41.5	41.5	-6.8
Total	0.4	15.1	-38.8	-38.3	-54.1
Excluding cocoa	16	19.1	8.8	30.2	-16.4

Source: World Bank data.

Whereas mean per capita income had reached CFAF 333,959 in 1980, it fell to just CFAF 209,411 in 1991. Even when compared with the preboom years, income is now lower (in 1975, per capita GNP was almost CFAF 300,000). In the 1980s per capita GNP declined by 2.4 percent annually. The situation is worse for private consumption. In 1991 mean private consumption was significantly lower in real terms than it was throughout the entire period. While real GNP declined by 2.4 percent annually between 1980 and 1991, real private consumption declined by 4.9 percent annually—compared with the 4.0 percent growth in real consumption toward the end of the 1970s.

These figures may overstate the decline in real incomes, if a significant shift of resources into the informal sector has taken place. National accounts data usually underrecord informal sector activities, and growth in such activities may have increased the underrecording of measured national output and consumption. However, data from the Côte d'Ivoire Living Standards Survey (discussed in the next section) also suggest a decline in real expenditures of a similar order in the national accounts (Grootaert 1993). These estimates, based on household data, include both formal and informal sector activities. Thus, the national accounts data give a reasonably accurate account of the decline in income and consumption, at least during the latter half of the 1980s.

Summary

The inadequacy of economic policy in Côte d'Ivoire can be viewed from two standpoints. The first is the inability of the government to achieve the intermediate objectives of economic policy—macroeconomic balance, resource reallocation, improved competitiveness. These are the nuts and bolts of economic policy. The second is the more fundamental objectives of economic policy—enhancing economic growth and development, improving the environment and quality of life, and alleviating poverty and deprivation. This brief review of the macroeconomic balances (as part of the nuts and bolts) during the 1980s tells a dismal story. Table 3.14 summarizes most of the relevant data on both the intermediate results and the more fundamental objectives. At the end of the decade, with the exception of monetary instruments and the rate of inflation, the imbalances were as much in evidence as they were at the beginning. The composition of the macroeconomic aggregates, and the immediate causes of the imbalances, have changed over the decade, but the fact remains: the adjustment efforts of the 1980s failed to correct the imbalances. There has been some success in reducing inflation and controlling the external deficit, attributable mainly to contractionary macroeconomic policies, which has led to import compression and a general decline in GDP, especially since 1987. The adjustment has also penalized investment at the expense of consumption expenditure. Private investment fell from almost

16 percent of GDP during 1978–80 to only 7 percent in 1987–91. Similar orders of magnitude hold for public investment. Savings performance has been weak, and export performance only marginally better. These indicators do not auger well for future growth.

The figures speak for themselves: the economic shocks to which the economy has been subjected, together with the limited and fettered adjustment response, have resulted in the most devastating social cost—declining standards of living and welfare. It has meant the abandonment of economic growth as an effective policy objective. How this has affected poverty, and the equity objective, is the subject of the next section.

Economic recession, fettered adjustment, and poverty

Given the abandonment of economic growth, Côte d'Ivoire represents a counterfactual case—showing how poverty might be affected when adjustment policy reforms are not applied effectively. The analysis that follows will show that nonadjustment has reduced average incomes, thereby increasing poverty alarmingly.[19] This "growth" effect in reverse dominates any analysis

Table 3.14 Macroeconomic indicators of adjustment, 1975–91
(annual averages)

Indicator	*Destabilizing period* 1975–77	1978–80	1975–80	*Partial adjustment* 1981–83	1984–86	1981–86	*Fettered adjustment* 1987–91
Intermediate results							
Real effective exchange rate (index)	104.8	128.8	116.8	110.4	106.5	108.5	124.8
Relative inflation rate (index)	99.3	115.4	107.4	110.2	102.3	106.3	95.5
Money supply growth (percent per year)	34.2	3.7	18.9	6.0	11.9	9.0	-2.2
Real interest (discount) rate (percent)	3.3	6.0	4.6	9.9	10.0	9.9	9.5
Fiscal deficit/GDP (percent)	-1.4	-10.6	-5.8	-11.9	-2.7	-7.3	-13.2
Balance of payments current account/GDP	-6.8	-14.6	-10.7	-14.9	-1.6	-8.3	-12.4
Final results			*(percentage)*				
Real GDP growth	5.3	5.3	5.3	1.6	2.4	2.0	-1.6
Private investment/GDP	13.5	15.8	14.6	14.1	8.5	11.3	7.1
Domestic investment/GDP	24.3	28.6	26.5	23.2	12.6	17.9	11.5
Domestic savings/GDP	28.2	25.3	26.8	19.3	23.3	21.3	15.4
Exports of GNFS/GDP	40.4	35.1	37.7	36.0	43.6	39.8	35.1
Imports of GNFS/GDP	36.4	38.4	37.4	39.9	32.9	36.4	31.2
Real growth rate of exports	-0.1	6.9	3.4	0.1	7.7	3.9	6.0
Real growth rate of imports	16.3	5.9	11.1	-8.4	6.6	-0.9	-4.5

Note: For definitions of variables, see appendix table 3B.1
Source: World Bank and IMF data.

of poverty in Côte d'Ivoire during the 1980s. Insofar as this analysis is confined to the historical record, however, it does not separate the effects of the shock (primarily the terms of trade decline) from the fettered policy response (expenditure-reducing policies). The data also suggest that groups that would normally benefit from structural adjustment—notably export crop farmers in the African context—have in fact suffered disproportionate losses due to the economic changes of the 1980s. Again, the analysis offers insights into scenarios that are counterfactuals to the adjustment case.

Although data on poverty in Côte d'Ivoire are not available for the entire decade, the Côte d'Ivoire Living Standards Survey does provide reasonably good household data for 1985–88. Information from a sample of 1,600 households was collected each year on a range of variables—income, expenditures, labor force activity, education, health, and anthropometry. These data, extending over a four-year period in which significant macroeconomic changes occurred, offer a rare opportunity to investigate the implications of economic shocks, recession, and adjustment for income distribution in general and poverty in particular. One problem with the survey has been the change in sampling procedures and sampling frame in 1987. Demery and Grootaert (1993) identify the nature of the sampling bias generated by these changes, and reweighed the data as necessary. The following review of the effects on poverty in Côte d'Ivoire relies heavily on an analysis of these data by Grootaert (1993).

Due to difficulties in measuring income through the Côte d'Ivoire Living Standards Surveys and similar household surveys,[20] per capita expenditures are taken as the indicator of welfare (and indeed are a proxy for income trends). The changes in nominal and real expenditure per capita in Côte d'Ivoire and each of five regions of the country are summarized in table 3.15. To compare expenditures across the region, an appropriate regional price index based on Grootaert and Kanbur (1993) is used. The consumer price index was used to adjust for price changes over time. For the period covered by the Côte d'Ivoire Living Standards Surveys (1985–88), the average inflation rate was 5.3 percent according to the consumer price index. Table 3.15 shows overwhelming evidence of a dramatic fall in household expenditures during the period covered (and especially in 1987–88). These trends are fully consistent with the national accounts data reviewed above.

From 1984 to 1986 Côte d'Ivoire benefited from favorable external price shocks, which, together with a concerted effort at changing relative prices, improved the macroeconomic balances and GDP growth. Yet thereafter the terms of trade returned to a downward trend, and the government in effect abandoned its structural adjustment program. In the crisis management that ensued, the government sought to reduce expenditures in an effort to control the macroeconomic imbalances, and GDP declined sharply up to 1991.

Table 3.15 Nominal and real per capita expenditures, by region, 1985–88

(CFA francs)

Region	*1985*			*1986*			*1987*			*1988*		
	Nominal	*Real value*	*Real index*	*Nominal*	*Real value*	*Real index*	*Nominal*	*Real value*	*Real index*	*Nominal*	*Real value*	*Real index*
Abidjan	376,108	376,108	100.0	335,698	312,859	83.2	410,220	372,361	99.0	332,938	288,708	76.8
Other cities	252,387	271,864	114.3	271,758	270,540	99.5	246,469	250,010	92.0	190,190	178,165	65.5
Rural areas												
East Forest	143,104	164,472	69.1	160,890	172,341	104.8	159,491	167,974	102.1	152,267	152,501	92.7
West Forest	187,120	239,134	100.5	163,782	204,457	85.5	138,380	169,776	71.0	120,225	143,947	60.2
Savannah	115,910	152,573	64.1	132,968	154,676	101.4	120,017	136,061	89.2	113,957	120,684	79.1
Côte d'Ivoire	213,634	237,853	100.0	216,173	223,905	94.1	212,191	216,965	91.2	178,051	173,072	72.8

Source: Grootaert (1993).

It is hardly surprising, therefore, that poverty increased throughout the period. The evidence is summarized in table 3.16, which reports three measures based on the class of poverty index suggested by Foster, Greer, and Thorbecke (1984).[21]

Between 1985 and 1986, poverty fell—marginally in most areas but more so in the East Forest. Poverty among the poorest groups fell noticeably (as reflected in the P_2 indexes),[22] suggesting that the combination of the favorable external shock and the initial attempts to improve tradables prices raised income among the poorest groups. But thereafter all indexes began to rise steeply—especially between 1987 and 1988, when GDP began to decline. For the country as a whole, the proportion of the population in poverty increased from 30 percent in 1985 to 46 percent in 1988. Poverty increased more in urban than in rural areas, so that the share of the poor in urban areas increased from 19 percent in 1985 to 25 percent in 1988. However, poverty in rural areas (apart from the East Forest) was also on the rise—especially in the West Forest, where poverty increased from 18 percent in 1985 to 55 percent in 1988.

To explore the relationship between these poverty trends and the adjustment programs of the 1980s, poverty indices can be decomposed in two ways. First, the effect of changes in *mean* expenditures can be separated from the influence of expenditure *distribution* changes. Second, the poverty index is disaggregated by socioeconomic group in order to assess the differential effects of macroeconomic events on the groups in society.

Growth and distributional effects

The methodology of separating out the effects of changes in mean expenditures (the growth component) from changes in the distribution of expenditure (the distribution component) is set out in Ravallion (1992) and Ravallion and Datt (1993). Grootaert (1993) applies this methodology to Côte d'Ivoire, and his results are summarized in table 3.17.

For the country as a whole, the growth effect is overwhelming. In fact, the effect of changes in the distribution of expenditures was negative between 1985 and 1988, meaning that the distribution of expenditures narrowed over the period. If mean expenditures had remained constant, poverty would have fallen by 20 percent. The negative influence of the distributional effect is true for all regions except Savannah. For this region, both the growth and the distributional effects increased poverty. The lesson of table 3.17 is clear: the declines in GNP were the most important determinants of poverty in Côte d'Ivoire during the latter half of the 1980s. And if poverty is to be reduced in the coming years, growth must be rekindled. But table 3.17 assesses only the early phase of income decline in the country. Since GDP growth was nega-

Table 3.16 Poverty indexes by region, 1985–88

	P_α indexes											
	1985			1986			1987			1988		
Region	P_0	P_1	P_2	P_0	P_1	P_2	P_0	P_1	P_2	P_0	P_1	P_2
Abidjan	0.034	0.009	0.004	0.166	0.035	0.012	0.074	0.019	0.009	0.139	0.023	0.006
Other cities	0.234	0.075	0.037	0.233	0.062	0.024	0.224	0.053	0.019	0.410	0.106	0.040
East Forest	0.479	0.155	0.069	0.395	0.115	0.045	0.435	0.111	0.041	0.494	0.145	0.062
West Forest	0.178	0.036	0.013	0.200	0.013	0.013	0.376	0.102	0.043	0.553	0.154	0.064
Savannah	0.502	0.183	0.088	0.481	0.058	0.058	0.578	0.197	0.093	0.652	0.258	0.131
Côte d'Ivoire	0.300	0.098	0.045	0.045	0.032	0.032	0.348	0.101	0.043	0.459	0.142	0.063

	Decomposition (percentage share by region)											
	1985			1986			1987			1988		
Region	P_0	P_1	P_2	P_0	P_1	P_2	P_0	P_1	P_2	P_0	P_1	P_2
Abidjan	2.3	1.8	1.6	11.0	8.4	7.8	3.9	3.6	3.8	5.2	2.8	1.5
Other cities	16.8	16.3	17.6	17.1	17.4	17.3	14.6	12.0	10.0	19.3	16.1	13.7
East Forest	37.1	36.8	35.3	31.8	33.7	34.5	29.3	25.8	22.4	25.5	24.1	23.3
West Forest	8.3	5.1	4.1	9.2	7.1	5.5	11.8	11.1	11.0	18.6	16.8	15.6
Savannah	35.6	39.9	41.4	30.9	33.3	34.9	40.3	47.5	52.9	31.4	40.2	45.9
Côte d'Ivoire	100.0	100.0	100.0	100.0	100.0	100.0	100.0	100.0	100.0	100.0	100.0	100.0

Note: Table is based on a poverty line of 128,600 CFAF annually.
Source: Grootaert (1993).

tive up to 1991 (and since cocoa and coffee prices fell further in 1989), it is likely that poverty levels have increased even above the 1988 levels reported here. These data are a chilling reminder of what the outcomes might be for the poor when governments fail to adjust to changing external circumstances in an orderly and planned manner.

Poverty among the socioeconomic groups

In disaggregating the P_α indexes, Grootaert (1993) distinguished eight socioeconomic groups (table 3.18). Poverty among all socioeconomic groups increased throughout the period, but the increases were far from even. Among the urban groups, it is clear that public sector employees bore the brunt of the recession (and fiscal contraction), with the incidence of poverty (P_0) increasing from just 5 percent in 1985 (representing just less than 2 percent of total poverty) to 21 percent in 1988 (or 6 percent of total poverty). Why poverty among this group should rise as much must be investigated further. The government has been reluctant to reduce real wages and salaries in the civil service—so why the increase in poverty among this group? Judging from the movement in the P_2 measure, this deterioration in living standards seems to have applied particularly among the lower-paid public sector workers. Lower-paid public employees may have been treated less favorably than better-paid civil servants, though this is conjecture at this point.

Table 3.17 Decomposition of 1985–88 changes in head-count index (P_0) by region and socioeconomic group

Category	*Growth component*	*Redistribution component*	*Residual*	*Total change*
Region				
Abidjan	0.076	-0.002	0.031	0.105
Other cities	0.213	-0.111	0.072	0.174
East Forest	0.046	-0.061	0.030	0.015
West Forest	0.355	-0.005	0.025	0.375
Savannah	0.146	-0.022	-0.018	0.150
Socioeconomic group				
Export crop farmers	0.213	-0.090	0.059	0.182
Foodcrop farmers	0.162	-0.037	0.031	0.186
Public sector employees	0.208	-0.001	-0.043	0.164
Private formal sector employees	0.102	-0.040	0.018	0.080
Informal sector employees	0.306	-0.042	0.016	0.280
Self-employed	0.123	-0.045	0.122	0.200
Inactive	0.126	-0.068	0.078	0.136
Unemployed	0.114	0.047	0.0181	0.342
Côte d'Ivoire	0.169	-0.06	0.049	0.158

Note: For details of decomposition, see text.
Source: Grootaert (1993).

Table 3.18 Poverty indexes by socioeconomic group, 1985–88

Group	1985			1986			1987			1988		
	P_0	P_1	P_2	P_0	P_1	P_2	P_0	P_1	P_2	P_0	P_1	P_2
P_α indexes												
Export crop farmers	0.366	0.094	0.038	0.354	0.099	0.037	0.477	0.150	0.063	0.548	0.179	0.087
Foodcrop farmers	0.434	0.144	0.065	0.411	0.121	0.048	0.473	0.132	0.055	0.590	0.196	0.087
Public sector employees	0.049	0.007	0.001	0.056	0.006	0.001	0.072	0.016	0.006	0.213	0.050	0.018
Private formal sector employees	0.071	0.014	0.005	0.096	0.009	0.001	0.061	0.012	0.004	0.151	0.025	0.007
Informal sector employees	0.262	0.075	0.028	0.401	0.097	0.028	0.364	0.090	0.040	0.542	0.183	0.093
Self-employed	0.262	0.104	0.058	0.287	0.077	0.03	0.333	0.084	0.033	0.462	0.127	0.052
Inactive	0.183	0.075	0.043	0.211	0.047	0.015	0.327	0.141	0.080	0.319	0.060	0.031
Unemployed	0.041	0.005	0.001	0.346	0.119	0.067	0.312	0.049	0.009	0.383	0.151	0.076
Côte d'Ivoire	0.300	0.098	0.045	0.299	0.082	0.032	0.349	0.101	0.043	0.459	0.142	0.063
Decomposition (percentage share by group)												
Export crop farmers	14.5	11.5	10.0	21.8	22.2	21.6	25.9	28.0	27.9	17.7	18.7	20.6
Foodcrop farmers	63.6	65.2	63.8	51.2	54.9	56.4	48.8	47.2	46.4	52.4	56.2	56.9
Public sector employees	1.7	0.8	0.3	2.4	1.0	0.4	3.0	2.4	1.9	6.2	4.8	3.8
Private formal sector employees	2.4	1.4	1.1	2.3	0.7	0.3	1.5	1.0	0.8	3.0	1.6	1.0
Informal sector employees	1.5	1.3	1.0	1.8	1.6	1.2	1.8	1.5	1.6	1.6	1.7	2.0
Self-employed	12.8	15.6	18.7	14.1	13.8	14	12.9	11.3	10.3	14.8	13.2	12.2
Inactive	3.3	4.2	5.1	4.9	4.0	3.4	5.6	8.3	11.1	2.5	2.8	2.4
Unemployed	0.2	0.1	0.0	1.5	1.8	2.7	0.6	0.3	0.1	0.9	1.1	1.3
Côte d'Ivoire	100.0	100.0	100.0	100.0	100.0	100.0	100.0	100.0	100.0	100.0	100.0	100.0

Note: Table is based on a poverty line of 128,600 CFAF annually.
Source: Grootaert (1993).

All other urban groups have also suffered. More than 54 percent of employees in informal sectors were in poverty in 1988. The self-employed were similarly affected. An interesting feature is the change in poverty among the unemployed category. In 1985 only 4 percent of the unemployed were below the poverty line. By 1988 the figure had risen to 38 percent. This suggests that unemployment changed from being a "search" phenomenon (in which better-off workers voluntarily spend periods of unemployment searching for higher-wage jobs) to being a manifestation of labor underutilization and involuntary unemployment. It appears that the unemployed increasingly have no alternative, reflected by the growing incidence of poverty among them.

Among rural groups, export crop farmers appear to have fared the worse of the two main groups distinguished. In 1985, 37 percent of export crop farmers were poor; by 1988, this figure has risen to 55 percent. The increase in poverty among food producers is not as great, and the share of this group in total poverty fell from 64 percent in 1985 to 52 percent in 1988. According to Grootaert, a significant decline in farm income was the main determinant of the increase in poverty among export crop framers. The Côte d'Ivoire Living Standards Surveys record a decline in farm income of more than 47 percent in the West Forest and 12 percent in Savannah. The same period saw a decline in the quantities of cocoa and coffee sold, which explains why the income of such groups fell so steeply in the four years covered by the survey. The area planted in coffee also declined sharply, although the area under cocoa cultivation increased.

These data clearly reflect the failure of the adjustment efforts to depreciate the real effective exchange rate and to improve the real income levels of exporters. Whereas poverty levels held steady between 1985 and 1986 (due to favorable world market conditions), the subsequent deterioration in the circumstances of exporters is due directly to the failure of key elements of macroeconomic adjustment. The evidence of the Côte d'Ivoire Living Standards Surveys is that export crop activities declined over the period, generating lower income, and creating greater poverty among export crop farmers. Yet, under a successful expenditure-switching adjustment scenario, this is the very group that should gain from relative price movements. The fact that this group has become noticeably worse off is a clear indication that the adjustment attempts in mid-decade failed because, among other reasons, they did little to change the underlying trend in relative price movements. It is likely that poverty among export crop farmers has increased even more since 1988, given the continued decline in terms of trade, and the continued appreciation in the real exchange rate.

Several conclusions can be drawn from this brief review of poverty trends in Côte d'Ivoire. First, nonadjustment has seriously eroded the living standards of all groups in Ivorian society. Poverty has become more widespread in the country, and all groups now contain a growing number of persons in poverty. Second, the decline in GDP makes eradicating poverty an impossible task, and dominated the poverty scenario during the second half of the 1980s. Third, while all groups have suffered, some experienced greater deprivation—especially low-paid public sector workers in urban areas and export crop producers in rural areas. The declining expenditures and income of the latter group conveys a powerful message about the failure of the adjustment efforts of the 1980s and its repercussions.

Human capital and social expenditures

This evidence of serious social cost incurred in the 1985–88 period is based on a particular measure of welfare—the total expenditures of households. Do other indicators of welfare suggest deprivation of the same order?

Basic needs. Table 3.19 summarizes the evidence reported by Grootaert (1993) on five basic needs indicators: three for educational outcomes (literacy and primary and secondary enrollment rates) and two for health outcomes (the percentage of ill household members who consulted either a doctor or a nurse, and the percentage of household members reporting preventive consultations, primarily prenatal care and vaccination). All measures are reported for the poorest groups (those whose annual per capita expenditures are below CFAF 75,000 in 1985 prices), the moderately poor (those whose annual per capita expenditures are between CFAF 75,000 and 128,600), and the nonpoor (those whose per capita expenditures are greater than CFAF 128,600).

The literacy rate has a momentum of its own (reflecting previous education history), and major changes in this indicator are not to be expected over such a short period. Although this is true for most groups and for the country as a whole, literacy among the poorest males fell quite dramatically and consistently each year (from just less than 23 percent in 1985 to less than 17 percent in 1988). This decline in literacy among the poorest males is likely to be due to changes in the composition of the poorest group. The least literate have clearly been most likely to fall into the poorest category during the period covered (Grootaert 1993).

The primary and secondary enrollment rates are more sensitive indicators of how recent economic changes affected educational outcomes. The net primary enrollment rate (the number of primary-school-age children enrolled in primary school as a percentage of all children of primary school age) reflects the effects of both temporary and permanent withdrawals from schooling. This rate was fairly constant for Côte d'Ivoire as a whole during the period (around 54 percent, except for 1987), and the same applies to most groups. However, enrollment among females in the poorest group of households fell noticeably. The net secondary enrollment (defined as the number of children of secondary school age currently enrolled in school as

Table 3.19 Social indicators, 1985–88
(percentage of group)

Indicator		1985	1986	1987	1988
Education indicators					
Literacy					
Very poor	male	22.8	19.9	18.2	16.8
	female	8.0	7.3	7.4	8.3
Moderately poor	male	26.7	31.3	26.3	32.9
	female	12.9	15.5	10.9	17.1
Nonpoor	male	45.1	45.1	49.8	49.7
	female	28.0	27.7	31.2	31.8
All		30.9	31.9	32.4	31.9
Net primary enrollment rate					
Very poor	male	31.7	35.6	34.1	31.0
	female	22.4	22.9	16.7	16.7
Moderately poor	male	51.1	49.3	48.2	54.3
	female	41.0	37.6	36.7	41.9
Nonpoor	male	66.3	64.2	78.0	74.0
	female	54.0	57.5	63.9	57.7
All		53.6	54.1	58.4	54.0
Net secondary enrollment rate					
Very poor	male	9.7	3.0	2.8	3.5
	female	5.3	2.0	4.5	1.2
Moderately poor	male	20.0	16.3	11.5	14.8
	female	9.8	5.2	4.1	9.0
Nonpoor	male	36.8	37.6	36.8	33.6
	female	18.8	25.6	22.9	21.1
All		22.9	25.2	22.3	19.1
Health indicators					
Percentage of ill people who consulted doctor/nurse					
Very poor	male	31.2	30.8	20.0	19.1
	female	30.2	28.0	15.5	16.2
Moderately poor	male	36.9	30.0	37.4	32.8
	female	36.2	30.6	34.0	31.3
Nonpoor	male	48.6	47.7	46.2	52.6
	female	50.8	51.8	48.4	54.8
All		45.8	43.9	40.6	41.3
Percentage of people who have preventive consultations					
Very poor	male	14.2	21.9	19.9	40.0
	female	15.6	27.2	26.1	47.3
Moderately poor	male	17.1	21.9	29.7	31.4
	female	18.1	23.6	33.3	35.9
Nonpoor	male	23.5	29.2	29.9	26.0
	female	25.8	30.7	37.2	32.8
All		22.3	27.9	32.1	32.8

Note: See text for definitions.
Source: Grootaert (1993).

a percentage of the total number of secondary-school-age children) indicates greater welfare loss over the period. The rate fell for most groups, especially for the poor. Secondary enrollment among the poorest fell to only 3.5 percent for males and 1.2 percent for females—a sad reflection of the difficult situation that poor households faced during the 1980s. These indicators also suggest that the poor will have few opportunities to escape poverty unless their human capital is enhanced far beyond that suggested by these data.

The proportion of ill persons contacting either a doctor or a nurse for treatment has declined marginally over the period. However, this masks critical differences among the groups. Between 1985 and 1988 the nonpoor were more likely to consult a practitioner when ill, while the poor (and especially the very poor) were dramatically less likely to do so. Grootaert (1993) reports that medical consultations were also increasingly less likely in rural areas, suggesting that access to health facilities has deteriorated.[23] However, the preventive health care indicators suggest a different trend—an increase in the percentage of persons (including the poor) who had preventive health care over the period. Why these indicators contradict each other is not clear. It may be that vaccination programs have been well targeted, and do not require the medical infrastructure necessary to support effective curative consultations.

These basic needs indicators do not show universal deterioration, but there are enough signs of increasing deprivation among the poor to suggest that fettered adjustment during the 1980s has constrained progress in human capital accumulation among the least privileged in Côte d'Ivoire. These outcomes are due to an interplay between demand factors at the household level (household income and opportunity costs that govern the choices of households about the education and health of its members) and supply factors, primarily the availability of effective service delivery (education and health). Declining income and higher opportunity costs are likely to have discouraged poor households from investing in education and health care for their members—but what of supply factors?

Basic needs inputs. As suggested earlier, the external constraints on the government created a largely internal adjustment effort, the outcome of which was a reliance on expenditure reduction. To what extent did this contractionary fiscal policy reduce expenditures in the social sectors, and thereby reduce the effective delivery of education and health services? As shown in table 3.20, nominal and real government expenditures on education and health increased during the 1985–90 period. Moreover, these sectors have been absorbing a growing share of total government expenditures (23 percent for education and 4.3 percent for health in 1990). Table 3.20 also indicates higher allocations to primary education at the expense of higher levels, which is usually a favorable indicator for the human capital prospects of the poor. Thus, the data in the table are encouraging, and in no way explain the downturn in basic needs outcome indicators among the poor.

These expenditure data do not necessarily measure effective service delivery, but may simply reflect increases in wages and salary costs in these sectors. As reported earlier, the share of wages and salaries in noninterest expenditures increased from 49 percent in 1975–80 to 54 percent in 1981–86 (and thereafter). In the education sector, the ratio of personnel to nonpersonnel expenditures increased from 1.4 in 1976 to 10.8 in 1988. Sahn and Bernier (1993) report that salaries accounted for 78 percent of total expenditures in the education sector in 1990, and 95 percent at the primary level. This tendency for wages and salaries to be more important at the primary level may explain the growing allocation of expenditures to the primary sector. However, it does not imply more effective delivery of educational services at this level. Sahn and Bernier (1993) suggest that high teacher

Table 3.20 Government expenditures on health and education, 1985–90

Category	*1985*	*1986*	*1987*	*1988*	*1989*	*1990*
Education expenditure						
(CFAF billions)	177.0	200.6	211.0	220.4	221.1	208.4
As percentage of GDP	5.6	6.2	6.8	7.2	7.5	7.7
As percentage of current expenditures	20.6	22.7	22.7	20.2	20.0	23.0
Memorandum items						
Real education expenditure (CFAF billions)[a]	177.0	188.9	231.6	236.4	236.2	248.0
Real education expenditure per capita (CFAF)	18,830	19,475	22,931	22,514	21,868	22,140
Composition of education expenditure (in percent)						
Primary	40.8	41.0	40.8	41.9	42.2	46.0
Secondary	34.6	31.3	31.3	31.4	30.9	28.8
Tertiary	17.4	17.9	17.6	17.3	17.4	13.7
Technical/vocational	7.3	9.7	10.4	9.4	9.5	11.5
Health expenditure						
(CFAF billions)	29.1	31.5	33.7	36.2	23.5	38.9
As percentage of GDP	0.9	1.0	1.1	1.2	1.3	1.4
As percentage of current expenditures	3.4	3.6	3.6	3.3	3.5	4.3
Memorandum items						
Real health expenditure (CFAF billions)[a]	29.1	29.7	37.0	38.8	41.1	46.3
Real health expenditure per capita (CFAF)	3,096	3,058	3,662	3,698	3,808	4,133

a. Deflated by services component of GDP deflator (1985 = 100).
Source: Grootaert (1993).

salaries (higher than in certain European countries) were responsible for the dominance of wage costs in the education sector: teachers constitute just one-third of the public sector work force, but 60 percent of the public sector wage bill. Thus, these considerations are a cautionary reminder that the expenditure data can be misleading. Although the education sector absorbed an increasing share of the budget during the fettered adjustment period, it is unlikely to have led to more effective service delivery if the increase in teacher salaries diverted funds from other key recurrent inputs (such as books and other materials) or from developmental expenditures (expanding the school network).

A similar cautionary note should be sounded in interpreting the health expenditure data. Sahn and Bernier (1993) describe the health care system of Côte d'Ivoire as biased strongly toward curative rather than preventive care. The share of the health budget devoted to hospital-based care rose from 40 percent in 1980 to more than 56 percent in 1986. They estimate that 54 percent of total recurrent expenditures and 61 percent of developmental expenditures were allocated to the tertiary level of the health sector in 1990. As with the education sector, Sahn and Bernier report a high share of salary and wage costs in total health expenditures. The 1990 figure for personnel costs in the budget (77.4 percent in 1990) is above the average for their sample of African countries (61.9 percent) and was a substantial jump over the shares recorded earlier in the 1980s, which fluctuated around 70 percent. They report that nonsalary expenditures in the health sector fell from CFAF 1,222 per capita in 1981 to just CFAF 670 in 1990, with adverse repercussions for material inputs and supplies.

Thus, the record for neither education nor health is encouraging. The problems facing the Ivorian government in its adjustment efforts—obliging it to follow an expenditure-reducing strategy despite persistently high wage levels—are likely to have had serious repercussions for the delivery of education and health services. Although the shares of these sectors in total government spending were protected throughout the fettered adjustment phase, it merely reflects the labor-intensive nature of these activities. The evidence suggests that service delivery has deteriorated.

Key policy issues

Having established the turn of events in the various episodes of adjustment during the 1980s in Côte d'Ivoire, and their consequences, we now make an assessment of the critical weaknesses. The key question here is what room for maneuver did the Ivorian government have in framing its adjustment policies in a way that differed from the historical record?

In this assessment of the attempts at macroeconomic adjustment in Côte d'Ivoire, three areas of policy failure are identified. The first concerns macroeconomic mismanagement in general, and specifically the government's failure to resolve fiscal problems. The second involves the severe constraints on exchange rate management, which have led to an undue reliance on expenditure-reducing policies. The third examines the implications of macroeconomic policy for private investment in Côte d'Ivoire, which declined markedly during the 1980s.

Public sector economic mismanagement

Our discussion of economic management during the 1980s is divided into two basic issues: the first concerns the commitment of the government to the adjustment programs and the seriousness with which it has approached these matters; the second focuses more narrowly on fiscal issues.

The commitment to adjustment. In much of this section, areas of inadequate policy action are identified. Explaining why the government failed to implement key reforms is certain to be extremely complex. Many of the answers, however, are to be found in the political economy of Côte d'Ivoire. Given the political expediencies and priorities of the government during the 1980s, its policy objectives were to stabilize the public finances and economy if possible without making fundamental reforms that would have upset the status quo and threatened powerful vested interest. Because of these objectives, the government was operating in quite a different paradigm from that which lies behind adjustment.

To understand why this was the case, one needs to explore further the complexities of Côte d'Ivoire's political economy. Van de Walle (1991) argues that there are particular features of the political economy which explain in large measure the failure of the government to implement key structural reforms. Two particular features of countries in the CFA franc zone must be highlighted: their urban social base, and the patrimonial roots of the political system. Van de Walle describes the regimes as resting not with the ballot box but with urban-based elites closely tied to the state. The political system is thus built on "prebendalism,"[24] and on securing political control over economic affairs. Any attempt to loosen the grip of the government on the functioning of the economy (in accordance with the free market paradigm) is thus likely to be inconsistent with the underlying political economy, and thus to be resisted. According to Van de Walle, this problem is clearly and acutely illustrated in the financial sector, where the government had a longstanding interest in controlling the allocation of credit (and thus rewarding its supporters). The fact that these credits have been allocated to poorly performing public enterprises and projects explains in large measure the poor state of the banking sector.

The key inadequacy of adjustment policy in Côte d'Ivoire has been the insistence on internal adjustment, with its seriously adverse consequences for growth and equity. The reasons for this insistence emanate from this underlying political system. Van de Walle (1991)argues that "none of the 14 countries in the Zone have sought to leave the Zone....African leaders have steadfastly supported convertibility at the current parity." He suggests two main reasons for this. First, there are specific advantages in an overvalued real exchange rate to groups that give support to the government (notably the urban elites, who benefit at the expense of rural-based farmers). "It is symptomatic," he argues, "of political realities in the Zone that governments have preferred to lower producer prices paid to farmers rather than cut salaries or lay off staff in the plethoric public bureaucracy." Second, membership in the CFA franc zone provides elites in the zone with some key political advantages. During times of recession, political control over the economy becomes even more important: mechanisms that enhance rent-seeking and patronage become critical to maintaining political support. For these reasons, Van de Walle argues, disturbing the economic arrangements of the zone would be politically risky. It is for these deep-seated political and economic reasons that the government has been slow in initiating fundamental change.

Failure to resolve fiscal problems. A concrete manifestation of the government's limited implementation of macroeconomic adjustment was its failure to deal sufficiently with its fiscal problems. While the fiscal deficit is the outcome of the complex interaction among economic, political, and social factors, three elements are highlighted in what follows: the debt overhang, wages and salaries, and government revenue.

The fiscal undiscipline in the latter half of the 1970s dominated subsequent events because expenditure levels during these boom years were financed primarily through foreign borrowing. The macroeconomic accounts have since been dominated by the servicing of this debt. Whereas at the end of the 1970s interest payments on public debt amounted to only about 2 percent of GDP, they had risen to 12 percent by 1991 (which is about equal to the fiscal deficit in 1991). Uncorrected, the debt burden will pass to future generations. For the present, the fact that the government is simply not servicing its debt but is financing it by accumulating arrears means that a large overall deficit is not critical. However, arrears cannot continue to be accumulated indefinitely, and there are signs that it is having fundamental repercussions on the economy at large, disrupting the financial sector and discouraging investment.

With hindsight, the macroeconomic problems of the 1980s would have been significantly less serious if the fiscal excesses of the 1970s had been avoided. Berthélemy and Bourguignon (forthcoming) suggest that excessive and inefficient spending by the government was the main determinant of the macroeconomic crises that dominated the 1980s. However, they also show that had private sector savings not fallen so rapidly, the investment program could have been financed without heavy external borrowing. In fact, our decomposition analysis reveals that the expansion in private sector consumption expenditures was also responsible for the growing external current account deficit at the end of the 1970s. And the decline in savings is readily explained by the severity of the external shock and the decline in profit income that ensued.

Debt service is not the only item in government expenditures that stands out in the fiscal accounts. Expenditures on wages and salaries have also increased relative to other expenditure items, and in relation to GDP. In 1985, when an overall fiscal deficit of just 1.5 percent of GDP was recorded, wages and salaries amounted to just over 8 percent of GDP, or 25 percent of total central government expenditure (appendix table 3B.2). By 1991 expenditures on wages and salaries increased to over 12 percent of GDP, and amounted to 35 percent of total expenditures (or 52 percent of primary expenditure and 60 percent of total public consumption spending). Public sector employment and earnings have thus been protected from the major burden of adjustment.[25]

While other expenditures have been cut somewhat, the main burden of adjustment has fallen on public investment expenditures. These declined from an average of 18 percent of GDP in 1978–83 to only 3 percent in 1987–91. The simple fact is that had public sector employees borne a burden of adjustment similar to that of the private sector (leaving public sector wages and salaries constant as a percentage of GDP over 1985–91), public investment could have been raised to almost 7 percent of GDP (roughly what it was in the middle of the decade). The failure of the government to control the wage and salary component of its expenditures is a tangible symptom of the constraints it faced in undertaking macroeconomic adjustment. In 1990 the government was forced to withdraw announced salary reductions because of massive public demonstrations against the policy.

The third feature of the fiscal imbalances of the decade is the revenue side of the accounts. Aside from the boom years of 1984–86, government revenue during the 1980s amounted to 25 percent of GDP, and somewhat less in the later years. Although these outcomes are satisfactory for a developing country, these were much lower figures than had been achieved under boom conditions. Funds derived from the Agriculture Price Stabilization Fund contributed handsomely to the exchequer in the late 1970s and again in 1984–85, but, by their nature, such revenues could not be relied upon as a basis for medium-term fiscal planning. By 1991 they contributed only 4 percent toward central government revenue, leaving a significant hole on the revenue side. Throughout the 1980s, tax revenue rarely exceeded 20 percent of GDP. Given the decline in the tax base, the government was exposed to the vicissitudes of export revenues and the world prices of a handful of primary commodities. One of the conundrums facing the government is that any attempt to raise tax rates may be counterproductive if doing so accelerates the informalization of economic activity and a contraction in the tax base.

The real exchange rate

The macroeconomic events of the 1980s in Côte d'Ivoire cannot be understood without reference to the major exchange rate appreciation that has dominated the scene since 1985. The government has been unable to reverse this appreciation given the policy instruments at its disposal.

An exchange rate appreciation in itself does not prove that the real exchange rate is overvalued, since an appreciation may be a result of an undervalued exchange rate in earlier years. Even if the real effective exchange rate has not appreciated since some base year when the rate was in equilibrium, this does not prove the absence of overvaluation, since the equilibrium rate itself may well have changed during the period. In particular, if the terms of trade faced by the country deteriorates, the equilibrium real exchange rate will depreciate. The constancy in the real effective exchange rate would imply growing overvaluation, since the equilibrium real effective exchange rate would have fallen over the period. In Côte d'Ivoire during the 1980s, the degree of overvaluation would be an outcome of these two forces: first, the increase in the actual real effective exchange rate, and second, the decline in the equilibrium real effective exchange rate brought about by the decline in the terms of trade, and by reductions in capital inflows, which occurred in the 1980s.[26]

The appreciation in the real effective exchange rate we have observed, therefore, must be interpreted with caution. For example, assume that the real effective exchange rate for 1985 represents the equilibrium real effective exchange rate (on the basis that the resource balance was in surplus (13 percent of GDP), and the current account was marginally in surplus (0.6 percent of GDP). Since then, the real effective exchange rate has appreciated by 43 percent (that is, up to 1991—see table 3.5). This does not mean, however, that the Ivorian real effective exchange rate is overvalued by 43 percent, since this would be the case only if the equilibrium real effective exchange rate had remained unchanged since 1985. Yet table 3.5 also shows that the terms of trade declined by 37 percent between 1985 and 1991, which means that the equilibrium real effective exchange rate is certain to have fallen.[27] This means that there is a greater degree of overvaluation than that indicated by the real effective exchange rate time series. This is one reason some observers—such as Boughton (1991, 1992) and Stolber and Vagenas (1992)—have placed the degree of overvaluation at modest levels. The former suggests that overvaluation is around 10 percent, while the latter estimate an overvaluation of only 7 percent (in 1990). These authors fail to take into account movements in the equilibrium rate in general, and particularly those originating from the terms of trade decline. The estimate of a 43 percent real exchange rate overvaluation in 1991 might therefore be considered a lower bound to the true degree of overvaluation.

Using a three-sector Salter-Swan dependent-economy model, Devarajan, Lewis, and Robinson (1993) have developed a simple methodology for estimating the degree of overvaluation which takes into account the induced change in the equilibrium real effective exchange rate brought about by terms of trade movements and changes in long-run capital inflows.[28] Using this methodology, Berthélemy and Bourguignon (forthcoming) have estimated the extent of real exchange rate disequilibrium in Côte d'Ivoire. They find that the answer depends critically on the choice of year to represent the equilibrium configuration. Taking the real exchange rate in 1978 as the equilibrium rate, they estimate that the Ivorian real exchange rate in 1987 was overvalued by about 50 percent, similar to the estimate of 46 percent in 1986 for Cameroon reported by Devarajan, Lewis, and Robinson (1993). Berthélemy and Bourguignon, however, question the choice of 1978 as an equilibrium year, given the fact that the terms of trade were then at their peak. Taking a longer view, and assuming that the real exchange rate in 1970 was in equilibrium, they estimate that the real exchange rate in 1987 was overvalued by only 15 percent (having been increasingly undervalued during the 1970s). This lower estimate of the real exchange rate overvaluation assumes that the net transfer of resources (on the capital account) in 1970 applies (in relative terms) to 1987. Taking into account the debt overhang and the consequent debt service commitments, the estimate of real exchange rate overvaluation should be higher than this estimate (recall that the equilibrium real effective exchange rate is also a function of capital flows).

However, even if it could reasonably be assumed that net capital flows can be reestablished at their relative values of 1970 (ignoring the debt service accumulation since), the estimate of a 15 percent real exchange rate overvaluation should still be regarded as an underestimate. This is because the methodology used is based on a full employment model (an extended Salter-Swan model), and assumes in effect that internal balance is maintained throughout. Our review of the events of the 1980s, however, suggests that nothing could be further from the case in Côte d'Ivoire. The adjustment in the external account of Côte d'Ivoire that took place during the 1980s has been a result of import compression, which in turn was brought about by a significant reduction in GDP and investment. In effect, external balance has been brought about through internal imbalance. And such adjustments are excluded from the Devarajan, Lewis, and Robinson approach. The real exchange rate can be considered overvalued by 15 percent as estimated by Berthélemy and Bourguignon only if lower output and investment levels are assumed to be a continuing feature of the Ivorian economy (as well as discounting the effects of increased debt service on capital flows, and assuming that net capital inflows are expected to be at the 1970 level in the foreseeable future). However, if the policy objective is to achieve both an external and an internal balance over the medium term, estimates of the degree of overvaluation of the real exchange rate must also reflect the need to raise levels of investment and GDP, which, other things being equal, will require a depreciation in the real exchange rate. For these reasons the degree of overvaluation is certain to be significantly higher than the 15 percent estimate reported by Berthélemy and Bourguignon.

With modest world inflation, it would take a considerable period of negative rates of domestic wage and price inflation to restore the real effective exchange rate to an equilibrium value. Overvaluations in excess of 40 percent simply cannot be addressed through internal adjustments, especially with domestic wage and price rigidities of the kind that have persisted in the Ivorian economy. Whereas there will be continued debate about the exact degree of overvaluation of the Ivorian real exchange rate, the simple facts that the real effective exchange rate has appreciated, that the terms of trade have declined, and that net capital inflows have declined all combine to reinforce the conclusion that at the end of the 1980s a serious competitiveness problem persisted for Côte d'Ivoire.

A key issue, therefore, in our assessment of adjustment in Côte d'Ivoire is why the government was unable to correct this serious macroeconomic distortion. The first and obvious reason is Côte d'Ivoire's membership in the CFA franc zone, with the exchange discipline that this entails. The tying of the CFA franc to the French franc has made exchange rate policy inflexible, and macroeconomic policy a hostage to fortune. In particular, the nominal appreciation of the French franc during the latter half of the 1980s has had serious repercussions for Côte d'Ivoire, since much of the country's trade was outside the franc zone, leading to a strong upward movement in the nominal effective exchange rate (this was also a result of devaluations among Côte d'Ivoire's competitors).

There can be little debate over this explanation of the nominal inflexibility underpinning the Ivorian case, and the limits that apply to relying on solely internal adjustments to restore the equilibrium real effective exchange rate. However, during the period under review, an alternative policy to a nominal depreciation was tried: a combination of export subsidies and import tariffs. In a two-commodity world, it can readily be shown that the combination of an export subsidy and an import tariff (both of which raise the domestic price of the tradable commodity) is an exact equivalent of a nominal depreciation. This theoretical equivalence was the foundation for the policy strategy in the mid-1980s. In the event, the policy did not succeed and was abandoned. Given the central importance of the exchange rate issue for the macroeconomics of Côte d'Ivoire, understanding why the policy failed is critical. In this assessment of the tariff plus subsidy scheme, we identify two major problems with the strategy: first, the technical issues that surround the policy, and second, the implementation problems.

Technical issues. Our first concern is to establish whether this policy strategy does, in fact, have a strong theoretical case. The problem with the international trade model that underpins it (the usual 2 x 2 x 2 case) is hardly appropriate for a country like Côte d'Ivoire. First, the assumption of just two sectors (exportables and importables) is not a meaningful assumption for most developing countries. In a model with three sectors (exportables, importables, and nontradables), Devarajan and de Melo (1987) assess whether such a policy would lead to a real exchange rate depreciation in every case. They find that because of its effect on the price of nontradables, the tariff plus subsidy scheme is likely to increase the fiscal deficit, and thereby lead to an appreciation in the real exchange rate. Second, the orthodox model ignores the incentives created in the tariff plus subsidy scheme for illegal trade (incentives that do not arise in the case of a nominal devaluation). O'Connell (1992) analyzes the implications of this critical difference between a devaluation and a tariff plus subsidy policy. The latter requires the existence of an administrative machinery to value trade flows and to assess the subsidy payable and the tariff chargeable. Such administrative costs are not incurred in the case of a devaluation.[29]

The emergence of illegal trade is likely to undermine the policy objectives of the tariff plus subsidy strategy directly. There are three mechanisms through which the use of the tariff plus subsidy policy can backfire and fail to achieve the equivalent of a devaluation. First, an increase in trade taxes is likely to reduce real incomes by drawing real resources into illegal activities (such as smuggling). O'Connell (1992) argues that the tariff plus subsidy policy can "end up appreciating the real exchange rate in terms of importables if the nontradables sector has a sufficiently low income elasticity of demand or a relatively high cross elasticity of supply with respect to the [tariff plus subsidy] rate." Second, other illegal activities (such as invoicing fraud) will increase export prices relative to import prices, and thus the tariff plus subsidy policy will not be uniform between the two tradable commodities (as the textbook might suggest). In raising relative exportables prices, the tariff plus subsidy policy will create distortions in resource allocation thatwould not arise from a devaluation. Added to this are the effects of expectations. It may be that economic agents will perceive tariffs as permanent, but export subsidies as temporary. This asymmetry in expectations might undermine any drive to encourage resource flows into exportables. Finally, illegal trade will increase the tendency for the fiscal deficit to increase (since revenues from trade taxes will be insufficient to meet the expenditure requirements of trade subsidies). This may add to the tendency for perverse movements in the real effective exchange rate to emerge.

In short, the incentives created for illegal trade can end up completely undermining the objectives of the exercise—increasing resource misallocations, increasing rent-seeking activities, and putting pressure on the fiscal deficit. These theoretical considerations are particularly relevant to the Côte d'Ivoire case. There is anecdotal evidence of widespread underinvoicing of imports, and there have been serious problems in ensuring prompt payment of export subsidies (given the fiscal constraints facing the government). The problems of implementing the tariff plus subsidy policy, therefore, arise in part from these conceptual and technical weaknesses of the policy.[30] In addition, there have been more practical difficulties with implementation, and it is to these that we now turn.

Implementation issues. The implementation of the tariff plus subsidy policy left much to be desired. Its financing over time was left indeterminate, which led to doubts in the private sector over its sustainability and permanence. Ivorian government officials never believed that the export subsidy would gain primary access to the budgetary resources (despite the creation of a special fund in the treasury, which at one point contained CFAF 16 billion). In theory, the additional revenue needed for export subsidy payments was to come from the application of import duties. However, as we have already observed, there was sufficient avoidance of such duties for the scheme to imply a serious fiscal commitment to it. At a time when the government was under pressure to reduce the fiscal deficit, such a policy lacked credibility from the start. Payment of the export subsidy was patchy, the distortions in incentives remained, and the system failed to have any impact on investment.

Would a nominal devaluation have helped? The evidence of the overvaluation of the real exchange rate suggests that had the government had the option of adjusting the nominal exchange rate when the crisis first revealed itself in the early 1980s, the adjustment effort would have been more successful. Lambert, Schneider, and Suwa (1991) use an applied general equilibrium model of the Ivorian economy to trace this counterfactual scenario—namely a sharp, once-for-all, nominal devaluation in 1981. They find that the devaluation has favorable effects on the macroeconomic balances, debt service, and income distribution. First, the devaluation is found to be effective in closing the external and fiscal deficits through the orthodox channels (increases in export volumes, decreases in imports, increased government revenues from the more buoyant economy). The lower fiscal deficit results in less borrowing and lower accumulation of debt (and debt service). Devaluation was also found to encourage increased private capital inflows, which further reduced public sector external borrowing. The debt overhang is considerably reduced as a result of a devaluation, and a much larger share of the debt is in the private sector. The simulated devaluation also improved income distribution and reduced poverty. It raised the incomes of smallholders and reduced unemployment. Using a general equilibrium interpretation of the economic history of Côte d'Ivoire, Lambert, Schneider, and Suwa have amply demonstrated how exchange rate inflexibility has fettered the adjustment efforts of the 1980s.

The collapse of private investment

The third key issue emerging from Côte d'Ivoire's experience of adjustment is the devastating decline in private investment—from almost 16 percent of GDP in 1978–80 to only 7.1 percent in 1987–91 (see table 3.14). The reasons for this disturbing outcome are complex, but the following factors are likely to have played important roles:

- *The availability of credit.* Credit has been limited due to the influence of fiscal deficits and the consequent debt overhang. In a survey of private enterprises (reported in Ruenda-Sabater and Stone 1992), a lack of access to finance was the single most important obstacle to the growth of the enterprise. It seems that each of the mechanisms used by the government to finance its deficits and to service its debt has crowded out private investment.

- *Labor market effects.* The public sector has crowded out the private sector by bidding away the most educated members of the labor force. Graduates are guaranteed civil service employment at highly favorable rates of remuneration (9 to 10 times GNP per capita). It is difficult for the private sector to compete with these salaries. At the same time, however, higher public sector pay has a knock-on effect for wages and salaries in the private sector, which makes it difficult to maintain competitiveness and create productive investment opportunities. Employers in the private sector also face several labor market interventions.
- *Inappropriate macroeconomic policies.* In particular, the overvaluation of the real exchange rate has discouraged private investors. Such overvaluation, combined with rigidities in the labor market, reduces the returns to investment in tradables activity. At the same time, the reliance on expenditure-reducing policies has significantly reduced the size of the domestic market, eroding investment opportunities in this area.
- *Public sector arrears.* Arrears have also undermined productive investment in the private sector. Financing the public sector deficit by accumulating arrears has adversely affected the liquidity position of enterprises, and seriously undermined the confidence of private investors in the future (Ruenda-Sabater and Stone 1992). The arrears problem is compounded by other related anomalies. For example, profit tax is imposed on firms on the basis of an entitlement to an export subsidy, rather than the receipt of the subsidy. Even if the subsidy is paid, it may create liquidity problems for firms. But if the subsidy is seriously delayed, or not paid at all, the government in effect taxes firms for income they do not receive (Ruenda-Sabater and Stone 1992).

Concluding observations

Côte d'Ivoire has been subjected to three groups of destabilizing shocks over the period covered in this study: first, unsustainable expenditure levels in the late 1970s brought about in part by the commodity price boom and access to low-cost external finance; second, terms of trade and real exchange rate shocks that occurred mainly during the second half of the 1980s; and finally, a plethora of policy-induced distortions and public sector influence, affecting production, trade, and exchange rates. Our review suggests that the policy responses to these destabilizing features of Ivorian economic history have been quite inadequate, relying almost entirely on an internal adjustment strategy that emphasized expenditure reduction, rather than fundamental structural adjustment.

Had the only source of destabilization been the unsustainably high level of public investment during the late 1970s, the policy response that occurred would have been appropriate, and might have been sufficient, to restore balance. An indication of this is the measure of success achieved prior to 1987. Thereafter, the deterioration in the barter terms of trade and the appreciation in the real exchange rate have rendered this policy response inadequate. Even without these further shocks in the latter half of the decade, however, there are serious doubts that the policy response taken would have been sufficient to regain a steady-state path of sustainable growth. This is because the domestic economy had become so distorted by trade and price interventions and direct government involvement in productive activities that the reliance on internal adjustment is likely to have been critically flawed. An internal, expenditure-reducing adjustment strategy can be truly effective only if there is sufficient flexibility and responsiveness in the economic system. For example, internal adjustment can be effective only if there is sufficient price and wage flexibility in the domestic economy. Therefore, at the very least, the policy response to the initial destabilizing events required that the rigidities and distortions in the domestic economy be corrected first. Otherwise the internal adjustment effort would be fettered by an insufficient response of the domestic economy.

The attempts to improve the functioning of the domestic economy are currently being addressed in earnest, but these improvements are certainly too late to rescue the internal adjustment strategy. This is because other events—the terms of trade shock and the appreciation in the real exchange rate—call for a different adjustment approach, one in which an equilibrating movement in the real exchange rate is brought about within a reasonable time frame. So far, the Ivorian authorities have not been able to bring about this change. The attempts in the mid-1980s to depreciate the real exchange rate (through a combination of expenditure reduction, export subsidies, and import tariffs) did not succeed.

Appendix 3A. Structural adjustment policy reform: design and implementation

Fiscal policy and economic management

Initial distortion. The fiscal deficit in 1980 was 12 percent of GDP, compared with a small surplus in 1977, due to an expansion in investment spending financed through foreign borrowing.

SAP reforms. Attempts were made to reduce the fiscal deficit by:

- linking investment expenditures,
- introducing a three-year rolling investment plan (loi program),

- bringing stabilization fund surpluses under the budget,
- improving reporting and appraisal procedures.

Assessment. The overall fiscal deficit was not closed during the decade. In 1991 it was 13 percent of GDP. Despite cuts in public investment from 18 percent (1978–83) to 3 percent (1987–91), the increase in debt service and wages and salaries (the latter from 20 percent of total expenditure in 1980 to 35 percent in 1991) has aggravated the fiscal deficit problem. However, the primary deficit has been closed.

Monetary policy

Initial distortion. As a member of the WAMU, Côte d'Ivoire's monetary policy is governed by rules restricting seignorage. Yet the government engaged in expansionary monetary policy in the early 1980s by utilizing public enterprise borrowing and by borrowing from abroad. The money supply grew by 19 percent annually between 1975 and 1980.

SAP reforms. Credit ceiling tightened under IMF guidance. WAMU rediscount rates released.

Assessment. Monetary expansion was arrested during the decade. The reduced availability of external borrowing meant that the WAMU rules tightened monetary discipline. Broad money growth fell to 10 percent annually between 1985 and 1991, and to –1.4 percent between 1986 and 1991.

Trade policy

Initial distortion. Major distortion in incentives and resource allocation caused by trade policy (tariffs and quantitative restrictions, and exchange rate overvaluation) and direct price controls.

SAP reforms. Adjustment programs attempted to remove quantitative restrictions with temporary import surcharges during transition and apply tariffs/export subsidies, yielding uniform effective protection rates of 40 percent. In this way, trade policy involved a liberalization component and an attempt to mimic a depreciation.

Assessment. This program succeeded only during its early years, especially 1985–87. Thereafter implementation was weak. Effective rates of protection were not uniform in any event, and quantitative restrictions were reimposed in 1987. System of incentives remains highly distorted.

Exchange rate policy

Initial distortion. Nominal exchange rates fixed to French franc; nominal rates stable during earliest period due to French franc stability. But real exchange rates appreciated due to domestic inflation, which was in turn due to commodity windfall and investment boom.

SAP reforms. No change in nominal exchange rate policy: CFA franc parity with French franc was to remain at FF = CFAF 50. Real exchange rate changes to be achieved through internal adjustment.

Assessment. Appreciation of French franc caused marked appreciation in real exchange rate after 1983; internal policy (fiscal/monetary restraint) unable to reverse appreciation. CFA franc was thus overvalued at the end of the decade.

Public enterprise reform

Initial distortion. During crisis period, public enterprises were well funded, but were inefficient and not subject to budget processes and accountability. Hence, they became a serious drain on exchequer finance.

SAP reforms. Policy reform sought to bring public enterprise activities under the discipline of the budget, introduce proper audits and accountability, and restructure inefficient enterprises. Under SAL III resource flows to the public sector were to be reduced by 30 percent (in 1986) and annually thereafter. Programs also sought to accelerate the privatization program, especially after 1990.

Assessment. Enterprise budgets were generally incorporated into central government accounting. Management audits were conducted as planned. Management practices in several public enterprises improved, but they remain inefficient, and enterprises continue to absorb public funds. As of 1991, those enterprise management problems continue to be addressed. Four enterprises privatized by 1991, and program to expand to 20 enterprises in 1991–93, and a further 30 enterprises in a second phase. In short, the privatization program, though late on the scene, is progressing satisfactorily. Existing enterprises continue to be a drain on the budget and to need assistance.

Financial sector reform

Initial distortion. Real interest rates were generally negative from 1975 to 1980. Credit market controlled by credit ceilings. Multiple interest rates in operation; a lower rate for crop credit. Overexpansions in the private banking sector.

SAP reforms. Most financial sector reforms were introduced in late 1980s. Interest rates were raised. Less reliance was to be placed on direct quantitative credit controls, and more on indirect instruments; direct sector credit controls were to be abolished; favorable TEP rates were to be abolished; and development banks were to be closely monitored, assisted and restructured, especially the BNDA. Insurance sector was also to be assisted.

Assessment. Real interest rates were positive throughout adjustment period, TEP effectively abolished, and interest rate structure simplified. Attempts to reconcile BNDA failed, and the government is arranging liquidation; other major commercial banks continue to be troubled, and require continual assistance; similarly, problems remain with insurance sector.

Appendix 3B.

Appendix table 3B.1 Key macroeconomic indicators, 1975–91

Indicator	*1975*	*1976*	*1977*	*1978*	*1979*	*1980*	*1981*	*1982*	*1983*	*1984*	*1985*	*1986*	*1987*	*1988*	*1989*	*1990*	*1991*
A. *GDP and sector growth*[a]	*(annual percentage change)*																
GDP at market prices	10.2	5.8	-0.2	13.9	2.9	-0.8	4.3	1.6	-1.2	-1.1	5.2	3.0	-1.2	-1.6	-1.0	-2.6	-1.8
Agriculture	9.4	6.0	-4.4	9.5	0.4	12.9	2.1	-1.4	-11.0	4.7	-23.0	4.8	1.1	10.1	7.4	2.3	0.1
Industry	14.5	15.5	10.0	19.1	8.0	8.8	10.0	-15.0	3.1	4.7	-18.3	8.7	14.1	-3.8	-4.5	-7.7	-9.2
Services	18.9	-22.5	-25.6	54.3	8.9	-22.0	9.8	22.9	12.0	-13.7	55.9	-0.7	9.0	-2.5	-24.8	18.4	5.5
Gross domestic investment	2.8	26.3	43.8	16.4	-7.0	18.5	-21.3	-13.7	-8.0	-52.1	40.0	-3.3	-11.8	23.6	-38.4	-11.6	0.0
Gross domestic income	4.6	15.0	12.6	8.2	-1.2	-4.5	-0.4	0.8	-0.7	3.6	6.0	4.5	-8.1	-4.4	-5.3	-7.5	0.4
Total consumption	13.3	5.6	1.3	16.3	4.1	-9.1	10.3	0.7	0.3	5.0	0.5	9.5	-4.1	-6.7	0.7	-8.8	0.0
Exports (GNFS)	-4.0	11.7	-7.9	5.7	2.3	12.7	6.9	1.4	-8.0	10.3	-0.4	13.2	1.3	-1.7	12.1	12.1	0.0
Imports (GNFS)	-2.7	25.7	26.0	14.7	-3.2	6.2	-5.0	-11.0	-9.3	-9.3	-2.4	31.5	-10.1	-5.8	0.5	-2.5	0.0
B. *Prices*																	
Consumer price index (1985=100)	35.3	39.5	50.4	56.9	66.4	76.1	82.8	88.9	94.2	98.2	100.0	106.6	112.2	120.7	122.5	120.6	0.0
Relative prices (1985=100)	114.8	112.5	96.6	91.0	87.6	85.6	87.4	88.6	91.7	97.1	100.0	93.0	94.6	93.7	98.8	102.3	102.4
Relative inflation (1985=100)	94.9	95.2	107.9	110.8	116.9	118.4	113.0	110.9	106.6	103.2	100.0	103.8	99.9	101.4	96.7	91.0	88.3
Real interest (discount) rate	2.8	3.2	4.0	4.6	5.3	8.0	8.7	11.1	9.9	10.3	10.5	9.1	9.5	11.5	13.5	13.3	0.0
C. *Terms of trade and exchange rate*																	
Terms of trade (1985=100)[b]	77.9	100.5	140.2	126.4	112.7	98.1	85.4	83.4	84.9	97.0	100.0	102.8	83.9	77.1	69.0	62.4	63.0
Real eff. exchange rate (1985=100)[b]	101.2	100.0	113.2	121.5	131.0	133.9	119.7	110.4	101.2	100.3	100.0	119.1	125.4	126.2	120.4	125.8	126.3

Nom. official exchange rate	224.3	248.5	235.3	209.0	201.0	225.8	287.4	336.3	417.4	479.6	378.1	322.8	267.0	302.9	289.4	256.4	278.6
D. External accounts[c]								*(percentage of GDP)*									
Curr. acct. balance (exc. off. grants)	-10.8	-6.0	-3.5	-11.1	-15.2	-17.5	-16.9	-13.8	-14.1	-1.5	0.6	-3.9	-10.7	-12.6	-13.5	-13.2	-11.9
Exports of GNFS	36.7	41.7	42.6	36.5	34.6	34.0	35.2	36.4	36.5	45.8	45.8	39.3	35.4	32.0	34.9	36.7	36.7
Imports of GNFS	36.6	36.2	36.3	37.4	37.7	40.1	42.3	39.3	38.2	34.3	32.6	31.8	31.0	29.2	31.8	32.2	31.9
Resource balance	0.1	5.5	6.3	-0.9	-3.1	-6.1	-7.1	-2.9	-1.7	11.5	13.2	7.5	4.4	2.8	3.0	4.4	4.8
E. Public finance								*(percentage of GDP)*									
Total expenditure	..	32.6	37.2	42.7	44.0	40.1	38.9	40.3	40.6	35.5	32.7	31.9	33.7	40.3	40.6	36.2	35.8
Total revenue	..	28.9	38.1	34.0	33.2	27.8	27.5	27.0	29.6	31.9	31.2	29.0	25.5	25.7	23.1	23.6	22.7
Fiscal deficit (-)/ surplus (+)	..	-3.7	0.9	-8.8	-10.8	-12.2	-11.3	-13.3	-11.0	-3.6	-1.5	-2.9	-8.2	-14.6	-17.6	-12.6	-13.1
F. Investment and savings[a]								*(percentage of GDP)*									
Gross domestic investment	22.4	23.0	27.3	29.8	28.0	28.2	25.9	23.2	20.6	10.9	14.6	12.2	11.7	15.1	10.3	9.8	10.5
Public investment	9.2	9.5	10.8	13.3	13.3	9.0	8.8	6.8	6.3	4.6	3.7	4.7	3.9	4.7	3.2	2.8	2.8
Private investment	12.8	12.7	15.1	16.3	13.8	17.1	15.5	14.9	11.9	7.7	9.7	8.3	6.7	7.2	6.8	7.0	7.7
Gross domestic saving	22.6	28.5	33.6	28.8	24.9	22.2	18.8	20.3	18.9	22.4	27.8	19.7	16.1	18.0	13.4	14.2	15.2
Gross national saving	14.5	18.9	25.0	19.2	14.5	10.0	6.8	8.4	6.7	10.8	14.3	7.7	2.6	4.6	-1.6	-3.0	4.0

.. Not available.
a. Constant 1987 prices.
b. Relative price index is the consumer price index (CPI) divided by the trade-weighted foreign wholesale price index (FWPI). The relative inflation index is the home country CPI divided by the trade-weighted foreign CPI. The real interest rate is the discount rate adjusted for inflation based on CPI (1985=100). The real effective exchange rate index is the nominal effective exchange rate multiplied by the ratio of CPI and divided by the weighted foreign wholesale price index. The nominal effective exchange rate is measured as a trade-weighted average for Côte d'Ivoire's 20 most important trading partners. An increase in the REER means an appreciation in the exchange rate.
c. External account GDP ratio is based on current CFA francs.
Source: World Bank and IMF data.

Appendix table 3B.2 Government financial data, 1976–91

(percentage of GDP)

Category	*1976*	*1977*	*1978*	*1979*	*1980*	*1981*	*1982*	*1983*	*1984*	*1985*	*1986*	*1987*	*1988*	*1989*	*1990*	*1991*
A. Total revenue	28.9	38.1	34.0	33.2	27.8	27.5	27.0	29.6	31.9	31.2	29.0	25.5	25.7	23.1	23.6	22.7
Total tax revenue	21.3	20.4	20.5	20.7	20.4	22.3	21.2	20.8	19.2	18.4	20.3	21.5	20.3	19.1	19.4	19.3
Direct	4.0	4.4	5.8	5.0	4.8	5.2	4.6	5.1	4.4	2.7	5.0	5.2	5.1	4.7	5.3	4.8
Goods and services	4.3	4.4	5.1	5.5	5.8	6.4	6.9	6.7	6.2	6.3	5.6	6.6	6.5	6.5	7.5	6.0
International trade	12.9	11.6	9.6	10.2	9.8	10.7	9.7	8.9	8.6	9.3	9.7	9.8	8.7	7.9	6.6	8.6
Imports	8.0	7.6	7.1	6.6	7.3	8.2	7.5	7.0	6.1	6.7	7.3	7.2	7.0	7.2	6.3	8.3
Exports	4.9	4.0	2.6	3.6	2.4	2.6	2.2	2.0	2.5	2.6	2.4	2.5	1.8	0.7	0.3	0.3
Nontax revenue	7.6	17.7	13.5	12.5	7.4	5.2	5.8	8.8	12.8	12.8	8.6	4.0	5.4	3.9	4.2	3.3
Price stab. fund	4.8	15.5	10.0	8.1	3.9	1.3	2.7	3.9	8.9	9.0	4.5	0.3	0.8	0.7	0.8	1.0
Surplus 1	0.0	0.0	0.0	0.0	0.0	0.0	0.0	0.0	0.0	0.0	0.3	0.3	0.8	0.7	0.8	1.0
Surplus 2	0.0	0.0	0.0	0.0	0.0	0.0	0.0	0.0	0.0	0.0	4.2	0.0	0.0	0.0	0.0	0.0
Other nontax revenue	2.8	2.1	3.4	4.4	3.6	3.9	3.1	4.9	3.8	3.8	4.1	3.7	4.5	3.3	3.4	2.3
Social security contributions	0.0	0.0	0.0	0.0	1.4	1.2	1.3	1.2	1.1	1.0	1.3	1.1	1.3	1.5	1.6	1.4
Other	0.0	0.0	0.0	0.0	2.2	2.7	1.8	3.7	2.7	2.8	2.9	2.6	3.2	1.7	1.8	0.9

B. Total expenditures	32.6	37.2	42.7	44.0	40.1	38.9	40.3	40.6	35.5	32.7	31.9	33.7	40.3	40.6	36.2	35.8
B1. Primary expenditures	31.1	35.7	40.7	41.3	36.8	34.0	32.9	31.8	25.6	23.3	25.1	26.7	31.8	30.7	25.7	23.5
Wages and salaries	6.4	7.1	7.3	8.1	8.3	9.0	9.5	9.8	8.9	8.3	8.3	10.9	11.6	12.0	12.6	12.4
Social accounts	0.0	0.0	0.0	0.0	0.6	0.7	0.8	0.8	0.8	0.9	0.8	0.8	1.0	1.3	1.4	1.3
Other current	9.9	6.5	10.1	11.3	10.4	9.6	8.6	8.3	8.0	7.0	11.3	9.2	11.2	8.8	7.7	6.9
Price stab. fund deficit	0.0	0.0	0.0	0.0	-0.7	-0.2	-0.5	-0.4	-0.1	-0.6	0.0	1.9	3.4	5.4	1.3	0.1
Investment	14.8	22.1	23.3	22.0	18.1	14.9	14.5	13.1	8.0	7.7	4.7	3.9	4.7	3.2	2.8	2.8
B2. Interest due on public debt	1.5	1.5	2.0	2.7	3.2	4.8	7.4	8.8	9.9	9.4	6.8	7.0	8.5	10.0	10.6	12.3
Domestic	0.0	0.0	0.0	0.0	0.0	0.0	1.2	1.4	1.7	1.3	0.3	0.5	1.0	1.0	1.3	1.1
External	0.0	0.0	0.0	0.0	0.0	0.0	6.2	7.4	8.2	8.1	6.4	6.5	7.6	8.9	9.2	11.2
C. Total expenditures	32.6	37.2	42.7	44.0	40.1	38.9	40.3	40.6	35.5	32.7	31.9	33.7	40.3	40.6	36.2	35.8
Current	17.8	15.1	19.5	22.0	22.0	24.0	25.8	27.3	27.5	25.0	27.2	29.8	35.6	37.5	33.5	33.0
Capital	14.8	22.1	23.3	22.0	18.1	14.9	14.5	13.1	8.0	7.7	4.7	3.9	4.7	3.2	2.8	2.8
D. Primary deficit (A–B1)	-2.2	2.4	-6.7	-8.2	-9.0	-6.5	-5.9	-2.2	6.3	7.9	3.8	-1.2	-6.1	-7.6	-2.1	-0.8
E. Overall financial balance (A–B)	-3.7	0.9	-8.8	-10.8	-12.2	-11.3	-13.3	-11.0	-3.6	-1.5	-2.9	-8.2	-14.6	-17.6	-12.6	-13.1

Note: Ratios calculated in current prices.
Source: IMF data.

Appendix table 3B.3 External trade balance of payments, 1975–91
(US$ millions)

Item	*1975*	*1976*	*1977*	*1978*	*1979*	*1980*	*1981*	*1982*	*1983*	*1984*	*1985*	*1986*	*1987*	*1988*	*1989*	*1990*	*1991*
Exports of goods and nonfactor services	1,465	1,970	2,737	3,026	3,233	3,577	2,869	2,798	2,491	2,995	3,160	3,659	3,485	3,247	3,286	3,640	3,498
Merchandise (fob)	1,239	1,735	2,412	2,616	2,723	3,013	2,435	2,347	2,066	2,625	2,761	3,187	2,950	2,691	2,808	3,120	3,011
Nonfactor services	226	235	325	410	511	564	434	451	425	370	399	471	535	556	479	520	487
Imports of GNFS	1,561	1,802	2,420	3,138	3,585	4,135	3,284	2,945	2,678	2,311	2,173	2,952	3,214	3,110	3,076	3,365	3,043
Merchandise (cif)	1,012	1,161	1,597	2,043	2,233	2,614	2,068	1,790	7,635	1,487	1,410	1,640	1,863	1,769	1,720	1,702	1,671
Nonfactor services	549	641	823	1,095	1,351	1,521	1,216	1,155	983	824	763	1,312	1,351	1,341	1,356	1,663	1,372
Resource balance	-96	168	317	-112	-351	-558	-414	-147	-127	684	987	707	271	137	210	275	455
(as a percentage of GDP)	0.1	5.5	6.3	-0.9	-3.1	-6.1	-7.1	-2.9	-1.7	11.5	13.2	7.5	4.4	2.8	3.0	4.4	4.8
Net factor income	-141	-158	-194	-309	-460	-563	-518	-507	-509	-494	-666	-648	-881	-923	-986	-1,046	-1,260
Factor receipts	39	28	42	60	59	63	46	46	47	38	40	68	78	72	35	44	18
Factor payments	180	186	236	369	519	626	564	553	555	531	706	716	959	1,035	943	1,133	1,278
Net current transfers	-184	-290	-345	-458	-576	-716	-495	-391	-320	-291	-279	-427	-501	-514	-470	-540	-328
Current account																	
Balance before official grants	-421	-280	-222	-879	-1,388	-1,836	-1,427	-1,016	-955	-101	42	-369	-1,111	-1,300	-1,246	-1,311	-1,132
As a percentage of GDP	-10.8	-6.0	-3.5	-11.1	-15.2	-17.5	-16.9	-13.8	-14.1	-1.5	0.6	-3.9	-10.7	-12.6	-13.5	-13.2	-11.9
Official capital grants	42	31	45	40	5	10	15	30	27	28	26	71	143	61	91	107	0
Balance after official grants	-379	-249	-177	-839	-1,383	-1,827	-1,411	-1,016	-929	-73	68	-298	-968	-1,239	-1,155	-1,204	-1,132

Long-term capital inflows	270	276	571	839	715	1,033	921	899	534	346	242	154	345	297	201	228	..
Direct investment	69	45	15	83	75	95	33	47	38	22	29	71	88	52	41	48	13
Net long-term borrowing	308	270	725	833	706	1,120	810	1,504	506	942	728	459	691	584	622	898	1,301
Other long-term inflows	-107	-39	-169	-77	-66	-182	78	-653	-10	-617	-516	-376	-434	-339	-462	-718	..
Other items	16	3	-275	165	339	682	113	-32	251	-299	-283	-225	119	206	113	508	3,308
Non-short-term capital	11	7	-227	198	418	759	212	3	405	-180	-367	289	752	1,011	885	896	3,308
Capital flows	0	0	0	0	0	0	0	0	0	0	0	-459	-646	-807	-1,173	-1,375	..
Errors and omissions	6	-4	-48	-32	-79	-77	-99	-35	-154	-119	84	-55	13	2	1,175	-28	..
Changes in net reserves	20	72	6	-62	92	-30	-119	-166	329	112	377	150	145	26	-27	-90	-141

.. Not available.
Source: World Bank data.

Appendix table 3B.4 Implicit GDP deflators and relative price indexes, 1975–91

Item	*1975*	*1976*	*1977*	*1978*	*1979*	*1980*	*1981*	*1982*	*1983*	*1984*	*1985*	*1986*	*1987*	*1988*	*1989*	*1990*	*1991*
GDP deflators																	
GDP at market prices	37.5	44.9	59.8	63.2	67.6	76.7	76.4	82.8	88.2	100.0	104.2	104.2	101.8	102.2	99.7	94.2	95.4
GDP at factor cost	37.8	45.7	62.4	66.1	70.8	83.0	83.8	89.1	92.0	100.0	104.4	109.7	102.6	104.2	102.5	96.7	95.5
Agriculture	34.7	37.9	54.2	61.1	67.7	69.8	75.0	75.4	82.6	100.0	96.6	104.5	114.6	114.0	107.8	99.9	97.9
Industry	49.5	54.9	63.8	67.5	70.6	69.9	66.8	96.8	98.9	100.0	118.2	116.9	109.6	110.3	108.0	116.4	114.8
Mining/quarrying	37.1	44.8	54.7	71.4	71.7	25.5	61.2	75.0	89.5	100.0	102.0	44.5	37.2	37.0	35.8	35.5	..
Manufacturing	52.4	57.0	68.4	74.3	79.1	77.7	73.6	111.7	114.5	100.0	..	..	..	..	..	..	..
Services	36.3	49.3	70.9	69.8	73.5	105.8	104.0	97.6	95.9	100.0	103.4	109.8	94.2	96.4	96.8	86.9	87.5
Price ratios																	
Agriculture/services	0.954	0.767	0.763	0.875	0.921	0.660	0.721	0.772	0.862	1.000	0.934	0.952	1.217	1.183	1.114	1.150	1.119
Industry/services	1.361	1.113	0.900	0.967	0.960	0.661	0.642	0.991	1.032	1.000	1.143	1.065	1.164	1.144	1.116	1.340	1.312
Mining/services	1.022	0.908	0.772	1.023	0.976	0.222	0.588	0.768	0.934	1.000	0.987	0.405	0.395	0.384	0.370	0.409	..
Manufacturing/services	1.443	1.157	0.964	1.064	1.075	0.735	0.708	1.144	1.194	1.000	..	..	..	..	..	..	..
Agriculture/industry	0.701	0.689	0.848	0.905	0.959	0.999	1.123	0.779	0.835	1.000	0.817	0.894	1.045	1.034	0.998	0.858	0.853

.. Not available.
Source: World Bank data.

Notes

1. The cutoff point for this study is 1991. Since then, several important policies have been implemented, and the government has made major strides in making needed institutional changes.

2. Other members of the West African Monetary Union are Benin, Burkina Faso, Mali, Niger, Senegal, and Togo. Boughton (1991, 1992) provides further details on the history and structure of the CFA zone and its monetary unions.

3. Understanding the relationship between the West African Central Bank and the French treasury is complicated by a similar arrangement with the Banque des Etats de l'Afrique Centrale (Central-African Central Bank). While the West African Central Bank has acquired a sizable overdraft on its operations account, the Central-African Central Bank has generally maintained large surpluses. It has been suggested that the French treasury takes the overall balance of both unions into account in considering the urgency of correcting an operations account imbalance.

4. Which of the two options is preferred is a moot point: financing through seigniorage and the inflationary tax, or financing through domestic arrears. The former taxes holders of money balances, and the latter "taxes" owners of enterprise capital.

5. Based on a multivariate analysis of the real exchange rate, Chamley and Ghanem (1991) conclude that both aggregate demand shocks and public expenditure appeared to be positively correlated with the real effective exchange rate. However, they were not confident about the robustness of the latter relationship.

6. The results they report for Côte d'Ivoire were based on an unpublished study by Achi Atsain and Allechi M'Bet (Centre for Economic and Social Research, Université Nationale de Côte d'Ivoire, Abidjan).

7. Recall that it was the unsustainably high level of investment expenditures that led to the destabilization and financial crisis in the first place.

8. This figure does not include "credits at risk," which are more difficult to define, but which would increase this measure of bad debt significantly.

9. The big four commercial banks—Société Générale de Banques en Côte d'Ivoire (SGBI), Banque Internationale pour le Commerce et l'Industrie de la Côte d'Ivoire (BICICI), Société Ivorienne de Banque (SIB), and Banque Internationale pour l'Afrique Occidentale/Côte d'Ivoire (BIAO/CI)—dominate the Ivorian banking scene. They account for 80 percent of net domestic credit.

10. Taxes on petroleum and tobacco, cocoa and coffee exports, and rice imports were raised, and value added tax was extended to the distribution sector.

11. Payment arrears were either directly or indirectly due to public sector arrears. Producers not paid by the government (such as exporters suffering from the Agriculture Price Stabilization Fund arrears) defaulted on their credit repayments.

12. Note that during these years the contribution of the price stabilization fund to government revenues was at historically high levels. As a proportion of GDP, these funds amounted to 15.5 percent in 1977, which, when combined with other taxes on international trade, amounted to 27 percent of GDP.

13. In the analysis that follows, changes in the resource balance are explained in terms of their proximate determinants, as defined in the national accounts identities. Because of the use of identities, caution should be applied in assuming causation.

14. These periods differ slightly from our representation of the periods of crisis, partial adjustment, and fettered adjustment, because the trade balance began to widen after 1985 (rather than after 1986).

15. Of course, the supply response need not have been due to adjustment policies, but simply to the fortuitous improvement in commodity prices.

16. Private consumption continued to increase, thus fueling the external imbalance, but not significantly.

17. It should be emphasized that the relative price measures used in the table are crude, and may not accurately reflect the tradable/nontradable relative price. For example, food production included under agriculture might be better considered nontradable, as would many manufacturing activities sheltered behind import controls.

18. These calculations are similar to (but not identical with) those reported earlier from Schiff and Valdés (1992).

19. This section draws heavily on Grootaert (1993).

20. In general, household surveys underestimate incomes (and savings), especially among higher-income groups.

21. The poverty index is defined as

$$P_\alpha = \frac{1}{n} \sum_{i=1}^{q} \left(\frac{Y_p - Y_i}{Y_p} \right)^\alpha$$

where Y_i is the expenditure of the *i*th individual ($i = 1,...q$), there being n in the population and q in poverty. Y_p is the poverty line. α is a parameter to be selected by the analyst.

22. For values of $\alpha > 1$, a higher weight is attached to the incomes of the poorest groups.

23. It is quite likely that service use by households depends in part on the quality of the service received—for example, the availability of medicine. If the service has deteriorated, households may be less likely to use it. The same considerations apply to education.

24. While patrimonialism is defined as the obtaining of a government position through a financial contribution, prebendalism is the obtaining of a sinecure through favor or patronage.

25. The evidence from the Côte d'Ivoire Living Standards Survey suggests that poverty levels among public employees have risen steeply, suggesting that public employment cuts have been directed primarily at the lower-paid.

26. Edwards (1989) demonstrates that the equilibrium real exchange rate will change as a result of changes in tariffs, government consumption expenditure, and long-term capital transfers from the rest of the world. The net effect of these changes on the equilibrium real exchange rate is certain to be complex, and to depend on whether the changes are (and are perceived to be) permanent or transitory. Edwards concludes that "generally speaking, it is not possible to know how the effect of import tariffs and terms of trade shocks on the equilibrium real exchange rate will be distributed through time."

27. It is unlikely that the increase in import tariffs over the period, which, all else equal, would appreciate the equilibrium real exchange rate, would have been sufficient to counteract the effects of the terms of trade decline.

28. Their model explains movements in the equilibrium real exchange rate in terms of these two factors alone, and ignores other fundamentals that determine the rate—tariffs, exchange controls, and real government consumption. Changes in these are likely to alter the equilibrium real exchange rate. Similarly, the method is static in approach, and does not address a number of dynamic issues (such as the effects of permanent versus temporary shocks). See Edwards (1989) and Williamson (1983).

29. There are other considerations that serve to restrict this exact equivalence of a tariff plus subsidy scheme to the textbook. The tariff plus subsidy scheme does not affect invisible trade, it does not change asset values or domestic interest rates, and it does affect fiscal deficits. In each of these respects, the policy differs from a nominal devaluation.

30. Conversely, some studies support the tariff plus subsidy approach, on the grounds that exporters are highly responsive to increased price incentives. Levy and Newman (1991) estimated supply responses in the Ivorian export sector and found that "exports respond positively to increases in export prices and negatively to increases in import prices." Although they argue that the tariff plus subsidy policy would go some way toward mimicking a nominal devaluation, they stop short of supporting the strategy as it was applied in the Côte d'Ivoire case—because they did not assess the budgetary implications of the policy, and because problems surrounded how the policy was implemented.

References

Berthélemy, J.C., and F. Bourguignon. Forthcoming. "Growth and Crisis in Côte d'Ivoire." A World Bank Comparative Macroeconomic Study. Washington, D.C.

Bevan, David, Paul Collier, and Jan Willem Gunning. 1990. *Controlled Open Economies: A Neoclassical Approach to Structuralism.* Oxford: Clarendon Press.

Boughton, James M. 1991. "The CFA Franc Zone: Currency Union and Monetary Standard." International Monetary Fund Working Paper 91/133. Washington, D.C.

———. 1992. "The CFA Franc: Zone of Fragile Stability in Africa." *Finance and Development* 29(4):34–36.

Chamley, C., and H. Ghanem. 1991. "Fiscal Policy with Fixed Nominal Exchange Rates: Côte d'Ivoire." Policy Research Working Paper 658. World Bank, Macroeconomic Adjustment and Growth Division, Country Economics Department, Washington, D.C.

Demery, Lionel. 1993. "Income and Expenditure Aggregates: Estimates from the Côte d'Ivoire Living Standards Surveys." Policy Research Working Paper. World Bank, Poverty and Social Policy Division, Washington, D.C.

Demery, Lionel, and Christiaan Grootaert. 1993. "Correcting for Sampling Bias in the Measurement of Welfare and Poverty in the Côte d'Ivoire Living Standards Survey." *World Bank Economic Review* 7(3).

Den Tuinder, B.A. 1978. *Ivory Coast—The Challenge of Success.* Baltimore, Md.: Johns Hopkins University Press.

Devarajan, S., and J. de Melo. 1987. "Adjustment with a Fixed Exchange Rate: Cameroon, Côte d'Ivoire, and Senegal." *World Bank Economic Review* 1(3):447–88.

Devarajan, Shantayanan, Jeffrey D. Lewis, and Sherman Robinson. 1993. "External Shocks, Purchasing Power Parity, and the Equilibrium Real Exchange Rate." *World Bank Economic Review* 7(1):45–64.

Edwards, Sebastian. 1989. *Real Exchange Rates, Devaluation and Adjustment: Exchange Rate Policy in Developing Countries.* Cambridge, Mass.: The MIT Press.

Foster, J., J. Greer, and E. Thorbecke. 1984. "A Class of Decomposable Poverty Measures." *Econometrics* 52(1):761–66.

Grootaert, Christiaan. 1993. "The Evolution of Welfare and Poverty under Structural Change and Economic Recession in the Case of Côte d'Ivoire, 1985–88." Policy Research Working Paper 1078. World Bank, Poverty and Social Policy Division, Africa Technical Department, Washington, D.C.

Grootaert, Christiaan, and Ravi Kanbur. 1993. "A New Regional Price Index for Côte d'Ivoire Using Data from the International Comparisons Project." Policy Research Working Paper 1080. World Bank, Poverty and Social Policy Division, Africa Technical Department, Washington, D.C.

Lambert, S., H. Schneider, and A. Suwa. 1991. "Adjustment and Equity in Côte d'Ivoire: 1980–1986." *World Development* 19(11):1563–76.

Lane, Christopher. 1989. "Monetary Policy Effectiveness in Côte d'Ivoire." Overseas Development Institute Working Paper 30. London.

Levy, V., and J. Newman. 1989. "Wage Rigidity: Micro and Macro Evidence on Labor Market Adjustment in the Modern Sector." *World Bank Economic Review* 3(1):97–117.

O'Connell, Stephen. 1992. "Uniform Commercial Policy, Illegal Trade, and the Real Exchange Rate: A Theoretical Analysis." *World Bank Economic Review* 6(3):459–79.

Ravallion, Martin. 1992. "Poverty Comparisons: A Guide to Concepts and Methods." Living Standards Measurement Study Working Paper 88. World Bank, Washington, D.C.

Ravallion, Martin, and G. Datt. 1991. "Growth and Redistribution Components of Changes in Poverty Measures—A Decomposition with Applications to Brazil and India in the 1980s." Living Standards Measurement Study Working Paper 88. World Bank, Washington, D.C.

Ruenda-Sabater, Enrique, and Andrew Stone. 1992. "Côte d'Ivoire: Private Sector Dynamics and Constraints." Policy Research Working Paper 1047. World Bank, Public Sector Management and Private Sector Development Division, Country Economics Department, Washington, D.C.

Sahn, David, and Rene Bernier. 1993. "Evidence from Africa on the Intrasectoral Allocation of Social Sector Expenditures." Cornell Food and Nutrition Policy Program. Ithaca, N.Y.

Schiff, Maurice, and Alberto Valdés. 1992. *The Political Economy of Agricultural Pricing Policy.* Vol. 4, *A Synthesis of the Economics in Developing Countries.* Baltimore, Md.: Johns Hopkins University Press.

Stolber, Walter, and Constanin Vagenas. 1992. "The Future of the CFA Franc: A Case for Currency Adjustment or More?" Union Bank of Switzerland Occasional Paper. Zurich.

Van der Walle, Nicolas. 1991. "The Decline of the Franc Zone: Monetary Politics in Francophone Africa." *African Affairs* 90:383–405.

Williamson, John. 1993. *The Open Economy and the World Economy: A Textbook in International Economics.* New York: Basic Books.

4

Ghana: frontrunner in adjustment

Chad Leechor

By customary criteria, Ghana's adjustment program has been a success. Policy reform has been extensive, despite opposition and institutional constraints. The benefits of adjustment have been large, visible, and widely shared. The results are all the more remarkable given the chaotic initial conditions and the external shocks sustained since reform began. But there is room for improvement. Today, Ghanaians still believe that doing business entails major political risks. Banks cannot mobilize adequate resources to make more credit available. Government employment practices keep wages artificially high. Supply response has been limited and confined largely to trading and services, which require relatively little time and commitment.

Before the 1983 reform, Ghana's economy had virtually collapsed. Economic infrastructure was no longer in working condition. Basic institutions had ceased to function. The incentive system was badly distorted. Under the circumstances, necessary measures involved not just policy change, but a substantial amount of physical and institutional rehabilitation. But the crisis did offer one advantage—it helped limit internal resistance to reform. Interest groups had little justification for maintaining the status quo. Rent-seekers could no longer find rents. A broad consensus for change prevailed.

But external conditions were less propitious. In 1983 Ghana suffered one of the most devastating droughts in decades. Furthermore, almost 1 million Ghanaians who had been working in Nigeria were sent home. This made the task of rebuilding a shattered economy even more difficult. But more serious shocks were yet to come. Starting in 1984 the world price of cocoa began a sharp descent and depressed Ghana's export earnings despite an increase in its export volume. At the same time, import prices rose steadily after a brief respite from the oil-market slump of 1985 and 1986. The cumulative terms of trade losses after 1987 were substantial.

Ghana's initial reform efforts focused on stabilization and liberalization. Fiscal discipline was introduced and sustained for nearly a decade. The thrust of fiscal policy was to reverse the decline in revenue, a trend that had lasted for more than a decade. Revenue collection rose dramatically between 1984 and 1987, and the resources enabled the government to pursue more expansionary policies without enlarging its fiscal deficit. The improved fiscal balance, maintained until 1992, allowed a greater degree of monetary restraint.

A measure of stability was achieved. In the preceding decade, inflation had averaged 66 percent annually, with wide fluctuations from year to year. During adjustment, the rate of inflation was brought down to an average of 26 percent—which, despite improved fiscal and monetary control, showed a persistence of high inflation. The main reason was Ghana's small monetary base (6 percent of GDP), which made the price level sensitive to monetary growth. The primary source of monetary expansion was an imbalance between local expenditures and domestic sources of revenue. Prior to 1990 part of foreign aid was converted into financing for local expenses, contributing to the expansion of reserves and a corresponding increase in the supply of money. Yet the distortionary effects of inflation have been mitigated by the liberalization measures. Particularly important has been the market-based exchange rate system, which minimizes the possibility of exchange rate distortion. Extensive price control has been removed, allowing relative prices to adjust under inflation. Interest rates have also been liberalized.

Major progress has also been made in the external sector. Massive overvaluation of the local currency has been quickly and decisively corrected. Quantitative restrictions and foreign exchange control have been phased out. Moreover, trade taxes have been reduced progressively in an effort to rationalize the incentive system. Trade volume has expanded significantly. In addition, prudent management of external debt has lowered the burden of debt services, while also building up foreign exchange reserves to an adequate level.

Foreign aid has played a major role. From the outset, it allowed Ghana to import the capital goods and supplies it needed for rehabilitation. Later on, foreign aid supplemented the meager export earnings to pay for imports and soften the impact of adverse shifts in the terms of trade. But the size and role of foreign aid have often been misunderstood. For instance, the amount has sometimes been considered excessive, although at its peak Ghana's net foreign aid was less than 5 percent of GDP, compared with an average of 8 percent throughout Sub-Saharan Africa. In addition, the losses due to Ghana's declining terms of trade have been substantial; since 1990 they have virtually offset the net aid flow (figure 4.1).

Foreign aid has served largely to facilitate policy change. By strengthening the bargaining position of those in favor of reform, the donor community represents an important constituency in the political process. In the absence of foreign aid, the adjustment program would have been far more modest. But the leverage of foreign aid is often exaggerated. Even when reform has been undertaken, donors are not well equipped to ensure that it is implemented effectively. Furthermore, internal political forces are generally the deciding factor, although donors may occasionally influence the outcome by throwing their weight on one side.

The adjustment program has clearly changed the economy. Growth has been restored. Since 1983 real income per capita has averaged 2 percent annually—in contrast to the 1970s when real income fell by a third. Evidence suggests also that the benefits of growth have been distributed broadly. Farmers and rural workers have benefited from improved producer prices for cocoa and the liberalization of trade for other cash crops. Real food prices (for cereals and roots) have fallen gradually. Furthermore, government expenditures on social programs rose significantly during the adjustment period. Social indicators show improvements across the board.

The extent and replicability of Ghana's experience have attracted much interest. Many believe that Ghana's adjustment performance has been exceptional by regional standards. But its performance largely reflects the depth of economic decline before reform. Over a longer time horizon, Ghana's record is not that distinctive. For example, between 1980 and 1990, real GDP growth in Ghana averaged 3 percent annually, behind nine other Sub-Saharan African countries, including Botswana, Burkina Faso, Burundi, Congo, Mali, and Mauritius, and comparable to six others, including Malawi, Senegal, Tanzania, and Zimbabwe.

Figure 4.1 Foreign aid and terms of trade deterioration, 1984–92

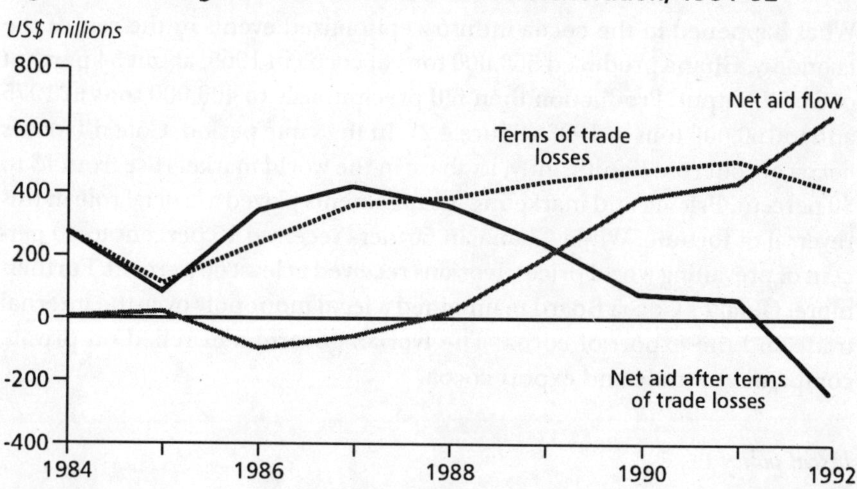

Source: IMF, *International Financial Statistics*; Government of Ghana.

The economy before adjustment

The images of Ghana in the early 1980s are hard to forget. As two observers put it:

> The economy had been largely devastated. Signs of collapse were everywhere....Roads acutely needed repair; much of the railways had ceased to function and the ports were in only slightly better condition. Power supply and telephone connections had broken down. Lack of imported spare parts had crippled much of the transport fleet and prevented repairs of the infrastructure (Chand and van Til 1988, p.11).

The calamity was not an isolated event in Ghana's history. Nor was it entirely self-inflicted. The most severe drought in decades hit Ghana in 1983. World prices for cocoa had already started their secular descent. In addition, more than a million Ghanaians who had been working in Nigeria during the oil boom were sent back home.

Exogenous shocks of this magnitude would have been difficult to absorb in any event. But the timing could not have been worse. Ghana's economy had already been weakened by years of declining output, accelerating inflation, and dwindling foreign exchange reserves. Even without the shocks, Ghana would still have confronted a major crisis from decades of economic mismanagement.

Cocoa as a microcosm

What happened in the cocoa industry epitomized events in the rest of the economy. Ghana produced 560,000 tons of cocoa in 1965, about 34 percent of world output. Production then fell precipitously to 400,000 tons in 1975 and to 160,000 tons in 1983 (figure 4.2). In the same period, Côte d'Ivoire's cocoa output rose significantly, its share in the world market rose from 13 to 30 percent. Pricing and marketing arrangements played a crucial role in this reversal of fortune. While Ghanaian farmers received 15 percent to 40 percent of prevailing world prices, Ivorians received at least 66 percent. Furthermore, Ghana's Cocoa Board maintained a legal monopoly over the internal trade and the export of cocoa. The Ivorian government relied on private companies to trade and export cocoa.

Fiscal policy

Prior to adjustment, government revenue fell from about 20 percent of GDP in 1970 to less than 5 percent in 1982. The decline occurred mainly as a result of overtaxing cocoa farmers, which depressed production and encouraged smuggling. In addition, the overvalued cedi (₵) lowered import taxes and had an adverse effect on revenue generally.

Government expenditures increased significantly from year to year, largely independent of the budget constraint. For instance, from 1972 to 1982 nominal government outlays rose from ₵587 million to ₵11,374 million. Current expenditures consistently exceeded the revenue collected. Capital expenditures and grants to public enterprises enlarged the deficits. Despite the shortfall in available resources, grants accounted for a significant share of total expenditures, ranging from 15 percent to 25 percent.

Government deficits represented a significant share of the economy in the 1970s. At the peak of the spending binge in 1976, the budget deficit amounted to 11.3 percent of GDP. For the decade, budget deficits averaged 7 percent of GDP.

Monetary policy

Highly accommodating monetary policies were pursued during the period. The monetary base, and thus money supply, grew primarily because the Bank of Ghana extended credit to the government to finance deficits (figure 4.3). In certain years—1979 and 1982, for instance—the primary source of monetary growth was direct lending from the Bank of Ghana to public enterprises. Net foreign assets played a minor role in monetary policy, whether as a contractionary or expansionary factor. In the late 1970s, large cocoa export earn-

Figure 4.2 Ghana's cocoa output and prices, 1975–90

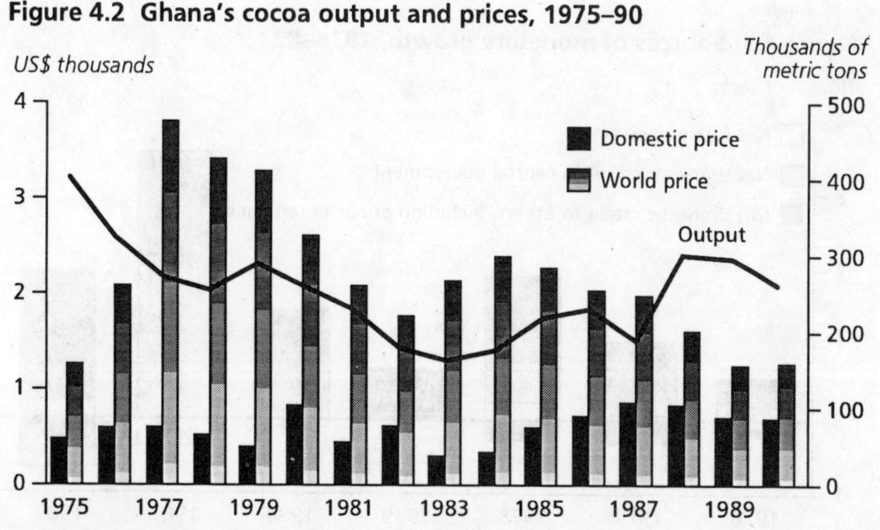

Note: Prices are in U.S. dollars per metric ton; domestic prices are converted using inflation-adjusted exchange rate.
Source: International Cocoa Organization; IMF, *International Financial Statistics.*

ings helped cover the rising import bill stimulated by government expenditures. In the early 1980s, as the external balance deteriorated, imports and foreign exchange were controlled extensively to slow the depletion of foreign exchange reserves.

Between 1972 and 1982, the monetary base expanded by an average annual rate of 40 percent. The stock of currency and reserves thus expanded from ₵352 million to ₵10,211 million. The loss of monetary control accelerated inflation, which reached 116 percent by 1977, from single-digit levels a few years earlier. During the same ten-year period, the consumer price index rose by an average annual rate of 53 percent, despite the extensive price and distributional controls of goods and services. The price level did not rise as quickly as the money supply in the late 1970s, reflecting the control mechanism. Eventually a convergence occurred, with some overshooting in the early 1980s as scarcities of goods became widespread.

Exchange rate policy

The loss of fiscal and monetary control would already have been costly to the economy. But the problem was then aggravated by the government as it attempted to suppress some of the symptoms, thereby preventing the necessary adjustments.

As inflation intensified in the 1970s, Ghana failed to make exchange rate adjustments. Devaluation was regarded as a political taboo—the Busia Administration had attempted it in 1971, but it led to urban riots and a successful military coup. The parallel-market exchange rate began to diverge sharply

Figure 4.3 Sources of monetary growth, 1976–82

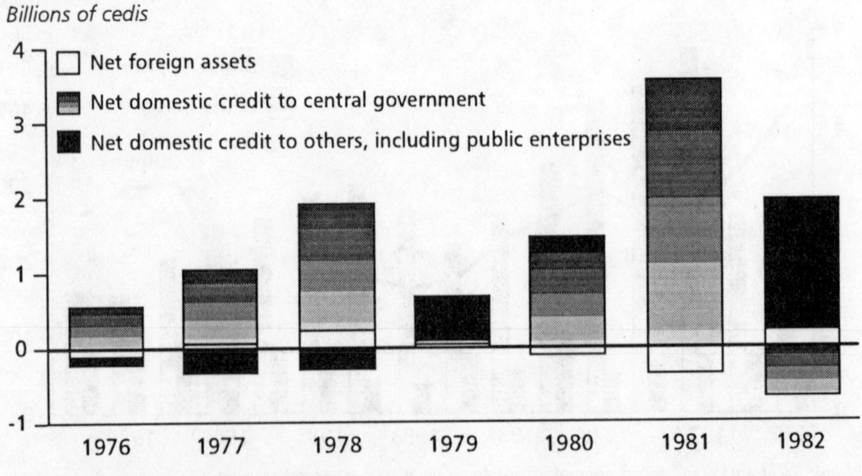

Billions of cedis

Net foreign assets
Net domestic credit to central government
Net domestic credit to others, including public enterprises

4, 3, 2, 1, 0, -1
1976 1977 1978 1979 1980 1981 1982

Source: IMF, *International Financial Statistics*.

Figure 4.4 Exchange rates, cedis per U.S. dollar, 1974–90

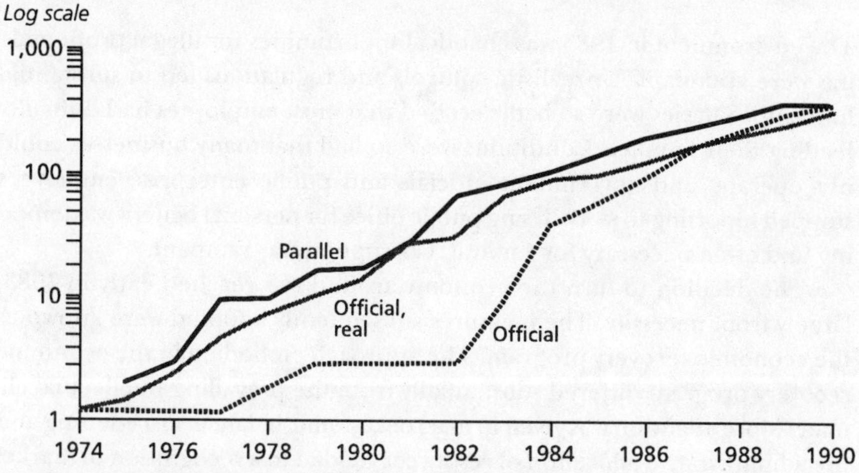

Note: The real official exchange rate is adjusted for the inflation differential between Ghana and the United States.
Source: IMF, *International Financial Statistics*; World Bank staff calculations.

from the official rate (figure 4.4.) In 1978 and 1979 the exchange rate was finally devalued from ₡1.15 to ₡2.75 per U.S. dollar. But the adjustment, while substantial by historical standards, was too little and too late relative to need. The concurrently high inflation quickly eroded the effect of the devaluation. The divergence between the black market and official rates continued to widen.

The parallel-market exchange rate may not be a good yardstick for judging policies. The black market could be subject to speculative manipulations and could carry excessive risk premiums. For this reason, an alternative comparator is provided—the official rate taken at the beginning of the period (1974) and successively adjusted by the extent to which cedi inflation (the change in the consumer price index) exceeded dollar inflation. This new measure yields the exchange rate that would maintain the relative purchasing power of the two currencies—hence the inflation-adjusted exchange rate. As shown in figure 4.4, the inflation-adjusted exchange rate tracks the black market rate closely, although some risk premiums are reflected by the latter.

If the inflation-adjusted exchange rate is used as a proxy for the appropriate exchange rate, then the deviation between the official rate and the inflation-adjusted exchange rate represents a measure of the exchange rate distortion. The extent of this distortion is presented in figure 4.5. By 1982 the overvaluation exceeded 1,000 percent of the official exchange rate. At that time, an exporter would get ₡2.75 for a dollar surrendered to the Bank of Ghana, but more than ₡60 in the black market.

Policy reform, 1983 through 1991

The environment in 1983 was chaotic. Opportunities for illegal profit-making were abundant. Unrealistic controls and regulations led to substantial hardship. Salaries were so badly eroded that most employees had difficulty feeding their families. Conditions were so bad that many businesses could not operate, and government officials and public enterprise employees stopped reporting to work. Using public office for personal benefit was tempting and often necessary for survival. Corruption was rampant.

The decision to turn the economy around was reached early in 1983, largely from necessity. The measures subsequently adopted were known as the economic recovery program. The approach embodied in the economic recovery program differed substantially from the prevailing intellectual climate. More attention was given to macroeconomic balance. Price-setting and the administrative allocation of resources yielded to a recognition of market forces. The rationale for the policy reversal appeared to be the realization that fighting corruption in the context of extreme scarcities and distortions was essentially a lost cause.

Initial efforts under the economic recovery program focused on stabilization. In the context of deferred adjustments in a badly distorted economy, stabilization was not a simple task. The magnitude of necessary price adjustments was colossal and could have created considerable dislocations in a fragile economy. A gradualistic approach was deemed necessary. In the meantime, economic production had to resume. Rehabilitation of infrastruc-

Figure 4.5 Overvaluation of the cedi, 1974–90

Percentage of official exchange rate

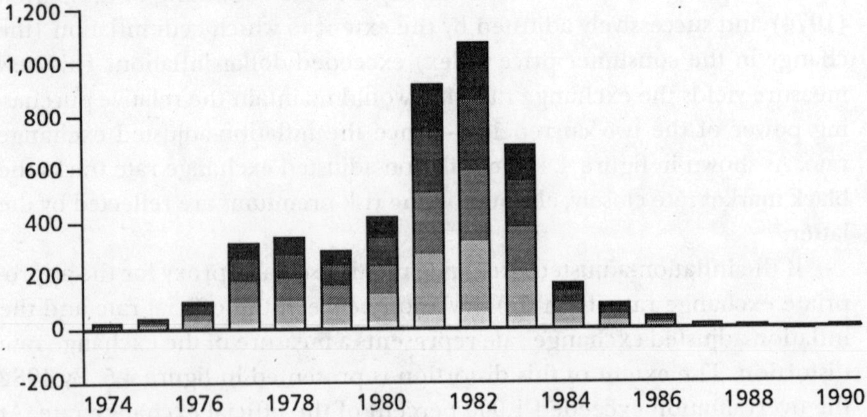

Source: IMF, *International Financial Statistics*; World Bank staff calculations.

ture was urgent. Foreign exchange was required to ensure the flow of essential imports. In addition, the government had to face the traditional stabilization tasks of controlling inflation and moderating fluctuations in interest and exchange rates.

Macroeconomic reform: design and implementation

Foreign exchange regime

Among the most significant and successful measures in the first stage (1983–87) was the exchange rate policy. Within the first year of the economic recovery program, the official exchange rate was devalued from ₵2.75 to ₵8.83 to the U.S. dollar. And that was just the beginning. Overvaluation was still massive. Several maxidevaluations, as they were known then, followed, depreciating the currency further to ₵90 per dollar by September 1986. The official rate was thus brought within 25 percent of purchasing power parity (figure 4.4.) Yet the black market rate was still about twice the official rate.

In September 1986 a major step was taken when a foreign retail auction was introduced. Initially the auction covered most trade transactions, excluding a few major items such as petroleum, cocoa, and essential imports. The auction system was subsequently modified extensively—the coverage of transactions was broadened, the introduction of foreign exchange bureaus legalized the remaining parallel market, and a wholesale auction system replaced the retail system. Throughout, the foreign exchange market functioned smoothly as the exchange rate adjusted to changing market conditions, and the overvaluation of the cedi was virtually eliminated. In April 1992 the wholesale auctions were abolished, and the central bank's management of the exchange rate has since taken place directly in the interbank markets.

Fiscal policies

Adjustment in the foreign exchange markets was supported by the economic recovery program's fiscal discipline. The key element of fiscal policy was resource mobilization. Revenue as a percentage of GDP rose from less than 6 percent in 1983 to 14 percent in 1986. Moreover, the increase in revenue did not come from the imposition of new or more onerous taxes. Tax policies were gradually restructured, with an emphasis on broadening the tax base and lowering rates. The top marginal tax rate on personal income, for instance, was cut successively from 60 percent in 1985 to 30 percent in 1991, while the standard deduction was raised substantially in real terms. Tax compliance improved, while collection efforts were strengthened. Tax bureaus were reorganized, and professional staff were extensively recruited. The sharp upsurge of revenue made it possible both to narrow the fiscal imbalance and to raise the level of expenditures (figure 4.6).

Thus, unlike adjustment elsewhere, the first four years of reform in Ghana saw a continuous expansion in government spending (the size and composition of public expenditures since the reform started is shown in figure 4.7). Yet the increased expenditures reflected a recovery from a sharp fall that had preceded the reform, rather than a net addition of new programs and services. Public sector pay, for instance, was raised significantly in this period to compensate for the large erosion up to that point. Starting in 1986, a program of civil service retrenchment was also implemented. Expenditures on social services and rehabilitation of infrastructure rose significantly, reversing the sharp decline before 1983.

Monetary policy

With improved fiscal discipline, monetary policy became more manageable. As the economic recovery program was implemented, the monetary base began to stabilize, and the rate of inflation fell significantly (figure 4.8). Yet, the initial success of the stabilization program complicated monetary management in new ways. External financial support for Ghana rose dramatically, allowing a replenishment of depleted foreign exchange reserves. Although the build-up of reserves was partly a policy choice, it was also necessitated by the government's financing of local expenses. In 1988 and 1989, for instance,

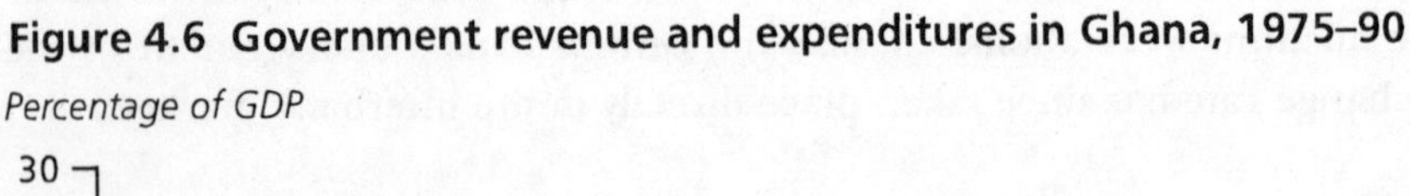

Figure 4.6 Government revenue and expenditures in Ghana, 1975–90

Percentage of GDP

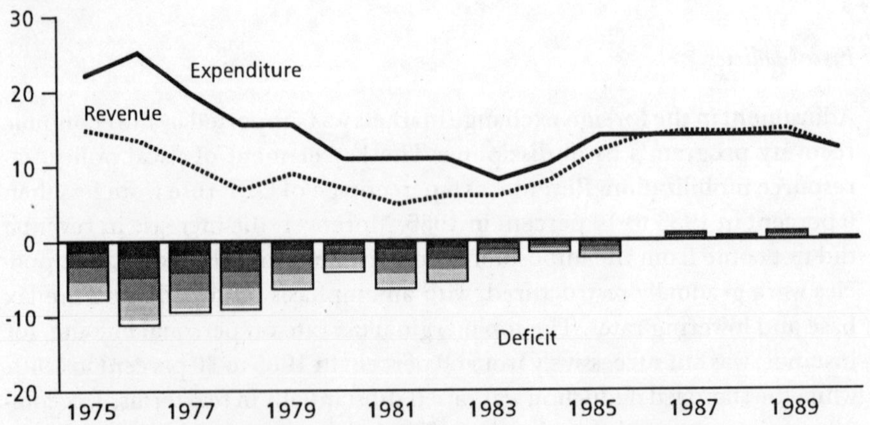

a. Narrow definition, including expenditures financed by foreign aid.
Source: IMF, *International Financial Statistics*, various years; World Bank staff calculations.

domestic spending in excess of domestic revenue was financed by the conversion of foreign aid. Foreign assets held by the Bank of Ghana became an important source of monetary growth, replacing the fiscal deficits of a few years earlier. But since 1989, domestic credit policy has been used aggressively to offset the growth of foreign assets (see figure 4.3). Initially the policy generated a small fiscal surplus. This was used to repay the government's debt to the Bank of Ghana to offset monetary growth. In subsequent years, repayments were increased, and domestic credit extended by the Bank of Ghana was reduced. Inflation fell to single-digit levels by the end of 1991.

Figure 4.7 Composition of government expenditures, 1984–91

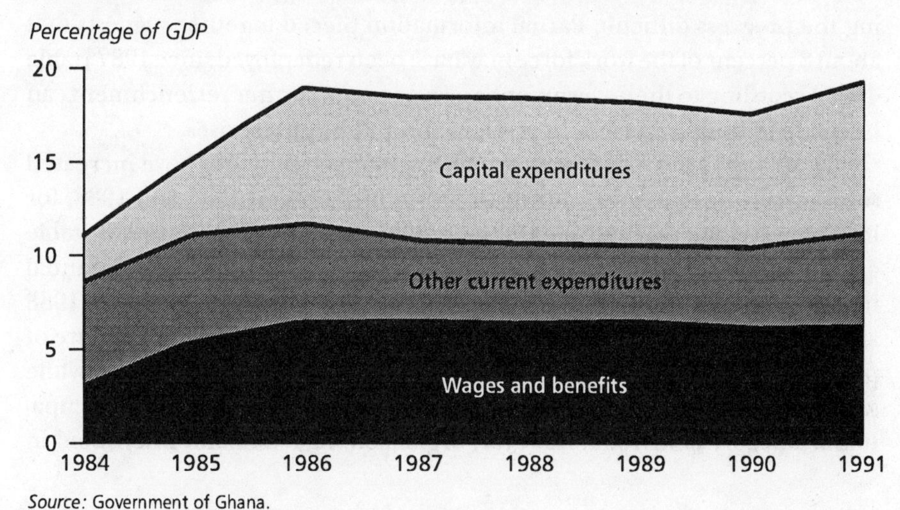

Source: Government of Ghana.

Figure 4.8 Inflation in Ghana, 1971–91

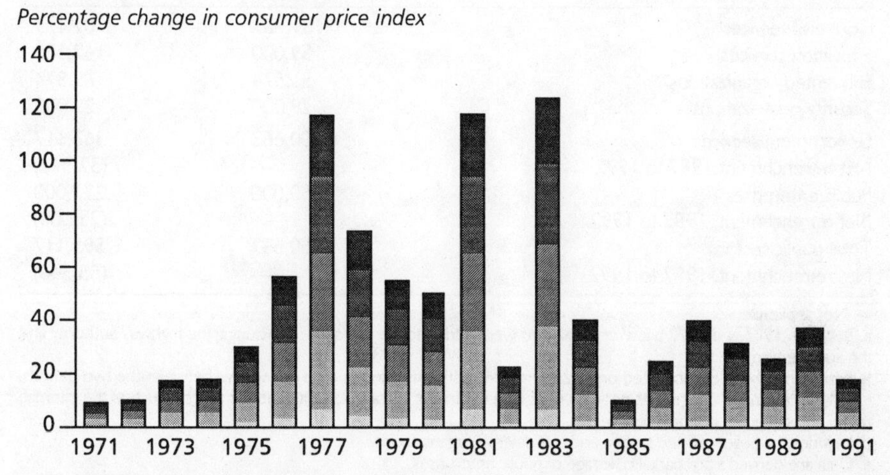

Source: IMF, *International Financial Statistics*; World Bank staff calculations.

Sectoral reform: design and implementation

Labor markets

Ghana's labor market is segmented, with an informal sector (rural and urban) and an organized modern sector. In the informal markets, wages are determined by market forces. In the organized modern sector, the government is the wage leader, accounting for about two-thirds of total employment.

Since the mid-1980s, the government has attempted to restructure the size of the public sector work force and its compensation. Some progress has been made toward retrenchment, but a severe shortage of data makes assessing the progress difficult. Partial information pieced together suggests that about 8 percent of the work force may have been redeployed since 1987 (table 4.1). According to the government's own account, further retrenchment can be made in both government services and public enterprises.

Despite pervasive overemployment, public sector wages have increased substantially in real terms during adjustment. Between 1983 and 1988, for instance, average real earnings in the public sector more than tripled (table 4.2). Again much of the increase sought to compensate for the substantial inflationary erosion that had occurred prior to adjustment. Between 1988 and 1992, the government attempted to link wage increases to a measure of productivity. Average real earnings were held more or less constant, while salary differentials were permitted to widen across grade levels and occupational categories. In 1992, however, organized wage demand intensified in

Table 4.1 Number of public sector employees, 1987 and 1992

Group	*1987*	*1992*
Core civil services[a]	131,089	102,173
Education services	159,000	167,370
Subvented organizations[b,c]	81,574	69,574
Security organizations[d]	29,000	29,000
Government services	400,663	368,117
Net retrenchment, 1987 to 1992	—	(32,546)
Public enterprises[e]	250,000	227,000
Net retrenchment, 1987 to 1992	—	(23,000)
Total public sector	650,663	595,117
Net retrenchment, 1987 to 1992	—	(55,546)

— Not applicable.
a. Between 1987 and 1972 a few organizations were added to the civil service, including the highway authority and the audit service.
b. Some employees of subvented organizations were transferred to the core civil service between the two periods.
c. Includes estimates of agencies not covered in the controller and accountant general's payroll, such as the internal revenue service and customs services.
d. Includes the police, armed forces, and civil defense organizations.
e. Data are derived from partial coverage of public enterprises.
Source: Government of Ghana; State Enterprise Commission (1992); Commander and Estrada (1992).

Table 4.2 Indexes of average real earnings and minimum wages, 1983–92
(1985 = 100)

Year	Average real earnings		Real
	Public	Private	minimum wage
1983	48	43	54
1984	67	77	56
1985	100	100	100
1986	..	..	103
1987	122	93	120
1988	160	188	91
1989	167	..	84
1990	164	..	79
1991	171	..	83
1992	270	..	117

.. Not available.
a. The 1992 indexes are estimated on the basis of average salary increase of 80 percent granted to government employees.
Source: World Bank; *Quarterly Digest of Statistics* (1991).

the months before the elections. In October 1992, the government agreed to raise the average government service pay by about 80 percent. Average real wages in the public sector have exploded by 500 percent since adjustment, or 20 times the gain in per capita GDP.

Trade reform

The aim of reform has been to rationalize the incentive system and improve the competitiveness of local producers. In the initial stage, the extensive quantitative restrictions and domestic price controls were removed and the foreign exchange regime was liberalized. Subsequently, price distortions arising from tariffs and protective taxes were reduced, as shown in table 4.3. Significant protection remained, however, in the form of protective features built into the sales tax and the excise tax; these were phased out by 1989. The special import tax, which covers a wide range of sensitive industries, has gradually been reduced from about 40 percent to 10 percent across the board in 1992.

Critics of trade reform have said that it has been too abrupt and too damaging to local industries. Yet this criticism fails to recognize the limited extent to which tariffs have been reduced under a policy that has been phased in over five to seven years. Considerable protection is still in place—averaging about 30 percent in nominal terms over world prices after accounting for tariffs and a surcharge (special import tax). However, removal of quantitative restrictions did significantly change the extent of protection after the first few years of adjustment. Fortunately, the change was accompanied by a series of massive devaluations, which worked to the advantage of local producers.

Along with the liberalization of imports, efforts have been made to promote exports. The first was to remove a variety of export duties. Export licensing was then abolished in 1990, and export procedures were made somewhat less cumbersome. A few export incentives were also introduced, including duty-free import of machinery and income tax rebates based on export sales. Yet major export constraints remain—particularly the nonfunctioning duty-drawback mechanism and the lack of access to export finance by private firms. The extensive control of public enterprises over marketing activities and logistical services further inhibits the country's export potential. Regulations of foreign investment, including restrictions on private firms' joint ventures with foreign partners, impede Ghana's finding a foothold in overseas markets.

Financial sector

Major financial sector reform has been undertaken since 1988, focusing on the banking system. Initial efforts were targeted at upgrading the financial position of commercial banks, many of which carried large portfolios of nonperforming assets of public enterprises. The government issued long-term bonds in exchange for the nonperforming assets, which were then put up for sale or liquidation. This restructuring enabled the banks to meet international standards of capital adequacy. Institutional development efforts and prudential regulations have been upgraded.

Commercial interest rates are no longer regulated. Sectoral lending requirements no longer apply. In 1991 the government announced its intention to divest its ownership of commercial banks. In addition, the government broadened its use of government securities as an instrument of indirect monetary control. In 1992 global and institution-specific credit ceilings were abolished in a switch to full-fledged open-market operations. At the same time, a variety of new financial institutions started operating in Ghana, including two private investment banks, two discount houses, and a leasing company.

Yet the financial system remains fragile. Resource mobilization is limited, constraining the scope of commercial lending. In recent years, more of

Table 4.3 Import tariffs, 1983–90
(percent)

Category	*1983*	*1984*	*1985*	*1986*	*1987*	*1988*	*1989*	*1990*
Concessionary tariff	10-20	10-20	20-25	10-20	10-25	10-25	0	0
Basic raw materials	25	25	25	10	15	10	10	10
Other raw materials	30	30	30	20	20	15	15	10
Capital goods	30	30	30	20	25	15	15	10
Consumer goods	30	30	30	25	35	20	20	20
Luxury goods	30	30	30	30	30	25	25	25

Source: GATT (1991).

the banks' assets have been absorbed by government securities sold for the purpose of mopping up excess liquidity. Nonbank intermediation is dominated by public enterprises, and as a result the volume of contractual savings has been relatively small and shown little expansion.

Agriculture

The agricultural sector has more than a 40 percent share of GDP. Sectoral reform started relatively late, toward the end of the 1980s. The extent of reform has been limited, except for exchange rate polices. Adjustments of the cedi under macroeconomic reform have significantly increased the prices of a variety of traded commodities, including cocoa and horticultural products. And for cocoa, the rate of export tax has gradually been reduced. Cocoa producers have thus received a higher share of world prices. But world cocoa prices fell substantially during the adjustment period—by more than 50 percent since 1986. Thus, real producer prices have fallen, as has cocoa production since 1989.

Agricultural reform focused on gradually reducing the government's involvement in the sector. Government farm estates and fertilizer plants are being divested. Subsidies for fertilizers and chemicals are being phased out. Export taxes and other trade restrictions are being reduced. Yet agricultural growth remains sluggish, at a pace well below growth in the rest of the economy. In part this stagnation reflects the declining trend in primary prices worldwide.

Role of the public sector

Reform has made little progress in several important areas, one of which is the rebuilding of government capacity in policy analysis and implementation. The limited institutional capacity reflects a failure of management, which tends to centralize decisionmaking and monopolize information. Capable staff are not fully utilized and are thus undermotivated. Budgetary procedures are hampered by technical and political constraints, which prevent the flow of authorized allocations. The civil service is unduly large, with inadequate supervisory and managerial oversight. Even after several rounds of retrenchments, Ghana's civil service remains one of the largest in Africa in relation to the country's population (figure 4.9).

Public enterprises

One of the most crucial shortcomings of the adjustment program is the restructuring of government commercial activities. Given previous developmental strategies that relied heavily on the public sector as a vehicle for growth,

Ghana had, and still has, more than 300 public enterprises, more than all other African countries except Tanzania. These enterprises have established their presence in virtually every sector in the economy. Moreover, they have considerable commercial advantages over private companies, including financial assistance, the use of government-owned commercial assets, special tax treatments and, in many industries, a quasi-monopolistic position. These enterprises thus threaten and deter private investment. Ghana's private investment is less than 8 percent of GDP, far below the level required for self-sustained growth, and less than half of average private investment in low-income developing countries.

The government has been ambivalent about public enterprise reform. In the first few years of adjustment, the government showed no intention of changing its role in commercial activities. However, it did acknowledge the excessive work force and the poor performance of public enterprises across the board. Its initial strategy was to upgrade the efficiency of the enterprises, rather than to allow competition from private companies. Little effort was made to instill the basic financial principle that the commitments of enterprises be met by the enterprises themselves, not by the taxpayers or by foreign aid.

As the losses of public enterprises mounted and their burden on the budget increased toward the end of the 1980s, the government began to reconsider its position. Efforts to streamline public enterprises were stepped up. The sale and liquidation of minor enterprises were attempted (table 4.4). Limited participation of private companies became a possibility. Yet as of late

Figure 4.9 Size of civil service in five African countries

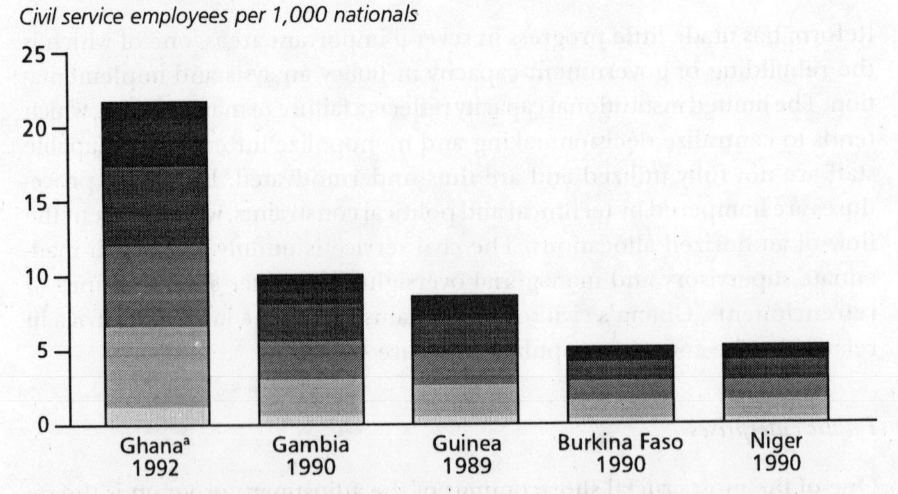

a. Includes the core civil service, educational service, and subvented organizations, but not parastatals.
Source: Government of Ghana; World Bank staff estimates.

1992, statements of intent far outnumbered actual measures. In March 1992, for instance, in a break with longstanding tradition, the government announced a plan to let private companies trade in cocoa within Ghana. However, cocoa exporting was to remain the exclusive right of the state-owned Cocoa Board. The Cocoa Board was also granted responsibility for licensing private companies. Real competition has not yet taken place.

Economic outcomes

Ghana has come a long way since 1983. Major price control and policy distortions have been corrected. A reasonable fiscal balance has been achieved. Its external position has been strengthened. In fact, during the adjustment period Ghana has prospered, despite a massive decline in the international prices of gold and cocoa. Moreover, structural reform will enable Ghana to respond more buoyantly to the external and policy shocks it will inevitably experience.

Productive sectors

Since 1984 Ghana has significantly upgraded its economic performance. Real GDP growth has averaged 5 percent annually, with per capita real growth of about 2 percent. In the same period, Sub-Saharan African countries have shown a GDP growth of less than 3 percent annually, with little per capita growth. At the global level, however, low-income countries as a group have grown at an annual rate of about 6 percent, exceeding the growth rate in Ghana and Africa as a whole.

Ghana's performance has been relatively steady over time. Aside from 1984, when a growth spurt occurred after the major drought, and 1990, when there was an oil shock and global recession, Ghana's growth has been very close to 5 percent annually. Growth at the sectoral level has varied more widely (figure 4.10). Services, which account for more than 40 percent of GDP, have shown rapid and consistent growth. Agricultural growth has been sluggish

Table 4.4 Public enterprises and divestiture, 1987–91

Item	*1987*	*1988*	*1989*	*1990*	*1991*[a]
Estimated number of public firms	329	329	314	291	266
Targeted for divestment	..	32	45	39	42
Actual divestment	..	..	15	23	25
Cumulative divestment	..	..	..	38	63
Liquidated	..	..	15	24	26
Sold	..	..	..	14	37

.. Not available.
a. Includes sales, liquidation, and management contracts.
Source: State Enterprise Commission (1992); World Bank data.

and uneven. Manufacturing, with a share of less than 10 percent of GDP, grew rapidly in the initial years of adjustment as the utilization of existing capacity increased. In more recent years, however, manufacturing production has stagnated, growing at an average of only 2.8 percent annually between 1988 and 1991. Mining, which attracts much interest from foreign companies, has shown consistent and strong performance.

By 1991 Ghana's economy was about 40 percent larger than it was in 1984. Much of the growth (77 percent) came from the service sector, especially trading. Industry contributed about 18 percent to the growth, including the mining subsector, which contributed 3.6 percent. Agriculture, the largest segment of the economy, made a relatively small contribution of 5 percent. This pattern of sectoral change is similar to that of many advanced, postindustrial economies in which production is being shifted to lower-wage countries. In Ghana, however, this pattern suggests a need to reexamine policy and other structural constraints.

The pattern of sectoral growth in Ghana is substantially different from that of neighboring Nigeria. In the case of Nigeria, postadjustment (1986–92) growth was derived equally from agriculture, services, and oil production. Industry made no major contribution during this period. The expansion of agricultural production was particularly dramatic. After a long period of stagnant and declining output before 1986, agriculture grew by an annual rate of 4.3 percent between 1987 and 1992. Adjustment of the exchange rate and the abolition of agricultural marketing boards provided the major impetus for the growth. In Ghana, where agricultural reform has been slower and more modest, output growth has been about half that of Nigeria.

Figure 4.10 GDP growth by sector, 1984–91

Annual percentage change in value added

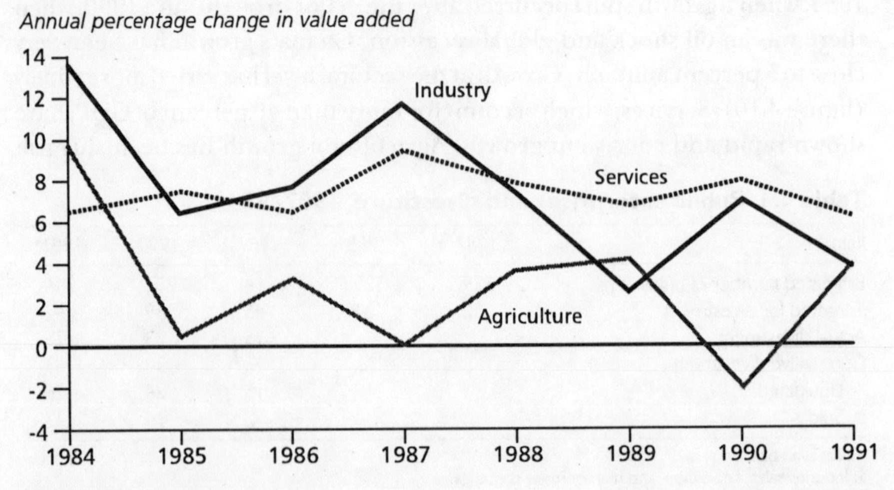

Source: Ghana Statistical Service.

Supply response in agriculture

Since agriculture is the dominant sector, its sluggish performance has been a drag on the economy. Its disappointing performance raises several questions. Is reform in the sector lagging behind reform in the rest of the economy? Have prices become less distorted and risen toward world price levels? What nonprice factors are still constraining the supply response? Does the sector have adequate capacity to adjust to changing incentives?

Aside from the exchange rate adjustments and changes in cocoa pricing policies, agricultural reform in Ghana started relatively late, about five years behind the overall adjustment program. Reform has sought primarily to reduce the role of public enterprises in the production, pricing, and distribution of agricultural inputs and outputs. As with public enterprise reform in Ghana generally, progress has been slow and limited in scope. Divestiture and liquidation of state-owned farms, processing plants, and chemical companies have started. Marketing and distribution control is being liberalized, although longstanding practices and traditions tend to change gradually. The infrastructure is being upgraded, but remains inadequate, particularly rural feeder roads and critical links with external markets. Marketing facilities and physical structures are underdeveloped and owned predominantly by the public sector, which limits the scope for attracting private investment. The combination of marketing and infrastructure constraints is reflected in the wide distribution margins observed for a variety of common items (table 4.5).

Available evidence on price incentives suggests that Ghanaian farmers respond promptly and significantly to price changes. For instance, the production of root crops and cereals is projected to rise by about 37 to 50 percent of a given increase in real producers' prices in the short run. Longer-run price elasticities of supply are considerably higher (table 4.6). Among tree crops, the supply response to prices is also significant. Cocoa production rebounded sharply due to the increase in producer prices between 1984 and 1989 (see figure 4.2), and a vast majority of cocoa producers undertook new plantings after the adjustment was initiated (Commander 1989).

Table 4.5 Ratio of retail to farmgate prices

Commodity	*Retail center*	*Producing center*	*Ratio*
Yams	Accra	SaLaga	1.61
Maize	Accra	Nhoshanza	1.56
Tomatoes	Accra	Akumadan	2.27
Goats	Accra	Bawku	1.76
Palm oil	Accra	Kade	2.26
Sheanut	Takoradi	Wa	3.30
Cocoa	Takoradi	Goasco	1.64

Source: Ghanexim.

The adjustment period in Ghana also coincided with a long-term cyclical downturn in world commodity prices. Ghana's principal crop was particularly hard hit; since 1984 world prices for cocoa averaged less than three-quarters of the prices in the preceding decade, and the slump deepened toward the end of the 1980s. World prices for other commodities also showed a cyclical decline—including gold, another major export. Domestic commodity prices in Ghana, including roots and cereals (the primary foodcrops), reflected this global trend. With the exception of the drought year (1983), real food prices have been falling since 1980.

An important element of Ghana's adjustment policies was to improve producer prices for cocoa. The government gradually but consistently raised the share of world prices received by cocoa farmers. Yet the effort was constrained by the necessity of maintaining the flow of revenue, by high marketing costs (to the public enterprise), and, most severely, by falling world prices. Starting in 1988 and continuing into 1993, the prices received by cocoa farmers began to fall again in real terms. Production also leveled off.

Thus, cyclical swings in global commodity prices have played an important role in depressing Ghanaian farm income and farmers' ability to adjust or diversify their sources of earnings. This constraint was exacerbated by limited progress toward rehabilitating the infrastructure and liberalizing marketing arrangements.

Foreign aid

An important aspect of Ghana's adjustment experience in the 1980s is the role of external assistance. Donors have played a major role in both shaping the adjustment program and financing the attendant costs. Soon after the economic recovery program was initiated, foreign aid increased dramatically. Net resources to Ghana under official foreign aid rose from about $270 million in 1984 to $385 million in 1986, and to $480 million in 1990.

Yet the size of this external assistance is not particularly large compared with that received by other African countries. As a share of GDP, the disburse-

Table 4.6 Regression estimates of agricultural supply response
(selected agricultural output)

Dependent variables	*Constant*	*Price (lagged one period)*	*Production (lagged one period)*	R^2
Cereals	-0.48	0.53	0.82	
	(0.26)	(0.32)	(0.38)	0.73
Root crops	0.53	0.37	0.16	
	(0.19)	(0.21)	(0.36)	0.71

Note: Figures in parentheses are estimated standard errors. Double-lag equations are used. Ten observations (1980–90) are used in each equation.
Source: World Bank staff estimates.

ment of official assistance to Ghana was about 10 percent in the late 1980s, considerably lower than in Malawi (20 percent), Senegal (25 percent), and Tanzania (more than 30 percent). On a per capita basis, the same picture emerges. Official assistance to Ghana was about $40 per person in 1989, somewhat higher than in Tanzania ($37) and Côte d'Ivoire ($34), but still lower than in Zambia ($48), Malawi ($49), and Senegal ($91).

As it turned out, foreign aid was much needed to offset Ghana's losses due to its declining terms of trade. Falling prices for gold and cocoa had lowered Ghana's foreign exchange earnings significantly in relation to its potential based on 1984 prices (see figure 4.1). Without foreign aid, the adverse terms of trade shifts would have seriously threatened the progress of the adjustment program. Nonetheless, the net incremental resources available to Ghana were much smaller than is generally believed. The net amount became insignificant after 1988, and the net aid flow actually fell short of terms of trade losses in 1992.

The more important contribution of foreign aid may have been toward policymaking. As with other countries, Ghana's decisionmaking process involves balancing the demands of various interest groups. Foreign aid has expanded the scope of policy considerations to constituencies that were not part of the policymaking circle or did not have adequate political power. For instance, correcting local currency overvaluation had been considered a political taboo for several decades prior to adjustment. Similarly, without foreign aid the groups favoring fiscal discipline and more liberal economic management might not have prevailed.

Yet the leverage of foreign aid is not as great as is generally perceived. The acceptance of aid-supported reform depends on how such reform affects local political and social expectations. Decisionmaking is governed by internal political considerations. Donors likely can make a difference only when the contest among interest groups is close. Moreover, the success of reform depends on the capacity of local implementation—as indicated by the limited progress toward restructuring the public sector's commercial undertakings. Vested interests, particularly political appointees in charge of vast public assets, still dominate decisionmaking, despite considerable support for reform from the donor community. Foreign aid has had little effect on addressing excessive public sector employment, the absence of financial discipline among public enterprises, and the overextended scope of government functions.

Is self-sustained economic growth possible?

Has Ghana reached a point where it can generate rapid growth without foreign aid? Its strong performance for a decade does not by itself confirm the possibility. Many countries, including neighboring Côte d'Ivoire, made similar strides toward self-sustained growth, only to suffer protracted declines afterward. Assessing the prospects for Ghana requires examining some of its fundamental features.

International experience shows that rapid and sustainable growth is commonly associated with a few observable characteristics. First, a country's savings and investment rate should be high, normally higher than the average for countries with a similar income level. Second, the country should have extensive links with world markets to facilitate the flow of capital and technology. Third, a country needs a stable economic environment, which limits the volatility of the exchange and interest rates.

Where does Ghana stand today in terms of these criteria? While much progress has been made, there is much scope for improvement.

Savings and investment

Domestic saving in Ghana has risen in recent years from about 5 percent of GDP to 8 percent of GDP (figure 4.11). The increase has brought the savings rate up to the level of the 1960s, which is still very low by international standards. For Sub-Saharan Africa, the savings rate has gone down in the past two decades, but the current rate is about 13 percent. In Asia, where rapid growth has often been observed in many countries, the savings rate is about 28 percent of GDP.

Despite low domestic saving, Ghana has in recent years been able to draw on foreign aid and maintain an investment rate of about 16 percent of GDP

Figure 4.11 Savings and investment, 1975–91

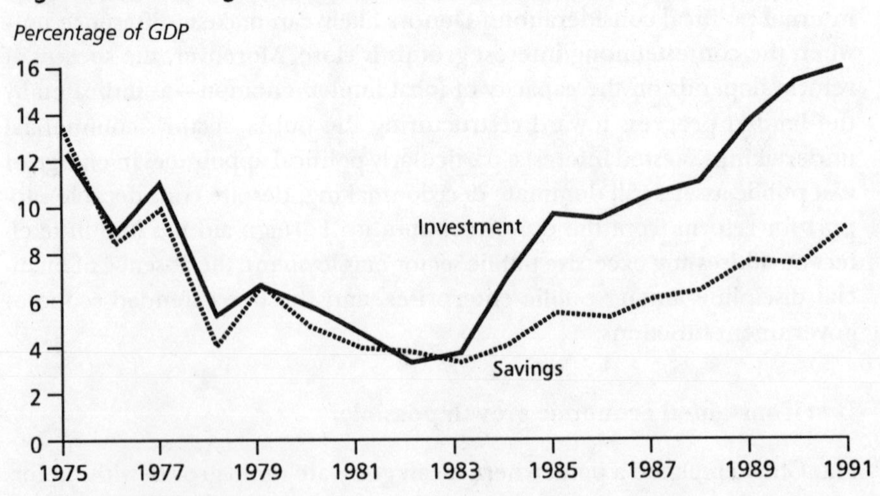

Source: Government of Ghana.

(figure 4.11). Half of the investment comes from government capital expenditures. The remainder is a combination of investments by public enterprises and private companies. Data on private sector investment are not readily available, but it clearly is not more than 8 percent of GDP.

Ghana's gross domestic investment is comparable to the average for Sub-Saharan Africa (15 percent of GDP). But it is still considerably lower than in low-income countries as a group (29 percent) and lower than in high-growth East Asian countries in the 1960s (22 percent). Furthermore, since the government's share in investment is large, the shortfall is due to a lack of investment demand in the private sector. This aspect of Ghana's adjustment experience requires further attention. After a decade of generally favorable adjustment efforts, private sector investment, normally the driving force for vigorous growth, has not been particularly strong (World Bank 1992).

Links with external markets

Ghana has long held a distinctive position in world markets as a leading exporter of quality cocoa and gold. Yet trade with the rest of the world is comparatively small. Ghana's measure of openness—the sum of its imports and exports as a share of GDP—has recently been about 40 percent, a significant expansion from a very depressed level prior to the adjustment program. While the degree of openness varies substantially from one country to another, many countries of similar size and endowments, such as Côte d'Ivoire, Malaysia, and Zimbabwe, show much greater integration with the world economy. For instance, Malaysia's trade volume exceeds its GDP.

The size of trade is determined largely by a country's ability to export and to attract foreign investment. Ghana's exports seem to have reached a plateau in recent years at about 18 percent of GDP (figure 4.12). Furthermore, the base of Ghana's exports is restricted to a few traditional items, including cocoa, gold, and timber, which still account for about two-thirds of total exports. Nontraditional exports have grown, but remain a small part of total exports at less than 6 percent (figure 4.13). Imports have also shown dramatic growth, reaching about 25 percent of GDP in recent years. But after aid-funded imports are excluded, the sustainable volume of trade (both imports and exports) is about 35 percent of GDP, considerably lower than the level for high-growth countries.

Economic stability

The adjustment program has made significant strides, particularly in the areas of fiscal discipline and monetary restraint. Yet inflation control has shown mixed results. The rate of inflation—as measured by the change in the consumer price index—was brought down to a single-digit level on a few occasions. However, it averaged 26 percent annually between 1984 and 1991, compared with a rate of about 6 percent among its trading partners. Inflation has been relatively high and volatile during the adjustment period. This volatility is reflected in the nominal exchange rates, domestic interest rates, and credit conditions in the economy.

The apparently paradoxical link between monetary restraint and high inflation can be explained by the absence of financial depth. The broad monetary aggregate (M2) in Ghana has been about 14 percent of GDP in recent years, implying that Ghana's financial depth is one of the lowest in the world. (Only Argentina and Uganda have less financial depth than Ghana.) This low level is due primarily to the unwillingness of the public to hold deposits in domestic banks. Furthermore, the monetary base (or high-powered money) is correspondingly small, representing about 6 percent of GDP in 1990.

Given the limited financial depth, even monetary increases that are small in relation to the economy can have a large impact on the price level. Consider for example, an expansion in the monetary base of 1.5 percent of GDP annually, a modest increase by international standards. In Ghana, however, this increase would translate into monetary expansion of about 25 percent. Over the medium term, this increase in the monetary base and money supply would translate into annual inflation of about 25 percent, the level observed during the adjustment period.

Figure 4.12 Exports and imports, 1975–91

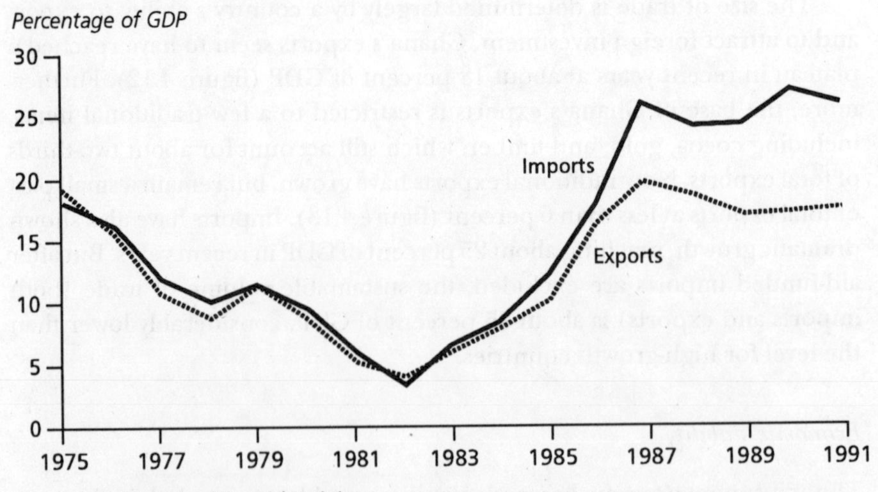

Source: IMF, *International Financial Statistics.*

Private sector development

To achieve rapid and self-sustained growth, Ghana must overcome several major obstacles to private sector development and public sector reform.

Building private sector confidence. The lack of confidence in the business environment among private sector actors has been frequently noted. Among Ghanaian business people, the terms often used to describe the business environment include "mistrust," "harassment," and "the absence of support." More erudite observers use such terms as "ambivalent attitude" or "issue of governance."

The confidence issue is in part a legacy of past policies. Serious economic mismanagement prior to the adjustment program had led to chaos and real hardship—both of which remain vivid in the collective memory. Even during the period of recovery, the economic climate was clouded by official actions that posed serious threats to private businesses. Properties were seized and people's lifetime savings were confiscated. Prosecutions of individuals were actively pursued under normal and parallel legal channels. Business opportunities were constrained by the presence of public enterprises with powerful political connections.

The adjustment program has nonetheless made considerable progress toward pragmatism. Despite a strong voice for maintaining the status quo, official control of many economic activities has been withdrawn, primarily in an effort to curb brazen forms of corruption. But convincing signs of a new

Figure 4.13 Composition of merchandise exports, 1984–91

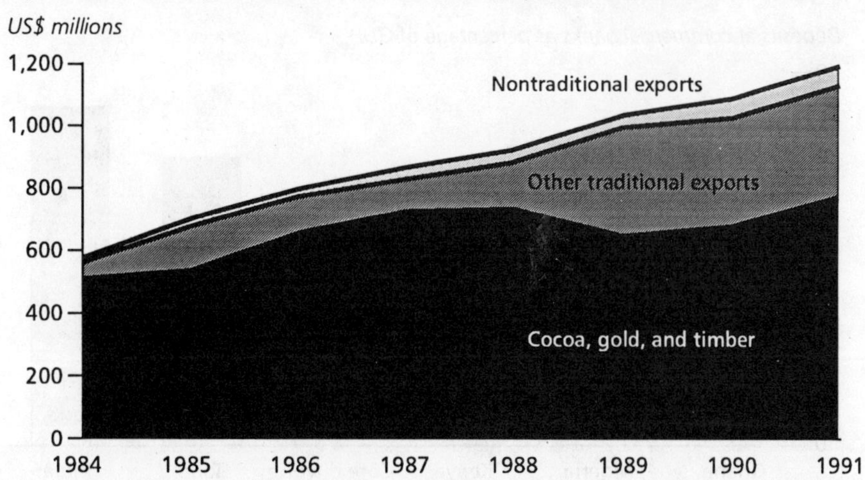

Source: Ghana Council of Export Promotion.

approach and a new partnership with private businesses have not been forthcoming from the government. The divestiture of government commercial undertakings has been slow and faltering.

The availability of credit. The absence of confidence shows up in the banking system. Deposits at commercial banks have represented about 8 percent of GDP in recent years, compared with an average of about 16 percent for Sub-Saharan Africa as a whole (figure 4.14). The failure to mobilize resources is in turn restricting the availability of credit and raising the costs of funds, with pervasive repercussions in the economy. Ghanaian business people throughout the country consider the difficult access to credit one of the most serious problems they face.

Since the adjustment process began in 1983, the level of credit available per unit of final output has declined. This decline is due in part to the direct control of domestic credit that was in effect until 1992. (Since 1990 greater reliance has been placed on the control of the monetary base through sales of government securities and the use of government repayment to the banking system.) Furthermore, a large proportion of the credit that is available goes to state-owned enterprises. Credit to the private sector has been extremely scarce. Compared with more dynamic economies—Thailand and Malaysia in the 1960s, for example—Ghanaian private businesses have about one-third or one-fourth as much credit to work with (table 4.7). The same situation applies to nonbank financial institutions. Outside the banking system, insurance companies and pension funds are the principal

Figure 4.14 Financial resource mobilization in selected countries

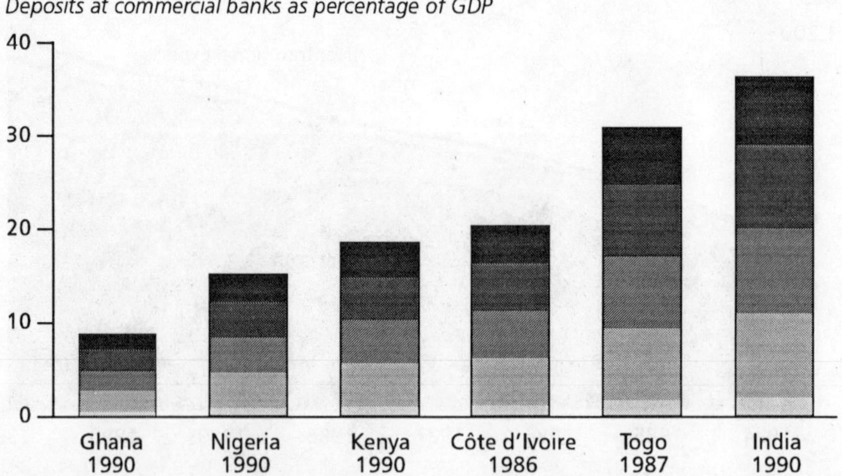

Note: Includes demand, savings, and time deposits. Most recent data available.
Source: IMF, *International Financial Statistics*.

Table 4.7 Banking system credit, Ghana, Malaysia, and Thailand, various years
(percentage of GDP)

	Ghana				*Malaysia*			*Thailand*		
Year	*Private sector*	*State-owned enterprise*[a]	*Total*	*Year*	*Private sector*	*State-owned enterprise*	*Total*	*Private sector*	*State-owned enterprise*	*Total*
1984	4.6	1.8	6.4	1964	13.2	0.0	13.2	13.4	0.0	13.2
1985	6.2	5.3	11.5	1965	12.7	0.0	12.7	14.2	0.0	14.2
1986	7.3	4.3	11.6	1966	13.2	0.0	13.2	14.2	0.0	14.2
1987	6.3	3.4	9.7	1967	14.3	0.0	14.3	15.5	0.0	15.5
1988	5.5	3.4	8.9	1968	16.4	0.0	16.4	16.1	0.0	15.1
1989	4.4	3.1	7.5	1969	15.8	0.0	15.8	17.0	0.0	17.0
1990	4.3	2.9	7.2	1970	18.4	0.0	18.4	18.1	0.0	18.1

Note: Table excludes claims on the central government.
a. Including Cocoa Board borrowing through cocoa bills.
Source: IMF, *International Financial Statistics*, various years.

intermediaries, and the private sector plays a minimal role in running the institutions and using the funds.

Labor markets. Wage rates and the quality of labor represent a major part of business decisions, particularly those of foreign companies. Wage rates in Ghana remain competitive by international standards. But this wage advantage is offset by the relatively low level of education and skills of the average worker. Furthermore, the poor quality of infrastructure and support services in Ghana tends to erode its competitive position.

Wages are also affected by public sector employment. More than half of employees in the modern sector work for the government and public enterprises. Government service alone employs about 360,000 persons, or more than 2 percent of the Ghanaian population, making it one of the largest civil services in Africa, even after several rounds of retrenchment (see figure 4.9). Within the public sector, compensation includes salaries, several in-kind allowances, generous end-of-service benefits, relatively secure tenure, and undemanding workloads due to overstaffing. These practices, when adopted by the largest employer in the economy, tend to limit the extent to which wages can adjust to changing market conditions. They also prevent Ghana from fully realizing its comparative advantage, following the relatively liberal trade and exchange regimes implemented during the adjustment period.

As of 1990 public enterprises employed more than 200,000 workers, or about one-fifth of the total work force in the modern sector. By the government's own account, there is considerable redundancy at all job levels across public enterprises. A recent review shows that four-fifths of the workers in some enterprises are unnecessary. The number of support staff is often several times higher than in comparable companies in the private sector. In addition to staffing redundancy, generous leave policies prevail. Junior employees receive thirty working days of leave annually. Higher-level staff are entitled to more.

The staffing of public enterprises has important fiscal implications. A dramatic example arose in 1992 when the government agreed to pay accrued end-of-service benefits, which had not been funded by the public enterprises. The amount was estimated at about 4.5 percent of GDP, although the full size of the workers' claims is not known. This added fiscal pressure arose in the context of a significant macroeconomic imbalance in 1992. The government planned to pay for the expenses over a period of three years.

But the underlying financial discipline necessary to prevent future fiscal costs may not have been achieved. The average pay for public enterprise employees is estimated to be 15 percent higher than for private companies (State Enterprise Commission 1992). Furthermore, the levels of pay and employment do not depend on the financial position of the enterprises involved. They are determined in a collective bargaining process in which representatives of the "owners" have much to gain in providing generous settlements.

Commercial assets. Public sector ownership of commercial properties is also pervasive. Local authorities and public enterprises control a substantial amount of commercial land and structures. The full extent of such control is difficult to document without a serious effort by the government. Available data suggest that it is extensive. According to information provided by 127 relatively large public enterprises in 1989, the fixed assets they owned and controlled represented about 94 percent of GDP. (Estimates of total fixed assets in the economy are not available, but they might be on the order of 8 to 10 times GDP.) Another 200 public enterprises also own and control commercial assets.

The impact of government ownership of land and commercial structures on private investment requires further research. What is clear, however, is that the supply of commercial properties is substantially more restricted than it would be without such extensive government ownership. In addition, entrepreneurs operating on rented premises have little incentive to make extensive investments to upgrade and develop the properties.

Addressing the presence of public enterprises. To private businesses and prospective investors, the existence of some 300 public enterprises is not a matter of indifference. Public enterprises have considerable competitive advantages. They have access to government debt and equity capital, with virtually no demands placed on them with respect to the rate of return. They do not pay rent on government-owned commercial properties. Furthermore, they are not expected to pay taxes, benefiting either from statutory exemptions or lack of enforcement (see the contribution of public enterprises to government revenue in figure 4.15).

To a private entrepreneur public enterprises are a significant threat. To overcome some of the disadvantages, many entrepreneurs understandably try to evade taxes, as evident from the highly publicized cases of prosecution. Even if successful, the benefits of tax evasion offset only a small part of the disadvantages. Clearly, private entrepreneurs have to seek out the activities and niches in which public enterprises have not already established a foothold. But their search may be in vain, since just about every business niche is occupied. In the presence of such competition, investment is the preserve of those with exceptional business acumen or those insensitive to risks. Ordinary law-abiding and risk-averse entrepreneurs probably would not invest in this environment.

Restricting monopoly power. Many legal barriers have been erected to restrict the entry of private companies. The most visible restriction applies to cocoa trading. Until 1992 private companies were not allowed to trade cocoa in competition with the state-owned Cocoa Board. Since 1992 private companies have been granted the right to buy and sell cocoa within Ghana—but exporting is still the exclusive province of the Cocoa Board. Yet even this opening in internal trading has been marred by the decision to rely on the Cocoa Board as the issuer of trading permits.

In the energy field, a few state-owned entities monopolize production, pricing, and distribution—the Ghana National Petroleum Corporation, the Volta River Authorities, and the Electricity Corporation of Ghana. Numerous

Figure 4.15 Private companies and public enterprises: share in work force and contribution to government revenue, 1988

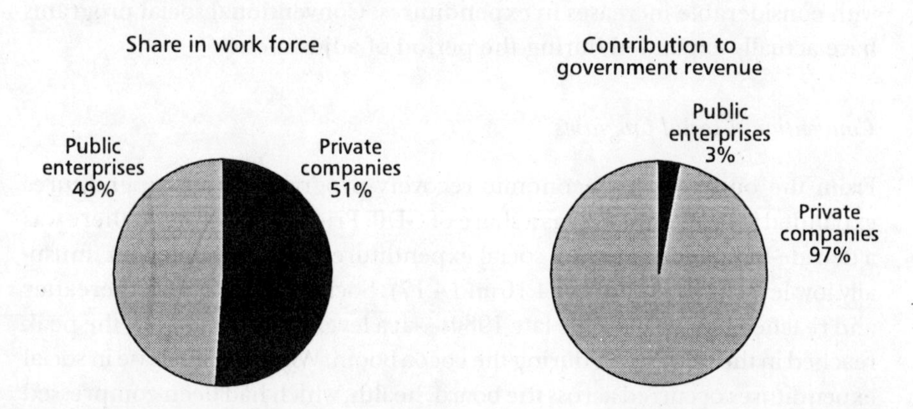

Source: World Bank data; Government of Ghana.

restrictions apply in other industries. In the insurance business, for instance, policies covering a public sector organization or its purchases can be written only by the government-owned State Insurance Corporation. The restriction allows the State Insurance Corporation to capture about 80 percent of the industry's revenue. Ten other private companies pick up what is left. Similarly, in the pension fund business a mandatory contribution of about 17 percent of each company's wage bill goes to the government-owned Social Security and National Investment Trust, which is the only pension fund in the country.

Social programs and adjustment

As in most countries in the region, the Ghanaian government supports an extensive array of welfare measures. Some programs are justifiable—for example, health and education programs carried out by designated agencies to serve the general public. But others are less viable and deserve greater policy scrutiny—such as maintaining the high rate of public sector employment and the variety of subsidies for goods and services. Taken together, the conventional and other welfare measures represent a significant share of public sector undertaking. The scale and character of welfare programs have major implications for the outcome of adjustment policies.

There is justifiable concern about whether adjustment policies hurt the poor disproportionately. Expenditure cuts are often necessary under adjustment, and the cuts often fall heavily on social programs. For the poor, who have no alternative access to basic services, reductions in social programs can have serious consequences. Yet this concern presupposes that social services are actually being delivered effectively—and this is not always true. Where the delivery of essential services is ineffective or wasteful, expenditure cuts would not necessarily impose an undue burden. Furthermore, adjustment and the attendant fiscal discipline do not necessarily involve expenditure cuts. Ghana's adjustment experience shows that fiscal discipline can be consistent with considerable increases in expenditures. Conventional social programs have actually expanded during the period of adjustment.

Conventional social programs

From the outset of the economic recovery program, social expenditures expanded in real terms and as a share of GDP. Prior to adjustment, there was a decade-long decline in real social expenditures, which reached an unusually low level in 1983 (figures 4.16 and 4.17). Social spending rose thereafter and reached a plateau in the late 1980s—at a level somewhat below the peak reached in the mid–1970s during the cocoa boom. While the increase in social expenditures occurred across the board, health, which had been compressed severely, received the greatest share increase.

Education. Along with increased expenditures on education, an extended program of educational reform was pursued, and expenditures within the subsector were reallocated. The preuniversity education cycle was shortened, and more a practical curriculum was introduced. Streamlined training programs, higher salaries, and a reduction in nonteaching staff improved the quality of teaching. A greater share of the education budget went to basic education, although the share remained low by international standards. The program helped increase enrollment at the primary and secondary school levels; primary school enrollment rose by about 10 percent between 1985 and 1989.

Figure 4.16 Social sector current expenditure, 1976–89

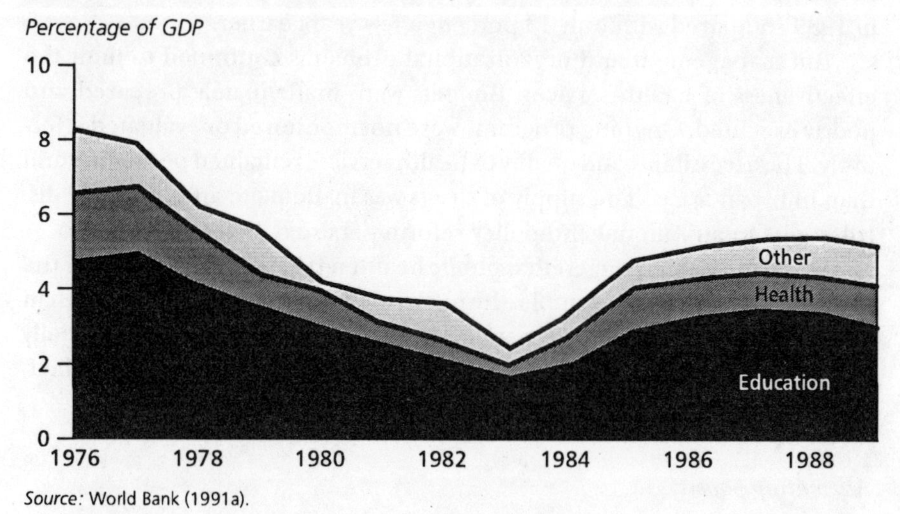

Source: World Bank (1991a).

Figure 4.17 Social sector capital expenditure, 1976–89

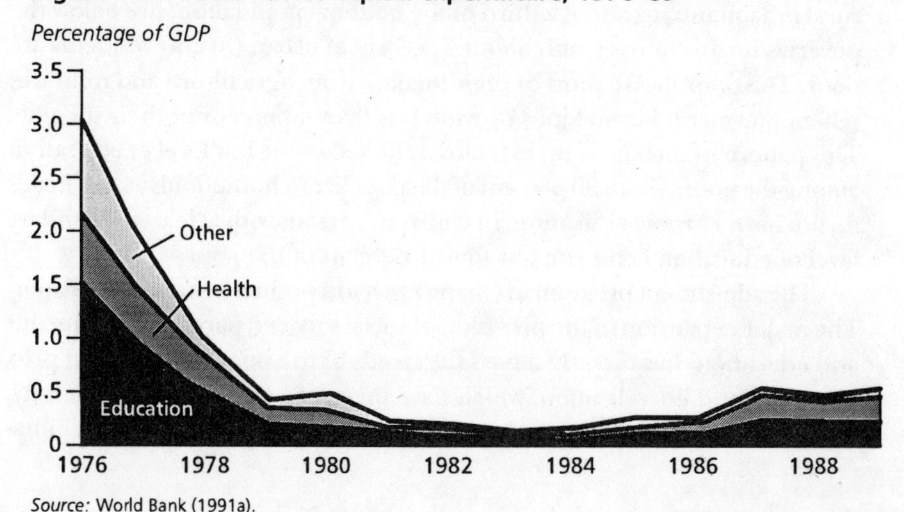

Source: World Bank (1991a).

The quality of education remains a concern. Functional literacy has been much lower than the rate of school attendance would imply. The low level of literacy reflects, in part, the linguistic diversity in Ghana and a general shortage of appropriate reading materials.

Health. To reverse the decline in health status of the population, the government embarked on a health reform program to improve the accessibility and quality of health services. Major emphasis was placed on rehabilitating existing facilities, increasing utilization, and expanding private sector involvement in care delivery. Significant progress was made in increasing immunization coverage and, to a lesser extent, establishing essential drug policies. For instance, 67 percent of children younger than one year were immunized in 1989 compared with only 13 percent a few years earlier.

But management and organizational problems continued to limit the effectiveness of health services. Budgets were inadequately prepared and poorly executed. Ongoing programs were not monitored or evaluated effectively. The accessibility and quality of health services remained poorer in rural than in urban areas. The supply of drugs was inadequate and unevenly distributed. Organizational and policy reform persisted, however.

Social indicators suggest that public health services improved during the adjustment period. For example, the infant mortality rate fell from more than 11 percent in 1980 to about 9 percent in 1989. River blindness was virtually eliminated. Moreover, the malnutrition rate among children was cut in half, while life expectancy rose from about fifty-two years to fifty-five years.

Alleviating poverty

In Ghana poverty is primarily a rural phenomenon. More than two-fifths of rural inhabitants, or about a third of the national population, live below the poverty line. In contrast, only about 4 percent of urban (Accra) residents are poor. The poor derive most of their income from agriculture and nonfarm self-employment. Formal jobs provide less than 4 percent of their income. This pattern of income sources is closely linked to the low level of education among the poor. About 80 percent of the poor live in households whose heads do not have a formal education. In contrast, persons with at least a secondary level of education comprise less than 1 percent of the poor.

The adjustment program in Ghana has had a positive impact on the poor. The major expansion in the provision of social services, particularly in health and education, has directly served the needs of the poor. Agricultural pricing policy and liberalization, which have increased farm income generally, have helped the poor in their largest source of income. Physical rehabilitation of infrastructure has revived trading and expanded the markets, improving conditions for the poor. Quality-of-life indicators, including child malnutrition, infant mortality, primary health care, and access to water, have all improved since the adjustment program started.

More direct antipoverty programs were also attempted. For example, with an outpouring of international support, the government in 1988 launched the PAMSCAD program, a program of actions to mitigate the social costs of adjustments. It was an ambitious and complex undertaking, involving seven sectoral ministries, thirteen public agencies, twenty-three distinct projects, and numerous designated activities. The intent was to provide quick relief to the poor throughout the country. While some progress was made, the impact was less than anticipated. The difficulty in targeting assistance to the poor stems from two factors. First, the poor are not concentrated in any particular area. Second, their consumption pattern does not differ distinctly from the pattern for the nonpoor. Furthermore, most of the measures under the program of actions attempted to overcome some of the shortcomings of similar programs implemented elsewhere. For example, program design called for avoiding simple transfers in favor of producing useful assets for local communities. In addition, the wages offered under the project were kept relatively low to avoid attracting the nonpoor. But these constraints generated new problems. Administrative procedures became cumbersome, and the response rate from the poor was lower than expected.

Nonetheless, the alleviation of poverty remains a key policy objective. The government is committed to providing a stable and progrowth environment. The expenditure pattern is gradually being shifted toward rural residents. The provision of conventional social services is being upgraded and is a high priority. Remedial actions to correct labor market rigidities, particularly those associated with formal and public sector employment, would provide further scope for alleviating poverty.

Implicit welfare

Ghana has a variety of public measures that provide special assistance to selected groups of people, including subsidies for certain types of goods and services (such as water, electricity, housing, and education). Assistance is also extended through the employment practices of government agencies and public enterprises that seek to protect the level of earnings and create employment, particularly at the lower organizational levels. These measures are similar to welfare measures elsewhere, although eligibility is not based on categorical criteria, such as old age, disability, or temporary unemployment. Nor are the measures targeted specifically at reducing poverty, since the vast majority of the beneficiaries are not poor relative to the rest of the population. On the whole, the assistance is directed at groups with political power—primarily employees in the public sector.

Jobs and pay. Aside from the self-employed, who are predominantly in agriculture, government agencies and public enterprises employ about twice as many people as the private sector (table 4.8). (Note that respondents to the surveys cited in table 4.8 did not always distinguish clearly between government service and public enterprises. Thus, the data on total public sector employment are more reliable than the data for its components.)

The penchant for hiring and the tolerance for redundancy are not unique to either the current administration or to Ghana. The sentiment is understandable and widely shared across the region. Many officials believe that the government's budget is so large that a few more workers here and there hardly matter. Furthermore, protection against job losses also extends beyond the public sector. Private companies are often told not to lay off workers. In a few major companies, redeployed staff have subsequently been rehired at the behest of the government.

Budgetary transfers to public enterprises. Closely linked to maintaining employment in the public sector is the regular budgetary support provided by the government to public enterprises. The transfers serve a variety of purposes—financing new projects, covering operational losses, paying for defaulted loans and, more recently, paying for the enterprises' unfunded liabilities. Some transfers are also made explicitly to help public enterprises' employees purchase homes and cars. In recent years, transfers have been in the form of implicit assistance through forgone taxes and uncollected dividends and interest. Recent estimates show that both direct and implicit transfers amounted to about 2 percent of GDP.

Such practices raise important policy questions. The most obvious question is their implication for macroeconomic stability. A serious commitment to fiscal discipline would call for not only a sharp reduction in the transfers,

Table 4.8 Distribution of employment
(percentage of work force)

Type of employment	*1984*	*1987–88*
Private companies	5.9	6.9
Government	5.7	12.1
Public enterprises	4.5	2.5
Self-employed	82.2	74.7
Others	1.7	3.8
Total	100.0	100.0

Source: 1984 Population Census; 1987–88 Ghana Living Standards Survey; World Bank (1989).

but also for an effort to extract reasonable financial returns on the huge "investments" made in public enterprises. Moreover, continuing support for public enterprises would seem to be inconsistent with pursuing a major program of divestment and, with the currently low level of private investment in the country in the presence of the commercial advantages enjoyed by the public sector, will merely depress private investment further.

Housing. As in most countries with a comparable level of income, housing is scarce and inaccessible to a large segment of the population, particularly those in urban centers. The government uses a two-prong strategy for meeting housing needs. One is to provide accommodations to civil servants at designated levels and posting assignments. Thus, housing is a component of civil service pay. In recent years, mortgage loans have been made available through the new public enterprise, Home Finance Corporation, primarily to assist public sector employees. No reliable information is currently available on the extent and scope of this form of assistance, whether in physical or financial terms.

The government also provides housing assistance through two major public enterprises—the State Housing Corporation and the Tema Development Corporation. The program develops and provides affordable housing to the public by offering prices that do not include land value and that are set below construction costs, and by setting rental costs below the cost of maintenance and management.

To support the State Housing Corporation and Tema Development Corporation, the government has transferred a vast amount of resources to the corporations. The Tema Development Corporation controls 40,000 acres of prime commercial and residential properties in the primary port city of Tema. The State Housing Corporation owns about 4,800 rental units and more than 8,000 acres of prime land, including 3,300 acres in Accra and Kumasi. The government also supports the corporations by subsidizing site development and construction materials. In addition, debt to private creditors and contractors is huge—an amount that has not been fully serviced and may eventually become the liability of the government. Both the Tema Development Corporation and the State Housing Corporation are technically insolvent, with substantial negative net worth.

Other goods and services. A significant amount of transfers occurs in the form of underpriced goods and services made available to the public through various government-owned enterprises. Consumer subsidies in the form of subsidized loans are particularly important for water, electricity, and tertiary education. In addition, a variety of producer goods, including chemicals and fertilizers, remain available at below-market prices or on favorable credit terms. The tariffs for electricity, for instance, represent about 20 to 70 percent of the long-run marginal costs, depending on the type of final users. In 1990 the implicit subsidies provided to electricity users alone were estimated at 2 percent of GDP.

Criteria for judging welfare measures

For national economic management, it is already quite evident that current welfare measures are expensive and undermine the conditions required for a stable economic environment that fosters growth and the alleviation of poverty. Some standards and principles must be established to allow policymakers to make independent evaluations. A few criteria may be useful:

- *Need.* Clearly, public assistance provided by a government should target demonstrated need. When need is not critical or when alternate sources of relief are available, public help should be curtailed. On this basis, a variety of subsidies could be phased out. For example, a graduated price schedule for water and electricity prices could be applied without hurting the poor. Excess employment in the public sector could also be reduced, with the budgetary saving devoted to better targeted poverty-reduction measures.
- *Effectiveness.* Even when needs are evident, the vehicles used to deliver services may not achieve the desired results. This is particularly likely when a public enterprise staffed by political appointees has responsibility for service delivery. The State Housing Corporation is a case in point. While failing the mandate to develop and maintain affordable housing for the public, the corporation also managed to exceed authorized expenditures and incur substantial debt. The ineffectiveness of existing enterprises is well documented.
- *Affordability.* When the need is clear and an effective vehicle is available, the cost-effectiveness of delivery mechanisms is an important consideration. With limited resources available from both taxpayers and foreign aid, constant vigilance in controlling costs is a necessity. Jobs in the public sector, for instance, represent an expensive way to transfer money to the poor. Through unions and collective bargaining, public employees are able to extract pay that exceeds their contributions. In contrast, well-defined and temporary public work offers pay levels that are not negotiable and that tend to attract those who have the greatest need for the cash or food.
- *Prioritizing competing needs.* Not all worthwhile programs can be implemented. Budgetary and administrative constraints imply that priorities must be set. In an ideal setting, need and the effectiveness of delivery mechanisms should be the basis for setting priorities. In reality,

political necessity understandably plays an important role. But whatever the actual selection criteria, spending agencies must clearly prioritize competing claims. The lack of clear priorities hinders achievement of worthwhile goals and intensifies the pressure to provide an even greater amount of assistance.

- *Market neutrality.* Implicit welfare measures often introduce distortions. The distortions may pertain to prices, factor mobility, or private mechanisms for achieving the same ends. In Ghana, perhaps the most important distortion is found in the labor markets. Because the government employs about one-half of the labor in the modern sector and pays them more than their productivity warrants, wages and labor mobility are restricted. It costs private companies more to set up business and compete for labor. This distortion has an important bearing on the sluggish economic performance and low private investment.

Final remarks

Clearly, trust and confidence must be restored to enhance the private sector's response. But a fractured relationship cannot be rebuilt overnight, or mended quickly. Winning trust involves doing things in a new way—establishing a consistent, sustainable policy to build credibility.

The key ingredient for restoring confidence is a commitment to fair play. At one level, fair play calls for eliminating the commercial advantages granted to public enterprises. Public enterprises must stand on their own, without tax preferences, the free use of government properties, priority access to credit, expenses that are passed on to the taxpayers, and monopolistic power created by legal barriers. At another level, fair play involves nondiscriminatory enforcement of the rule of law. Today, private businesses are still concerned about losing property and being subject to arbitrary tax audits. Further breaches of confidence must clearly be avoided. In addition, proactive measures involving constructive dialogue with the private sector and the restitution of previously nationalized assets (as in Uganda) would accelerate the healing process. A good beginning has been made in recent years with the creation of the private sector advisory group—a new participant in and contributor to national policy deliberations.

Rapid growth also requires that government services be delivered more effectively. But improving services is an immense task. First, the scope and functions of the government must be reviewed. Since many of the functions are primarily welfare measures rather than essential services, there is room for curtailment. Second, the current work force must be reduced significantly, at least to bring it closer to the level of other African countries. These efforts must be supplemented with transitional assistance—though not at the level of current severance benefits, which, by imposing high short-term fiscal costs, may have impeded the necessary medium-term adjustment of the work force. Third, the culture of management must be changed by redelegating authority, and results must be evaluated and monitored closely.

Such reforms would inevitably create winners and losers. The winners would be the general public, particularly the private sector. Producers would profit, too, from better access to businesses now restricted to public enterprises. They would also benefit from better access to credit once preferential treatment for the public sector is removed. Consumers would benefit from the greater number of producers, as greater competition will keep prices down. And everyone would benefit from tighter control over public finance and lower inflation. On the whole, however, the winners in this scenario do not represent a unified coalition. Their interests are widely dispersed. Thus, as a political force, they are not in a position to demand quick actions.

In contrast, the potential losers under the reforms are politically powerful. They include well-connected political appointees in public enterprises, who have substantial interests at stake. They include redundant workers in the public sector with vocal and well-organized unions. As a lobbying group, the potential losers could effectively oppose the reforms or more subtly circumvent the necessary changes. To make progress, the reform strategy must account explicitly for the losers, the magnitude of their losses, and how the transition might be managed.

The choices fall in the realm of political economy. Ultimately, success will depend on the level of political will. The reform agenda involves a tradeoff between personal gain and the public interest. Decisionmakers must choose between immediate benefits that would accrue to colleagues and friends and more remote gains that would benefit the general public. Precedents suggest the former option is likely to be selected. However, Ghana's experience suggests that there is room for cautious optimism. Previous reforms of the foreign exchange regime, import licensing, and price controls show that the public interest can prevail.

References

Abbey, J.L.S. 1990. "Ghana's Experience with Structural Adjustment: Some Lessons." In James Picket and Hans Singer, eds., *Towards Economic Recovery in Sub-Saharan Africa.* London: Routledge.

Alderman, Harold. 1991. *Downturn and Economic Recovery in Ghana: Impacts on the Poor.* Cornell Food and Nutrition Policy Program Monograph 10. Ithaca, N.Y.

Bacha, E. 1992. "External Debt, Net Transfers and Growth in Developing Countries." *World Development* (U.K.) 20(8):1183–93.

Chand, Sheetal K., and R. van Til. 1988. "Ghana: Toward Successful Stabilization and Recovery." *Finance and Development* 25(March):11–17.

Chhibber, Ajay, and S. Fischer, eds. 1992. *Economic Reform in Sub-Saharan Africa.* A World Bank Symposium.Washington, D.C.

Chhibber, Ajay, M. Dailami, and Nemat Shafik, eds. 1992. *Reviving Private Investment in Developing Countries: Empirical Studies and Policy Lessons.* Amsterdam: North-Holland.

Clark, Leith J., and Michael F. Hojchie. 1991. "The Political Economy of Structural Adjustment in Ghana." University of Western Ontario, Department of Economics, London, Ontario.

Commander, S., ed. 1989. *Structural Adjustment and Agriculture: Theory and Practice in Africa and Latin America.* London: Overseas Development Institute.

de Merode, Louis. 1991. "Civil Service Pay and Employment Reform in Africa." World Bank, Africa Technical Department, Washington, D.C.

Duncan, A., and J. Howell, eds. 1992. *Structural Adjustment and the African Farmer.* London: Overseas Development Institute.

GATT (General Agreement on Tariffs and Trade). 1991. *Trade Policy Review Mechanism: Ghana.* Geneva.

Ghana, Ministry of Transportation and Communications. 1991. "Commodity Transport Case Study." Prepared by Ghanexim Economic Consultants. Accra.

Green, Reginald. 1987. "Stabilization and Adjustment Policies and Programs: Ghana." World Institute for Development Economics Research, Helsinki.

Helleiner, G.K. 1992. "The International Monetary Fund, the World Bank and Africa's Adjustment and External Debt Problems: An Unofficial View." *World Development* (U.K.) 20(6):779–92.

Huq, M.M. 1989. *The Economy of Ghana: The First 25 Years Since Independence.* New York: St. Martin's Press.

Husain, Ishrat. 1992. "Comments on Professor Helleiner's Paper." World Bank, Africa Region, Washington, D.C.

Jebuni, C.D., A. Oduro, Y. Asante, and G.K. Tsikata. 1992. "Diversifying Exports: The Supply Response of Non-Traditional Exports to Ghana's Economic Recovery Program." University of Ghana, Department of Economics, Accra.

Jeffries, Richard. 1992. "Urban Popular Attitudes Towards the Economic Recovery Programme and the PNDC Government in Ghana." *African Affairs* (U.K.) 91:207–26.

Kapur, Ishan, Michael Hadjimichael, Paul Hilbers, Jerald Schiff, and Philippe Szymczak. 1991. *Ghana: Adjustment and Growth, 1983–91.* Occasional Paper 86. Washington, D.C.: International Monetary Fund.

Killick, Tony. 1978. *Development Economics in Action: A Study of Economic Policies in Ghana.* London: Heinemann.

Kusi, Newman K. 1991. "Ghana: Can the Adjustment Reforms Be Sustained?" *Africa Development* (Coderria, Senegal) 16(3-4):181–206.

Lang, K. 1992. "Ghana: The Role of External Assistance." World Bank, Western Africa Department, Washington, D.C.

Leechor, Chad. 1991. "Ghana: Ending Chaos." In Ajay Chhibber, Mansoor Dailami, and Vinod Thomas, eds., *Restructuring Economies in Distress: Policy Reform and the World Bank.* New York: Oxford University Press.

Patillo, C.A. 1991. "Public and Private Investment in Ghana, Chile, and Malaysia." World Bank, Western Africa Department, Washington, D.C.

Roemer, Michael. 1984. "Ghana, 1950–1980: Missed Opportunities." In Arnold C. Harberger, ed., *World Economic Growth: Case Studies of Developed and Developing Nations.* San Francisco, Calif.: Institute for Contemporary Studies Press.

Sarris, Alexander, and Hadi Shams. 1992. "Ghana under Structural Adjustment: The Impact on Agriculture and the Rural Poor." International Fund for Agricultural Development, Studies in Rural Poverty 2. New York.

Sowa, N.K., A. Bach-Nuakoh, K.A. Tutu, and B. Osei. 1992. "Small Enterprises and Adjustment: The Impact of Ghana's Economic Recovery Program." University of Ghana, Department of Economics, Accra.

State Enterprise Commission. 1992. "Program and Employment Structures in State-owned Enterprises." Government of Ghana, Accra.

Toye, John. 1990. "Ghana's Economic Reforms, 1983–87: Origins, Achievements and Limitations." In James Picket and Hans Singer, eds., *Towards Economic Recovery in Sub-Saharan Africa.* London: Routledge.

Younger, Stephen D. 1991a. "Aid and the Dutch Disease: Macroeconomic Management When Everybody Loves You." Cornell Food and Nutrition Policy Program Working Paper 17. Ithaca, N.Y.

———. 1991b. "Monetary Management in Ghana." Cornell Food and Nutrition Policy Program Working Paper 8. Ithaca, N.Y.

World Bank. 1989. "Ghana: Structural Adjustment for Growth." Western Africa Department, Washington, D.C.

———. 1991a. "Ghana: Progress on Adjustment." Western Africa Department, Washington, D.C.

———. 1991b. "Ghana: Public Enterprise Reform." Western Africa Department, Washington, D.C.

———. 1992. "Ghana 2000 and Beyond: Setting the Stage for Accelerated Growth and Poverty Reduction." Western Africa Department, Washington, D.C.

5

Kenya: patchy, intermittent commitment

Gurushri Swamy

Kenya started the 1980s with many more favorable economic features than other Sub-Saharan countries. The structure and dynamism of the economy in the late 1970s evolved out of the favorable policy environment of the past. But economic management deteriorated in the late 1970s, which resulted in the intensification or emergence of a number of major distortions. During the 1980s progress was measurable and significant in only a few areas, and the economy's momentum of the first two decades of Independence slowed considerably. As one commentator writes, "Few country lending experiences have given the [World] Bank so much cause for frustration" (Mosley 1991). That frustration stemmed from three sources.

First, the stated policies—which were broadly in line with the World Bank's recommendations—were undermined by implementation that was often lethargic and sometimes contrary to the stated policies. The fourth plan document (1979) enunciated a more open strategy for the industrial sector. In 1982 the Kenya Government Commission on Government Expenditures clearly indicated that greater discipline and efficiency were necessary, and that the gross misuse of government resources should be curbed. The Sessional Paper of 1986 contained policy statements on reforming agricultural marketing, reducing protection to industry, and controlling public spending. But the first adjustment attempt (1980–84) was marked by a total lack of compliance, partly because of design and timing problems, but also because the commitment to the stated policy changes was limited to a small coterie of top civil servants. Trade reforms were not carried out, and grain marketing was not liberalized. Even in the second period of adjustment (1985–91), when much more effort went into building a broader consensus, the pace was incremental, and the commitment of top officials waxed and waned. Overall, despite a fairly stable political climate, commitment was patchy and intermittent throughout.

Second, the lack of transparency in the implementation of reforms often dampened or nullified the structural reforms that were undertaken. Although almost all imports were in principle liberalized, or "automatically licensed," supervisory reports indicate that in practice there was a lack of automaticity and transparency, and undue influences restricted imports that competed with domestic production. Although an auction market for government paper was created, financial institutions typically took up most of that paper by "arrangement." And although the banking laws and the supervision apparatus were strengthened, political considerations prevented effective prudential oversight, which led to a banking crisis. Similarly, the process of budget rationalization was often bypassed, and controls on movement of grain were reinstituted after a period of relaxation.

Third, during the first phase of adjustment, the designs of the structural adjustment loans in the early 1980s and the first agricultural sector adjustment loan in 1986 were faulty, at least in retrospect. A fairly rapid pace of trade liberalization was postulated when the country was attempting to control one of its worst financial crises. In addition, the design of the grain marketing conditionality contained a basic flaw—market liberalization was seen to occur simultaneously with increases in official procurement prices. Each loan was fettered with too many conditions that were too general, focusing on studies and action plans partly because of inadequate sector understanding (sectoral work on industry and trade was dated) and partly because of political considerations. The World Bank also released credit tranches when conditionalities were met more in letter than in spirit.

The adjustment program in the second half of the 1980s benefited from greater experience and preparation in some areas. Instead of grouping many reforms in one operation, the adjustment agenda was parceled into sectoral programs. The design of the reform programs in trade liberalization and export development was based on updated information. In recognition that trade liberalization was not going to be completed within the time frame of a single credit, progress was monitored under the export development credit that followed. And moves on the exchange rate were monitored through IMF programs. The relative success of the trade liberalization program is due to better design and to intensive supervision.

The lessons of the early 1980s were not, however, fully internalized in the policy dialogue on agricultural sector reform, where progress remained frustratingly slow. There was even some reversal, with the recent reinstitution of grain movement controls. The conditionality on reducing the role of the grain marketing parastatal remained vague. In the second structural adjustment loan (1982), the condition was to "undertake a review of maize marketing and implement its recommendations." In the agricultural sector adjustment loan (1986), the National Cereals and Produce Board (NCPB) was one of the three parastatals to be restructured, including a write-off of debt to reduce its claims on the budget. Because this restructuring never happened, the second agricultural sector adjustment loan (1990) asked for performance contracts to raise the National Cereals and Produce Board's efficiency. And conditions continued to be imposed for studies, plans, and exchanges of views. The second agricultural sector adjustment loan had the following second tranche conditions: to finalize studies on increasing the efficiency of private fertilizer imports and on minimizing the distortions from aid-financed fertilizers, to complete a food security plan (started under the first loan), and to prepare a drought contingency plan. Perhaps the World Bank bought into a far too gradual pace of reform knowing that the government lacked conviction and political will. The design and dimensions of reforms in this area were too limited to achieve significant restructuring of the sector, and political interests sabotaged the program.

Another major flaw was that the second attempt at adjustment was made in the face of growing financial undiscipline. IMF programs were not adhered to, the fiscal balance deteriorated steadily, and inflation accelerated. Adjustment was affected differently than in the earlier period when reforms became hostage to a stringent stabilization program. Fiscal undiscipline in the second half of the 1980s made trade and financial sector reform difficult in a different way: rather than fiscal policy defending a certain exchange rate, the exchange rate was forced to continuously catch up with higher inflation. Independent monetary policy and the move toward indirect instruments of monetary control were made far more problematic because of the large financing requirements of the government. In retrospect, this experience underscores the difficulties of implementing structural reforms in the context of either financial laxity or extreme stringency. A relatively stable environment seems essential. Such an environment was not present during much of the 1980s.

The lack of sufficient attention to the control of financial balances threatened to undercut the World Bank's lending program altogether. In the late 1980s, some second-tranche releases of sector credits were made, even though medium-term macroeconomic stability was clearly in question. But the World Bank soon found itself in the position of being unable to justify such releases. At the consultative meeting of November 1991, donors also expressed concern with the lack of transparency and accountability in the use of public funds. In September 1992, the World Bank decided to postpone disbursements of the second tranches for ongoing operations because several sector-specific conditions had not been met and, most important, the macroeconomic program was completely off track. In December 1992, it canceled the second tranche of the second agricultural sector operation because of the reimposition of grain movement controls.

In the first few months of 1993, the Kenyan government completed many of the structural reforms required under the sectoral loans (with the important exception of removing grain movement controls). But it was unable to maintain a satisfactory macroeconomic framework despite a "shadow program" agreed to with the IMF. Although growth in government expenditures and credit to the government slowed temporarily, this was offset because the central bank allowed many delinquent and distressed financial institutions to borrow heavily from it, rapidly increasing the money supply. It was not until April 1993 that a satisfactory agreement to control the deficit and the financial intermediaries was reached, and the World Bank could contemplate releasing the second tranches. By this time, the foreign exchange situation had become so strained that the government had reversed some of its earlier reforms. It is yet to be seen whether the government will implement the measures necessary to restore and maintain financial stability. But it is clear that the World Bank and the country paid a price in continuity of reform and country dialogue.

The economy before adjustment

Good performance indicators

At the outset of the 1980s, Kenya had a distinctly more favorable economic structure and better incentives and institutions than most other countries in Africa. Since Kenya's Independence in 1963, both its political leadership and its development strategy have shown remarkable continuity. The strategy was based soundly on agricultural development, particularly of smallholder agriculture. It helped the GDP grow by 6.6 percent annually in the first decade after Independence, with agriculture growing at nearly 5 percent annually. Although the oil price shocks slowed growth in the 1970s to about 4 percent annually, GDP growth was still above the average for low-income countries. Savings and investment in Kenya were relatively high for its per capita income level; both had approximated 20 percent of GDP during the 1970s. The incremental capital-output ratio, while having risen from 3 in the 1960s to 4 between 1972 and 1977, was not unreasonable, particularly given the oil price shock in the early 1970s. The tax-revenue ratio had increased from about 12 percent in 1966–67 to 21 percent in 1979–80, and the current fiscal account had produced a surplus of 2.5 to 4 percent of GDP annually for the investment program. Public and private investment in human capital formation yielded education and health indicators well above the average for Sub-Saharan Africa. Primary school enrollment was not far from universal. A life expectancy of 55 years and an infant mortality rate of

83 per thousand live births in 1980 were significantly more favorable than the average for Sub-Saharan Africa.

The structure of production also changed significantly after Independence. The government distributed a considerable amount of high-potential and medium-potential land that had belonged to large farmers to smaller farmers and encouraged cultivation of tea, coffee, and hybrid maize, and dairy farming.[1] The smallholders' share of coffee and tea production increased from practically nothing in 1955 to 40 percent and 70 percent respectively in the early 1980s. Between 1965 and 1979, the small-scale farm area under improved varieties of maize increased about fortyfold. The impetus for smallholder activities helped rural income grow by 5.2 percent annually from 1974 to 1982, much of it in nonfarm activities. Growth of income was probably just as strong in the earlier years. Collier and Lal (1984) estimated that, in the Central Province, rural income per adult equivalent increased 3.8 percent a year during 1963–74, and Crawford and Thorbecke (1978) estimated that the incidence of poverty was reduced from 50 percent of the smallholder population to 22 percent.

Although a dualistic farming sector continued to exist (about 3,500 large farms accounted for 39 percent of cultivable area in 1979) as influential Africans bought ranches, large farms, and estates from departing Europeans, small farmers were not neglected or taxed. Because the large-farmer lobby was influential, prices paid for major export crops, maize, and wheat were near world prices and crop development support was extensive. Smaller farmers benefited from both. Moreover, traditional export crops were not taxed explicitly, and a diversified tax structure supported a sustained high tax effort.[2] All in all, in this largest sector of the economy—which provides the livelihood of the majority of Kenyans—there had been remarkable transformation and growth, unlike in most countries in the region.

The economy was also beginning to see favorable demographic trends. Buoyed by favorable income growth in rural areas and improved health conditions, the rate of population growth initially increased from 3.0 percent annually at Independence to 3.8 percent by the end of the 1970s, and the fertility rate increased from 6.8 to 7.9. However, during the 1980s, fertility began to decline, falling to 7.7 by 1984 and 6.7 by 1989. Because the government did not offer extensive family planning services until the mid-1980s, the demographic transition is explained by other factors, such as the increase in education of women, the rising private costs of education, the modernization of Kenyan society, and the economic growth of the 1960s and 1970s. Of course, given the dynamics of population growth, the full effects of a fertility decline will not be felt for many decades. The government must in the meantime address the pressures imposed by the growth of population on arable land, social services, and productive employment. Nevertheless, Kenya is one of the few countries in Africa in which the demographic transition started in the early 1980s.

Less favorable performance indicators

Performance in other areas of the Kenyan economy was less buoyant, and the economic structure became badly distorted. An uneasy yet mutually accommodating relationship between Asian-Kenyan entrepreneurs and African Kenyans in political power created a highly protected, uncompetitive, and oligopolistic industrial structure. The structure served the economy well shortly after Independence, and, fueled by the rise in rural income and by regional trading arrangements, industry grew at a rate of nearly 10 percent annually between 1964 and 1978. But the customs union with Tanzania and Uganda began to collapse in the mid to late 1970s, and as the sector became more insular, industrial growth decelerated in the 1980s. By 1985 the share of imports in domestic supply had fallen from its 1972 level of 44 percent to 19 percent, accompanied by a decline in the share of exports in gross output. Import substitution came to account for two-thirds of growth in the expanding subsectors, while several industries actually contracted. Gross investment in manufacturing fell heavily, declining in real terms to less than half of its 1978 level by 1985—suggesting disinvestment. The limits to import substitution, the collapse of the regional trading arrangements, and the surge of vandalism against Asian Kenyans in the wake of the attempted coup in 1982 all hastened the decline in investment. And inside the sector, the growing pervasiveness of the import licensing system and regulations on business activities in Kenya created enormous opportunities for rent-seeking and for executive discretion.

By the early 1980s, the public sector was overextended. The "Kenyanization" of industry and the desire to industrialize rapidly had created massive public sector ownership, not only in such traditional activities as utilities and transport, but also in distribution and manufacturing. Traditional suspicion of Asian traders and the interest of large farmers had combined to create marketing parastatals, most notably the National Cereals and Produce Board, which could support high producer prices in good times and in bad. Over the years, these parastatals drained the budget and, indirectly, the banking system. Meanwhile, controls on grain movements generated rents for those who granted and obtained licenses. At the same time, the civil service had expanded tremendously, primarily at the lower grade levels. Although real wages stagnated or fell, the sheer increase in numbers meant that the total wage bill remained high. With its protected industrial structure and bloated public sector, the Kenyan economy was not unlike many others in the region.

The overextension of the public sector showed up in economic inefficiency. The government had changed in the early 1980s from being a net provider of investment funds to being a net user of private savings to finance its investment and consumption expenditures. The surplus in the current budget dwindled to zero, and the economic classification of the budget showed that a large share was taken up by wages and salaries with little left to fund nonwage operational and maintenance expenditures. At the same time, the incremental capital-output ratio (ICOR) increased dramatically from 3 to 4 in the early 1970s to 9 to 15 by the early 1980s, suggesting that expansion of the public sector's role in the economy, including the support of poorly justified projects by government financial institutions, had been highly unproductive.

Several other macroeconomic indicators were also poor throughout the 1970s and into the 1980s. Kenya suffered severe external terms of trade shocks—a decline of 22 percent during 1972–75 (the first oil price shock), an increase of 53 percent in the next two years (a coffee boom), and a drop of 28 percent by 1980 (the end of the coffee boom and the second oil price shock). These shocks were compounded by poor macroeconomic management, breaking the tradition of fiscal responsibility and prudent monetary policy during the first ten years after Independence. By 1979–80, the public-expenditure-to-GDP ratio had increased from its 1973–74 level of 24 percent to more than 31 percent, fueled largely by increases in school enrollment, defense expenditures, and investment in national entities, such as Kenya Airways and Kenya Railways. The budget deficit increased—from 3 to 4 percent in the early 1970s to around 10 percent by 1981. Inflation, which had averaged 3 percent in the first ten years after Independence, accelerated to 13 percent in 1981 and 22 percent in 1982. Kenya had adjusted its administered interest rate structure only marginally since 1973, and interest rates ranged from mildly to strongly negative. The current account deficit as a percentage of GDP increased from about 4 percent in the early 1970s to 14 percent in 1980. Although the deficits were offset largely by long-term concessional capital flows, borrowing on relatively hard commercial terms expanded sharply, increasing the debt service ratio from less than 4 percent in 1977 to 13.2 percent in 1980. Macroeconomic management was quite aggressive in exchange rate depreciation. The Kenyan shilling was linked to the dollar from 1971 to 1975 and to the special drawing right (IMF basket of currencies) since then. With discrete periodic devaluations, the real effective rate, as calculated by the IMF, depreciated nearly 30 percent from 1972 to 1980.

The structural adjustment program

It was almost by accident that Kenya came to the World Bank for quick-disbursing money. Although severe structural distortions were building throughout the 1970s, the critical trigger point was the financial imbalances created by the terms of trade shocks and by fiscal undiscipline. The country first sought out the IMF, as it had on two occasions since 1975. Terms for a standby agreement were agreed upon in August 1979, but disbursements were delayed for a year because the ceilings on government borrowing from the central bank proved untenable. With this delay, the government needed quick-disbursing money urgently—which happened to coincide with the World Bank's decision to move into medium-term balance of payments support, essentially to help countries adjust to the oil price shock. A planned industrial sector loan was converted into a structural adjustment loan in the expectation that it would effect a quick response in exports. The response did not materialize. Worsening economic conditions forced the government to return to the IMF in 1982 and to request a second structural adjustment loan from the World Bank. Despite the fact that reform under the first structural adjustment loan was proceeding more slowly than planned, the second structural adjustment loan was ambitious—picking up the largely unfinished agenda on trade reform and addressing reforms in grain marketing, interest rates, energy, and even family planning.

Although the economy stabilized between 1982 and 1984 (at the expense of growth and consumption), little or no progress was made toward structural adjustment. There were design and timing problems, but the lack of compliance can also be traced to the absence of commitment among all but a small coterie of top civil servants.[3] This group clearly underestimated the strength of the vested interests. Perhaps it also overestimated the World Bank's willingness to enforce its conditionalities—the second tranche of the second adjustment loan, although delayed nine months, was released despite questionable implementation of the agreed program. The unsatisfactory implementation led to a pause in adjustment lending, and nearly four years passed before another attempt. Given the limited implementation capacity of the government, and in the hopes of building a greater consensus, it was decided that adjustment should proceed on a sectoral basis with support from the World Bank, with the IMF monitoring the macroeconomic balances.

Accordingly, adjustment programs were developed in agriculture (supported by two sector loans in 1986 and 1990), industry (1988), the financial sector (1989), export development (1990), and education (1991). The period from 1986 to 1991 (extended to 1992 when relevant) constitutes the core adjustment program as discussed in this chapter (see appendix 5A).

The most notable success has been the slow but definite progress toward reducing the protection given to the industrial sector. Automatic licensing was extended progressively to different import schedules, and tariffs were lowered significantly. These measures were supported by a substantial real exchange rate depreciation that more than reflected terms of trade changes, and by the decontrol of prices on most nonfood commodities. With the introduction of foreign exchange bearer certificates and export retention schemes in 1991–92, a legal parallel market for foreign exchange was created—and Kenya reached a stage where it could delicense import and foreign exchange transactions completely. With progressive import liberalization and the evolution of foreign exchange markets, premiums in the parallel markets for foreign exchange reached a historical low by late 1991, and deposits abroad grew rapidly. These developments suggest that the rents generated earlier by the licensing system were reduced substantially. (However, the official exchange rate was allowed to appreciate in 1992, and the premium in the legal parallel markets increased.) Several export development efforts began or intensified around 1988—an export compensation scheme, a manufacturing-in-bond scheme, and, most recently, an import duty and value added tax exemption scheme. An export processing zone is being built near Nairobi. On the whole, it is too early to assess the impact of these efforts. But a 10 percent annual increase between 1985 and 1991 in the quantum index of manufactured exports on the heels of a decade of stagnation can reasonably be attributed to import liberalization measures and currency depreciation that reduced the antiexport bias.

Even in industrial sector reform—in which the reduction of protection was one successful component of the adjustment program—three large lacunae remained. First, tariffs on imports of some competing goods were still quite high. Second, and more important perhaps, import licensing, even when automatic, created delays, uncertainty, and too much discretion. In particular, parastatals continued to be unofficially protected by their monopoly position, higher tariffs, prohibitions on competing imports, and ad hoc duty exemptions on raw materials. Even with these advantages, all indicators of efficiency and growth show that the parastatal sector lagged well behind the rest of the economy. Third, fundamental legal and regulatory constraints, including nebulous property rights and unclear procedural recourse, affected private entrepreneurs. Laws and regulations on competition were poorly enforced, encouraging the buildup of market power.

In the agricultural sector, the commercial import of fertilizers was delicensed, and fertilizer prices throughout the distribution chain were decontrolled. But aid-financed fertilizers continued to be allocated in nontransparent ways. Furthermore, the government disengaged from output marketing in only a few minor crops. The National Cereals and Produce Board continued to be a major drain on the budget, despite direct and indirect efforts to reduce its scale of operations. Its pricing policies enabled it to outbid private traders in the primary markets and undercut them in the secondary market. The retail prices of food commodities were still controlled, primarily in the urban areas, conferring an undifferentiated subsidy on urban consumers. Efforts to increase the share of nonwage expenditures in the sector were largely unsuccessful, threatening the effectiveness of such programs as the training-and-visit extension system—which is critical to increasing land yields in a country with increasing population pressure on available arable land.

Fiscal management was uneven. By the late 1980s, the stabilization trend of the early years of the decade was completely reversed. By fiscal 1991, the budget deficit was as high as in fiscal 1981, and the financing of large deficits that reemerged through domestic borrowing and money creation was inflationary, and it progressively crowded out the private sector. Despite the initiation of a "budget rationalization" program in 1985, the share of nonwage expenditures declined, primarily because of civil service salaries and domestic debt servicing. The external accounts also deteriorated in the late 1980s, partly because of a decline in terms of trade. The country's debt increased by 50 percent during this period, and despite a general softening of terms, the debt service ratio reached 30 percent, compared with 13 percent in 1980.

In the financial sector, an increase in real interest rates was sustained, with virtual liberalization in 1991. But continued fiscal laxity turned this achievement into a mixed blessing. The large budget deficits that reemerged were financed by "arranged" placement of government securities with financial institutions at increasing interest rates. Consequently, the government's domestic interest payments grew nearly twice as fast as its domestic debt, doubling the share of interest payments relative to GDP. At the same time, the formal credit markets remained segmented—credit ceilings continued for the private sector, a real secondary market for government paper did not develop, parastatals continued to have priority access to credit, and development finance institutions, including the agricultural credit agencies, remained insulated from the rest of the financial sector. Thus, liberalization of interest rates in one sector did not ensure the efficient allocation of financial resources. Further, distressed banks were not restructured successfully—in fact, their numbers grew. While prudential and regulatory mechanisms were strengthened, political interference stifled their implementation and led the country into a banking crisis in the early 1990s.

Social sector reform, although headed in the right direction, had barely begun. As mentioned earlier, social sectors received relatively high funding from the government. Thus, social sector reform was focused on equitable and efficient resource allocation to meet the demands of a growing population, and on improving cost recovery.

Macroeconomic reform: policy and implementation

The two oil crises in the 1970s led to a sharp deterioration in terms of trade. Additionally, in the wake of the coffee boom of 1977–78, fiscal discipline eroded. As a result of these developments, Kenya was characterized by large financial imbalances in the early 1980s. In 1981 the excess of domestic demand over domestic product was 11.4 percent of GDP, and the current account deficit was 12.5 percent of GDP. The total absorption of foreign savings (including grants), which financed over 40 percent of domestic investment, was 13.3 percent of GDP. The budget deficit was 10 percent of GDP, and inflation was over 20 percent. The high current account deficits of the late 1970s and early 1980s were financed by a record level of borrowing from private sources, which caused the debt service ratio to increase by more than 10 percentage points to over 25 percent during 1980–83. These financial imbalances were unprecedented and unsustainable.

The period 1980–84 was characterized by a steady reduction in excess demand—the excess of domestic expenditures over income fell from 11 percent to less than 2 percent. This reduction was achieved mainly by reducing the budget deficit, and by sharply reducing expenditures, including public investment (figure 5.1). The reduction in excess demand was supported by decelerating monetary growth, rising interest rates, and tightening import controls. As a result, by 1984 real domestic demand was 5 percent less than

Figure 5.1 Kenya's fiscal and external accounts, 1981–91

Percentage of GDP

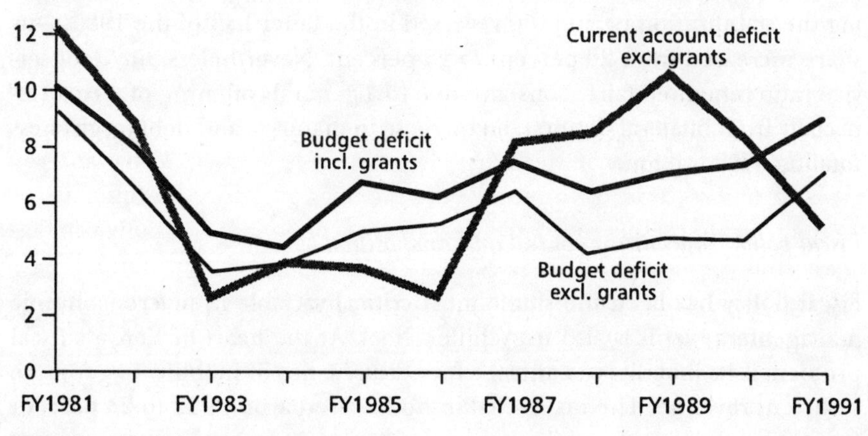

Source: World Bank data.

in 1980 despite a population increase of 17 percent and further deterioration of external terms of trade. The budget deficit and the current account deficit declined to about 4 percent of GDP, inflation decelerated to 10 percent, and interest rates turned positive in real terms. This was achieved without any significant increase in revenues or exports; in fact, the revenue-GDP ratio declined, as did export volume. Kenya was among the minority of countries that successfully reduced financial imbalances toward sustainable levels, although at considerable cost—the reduction of consumption, investment, and imports.

Macroeconomic management in the latter half of the 1980s was uneven—essentially reversing the progress made from 1980 to 1984. The ratio of the budget deficit to GDP clearly increased (see figure 5.1), reaching by 1991 the level of the early 1980s. The inflationary financing of large deficits through domestic borrowing and money creation crowded out the private sector. Inflation accelerated to 20 percent in 1991 from its 1986 rate of less than 7 percent. Because banks continued to finance the government's generally loose fiscal stance, the share of domestic credit available to the private sector fell steadily from 75.4 percent in 1980 to 56.6 percent in 1990. Credit ceilings on lending to the private sector, and involuntary finance to the government through de facto requirements that bank and nonbank institutions invest heavily in government paper, also contributed to the decline.

A similar picture emerges from an examination of the external accounts. After falling to less than 3 percent in 1986, the ratio of the current account deficit to GDP increased in 1989 to levels nearly comparable to those of the early 1980s before declining again (see figure 5.1). Part of the explanation is found in the external terms of trade, which, despite substantial improvements during a few years, declined for most of the 1980s. These trends increased the country's outstanding debt by 50 percent during the period. The reduction in the share of borrowing from private sources during the stabilization period was reversed in the latter half of the 1980s—its share increased from 20 percent to 25 percent. Nevertheless, the debt service ratio remained fairly constant, due to a general softening of terms (especially from bilateral donors), an increase in maturity, and debt forgiveness totaling $752 million.

Fiscal policy: expenditure control and composition

Fiscal policy has been the single most critical variable in macroeconomic management, yet it is also its Achilles' heel. At the heart of Kenya's fiscal problem is its inability to control expenditures, not its inability to generate sufficient revenue. The tax-to-GDP ratio hovered around 22 to 23 percent for most of the decade, while the ratio of recurrent expenditures increased dramatically. The inability to control expenditures was due in part to how the composition of expenditures was structured, but also in part to a general lack of discipline in expenditure allocation and execution.

The structural components caused either downward inflexibility in expenditures or an upward pressure. Downward inflexibility characterized, for example, the civil service wage bill, which accounted for 6 percent of GDP during the 1980s. Upward pressure came from the growing demands of teacher salaries and interest payments, particularly on domestic debt of the central government and the parastatals (table 5.1). These problems cannot be resolved quickly or easily—but the government did not make even the smallest dent in the 1980s. The escalating share of these payments severely reduced the share of the nondefense, nonwage expenditures, and it limited the allocations to the education and health sectors.

Fiscal policy was also thwarted by the absence of clear expenditure priorities and the political will to control expenditures. One result was that expenditure ceilings set by the treasury were repeatedly violated. Government functions also proliferated. With a sharp increase in the number of departments and divisions, coordination became unwieldy. Much of the proliferation came after the district focus program was adopted in 1983, under which all central government functions were fully represented at the district level.

The structural problems associated with expenditure control in the government were pervasive. Yet the government focused only on budgetary processes. In 1985 it launched the budget rationalization program to intro-

Table 5.1 The composition of current expenditures, 1981, 1985, and 1990

(percentage of GDP)

Economic classification	*1981*	*1985*	*1990*
Wages and salaries	6.0	6.1	6.0
Teachers' salaries	2.8	3.2	3.9
Total	8.8	9.3	9.9
Nonwage expenditures	8.5	6.7	6.3
Defense-related	2.8	2.1	2.6
Non-defense-related	5.7	4.6	3.7
Interest	2.4	4.1	5.4
Domestic	1.3	2.6	3.6
Foreign	1.1	1.6	1.8
Transfers to state enterprises	0.8	..	..
Other	..	..	..
Sectoral distribution (total expenditure)			
Education	6.1	5.5	6.4
Health	2.3	1.7	1.7

.. Not available.

Source: IMF, *Statistical Abstracts* and *Economic Surveys*; World Bank staff estimates.

duce better planning and discipline into resource programming and expenditure, seeking a greater balance between developmental and current spending, and between wage and nonwage spending. The budget rationalization program also sought to target scarce managerial and financial resources on a smaller number of critical "core" investment projects.

The budget rationalization program achieved some success in procedural areas. For example, ministries began to issue a forward budget circular that requests submissions well in advance of the forward budget period and imposes ceilings on expenditures, including wages and salaries. One provision of these circulars attempts to impose planning and budgetary discipline—stating that "projects and programs not included in the first year of the forward budget will not be considered for inclusion in the draft estimates for the next fiscal year." Within these parameters, ministries prioritized their submissions to the treasury. In turn, the treasury began to monitor central government expenditures more effectively.

Yet the budget rationalization program did not improve resource allocation. Between 1981 and 1986, nonwage operations and maintenance expenditures declined from 36 percent to 26 percent of total recurrent expenditures. After the budget rationalization program was introduced, the share of these expenditures declined further to 22 percent. Lacking nonwage funds, the ministries relied increasingly on the development budget—particularly its donor-financed component—to finance their recurrent expenditures. The share of recurrent expenditures going to civil service payments remained high, and that of interest payments and teacher salaries increased. It became clear that without more fundamental reforms, mere procedural reform was ineffective. Investment targeted at core projects to ensure that they were fully funded also came up short. One of the problems was determining what a core project is, particularly given that much of the investment budget was donor-financed. But even when a core project was "defined," allocations were substantially less than agreed upon.[4]

Fiscal policy: revenue generation and composition

As mentioned earlier, Kenya's revenue generation efforts compare favorably with those in lower- to middle-income countries. Its structure of taxes is more mature than in most Sub-Saharan countries—it is more diversified and does not rely heavily on international and production taxes. The elasticity of revenues with respect to GDP has been estimated at 0.8 to 1.1, which is relatively good, although the government has often introduced discretionary measures to maintain the high ratio of revenue to GDP.

Rather than raise additional revenue relative to GDP, the tax reform program sought primarily to simplify the tax structure, lower high tax rates that may encourage evasion and discourage investment, strengthen tax administration, and increase the use of user charges, particularly in health and education.

Efforts to simplify the tax structure and reduce unduly high rates focused on the import tax structure and on company taxation. The government was successful in reducing both the company income tax (from 52 percent in 1989 to 37.5 percent in 1992) and the average unweighted import tariff (as part of the trade liberalization process; see box 5.1). In 1990 the government also introduced a uniform, 18 percent value added tax on the outputs and inputs for several products. The coverage was broadened to cover more products and services as well. Also in 1990, the government sought to improve tax collection by introducing the tax modernization program, an attempt to strengthen the analytical capacity and operational efficiency of the tax departments and to computerize the tax system.

Monetary policy and deficit financing

As is the case in many developing countries, in Kenya the central bank has limited scope for designing and implementing monetary policies independent from the Treasury's financing needs. It is forced to accept such financing requirements and then to discharge its remaining responsibilities residually.

During the stabilization period of 1981–84, the sharp decline in deficit financing requirements was reflected primarily in a decline in foreign borrowing; domestic financing changed only slightly (table 5.2). The share of the private sector in domestic credit fell sharply (from 67 percent to 61 percent); part of the stabilization was thus made possible by crowding out the private sector. During the second half of the 1980s, when large budgetary deficits reemerged, all forms of financing increased, and credit to the economy expanded at a much faster rate. Still, the share of the private sector

Table 5.2 Financing of budget deficits, 1981–91
(change in ratio)

Item	*1981–84*	*1984–91*
Budget deficit/GDP (excluding grants)	-5.8	+4.5
Financing		
Grants/GDP	-0.1	+1.2
Foreign borrowing/GDP	-4.7	+1.7
Domestic financing/GDP	-1.0	+1.5
Inflation (change in rate)[a]	-11.1	+4.7
Growth of real domestic credit (annual percentage)	3.4	5.6
Change in share of private sector in total credit	-6.3	-2.8

a. From December to December.
Source: IMF, *Statistical Abstracts* and *Economic Surveys;* World Bank staff estimates.

continued to decline. Thus, the increase in domestic financing had predictable effects—accelerated inflation and continued tightening of access to credit by the private sector. Econometric work (covering the period 1965–88) substantiates the crowding out effect. Mwega and Killick (1990) estimated that an increase of KSh 1 million in banking system credit to the public sector resulted in a reduction in credit to the private sector of KSh 0.36 million.

From 1986, monetary policy reform sought to shift from direct instruments of control (credit ceilings on private sector credit, fixed interest rates on government paper, and compulsory secondary liquidity requirements) to more indirect instruments (reserve ratios, variable liquidity ratios, and liberalized, market-based interest rates). Reform was also targeted at improving the central bank's control over the growing number of near-bank financial intermediaries that were able to circumvent restrictions on interest rate and credit ceilings. In conjunction, coordination between the treasury and the central bank was to be improved—both to implement monetary policy and to stabilize external shocks more effectively.

The successful reforms were in interest rate liberalization. From 1984, maximum rates on commercial loans were positive in real terms. Over the years, the interest rate ceilings on commercial loans moved closer to the near-bank financial intermediaries' rates. In April 1990 the government went a step further, abolishing all charges and fees from the ceiling on commercial bank loan rates; effective rates could thus exceed the ceiling significantly. In July 1991 an auction market for government bills and bonds was established.

Other reform measures included the introduction of cash reserve ratios (6 percent since 1986), and the imposition of 20 percent and 24 percent liquidity ratios on commercial banks and near-bank financial intermediaries respectively, consisting of cash—deposits with the central bank and other domestic banks—and treasury bills; the latter must constitute at least 50 percent of liquidity requirements. The government also instituted a rediscount window that allowed treasury bills and other government paper with three months or less to maturity to be discounted. The central bank discount rate was set at 1.5 to 2.5 points above the latest treasury bill rate.

It appears that progress in monetary policy reform was a mix of old and new measures, but direct controls on private credit, pressure on commercial banks and near-bank financial intermediaries to hold treasury bills above the liquidity requirement, and pressure on government-owned funds (such as pension and social security funds and insurance companies) to buy long-term government paper remained the main instruments. The "arranged" placement of securities hindered the emergence of a true secondary market for government paper. The only market was for bonds nearing maturity (which can be used as bank reserves) traded by a few large banks as part of their money market activities. While this policy probably enabled the government to pay a lower interest rate on its borrowing than would have been necessary in a truly open market, large fiscal deficits contributed to an increase in the government's domestic interest burden, which tripled as a share of GDP during the 1980s (see table 5.1).

Trade reform

Import liberalization

Import liberalization has a checkered history in Kenya, and significant and sustained progress was made only in the past few years. Import substitution behind protective barriers and "Kenyanization" through state participation were the main principles of industrialization in Kenya. The beginnings of industrial protection (particularly for manufacturing) date back to the post–World War II period, when the government erected a structure of protective tariffs tailor-made to the particular transnational it was trying to attract. In 1963 Kenya became part of the customs union with Uganda and Tanzania, straining the perpetuation of the system of favors through tariffs. Rather, selective import quotas replaced tariffs as the primary instrument of protection. The system continued even after the dissolution of the customs union in 1977. The fourth development plan (1979–84) subsequently recognized that the industrialization strategy would have to move to a more outward-oriented approach. To that end it called for removing quantitative restrictions, reducing tariffs and their dispersion, and establishing a flexibly managed exchange rate to support import liberalization and export promotion.

Between 1980 and 1984, the fourth plan strategy formed the basis for two trade reforms—the phased replacement of quantitative restrictions with equivalent tariffs, and the subsequent tariff rationalization to provide a more uniform and moderate structure of tariff protection. Yet after an initial round of liberalization, the government halted its reform progress and actually regressed, reintroducing import controls for some items when the balance of payments deteriorated. Moreover, to the extent that quantitative restrictions were removed, tariffs were raised on restricted items, some to over 100 percent. In addition, during the extreme foreign exchange crisis of 1982–84, tariffs were increased by 10 percent across the board.

This episode of import liberalization was not successful for several reasons. First, the attempts at liberalization coincided with a period of macroeconomic crisis followed by rapid stabilization, and trade policy became hostage to the needs of stabilization. The central bank was justifiably concerned that the removal of quantitative restrictions would result in loss of control over the balance of payments, given a low level of reserves. Second, there was no movement on the real exchange rate: small nominal devaluations were overwhelmed by high inflation during this period. An increase in the rate of export compensation, designed to compensate for lack of improvement on the real exchange rate, did not function very well. There was a paucity of data for design of reforms—the most recent estimates of effective protection were for 1968—and the program was launched before the necessary homework was completed. As a result, the imposition of high tariffs on some goods and reduction of tariffs on others were done in an ad hoc manner.

Yet the government did make some progress. The share of imports under the quota-free category increased from 24 percent in 1980 to 48 percent in 1985. The average tariff rate was lowered by about 8 percent. And a more transparent, less arbitrary system of import licensing was established, in which import items were allocated to either an unrestricted list (schedule I) or a restricted list (schedule II).

In 1988 another attempt was made to liberalize imports. The reform program sought first to reclassify imports into five categories: schedule I (unrestricted licensing), II, and IIIA, IIIB, and IIIC, with progressively stricter licensing requirements. Over the years, progress toward delicensing imports was fairly dramatic. Automatic or unrestricted licensing was extended to schedules II, IIIA, and IIIB. By 1991 quantitative restrictions affected only 22 percent of all importable items, compared with 40 percent in 1987, and they affected only 5 percent of imports, compared with 12 per-

Box 5.1 Progress in trade liberalization

During most of the post-Independence period, Kenya's trade regime was oriented toward import substitution. Domestic industries were protected by tariffs and import quotas, and several public sector enterprises enjoyed monopoly status in commercial activities, including international trade. Not surprisingly, manufacturing exports declined significantly as a share of total exports, even though external circumstances were generally favorable to these goods. Recent reforms have sought to encourage export development and improve the efficiency of domestic production by exposing domestic producers to foreign competition.

Under the Industrial Sector Adjustment Program and the Export Development Program, protection has become more transparent; with tariffs replacing quantitative restrictions. There has also been a lowering of tariff rates, a reduction in tariff dispersion, and, consequently, a fall in protection. The table below shows the decline in economywide average tariffs. The reform-induced declines in average tariffs are greater when imports previously protected by quotas are excluded. Though maximum tariff rates have fallen substantially, most of the reduction in the level of manufacturing protection has been accomplished through a reduction in the production coverage of quantitative import controls. For instance, the quantitative controls (schedule IIIC) covered most manufacturing production in fiscal 1986. This coverage fell to 79 percent in 1988, 45 percent in

cent in 1987. These shares fell further when several items were moved from IIIC to IIIB in July 1991, so that the only goods left in IIIC were those restricted for health or public safety reasons. Moreover, while quantitative restrictions covered most of the manufacturing production in 1985–86, they covered only 28 percent in 1990–91. Thus, the reform effort to remove licensing controls was more far-reaching than during the earlier attempt at liberalization (box 5.1).

Tariff reform was also generally impressive: the highest tariff rate was reduced from 135 percent to 60 percent, the number of tariff categories was reduced from 25 to 12, and tariff rates on noncompeting imports were lowered. These measures were counterbalanced somewhat by the increase in some tariffs to ensure protection when automatic licensing was introduced, and when items were moved from the most restricted list to automatic licensing. Overall, production-weighted tariffs fell from 62 percent in 1989–90 to 45.5 percent in 1991–92.

The second attempt at import liberalization was relatively successful for several reasons. In the intervening three years between the two attempts, a sector study by the World Bank developed a solid understanding of the structure of industry and its effective protection, and yielded a detailed design of components of reform, based on discussions with an interministerial committee. Considerable effort went into building a more genuine commitment

1990, and 28 percent in 1991. The reduction in protection was not uniform across the manufacturing sector: in June 1989 reductions occurred mainly in the paper and iron and steel subsectors, in June 1990 in food manufacturing, and in June 1991 in textiles and automobiles. However, the numbers understate the actual change in nominal protection relevant to domestic manufacturing. Tariffs on competitive imports fell by much more than the average. This is evident from the larger reductions in production-weighted tariffs, which fell from 61.8 percent in 1990 to 55.5 percent in 1991 and to 45.5 percent in 1992.

Box table 5.1 Economywide average tariffs, fiscal 1985–92
(percent)

All schedules	*1985*	*1988*	*1989*	*1990*	*1991*	*1992*
Unweighted	40.0	39.6	41.3	41.0	38.8	34.0
Import-weighted	..	29.6	27.3	24.5	22.0	20.4
1990 schedules I, II, IIIA, and IIIB						
Unweighted	—	—	—	34.5	29.5	25.9
Import-weighted	—	—	—	28.9	20.2	18.7

— Not applicable.
.. Not available.
Source: World Bank–UNDP (1993).

on the part of the government. The reforms were sequenced and implemented with careful coordination with exchange rate changes. Later, the liberalization process was complemented by other initiatives in export promotion, and by an improved incentive structure resulting from price decontrol.

But the liberalization process was not complete. Although the tariff rates introduced with automatic licensing were generally less than the estimated equivalent tariffs, they were on the higher end and needed to be lowered to reduce effective protection further. Moreover, the import licensing system was not entirely dismantled and was subject to considerable executive discretion. For example, even for items eligible for automatic licensing, foreign exchange authorizations were to be obtained, and foreign exchange was released only with a lag. From time to time, depending on the level of reserves, these licenses and authorizations took longer to obtain or were denied.[5] A 1992 World Bank survey on the costs to firms of annual licensing requirements (equivalent to a 5 percent tax on turnover) indicated that import licenses were the main determinant of licensing burden. Equally vexing were the continued ad hoc import duty exemptions to nonexporters—encouraging favoritism and discrimination, and diminishing revenue.

Table 5.3 Key incentive indicators, 1982–92

(percent and indexes, 1982=100)

Indicator	*1982*	*1984*	*1986*	*1988*	*1990*	*1992*
External sector						
Effective exchange rates[a]						
Nominal	100.0	97.4	82.9	73.6	69.3	55.1
Real	100.0	101.9	87.1	72.5	61.8	60.9
Terms of trade	100.0	109.9	103.4	88.4	71.0	..
Average import tariffs (percent)						
Unweighted	0.0	41.0	38.8	41.3	38.8	..
Import-weighted[b]	0.0	0.0	24.3	27.3	22.0	..
Domestic economy						
Real wages[c]						
Private sector	100.0	83.8	83.9	89.0	83.7	..
Public sector	100.0	85.3	87.5	88.3	77.8	..
Inflation (annual percent)[d]	22.2	9.0	5.6	12.3	15.8	27.3
Real interest rates (annual percent)						
Deposits	-10.0	2.7	5.6	-2.0	-2.1	-10.1
Loans	-7.7	5.3	8.4	2.7	3.0	-6.6

.. Not available.
a. IMF index.
b. Weighted by 1989/80 import values; estimates are for fiscal years (e.g., 1987 refers to 1987/88).
c. Upper ends of average commercial bank three- to six-month deposits and unsecured loans and deposits.
d. Revised Nairobi consumer price index since 1987.
Source: IMF, *Statistical Abstracts* and *Economic Surveys*; World Bank staff estimates.

Figure 5.2 Parallel market dollar premium, 1987–93

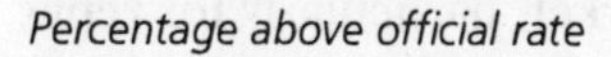

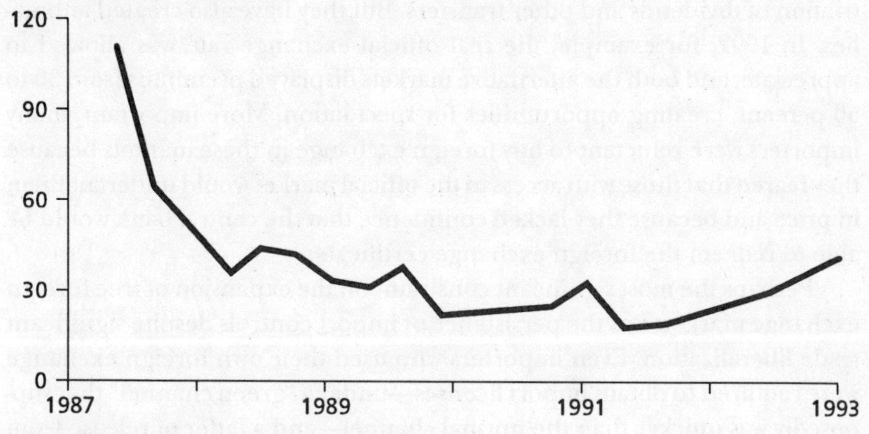

Note: Data not available for April 1991 and January 1992.
Source: World Bank data.

Exchange rate management

The management of the exchange rate in Kenya in the second half of the 1980s was effective. The Kenyan shilling was pegged to the special drawing rights basket of currencies, with weights reflecting Kenya's trading pattern. Since the outset of stabilization in the early 1980s, the government pursued a flexible exchange rate policy (table 5.3). Although the real exchange rate remained relatively constant between 1982 and 1985, it depreciated by more than 40 percent in the second half of the 1980s (by more than the decline in the terms of trade), and the black market premium declined from 110 percent in late 1987 to 17 percent in the third quarter of 1991 (figure 5.2). In October 1991, taking a significant step toward creating a legal free market for foreign exchange, the government issued foreign exchange bearer certificates. Under the system, anyone changing foreign currency not derived from exports was entitled to a certificate that could be exchanged for foreign exchange in the future at the ruling exchange rate. In addition, if it had been held for more than three months, additional foreign exchange equivalent to the London interbank offer rate (LIBOR) applied to the face value of the certificate could be bought. In August 1992 a 100 percent export retention scheme was introduced for exporters of nontraditional goods; in November 1992 this was expanded to cover exporters of traditional crops at a rate of retention of 50 percent. The retained foreign exchange was freely tradable but had to be used for "approved transactions," which had to take place within the banking system.

The markets for foreign exchange certificates and export-retention earnings were clearly an alternative to the official market, particularly for repatriation of dividends and other transfers. But they have also created anomalies. In 1992, for example, the real official exchange rate was allowed to appreciate, and both the alternative markets displayed premiums from 30 to 50 percent, creating opportunities for speculation. More important, many importers were reluctant to buy foreign exchange in these markets because they feared that those with access to the official market would undercut them in price and because they lacked confidence that the central bank would be able to redeem the foreign exchange certificates.

Perhaps the most significant constraint on the expansion of free foreign exchange markets was the persistence of import controls despite significant trade liberalization. Even importers who used their own foreign exchange were required to obtain import licenses—under a "green channel" that supposedly was quicker than the normal channel—and a letter of release from the Ministry of Commerce. This structure allowed for manipulation, uncertainty, and discretion.

Export promotion

During much of the 1980s, a significant antiexport bias on nontraditional goods prevailed, essentially for manufactures—the effective duty on imports was significantly higher than the subsidy on nontraditional exports. The export compensation scheme that had been operational since 1974 was largely ineffective, marred by frequent changes and delays, and benefiting only a few large exporters—four top exporters received the lion's share of payments. The flat 20 percent rebate overcompensated or undercompensated various exporters, and because the rebate was made arbitrarily, it left out a large number of potential exporters.

In 1988 the government introduced the manufacturing-under-bond scheme, allowing customs authorities to waive import duties and taxes on imported materials used as input for the production of export goods. Yet the fact that this facility was available only to export specialty firms limited its attractiveness, as did its cumbersome procedures and high costs. In 1990 a more general import duty/value added tax exemption scheme based on a negative list was introduced, whereby eligibility would be expanded and exemptions would be based on specific export contracts or previous export performance.

These specific tax exemption measures were complemented by regulatory reform to centralize and consolidate several licensing procedures for exports and general trade, and by simplified procedures for new investments. In 1990 construction of an export processing zone near Nairobi began. Its users will receive other advantages—an exemption from income tax for ten years, unrestricted foreign ownership and employment of foreigners, and complete control over foreign exchange earnings.

It is too early to assess the impact of these measures. A greater number of firms began to use the manufacturing-under-bond scheme, and the demand for the tax exemption scheme increased. The export processing zone was not yet operational, but three other privately owned export processing zones emerged and became operational.

The import liberalization measures of recent years reduced the antiexport bias; also, the more aggressive management of the exchange rate probably increased the absolute profitability of exports. These developments—rather than the more recently introduced export promotion measures—are likely to have been the prime determinants of the 10 percent growth in the quantum index of manufactured exports between 1985 and 1990.[6]

Price decontrol and regulatory policy

Price controls in Kenya predate World War II. However, the first formal legislation was the Price Control Ordinance of 1956—later renamed the Price Control Act of 1972—which also served as the model for the current price control framework. Although the range of price-controlled commodities was revised, its procedures and regulations were incorporated largely "as is" into the Restrictive Trade Practices, Monopolies, and Price Control Act of 1988. This act applied to both private and public sector enterprises, but did not cover infrastructure services, the prices of which were controlled by the relevant line ministries. Price controls operated at both the production and the retail levels, depending on the commodity. Price controls on staple foods were imposed to protect lower-income groups, while the main reason for price controls on manufactures was to protect against monopolistic pricing practices.

Prices have been decontrolled extensively, especially since 1986. Between 1983 and 1991, the number of controlled products under the general order fell from 56 to 6, and those under the specific order fell from 87 to 29. Price decontrol was a continuous process, and the government nimbly seized the right market and political opportunities. Price decontrols were geared primarily toward manufactured goods, while controls on consumer prices of staples continued to exist, except on such items as sugar and milk. However, cost-plus pricing (based on outdated data) continued to guide price setting for prices still controlled in the manufacturing sector, and there was no provision for automatic adjustment for inflation or for price changes for intermediate inputs. Nor had a procedure been established for appeal. Prices were set for each enterprise, and delays in price changes increased during the 1980s.

A legal and regulatory framework that provides clarity, certainty, and predictability is necessary to give the private sector enough confidence to enter economic activities. In addition, laws must be framed and enforced so that the transaction cost of arriving at and renegotiating various contracts is reasonable. The minority population of entrepreneurs of Asian origin in Kenya should perceive that they have access to a "level playing field." Welcome but muted efforts have been made since 1986 to improve the legal and regulatory setting—establishing a one-stop office in the Investment Promotion Center to simplify and hasten approval of new investments, simplifying trading (including export) procedures, and allocating foreign exchange for repatriation. But these measures—modifications, really—have not addressed the fundamental legal and regulatory constraints that affect private entrepreneurs. For example, in approving the acquisition and subdivision of urban land, local authorities often asked for the surrender of the freehold title in exchange for 99-year leasehold titles. Moreover, the minister of finance could arbitrarily approve takeovers, set prices, order divestitures, appoint or dismiss board members and trustees, and overturn the decisions of regulatory bodies. Guidelines for determining violations of labor and employment laws were also absent—and the arbitrariness of import duty exemptions has already been discussed.

But the most critical constraints on private sector competition and economic efficiency were the laws governing entry, exit, and operational flexibility. Although competition policy had been set in legislation, the existence of market power, extensive vertical integration, and a highly concentrated wholesaling system suggests that enforcement was weak. Important market segments in the Kenyan economy were controlled by single monopolies, generally parastatals, or by just a few producers. Nearly 60 percent of sales in the economy were estimated to occur in oligopolistic markets; in manufacturing, the share was about 40 to 50 percent. Moreover, most manufacturers were prohibited from marketing directly to retailers or the public, thus protecting the marketing power of parastatals—and nowhere was this more pervasive than in the agricultural sector. Exit laws were essentially "winding-up" policy—focusing on the disposition of assets without any provision for interim legal protection to reorganize. In practice, adjudication took four to ten years, placing enterprises in limbo as their operations came to a standstill and their assets were tied up.

Finally, empirical work indicates that licensing requirements imposed significant monetary and transaction costs on firms (table 5.4). A survey of enterprises showed that the cost of annual licenses—including direct license fees, agent fees and bribes, and transaction costs for enterprise staff time—was very high both as an absolute amount and as a proportion of sales. Moreover, the relative cost of licenses varied inversely with the size of the enterprise, with small firms paying as much as 9.4 percent of their turnover. Compounding these costs was the proliferation of business licenses required by local authorities.

Financial sector policy and reform

The financial system in Kenya in the mid-1980s was fairly well developed, comprising 24 commercial banks, 54 near-bank financial intermediaries, 207 hire-purchase companies, 32 societies, 53 insurance companies, and more than 1,000 savings and credit cooperative societies. In addition, there were 10 development finance institutions, a large post office savings bank, and a national social security fund. The formal financial system had mobilized domestic financial resources effectively: M2/GDP was around 30 percent—about the same as in other medium-growth developing countries—an increase from 24 percent in 1968.

In the early 1980s concerns about a large foreign presence in the system prompted a relaxation in licensing requirements, and small, locally owned banks, building societies, and near-bank financial intermediaries proliferated. Anomalies in the banking law also made it possible for commercial banks to set up near-bank financial intermediaries, and thus circumvent restrictions on banking activities and interest rate ceilings. Indeed, because near-bank financial intermediaries were not subject to statutory reserve requirements and were allowed to borrow and lend at higher rates, they attracted deposits away from commercial banks. Many of these new institutions were promoted actively with funding deposits from the political and administrative elite, particularly those responsible for state-owned enterprises. In the absence of

Table 5.4 Annual license requirements and costs, 1992

Item	*Overall*		*Small firms*		*Medium-size firms*		*Large firms*	
Number, regular	4.5	(1.3)	2.9	(0.6)	4.0	(0.5)	9.7	(1.3)
Number, specific (import/export)	10.2	(3.4)	1.2	(3.4)	3.8	(2.3)	38.9	(1.7)
Total	15.1	(2.4)	4.3	(1.2)	8.0	(1.2)	49.0	(1.4)
Full cost (KSh thousands)	124.3	(3.1)	16.1	(3.7)	95.0	(2.8)	450.4	(1.6)
Transaction cost (work hours)	223.0	(14.8)	69.0	(1.7)	89.7	(1.7)	816.0	(2.8)
Full cost/sales (percent)	5.2	(3.0)	9.4	(2.3)	1.8	(1.7)	1.2	(2.6)
License markup[a] (percent)	66.0	(4.9)	30.5	(2.1)	102.3	(5.1)	84.6	(2.1)

Note: The left entry in each cell is the mean value. The coefficient of variation is provided in parentheses. Mean values reported in the table are statistically significant at the .05 level unless otherwise noted.
a. Defined as full cost/direct cost minus one.
Source: World Bank data.

prudential regulation and with poorly enforced regulations on capital and reserves requirements, four commercial bank groups that owned prominent near-bank financial intermediaries failed in 1986. By 1989, 4 other commercial banks and 24 near-bank financial intermediaries were in trouble, 7 of which appeared to be insolvent. If liquidated, these 28 institutions would have losses ranging from an estimated $105 million to $178 million.

The credit market was more segmented than appeared, given the number and range of financial institutions.[7] Four large commercial banks operated as a "gentleman's club," retaining strong ties to multinational and blue chip companies, and adhering to conservative lending practices. The rest were weak; to survive, they sought out new, risky business. Under significantly weak prudential supervision, and since the near-bank financial intermediaries were subject to higher interest rate ceilings than were commercial banks, the financial intermediaries could undertake riskier ventures. Six development finance institutions set up by the government in the 1960s and 1970s directed credit to specific sectors for long-term investment. They were largely unprofitable and unsustainable, suffering serious portfolio problems. In the agricultural sector, influential large farmers preempted the resources of the Agricultural Credit Corporation and rarely paid them back—in essence being subsidized heavily by the budget. And credit to the private sector was limited by the government's preemption of credit for financing its budget deficits and those of its parastatals, such as the National Cereals and Produce Board.

The government amended the banking laws in 1989—narrowing the regulatory gap between classes of institutions, imposing more stringent licensing requirements on banks and near-bank financial intermediaries, increasing minimum capital requirements, establishing the Deposit Insurance Fund, setting guidelines for loan provisioning and minimum financial disclosure requirements, and increasing penalties for violation. The government sought to strengthen the central bank's technical and managerial capacity to inspect, monitor, and supervise the financial system. And, in the first phase of the reform initiative, nine small banks were restructured.

The legislative reform measures had little impact. The technical capacity of the supervisory department of the central bank was improved, but political forces continued to weaken its enforcement, even as the number of banks and institutions in difficulty grew. It was estimated that 11 banks and 20 near-bank financial intermediaries, accounting for about 25 to 50 percent of nonperforming loans and for about 60 percent of total assets, were in distress in 1992. The consolidation and restructuring of nine banks was delayed and undercut by political factors to the extent that the institutions were stripped of their assets. The consolidated bank itself became a troubled institution. In retrospect it appears that most depositors had already shifted their deposits to the stronger institutions, and the large depositors were paid off in equity or bonds. A large number of banks and near-bank financial intermediaries continued to operate with capital ratios well below the required minimum, and required cash and liquid asset ratios were widely ignored, with supervisory penalties conspicuously absent.[8]

The effects of interest rate liberalization in the banking sector on monetary policy have already been discussed. In a broader sense, the reform program did not reduce the rigidities in the allocation of credit; thus, interest rate liberalization had little effect on improving the efficiency of credit allocation, which would be the primary objective. As discussed earlier, there is no clear evidence that interest rate liberalization generally increased either the profitability or the solvency of financial institutions. It probably did help improve the profitability of a few already solvent banks, but higher interest rates did not support the profitability of the large number of distressed commercial banks and near-bank financial intermediaries because their clients were not servicing their debts anyway.

Agricultural marketing reform

Kenya was one of the few African colonies in which Europeans became involved in land ownership, agricultural production, and exports. The pattern of land ownership and produce marketing from colonial days continued in some ways—for example, dualistic land ownership and marketing structures. Between 1931 and 1959, about 3 million hectares of high-potential and medium-potential land were set aside for exclusive occupation and cultivation by Europeans, and these farmers provided most of the country's exports of food and beverage crops. Under pressure from white settler farmers, the government established a system of marketing boards that paid at least the export price—and often well above—for all crops. African farmers limited to nonscheduled areas were not allowed to grow cash crops or keep grade cattle. The net effect was a rigid, dualistic agricultural system of land ownership, production, and marketing.

Of course, some of the features of this system changed. Before Independence the colonial government began to encourage smallholder production of cash crops, a process that the government hastened considerably after Independence. The government bought, subdivided, and settled smaller farmers on about half a million hectares in settlement schemes. Indeed, the distribution of land to and support for smallholder farmers was the basis for the excellent performance of Kenyan agriculture in the 1960s and 1970s. Nevertheless, the strongly dualistic nature remained, with two attendant features. First, in all but a few years, the prices paid to producers of the major food and export crops were maintained in real terms and as close to import or export parity as appropriate (table 5.5). There was little discrimination against agriculture in this respect, although the protection given to industry and an overvalued exchange rate in some years meant that the terms of trade for agriculture were less favorable than they would have been otherwise.

Second, the presence of the grain marketing parastatal—the National Cereals and Produce Board—continued to be pervasive, despite the recommendations of at least seven commissions since 1942 to reduce the role of the state in grain marketing. Interdistrict movement of grain continued to be controlled. Large maize farmers benefited from guaranteed high prices, while many bureaucrats gained rents from issuing permits for grain movement. Direct state participation in and restrictions on private sector marketing and production extended to other agricultural commodities as well. The government directly marketed several import substitution crops monopolistically: wheat, rice, cotton, sugar, and milk. In all cases, restrictions or outright bans were imposed on private sector participation.

The sustained, relatively high producer prices for maize, together with smaller increases in the price at which the National Cereals and Produce Board could sell to millers and the high marketing costs of the parastatal, had predictable effects on the budget (table 5.6). Also worth noting is the sevenfold increase in the deficit per ton of maize handled—explained in part by the rapid expansion of cereals and board depots in the late 1970s and early 1980s, and a threefold increase in staff between 1980 and 1987. In addition, by 1987 the National Cereals and Produce Board had accumulated debt exceeding 5 percent of GDP, which was "written off" or taken over and paid off by the government in 1988–89.

As with output pricing, controlled input prices reflected import parity. For example, the pricing formula for fertilizer added margins and transport costs to a reference price based on import prices, seed prices were based on the costs of production, and the price of agricultural chemicals was not controlled. The licensing of fertilizer imports was the main problem—in the guise of administering technical standards and coordination with donor-financed

Table 5.5 Producer prices in Kenya, 1984–85 and 1991–92

Product	*1984–85*	*1991–92*
Maize		
Percentage of import parity	73.2[a]	69.9
Percentage of export parity	155.7	128.8
Coffee (percentage of export price)[b]	91.3	89.5
Tea (percentage of export price)[b]	84.4	88.6

a. Figure for 1983, since there were no exports in 1984.
b. These are average prices. Smallholders obtained about 80 percent of the price obtained by estates because of differences in quality and, in the case of coffee growers, deductions by the cooperatives.
Source: World Bank data; author's estimates.

Table 5.6 National Cereals and Produce Board operations, 1983–84 and 1991–92

Item	*1983–84*	*1991–92*
Producer price of maize (KSh/ton)	144	300
Price to millers (KSh/ton)	208	359
Gross margin/producer price (percent)	53.5	19.7
National Cereals and Produce Board deficits (K£ millions)[a]	12.8	70.9
Deficit/current government expenditures (percent)	1.3	2.3
Deficit per ton handled (KSh per ton)[b]	11.4	74.3

a. Before finance charges.
b. Sales and purchases.
Source: World Bank data; Egerton University (1992); author's estimates.

imports, the government restricted import licenses to a fairly small number of importers. The result was uncertainty over supplies and poor timing. In addition, price controls down to the retail level reduced supplies and penalized cereal-producing smallholders, who did not have access to institutional suppliers such as the coffee cooperatives.

Output marketing

The reform program sought to disengage the government from marketing (and in some cases, processing). Unfortunately, the process was slow and tangled; only dubious success was achieved, and that with minor crops. Milk prices were decontrolled, and restrictions on private sector processing and marketing removed. In 1987–88, the government eliminated the cotton marketing board's monopoly on paper, and approved the divestiture of its gins and its restructuring as a regulatory agency. No further progress was made. The government also decided to divest its bacon factory and the Kenya meat commission. While staff were laid off initially, the commission resumed operations in 1989. In the sugar sector, no decisions were reached, pending the completion of a subsectoral study.

The saga of attempts to reform the marketing of maize, the most important foodcrop, could fill many pages. Grain market reform had the stated aim of having all domestic trade managed by private merchants with deregulated prices. Various studies indicated that the National Cereals and Produce Board had a role—one limited to holding minimal amounts of strategic reserves for smoothing sharp increases in consumer prices in poor harvest years. In addition, the National Cereals and Produce Board would be a buyer of last resort, maintaining floor prices for producers. The food security and stabilization role thus envisaged for the National Cereals and Produce Board would be quite limited—if its monopoly on internal trade and on imports and exports were removed, private trade would be able to assume most of these functions.

Both design flaws and a lack of commitment impeded reform. The design flaw was the inconsistency between fixing the purchase price close to the import parity price and reducing the role of the National Cereals and Produce Board to being a buyer of last resort. A price set close to import parity is likely to encourage most farmers to choose to sell to the cereals board. Indeed, the parastatal then becomes a purchaser of (the farmers') first choice, leading to the accumulation of stocks purchased at prices too high to make export profitable. This occurred repeatedly in the 1980s. In the early 1980s, grain reserves for several years were 40 to 60 percent higher than the desired level of 270,000 tons. Later in the decade, when the desired level was increased to 560,000 tons, actual stocks were still often 60 to 70 percent higher, even after significant exports. If the reform program sought to reduce the role of the cereals board, the most potent instrument was the reduction in the purchase price, perhaps closer to export parity. Although terms such as "flexible pricing" and "improved pricing methodology" were cited in policy documents, purchase price reduction was never an explicitly stated objective.

Instead, other solutions to the problem were attempted—the quantity of maize allowed to be moved without permit was raised from 2 bags to 44 bags, 70 percent of the board's buying centers were closed, and millers were allowed to buy an increasing share of their requirements directly from traders rather than from the National Cereals and Produce Board. The cereals board was also "restructured," which included a debt write-off in 1988.

Evaluating the effects of these efforts is problematic, since defining and measuring what is actually happening in practice is difficult. Some preliminary evidence does seem to indicate that during 1988–91, when movement controls were eased, private trade was able to equalize interregional price disparities by raising prices in surplus areas and reducing them in deficit areas. The operating margins of private trade were clearly lower than those of the National Cereals and Produce Board. At the same time, the cereals board purchases were lower than in previous years, suggesting that its role in the market declined. But the trend was quickly reversed when movement controls were reimposed in 1992 and the procurement price was jacked up to 110 percent of import parity. At the same time, by reopening buying centers and offering maize to millers at a subsidized price, the government undercut its own decision to encourage millers to buy directly from the market.

The impact on the National Cereals and Produce Board's finances is also unclear. Despite the debt write-off and closing of buying centers, the average cost of a bag of maize handled by the cereals board remained high. Staff reduction targets were not met, and the cereals board was still unable to cover its cost of operation, as indicated by growing deficits. In addition to a programmed transfer from the central budget in 1991–92, for example, a further subsidy became necessary—about 2 percent of all current expenditures.

Fertilizer marketing

Complete decontrol of prices at all levels since 1990 has increased the number of fertilizer retailers at interior locations—thus increasing availability, particularly at the retail level, where margins had been badly squeezed in the past. In 1991 fertilizer imports were transferred from schedule II to schedule I and became unrestricted. It is unclear whether this move increased the number of licensed importers. Estimated fertilizer use declined between 1989 and 1991. Donor-financed fertilizers, which account for about 60 percent of annual imports, continued to be "allocated" in a process that was neither transparent nor coordinated with private demand for fertilizers. This, together with continued uncertainties about import licensing and foreign exchange allocation and the continued domination of the market by government-owned distributors, appears to have discouraged private traders.

Public enterprise reform

The government held equity in about 250 commercially oriented enterprises producing goods and services for profit; in over half, the government was the majority equity holder. Equity was held directly in about 50 enterprises; equity in the rest was held through government-owned development finance institutions. The single largest economic activity of parastatals was manufacturing; in 1990, 60 percent of the enterprises were in manufacturing and mining, 18 percent in distribution, 15 percent in finance, and the rest in transport, electricity, and other services. Between 1986 and 1990, the parastatal sector accounted for 11 percent of GDP.

While GDP grew overall by 5 percent between 1986 and 1990, value added in the parastatal sector grew at only 0.5 percent annually—with negative growth in the manufacturing and mining sectors. (Table 5.7 provides indicators of the economic and financial performance of the public enterprise sector and its relationship to the rest of the economy.) Based on a sample of parastatals and private enterprises, it is estimated that total factor productivity growth during this period was negative for the parastatal sector, compared with 5.4 percent for the private sector; the growth of labor inputs was half that of the private sector, while the growth of capital inputs was twice as high, indicating an inefficient use of resources. Excluding the profits of the central bank, net inflows to the central government budget were either significantly negative (–0.9 to –1.1 percent of GDP) or near zero.

While economic inefficiency was the most disturbing characteristic of the parastatal sector, its effects on the budget and external accounts were not negligible. The sector accounted for more than a third of the government's net lending and equity operations and contributed little revenue: in fact, unremitted taxes—those collected but not remitted—were estimated to have been 0.5 percent of tax revenues in 1991. The sector ran a net trade deficit of 28 percent of the total trade deficit. While the sector did not greatly increase the external debt and debt service burden, the efficiency with which these funds were used is at issue. Furthermore, the government often assumed the debt and debt servicing obligations of parastatals, which often borrowed externally without clearance from the treasury.

Parastatals do not appear to be a burden on the banking system. But their demand on or lack of contribution to budgetary revenues indirectly increased the government's own budget deficits and its demands for credit. Too, close ties seemed to exist between parastatals and distressed banks—distressed banks held an estimated 85 percent of all parastatal deposits, due to a government directive that parastatals place their deposits there and with near-bank financial intermediaries. Conversely, it also appeared that loans to parastatals were a source of loss for the distressed banks. Thus, although the aggregate figures did not exhibit a dangerous interdependence, the link between poorly performing parastatals and the subset of distressed banks was in fact quite close.

Table 5.7 Performance indicators of the parastatal sector, 1986–91

Efficiency indicators	*Value*
Total value added (annual percent)	0.5
Value added in manufacturing (annual percent)	-0.1
Change in total factor productivity (annual percent)	-1.7
Growth rate of labor use/growth rate of labor in private sector (ratio)	0.6
Growth rate of capital inputs/growth rate of capital in private sector (ratio)	2.1
Relationship to budget and external accounts	
Net lending and equity to parastatals/overall net lending by government (percent)	35.4
Profits, interest and dividend payments/tax revenue (ratio)	3.7
Parastatal external debt/public and publicly guaranteed debt (1990; percent)	17.0
Parastatal external debt servicing/total (1990; percent)	25.5
Net exports of parastatals/total net exports (percent)	-27.9
Relationship to banking system and near-bank financial intermediaries	
Parastatal deposits/total commercial bank deposits (ratio)	6.7
Parastatal deposits/total near-bank financial intermediaries deposits (ratio)	10.0
Parastatal credit/commercial bank credit (ratio)	6.0
Parastatal credit/near-bank financial intermediaries credit (ratio)	1.3

Source: World Bank data.

Finally, the parastatal sector strengthened the monopolistic and oligopolistic structure of industry. Monopolies were usually parastatal firms granted such power through legislation or administrative decree. They could exercise this power in sales or purchases, the latter through marketing institutions and boards. Oligopolies sometimes consisted of a combination of private and public firms. Parastatals were often protected by higher tariffs, effective (although not officially gazetted) prohibition on competing imports, and ad hoc exemptions on import duties on capital and intermediate goods.

Although several attempts were made to restructure the public enterprise sector, progress has been made only recently. In late 1991 the government announced its intention to divest its interest in a preliminary list of 207 enterprises, while retaining ownership of 33 strategic enterprises. Of the 207, it selected only 10 for privatization by 1995. Five have actually been privatized or brought to the point of sale. Furthermore, five majority-owned public enterprises, which accounted for the bulk of government transfers, were to be restructured, including railways, the port authority, the tea development agency, posts and telegraphs, and, again, the National Cereals and Produce Board. This was a modest beginning. And it is unclear whether all of the 33 enterprises to be retained in the public sector have "strategic" importance. But the greatest source of skepticism is the inclusion of the National Cereals and Produce Board in this list—it is targeted for yet another round of "restructuring."

Civil service reform

In 1990 the mainstream civil service employed more than a quarter million people—or about a quarter of urban wage employment. In the 1980s civil service employment growth slowed to an average of 4.8 percent a year after a spurt of 10 percent a year during the 1970s. Several policy measures have reflected the strong pressures to create jobs—guaranteed employment for university graduates and the tripartite arrangements of 1964, 1970, and 1979–81, which called for employment increases in the public sector by 15 percent, 10 percent, and 10 percent, respectively. Further, ad hoc absorption of staff from the agencies of the East Africa Community and the census operations of 1979, and a large number of "works paid" employees hired under development projects, have increased employment. As may be expected, the composition of the civil service is biased heavily toward low-skilled employees; only 11 percent are in the middle- or upper-management cadres.

It can be difficult sometimes to judge whether the expansion of public employment is justified by the corresponding increase in the real value of government services provided. However, if one takes GDP growth as a rough indicator of demand for government services and assumes no decline in average productivity of civil servants, then increases in government employment far exceed the increase in demand; the rate of increase in government employment was twice that of GDP.

This steady growth in civil service employment was accompanied by stagnation or regression in the salaries and wages paid to civil servants. During the 1980s, in particular, average real wages declined by over 15 percent, compared with a 7.3 percent decline in the private sector. The government's wage policies helped hold the total civil service wage bill in check even while employment expanded—and in fact served as the (moderate) wage leader for the entire modern sector. However, the slow growth in real wages was distributed unevenly—lower wage grades received larger percentage increases. Together with a "grade creep," this led to a compression of salary scales, reducing the attractiveness of government jobs for professionals and the highly skilled, as reflected in high vacancy rates at these levels.

In sum, overstaffing was not dealt with effectively. While the government occasionally declared hiring freezes and supposedly abandoned its practice of giving jobs to all university graduates and graduates of other training programs, these policies were not systematically implemented. In any case, overstaffing occurs predominantly at the lower grade levels, so that reduction in size at this level is likely to be more important than restriction of university graduates.

Social sector policies

Education

Kenya's educational system expanded rapidly—in part in reaction to the highly restrictive and unequal educational practices of the colonial government and in part to accommodate the extraordinary growth in the school-going population. And its basic indicators are some of the best in Africa: a 99 percent primary school enrollment rate, an enrollment rate of 48 percent among females, and an adult literacy rate of 60 percent for males and 40 percent for females. Public expenditures on education are also among the highest in Africa—at 6 percent of GDP. Some 57 percent of public recurrent expenditures go to primary education; the spirit of Harambee, or "Let's pull together," has brought parents into the funding fold—they bear 56 and 73 percent shares of the capital (and some recurring) costs of education at the primary and secondary levels.

Despite the additional funds from parental sources, public expenditures on education grew as a share of GDP (see table 5.1) and comprised 40 percent of the budget by fiscal 1991. Public recurrent expenditures financed primarily teacher salaries—real salaries declined but the number of teachers grew at a faster rate than enrollments, so that the average class size was unusually small. At the same time, the dropout rate was very high: roughly half of all children who began primary education failed to complete it. Thus, there is room for improvement.

Only 1.3 percent of the eligible population was enrolled at the university level. Yet this subsector took up 72 percent of capital expenditures and 18 percent of recurrent expenditures in the late 1980s (an increase from 11.8 percent in 1985). Until recently 30 percent of university spending went for student boarding and other allowances. Recent structural changes that made admission easier, and the fact that cost-sharing is substantially lower than in basic education, contributed to a very high private demand. In the last five years, the number of public universities increased from one to six.

Kenya faces different financing issues than most other African countries, where scant public spending on education must be increased. In particular, Kenya must address the high and rising budget share of education and its biased distribution toward universities. Three broad measures are paramount: limiting the growth of teachers at the primary level, lowering dropout and repeat rates, and containing the public resource demands of the secondary sectors, particularly of universities. The first measure entails three reforms: increasing class size and teacher workloads, limiting the intake of teachers colleges, and halting the recruitment of untrained teachers. Allocating public resources more equitably would entail introducing direct charges and recovering the full cost of food and boarding, and reforming the student loan scheme at the university level. Public universities should also be consolidated, and new admissions restricted for a period of time.

In the year since the adjustment program was initiated, quantitative limits on the number of teachers on the payroll and the number and mix of trainees accepted into training colleges were exceeded. At the university level, admission targets were adhered to, direct charges were instituted along with need-based grants, and some aspects of the student loan scheme (still available to all students) were restructured to reduce the amount of personal allowances.

Health

As in education, health indicators improved dramatically after Independence—life expectancy increased from 42 to 58 years, the crude mortality rate declined from 20 to 11 per thousand population, and infant mortality declined from more than 200 to 110 per thousand live births. The coverage of immunization programs has also grown, and dropout rates have declined.

At the same time, AIDS has become a significant public health problem. About 200,000 Kenyans are now estimated to be HIV-positive, and about 2,500 new AIDS cases are diagnosed annually.

Historically, the bulk of the ministry of health budget was allocated to secondary and tertiary hospital services, leaving few funds for rural health facilities. And although the allocated share of preventive services and rural health services increased in the late 1980s by 7 and 11 percentage points, it remained low in relation to need. Furthermore, actual expenditures for preventive and rural services fell short of allocations—by about 19 to 24 percent—while actual spending for curative services was well above 100 percent of allocations. The share of recurrent expenditures devoted to nonwage expenses such as medical supplies has also declined steadily, from about 28 percent in the 1970s to 20 percent in the late 1980s. Only limited user charges were in effect until 1989. Moreover, inadequate maintenance—a systemic problem—affects rural health facilities in particular. A survey in 1981 showed that less than half of Kenya's rural facilities had a reliable water supply and 65 to 70 percent were unacceptably run down.

To meet the increase in demand in the face of tight resources, the government has sought to mobilize additional resources and to ensure that facilities are used more efficiently. In December 1989 the government introduced outpatient and inpatient user charges at all public sector facilities except dispensaries; in July 1990 it introduced reforms to the national hospital insurance fund, a parastatal covering primarily wage earners and their families. User chargers were accompanied by waivers based on ability to pay and incentives to facilities that allowed them to keep part of the revenue they generated. The reforms to the insurance fund made contributions proportional to income and increased the coverage.

After the imposition of user charges, attendance at facilities fell, but they soon returned to their previous levels with one important exception—attendance increased at dispensaries and health centers, and declined at hospitals. This was a desirable outcome. However, public concern about the continued inadequacy of facilities and the perception that the waiver system was not functioning properly forced the government to reduce or suspend some charges three months later. This withdrawal reduced cost-sharing revenues by about 50 percent and eliminated the incentive to seek care first at a lower-level facility. Then, in 1992 fees were reintroduced progressively from the national hospital in Nairobi to district hospitals and health centers. And the waivers system was strengthened and expanded. The government also increased its budgeted and actual recurrent spending by 30 percent between fiscal 1989 and 1992, and the share of total health expenditures increased from 7.6 percent to more than 8.5 percent.

The outcomes of structural adjustment

Impact on intermediate variables

Much of the stabilization gain of the early 1980s was lost in the late 1980s—the budget deficit increased almost to the levels of the crisis period, and high inflation reemerged (table 5.8). While the gains in reducing the external deficit were not entirely reversed, the increased and high debt service ratios indicate the precariousness of the external balance.

Progress was made in maintaining positive interest rates and in real exchange rate depreciation. With the removal of price controls, and the maintenance of producer incentives in agriculture, the overall incentive structure was reasonably undistorted in the late 1980s.

Macroeconomic and sectoral outcomes

From 1980 to 1984 the economy experienced a low growth rate due largely to stabilization policies that cut expenditures sharply—resulting in a decline in the excess of expenditures over income from 11 percent of GDP in 1980 to 1 percent in 1984–85 (table 5.9). Moreover, the low efficiency of investment in the late 1970s led to a high incremental capital-output ratio and a negative rate of productivity growth during the early 1980s.

After the slowdown in the first half of the 1980s, growth resumed and investment reflected greater efficiency in the late 1980s. The increase in efficiency can be attributed to a decline in the rate of (unproductive) investment between 1980 and 1984—much of it in the public sector, where the

Table 5.8 The effects on intermediate variables, 1976–91

		Adjustment period	
Intermediate variable	*Crisis period (1976–81)*	*Phase I (1981–84)*	*Phase II (1985–91)*
Change in fiscal deficit/GDP (percentage points)	5.7	-5.8	4.5
Inflation rate (change in rate)[a]	3.3	-11.1	4.7
Real average interest rate (loans)	-2.1	-0.3	4.6
Real effective exchange rate (percentage change)	-16.9	5.7	-42.3
Change in current account/GDP (percentage points)	9.9	-8.2	4.0[b]
Debt service/exports average (percent)	8.0	26.0 to 28.0	30.0

Note: A minus sign indicates a decline in deficit or rate.
a. December to December.
b. 1984–90.
Source: IMF, *Statistical Abstracts* and *Economic Surveys*; World Bank staff estimates.

ratio of public fixed investment to GDP declined by 1.6 percent. The public sector maintained a lower rate of investment in the late 1980s.

Yet, despite the decline in the share of public investment, the sector's claims on private sector savings grew. By the early 1980s, the central government had changed from a net saver in the late 1970s to a consumer of private savings. By the late 1980s and early 1990s, the position deteriorated steadily. After a sharp decline in and imprudent use of foreign savings in the mid-1980s, external resource use increased to 4.6 percent in the late 1980s. The conclusion is that while some public sector adjustment occurred, primarily as a reduction in the rate of public investment, it was inadequate in terms of placing demands on both the private sector and foreign savings.

Table 5.9 Macroeconomic and sectoral outcomes, 1975–91

		Adjustment period	
Item	*Crisis period 1975–80*	*Phase I (1980–84)*	*Phase II (1985–91)*
GDP growth (annual percent)	5.6	2.1	5.0
Gross investment/GDP	28.8[a]	23.8	20.0
Incremental capital-output ratio (annual averages)[b]	..	10.8	4.2
Total factor growth/productivity (annual percent)	..	-0.3	1.9[c]
Sectoral GDP growth (annual percent)			
Agriculture	2.6	2.8	3.5
Industry		2.1	5.0
Manufacturing	7.6	3.7	5.3
Services	..	4.1	5.1
External trade			
Export growth (annual percent)	0.5	-3.4	4.8
Growth of volume of manufacturing exports (annual percent)	-4.1	-8.7	10.5[c]
Nonoil imports/GDP	22.5	18.0	19.1
Domestic exports/GDP	20.6	16.6	13.4
Manufacturing imports/domestic supply	44.3[d]	26.8	19.1
Manufacturing exports/output	22.6[d]	13.3	6.1
Savings and investment (percentage of GDP)			
Fixed investment	23.2[a]	21.6	19.4
Public	10.4[e]	8.8	8.1
Private	12.6[e]	12.8	11.3
Financing			
Central government savings	2.8[a]	-1.1	-1.5
Private sector savings	18.2[a]	20.2	21.9
Foreign savings (grants and net borrowing)[d]	9.0	1.4	4.6

.. Not available.
a. 1977–79.
b. Average of incremental capital-output ratios for 1980–84 and 1985–90.
c. 1985–90.
d. 1972.
e. Shares based on 1979 data.
f. The data are averaged differently to sharpen the changes; the first period refers to 1978–81, the second to 1982–86, and the last to 1987–91.
Source: IMF, *Statistical Abstracts* and *Economic Surveys*; World Bank staff estimates.

A growth in private sector savings was directed into financing the government deficit rather than private investments; indeed, the private investment effort slowed throughout the 1980s. This may be indicative of the stagnation to be expected in the early years of adjustment. Yet it may also reflect a continued reluctance to invest in the face of regulatory and other nonprice barriers and, more recently, political uncertainties.

Adjustment focused heavily on the external sector. Import liberalization was substantial. The ratio of imports to GDP has increased since the mid-1980s, but not the share of imports in the domestic supply of manufactures (table 5.9). In fact, this share was lower in the latter part of the adjustment period than initially, suggesting that manufacturing sector imports were not liberalized to the same extent as other imports.[9]

For exports the picture is less clear. The export-to-GDP ratio continued to decline, as did the ratio of manufactured exports to output—suggesting that a significant increase in export orientation did not occur. At best, exports grew at the same rate as GDP in the second half of the 1980s. But this overall result is due partly to the still relatively large share of primary commodities in the export structure, for which growth was modest. The rate of manufactured exports increased sharply, particularly in the past few years, suggesting that production may be shifting from supply for mainly domestic markets to exports of manufacturing. But the small share of manufactures in merchandise exports—about 20 percent—has little impact on the export-GDP ratio.[10]

In agriculture, the rate of output growth, while lower than in the years following Independence, is still quite respectable. The delicensing of private imports of fertilizer and decontrol of its price could be expected to have a direct effect on production, although the direction of the effect is theoretically ambiguous: price decontrol and thus higher prices might suppress demand, wider availability may reduce prices and increase usage. So far, neither has occurred. Usage showed an increase until 1990, and a significant decline in the next two years. The failure at rationalizing public expenditures (including a restructuring of the National Cereals and Produce Board) suggests that priority investments are underfunded, as are critical agricultural services.

Adjustment and aid

This discussion of the reform process brings us logically to another question about Kenya: whether aid (including the World Bank's) has been so generous as to encourage the government to avoid substantial reform. This question is difficult to assess. At the aggregate level, the net disbursement of official development assistance per capita to Kenya in 1990—at $41—was less than that for other "favored" African countries, such as Tanzania ($47.1),

Burundi ($48.8), and Malawi ($56.3). Yet it was substantially higher than net disbursements to Ghana ($31.2), Africa's best performer. Much the same picture emerges for net official development assistance as a share of GDP. At 11.1 percent, Kenya's share is higher than Ghana's (7 percent), but much lower than that of other countries (48 percent for Tanzania, and about 26 percent for Malawi and Burundi). Without making too much of these numbers, one can probably say that while the resource use and policy reform behavior of Kenya makes it less deserving of the aid it obtained than, say, Ghana, Kenya does not exhibit the same extent of aid dependency as other donor favorites in the region. At the same time, it does appear that generous project funding by several donors has led to a public investment program that, while declining as share of GDP, is not well prioritized. Even more critical, the growing reliance on grants and counterpart funds has also undoubtedly contributed to higher consumption expenditures by the government, particularly on the civil service.

A more specific question: Has the World Bank's policy-based lending to Kenya in the 1980s allowed it to undertake adjustment or to postpone it? Here, too, the answer is mixed. The most successful area of reform has been trade liberalization (and exchange rate depreciation)—and to a lesser extent export development. The link between trade reform and the increased demand for foreign exchange that it generates (at a given exchange rate) is quite direct, and it would be right to conclude that the reforms would not have occurred had the World Bank not kept up steady lending. At the same time, it is arguable that the budget support provided by these funds helped postpone many critical reforms—civil service reform, parastatal divestiture (including the National Cereals and Produce Board), and social sector reform.

Appendix 5A. Policy reform in Kenya: design and implementation

Fiscal policy and management

Initial distortion. In the early 1980s, financial imbalances and inflation were high. The budget deficit ran at 9 percent of GDP, the current account balance at 12.5 percent of GDP, and gross investment at 30 percent of GDP (financed half by foreign savings). There was a large expansion in public investment in the 1970s.

Reforms. There was sharp deflation during 1980–84, through the reduction of the budget deficit (4 percent), import compression, tight monetary policy, and a decline in public investment. The budget rationalization program was introduced in 1985 to increase operations and maintenance expenditures and prioritize investment expenditures.

Assessment of progress. During 1985–91 the deflationary trend was reversed. Financial imbalance increased to levels of the early 1980s. Budget rationalization was unsuccessful; the proportion of funding for operations and maintenance fell from 36 percent in fiscal 1981 to 26 percent in fiscal 1986 and to 22 percent in fiscal 1991.

Monetary policy

Initial distortion. In the early 1980s, the banking system financed large budget deficits; there were direct controls on credit to the private sector and negative interest rates.

Reforms. Growth in credit during the stabilization period, 1980–84, slowed. There were positive interest rates, but continued controls on credit to the private sector, whose share declined by 6.3 percentage points. There were also attempts to shift to indirect instruments of monetary control starting in 1989—such as introducing an auction for government paper and activating reserve and liquidity ratios.

Assessment of progress. There was a reversal of trends in monetary growth in 1985–91, and a continued decline in the share of private sector credit (by 2.8 percentage points). The shift to indirect instruments was not successful. The auction market was limited; direct credit controls and placement of government securities continued to be the main instruments. Higher interest rates contributed to an increase in domestic debt service payments as a share of GDP, from 1.3 percent in fiscal 1981 to 3.6 percent in fiscal 1990.

Exchange rate management

Initial distortion. The Kenyan shilling was tied to the U.S. dollar from 1971 to 1975 and to the SDR since 1986. Discrete devaluations depreciated the real exchange rate during the 1970s.

Reforms. There was active management of the exchange rate through much of the 1980s. In 1992 tradable foreign exchange certificates and export retention schemes were introduced.

Assessment of progress. In 1980–84 the real exchange rate appreciated, but there was real depreciation during 1985–91, compensating more than fully for the terms of trade changes and domestic inflation. The black market premium declined. A second legal free market for foreign exchange started functioning. In 1992, however, the official rate appreciated, and the legal parallel markets carried premiums of 30 to 50 percent.

Import liberalization

Initial distortion. Local goods were highly protected by quantitative restrictions, high tariffs, and bans. The breakup of the East African Community in 1977 intensified inward orientation.

Reforms. During 1980–84 a first attempt was made to remove quantitative restrictions and reduce tariffs. A second attempt was made during 1988–91.

Assessment of progress. The first attempt was unsuccessful, and import liberalization became hostage to stabilization needs. The second attempt was relatively successful. By July 1991 the only items protected by quantitative restrictions were for health or public safety; all other items were licensed "automatically." In practice, even for items eligible for automatic licensing, permits were (and still are) delayed and foreign exchange authorizations were obtained. This also applied to imports financed with own funds. The average import-weighted tariff was reduced from 30 percent in 1984–85 to 20 percent in 1991–92. Tariffs on competing imports fell faster. The import-GDP ratio increased slightly.

Promotion of nontraditional exports

Initial distortion. There was an antiexport bias despite the export compensation scheme, which functioned poorly.

Reforms. A manufacturing-under-bond scheme was introduced in 1988, followed by an import duty/value added tax exemption scheme in 1990. Establishment of an export processing zone was expected to be completed in 1993.

Assessment of progress. Manufacturing-under-bond and import duty/value added tax schemes were popular, but it is too early to assess their impact. Manufactured export growth picked up (10 percent a year increase during 1985–91), attributable mainly to import liberalization and exchange rate depreciation.

Liberalization of domestic prices and trade

Initial distortion. Agricultural output and input pricing was *not* distortionary, but maize trade was controlled by parastatal and movement controls. Retail prices were controlled for basic commodities. Manufactured goods' prices were controlled, and parastatals controlled wholesale trade in a number of goods.

Reforms. Prices for most manufactured goods and many staple foods were decontrolled; maize and wheat prices were not decontrolled. There was some relaxation of grain movement controls and controls on direct sales to millers.

Assessment of progress. Relaxation of food marketing controls has not resulted in true liberalization—the parastatal remains the major actor. Recently, movement controls were reimposed. Wholesale trade in some manufactures continued to be controlled by parastatals (for example, the Kenya National Trading Corporation).

Financial sector

Initial distortion. There were large numbers of banks and near-bank financial intermediaries, but concentration and segmentation were high. A poor licensing and regulatory framework led to financial distress. There was an unhealthy cross-relationship with parastatals.

Reforms. The banking laws were amended to improve licensing and regulations and to strengthen the central bank's technical and managerial capacity. Nine small institutions were restructured.

Assessment of progress. The laws were poorly enforced, leading to a financial sector crisis in the early 1990s. The number of distressed institutions increased; restructuring was unsuccessful. Excessive political interference and links with parastatals continued.

Public enterprise reform

Initial distortion. There was a large parastatal sector (about 250 enterprises) accounting for 11 percent of GDP, overwhelmingly in manufacturing. Economic inefficiency, monopoly status, and budgetary drains characterized the sector.

Reforms. In late 1991 the government announced its intention to divest its equity in 207 enterprises. Ten were selected for privatization by 1995; five were brought to the point of sale.

Assessment of progress. A modest beginning.

Labor and wage policies

Initial distortion. Labor policies toward the private sector were flexible and pragmatic despite extensive unionization and collective agreements. The only significant restrictions were on permanent retrenchment. Public sector employment (25 percent of the urban labor force) grew by 10 percent a year during the 1970s, mainly at the lower grades. Employment was guaranteed to all university and training program graduates. Real wages fell during the 1980s.

Reforms. None.

Assessment of progress. None.

Social sector policies

Initial distortion. There was high private and government spending (6 percent of GDP) on education. By the early 1980s, primary school enrollment was universal, but public expenditures were biased toward secondary levels and teachers' salaries, with low internal efficiency. There were good health indicators—some of the best among low-income countries. But tertiary care and large urban hospitals took a disproportionate share of resources, with poor cost recovery.

Reforms. Reforms since 1991 attempted to limit the growth of the teaching force, increase class size, and increase cost recovery at the university level. In 1989 graduated user charges were introduced for certain services and amenities, facilities were allowed to keep 75 percent of collections, and waivers were allowed for those unable to pay.

Assessment of progress. The government maintained its expenditures (as a share of GDP) and has not discriminated against the sector. But it has not been able to restrain growth of the teaching force. Cost recovery has increased. The program of user fees was poorly implemented; some features have been abandoned, others reintroduced. The impact is unclear.

Notes

1. The Million Acre Settlement Scheme introduced in 1961 and other minor settlement schemes settled over 34,000 families on 430,000 hectares. The Shirika program started in 1971 had settled more than 100,000 hectares by 1976. Altogether, about one-third of the large-scale mixed farm area was officially subdivided.

2. Coffee and tea farmers received about 90 percent of the world market prices on average. However, small coffee farmers received lower prices essentially because of deductions made by inefficient cooperatives. The price paid for maize was about 75 percent of the import parity price in the 1980s but well above the export parity price. Here, too, late payments by the cereal marketing board have caused delays in some years.

3. Mosley (1991) notes that "the Ministry of Finance, in 1982, was firmly in the hands of Harris Mule with backing from Ndegwa and Nyachea. It was ... these technocrats within the Kenyan government who saw in this period of economic crisis an opportune moment for pushing through a comprehensive reform package."

4. For example, in the agricultural sector, where attempts at budget rationalization were most persistent initially, the Ministry of Agriculture excluded about 10 percent of its projects, which it judged as having lower priority, while the Ministry of Livestock Development discarded about 20 percent of its projects. A subset of 33 was then defined as "core projects" for priority full funding in 1991–92. However, actual allocations were substantially lower—56 percent of the development budget compared with 69 percent. On recurrent expenditures, there was a decrease of 6 percent compared with a targeted increase of 4.4 percent. Ironically, noncore projects fared better.

5. For example, the average lag from license application to allocation fell from six months in 1988 to about four weeks in early 1991. But soon, the time taken lengthened to more than ten weeks; importers reacted by submitting multiple applications, then the government returned all applications for resubmission.

6. Among nontraditional exports, the rapid growth of horticultural exports preceded the import liberalization program begun in 1988. During 1981–89, the volume of horticultural exports grew more than sevenfold. As a private sector activity, this subsector was able to prosper essentially because of minimal regulation by the Horti-

cultural Crops Development Authority, a parastatal that has concentrated on promotional efforts rather than actual involvement in marketing.

7. The Hirschmann index, which measures concentration on a scale of 0 to 1 (maximum concentration), was estimated for the bank and near-bank sectors for end-1991. This statistic indicated that the strength of competition in the industry was similar to that in a market characterized by about 5 equally sized banks, rather than the 28 that actually exist. For the nonbank financial institutions, it was as if there were 13 equally sized institutions, rather than the 56 that actually exist.

8. For example, during 1991, 6 to 10 banks had liquidity ratios below the minimum, and as many as 24 to 29 nonbank financial institutions did not meet the requirements.

9. An examination of the annual ratios shows that after reaching a low of 19 percent in 1985, it increased slightly to an average of 20.3 percent during 1986–90, before declining to 17.3 percent in 1991.

10. It is more difficult to explain why the ratio of manufactured exports to output has fallen, despite growth of exports twice that of output. An examination of annual ratios shows that after falling to a low of 5 percent in 1987, the ratio increased to 7.5 percent in 1991.

References

Collier, Paul, and D. Lal. 1984. "Kenya: Why Poor People Get Rich, 1960–79." *World Development* 12(10):1007–18.

Crawford, E., and E. Thorbecke. 1978. *Employment, Income Distribution, Poverty Alleviation, and Basic Needs in Kenya.* Geneva:ILO.

Egerton University. 1992. *Proceedings of Conference on Maize Supply and Marketing under Market Liberalization.* Nairobi, Kenya.

Mosley, Paul. 1991. "Kenya." In Paul Mosley, Jane Harrigan, and John Toyle, eds., *Aid and Power: The World Bank and Policy Based Lending.* London: Routledge.

Mwega, F.M., and Tony Killick. 1990. "Monetary Policy in Kenya, 1967–88." *East African Economic Review* 6(2).

World Bank–UNDP. 1993. *Kenya: Challenge of Promoting Exports.* Washington, D.C.: World Bank.

6

Nigeria: ownership abandoned

Rashid Faruqee

Nigeria took bold steps early on in a few key policy areas of its structural adjustment program—reforming the exchange rate, liberalizing trade, and abolishing commodity boards. Although devaluation was widely deemed a sign of weakness, the initial reforms devalued the naira by 66 percent. Import liberalization wiped out the biggest source of rents for the politically powerful. And the abolition of commodity boards executed with one stroke a crucial reform that took many adjusting countries several years to carry out.

Several factors made this impressive beginning possible. The military government could initiate the reforms without worrying about how they might hurt some groups. The reform tasks were formulated by a generally competent technical group after much preparation. And the political changes that were announced as the economic changes were made garnered acceptance of the reform.

The initial acceptance of Nigeria's structural adjustment program shows that able leadership and public debate and discussion can overcome domestic opposition to reform. Even at the start, some compromises were needed to put the program in place. After the initial announcement bang, affected groups mounted opposition—forcing reversals of the petroleum price increase and concessions on the tariff schedule—and the government lost its determination and ability to overcome political opposition and keep the reforms on track.

This political context of reform in Nigeria proved to be more complex than either the World Bank or the government expected. The complexities arose from two factors. First, some of the reforms reduced the income and rents of those who were expected to carry them out. Second, the political leadership, including the military, had a short-run outlook that foreclosed thinking about benefits in the medium and long run.

Nigeria's adjustment program, however incomplete, has produced clear positive results, although part of the outcome is also due to resource flows and some debt relief. The decline in GDP growth has been reversed: from –2 percent annually during 1980–86 to more than 5 percent during 1986–91. The ratio of investment to GDP, although still lower than in 1981–83, has improved since the crisis years. Nonoil exports grew in the early years of the adjustment program. Agricultural production responded more than manufacturing. But the outcomes in other areas are not as encouraging. Perhaps most important of all, stabilization has proven too elusive in Nigeria. And pursuing structural changes on several fronts simultaneously is all the more challenging when a vast cadre of civil servants is either unable or unwilling to manage the implementation of the reforms.

Obtaining the commitment to sustain reforms, rather than just launch them against political opposition, is much more difficult. Nigeria regressed in 1988 when mounting opposition to austerity measures gathered momentum and unnerved the political leadership. Another serious attempt to put the reform program back on track in 1989 could not be sustained because of mounting political pressure and the new oil boom during the Gulf war. Part of the problem was that structural reform—to ensure a more efficient, diversified economy—would take more time than originally anticipated. And the supply response was slower than stipulated. The result: the government lost its determination and ability to overcome political opposition and keep the reforms on track.

The economy before the structural adjustment program

Since Nigeria's independence in 1960, the economy has been transformed from a subsistence agrarian society into a largely monetized economy—fueled particularly by the discovery and exploration of oil fields in the early 1970s. The transformation consists of three periods: 1973–78, 1979–83, and 1984–86, coinciding with an oil boom under military rule, an oil boom under civilian rule, and the Buhari regime (prior to Babanginda's takeover).

1973–78: an oil boom under military rule

The oil boom in the early 1970s had a pervasive effect on the growth and development of the economy. Oil quickly became the dominant sector of the economy, accounting for more than 90 percent of exports, and the main source of revenue. Between 1972 and 1974, federal revenue from oil increased fivefold, constituting 80 percent of total revenue. Oil revenue grew more modestly during the remainder of the period (1975–78), when OPEC rules required Nigeria to cut oil production. Nigeria's new wealth radically affected the scope and content of investment, production, and consumption patterns, the government's approach to economic management, and the policies and programs implemented. Federal expenditures increased rapidly, doubling between 1973 and 1974, and again between 1974 and 1975. Much of this increase in government expenditures went to investment. Measured at 1984 prices, the share of investment in GDP increased from less than 12 percent in 1971 to more than 25 percent in 1977.

The growth in oil revenue was absorbed largely by public sector spending, particularly on the infrastructure. The increase in public expenditures went largely to improving transportation and social services, in part to ameliorate the effects of the 1969 civil war. Transportation facilities, especially roads and ports, were expanded significantly, as were educational opportunities (the primary school enrollment doubled from 35 percent in the early 1970s to 70 percent in the latter part of the decade). Yet many public projects were undertaken without the requisite analysis of their long-term financial viability and the efficiency with which such projects were implemented in the past.

The rapid growth of the public sector—and the construction boom that accompanied the massive investment program—altered the prevailing pattern of relative prices and wages and changed the underlying structure of the economy. High wage and price increases secured the resources needed to accommodate the demand in nontraded goods, but they depressed the nonoil traded goods sectors. An exchange rate policy that allowed the naira to appreciate with rising oil revenues in combination with rising domestic costs meant a sharp deterioration in international competitiveness. The negative impact of these policies on agriculture was particularly severe.

Notwithstanding a rapid increase in public expenditures, the growth in oil revenue was sufficient to maintain a federal budgetary surplus; yet in 1976, expenditures began to outpace revenue. State budgets also began to show deficits. And as expenditures of the federal government outpaced revenue, federal transfers to states declined from about 40 percent of federal revenues in 1973 to about 20 percent in 1979. Moreover, in the nontraded goods sector, wages were inflated to keep pace with the wages offered in the construction and service sectors. Meanwhile, the value of the real exchange rate increased by more than 100 percent from 1973 to 1978. As the naira appreciated with the growth in oil revenue, exports were placed at a particular disadvantage.

The foreign exchange generated by oil revenue was used to increase the supply of tradables. Yet the demand for imports was greater than could be supported solely by oil earnings, and Nigeria borrowed significantly during this period to purchase overseas goods (an average annual external borrowing of about $570 million). Economic problems began to surface in

1978, but a second oil boom in 1979 lent confidence that oil revenue would in fact be a sound basis for planning and sustaining public sector consumption and investment.

1979–83: an oil boom followed by a crisis under civilian rule

The second oil revenue boom coincided with civilian government under President Seghari. Yet the economic problems that had begun to surface in 1978 continued in other ways. In 1980–81 the terms of trade, which had remained relatively constant through 1979, doubled from their 1976 level (figure 6.1). And record oil revenue prompted the government to increase public expenditures—leading eventually to a deficit in 1980. Overall growth in GDP was only 4.2 percent in 1980. Agricultural GDP grew by 6.4 and industrial GDP by 7.3 percent, but petroleum sector GDP declined by 11.6 percent. Moreover, exports fell by 9.5 percent, while imports grew by 27.2 percent. In 1981 oil prices fell precipitously. Thus, severe terms of trade variations led to extraordinary fluctuations in real income. Whereas real income had increased by 200 percent between 1972 and 1980, it had declined by almost 60 percent by 1983 from its 1980 peak level. Because the oil boom could not generate enough revenue to keep pace with public expenditures and real income declined, the government was forced to run a budget deficit and increase its borrowing. By 1983 the federal budget deficit amounted to 12 percent of GDP.

The government financed its external and fiscal imbalances by incurring debt, depleting international reserves, and going into arrears in external payments. Yet the prevailing view of the Seghari government was that the

Figure 6.1 Terms of trade shock, 1976–91

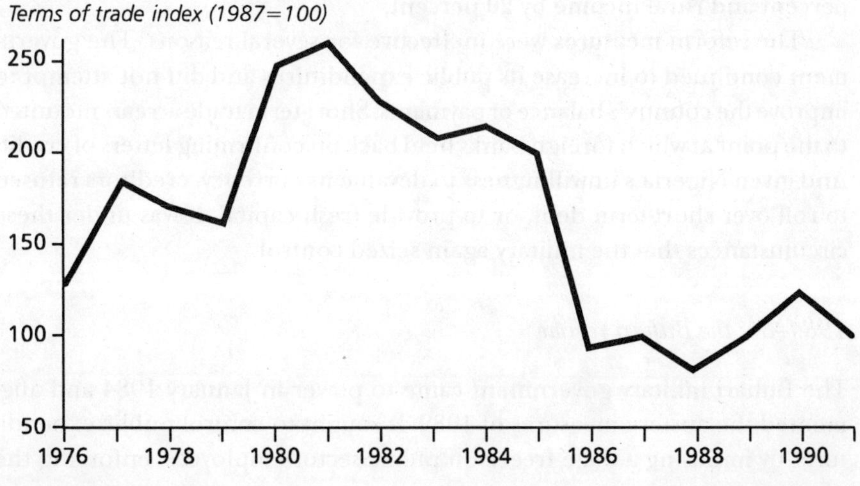

Terms of trade index (1987=100)

250
200
150
100
50
1976 1978 1980 1982 1984 1986 1988 1990

Source: World Bank data.

downturn was temporary and that maintaining a high level of investment with foreign borrowing was justified. Unfortunately for Nigeria, real world interest rates turned positive when its terms of trade started to deteriorate. Because additional debt could be contracted only at variable interest rates and at shorter maturities, credit conditions became harsher. In the early 1980s, real interest rates reached 20 percent. Given the poor rates of return on investment in Nigeria (as proxied by the negative GDP growth rate in that period), Nigeria clearly undertook excessive external borrowing.

Despite the precipitous drop in oil revenues, the real exchange rate continued to appreciate. Although the naira depreciated by 27 percent against the U.S. dollar between 1981 and 1983, the nominal effective appreciation rate was 12 percent—increasing the appreciation rate to about 40 percent in real terms. Because the distorted exchange rate prevented the government from allocating resources efficiently to purchase imports, it established several measures and stringent trade controls in the Economic Stabilization Act of 1982. Among the measures were the rationing of foreign exchange, a restriction on import licenses, an increase in duties, and the initiation of an import deposit program. Public investment was also cut drastically, and gasoline prices and tariffs were increased.

Despite the austere measures, the economy reached a crisis in 1983–84 when oil prices declined precipitously by 45 percent from their 1980 level. The GDP growth rate in 1983 was –6.7 percent; nonoil sector growth fell to –9.3 percent and petroleum sector growth to –2.5 percent. External and fiscal imbalances emerged. The external current account deficit grew to 6 percent of GDP in 1983, and Nigeria's indebtedness impeded its access to foreign capital. The budget-deficit-to-GDP ratio reached 13 percent in 1983. By 1983 per capita private consumption in real terms was 20 percent below its 1978–79 level. Between 1980 and 1984, urban income declined by 34 percent and rural income by 20 percent.

The reform measures were ineffective for several reasons. The government continued to increase its public expenditures and did not attempt to improve the country's balance of payments. Short-term trade arrears mounted to the point at which foreign banks held back on confirming letters of credit. And given Nigeria's unwillingness to devalue its currency, creditors refused to roll over short-term debt, or to provide fresh capital. It was under these circumstances that the military again seized control.

1984–86: the Buhari regime

The Buhari military government came to power in January 1984 and augmented the austere measures of 1982. It sought to control public expenditures by imposing a wage freeze on public sector employees, enforcing the redundancy of a large number of civil servants, and requiring user fees in the education and health sectors. These measures made a dent in Nigeria's budget deficit, which declined from 13 percent of GDP in 1983 to about 3 percent in 1984. Yet the Buhari regime continued to fund inefficient parastatals, while cutting funds for maintaining infrastructure and equipment.

The decline in public expenditures had its severest impact on the construction and service sectors, but employment and production also declined sharply in most other sectors of the economy. Capacity utilization declined and plant closures were widespread as the access of the import-dependent industrial sector to imported inputs was sharply curtailed. Imports declined by 22.7 percent in 1984; nonoil exports declined by 44.2 percent.

Accompanying the declines in imports and exports was a significant rise in domestic prices and an increase in inflation to 40 percent. Domestic savings and investment also declined; investment fell to 12 percent of GDP, down from 24 percent in 1981. Private investment suffered a more drastic decline, accounting for only 25 percent of total investment in 1985, compared with 50 percent in the 1970s. External debt service requirements on private debt and rescheduled arrears reached 34 percent of exports of goods and nonfactor services in 1985—tripling debt service requirements from the 1982 level.

By 1985 the distortions in the economy were pervasive and serious. The exchange rate was grossly overvalued, and despite the oil revenue boom, the budget deficit again rose to an average of 7 percent between 1980 and 1985. Moreover, despite efforts to control the budget deficit, public sector funding again burgeoned, and the number and size of public enterprises increased sharply. Some of the reforms introduced by the Buhari regime did not include fundamental structural changes that were necessary—particularly the devaluation of the naira, import liberalization, and key reforms proposed by the World Bank and the IMF. More specifically, the government chose not to privatize public enterprises, as had been suggested by the World Bank and the IMF, and rather than rationalize the import regime, it made import controls more stringent. Significant differences thus emerged between the Nigerian government and its creditors, especially the World Bank and the IMF.

In August 1985 the Babangida government came to power and, spurred by another precipitous drop in oil prices, proclaimed a fifteen-month period of national economic emergency as of October 1985. By 1986 the terms of trade had plummeted in the face of the decline in the real price of oil, representing only 35 percent of their 1980 level. Furthermore, without proper accommodation to multilateral lending institutions, the prospects for further credit were bleak. These events set the stage for the structural adjustment program.

Origin, design, and implementation of the structural adjustment program

One of the measures initiated by the Babangida government was a national debate about whether Nigeria should implement the policy reforms necessary to secure IMF support. The debate was ostensibly to build political legitimacy by showing the willingness of the new government to eschew the authoritarian approach of the previous regime. It was coordinated by government representatives, universities, the central bank, and the civil service.

Yet the debate clearly indicated strong opposition to the policy reforms required by the IMF. In particular, the business community was concerned that trade liberalization would prevent it from competing with imports. Others were skeptical that the IMF funds would be used for their intended purpose. And nationalistic forces opposed the imposition of reform measures by an external entity—particularly devaluing the naira.

The Babangida government accepted the outcome of the national debate by rejecting the IMF loan. Yet the government seemed willing to compromise by expressing its intention to undertake a structural reform process. In 1986 the Babangida government submitted a reform budget that contained a package of export incentives incorporating trade liberalization, but without a change in the import licensing system. The petroleum subsidy was reduced by 80 percent, and a commitment was made to privatization. Moreover, the government had balanced the budget. Although an exchange rate adjustment was mentioned, the naira was not devalued; rather, a levy was imposed on imports.

Nigeria's creditors, and the World Bank and the IMF, did not accept the package of reforms in the absence of devaluation measures. Thus, in August 1986 the government announced its structural adjustment program, whose central feature was a two-tier system to devalue the naira. Consistent with its previous stance, the government did not accept an IMF loan. Meanwhile, the World Bank and the London and Paris Clubs agreed to new loans and the rescheduling of old debt.

Several factors propelled structural adjustment and devaluation. First, Nigeria's plummeting oil revenue was jeopardizing the country's economic stability, and devaluation would boost the government's naira revenue in the short term. Second, given Nigeria's precarious relationship with its creditors, debt reschedulings would be acceptable to its creditors only under conditions defined clearly in an adjustment program. Third, Nigerian policymakers were becoming increasingly aware that the state intervention approach was not an effective development strategy. And fourth, a core group of leaders was persuaded that a new development strategy—one that turned away from government-led growth—was now most desirable. Too, people accepted interim hardship from the austerity program in the hope that broadly based political reforms would create a more equitable distribution of growth benefits at the end of the interim austerity—and, in so doing, preclude the corruption that had marked earlier regimes.

Declaring its intention to make a transition to civilian rule, the Babangida government had to retain the support of the military, which would be affected adversely by both the transition to civilian rule and the devaluation of the naira because it was a large net importer and had access to goods subsidized by the government. The Babangida government reportedly obtained the military's support by granting it exceptions to alleviate some of the impacts of the structural adjustment program. Moreover, the Babangida government had eliminated one of the main points of concern—the appearance of outside interference.

The structural adjustment program began in July 1986 and originally was to end in June 1988. The government, however, reaffirmed its commitment to continue to pursue the basic elements of the structural adjustment program until the program's objectives were fully attained.

Ceding ownership

The Babangida government shrewdly distinguished between borrowing from the IMF and initiating an economic reform program. It thus created general support for a program that was "made in Nigeria by Nigerians," a source of national pride that the program was not dictated by outside agencies. The overall design of the adjustment program was comprehensive, stressing the key reforms required to correct serious distortions or problems in the exchange rate, fiscal performance and monetary policy, trade policies, price regulation, and parastatal performance.

Although implementation started well, it soon slackened, and even regressed. Political factors, interacting with fluctuating oil revenue, contributed to this phenomenon. Fluctuations in the oil revenue (due to changes in the oil prices) not only had a direct effect on economic outcomes, such as growth, but also had an indirect effect through influencing economic reform policies. As noted earlier, when oil revenue booms took place before (under both military and civilian rules), the government pursued expansionary policies. Similarly, after 1986 the fluctuating oil revenue had some effect on how the reform program was pursued. The implementation record can be broken into four distinct phases.

July 1986 to December 1987. During the initial period, crucial reforms were implemented fairly effectively. In one stroke the naira was devalued, the import licensing system was eliminated, and the commodity boards were abolished. Several institutional and political factors contributed to this initial reform momentum: a highly centralized institutional set-up and extensive preparation, which permitted coordination by a small, relatively unified and technically competent economic team; the absence of phase-in periods, and the government's strong posture; and the public's acceptance of the close link between economic and political reforms.

January 1988 to early 1989. In January 1988 the program stalled, and in some areas, such as controls on the budget deficit and the growth of money supply, it even regressed. This stall in implementation was due to several factors: acceptance of moderate inflation to stimulate growth, apprehension over growing labor and student unrest, and rising food prices. Fiscal and monetary discipline also fell apart. Among other things, the government proposed a $600 million reflationary fund, lower (regulated) interest rates, and backing away from a proposed petroleum price increase.

Early 1989 to May 1989. Beginning in early 1989, the Bretton Woods institutions pressured the government into returning to tighter fiscal and monetary policies in the 1989 budget. Yet by now, rent-seeking interest groups, who lost out during the initial period of the structural adjustment program, had resurfaced and undermined the reform process. For example, the closure of several inefficient industries prompted the Manufacturing Association of Nigeria to seek and obtain greater protection. The government also lost much ground on trade liberalization to large agricultural interests by increasing the number of items under import bans. Too, the government fell prey to political pressure to increase public spending, and resorted to extrabudgetary spending. And economic and political reforms were no longer mutually supportive. In fact, in May 1989 Nigeria experienced serious riots against the structural adjustment program.

June 1989 to the end of 1992. By June 1989 the government was focusing more on political reforms than on economic reforms. Consequently, the quality and consistency of economic policymaking declined markedly. The last phase of the implementation coincided with the oil boom from the Gulf crisis of 1990–91. The government totally yielded to political pressures, and despite repeated official pronouncements that it would continue with reforms, it could not sustain the original objectives of the structural adjustment program and instead implemented ad hoc policies to meet short-term expenditures. The most serious issues were unrestrained public spending and irresponsible fiscal behavior. For example, the recent incremental revenue from higher oil prices was spent on major investment projects or on political transition programs—all outside established budgetary procedures and often in the absence of transparency. Overall, since 1990 the government has fallen even further behind in implementing the reform program set out under the structural adjustment program.

Key elements of the structural adjustment program of 1986

But what was the design of the structural adjustment program of 1986? The centerpiece was a market-based exchange rate and liberalization of trade—removing most import bans, developing a new tariff schedule, and implementing policies to increase export growth. The structural adjustment program and the supporting World Bank loan helped finance the foreign exchange gap that had accumulated in 1986–87 from the decline in oil revenue. The World Bank made a Trade Policy and Export Development Loan of $452 million, and the IMF approved a standby arrangement of SDR 650 million, although the drawings were made under this facility. Also, additional financial assistance in the form of dept reschedulings and new money from the Paris and London Clubs accompanied adoption of the structural adjustment program. Appendix 6A provides a formal summary of the main elements of the structural adjustment program. Here they can be highlighted as follows:

- The adoption of tight fiscal and monetary policies to reduce inflationary pressures and to rationalize public expenditures, including public investment programs.
- The dismantling of exchange controls and the adoption of a market-determined exchange rate policy.
- The liberalization of the trade regime, the rationalization of customs tariffs and excise duties, and the abolition of price controls.
- Financial sector reforms.
- The privatization and commercialization of public enterprises and the abolition of marketing boards.

Macroeconomic policy reform: design and implementation

Fiscal policy and management

Fiscal management and public expenditure reforms. The government's fiscal policy and public expenditure reforms were a critical element of the adjustment program. The structural adjustment program called for reducing the relative size of the public sector and reallocating public expenditures toward infrastructure and human resources. Federal budget deficits were to be brought below 4 percent of GDP by 1988, focusing particularly on reducing civil service wage employment and limiting transfers to parastatals. The structural adjustment program sought to rationalize budgetary processes, particularly the systems for renewing budget proposals and monitoring and accounting of expenditures. Economic appraisal was also to be used to determine public investment programs, and funding priority went to projects with proven financial viability and low completion costs (discussed later).

IMPLEMENTATION. In 1986 the government closed its deficit, largely because devaluation increased naira-denominated oil revenue. The inflow of funds from multilateral institutions and other creditors alleviated some of the pressure on the budget, albeit temporarily. Yet recurrent expenditures exceeded budgeted expenditures, and attempts to control expenditures were of little consequence.

To address the impact of the structural adjustment program on the populace, the government introduced a reflationary budget for 1988. Among the new expenditures were transit subsidies, meal subsidies, and training for civil servants. Total spending increased by more than 30 percent, and the 1988 budget led to a deficit of 11.4 percent of GDP. Rapid inflation ensued, forcing the curtailment of budgetary releases in mid-1988. Not only was the reflationary budget of 1988 the first major policy backslide but it also undermined progress in other areas of reform.

The 1989 budget attempted to get back on course by imposing strict limits on expenditures. However, demonstrations and riots in opposition to the structural adjustment program prompted the government to make some extrabudgetary concessions—raising the minimum wage, unfreezing wages in the civil service, and removing the ban on civil service recruitment. Despite these expenditures, the budget deficit declined dramatically as the currency depreciated and the government received a naira windfall. In 1990 fiscal discipline broke down once more as the government renewed extrabudgetary spending. Moreover, established budgetary procedures were bypassed, and the strategic planning processes that had been established under the structural adjustment program were largely ignored. Of major concern was the expenditure of oil revenue without any apparent budgetary authorization. Fiscal indiscipline persisted into 1991.

ASSESSMENT. Public expenditure management has been ineffective for several reasons. Spending decisions and the rationale for spending patterns have lacked transparency, and the government yields too easily to pressure for greater spending, even when it recognizes the undesirability of doing so. The commitment to fiscal discipline and adherence to rules and established procedures seem to be weak or irregular. The government also continues to emphasize capital-intensive projects whose economic justification is highly uncertain. But also crucial is that it has not yet devised a strategy for making an effective macroeconomic response to the major peaks and troughs in government revenue from oil.

Public investment program reform. In mid-1985 the Projects Review Committee of the government of Nigeria made candid recommendations (in the "Onosode Report") for undertaking strategic planning in the public capital investment program based on quantifiable economic criteria. The report went on to suggest that existing projects be completed and that all new investments cease, given the absence of strong evidence of their technical and financial effectiveness. The structural adjustment program subsequently incorporated requirements that proposed public investments be documented properly to enable the government to determine their economic rate of return. As another measure, the adjustment program introduced a three-year rolling plan for public investment for the period 1990–92, which seeks to make the scope and content of investment projects conform to efficiency considerations.

The rolling plan requires that projects be approved before any expenditures can be incurred. On paper the plan prioritizes "core" projects and identifies a set of "noncore" investment projects that should not be funded in the absence of available resources. In reality, the structural adjustment program still failed to rationalize the public investment program: costs and benefits and alternative financing strategies were not tested; foreign financing sources for projects did not seem to have the same opportunity costs as domestic budgetary revenues; and the practice of ad hoc, off-budget provisioning for major projects continued. A review of the current plan shows a serious anomaly between project costs and financing sources. The core investment program includes at least a dozen import-intensive megaprojects that will require resources beyond the government's capacity. As detailed in box 6.1, the government has continued to pay as it earns for large federal, ongoing and planned projects and programs.

Tax reform. The structural adjustment program did not initially incorporate specific tax reform measures, but rather stressed the need for institutional, administrative, and structural changes in the tax system to realize the potential of Nigeria's nonoil revenue sources. In particular, it called for addressing the present disposition of taxation between the federal and state governments, and the consequent fragmentation and inefficiency of tax administration. The World Bank collaborated with the government to study the policy and administration of direct taxation and recommended simplifying and limiting the progressivity of the income tax rate, the structure of allowances and exemptions, the corporate income tax rate, and the structure of the federal taxation revenue department.

The structural adjustment program reduced the corporate income tax rate, improved tax collection procedures by introducing withholding taxes on interest income, and rationalized dividend taxation. The federal inland revenue department has also been reorganized to emphasize functional planning and to improve computerized capacity, and a series of international tax treaties have been signed.

Assessment of fiscal reforms. Overall, the *design* of fiscal policy and management reforms was sound; reform objectives have often been reflected in government budgetary documents. Yet the government has not consistently controlled budget deficits (table 6.1). Much of its lackluster performance stems from the reflationary budget of 1988, when the government attempted to appease opposition to the structural adjustment program by compromising on extrabudgetary expenditures. This lapse quickly undermined progress

Box 6.1 Irresponsible public investment

The following is a summary of observations drawn from the World Bank's public expenditure management report on projects and programs in the federal government investment portfolio.

Agriculture. The allocation in the 1992 budget for *fertilizer,* the largest item in the capital allocation for the Ministry of Agriculture, is N 0.6 billion, but the actual total procurement cost is estimated at N 3.4 billion, and extrabudgetary allocations will be required. Of the eleven ongoing *large-scale irrigation projects,* for which N 181 million has been allocated, only three, representing N 63 million of the allocation, are deemed viable. *Public grain storage facilities,* a component of the Federal Strategic Grain Reserve Program costing N 1.6 billion, are not fulfilling the goal of stabilizing food prices and enhancing the food security of the poor. Under capital supplementation N 150 million has been set aside for project execution by a newly established agency, the *National Agricultural Land Development Authority (NALDA),* whose mandate is to address the chronic problems of underutilized farm land and rural labor and the high cost of land development. This mandate duplicates the activities of other agencies.

Water supply. The *National Water Rehabilitation Fund Project* is supported by a World Bank loan in the amount of $240 million and requires an estimated N 5 million per year in counterpart funds from the government until 1996. Each year, however, federal contributions have been inadequate—N 3 million in 1992 and N 4 million in 1991—representing a possible widespread external financing problem. The River Basin Development Authority's *borehole programs* are performing poorly.

Oil and gas sector. The total investment planned for the 1991–95 period would require about $20 billion, with almost $13.5 billion to cover joint ventures. Several large projects do not have specific allocations in the plan document, but are funded from extrabudgetary sources. The Nigerian National Petroleum Corporation's *Pipeline Phase III* project ($550 million) is uneconomic and should be abandoned. Rehabilitation of existing refineries, such as Warri, Port Harcourt, and Kaduna, are high-priority but underfunded. The NNPC estimates in other areas. Although the government has implemented several potentially useful reforms in public expenditure programming (a system for centralized oversight has been established and a rolling plan introduced in principle), these procedural changes have seemingly had little effect on actual budgeting practices and outcomes. Spending outside the budget or circumventing established procedures continues to resemble pre-adjustment spending patterns.

Several factors account for the persistently ineffective fiscal policy management under the structural adjustment program. One is that large projects continue to be financed outside the budgetary process, and public enterprises are not brought under the review of the budget and its discipline. For ex-

the cost of constructing a new *export terminal* for the second Port Harcourt refinery at $340 million, which World Bank staff estimate could be cut by two-thirds. Construction of this terminal would not be well timed as output from the new Port Harcourt refinery would need to be diverted to the domestic market due to inefficient operation of other refineries. The oversized $1.14 billion project *Petrochemicals Phase II* is economical only on a sunk-cost basis. There is no budgetary allocation for this project even though expenditures are being incurred each year. The doubtful economic viability of the *liquid natural gas project,* originally estimated to cost about $2.5 billion, is fast approaching $4 billion due to delays in signing agreements with purchasers. This project also has no capital allocation in the federal budget.

Power. Installed capacity is about 5,600 megawatts; however, only 2,700 megawatts are available. No new investment is required until at least 1995, yet the Nigerian Electric Power Authority is planning to construct a new generating plant in 1994, a 300-megawatt gas turbine plant at Geregu at a cost of $135 million. NEPA's current investment program is about $300 million per year—too large given its financial condition and the sector's investment requirements.

Steel. The Ajaokuta steel plant had already cost more than $3 billion by the end of 1990, and capital costs are expected to be four times higher than those of new, competitive plants.

Aluminum. Initial estimates placed the capital costs of the aluminum smelter project at Ikot Abasi at $1.2 billion, making this project 60 percent more costly than comparable projects elsewhere in the world. The government had already expended $450 million by early 1991.

Abuja. The federal budget allocation for the new capital in 1991 was N 345 million and in 1992 N 465 million—both unlikely reflections of actual expenditures. The government has not assessed its plan to transfer to Abuja; nor has it identified priority expenditures or completed ongoing projects before undertaking new investments.

ample, the Nigerian National Petroleum Corporation operates as a parastatal outside of federal budget review procedures, and accountability is absent. Large losses by parastatals, which have been reluctant to increase user fees, have contributed to larger fiscal deficits. Similarly, the impact of reforms on public investment programs has been negligible, and returns on public investment have been poor. Most large-scale capital projects have not been cost-effective, due to such factors as inappropriate technology (and often location), long delays in completion, and overcharging by foreign suppliers or contractors. Inefficiency is most evident in the Ajaokuta steel complex—it will be a net loser of foreign exchange even on a sunk-cost basis. These two factors—the absence of accountability and poorly informed investment—are crowding out investment in the private sector.

The government's effort to achieve fiscal stability by smoothing fiscal spending during the peaks and troughs of oil revenue and sterilizing money supply increases from higher oil revenues has been unsuccessful. Tight fiscal and monetary policies were pursued. However, stabilization efforts were impeded in 1990, when the government initially kept windfall oil revenues in its stabilization account but later spent the naira counterpart funds. Inflation increased in the first part of 1991 by more than 30 percent on an annual basis. Thus, the government has continued the weak stabilization efforts made by previous administrations in the face of windfalls.

Another problem has been the inadequate capacity of the civil service to implement fiscal policy reforms. Despite the 1988 civil service reforms to improve accountability and managerial efficiency, the civil service consists of a large tier of lower-level employees and a small layer of senior-level staff overburdened by the requirements of reform. Moreover, salaries did not keep pace with the fivefold increase in prices from 1982 to 1990.

Finally, the excessive debt burden has aggravated fiscal management. Nigeria must pay roughly 5 percent of its GDP as debt service—one of the highest shares among developing countries. These debt service obligations exacerbate fiscal indiscipline and excessive spending. In fact, the primary balance

Table 6.1 Selected macroeconomic indicators, 1980–91

Indicator	*1980–85 (average)*	*1985*	*1986*	*1987*	*1988*	*1989*	*1990*	*1991*
Budget deficit as a share of nominal GDP (percent)	-7.0	..	-6.8	-8.3	-7.6	-4.6	-2.8	-6.0
Real interest rate	-3.0	..	10.7	-37.0	-8.3	-33.6	1.9	2.4
Index of real effective exchange rate[a]	..	167.8	91.6	29.3	34.8	31.0	28.7	24.2

.. Not available.
a. 1980 = 100.
Source: World Bank data; IMF, *International Financial Statistics.*

from 1986 to 1991 averaged about 3 percent, against an overall balance of –6 percent. This debt obligation, along with excessive spending in some areas, led to deficit financing and necessitated cuts in high-priority expenditures—such as the infrastructure and social services.

Monetary policy

Reform. Since Independence, Nigeria has gained rather significant financial depth. Its financial system has become relatively more developed than those in most developing countries, consisting of more than 110 commercial and merchant banks, several financial institutions, more than 100 insurance companies, nearly 1,000 pension funds, 7 stock exchanges, and several specialized financial institutions. In response to an M2-to-GDP ratio that had increased from 9 percent to 23 percent between 1960 and 1990, the structural adjustment program included tight monetary policies to control wage and price pressures from devaluation. One of the policies was to restrain domestic credit while also liberalizing interest rates. The structural adjustment program sought to develop more market-oriented financial systems to support resource mobilization and allocative efficiency.

Implementation. Monetary policy under the structural adjustment program has been uneven and generally ineffective. With the reflationary budget of 1988, the growth in money supply (39 percent) far exceeded the monetary target. In 1989, in the face of unabated inflationary pressures, the central bank again implemented strict monetary policies. The federal, state, and local governments and the parastatals were required to transfer their deposits from the banking system to the central bank, thereby causing a sharp drop in liquidity. M2 fell by 10 percent, and the required transfer of deposits had the desired impact on liquidity and prices. Overall, however, this stop-and-go monetary policy has been expansionary: from an average annual growth in broad money of 11 percent between 1981 and 1986, the rate of growth tripled between 1987 and 1991.

The unstable interest rates of the pre-adjustment period have continued (table 6.1). In August 1987 lending and deposit interest rates were deregulated, generating a dramatic decline in real rates, since nominal rates barely moved to compensate for inflation. Yet when tight monetary policy and a marked slowdown in inflation occurred in 1989, real deposit and lending rates became higher, creating political pressure to reinstitute controls for the advantage of selected borrowers. In January 1991 interest rates were again regulated. Yet even when interest rates have been deregulated, the central bank has encouraged banks to offer lower than market-determined rates. The expansion in money supply points to the absence of sufficiently tight monetary policy and lack of indirect monetary policy controls such as money markets and variable reserve ratios. Only in late 1989 did the central bank start the open-market tendering of treasury bills which led to a more market-oriented interest rate. Even when interest rates were deregulated, the central bank encouraged banks to offer lower than market-determined rates. This tinkering with the market limited the impact of interest rate policy, as has the government's unwillingness to allow interest rates on its debt to be subject to market forces.

The structural adjustment program also exercised monetary policy by imposing credit ceilings on individual banks. Moreover, sector-specific credit targets were reduced to two sectors: agriculture and manufacturing. Agriculture was to account for 10 percent of merchant bank loans and 15 percent of commercial bank loans. Meanwhile, the manufacturing sector was allocated 40 percent of merchant bank loans and 35 percent of commercial bank loans. At least 15 percent of bank loans were set aside for small-scale enterprises wholly owned by Nigerians.

Assessment. The structural adjustment program included appropriate monetary policies, yet their implementation has been poor. The post-1986 period has seen wide fluctuations in the supply of money, leading overall to an unprecedented expansion. Monetary policy was abandoned first in 1987–88, when the money supply increased by an average of 28 percent. Then, despite monetary controls that led to a slowdown of 10 percent in money supply growth in 1989, broad money increased by 40 percent in 1990. At this time the controls were abandoned—and the gap between the official and the parallel exchange rates widened. The monetary expansion has been due to the government's inability to sustain the sterilization of foreign exchange inflows while implementing its stabilization program. Too, the government's interest rate policy has been varied. Real interest rates have fluctuated since early on, due alternately to political pressures to regulate the rates and to monetary necessities to liberalize them. In January 1992 the government liberalized interest rates. The varied interest rate policy illustrates how the government has deviated from the structural adjustment path under political pressure. The government has also pursued various but inconsistent credit ceiling policies.

Exchange rate management

Reform. The focal point of the structural adjustment program was a market-determined foreign exchange rate. Prior to the structural adjustment program the demand for foreign exchange far exceeded the available supply, and the quantity of foreign exchange was subject to arbitrary rationing.

The structural adjustment program established a floating exchange rate mechanism tied to market-determined forces. The system was introduced in phases, and consisted of two tiers. The first tier was an officially administered rate, which applied to all public service transactions. The second-tier rate, applied to all other market transactions, was determined by auction—the second-tier foreign exchange market—under the aegis of the central bank and funded by oil revenue. The reform sought to curtail demand for imports, encourage capital inflows and nonoil exports, and eliminate the distortions imposed by the import licensing system—but above all to provide a realistic exchange rate for the domestic currency.

Implementation. When it was implemented in September 1986, the second-tier exchange rate system led to a 66 percent devaluation. In October the auction method was changed, and the amount of foreign currency available was increased. The naira appreciated by 45 percent. The exchange rate then remained stable for several months.

In July 1987 the market-determined (second-tier) exchange rate was unified with the official first-tier rate, and the second-tier foreign exchange market was replaced with the foreign exchange market; nonetheless, two separate exchange rates existed. Every two weeks, the central bank determined an auction rate for banks, the government, official foreign exchange dealers, and some importers. All other purchasers obtained foreign exchange at an interbank rate determined by market forces. In the latter half of 1987 the gap between the auction rate and the parallel market rate widened, reaching more than 50 percent by early 1988. Despite the growing gap between the official auction rate, which was an attempt to suppress depreciation, and the interbank market rate, which responded freely to market signals, both rates depreciated. The primary determinants were the rapid expansion of the money supply and the fiscal impact of the reflationary budget of 1988. Yet by early 1988, tighter fiscal and monetary policies helped reverse the trend.

Then in 1989 the government replaced the auction with the interbank foreign exchange market, allowing the central bank to determine the exchange rate on a daily basis. In the first quarter of 1991 both the auction and the interbank rates depreciated quite sharply, and the gap between the two widened considerably. The immediate cause was the higher public spending, which came as a result of pressures arising from a mini oil boom in 1990–91 that permitted a large increase in money supply. The central bank's role in the bidding process led to a brief appreciation in the nominal rate between late 1991 and early 1992, and the gap between the official rate (N 9.8 per U.S. dollar) and the parallel market rate (N 18.5 per U.S. dollar) widened. In March 1992 the central bank finally realized its goal—a uniform exchange rate system. Unification reduced the politically unpopular intervention in foreign exchange sales by the central bank.

Assessment. Exchange rate reform has been one of the most important achievements of Nigeria's program. What has been most remarkable is the sustained devaluation of the naira's external value between 1985 and 1992 (table 6.1). From 1988 to 1992, the quarterly average of the naira exchange rate per U.S. dollar depreciated by 27 percent, 58 percent, 61 percent, 67 percent, and 83 percent over the 1987 base period. Why is the depreciation so rapid, and to what extent has a realistic exchange rate been attained? The answer to the first question lies in the unmet demand for foreign exchange. The demand-supply gap expanded rapidly, from a mere $360 million in the first ten months of the second-tier foreign exchange market to $15 billion in 1989 and $17.5 billion in 1990. Much of this demand has been speculation, generated by the monetary expansion and the controlled interest rate policies. The dramatic decline in the exchange rate almost made it competitive, but intermittent efforts to regulate the exchange rate have caused it to deviate significantly at times from an equilibrium rate as reflected in the observed divergence between the official and the parallel market rates.

The crucial determinant of this continuous decline is the monetary policy. Contrary to structural adjustment program goals on paper, an expansionary money supply continued—banks failed to comply with credit limits, the government engaged in deficit financing, and further, it imposed a cap on interest rates, which encouraged the private sector to bid for foreign exchange with loan money. Overall, the exchange rate reform, although significant if compared with initial conditions, was undermined by a lack of consistency in implementation and by contradictory movement (or development) in other policies, such as increasing the fiscal deficit and putting a cap on interest rates.

Liberalization of international trade

Import reform. Prior to the structural adjustment program, trade policy consisted of quantitative import controls imposed by comprehensive licensing systems, and prohibitions. In an effort to create a business environment conducive to the efficient production and distribution of goods, the structural adjustment program liberalized trade. Several public sector trade corporations were abolished. As the second-tier foreign exchange market was introduced, import prohibitions were eased (the number of affected commodities was reduced from 74 to 16), and the import licensing system and the 30 percent import surcharge, introduced in January 1986, were abolished. Customs and excise tariffs were restructured so that the average unweighted nominal rate of protection fell from more than 33 percent to about 23 percent. Of course, producers were concerned that the new tariff structure would offer them less protection.

The 1988 government budget introduced a new tariff structure that provided a 28 percent average tariff level. While this level was higher than the level under the interim tariff schedule, it was still lower than the 33 percent level prior to the structural adjustment program. Yet the structural adjustment program did specify import duty rates for a seven-year period (1988–95), allowing producers and consumers to rely more confidently on a sustained tariff structure. And although the average tariff rate should increase marginally throughout the seven-year period, the overall tariff schedule exhibits less dispersion than the interim tariff, because it reduces intersectoral differences in tariff levels. Still, the structure of protection for trucks, metal and metal products, buses and automotive spare parts, cotton, textiles and yarn, and packaging materials has been fraught with anomalies.

Import implementation. The new tariff structure is operational, but the evasion of duties is fairly widespread. By unifying customs duties for producer inputs for all regions, the structural adjustment program has dominated the general concessionary duty rates for imports of certain inputs for selected categories of producers. Similarly, favorable duty exemptions for parastatals and the government have been curtailed. The new tariff regime has improved collection procedures for imports, thus generating greater revenue.

The structural adjustment program has also introduced an implicit landing charge into import duties, similar to the excise duty on comparable locally produced goods. Although the landing charge seeks to ensure that revenue taxation on consumption is protection-neutral, the charge is not always consistent with the excise duty and is not applied explicitly. Since import bans were curtailed in 1986, only minor changes have been made. In 1989 several items were exempted from the prohibitions, including cigarettes and jewelry, while others were added. Import duties on commercial vehicles were also reduced in 1989 and were subsequently eliminated altogether to allow low-income groups access to transportation.

Export reform. The structural adjustment program's export policy reforms sought to support growth and diversification of exports, particularly manufactured goods. To do so, it reformed the exchange rate system in an effort to promote exports, abolished most export bans, and introduced a duty drawback scheme.

Export implementation. The structural adjustment program sought primarily to increase nonoil exports. With the establishment of the second-tier foreign exchange market, exporters were allowed to retain 100 percent of their export earnings in the form of domiciliary accounts. As noted earlier, the foreign exchange market replaced the second-tier foreign exchange market, and in 1992 the exchange rates were unified and allowed to move freely according to market conditions. The massive devaluation of the naira increased the relative price of tradables, creating strong price incentives for exports. The government eliminated most export bans, abolished export licensing, removed export duties, and simplified export procedures. The six agricultural commodity boards that wielded monopoly power were abolished.

The duty drawback/suspension scheme was an important element of the government's export incentive plan. Duty drawbacks were granted to several manufacturing exporters, but verifying the import and export transactions has made implementing the scheme difficult. The central bank operates a refinancing and rediscounting facility that provides financial assistance to exporters. In 1988 it provided banks with more than N 500 million, largely to facilitate cocoa exports. Yet since 1988 prohibitions on certain crops and their derivatives have been reintroduced, either to avoid domestic shortages of these crops or to process them for export.

Assessment. Trade liberalization proceeded initially with little opposition. For example, the government was able to easily remove the import licensing system, because substantial abuses under the previous government had discredited the system. Similarly, irregularities with previous mechanisms for allocating foreign exchange discredited that system.

Yet the tariff structure was revised when some manufacturers expressed concern about the effect of the new trade regime on their import substitution enterprises. In the end, the government sought to give them greater protection from imports and imposed bans on several items that had previously been imported. The consolidated import prohibition list covered about 30 percent of agricultural and 20 percent of industrial products in 1989, targeting items produced domestically—including most food products, major grains, processed wood, textile fabrics, and vegetable oil. In December 1989 meat, chicken, and fish were added to the list.

Overall, trade and tariff policy reform has been inconsistent. Some reforms have stalled; others have even regressed. Import liberalization and the rationalization and harmonization of the tariff structure have not been fully realized. In particular, tariff rates have been modified frequently and have often incorporated landing charges, equivalent to excise duties on domestic products, thus compromising the transparency of the system. Excise duties and other import surcharges are changed at the discretion of the customs officials who collect them, which, according to one estimate, increased the average nominal rate of protection from 23 percent at the outset of the structural adjustment program to 28 percent in 1988 and to 45 percent in 1991.

Sectoral reform: design and implementation

Liberalization of domestic prices, markets, and trade

Reform. A key element of the structural adjustment program is price liberalization. Prior to the structural adjustment program, price distortions in agriculture were major determinants of the sharp decline in domestic and traditional export production.As a result, the six existing agricultural commodity boards were abolished in an effort to give private individuals, groups, companies, and processors access to the internal and external markets for all agricultural commodities. Also prior to the structural adjustment program, many manufacturing commodities were subject to price and distribution controls that were applied and enforced primarily at individual factories, enabling traders to absorb rents arising from the differential between the market price and the controlled price. In 1987 private enterprises were allowed to establish their own prices, thus taking these rents away from traders.

Implementation. The abolition of commodity boards was a bold step. Yet the government has maintained price controls on some goods produced by parastatals—most notably fertilizer and domestic petroleum and gas products. Furthermore, informal control mechanisms continue. In fact, the government has pressured some manufacturers and associations to roll back prices. The government has also continued to provide substantial subsidies for fertilizer and petroleum products—and has in fact increased them.

In 1988–89 restrictions on foreign ownership were relaxed significantly, and foreign investment activity is now permitted automatically for investments of more than N 20 million. The investment development coordination committee was established as a one-stop shop for foreign investment, facilitating the repatriation of profits. However, restrictions on foreign participation in selected sectors remain—garment manufacturing, radio and television set assembly, commercial transportation, and retail trading. Yet despite the greater freedom for foreign investment, investment growth is impeded by continued infrastructural deficiencies, government policy reversals, and uncertainty about the sustainability of adjustment under civilian rule at the end of 1992.

Assessment. Domestic agricultural trade and markets have been liberalized substantially, thus markedly improving the incentive system for agriculture. Yet progress in lifting restrictions on and abolishing subsidies in other markets remains far from satisfactory. For instance, the investment development coordination committee deals only with new enterprises, thus discriminating against existing enterprises that may be in a better position to undertake new investment. Moreover, foreign participation in insurance, mining, banking, and petroleum prospecting cannot be expanded above current levels. And the continued increased subsidies for fertilizer provide a lesson about how political forces and powerful interest groups can block or thwart reforms. For example, in northern Nigeria, which is the most prominent beneficiary of fertilizer subsidies, strong political forces have blocked any attempt to cut or abolish fertilizer subsidies.

Financial sector

Reform. The structural adjustment program did not initially address financial sector reforms. However, one of its goals was to establish a market-oriented financial system that would support the mobilization of financial savings and encourage the more efficient allocation of financial resources. The structural adjustment program thus called for reforming the old system of fixed credit allocations, subsidized and regulated interest rates for priority sectors, and term finance provided by development finance institutions.

Implementation. Not until 1988 did the government focus on the portfolio problems of the banking system, take measures to strengthen banking supervision, and carry out several portfolio audits. A deposit insurance system was then established in 1989, and in October 1990 new banking standards and tightened minimum capital requirements were introduced. New prudential regulations conforming to the evolving international standards became effective as of 1990.

Some of the most important banking system reforms were undertaken in 1991, including prudential regulations and accounting standards for banks. The central bank was also made more independent of the ministry of finance, and its supervisory capabilities were strengthened. The new prudential regulations should facilitate monitoring the financial status of banks more closely and weed out bad loans and financially inefficient banks.

Assessment. Because the reforms in the financial sector are relatively recent, it is difficult to assess their effectiveness and impact. Despite the reforms, Nigeria's financial system clearly continues to suffer serious problems. Fiscal policy is the root of the problems (constraining the positive effects of monetary policy), as is the government's inability to undertake stabilization measures to offset oil revenue shocks adequately. Equally problematic is the continuous noncommercial interference in the banking system: government agencies currently control or have a majority ownership in about 80 percent of commercial bank assets and 45 percent of merchant bank assets. Many traditional foreign banks are ceasing operations in Nigeria, and new foreign entrants into the market operate within a narrow niche. Only a few reputable international banks are reportedly able to provide high-quality banking services in Nigeria, and new banks are restricted from expanding their market share.

Public enterprise reform

Design. The structural adjustment program established four criteria in an effort to rationalize and commercialize public enterprises: (1) enterprises that can be fully operational on a commercial basis would be privatized; (2) those that can be partially privatized would no longer receive operating subsidies; (3) those that can be partially or fully commercialized but can continue to be owned by the government would be required to operate without government subventions; and (4) those that can be fully public entities would continue to receive public support, with user fees implemented as appropriate.

Implementation. After extensive preparatory work in 1988, the federal government of Nigeria issued a decree mandating the testing of 145 federal parastatals for full or partial privatization and commercialization. Some 111 enterprises were targeted for privatization by the end of 1991. By March 1992, 68 parastatals were fully or partially privatized.

The mode and scope of commercialization have varied widely. For example, although the Nigerian National Petroleum Corporation was commercialized, it is still subject to government-set fuel prices, and its investment decisions are still dictated by noneconomic criteria; its weak operational performance is manifest. Although the Nigerian Electric Power Authority has become a commercial enterprise, it still retains a monopoly on generation and distribution, and tariffs are set well below the supply cost. Moreover, metering and billing are inadequate, which reduces revenue by 25 percent. And Nigeria Telecommunications Limited is still struggling through the commercialization process. Although international tariffs have increased and contracted items have been opened up to international competition, other measures must be implemented to make the telecommunications sector fully commercialized.

The impact of the structural adjustment program on government financing of parastatals is difficult to ascertain precisely, because comprehensive information on government financial subsidies for public enterprises in the social, agricultural, and infrastructure sectors is absent. A large portion of government expenditures in these areas is at the state and local levels, where expenditure data are limited.

Assessment. The overall budgetary impact of the public enterprise reform program to date has been minimal. Government divestiture of its equity under its privatization program has been negligible thus far, and it is still too early to assess the efficiency gains of the reforms already implemented. The government has seldom used performance contracts, which can be of considerable value to clarify and to achieve the long-term goals of public enterprises that stay in the public sector.

Labor and wage policy

Reform. With few exceptions, the labor market in Nigeria operates without serious restrictions. The government interferes only by setting minimum wages in nominal terms. Yet the minimum wage has not been binding because market–clearing prices have been higher. Hence, the structural adjustment program did not include any explicit policy reforms on labor and wages. However, other policies have had an effect on labor and wages.

Implementation. The implementation of other adjustment policies seems to have had a favorable impact on employment. Export prices rose relative to wages, raising the demand for labor in that sector. The labor market responded with a decline in urban unemployment from 10 percent in the preadjustment period to 8 percent in March 1988. The decline reflected the growth of the informal sector and a migration of workers to the rural agricultural areas—consistent with emerging incentives and rural opportunities. Employment in the rural sector also improved slightly. Overall, unemployment fell from 6 percent in 1986 to 4 percent in 1989, but statistical evidence indicates that employment grew by slightly more than 3 percent annually after the inception of the program—a growth rate almost sufficient to absorb the growing number of workers in the labor force.

Real wages in Nigeria have declined since the early 1980s. By 1987 the index of rural and urban wages was less than half the 1980 level. In 1988 federal civil service wages increased by 27 percent—after having been frozen since 1982. The increase was quickly eroded by inflationary tendencies in 1988 and into the early part of 1989. Because private sector wages in urban areas usually follow public sector wages, most urban private sector wages have stayed the same in real terms during the adjustment period. A 1990 World Bank report indicates that since the inception of the structural adjustment program, rural wages have increased, but most urban wages, particularly those in the public sector, have remained stagnant or declined.

Social sector policies

Reform. Between 1975 and 1986 the health care sector expanded significantly. The number of doctors increased about fourfold, the number of hospital beds doubled, and the number of nurses and midwives tripled. But in the mid-1980s health care facilities began to deteriorate, and health care funding was curtailed severely, due to the decline in oil revenue. Moreover, a decline in available foreign exchange sharply curtailed drug imports. A similar trend beset education and water supply, with new capital spending coming to a halt. The adjustment policy was to increase the relative share of public expenditures on human resources in relation to commercially oriented activities. In the later adjustment period, the government sought to minimize the negative social consequences of the adjustment by providing employment programs in the public sector, transport subsidies, and special allowances for civil servants. But these efforts have been largely ad hoc and not well designed.

Implementation. As health care resources have declined, so too have the quality and availability of services; in response, individuals and families have bypassed the public health system. Likewise, the education system now faces deteriorating facilities, a shortage of instructional materials, and high pupil-teacher ratios.

State and local governments are responsible for providing primary and secondary health care. For state-level budgets, the depreciation of the exchange rate meant that they received a higher share of naira earnings from the federal government, whose naira revenue rose after the new foreign exchange regime was introduced. A new system for allocating oil revenue among the federal, state, and local governments has recently been implemented—a system that will provide more resources to the states. The additional funds available to the states should help them to restore some of the social sector programs and services.

Assessment. The government wanted to protect the relative size of social expenditures, particularly in health and education, although this was not explicitly included in the declared policy goals of the structural adjustment program. The government was not quite successful. In 1988 the share of total public expenditures for education was only about one-half its share in 1980 (UNDP and World Bank, *African Development Indicators,* 1992), and its share during the structural adjustment program is smaller than in the pre-adjustment crisis period. As a share of total federal expenditures, health care fares somewhat better—remaining at about 2 percent from the mid-1980s to 1990.

Furthermore, the adverse effect of the fiscal indiscipline was compounded by the federal government's recent shift of responsibilities to lower levels of government. In theory this move is desirable: government can respond more effectively at the local level to the health and education needs of the people. But responsibilities were decentralized with little preparatory time for the local levels to assimilate and delegate their new responsibilities. With the

With the recent change in oil-revenue sharing that will provide more funds to state and local government, social service entities should be able to discharge their responsibilities more efficiently.

Outcomes of the structural adjustment program

Macroeconomic reform

Nigeria's adjustment program had a positive impact on aggregate output. By 1988 output rebounded from its limited 2 percent growth in 1986 to growth at almost 9 percent, spurred primarily by an increase in agricultural production. Between 1989 and 1991 overall GDP growth averaged 5.8 percent annually, dominated by the oil sector. Three key factors explain the robust growth of GDP while the progress of reform has generally been unsatisfactory. First, oil production and exports are not affected by public sector inefficiency and other policy distortions. Second, the private sector, especially the agricultural sector, has performed well, partly because some key reforms have vastly improved the incentive structure and partly because some regulations have not been enforced and distortions have not materially affected the private sector and agriculture. Third, capital has been used more efficiently and investment has increased somewhat.

Outcomes according to other macroeconomic indicators are not as impressive and generally reflect inconsistent, stop-and-go progress in the reform program. The fiscal and monetary restraint envisaged by the structural adjustment program was pursued at the outset, creating low inflation in 1986 (6 percent, due also to a good harvest and low food prices) and a moderate 11 percent inflation in the following year. But the reflationary budget of 1988 was the turning point, and inflation soared. Although some monetary contraction policies were pursued in 1989, their effect was shortlived. Overall, the structural adjustment program has not yet fully stabilized the growth of money aggregates and prices.

Nigeria's exports are still dominated by oil, despite strong policies to achieve broader growth and diversification. Between 1986 and 1988 oil export revenue remained steady. In 1989 oil export revenue increased, and a further windfall occurred in 1990. Nonoil exports increased early on, but fell back to 1985 levels and remained constant between 1989 and 1991. As a result of demand management policies tightening imports and some recovery in oil exports, improvements in the balance of payments first appeared in 1989, and the current account was balanced for the first time since 1980. In 1990 the Gulf war led to higher oil prices, further improving the balance of payments and creating the largest surplus in the current account. Yet the surplus could not be sustained in 1991, because of a once again increased budget deficit and rapid growth of money supply, along with receding oil prices after the Gulf war; the overall balance of payments deficit increased fourfold from its 1990 level.

Nigeria borrowed heavily during the oil boom, but it also continued to do so thereafter, in order to compensate for declining oil revenue. Nigeria's debt was mostly nonconcessional, with expensive servicing costs in the face of rising interest rates. Nigeria's large debt overhang was a challenge to the structural adjustment program. Consequently, debts were rescheduled and some debts were reduced: with the limited amount of net borrowing, progress has been made toward consolidating debt and resolving all service arrears.

Aggregate output. Evidence suggests that the structural adjustment program had a significantly positive impact on aggregate output (table 6.2). Because the structural adjustment program was implemented in the last quarter of 1986, the observed growth in 1986 was limited—only about 2 percent of GDP in real terms. In 1987 a decline in crude oil output and weather-induced declines in agricultural production masked the positive effects of the structural adjustment program, and GDP remained more or less at the same level that year. In 1988 output rebounded, and GDP grew by nearly 10 percent. This growth was led by the spurt in agricultural production, which will be reviewed later. Higher producer prices prevailed for the traditional export crops. The decline in nonoil, nonagricultural output of 15 percent from 1982 to 1986 was partially recouped during the 1987–89 period. Between 1989 and 1991, overall GDP growth averaged 5.8 percent each year, dominated by the oil sector. The provisional estimate for GDP growth in 1992 is 4.6 percent.

Table 6.2 Real growth of GDP, 1980–91
(percent)

Year	*Rate of growth*
1980	4.2
1981	-10.7
1982	-0.8
1983	-6.7
1984	-4.3
1985	9.3
1986	1.7
1987	-0.2
1988	9.8
1989	6.7
1990	5.6
1991	5.1
Average, 1980–85	-2.6
Average, 1986–91	5.4

Source: World Bank data.

The 5.5 percent growth in GDP calls into question how the economy could attain this rate despite its uneven, lackluster reform performance. Three explanations stand out. First, as noted earlier, the pre-adjustment crisis period coincided with a precipitous decline in oil revenue, and growth during the adjustment period was due largely to the recovery of oil production and revenue—as was true of the high rate of GDP growth after 1989. Of note here is that oil production and exports are managed quite efficiently by the oil enterprise; similar efficiency in oil revenue management seems to be absent.

Second, although major components of the reform program faltered, key reforms (such as the exchange rate regime) allowed the private sector, especially smallholder agriculture, to flourish. A review of the sectoral outcomes (presented later) suggests that the reforms had a strong positive impact particularly on agricultural output growth, which was also helped by the good weather. Too, the private sector in Nigeria is robust and, despite inefficiencies and distortions in the public sector, managed to grow at a reasonable rate. Some of the adjustment reforms helped, as did import bans (though partially enforced) and high tariffs. A sector-specific analysis of national accounts indicates that, between 1986 and 1991, value added in the agriculture, petroleum, and service sectors grew annually by an average of 4.8, 3.6, and 6.1 percent, respectively; these percentages contrast sharply with the percentages for the 1980–85 period (0.4, –4.4, and 0.8 percent, respectively). Thus, each of these major sectors contributed to growth, and growth in two of the sectors, agriculture and services, was led by the private sector.

Third, investment trends help explain the robustness of GDP growth as the reforms faltered. If investment growth is strong (particularly in the private sector, since public investment remains inefficient), GDP growth can be fairly high. As analyzed later, total investment recovered somewhat during the structural adjustment program, but the investment-to-GDP ratio still remains low. Even a low investment-to-GDP ratio can yield a good rate of growth if investment efficiency improves markedly. Some evidence of that improvement exists.

Inflation. Stabilization has not been fully achieved and has adversely affected inflation. Despite a comparatively low inflation rate in 1986 and 1987 (due to good harvests), average inflation between 1986 and 1991 was 24 percent, compared with an 18 percent rate between 1980 and 1985 (table 6.3). The fiscal and monetary restraint envisaged by the structural adjustment program was either abandoned or not pursued vigorously from the outset. Credit to the federal government increased by 12 percent in 1987. Although net foreign assets fell by 39 percent, net credit to the private sector remained relatively strong, all of which increased the supply of money by 23 percent in 1987. While the inflation rate was moderate in 1987, the reflationary budget of 1988 led to some of the largest inflation rates ever in Nigeria. During 1988 prices started to respond to monetary developments with a lag. Policy slippages of 1988 and the subsequent increase in the budget deficit led to an increase in monetary aggregates, and the inflation rate reached nearly 55 percent that year.

In 1989 the government sought again to stabilize the economy and curb the high rate of inflation by introducing drastic monetary control—for example, increasing the discount rate to raise the liquidity ratio, and transferring public sector deposits. The effect of monetary contraction was not felt until 1990, when the inflation rate declined to just over 7 percent. However, in 1990 broad money expanded again by nearly 40 percent, most in the latter half of that year. This was due to an increase in overall financial credit to the government (by about 15 percent) and an increase in borrowing by the private sector from the financial system (by about 20 percent). The inflation rate rose to 13 percent in 1991, and as noted earlier, the current account deficit widened once again.

Overall, the adjustment policies stabilized the growth of money aggregates and prices only during the initial year of the program. After the reflationary budget of 1988, the inflation rate increased sharply, and the monetary squeeze and some fiscal austerity in 1989 had only a temporary effect. That the structural adjustment program has not stabilized monetary

Table 6.3 Money supply and the rate of inflation, 1980–91
(billions of nairas, except where otherwise specified)

Year	*Total net domestic credit*	*Net domestic credit to government*	*Net domestic credit to private sector and other*	*Money plus quasi-money*	*Inflation (percent)*
1980	8.8	1.8	7.0	14.4	10.0
1981	15.0	5.8	9.2	15.2	20.8
1982	20.8	10.1	10.7	16.7	7.7
1983	26.8	15.2	11.6	19.0	23.2
1984	29.5	17.4	12.1	21.2	39.6
1985	30.8	17.7	13.1	23.2	5.5
1986	34.5	17.9	16.6	23.6	5.7
1987	41.9	19.8	22.1	28.9	11.4
1988	52.7	25.3	27.4	38.4	54.5
1989	45.8	17.5	28.3	44.3	50.4
1990	52.8	19.0	33.9	62.1	7.4
1991	73.8	31.2	42.6	82.7	13.0
Average annual growth rate, 1980–85 (percent)	58.0	164.0	31.0	27.0	18.0
Average annual growth rate, 1986–91 (percent)	36.0	29.0	43.0	58.0	24.0

Source: Central Bank of Nigeria; IMF, *International Financial Statistics*.

policies is particularly manifest in the rapidly depreciating exchange rates and the growing gap between the official and the parallel exchange rates.

Investment and savings. Prior to the structural adjustment program, the Nigerian economy did reasonably well during the oil booms. When windfall savings were relatively high, investment expanded significantly. When domestic savings fell short of investment, foreign savings complemented domestic savings to finance investment. In itself this practice would not have been bad for the country, but the quality of investment was poor, not only creating the debt overhang, but also leading to the poor growth performance of the economy. Aggregate investment increased dramatically in the 1970s, peaking around 1979. During 1980 and 1981 the investment share declined, though it still remained high by historical standards. After 1983 the investment share fell drastically, while GDP growth went up steadily. In the 1982–85 crisis period, GDP growth and investment moved in opposite directions, which is a clear indication of the dismally poor quality of the investment at the time of the oil boom.[1]

The structural adjustment program has clearly improved the efficiency of investment, as evidenced by the movement of investment shares and GDP growth (figure 6.2 traces the investment shares of GDP and GDP growth rates). While the investment shares and GDP growth clearly moved in opposite directions before 1986, they have since moved more in parallel. If measured at 1984 prices, investment shares are still declining. However, since 1986 GDP growth has been increasing, clearly showing the efficiency component of

Figure 6.2 Investment and GDP growth, 1976–91

Percent (GDP growth in 1987 prices)

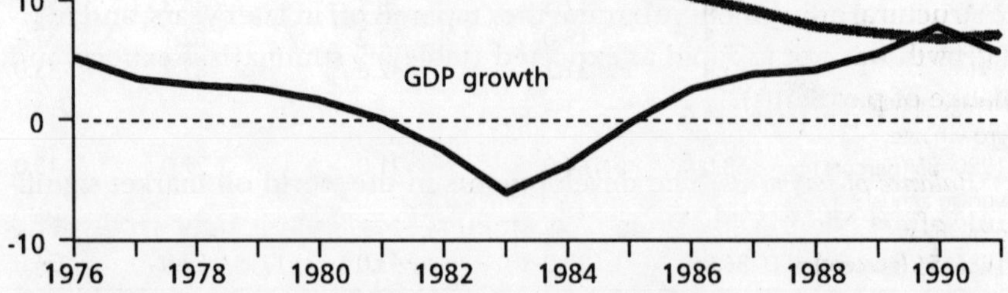

Source: World Bank data.

Table 6.4 Investment as a share of GDP, 1973–90
(percent)

Type of investment	*1973–80*	*1981–83*	*1984–86*	*1986–90*
Private	..	4.67	1.67	3.70
Public	..	11.37	5.70	8.70
Total	18.5	16.03	7.37	12.40

.. Not available.
Source: World Bank data for 1973–80; International Finance Corporation data for 1981–90.

investment after 1986. Growth in GDP during the structural adjustment program can thus be attributed in part to the increased efficiency of investment. Shares of investment have risen slightly from the crisis period (table 6.4), but Nigeria has not yet attained the rates it had experienced in the first half of the 1970s.

The trend is similar for domestic savings. The rate of savings rose markedly during the oil boom period, but plummeted between 1984 and 1986. After the structural adjustment program was implemented, the savings rate remained depressed, and as with investment, the savings rate will recover only when growth in aggregate GDP can be sustained.

Export growth. A key objective of the structural adjustment program is to create export growth and diversification. Despite strong export-supporting policies, nonoil exports have not picked up, and Nigeria continues to rely heavily on oil exports. Progress toward diversifying the productive base and increasing recorded oil exports to $1 billion has not been realized. This outcome exists despite the fact that exporters were able to reap the parallel market premium at a time when the premium was high. One point is that the unofficial production for export markets seems to be considerable. Although dependable estimates are unavailable, one study estimates that Nigerian textiles now supply as much as 30 percent of the needs of the low-income group in the West Africa subregion (Mosley 1992). The same study also estimates that about one-half of Nigerian cloth consumption in the early 1980s was coming from neighboring countries, particularly Côte d'Ivoire and Cameroon. Although agricultural exports grew rapidly in the early years of the structural adjustment program, they tapered off in later years, and overall growth was not as rapid as expected (table 6.5 summarizes exports and balance of payments).

Balance of payments. The developments in the world oil market significantly affect Nigeria's balance of payments—particularly debt service and capital inflows. In 1986 oil accounted for more than 90 percent of total exports, but the value of oil exports declined to $6.4 billion, only about 25 percent of their value in 1980. The overall balance of payments deficit in 1986 reached an all time high of $8.5 billion. In 1987 oil prices and exports increased, as did nonoil export earnings. Imports of goods and services also declined considerably after the 1986 devaluation, reducing the overall deficit somewhat. With oil prices again weakening in 1988, earnings dropped to 1986 levels. Imports again declined in real terms during 1987 (by 29 percent), and dropped by an additional 4 percent in 1988. Current account deficits during these years were financed through external reserves and interest arrears.

Due to the continuous compression of imports and some recovery in oil exports, the balance of payments improved somewhat in 1989, and the current account was balanced for the first time since 1980. The balance of payments again improved in 1990, because the Gulf war led to higher oil prices. Thus, the current account had a surplus of $2 billion, and the overall deficit was reduced by nearly 70 percent in 1990. In 1991 a sharp, nearly fourfold increase in the balance of payments deficit was again recorded, because exports fell on weaker oil prices and import spending accelerated strongly.

Overall, the structural adjustment program has had only a slight impact on the balance of payments. The record deficit of 1986 has been reduced but a substantial current account deficit continued until 1989, when the current account was balanced for the first time. Although the oil price has been the prime determinant of the balance of payments, stabilization policies did help in reducing the external imbalance. Devaluation compressed import demand—which has helped reduce the overall balance of payments

Table 6.5 Exports and overall balance of payments, 1980–91
(US$ billions)

	Exports			Current account	Overall
Year	*Petroleum*	*Other*	*Total*	*balance*	*balance*
1980	25.0	1.0	26.0	4.5	4.5
1981	17.2	0.6	17.8	-5.9	-6.2
1982	11.9	0.3	12.2	-6.7	-5.3
1983	10.0	0.4	10.4	-5.0	-5.8
1984	11.6	0.3	11.9	-1.0	-0.4
1985	12.2	0.4	12.6	-0.2	-0.1
1986	6.4	0.4	6.8	-4.4	-8.4
1987	7.0	0.5	7.5	-1.7	-4.3
1988	6.4	0.6	7.0	-2.6	-4.9
1989	9.4	0.4	9.8	0.0	-1.5
1990	13.5	0.4	13.9	2.0	-0.6
1991	11.7	0.4	12.1	0.0	-2.3
Ratio of 1985 to 1980	0.5	0.4	0.5	-0.0	-0.0
Ratio of 1991 to 1986	1.8	1.0	1.8	0.0	0.3

Source: IMF staff estimates.

deficit. Progress toward diversifying exports and achieving nonoil export growth has been slight. The largest surplus in the current account came in 1990, with the oil price hike induced by the Gulf war. By 1991 the current account no longer contained a surplus, and the overall deficit increased fourfold from its 1990 level.

External debt. During the oil boom years in the early 1970s, Nigeria borrowed heavily from the international capital market. Later, when oil revenue fell, it continued to borrow in an effort to compensate for the loss. Nigeria's debt is primarily nonconcessional, and it has been forced to meet expensive servicing costs in the face of rising interest rates—particularly difficult when the country's oil revenues were declining. Nigeria's large debt overhang created a difficult implementation environment for the structural adjustment program. Since 1986 Nigeria has paid an average of 5 percent of GDP in debt service, equivalent to 21 percent of export earnings and 25 percent of federal expenditures.

What impact has the structural adjustment program had on the external debt burden? Some relief has come through debt rescheduling. Yet as shown clearly in table 6.6, Nigeria's debt has grown in the adjustment period from the rescheduling of guaranteed and nonguaranteed trade arrears, promissory notes, the capitalization of interest on long-term debt, and adjustment valuation. Of the additional stock of outstanding debt, less than 5 percent has come from net borrowing. But despite the overall debt burden, progress

Table 6.6 Evolution of debt outstanding, 1980–91
(US$ millions)

Year	*Net borrowing*	+	*Revaluations*	+	*Rescheduling and reductions*	=	*Total flows*	*Public debt outstanding*
1980	1,122		-105		0		1,017	4,284
1981	2,256		-178		0		2,078	6,362
1982	2,917		-173		0		2,744	9,106
1983	1,723		-569		1,920		3,075	12,181
1984	-302		-832		345		-788	11,393
1985	-1,075		1,406		1,416		1,747	13,139
1986	94		1,646		4,277		6,017	19,156
1987	991		3,070		5,247		9,308	28,464
1988	357		-1,387		1,624		594	29,058
1989	871		-81		1,146		1,937	30,994
1990	-543		2,221		-87		1,592	32,586
1991	-91		41		716		666	33,253
1980–85	6,641		-451		3,681		9,873	—
1986–91	1,679		5,510		12,923		20,114	—
Total	8,321		5,060		16,605		29,986	—

— Not applicable.
Source: World Bank data.

has been made toward consolidating debt, and all service arrears have been resolved through rescheduling, consolidation, and some reductions.

Productive sectors

Agriculture. In agriculture, the structural adjustment program sought largely to change the incentive and price structure to enhance agricultural production, raise rural incomes, and make the regional mix of crop production more efficient. As noted, the key measures were trade liberalization, exchange rate reforms, and the abolition of the commodity boards. But special interest rates on rural loans were also removed, and agricultural credit was made more widely available. Although not consistent with the structural adjustment program's liberalization policies, selected imports were banned to promote domestic production.

The structural adjustment program has affected different products in different ways. For instance, the production of two key foodcrops, cassava and maize, increased rapidly as production technology became more sophisticated. But the adjustment policies set these technologies to use, because they freed up labor in the rural sector. In a recent report by the central bank, an aggregate picture of the movement of real prices and growth is based on two broad categories—export crops and foodcrops. The central bank data[2] show that both food and export crop production has risen since 1986—the average index of export crop production by nearly 45 percent, and foodcrop production by 60 percent (table 6.7). Yet, whereas the impact of the struc-

Table 6.7 Agricultural prices and output, 1980–90
(1980 = 100)

	Export crops		Foodcrops	
Year	Real prices	Production	Real prices	Production
1980	100	100	100	100
1981	89	94	116	102
1982	95	88	120	112
1983	79	78	112	94
1984	65	118	131	125
1985	78	110	110	137
Structural adjustment period				
1986	99	102	93	153
1987	241	103	69	145
1988	185	155	105	193
1989	147	170	89	216
1990	125	179	76	212
Averages				
1980–85	84.3	98.0	114.8	111.7
1986–90	159.4	141.8	86.4	183.8

Source: Central Bank of Nigeria.

tural adjustment program on export crop prices was significantly positive, the central bank's foodcrop price index actually went down. But such nonprice factors as the availability of imported technology, improved infrastructure, and the weather may be more important determinants of the difference. In 1987–88, the shifts in demand for locally produced food related to the structural adjustment program, as well as the effect of the 1987–88 drought, led to an increase in food prices (table 6.8).

For cash crops, the market-determined exchange rate led to large domestic price increases in 1987–88, often of 100 to 200 percent above the 1986–87 prices. The demise of the commodity boards allowed farmers to reap the benefits of the price increases. By 1988 domestic prices for cocoa, palm oil, and cotton were within 10 percent of the border price; before the structural adjustment program, they were much further below. For cotton, the ban on imported inputs for the domestic textile industry was a boon to production, increasing the acreage under cultivation by 50 percent in 1986–87. Table 6.9 illustrates the significant increase in export value of cotton and rubber during 1986–90.

The structural adjustment program thus removed several key structural barriers to agricultural production. As a whole, the sector has responded well to the new incentive structure effected by the structural adjustment program. Total agricultural output grew by more than 4 percent in the five-year post-adjustment period, compared with near stagnation in the five-year period before adjustment. In export agriculture in the pre-adjustment period, a combination of depressed prices due to macroeconomic policies and a

Table 6.8 Real prices of major food commodities, 1980–90
(1980 = 100)

Year	*Maize*	*Yams*	*Rice*	*Cassava (gari)*	*Sorghum*	*Millet*
1980	100	100	100	100	100	100
1981	131	116	107	128	107	100
1982	99	129	75	134	135	121
1983	89	106	71	145	131	91
1984	91	97	87	100	204	122
1985	142	68	108	68	131	96
Structural adjustment period						
1986	128	75	99	53	94	63
1987	41	39	87	65	82	59
1988	82	72	102	104	139	103
1989	79	67	102	82	113	70
1990	55	59	95	71	91	67
Averages						
1980–85	108.7	102.7	91.3	112.5	134.7	105.0
1986–90	77.0	62.4	97.0	75.0	103.8	72.4

Source: Central Bank of Nigeria.

marketing system dominated by the public sector virtually eliminated some crops from export (cotton, groundnuts, and palm oil) and drastically reduced other crop exports (cocoa, rubber, and palm kernel). In the post-adjustment period, cotton and groundnut exports revived, and import substitution in such crops as palm oil increased. More important, domestic food production increased between 1982–85 and 1986–90; the grain equivalent tonnage of all domestic foods increased by more than 31 percent, yielding an annual growth rate of nearly 5 percent.

On the downside for farmers, the structural adjustment program has increased the price of inputs. For foodcrops, prices rose for such inputs as pesticides and herbicides and minor farming implements. Yet their increased cost was compensated for by the easing of the labor constraint after the structural adjustment program. In addition to the purchased inputs, the tree crops sector must also replace plants and machinery. Although fertilizer is heavily subsidized, the absence of adequate supplies when they are required remains problematic. However, farm budget analyses of several crops (sorghum, cotton, millet/cowpea, and maize/sorghum) indicate that net real returns to farming, especially net real returns to family labor, have increased at least three to four times between 1983–85 and 1991.

Industry. The industrial sector consists largely of the core industrial projects controlled by the public sector, and the manufacturing sector. The federal government established the core industrial projects primarily to provide basic inputs for downstream industries. Many of the core industrial projects were the product of the oil boom and all of them reflect the inadequacy of the public sector in producing marketable goods and services. The performance of core industrial projects was grossly inefficient before the structural adjustment program and has remained so.

The manufacturing sector grew rapidly in the 1970s: from 4 percent of GDP in 1973 to 13 percent in 1983. This growth was ascribed to increases in investment supported by oil revenue, rather than to productivity gains.

Table 6.9 Value of selected cash crop exports, 1986–90
(US$ millions)

Commodity	*1986*	*1987*	*1988*	*1989*	*1990*
Cocoa	265.0	375.0	325.0	197.1[a]	181.4[a]
Cotton	0.2	0.7	8.3	..	..
Rubber	21.6	24.2	52.3	88.5[a]	48.6[a]
Palm kernels	5.0	8.0	15.0	16.0	..

.. Not available.
a. Estimated.
Source: Central Bank of Nigeria; World Bank staff estimates.

However, expansion into the early 1980s was largely import-dependent, encouraged by tariff-distorted incentives. Assembly-type activities that relied heavily on imports predominated in the manufacturing sector and contributed little to local value added or employment. Domestic valued added amounted to only 14 percent of the value of gross output, and more than two-thirds of raw material was imported. The export of manufactured goods was virtually nonexistent. As foreign exchange became scarce, capacity utilization declined.

The structural adjustment program sought to correct the distorted incentive structure that encouraged excessive dependence on imports. The short-term strategy of the government was to provide a sharp injection of imports to enable production to recover. The medium-term objective was to develop local technology, raw materials, and intermediate inputs. The structural adjustment program sought to provide the enabling conditions for achieving these goals by creating a realistic foreign exchange rate, liberalizing trade to make necessary imports more accessible, removing ex-factory price controls, and creating an appropriate tariff structure.

Manufacturing production. Manufacturing output increased by 5.1 and 12.9 percent in 1987 and 1988, compared with a decline in manufacturing output of 3.9 percent in 1986. The significant growth is attributed to local sourcing of domestic inputs for manufacturers of food and beverages, soap and detergents, tires and tubes, textiles, and clothing.

The results of a World Bank survey of selected manufacturing enterprises indicate the impact of the structural adjustment program on a subgroup of firms. Based on a survey of 100 enterprises in the main industrial areas of the country, the performance of the sector has improved—growing at 5 and 8 percent in 1987 and 1988, respectively. The scarcity of foreign exchange in the first six months of 1989 caused stagnation in the sector. The improved foreign exchange position in the latter half of 1989 was offset by tight credit constraints.

Among the subsectors that benefited from the foreign exchange and trade reforms were domestic-resource-based industries—including wood products and furniture, textiles, rubber, minerals, and certain food products (table 6.10). The textile subsector performed markedly well—more than doubling production between 1986 and 1989, on the heels of a decline of 40 percent between 1981 and 1986 (table 6.11).

In contrast, the import-intensive and low domestic value added subsectors such as electronics and vehicle assembly did not perform well, largely because their previous survival had depended on an overvalued exchange rate and heavy protection from imports.

Manufacturing capacity utilization. The World Bank's survey results indicate that capacity utilization increased from 42 percent in 1986 to 50 percent in 1988, but declined thereafter. Data from the Manufacturers' Association of Nigeria indicate that capacity utilization fell to 31 percent in the first half of 1989, recovered in the second half of the year, and rose to 38.5 percent in 1990. High capacity utilization is evident in subsectors that are domestically resource intensive, whereas low capacity utilization occurred in import-intensive subsectors (see table 6.10). According to the World Bank survey, the highest capacity utilization—from 64 to 80 percent—was found in textiles, rubber, and nonmetallic mineral products. The capacity utilization of electronics and electrical enterprises was much lower—about 26 percent. In vehicle assembly plants, capacity utilization fell to as low as 7 percent. A direct relationship exists between capacity utilization and the use of domestic inputs. Capacity utilization among firms that responded to the new incentive structure by using domestic inputs tended to be higher.

Investment. The World Bank survey results indicate that manufacturing investment in the post-adjustment period has been quite limited, although respondents noted plans to make investments in the future. Hence, output has grown because existing capacity has grown, not because new investment has started to grow. Yet it is uncertain how much additional growth can be obtained from existing investments that fall into disrepair as they lie idle.

Exports. Exports of manufactured goods have not increased as would be expected with the simplification of export procedures and the devaluation

Table 6.10 Average capacity utilization rates and local sourcing of raw materials, 1986–88
(percent; weighted average)

Subsector	Capacity utilization 1986	Capacity utilization 1987	Capacity utilization 1988	Share of raw materials from local sources 1988
Food, beverages, and tobacco	44.2	50.9	55.7	50.6
Nonmetallic mineral products	81.1	83.2	79.3	80.4
Wood products and furniture	37.0	42.8	53.7	85.1
Electrical and electronics	37.3	37.8	27.3	12.3
Domestic and industrial rubber	59.2	69.0	79.0	34.4
Paper products and printing	3.2	19.3	22.2	26.0
Leather products	50.4	50.4	49.5	79.8
Textiles	47.9	56.8	79.1	42.6
Basic chemicals and pharmaceuticals	15.5	21.3	35.3	4.2
Engineering industries	30.0	25.0	20.0	22.2
Aggregate average (percent)	42.5	47.4	50.6	43.7

Note: Weighted by firm value of output and subsectoral value-added weights.
Source: World Bank data.

Table 6.11 Manufacturing production, quarterly average, 1974–89
(1972 = 100)

Product	*Average 1974–83*	*Average 1984–86*	*Average 1987–89*
Sugar and confectioneries	98.8	40.1	43.8
Soft drinks	729.0	755.5	1,047.3
Beer and stout	445.7	508.7	492.4
Cotton textiles	211.5	86.0	143.5
Synthetic fabrics	1,204.5	548.8	4,359.3
Footwear	106.8	41.9	23.1
Paints and allied products	349.4	186.8	162.3
Refined petroleum	311.3	270.5	341.2
Cement	182.2	231.1	328.2
Roofing sheets	180.9	308.1	189.2
Vehicle assembly	2,641.3	887.5	281.9
Radio changers and television sets	321.5	176.9	339.2
Soaps and detergents	454.2	294.4	196.3
Total	363.8	313.6	484.7

Source: Central Bank of Nigeria (1992).

of the naira. One of the reasons is that official statistics underestimate exports, particularly in the presence of unofficial trading with neighboring countries, for example, for such consumer goods as textiles and soap.

Employment. Employment in the manufacturing sector declined despite increased output and lower wages because private firms have streamlined operations in order to control operating costs. The overall structure of employment has changed, with the greatest decline evident among expatriate employees and unskilled workers. With the contraction in formal sector employment, the informal sector appears to have grown. The limited evidence available suggests that the number of skilled workers and professionals has not declined, and may in fact have increased.

Import bans on manufacturing. Approximately one-third of industrial value added remains protected by import bans. In some instances, smugglers circumvent the bans; in other cases, import bans on certain textiles impede export production. For manufacturing the bans affect beverages, bakery products, garments, and wood products.

Social sector

Poverty is fairly widespread in Nigeria. Based on a 1985–86 household survey, the Nigeria Food and Nutrition Sector Report has estimated that about 18 percent of the population is food-insecure. Unfortunately, no reliable and comparable data are available from other years (particularly recent years) to show the trend in poverty in the post-adjustment years. Furthermore, the impact of austerity measures due to the decline in oil revenues can blur the impact of austerity measures imposed by structural adjustment. The weakening of oil markets reduced Nigeria's export revenue in real terms, simultaneously reducing per capita income. In 1987 GNP per capita was estimated at $370, which is much lower than the $850 in 1982–83, due in part to the overvaluation of the naira. Even when previous naira devaluations are accounted for, the consequent drop in per capita income is substantial and reflects a growing hardship on a large section of the population. Since 1987 GNP per capita has increased, and if it can be assumed that the structural adjustment program did not materially change the income distribution, the poor would not be worse off in 1991–92 in comparison with 1986–87. However, they still could be worse off compared with the oil boom years of the early 1980s. In the absence of relevant counterfactuals (that is, estimates of poverty in the absence of the structural adjustment program), the worse-off situation during the adjustment years in comparison with the oil boom years could be inappropriately ascribed to the structural adjustment program. Since per capita income growth was positive during the adjustment years, the relevant question is how income distribution was affected by the structural adjustment program.

Among the direct results of the structural adjustment program—and most significant—was the distributional effect of the exchange rate reform. The transfer of monopoly rents from those who had privileged access to foreign exchange before the structural adjustment program was significant. In the agricultural sector, producers of cash crops gained during the initial period, but foodcrop producers initially faced higher input costs without higher output prices. Food prices recovered only after 1988. The retail prices of all foodcrops increased between 1986–87 and 1989–90, in part because unusually good harvests allowed food prices to hit record low levels in 1986 and 1987. Higher food prices in recent years have imposed greater hardships on some people. While food prices rose at a much faster rate than nonfood prices in 1988, the two rose at about the same rate in 1989 and 1990. Overall, the real price of food actually declined during the adjustment years (see table 6.7), and the net impact on the poor should be positive, although recent increases may have caused some hardship. The critical factor is the real income of the poor—whether it has remained the same or increased. The position of the poor actually improved during the structural adjustment program. Since the production of food also increased (table 6.7), the net position of food producers should be positive or neutral.

Urban dwellers were generally hit harder by the austerity program, which began before the structural adjustment program, because of resource scarcity. Although, as noted earlier, the real incomes of some self-employed urban groups (artisans and businessmen) improved somewhat, most urban wages declined or remained stagnant since 1986. The real incomes of civil servants appear to have declined by about one-half between 1984 and 1989. On the other hand, real income in rural areas increased by about 40 percent between 1985 and 1989 according to a food security and nutrition report of 1990. Thus, one clear impact of the structural adjustment program is the change in the relative income position of rural and urban areas. During the 1970s—especially after the first oil boom—urban income improved, and the gap between urban and rural incomes widened. During the 1980s the urban and rural income gap narrowed from about 58 percent in 1980–81 to about 8 percent in 1984–85. In 1985–86 the gap was almost totally closed, and the gap reversed in favor of rural areas after 1986.

Although the oil boom had a limited impact on the lives and well-being of most people in Nigeria, there is some indication that living conditions improved, in some respects and for some people, during the oil boom years. For example, the primary school enrollment rate increased from 42 percent in 1960 to 98 percent at its peak in 1978–80.

With the end of the oil boom and the beginning of a crisis between 1984 and 1986, some indicators of well-being showed a decline, while a few remained constant or even improved slightly (table 6.12). For example, primary school enrollment rates fell to about 80 percent in 1985–86. After the structural adjustment program was initiated, some welfare indicators stagnated or declined somewhat. The adult literacy rate, primary school enrollment ratio, and secondary school enrollment ratio show a continued downward trend since the crisis years. However, health and welfare indicators continued to improve: life expectancy continues to rise, and infant mortality rates continue to decline.

The progress in welfare and health indicators seems to be consistent with other available data on access to water and with social expenditure data. Access to safe water seems to have improved from 41 percent in 1986 to 46 percent

Table 6.12 Social indicators, selected years, 1978–90

Indicator	*1978–80*	*1984*	*1985*	*1986*	*1987*	*1988*	*1989*	*1990*
Life expectancy (years)	47.3	49.3	49.7	50.1	50.5	50.8	51.2	51.5
Infant mortality (deaths per 1,000 live births)	120.0	110.4	108.5	106.7	104.9	102.8	100.6	98.5
Adult illiteracy (percent)	66.0[a]	..	57.0	..	..	..	49.0	49.3
Primary school enrollment ratio	98.0	81.0	82.0	..	68.0	72.0	70.0	..
Secondary school enrollment ratio	15.7	..	29.0	..	26.0	21.0	19.0	..

.. Not available.
a. Refers to 1980 only.
Source: World Bank, *World Tables 1992;* UNDP and World Bank, *African Development Indicators,* 1992; World Bank data; World Bank, *Social Indicators of Development 1991–92.*

in 1988. Similarly, although total federal expenditures on health in 1990 were about 40 percent of their value in 1981, health care expenditures show a constant trend—remaining at about 2 percent of total government spending in the mid-1980s until now. The continued effect of fiscal austerity and the decline in oil revenue led to a decline in the absolute and relative size of some social expenditures. In 1987–88 education received only one-half of what it received in 1980.

In conclusion, Nigeria's adjustment experience clearly demonstrates the benefits and the challenges of implementing structural adjustment. On the benefit side, the structural adjustment program has made it possible for the economy to reverse the decline and achieve a reasonable rate of growth. The challenges are evident from the lack of sustained progress on the reforms. A comprehensive structural reform program requires pursuing structural changes on several fronts simultaneously. Some elements of the reform program proceeded more effectively and tenaciously than others. Perhaps most important of all is the attainment of stabilization—a goal that has proven difficult in Nigeria. Attaining multiple targets simultaneously is even more challenging in a situation where the core group of civil servants is either unable or unwilling to effectively manage implementation of complex reforms. Nigeria's adjustment experience, however, proves that the results and impact of the program would have been even more impressive, and would be sustainable, if the progress of the reform were consistent and uniform.

Appendix 6A. Initial distortions and policy progress under the structural adjustment program (SAP)

Fiscal policy and management

Initial situation/distortion. The fiscal deficit in 1986 was about 7 percent. During the oil boom, public investment growth reflected the basis for capital-intensive projects. Public enterprises, before the SAP, were vehicles to distribute oil riches and generate business and employment for selected groups.

SAP reform. SAP reforms aimed at reducing the deficit to 4 percent by 1988 and improving budgetary planning and control through:

- A three-year rolling plan of public investment.
- Bringing the state and local governments within the context of a macroeconomic framework.

Assessment of progress in reforms. Overall progress in achieving fiscal policy goals is poor. The fiscal reform objective was essentially abandoned by the 1988 budget, and a number of the reforms were only on paper and not seriously pursued. The 1989 budget made another attempt to return to lighter fiscal policies, but the attempt was not sustained.

Monetary policy

Initial situation/distortion. With a significantly developed financial system, Nigeria's financial depth as measured by the relative size of M2 increased over time. Broad money accounted for 9 percent of GDP in 1960, but by 1990, M2 increased to 23 percent of GDP. Nigeria experienced unprecedented monetary expansion in 1986.

SAP reform. The SAP aimed at reversing the expansionary budget, reducing inflationary pressures, and emphasizing a more market-oriented financial system. The SAP included tight monetary policies to contain wages and prices in the face of devaluation. In 1989 the central bank implemented restrictive monetary policies.

Assessment of progress in reforms. The monetary restraint pursued since 1986 was abandoned in 1987–88 when money supply increased by 28 percent per year. In 1989 attempts to slow money supply growth resulted in an 11 percent decrease. But this monetary control was not sustained, and in 1990 broad money increased by 40 percent. The monetary expansion was due to the government's failure to ensure sustained sterilization of foreign exchange inflows.

Exchange rate management

Initial situation/distortion. By mid-1986 the naira became highly overvalued. The black market rate was N 3 to US$1, against the official rate of N 1 to US$1.

SAP reform. Exchange rate reform was carried out in phases: secondary foreign exchange market (12/85); unified foreign exchange market (7/87); interbank foreign exchange market (12/88); abolition of foreign exchange auction (3/92).

Assessment of progress in reforms. Overall progress in foreign exchange reform was good, but lack of reforms in fiscal policies and monetary control nullified the progress to some extent. Excess liquidity, weak implementation capacity, and interest group pressure were causes of the government's failure to stabilize the exchange rate and domestic inflation.

Liberalization of international trade

Initial situation/distortion. Trade policy was characterized by excessive import controls enforced through licensing systems and prohibitions. The exchange rate was overvalued, discouraging exports and keeping export prices low. Oil was the dominant export commodity and major source of export revenue.

SAP reform. The SAP aimed at creating a business environment conducive to production and distribution of goods by introducing a second-tier foreign exchange market, to ease import prohibitions; reducing imports under prohibition from 74 to 16; eliminating the 1986 import surcharge of 30 percent; and restructuring customs and excise tariffs. Early in the SAP the devalued naira gave strong price incentives for exports. The government introduced an export incentive plan that eliminated bans, abolished licensing, removed duties, simplified procedures, and established a duty drawback/suspension scheme.

Assessment of progress in reforms. The new tariff structure is operative, but evasion of duties is pervasive. Favorable duty exemptions accorded to the government and concessionary rates of duty for selected categories of producers were either curtailed or terminated. A landing charge was introduced into import duties. Overall, reform in trade and tariff policy has not progressed consistently. Nevertheless, with the introduction of a system of protection based on tariffs and a more realistic exchange rate, the private sector has entered the trade market and there has been a subsequent increase in exports.

Liberalization of prices and domestic trade

Initial situation/distortion. Price distortions in agriculture were major contributing factors to the decline in domestic export production. The commodity boards continued to set domestic prices on goods, maintaining a monopoly on exports. As in manufacturing, many commodities were subject to price and distribution controls.

SAP reform. Price liberalization led to the abolition of six commodity boards in 1986, which opened markets to private individuals, groups, and companies. In 1987 price controls were lifted and private enterprises could set their own prices. In 1988–89 restrictions on foreign ownership were relaxed.

Assessment of progress in reforms. Price regulations persist on such items as fertilizer, petroleum, and gas. Subsidies, an area of little progress, still exist and have even increased on fertilizer and petroleum products. The impact of price liberalization has been moderate. Progress has been made in liberalizing domestic trade and markets and in improving incentives, but implementation remains inconsistent. Restrictions on foreign participation were relaxed in 1988–89, but remain in many sectors.

Financial sector reforms

Initial situation/distortion. The prior financial system had fixed credit allocations, and subsidized and regulated interest rates for priority sectors, as well as term finance provided through finance institutions.

SAP reform. In 1988 the government focused on portfolio problems of the banking system. A deposit insurance system was established in 1989. New standards and minimum capital requirements were introduced in October 1990. New prudential regulations and accounting standards for banks became effective in 1990. The central bank became more independent.

Assessment of progress in reforms. Reforms are new and the effectiveness of implementation cannot yet be easily determined. The conduct of fiscal policy has caused serious problems in the financial system. Oil shocks are not adequately offset by stabilization measures. Government control and barriers to quality banking inhibit new international entrants.

Public enterprise reforms

Initial situation/distortion. Identification of the levels of privatization of public enterprises was sorely needed at the outset of the SAP formulation. The government needed to distinguish between full and partial privatization and record levels of subsidies for public enterprises.

SAP reform. The federal government issued a decree in 1988 to test 145 federal parastatals for privatization and commercialization. By end-1991 (or into 1992), 111 enterprises had been targeted to be privatized. Efforts to commercialize public enterprises and open competition by increasing international tariff and other measures are under way.

Assessment of progress in reforms. The budgetary impact of privatizing public enterprises is so far small, and divestiture of government equity through privatization negligible. Public enterprise reform goals and clear institutional responsibilities still need to be defined.

Labor and wage policy reforms

Initial situation/distortion. Before the SAP, unemployment rose to 11 percent in urban areas. Export prices rose relative to wages and raised the demand for labor. Since 1982 federal civil service wages have been frozen. Prior to the SAP, there were no serious restrictions or interferences in the labor market except for setting minimum wages.

SAP reform. The SAP policies did not include reforms specifically geared toward labor and wages. However, other policies in the SAP indirectly affected employment and wages.

Assessment of progress in reforms. The labor market responded to policies and incentives, and urban unemployment declined to 8 percent (3/88) due to informal sector growth and migration of workers to rural areas. By 1989 unemployment declined to 4 percent—9 percent in urban areas and 3 percent in rural areas. By 1987 the rural and urban wage index was less than half the 1980 level. In 1988 civil service wages increased 27 percent but the increase was not sustained due to the 1988 inflationary budgets.

Social sector policies

Initial situation/distortion. Since the mid-1980s, cutbacks due to decreasing oil revenues caused facilities to deteriorate while demand for services increased. Drugs could not be imported due to declines in foreign exchange. Enrollment doubled during this pre-SAP period, straining resources.

SAP reform. Under the SAP, the government intended to increase the share of public expenditures for human resources. As the SAP progressed, the government took steps to mitigate the negative effects of adjustment.

Assessment of progress in reforms. The government did not succeed in protecting public expenditures on social sectors during the early SAP. Education spending decreased from 21 percent in 1981 to 13 percent in 1988. The government decentralized responsibility to the local level too abruptly to have a positive effect. The SAP is intended to improve the state and local governments' ability to manage their resources efficiently. The government's efforts to alleviate the burden of the SAP have been wasteful.

Notes

1. Gross estimates of the incremental capital-output ratio (ICOR) for the different periods underscore this point. During 1982–85, the ICOR became negative, whereas during early 1990, when investment shares were the lowest, the ICOR figures are the most satisfactory—less than 2.

2. The data on agricultural production in Nigeria from different sources vary a great deal, and it is often extremely difficult to reconcile the difference. Here, we are using the central bank's data, because it just completed a major study that seems to have constructed the production indices carefully. However, it should not be surprising if the central bank's production index varies somewhat from what is indicated by such other sources as the Federal Office of Statistics.

References

Central Bank of Nigeria. 1992. *Annual Report and Statement of Accounts.* Lagos.

Husain, Ishrat. 1992. "Structural Adjustment in Sub-Saharan Africa: The Record, Lessons, and Prospects." Paper presented at seminar on Structural Adjustment in Low-Income Countries, Oxford, U.K., March 22–24.

International Monetary Fund. Various years. *International Financial Statistics.* Washington, D.C.

Mosley, Katherine P. 1992. "Seizing the Change: Economic Crisis and Industrial Restructuring in Nigeria." In Julius E. Nyang'oro and Timothy M. Shaw, eds., *Beyond Structural Adjustment in Africa.* New York: Praeger.

Olukoshi, Adebayo O. 1989. "Impact of IMF-World Bank Programmes on Nigeria." In Bade Arimode, ed., *The IMF, the World Bank, and African Debt.* Vol. 1, *The Economic Impact.* London: Zed Books.
Olukoshi, Adebayo O., ed. 1993. *The Politics of Structural Adjustment in Nigeria.* London: James Currey, Ltd.
UNDP and World Bank. Various years. *African Development Indicators.* Washington, D.C.: World Bank.
World Bank. 1992. *Social Indicators of Development 1991-92.* Baltimore, Md.: Johns Hopkins University Press.
———. Various years. *World Tables.* Baltimore, Md.: Johns Hopkins University Press.

7

Senegal: stabilization, partial adjustment, and stagnation

Mustapha Rouis

The results of the adjustment process pursued in Senegal have been modest, often falling well short of the targets in the government's medium-term financial program and in the policy framework papers. To achieve international competitiveness in the face of nominal exchange rate inflexibility, Senegal has attempted to correct both external and internal imbalances by reducing domestic expenditures, adjusting internal prices and wages, and adopting second-best trade policies. This deflationary policy has led to severe fiscal compression and cuts in public spending on priority areas. Inadequate administrative capacity has severely limited the effectiveness of second-best trade policies, and no credible incomes policy has been pursued. Consequently, the internal adjustment process has not produced the necessary depreciation in the real exchange rate; thus, the performance of exports has been disappointing, as has the ability of domestic industry to compete against imports, and private investment has declined. Deflationary policies to maintain domestic inflation below international inflation are not likely to achieve real depreciation over time. Thus, with a two percentage point annual inflation differential between Senegal and its main trading partners, it would take Senegal fifteen years to reduce relative production costs by one-third in real terms. Moreover, austerity programs cannot be implemented steadily for several years running. The best option available for Senegal is to depreciate the exchange rate quickly and substantially.

The financial stabilization achieved so far by Senegal is fragile, and it is doubtful whether it provides an adequate basis for longer-term sustainable growth. It has led to a conflict between fiscal imperatives that have necessitated higher taxation and competitiveness imperatives that have necessitated reducing the costs of production. It has also reduced public investment, operations and maintenance expenditures, expenditures on human resource development, the provision of adequate public services, and (relatedly) private investment—all crucial elements for longer-term development. While gains in income growth and in the social indicators associated with a more efficient utilization of capital and a reduction in spending are desirable, these are essentially short-term benefits.

Lessons and recommendations

Public sector management

Public sector management has improved, but public resources continue to be misallocated. Wages and salaries continue to be disproportionate to expenditures on maintenance and operations, as well as investment, and unless the size of the civil service wage bill is reduced drastically, both the fiscal position and the productivity of the civil service will deteriorate rapidly. Notwithstanding the mismanagement of civil service recruitment, the voluntary departures program had a good start and should be pursued. The cost of the program should be reduced and its financing should come from savings generated by a reduction in the number of civil servants—and not, as at present, solely from external sources.

While intersectoral allocations appear satisfactory, intrasectoral allocations remain a problem in agriculture, education, and health. Expenditures on irrigation were made at the expense of extension and research services. Those on higher education were made at the expense of primary education, and those on the curative health system were made at the expense of preventive health care. A beginning is being made with sectoral reforms for agriculture, for which a proposed reform program is under discussion with the World Bank and major donors. The adjustment process has not yet dealt with the social sectors comprehensively: a good start in reforming the social sectors has been made in the health sector with the First Human Resources Development Project; but little has been done in the education sector—a sector that urgently needs restructuring. With the completion of the public expenditure review study and the higher education sectoral study, a good analytical base now exists to enable the government to embark on restructuring the education system. To achieve the social targets delineated in government medium-term programs, resources should shift toward primary education and basic health care. But given the scarcity of resources, alternative ways must be found to deliver key services. In this respect, the private sector must be allowed to play an increasingly important role.

More vigorous shrinking of the state enterprise sector is imperative. The recent progress in privatizing public enterprises in Senegal can be attributed to a shift toward pragmatism in government strategy. The strategy gave equal emphasis to divestiture and other forms of privatization, such as contracting out and franchising. It also gave priority to profitable and viable enterprises over those that were financially unsound. The recommendation is that this strategy be pursued vigorously, and that key enterprises, including the groundnut oil processing company and the utility companies, be next in the privatization process.

The design of the adjustment program must account for the longer-term objective of alleviating poverty and address the temporary social costs of adjustment. In Senegal these objectives were pursued in an ad hoc manner, rather than as part of the overall macroeconomic framework. In other words, little effort has been made to build antipoverty objectives into the ex ante design of the adjustment program—due largely to the absence of information on the people expected to suffer the most from the reforms. With the completion of household surveys that will provide better data on various social groups, particularly the poor, social aspects are expected to be integrated more fully into the overall framework of adjustment.

Dependence on external aid

Senegal's reliance on external budgetary assistance has increased substantially over the years. This reliance, combined with the lack of hard donor conditionality, accounts for the postponement of difficult economic and social changes in Senegal, such as the downsizing of the civil service, the adoption of a more liberal labor code, and the restructuring of the agricultural rice sector. External budgetary assistance is viewed by some Senegalese officials as an "entitlement" to be counted on for years to come in the same way as tax revenues. The lack of real sanctions by donors may well have been a major factor in Senegal's slow progress in adjustment. Further adjustment support for Senegal should be selective and conditional on the implementation of upfront key policy measures—over time, external assistance should shift back to investment.

The enabling environment

While macroeconomic stabilization and relative price reforms are necessary, a healthy business environment is essential for a quick recovery of private investment and growth. As defined in the World Bank's third report on adjustment lending, the business environment encompasses the degree of certainty about government policies, the quality and sophistication of the legal and regulatory framework, the condition of the physical infrastructure, and the efficiency of labor and financial markets. While progress has been made in all four areas, only in the financial sector has it been satisfactory. With the government's preoccupation with short-term financial crises, fiscal policies became unpredictable, and, in some cases, policies were simply reversed. The mutual distrust between government officials and private businessmen rendered the design and implementation of reforms difficult. But the legal and regulatory framework remains problematic: while progress has been made in improving the incentive system (by revising the investment code and establishing a one-stop investment window), reducing the cumbersome control system of the public enterprise sector (shifting controls from a priori to a posteriori), and reforming the tax administration system, the judicial system is not working efficiently. The physical infrastructure is deteriorating in the absence of adequate resources for maintenance and operating expenses. The deficiencies of the labor market and competitiveness policy are among the highest priorities for reform. Where Senegal has introduced legal changes, the attitudes of civil servants and the labor unions toward the private sector have remained hostile. The recommendation is that future adjustment programs focus more on the enabling environment.

Government commitment

For any program to be implemented successfully, it must be owned by the government and must be accompanied by consensus-building efforts among the various interest groups. This cooperation has not always been the case in Senegal, despite the good intentions of the government and donors, including the World Bank. The government's resolve to pursue the actions called for by the structural adjustment program appears to have weakened, particularly after the 1988 election, when the program became increasingly biting. Although the commitment to adjustment appears to be strong at the highest official level, in practice the authorities are increasingly reluctant to oppose the interest groups that have had the most to lose from the reforms. These groups are primarily the labor unions, the civil service, and religious leaders (*marabouts*).[1]

The adjustment process and sequencing

Stabilization has been easier than structural adjustment in Senegal, and the latter is far from being complete. Although the third report on adjustment lending classifies Senegal as an intensive adjusting country—with four structural adjustment loans, two sector adjustment loans, and an IMF extended structural adjustment facility program—key structural areas remain to be addressed, including higher education, the labor market, the wage bill, and the legal environment. In addition, the real exchange rate remains significantly overvalued.

The packaging and sequencing of the reform measures are as critical as the policy content of the adjustment program itself. The sequencing of the reforms has been far from ideal. In addition to the absence of a real exchange rate policy, the decision to liberalize external trade before establishing an effective tax administration, eliminating labor rigidities, and reducing the cost of production reflects an insufficient consideration of the sequence of reforms. Similarly, the decision to proceed with the civil service departure program before establishing a data base on wages and civil servants and a monitoring system also reflects a deficient sequence of reforms. Finally, the privatization of public enterprises should have been initiated as soon as a good regulatory and incentive framework was in place.

The move toward adjustment

Senegal is a small, semi-arid Sahelian nation with a population of 7.6 million, predominantly rural. Its natural resource endowments are limited. The mainstays of the traditional economy remain millet cultivation and nomadic cattle raising for domestic consumption, and groundnut cultivation for export. The modern sector includes fishing, phosphates, chemical industries, and tourism and is concentrated in Dakar and on the coastal belt. At the current overvalued exchange rate, the 1991 per capita income of $720 places Senegal almost at the bottom of the lower-middle-income economies.

At Independence in 1960, Senegal inherited a relatively well-developed physical and social infrastructure due to the prominent role Dakar played as the capital of the large French West African colony. Senegal has enjoyed a high profile in African affairs and until recently, has been the only Sahelian country with a lively democratic system, including a vocal press. This system has helped Senegal mobilize substantial external resources over the years. Yet Senegal also has a long tradition of "African socialism," with widespread government intervention in the economy, and regulatory controls. Traditional values still play an important role in social, economic, and political spheres.

Although Senegal inherited a sound physical and social infrastructure, its need for structural economic changes also first became apparent in the early years of Independence, when Senegal lost its large French West African market and found itself with oversized industries and an excess of highly paid civil servants. Macroeconomic imbalances appeared as early as 1966, when groundnut exports suddenly lost their guaranteed French market and had to compete in the world markets. The government was slow to recognize the need for structural changes. To make matters worse, the government responded to a short-lived commodity boom in the early years of the second half of the 1970s by borrowing heavily from foreign commercial banks in the expectation of returning to more favorable terms of trade. A 1987 World Bank economic report on Senegal observes that "adjustment became unavoidable at the end of the 1970s, when a combination of poor financial and investment policies, worsened terms of trade and successive droughts plunged an already weakened economy into a severe crisis."

The crisis is evident from general statistics between 1960 and 1980. Senegal's economic performance was dismal even by Sub-Saharan African standards. GDP grew on average by 2.1 percent annually against a population growth rate of 2.8 percent. Senegal experienced the lowest GDP growth rate of any African state not affected by war or civil strife. Until 1966, economic management was relatively sound, and the economy grew at about 3.5 percent annually during 1960–66. Between 1967 and 1974, when the world oil price quadrupled, GDP grew by only 1.3 percent annually, and groundnut production fell by almost half. During this period, Senegal actively pursued a nationalization policy and an industrial import-substitution policy. Between 1978 and 1981 Senegal experienced two major droughts together with a substantial fall in world groundnut prices and, correspondingly, a GDP growth rate of 0.8 percent a year. By the end of this period, all key economic indicators reflected serious financial and structural imbalances. The fiscal deficit and the current account deficit reached 12.5 percent and 25.8 percent of GDP, respectively. Savings were negative—that is, total consumption exceeded GDP. The inflation rate rose to 12 percent. The total stock of debt represented 67.4 percent of GDP, and the scheduled debt service represented 18.5 percent of total exports of goods and nonfactor services.

In the late 1970s the government began to recognize the shortcomings of its ambitious nationalization policies and public sector development plans. In December 1979 it announced its medium-term (1980–84) program for economic and financial adjustment. The program, designed in close collaboration with the World Bank and the IMF, sought to stabilize the financial situation, raise public savings, increase investment in the productive sectors, liberalize trade, and reduce the state role in the economy. Yet, because the government did not implement the agreed upon measures, the IMF shifted its three-year extended fund facility arrangement to a simple one-year standby after only a year, and then cancelled it in 1983. Similarly, after approving its first structural adjustment loan in 1980, the World Bank cancelled its second tranche in 1983.

Renewed efforts were launched in 1984 with the same broad policy objectives in mind. The first meeting of a Consultative Group for Senegal was organized by the World Bank in December 1984, after which Senegal prepared a medium-term adjustment program for 1985 to 1992, which was endorsed by the donors. This meeting was followed by a second Consultative Group meeting organized in 1987. Since 1980 the government's adjustment effort has been supported by four World Bank structural adjustment loans (1980, 1986, 1987, and 1990) and two sector adjustment loans (for the financial sector in 1989, and for the transport sector in 1991), and by a series of IMF arrangements (extended fund facility in 1980, followed by five standbys, a two-year structural adjustment facility, and a three-year extended structural adjustment facility). Along with Kenya and Turkey, Senegal was the first country to receive an adjustment credit or loan from the World Bank. Five policy framework papers were approved by the World Bank and IMF boards between 1986 and 1991. Senegal has been a recipient country of the Special Program of Assistance since the program was established in 1988.

The adjustment program in Senegal has been supported generously by the donor community, either directly or as cofinancier of Bank operations. Between 1981 and 1991 adjustment support accounted for nearly two-thirds of the official development assistance disbursed to Senegal, and the total assistance to Senegal represented 4.3 percent of the total amount received by Sub-Saharan Africa. (Senegal's share in the region's population is 1.5 percent and in GNP 0.3 percent.) In 1991 net aid flow per capita to Senegal amounted to $84, or 12 percent of GDP per capita.

Underlying macroeconomic and sectoral issues

Real exchange rate and competitiveness

In the past two decades, Senegal has witnessed a swing in its terms of trade with no overall trend, high inflationary rates, and low productivity gains. Between 1981 and 1986 domestic prices rose by 4.5 percent more than the domestic prices of Senegal's trading partners; they have declined somewhat since then. These developments, together with the sharp real currency depreciation of non-CFA neighboring countries and the depreciation of the dollar since 1985, have severely eroded Senegal's competitiveness and exacerbated trade imbalances.

The movement in the real effective exchange rate (see the Côte d'Ivoire chapter for theoretical background), a commonly used measure of competitiveness,[2] shows that, despite the growing competitiveness of other developing countries (Sub-Saharan Africa, Latin America, and heavily indebted middle-income countries), the competitiveness of the CFA zone, including Senegal, was actually worsening, even in the face of internal adjustment programs. The real effective exchange rate in Senegal depreciated in foreign currency terms by 14 percent between 1980 and 1984, and then appreciated by 20 percent between 1985 and 1991 (table 7.1). The appreciation of the real effective exchange rate during the second half of the 1980s is due to the appreciation of the French franc vis-à-vis the U.S. dollar and the naira. The real exchange rate vis-à-vis Ghana, Nigeria, and China, against which Senegal's exports compete, has appreciated substantially, particularly since 1985.

The relationship between the real exchange rate and the real trade balance is also shown in table 7.1. While the real effective exchange rate in Senegal appreciated by 20 percent between 1985 and 1991, the trade balance had improved by 6 percentage points of GDP. A closer examination of the disaggregated data provides an explanation in line with theory. The improvement in the trade balance was due to a drop in exports by nearly 5 percentage points of GDP (in line with expectations) and a drop in official imports by 11 percentage points of GDP. The latter was due directly to drastic cuts in public expenditure programs—particularly investment—and to low growth.

The strategy for industrial development in Senegal had historically concentrated on import substitution, with the exception of a few industries engaged in exports of fish, phosphates, and groundnuts. This strategy had reached its limits by the mid-1980s, and, due to an underlying policy of high import protection, had discouraged the development of exports and encouraged fraudulent imports. Until the reforms of 1986, import protection was effected with extensive nontariff restrictions (quantitative restrictions, monopolies, and prior import authorization) and high and uneven nominal tariffs. In 1986, to improve the competitiveness of the industrial sector, the government implemented a comprehensive industrial reform program that sought to rationalize and liberalize its trade policy (discussed in the section on the design and implementation of macroeconomic reform).

Table 7.1 Real effective exchange rate, selected years, 1970–91
(1985 = 100)

Year	*Real effective exchange rate*	*Real exchange rate (French franc)*	*Terms of trade*	*Current resource balance (percentage of GDP)*
1970	93	78	103	-4.6
1975	122	97	100	-5.2
1980	103	92	95	-14.5
1981	91	88	101	-19.3
1982	93	93	88	-12.3
1983	92	93	86	-12.3
1984	90	92	98	-9.5
1985	100	100	100	-11.2
1986	126	109	106	-5.4
1987	134	105	103	-5.6
1988	121	98	102	-5.0
1989	114	93	107	-5.2
1990	122	94	106	-4.7
1991	120	94	103	-4.9

Note: An increase in the index indicates appreciation. The index is calculated from official exchange rates deflated by the wholesale price indexes. The real effective exchange rate is calculated using trade-weighted data for Senegal's 20 most important trading partners; the weights are those calculated by the IMF using the methodology described in "A Revised Weighting Scheme for Indicators of Effective Exchange Rates," IMF WP/87/87, which provides for the inclusion of countries that are competitors in export markets but that do not trade directly with the country concerned.

Source: World Bank estimates.

Labor and wage policy

Before the labor and wage reforms of 1986, the modern labor market had been regulated heavily by the government and suffered from a highly adversarial system of industrial and labor relations.[3] The government regulated hiring and firing practices and wage rates through various labor laws—particularly the labor code, the 1981 collective bargaining system,[4] and the civil service statutes. Although these regulations sought to ensure the welfare of workers, they instead led to higher production costs, low productivity, and limited investment and job creation. In effect, the government's income policy was contrary to its internal adjustment strategy.

As in other African countries, modern sector wages in Senegal are influenced largely by wages paid by the government, which in 1986 employed 68,000 of a total modern sector employment of 131,000 (Berg and associates 1990). Real civil service salaries and wages in the modern sector had declined between 1980 and 1985—but were still relatively high in comparison with other countries. Yet, to compensate for the decline, the government progressively increased salary and wage supplements and benefits, which by 1986 increased to 25 to 30 percent of the wage bill.[5] For the entire industrial sector, Svejnar and Terrell (1988) found that total factor productivity had declined annually by 5 to 7 percent in the 1980–85 period.

Because employers could not lay off workers without an elaborate and time-consuming process of government approval, they relied more heavily on temporary rather than permanent workers. But even temporary labor was problematic. Having fought for the country's independence, the labor unions remained influential, although their position weakened after 1976, when trade union pluralism was reintroduced (Ka and van de Walle forthcoming). The tripartite union-employer-government system was one of deep mistrust, especially between the unions and employers. In the civil service the government policy of guaranteeing job security and wage security had contributed significantly to an oversized and less productive civil service.

The banking sector

Senegal's banking sector crisis has been due to an array of factors. One of the most critical has been the government's willingness in the past to guarantee the borrowing of uneconomic public enterprises. Of the CFAF 144 billion of bad debts held by failing banks, more than 20 percent were government-guaranteed loans. These loans allow the government to circumvent the 20 percent limit on its borrowing from the central bank. These were considered risk-free. Yet when the government failed to honor its guarantees, they had a destabilizing effect on bank balance sheets. The government's interference is also evident in the national credit committees' discretionary power to fix bank-by-bank credit ceilings—which, because weaker banks receive higher credit ceilings than stronger ones, prolongs the life of sick banks at the expense of those that are financially sound. Also, the complexity of the legal framework made it difficult for banks to collect bad debts.

The ineffectiveness of bank credit management has also perpetuated the banking crisis. Crop marketing credits were particularly problematic. Crop credits are short-term advances that finance the full collection cost of agricultural products from producers through final sale. Since reimbursement is generally expected within the year, credit ceilings have not been applied. But, serviced only sporadically, these nonreimbursed crop credits have tended to accumulate, absorbing much of the annual increases in credit ceilings, and crowding out the productive sector. ONCAD, Senegal's defunct groundnut marketing and processing agency, is a case in point. Its dissolution in 1982 left the National Development Bank holding nonreimbursed claims of CFAF 94 billion. The major local banks were obliged to assume shares of the outstanding balance. Thus, in 1982 ONCAD's refinancing became a source of balance sheet problems for the banks and, of course, crowded out other borrowers.

Managerial and operational control has been ineffective, due largely to the division of responsibility between BCEAO (the regional central bank responsible for inspection) and national authorities (responsible for overseeing the implementation of corrective measures). Some banks had not been visited by the BCEAO for several years. Even when BCEAO recommended sanctions, the government often did not comply. Thus, prudential regulation eroded. Problems began emerging when political pressure forced banks to lend to failing public enterprises through government guarantees and BCEAO rediscount facilities.

The disregard of rules applying to liquidity positions and the absence of applied accounting standards have further eroded the control of banks. BCEAO failed to enforce sanctions on banks. Consequently, these banks continued to credit accrued but unpaid interest on nonperforming loans, making the balance sheets of weaker banks look stronger than they actually were. The problem banks also had preferential access to BCEAO rediscounting, making their balance sheets deteriorate even further. The BCEAO also used a money market mechanism whereby healthy banks—those with excess liquid deposits—were constrained by restrictive credit ceilings and forced to lend their excess liquidity to sick banks. Thus, liquidity problems surfaced only when the banks were finally unable to honor checks drawn upon them. The distressed banks had to borrow from BCEAO. (Table 7.2 shows the breakdown of ailing and healthy banks in Senegal as of September 30, 1988.)

Public enterprises

Nationalization and the creation of new agencies had expanded the government's public enterprise sector in the 1970s. But several deficiencies—soft budget constraints, lax hiring policies, and the absence of performance incentives for managers—softened the sector, and reforms became critically needed.

In 1986 the sector as a whole (including the banking sector) consisted of 85 enterprises—25 classified as noncommercial or administrative entities. The sector accounted for 29 percent of total investment in the economy, 17 percent of total employment, and 7 percent of GDP. The net losses of the sector after taxes and before subsidies represented about 2 percent of GDP and 9 percent of government revenue. The government's equity share in the sector was 72 percent. The financial performance of the nonfinancial public enterprises was poor, calling for budgetary subsidies. In addition to these budgetary transfers, the sector enjoyed other explicit transfers, such as loans from the treasury and debt servicing, and implicit transfers, such as tax exemptions, loan guarantees, preferential interest rates, and distortions from price controls. These enterprises accounted for the bulk of the credits to the economy (95 percent of long-term credits, 15 percent of medium-term, and 25 percent of short-term over the period 1985 to 1987). Many of these loans were nonperforming, thus perpetuating the banking sector crisis.

Fiscal policy and management

As in most countries undergoing adjustment programs, Senegal attempted to use its fiscal policy as a primary instrument for reducing aggregate demand and correcting major disequilibria in the economy. Yet the fiscal policy framework in Senegal is affected by several conflicting factors that both complicate the design of the reform program and render an assessment of its performance more difficult. Some of these factors are specific to Senegal; others are related to the rules that regulate fiscal and monetary policies within the West African Monetary Union, of which Senegal is a member.

Table 7.2 Summary of the banking system's situation, 1988
(CFAF billions)

Item	*Distressed banks*	*Sound banks*	*Total*
Loan portfolio	323	166	489
Nonperforming loans	233	6	239
Capital and reserves	36	29	65
BCEAO refinancing	167	30	197

Source: World Bank estimates.

Because Senegal belongs to the West African Monetary Union—which among other things regulates the money supply by adjusting credits—it has relied on fiscal policy for its adjustment efforts. While the French treasury's "operations accounts" gives West African Monetary Union countries financing guarantees for their balance of payments shortfalls, the BCEAO has adopted a safeguard feature to prevent monetary expansion—a statutory act whereby the maximum level of BCEAO advances to the government may not exceed 20 percent of the previous year's ordinary budgetary receipts. While this overdraft rule can be circumvented in some instances, the rule does impose a limit on the financing of government deficits from the central bank. Thus, while Senegal's membership in the West African Monetary Union may help limit the threat of inflation, the system is prone to liquidity crises.

The structure of the public sector in Senegal further complicates how public finances are managed. In addition to the consolidated central government operations, the treasury maintains diverse special and correspondent accounts. Until July 1991 these accounts were not integrated into the budget and were not subjected to normal budgetary procedures. Thus, the absence of effective control over these accounts could lead to large annual variations in the treasury's liabilities for them. The design and management of fiscal policy has also been made more complex by the close association between key fiscal measures and the industrial policy, particularly tariff reforms and production costs.

Some of this policy complication reflects the conflicting objectives of donors, particularly between those focusing largely on stabilization policy, which sought to mobilize revenue at the expense of promoting growth, and those emphasizing longer-term issues, such as reducing the cost of key inputs and the corporate tax rate. Also, it can be argued that the large inflow of official assistance from multilateral agencies and bilateral donors (particularly France) made it possible for Senegal to postpone "hard-budget" choices.

Major policy reforms, 1980 to 1991: design and implementation

Summary of progress

Overall, Senegal's performance in implementing its adjustment program has been mixed. Figure 7.1 shows the major reforms that have been undertaken and their status. Senegal has made strides in monetary and credit policy, pricing and trade policy, and financial sector policy—indeed, Senegal was one of the first CFA countries to undertake such far-reaching financial sector reform. But two caveats are in order here: the government recently reversed its important protection policy, and it has not aggressively recovered bad debts from the banking sector, hesitating to pursue the large debtors.

Figure 7.1 Implementation status of major policy reforms in Senegal, 1980–91

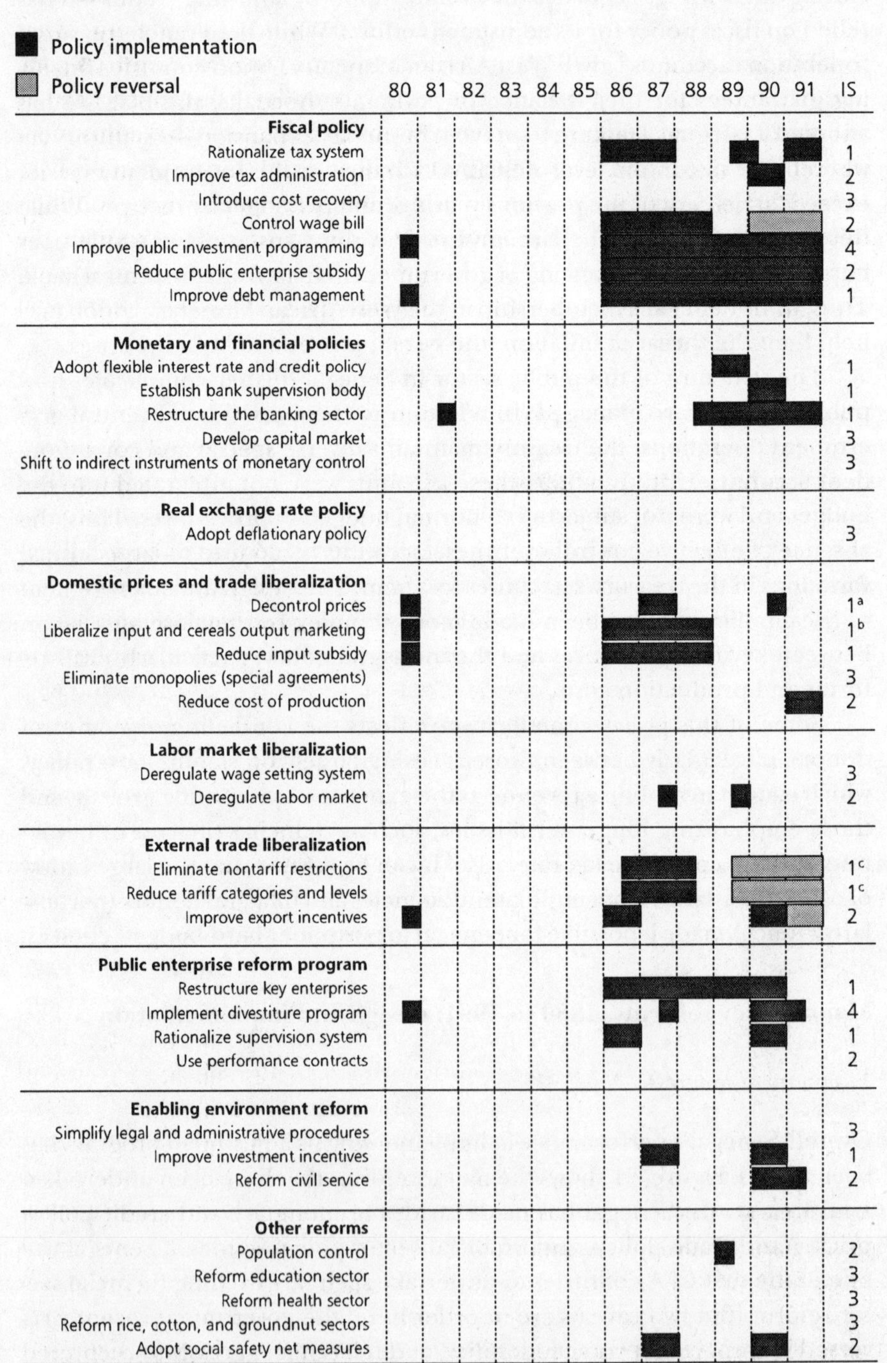

Note: IS is implementation status. 1 = implemented; 2 = not effectively implemented; 3 = not implemented; 4 = continuous.
a. Prices on 14 items remain controlled. b. Rice market remains controlled. c. Gradual policy reversal.
Source: World Bank staff.

The financial reform agenda is unfinished primarily in monetary policy, where a market-based system of money and credit management must be established.

Senegal's exchange rate policy has been a major disappointment, as has its labor and wage policy. Both are critical to improving the country's competitiveness in the world market. The real exchange rate has appreciated by at least 20 percent in foreign currency terms during the partial adjustment period. The labor market has been partially liberalized (hiring practices have been liberalized, and constraints on using temporary employment contracts have been partially relaxed). A labor code has been drafted to eliminate the rigidities in the labor market, but has not yet been enacted into law. And given the persistence of the rigidities in the labor market, labor costs remain a serious impediment to investment, growth, and competitiveness.

On the fiscal front, the government has implemented several reforms to simplify the tax structure (introducing a global personal income tax and assessing a single tax on corporate income), modernize the tax administration system, and mobilize resources by widening the scope of the value added tax. The government also introduced expenditure control in investment. Yet it has tended to focus on the financial short term, relying on windfall revenue from the petroleum imports and introducing numerous ad hoc tax measures, but ignoring more structural issues. Revenue has been mobilized and resources allocated at the expense of competitiveness and long-term growth. In expenditures the government has reduced investment and allocations to operations and maintenance, but protected wages and salaries, thus jeopardizing future growth and employment. In sum, the required fundamental restructuring has not been achieved. Five fiscal reforms are still key: strengthening tax administration (particularly customs), reducing dependence on petroleum revenues, reducing the wage bill, controlling transfers to public enterprises, and raising investment and operations and maintenance spending.

Sectoral reform also met with mixed success. The agriculture reform program has liberalized domestic trade, decontrolled the prices of most commodities, and eliminated input subsidies—but rice import controls remain a major issue, and producer prices for cash crops—groundnuts and cotton—continue to have no direct relationship to world prices. The domestic market for most commodities has been liberalized as a necessary condition but an insufficient remedy for turning agricultural production around. Agricultural development continues to be constrained by overvaluation of the real exchange rate and unfavorable terms of trade for groundnut oil and cotton.

The industrial reform program—which was to have been a comprehensive and well-sequenced effort—has been implemented only partially. Domestic and international trade has been liberalized, and most domestic prices have been decontrolled, but the government has recently begun to reverse its trade policy—primarily for fiscal reasons, but also to protect industry and to compensate for the appreciation of the real exchange rate. Crucial reforms—labor market deregulation, a stronger legal and administrative environment, lower energy prices, and export subsidy schemes—have been implemented late in the adjustment process, and again only partially. Among the measures to improve the regulatory environment, the investment code has been revised and investment procedures simplified. The industrial program has been reduced thus far to a policy of price and trade liberalization.

Public enterprise reform has been slow and uneven. Divestiture, which is nearly complete in the financial sector, has been slow with nonfinancial public enterprises. The progress made in the divestiture program is very recent—three-quarters of the public enterprises divested, translating into about 80 percent of assets and government equity, have been privatized and liquidated since 1989—and is due to the government's adoption of a more pragmatic strategy. The restructuring and rehabilitation of public enterprises have also been limited and in most cases confined to the signing of contract programs and "letters of mission" between the government and the concerned public enterprises. Contract programs have improved the transparency and accountability of the two contracting parties—not a small achievement—but have failed to achieve performance objectives largely because of the government's unwillingness to meet its financial commitments. The accumulation of financial arrears between public enterprises and the government and among public enterprises has been a serious problem. The problem seems to be less acute now because concurrent preventive measures have been introduced.

In education and health only a limited number of reforms have been implemented. The unfinished reform agenda calls for reducing the imbalances between primary education and higher education, and between basic health care and a curative health care system. Reform programs for higher education and health are currently under active consideration by the government.

As with other programs in CFA adjusting countries, the *design* of Senegal's adjustment program lacks an important policy instrument—the nominal exchange rate. The absence of an exchange rate as one of the major adjustment tools has complicated the design of the program and makes its full implementation difficult to guarantee. The deflationary policy that Senegal adopted relied more on demand management, and less on supply incentives.

Yet, aside from the real exchange rate issue, program design has improved steadily as Senegal has gained more adjustment experience. The shift from fundamental but complex macroeconomic reform to sector-specific adjustment programs is under way. Senegal chose to implement a series of selected well-focused programs to avoid overburdening its administrative capacity. It pursued this strategy by dividing the wide-ranging requisite policy changes into manageable packages, or sector adjustment loans—for example, in banking, human resources, and transport—that were supported by the World Bank and key donors.

As discussed in the introduction to this chapter, the *sequencing* of the reforms has certain flaws. The reform program addressed the following policies chronologically: a reduction in internal and external imbalances, the liberalization of agricultural marketing and then trade, public sector management efficiency (including public enterprises and the civil service), wage and labor market deregulation, population growth, banking sector restructuring, and transport sector rehabilitation. The sequencing and coherence of these various components of the reform program have been monitored closely through the policy framework paper process. And the evidence indicates that, because of the overvalued exchange rate, several more fundamental measures should have been pursued to provide a stronger base for sustainability. Particularly lacking has been progress on human resource reform—most notably education.

Some additional words about "ownership." As mentioned in the introduction, the momentum of the government's *commitment* to the reform program seems to have foundered after the 1988 election, when political pressure weakened the technocrats' influence. Government commitment to the reform program seems to depend on three key elements: the degree to which there is consensus-building among the interest groups, the strength of institutions in charge of formulating and coordinating the reform program, and the nature of the reforms themselves—the more politically and socially difficult these are, the more reluctant government is to implement them fully. Over time, policy measures tend to be discussed widely with concerned parties, and publicly debated. A case in point is the revision of the labor code, which involved extensive discussion between the government, the labor unions, and the employers unions, and, more recently, the discussion of the higher education sector. Notwithstanding this effort, the involvement of the private sector in the design of the reform program has been far from satisfactory.

Macroeconomic policy and management

Fiscal policy and management reform. Fiscal policy reform in Senegal covers a broad range of objectives—all to improve government financing and revenue. Senegal began the 1980s with an overall budget deficit of 12.5 percent of GDP, a primary deficit of about 10 percent of GDP, and total public expenditures of 32 percent of GDP. The civil service wage bill, by far the largest expenditure item, accounted for 40 percent of total expenditure. The key fiscal initiative was to increase revenue by enhancing the buoyancy of the tax system. In line with the recommendations of an IMF fiscal mission to Senegal in May 1985, the government's fiscal reform program sought to modernize the tax system, create a more effective and less distorted tax regime, and widen the tax base.

The government has also pursued a restricted expenditure policy. Although it recognized the need for a two-pronged strategy—controlling the wage bill and limiting transfers to public enterprises—policy measures were mostly ad hoc, and it was not until 1990 that the government adopted a coherent civil service program. Too, fiscal reform has failed to work toward improving the financial performance of public enterprises, thus perpetuating their budgetary burden and inefficiency. With a few exceptions (road maintenance and the recruitment of primary school teachers), nothing was done specifically to protect key social sectors, reduce operations and maintenance, and build a core public investment program.

Another important initiative of the fiscal reform program was improving the public investment program. In 1986 a three-year "rolling" public investment program was adopted, and it has since been updated on an annual basis. The public investment program reform package sought to make investment projects consistent with the macroeconomic framework and sectoral priorities; improve project preparation and appraisal; provide systematic monitoring of the physical and financial aspects of projects; incorporate the investment budget into the government's overall budget; and strengthen the technical ministries' capacity to identify, prepare, and monitor their respective projects.

The third key initiative was improving the external debt management system. A computerized debt management system was established with International Development Association–financed technical assistance to provide data on outstanding debts, arrears, and scheduled debt service and to issue computerized payment orders. To improve the structure of its external debt, the government also sought to discontinue commercial borrowing, curtail public guarantees to private borrowers, and stop the transfer of proceeds from debt relief negotiated by the government to the final borrowers.

The progress of the fiscal reforms has varied across policy areas. As part of its wide-ranging tax reforms, the government introduced a general tax code in early 1987 to change specific duties to an ad valorem basis and expanded the value added tax to the trade and construction sectors. In 1991 the value added tax was generalized to services and the transport sector, and the value added tax rates were revised to simplify and reduce their structure. To reform foreign trade taxation, the government simplified the tariff structure and lifted quantitative restrictions. In September 1989 the government instituted a withholding tax on professional and property income and a global tax on personal income—replacing a variety of schedular taxes—and in January 1990 it placed a single tax of 35 percent on corporate income. In another effort to widen the tax base, the fiscal cadastre for the Dakar region was completed, although follow-up measures to institute the tax have been delayed. Finally, efforts have continued to be made to raise tax revenue from the informal sector.

In conjunction with modernizing the tax system, the government has also sought to mobilize additional revenue through a number of measures.[6] The implementation of the plethora of new measures was particularly taxing on the limited administrative capacity, and the government tended to focus more on short-term than on structural issues. The new measures also created additional distortions to an already elaborate tax system. The predominance of short-term revenue considerations over measures to promote longer-term growth has prevented a meaningful reduction in energy costs and hampers the sustainability of the customs tariff harmonization and reduction.

Measures to reduce the size of the civil service and control the wage bill slipped seriously—and thus the wage bill still represents the lion's share of government revenues and recurrent expenditures. The lack of progress toward controlling direct and indirect subsidies to public enterprises reflects the complexity of this sector and the lack of government commitment to politically sensitive policies to reduce the amount of transfers from the budget to this sector.

Public investment program management has improved; in particular, conflicts between capital investment and sector strategies have been eliminated. Projects are also generally better prepared. Institutional capacity-building must continue to be strengthened, else progress thus far will be threatened. To do so, technical ministries must identify and prepare projects in their respective sectors more effectively, and coordination between the public investment program and treasury staff must be enhanced so that the budget clearly reflects the recurrent costs and debt implications of the public investment program. Without this coordination, allocations for operating and maintaining new projects will be insufficient, thus yielding poor rates of return.

Although the financial position of the government improved during the 1980s, the impact of some reform measures has been reduced drastically because of poor implementation. For instance, proceeding with the liberalization before effective tax administration was established and stabilization results were consolidated reflects inefficient sequencing. Also, efforts to combat underinvoicing through computerized customs declaration have yielded few significant results, given the absence of concrete efforts to enhance the functioning of the value assessment section, without which underinvoicing goes mostly undetected. Deficient revenue mobilization and wage bill control affected other expenditure items, undermining fiscal adjustment further.

Monetary policy reform. Within the institutional framework described in box 7.1, Senegal's monetary policy is threefold: managing overall demand to correct external imbalances; gaining a competitive advantage by keeping the level of inflation below that of major trading partners; and strengthening the management of liquidity and supervision of banks. While the government addressed the first two objectives primarily by pursuing restrictive credit policies, it implemented a more comprehensive set of measures in the banking sector, including the introduction of market-determined interest rates.

In September 1989 Senegal and other members of the West African Monetary Union adopted a comprehensive reform of monetary policy instruments that replaced the administrative controls over money and credit with an indirect and market-oriented system of monetary instruments. In particular:

- The preferential rediscount rate was abolished; the central bank's refinancing rate was set above the money market rates—at levels slightly higher than those for the French franc—and banks were given more flexibility in determining their rates on deposits and loans.

Box 7.1 Framework for monetary policy in West African Monetary Union countries

Monetary policy in Senegal is influenced heavily by its membership in the West African Monetary Union (WAMU), whose membership includes Benin, Burkina Faso, Côte d'Ivoire, Mali, Niger, Senegal, and Togo. Established in 1962, WAMU was substantially reformed in 1973–75 and again in 1989. Five essential provisions characterize the operation of the monetary union. First, the member countries share the CFA franc, whose convertibility into the French franc at a fixed exchange rate is supported by an overdraft facility through the operations account with the French treasury. In return for France's support, the member countries, through the BCEAO, agree to deposit the equivalent of at least 65 percent of their foreign exchange holdings in the operations account. Second, a uniform interest rate structure applies throughout the zone. Third, uniform ceilings on bank lending margins are fixed to the common interest rate structure. Fourth, common limits are set for government borrowing from the BCEAO, which, except for temporary overruns, could not exceed 20 percent of the previous year's fiscal revenues. Fifth, one zonewide interbank money market was established in July 1975 to help recycle the excess liquidity of deposit-money banks within the union and to curb capital outflow (deposit-money banks are not authorized to maintain deposits abroad in excess of their working balances).

- Conditions for access to central bank refinancing were tightened, and crop credit will be refinanced by the central bank only if it is within general refinancing limits and under the overall credit ceiling of the commercial banks.
- Rigorous controls were placed on state guarantees for borrowing by public and private enterprises. Government-guaranteed nonperforming loans will be imputed to the overall credit ceiling set for the government.
- The system of sectoral credit allocation was eliminated, and prior authorization will be used only as a qualitative credit control instrument.
- The BCEAO's bank inspection and supervision were sharply reinforced with the creation of the unionwide bank supervision body (*Commission bancaire*).

In a subsequent phase of reforms, reserve requirements may be introduced. During the transitional period, monetary and credit policy will continue to be based primarily on interest rate policy and overall credit ceilings.

Monetary and credit policy reform has been implemented forcefully and according to schedule—due largely to the heavy involvement of the BCEAO and in recognition that confidence in the banking sector had to be reestablished after ailing banks were liquidated. With minor differences, most of these reforms applied to all members of the union, making their implementation

The main monetary and credit policy instruments used by the BCEAO are national and bank-to-bank credit targets; a ceiling on access to central bank financing to maintain aggregate demand at a level consistent with balance of payments and domestic growth objectives; a rediscount rate; the interbank money market; and a liquidity ratio.

Given the openness of the monetary union, the fixed exchange rate regime, and the necessity of maintaining the debit balance of the operations account at an acceptable level, the BCEAO sets an overall credit target consistent with the final target for the individual country's level of net foreign assets. Using this overall national ceiling, the national credit committee of each member country establishes objectives for money and credit—based on external reserves and in light of prospective trends in production and prices—and the proposed ceiling for access by the government and the financial sector to central bank refinancing. This formulation comprises a target for net credit to the government, an indicative ceiling for crop credit, and ceilings for ordinary credit for the rest of the economy.

Monetary policy is conducted by controlling credit. As part of the reforms initiated in 1989, the BCEAO is considering introducing new monetary management tools, such as reserve requirements.

more universal. The reforms have created a sounder environment in which the government stems its interference in credit allocation. The government has begun to rely less heavily on borrowing from the banking sector, due to stricter controls on government borrowing through state-owned enterprises.

By adhering to a restrictive monetary policy in the past few years, the BCEAO has helped improve Senegal's external accounts.[7] Yet this policy has severely constrained domestic credit to the rest of the economy. From 1986 to 1991 credit to the nongovernment sector increased by an average of only 0.7 percent annually (in terms of money supply at the beginning of the year); in real terms, it declined substantially. The money supply (M2) has followed a similar trend, although the decline has been less severe. Given these trends, the ratio of M2 to GDP—one measure of the degree of financial deepening—has fallen from 0.28 in 1984 to 0.23 in 1991 (table 7.3).

In the context of the fixed exchange rate, BCEAO policies seemed to be appropriate for maintaining a sustainable external position, particularly because the fiscal situation could not be controlled. It is questionable whether this policy can be maintained without adversely affecting economic growth. The policies have successfully controlled the rate of domestic inflation, which has stabilized at less than 3 percent in recent years. Better inflationary control has helped Senegal recover a certain degree of competitiveness.

One of the results of monetary and credit sector reform has been liberalization of the interest rate structure. By eliminating the preferential discount rate—which formerly applied to agriculture, the export sector, small and medium-size companies, and residential construction (for first-time buyers or builders)—and by liberalizing margins and commissions, the government has kept lending rates for prime borrowers at 16 to 18 percent, while maintaining the official inflation rate at less than 3 percent. Bank lending continues to reflect the preference for short-term trade-related activities at the expense of longer-term investment projects, thereby undermining the growth

Table 7.3 Summary of monetary indicators, 1984–91
(annual percentage change, except M2/GDP)

Year	*Credit to government*[a]	*Credit to economy*[a]	*Money (M2)*[a]	*Nominal GDP*	*Ratio of M2 to GDP*
1984	5.5	2.0	5.2	8.1	0.28
1985	7.5	8.6	4.5	13.4	0.26
1986	1.6	1.3	11.2	12.5	0.26
1987	-1.7	3.5	0.2	6.1	0.24
1988	2.3	9.6	0.5	7.3	0.23
1989	-7.2	1.3	10.3	0.1	0.25
1990	-5.2	8.6	-4.8	7.0	0.22
1991	0.6	-4.3	5.8	2.5	0.23

a. Change in percentage of the money supply at the beginning of the period.
Source: BCEAO and IMF staff estimates.

prospects of the economy. Between 1985 and 1991, the share of short-term lending increased from 60 to 67 percent of cumulative bank lending, while loans to industrial projects have fallen from 22 percent to less than 15 percent.

The conduct of monetary and credit policy in Senegal has been designed and implemented in a firm, timely, and consistent manner. These measures have helped keep inflation low, curtail overall domestic demand, provide the basis for a more robust banking sector, and restrict government intervention in credit allocation. Yet they have not created the foundation for sustainable growth.

Trade policy reform. The objective of the trade reform program was to harmonize effective protection. It was to be implemented in two stages over a two-year period (July 1986 to July 1988). In the first stage in 1986, the government was to freeze the number of products subject to quotas, eliminate quantitative restrictions for a list of goods not produced in Senegal and for categories of goods of one subsector, reduce import duties for 15 groups of products (from 90 percent to 65 percent), and strengthen the export subsidy and duty drawback schemes, thus ensuring equivalent incentives across manufacturing sectors. In the second stage in 1987, the government was to eliminate most quantitative restrictions, as well as all reference prices *(valeurs mercuriales)*, except when underinvoicing or dumping were common practices; narrow the tariff rate band further; and strengthen the key industrial export institutions—that is, restructure the export insurance agency and the external trade agency. The main objective of these reforms was to reduce excessive tariff protection and to consolidate the tariff structure within a limited band (consisting of four customs duty rates).

Contrary to the experience in non-CFA countries, the removal of quantitative restrictions was not followed immediately by high tariffs, because the protection level in Senegal was already high enough, and, given the peculiar geographic location of the Gambia, any additional increase would merely have intensified the degree of fraud. Yet, although the schedule was largely adhered to, it can still be argued that the sequencing and pace of trade reform were less than optimal in Senegal. The implementation period (twenty-four months) was too short to allow the manufacturing firms to prepare themselves for stiff external competition. Moreover, the timing of the critical accompanying measures was problematic. The industrial policy reform called for reducing the cost of production in Senegal—liberalizing the labor market, reducing energy costs, and improving the regulatory environment. In retrospect, the labor market issue was not addressed effectively, the energy cost was only slightly reduced three years after trade was completely liberalized, and the regulatory environment was only recently addressed in a meaningful way.

Trade measures for opening up the economy proceeded largely on schedule. However, in the absence of the accompanying measures necessary to reduce the cost of business in Senegal, as well as in the face of significant real exchange rate depreciation in competing countries (including the Gambia), the industrial sector met increasing competition from imported goods. Light manufactures such as textiles, shoes, batteries, and matches, whose smuggling was somewhat controlled through quantitative restrictions, became totally exposed to competition. Under the pressure emanating from these industries, the government reintroduced several protection measures in mid-1989, including tariff exemptions for imported inputs necessary for producing textiles, matches, and batteries.

The government reversed its protection policy by raising customs tariffs, partly to restore protection for subsectors threatened by external competition and partly to increase tax revenue. It should be recalled that the government experienced major revenue shortfalls in fiscal 1989, and not necessarily because trade was liberalized. Customs duties (*droits de douane*) were raised from 10 percent to 15 percent in 1989, and a levy of 3 percent was imposed on most imports a year later (*timbre douanier*). Thus, the average nominal duty rate, which declined from 60 percent in 1985 to 35 percent in mid-1988, was raised to its current level of 43 percent. Moreover, to combat underinvoicing, the government introduced minimum customs tax assessments on a large number of imports and broadened the use of reference prices. Thus, the manipulation of tariff rates in order to mobilize revenue and protect industry, combined with the introduction of minimum customs assessments, basically reversed most of the tariff reforms achieved between 1986 and 1988. In fact, Senegal's protection system may have become more complicated by 1992 than it was during the prereform period.

Table 7.4 provides rough estimates of the effective rates of protection from 1985 to 1991 and shows clearly the reversal in government trade policy.[8] On average, the effective protection rates declined from 165 percent in 1985, before the reforms, to 89 percent in mid-1988, when most quantitative restrictions were eliminated and nominal tariffs were at their lowest levels. They increased to 98 percent in 1990 after the series of changes discussed earlier.

Table 7.4 Indicators of import protection, 1985–91

Indicator	*1985*	*1986*	*1987*	*1988*	*1989*	*1990*	*1991*
Average effective rate of protection (percent)	165.4	111.0	111.0	89.3	94.6	97.7	..
Customs receipts (CFAF)	73.4	80.0	83.4	74.3	91.1	104.1	115.0
Effective tariff rates (percent)[a]	18.1	23.0	25.6	23.0	25.2	28.6	30.3

.. Not available.
a. Defined as customs receipts as a percentage of imports of goods (cif).
Source: World Bank staff estimates.

In addition to these higher protection rates, recent changes reintroduced wide distortions in the incentive system among some industrial subsectors. Based on the same table, evidence about the impact of the trade reforms on customs receipts is not conclusive. Customs receipts increased by nearly 13 percent in nominal terms between 1985 and 1987, declined by that much in 1988, and then increased by 16 percent annually between 1989 and 1991. The increase during the latter period seems to have resulted from the effort to reduce tax exemptions rather than from tariff increases.

Domestic trade liberalization and implementation. Like other African countries, Senegal intensified direct government intervention in agriculture and manufacturing pricing and markets in the 1960s and 1970s. During its first phase, the adjustment effort attempted to reverse this situation and had achieved some success. In agriculture, pricing policy was used as the primary vehicle for stimulating production and shifting income in favor of rural producers.

SUBSIDIES AND PRODUCER PRICES. By the end of 1988 major subsidies in the agricultural sector were reduced or phased out, producer prices of foodcrops were liberalized, producer prices of cash crops were reduced slightly, and input distribution markets were liberalized. Fertilizer subsidies were eliminated for all commodities except cotton. Despite being adjusted from time to time, producer prices for groundnuts, cotton, and rice remained delinked from the world market prices.[9] A major study on agricultural prices and incentives was undertaken in 1988, but its recommendations were never implemented, particularly a proposal to adjust the groundnut producer price to the world market price. Nevertheless, budgetary constraints necessitated reducing the groundnut producer price in 1988.

CONSUMER PRICES. The prices for all but 16 consumer goods had been decontrolled in 1987 and 1988, and the office in charge of price controls was abolished in 1990. For manufactured goods, prices were decontrolled in conjunction with the elimination of quantitative restrictions on imports. In addition, an effective price information system was set up for local cereals. For rice, the government reduced the consumer price further than was desirable. The consumer items for which prices remained under control were sugar, salt, tea, wheat, flour, pharmaceutical products, cement, electricity, petroleum products, water, transportation, broken rice, tomatoes and tomato concentrate, and cooking oil. The government's rationale for controlling the prices of these items was that it was for social and strategic reasons.

In energy the government instituted a simpler and more transparent pricing and taxation system for petroleum products in 1991. This system set ex-refinery prices at import parity, plus a fixed handling fee paid to the local refinery company to account for the relative inefficiencies under which it was operating. Prices to distributors were derived from ex-refinery prices in which import duties and taxes were added together. Consequently, for the first time since 1986, domestic prices were reduced in July 1991 by 5 to 25 percent, with the higher reductions applying to industrial petroleum inputs. The distribution of petroleum products and their prices have not yet been deregulated.

MARKET DEREGULATION. Most restrictions on the domestic marketing of cereals other than rice have been removed, thus creating a well-functioning market with many participants. The role of the rural development authorities (SRDRs) was significantly curtailed in recent years, the public enterprise for input supplies (SONAR) was liquidated, and import controls on fertilizers were phased out. The distribution and collection of groundnut seeds were privatized, as was the primary marketing of groundnuts. The monopoly of the public enterprise SERAS on skins and hides was abolished (and the enterprise was later privatized).

Other reforms envisaged by the government included limiting market intervention by the food security commission, separating the rice operation from the *Caisse de péréquation et de stabilisation des prix* (CPSP), and allowing private importers to participate in rice importation and trade. Of these actions, the only measure implemented effectively was limiting intervention by the food security commission. In the rice sector, the government felt compelled to manage the distorted domestic prices to justify almost complete control of the activity by the public sector. In the groundnut sector, domestic primary marketing costs were reduced and the private sector was allowed into marketing in 1987. The sugar sector, consisting of a private company (CSS), enjoys a production and imports monopoly under a long-term convention with the government, which runs to the year 2000. The rice subsector has remained inefficient and has distorted the entire domestic cereals sector in favor of rice, to the detriment of locally produced maize, sorghum, and millet, whose production costs are far less expensive. The government also abandoned the principle of special agreements (*conventions spéciales*).

Labor and wage policy reform and implementation. A major element of adjustment in Senegal was to improve the functioning of the labor market. Strong labor market rigidity, high wages, and low productivity were impediments to new investment and the creation of employment. However, reform was limited to abolishing the labor office in 1987 and, consequently, liberalizing hiring practices; also, constraints on using temporary employment contracts were relaxed partially. The maximum period for such contracts was extended from six to twelve months. An attempt to revise critical provisions in the labor code had failed, and the modified code was not approved by the National Assembly due to deep-seated vested interests in the unions and the fear of triggering social unrest on the eve of the 1988 general election.

In 1989 the use of temporary labor was relaxed further. For all firms the maximum period for these contracts was extended to five years, and for firms in the industrial free zone and those benefiting from the investment code the period was unlimited. Both the general payroll tax (*contribution forfaitaire*) of about 3 percent and the income tax normally paid by employers were eliminated in 1989 for new and expanding firms. A tripartite committee composed of the government, employers associations, and labor unions was formed in January 1990 to examine existing labor legislation and industrial regulations. Thus, based on an in-depth study of the labor market in Senegal by the International Labour Organisation in 1990, the government decided that the labor code should be revised completely, rather than a few articles of the code modified. To maximize support for adopting a new labor code, the government informed and educated the public and the unions about the importance of liberalizing the labor market. The labor code has now been revised and submitted to the National Assembly for ratification. Among the key changes are that the different industry-specific wage scales have been made independent of the minimum wage, collective bargaining has been encouraged at the firm level, and firing practices have been liberalized.

In the public sector, the government also abolished automatic recruitment from training schools, downsized the civil service through a voluntary departure program, rationalized the wage benefits, and froze the minimum wage. With the exception of the latter, which also applies to the private sector, none of the other measures has been implemented effectively. Legal labor market rigidities still exist in Senegal, although compliance with them is becoming less effective with the expansion of the informal sector. In the civil service, real average salaries declined by 30 percent from 1980 to 1985, and then increased by 24 percent from 1985 to 1990 (table 7.5). But it was the more highly paid civil servants who saw their real wages decline faster. The salary differential in the civil service has narrowed from 1:8 in 1980 to 1:6 in 1990. Wages in the informal sector are believed to be a third of prevailing wages in the formal sector.

The partial approach to labor market reform has been ineffective. Yet although the comprehensive and less confrontational approach recently followed has not yet yielded results in the context of the internal adjustment strategy pursued by Senegal, it has enhanced public awareness about and government ownership of the reform program (box 7.2).

Sectoral and institutional reform

Banking sector reform. Of all the reforms undertaken by Senegal in the 1980s, banking sector reform—in which 7 of the country's 15 banks were closed—must be considered the most successful reform. This achievement owed a great deal to the very active role of the BCEAO, whose views on bank restructuring were very close to those of the foreign donors involved in the operation. Also, after some hesitation at the start, the government showed great political courage in closing several of the country's public banks, with the accompanying short-term negative impact on employment. The commonality of approaches and close coordination among donors played an important role in the success of the reform. It is important to note that Senegal was one of the first countries in the region to undertake such a significant reform of the financial sector.

In October 1987 the government consulted the IMF, the World Bank, and bilateral donors (France and the United States) with a view toward restructuring the ailing banks. BCEAO saw the extensive banking crisis in several member countries in late 1988 as an opportunity to restructure the banking sector and to lay a foundation for developing modern, responsible capital markets. While the restructuring or closing of the ailing banks was the more spectacular aspect of the reform, more important changes took place in policy that affected the general operational components of banks. The reform program consisted of six measures:

- A drastic restructuring of distressed banks that with the injection of additional capital would experience a positive net worth and meet minimum capital adequacy requirements (BIAOS and USB).

Table 7.5 Indexes of civil servants' real wages and salaries, 1980–91
(1980 = 100)

Year	Minimum wage	Civil servants' salaries		
		Minimum	Maximum	Average[a]
1980[b]	100	100	100	100
1981	99	94	94	94
1982	91	88	81	85
1983	94	85	74	81
1984	85	76	66	78
1985	78	70	59	70
1986	74	66	55	72
1987	77	69	58	77
1988	78	70	59	81
1989	85	76	59	86
1990	85	76	60	88
1991	87	..	..	..
Change 1980 to 1985	-21.7	-29.7	-41.3	-29.9
Change 1985 to 1990	8.6	7.4	0.4	24.2

.. Not available.
Note: Deflated by the consumer price index for the average Senegalese family.
a. The difference between the earnings (represented by this column) and rates data (represented by the two preceding columns) can be explained by promotions and fringe benefits.
b. Fiscal 1980–81.
Source: World Bank staff estimates.

- The closure of distressed banks for which no substantial injection of new capital was expected (BNDS, SOFISEDIT, SONAGA/ SONABANQUE, ASSURBANK, and BSK).
- A sharp reduction in abusive practices, such as forced crop credits and government guarantees on parastatal borrowing, and a reduction in government ownership in financial institutions to less than 25 percent.

Box 7.2 Government ownership: two different strategies for revising the labor code

The manner in which the government attempted to revise the labor code provides a useful lesson for the design of future reforms in Senegal and elsewhere. In 1987 the approach adopted by the government consisted of directly tackling selected articles in the labor code that deal with hiring and firing (Articles 35 and 47). There was little, if any, discussion with the social partners concerned (the employers association and labor unions). No public discussion of the merit of these reforms took place. The end result was that the revised code was not adopted by the National Assembly; it was seen as being imposed by the donors.

In 1990 the approach was to revise the code completely. And the social partners have been involved in all stages of the process: analytical work, discussion, and drafting. The initial preparatory work was facilitated by an ILO expert, who had established good rapport with the unions and the employers association. The outcome of this effort was the formation of a tripartite committee—comprising government, unions, and employers—to work with another international expert to revise the code. Terms of reference for the consultant were cleared by all parties concerned, as was the selection of the consultant. A very experienced consultant was selected, who also happened to have easy access to the head of CNTS (the main labor union) and the president of Senegal. Parallel to this effort, ILO was also commissioned to carry out an in-depth study on the wage-setting system in Senegal. The study served as a valuable input into the process of revising the code.

When the revised code was drafted, the government undertook a six-month public campaign led by high government officials to sensitize public opinion to labor market flexibility and liberalization. Thus, a first public debate was held in March 1991, a presentation of the issue at the National Assembly was made by the Prime Minister in June, and an employment symposium and a workshop for the labor inspectors were organized in July. The revised code was submitted to the National Assembly in September 1991, but has not yet been approved.

Revising the code was a lengthy and time-consuming process, taking about two years between the establishment of the tripartite committee and the submission of the revised code to the National Assembly. Nevertheless, Senegal has ownership of the new code, not the World Bank or outside consultants. Those who will benefit from and oversee the implementation of the code have been directly involved in the preparation and revision process.

- Substantial reforms in credit policies and in bank legislation, supervision, and practices (bank-by-bank credit ceilings, sectoral credit targets, prior authorization mechanisms, and interest rate policies).
- Recovery of bad debt.
- Studies of grass-roots mutual credit schemes.

In June 1989, after two years of attempting to save most of the development banks,[10] the government adopted a comprehensive strategy to restructure the banking system. The strategy called for maintaining only banks that, after restructuring, could become profitable, solvent, and liquid; privatizing banks to reduce government interference in bank management and limiting the government's equity share in banks to a maximum of 25 percent; and developing a global financing plan whose projected annual government contributions would be compatible with the government budget.

When shareholders agreed to rehabilitate the banks under their control, the strategy called for restoring the banks' financial situation through shareholder equity or quasi-equity contributions to offset losses and recapitalizing the banks to a level compatible with sound banking standards. In addition, staffing was to be reduced, expensive branch networks pruned, and managerial changes introduced. When the financial requirements for rehabilitating a bank would be beyond the resources of its shareholders, as in government-owned or -controlled banks, the balance sheet was to be split into a "sound balance sheet" that represented the performing loans and a "liquidating structure" that represented nonperforming assets. This procedure applies to five government-controlled banks.

The reforms were designed to curb the abuse of crop credits and government guarantees on parastatal borrowing that in the past had jeopardized bank profits. They were also to provide a market-oriented determination of interest rates (patterned after Paris rates) and to widen banking margins—all of which to improve the profitability of banks. In 1989 the West African Monetary Union Council of Ministers decided that measures should be introduced to make the bank-by-bank credit ceiling allocations more flexible. The system of credit objectives targeted to sectors designated as "priority" was eliminated. The prior authorization mechanism required for loans of more than CFAF 70 million was raised to CFAF 300 million. The Council of Ministers agreed that the BCEAO would channel all rediscounting needs through the money market, which it would continue to intermediate at the administratively determined rate; and meet the demand for borrowing in excess of money market deposits through a last-resort facility of the central bank.

There were two banks associated with private Senegalese investors whose foreign majority shareholders wanted to stay in business during the restructuring period: BIAOS (65 percent owned by the French BIAO Group) and MASSRAF (partly owned by Saudi Arabian interests). The government closed four of the five development banks and two commercial banks in which it had majority ownership. In addition, it sought to prevent the recurrence of past practices, by directly and indirectly reducing its capital share in all banks (except CNCAS, where no suitable buyer can be found) to a maximum of 25 percent, which is less than required to be a blocking minority. In short, with minor exceptions, the bank restructuring process was completed more or less on schedule.

BCEAO has been responsible for making changes in the banking legislation and supervision. It has successfully implemented the proposed reforms. To reform bank supervision procedures, it formed a West African Monetary Union zonewide control commission on October 1, 1990, with supranational authority; it then revised banking laws and regulations to prevent the recurrence of past excesses and bring them in line with practices in other countries. The BCEAO obtained support from France and the IMF to strengthen its inspection department.

In contrast to the government's prompt and courageous decision to close several banks, efforts toward debt recovery have been weak and erratic. As of the end of 1989, government estimates indicate that approximately CFAF 32 billion (about $100 million) of the CFAF 144 billion (about $450 million) of nonperforming credits of the banks to be restructured could ultimately be recovered in the period from 1990 to 1993. This amount would repay depositors whose assets were frozen when the banking sector was restructured and enable the government to service the debt it incurred to undertake the reform program. In this connection, the government established a recovery agency staffed in part by personnel laid off by the restructured banks, and charged with recovering the bad loans of the restructured banks by seizing debtors' assets, rescheduling loans, and pursuing other arrangements. To recover the bad debt and to ensure progress, an independent auditor prepared a data bank of all delinquent debtors of the banks being restructured. Progress on recovery has been followed by a committee established by the Ministry of Finance.

Implementing these measures has taken longer than necessary. The government's hesitancy to pursue the large debtors, most of whom are politically well connected, accounted for this lack of success. The implications of these developments are more significant than is the forgone revenue from debt recovery. The fact that large debtors continue to be perceived to be above the law explains in part the reluctance of banks to commit important sums for long-term investment projects.

The total cost of banking system reform was estimated at CFAF 275 billion. Of this, about CFAF 198 billion has already been secured through the consolidation of CFAF 146.5 billion from BCEAO on concessional terms, a sector adjustment loan of CFAF 31.7 billion (IDA plus cofinanciers), and the recovery of bad debts, estimated at CFAF 20 billion. The remaining CFAF 77 billion is expected to be covered from a further BCEAO consolidation and the ongoing recovery of nonperforming loans.

Public enterprise reform. Although the Senegalese were late in formulating a clear public enterprise sector strategy, the sectoral reform program has been comprehensive and based on detailed analytical work. The World Bank prepared two sectoral reports in 1981 and 1989 to assist the government in formulating an overall framework for reform. Several audit reports and specific policy studies were also carried out.[11] Two specific bank technical assistance projects were approved in 1977 and 1983, targeted at institution building and information management at both the enterprises and the supervisory agencies.

Public enterprise reform in Senegal dates back to the late 1970s, but in 1986 it became part of the government's medium-term economic and financial rehabilitation program, supported by three structural adjustment loans, a financial sector adjustment loan, and a technical assistance project.[12] The objectives of Senegal's reform policy are no different than those pursued by other countries—to restrict government intervention in enterprises that could be managed more effectively by the private sector, and to improve the government's ability to manage the public enterprises that remain under its control. Until 1985 government strategy had not been articulated. The first structural adjustment loan reaffirmed the end of the nationalization policy, the strong ex ante supervision of public enterprises, and the establishment of a system of contract plans, a new measure to help public enterprises develop a medium-term strategy and to clarify the relationship between the government and individual enterprises.[13] In 1985 government strategy called for privatizing and liquidating selected public enterprises, improving the management and performance of those that remained in the public sector, simplifying sectoral control procedures, and improving portfolio management information. In 1989 this strategy was refined and continued.

Since 1990 strategy has shifted from attempts to privatize nonperforming public enterprises to efforts to start with profitable enterprises and strengthen the process of privatization—a policy that has made the process more transparent. The government has imposed greater financial discipline by hardening the budget constraints of commercially oriented public enterprises (reducing operating subsidies, settling cross-debts, eliminating implicit subsidies, and eliminating overdraft facilities). Public enterprises must restructure or face liquidation. Overdrafts were eliminated to close a loophole for public enterprises that still enabled them to comply with the reduction in direct subsidies. One important shortcoming of the design of the reform program is the large number of small enterprises that were to be privatized (which distracted the government from focusing on major enterprises) and the large number of contract plans that were to be signed in a relatively short period. It can be argued that privatization could have been speeded up had the regulatory and incentive framework been reformed to create a favorable environment for private sector investment.

On the institutional and legal front, the government's approach throughout most of the 1980s was focused too much on perfecting instruments of control and strengthening oversight agencies. Recently, the government has shifted its approach. It created and later strengthened a focal parastatal agency (DRSP), the only agency outside the Finance Ministry responsible for formulating, managing, and monitoring the reform program for public enterprises. The agency is also responsible for supervising contract plan implementation, strengthening the public enterprise unit in the treasury by giving it greater authority in financial decisionmaking, curtailing the roles of other supervisory agencies to a posteriori compliance monitoring, and improving the composition of the board of directors.

Implementation has been uneven—good to fair on the legal, institutional, and rehabilitation fronts; fair to poor on the financial front; and, until quite recently, poor on the privatization front. Public enterprise reform has been plagued by significant delays—a clear indication of the complexity and institutional nature of the issues and the government's hesitancy to tackle tough reforms, particularly those affecting the treasury and vested interests.

The government has changed the law on the organization and control of the public enterprise sector, but it has not yet issued the decrees required for its enforcement. Agencies that implemented the program have been streamlined and rationalized. Twenty-four (of 44 planned) contract plans and "letters of mission" have been signed by the government and selected public enterprises. While contract plans have improved the transparency between and accountability of the two contracting parties—not a small achievement—they have not been successful in enforcing compliance with the financial obligations. As Nellis (1989) notes, "tariff regimes have been specified, investment programs stated, noncommercial operations costed out and compensation arranged for, and operating subsidies set—but in case after case the government has proven unable or unwilling to honor the financial commitments agreed upon; and the agreements have had to be repeatedly and extensively revised, or fallen into abeyance." Only 10 of a programmed 27 public enterprises have been restructured and rehabilitated.

On the financial front, the government has implemented the reforms in "letter but not spirit." Indeed, while the government reduced direct subsidies to public enterprises, the enterprises have resorted to commercial bank overdrafts and government guarantees for borrowing, thus precipitating the financial crisis of the banking system and accumulating arrears when the overdraft facilities have no longer been possible. The settlement of cross-debt arrears between the government and public enterprises has been carried out twice, in 1986 and 1989, but the problem reappeared because preventive measures were not implemented concurrently. The arrears at the end of 1989 were large, and their impact on the working capital and tax payment of public enterprises was significant. Settling these arrears was complex, and the process cannot be repeated indefinitely—and unless preventive measures similar to those adopted in 1991 are in place, the problem will recur.[14] As a good start, the government focused on the three utility companies (water, electricity, and telephone), apparently with some encouraging success.

Table 7.6 and figure 7.2 show the performance of the divestiture program for both financial and nonfinancial public enterprises. Over the entire reform period, the government has liquidated 21 public enterprises (most of them virtually defunct) and totally or partially privatized 26 others (most of which were small and unimportant)—together representing 42 percent of the total number of public enterprises in the sector. In terms of assets and government equity, however, they represent only 19 percent and 11 percent of the sector, respectively. The disproportionate percentages reflect the fact that the three utility companies (electricity, water, and telephone) were not

Table 7.6 Divestiture program, 1980–91
(percent)

Divested enterprises/ type of divestiture	*Enterprises as share of total in subsector*	*Enterprises' assets as share of total in subsector*	*Government equity*	*Government equity as percentage of assets*
Nonfinancial	36	12	6	38
Privatized	21	9	5	40
Liquidated	15	3	1	33
Financial	79	88	79	44
Privatized	36	46	31	32
Liquidated	43	42	48	57
All	42	19	11	41
Privatized	23	12	6	37
Liquidated	19	6	4	48
Divestitures supported by:				
Structural adjustment loan IV	25	10	5	37
Financial sector adjustment loan	6	5	4	51
Memo: Breakdown of all public enterprises (divested and nondivested)				
All public enterprises	100	100	100	72
Nonfinancial	88	91	94	74
Financial	12	9	6	49

Note: Data may not add up due to rounding.
Source: World Bank data.

Figure 7.2 Senegal public enterprise divestiture program

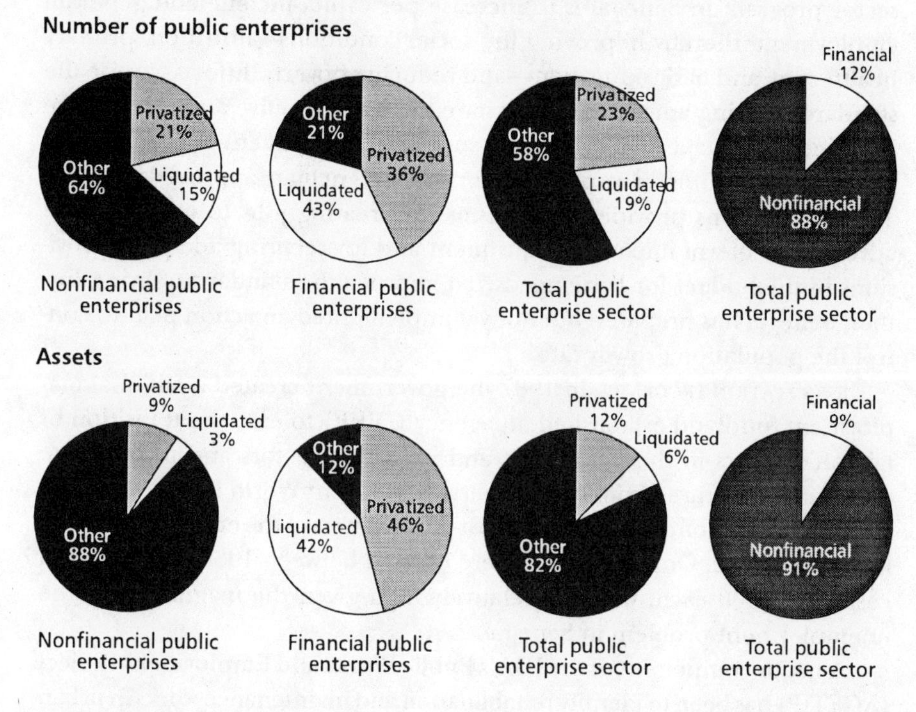

Source: World Bank staff estimates.

part of the divestiture program. They alone account for 33 percent of the sector's assets and 46 percent of government equity. A breakdown of the public enterprise sector shows that the divestiture process is 80 to 90 percent complete in the financial subsector, but far from being complete in the nonfinancial—36 percent in terms of numbers, 12 percent in assets, and 6 percent in government equity. In total, privatization has brought nearly CFAF 19 billion in cash to the treasury—70 percent from the sales of shares and 30 percent from dividends.

Progress in the divestiture program is very recent. Of the public enterprises privatized and liquidated, representing 80 percent of the assets and government equity, about 75 percent were divested between 1989 and 1991. There are several reasons for this recent positive development: the focus on profitable companies, the budgetary financial squeeze on public enterprises, and the improved transparency of the privatization process. Had the government not insisted on certain conditions (higher prices and no reduction in personnel), and had the enabling environment of the private sector (including a secondary market) been in place, the privatization performance would have been much better.

Social sector reform and implementation. The primary objective of the social sector program in Senegal is to increase per capita income and generate employment, thereby improving the social conditions—nutrition, primary health care, and basic education—and reducing poverty. Efforts to raise the standard of living among the poor have been more active and direct since 1987 in the context of World Bank–supported adjustment operations (including the first human resource sector adjustment loan, approved in 1991). These operations provide mechanisms for creating jobs to minimize the adverse short-term impact of adjustment and for securing adequate provisions in the budget for basic needs. To improve the standard of living further, Senegal has prepared but not yet implemented an action plan to control the population growth rate.

JOB CREATION PROGRAMS. In 1987 the government created a national employment fund and established an agency (DIRE) to ease the transition of laid-off workers in the parapublic and industrial sectors and to stimulate voluntary departures from the civil service. A recent World Bank evaluation of this program concluded that the cost-effectiveness of the employment fund has been mixed. Only 1,500 jobs were created between 1988 and 1991 at a cost of $11,000 each, which is relatively high given the magnitude of the unemployment problem in Senegal.

A major component of the IDA's Public Works and Employment Project (AGETIP) has been to identify rehabilitation and maintenance works in urban areas to be undertaken by small contractors with labor-intensive methods. The project has created 2,000 person-years of temporary employment over a two-year period. Apart from its success at easing the initial employment costs of adjustment, the project has helped increase the long-term skills of both small contractors and their temporary employees.

PUBLIC EXPENDITURE RESTRUCTURING. While the adjustment effort has sought to improve the composition of the investment program since 1986, it has only recently emphasized restructuring the government budget to ensure that resource allocations to primary health care and primary education are adequate. The voluntary departure program has sought to preserve adequate recruitment of primary school teachers and to protect allocations to social sectors during budgetary cuts. The results of the recent public expenditure review indicated that, while the health subsector benefited from the restructuring of expenditures toward primary health care during the 1980s, not much restructuring took place in the education subsector.

In the health subsector, real recurrent expenditures were the hardest hit, dropping by 21 percent between the first and the second halves of the 1980s (table 7.7). The total amount allocated to the health sector under the recurrent budget has fallen considerably, from 0.9 percent of GDP in 1980 to 0.6 percent in 1988. The balance between salaries and wages and materials and supplies continued to deteriorate, with the ratio rising from 2:1 in

1982 to 3:1 in 1989. The public expenditure review provides ample evidence that the adequacy and quality of health delivery services in the public sector has deteriorated significantly over the past decade. One positive development in health expenditures has been the increase in the share of total recurrent and investment expenditures on primary health care, from 48 percent in 1981 to 62 percent in 1989. Relatedly, the regional balance of per capita health expenditures has improved.

In education, recurrent expenditures remained constant in real terms during the 1980s. However, higher education experienced an increase at the expense of primary education, compounded by the fact that nonwage recurrent expenditures were squeezed hard, dropping to just about 10 percent of the wage cost. Thus, the quality of education services deteriorated at all levels. Expenditures in the sector were weighted excessively toward higer education during the latter part of the 1980s. These figures do not fully measure the failure of education policy, because they mask high wastage and failure rates, especially at the university level. Costs per student show vast disparities, with those at the university level 18 to 20 times the cost of elementary education. This compares unfavorably with countries with better education systems.

Institutional and legal reform and implementation. Several institutional and legal reforms have been discussed, including the revised labor code and greater public sector managerial efficiency. This section discusses the reforms

Table 7.7 Allocation of resources to social sectors, 1980–90
(real index, 1980 = 100)

Allocation	*Annual average*		*Percentage change*	
	1980–85	*1986–90*	*Total*	*Annual*
Total recurrent expenditure	108.2	98.5	-9.0	-1.9
Education	96.3	96.5	0.2	0.0
Higher education	88.7[a]	95.5	7.7	1.5
Wages	96.4	102.1[b]	5.9	1.1
Health	90.7	71.6	-21.0	-4.6
Wages	90.1	77.3[b]	-14.2	-3.0
Total investment	85.1[c]	58.7	-31.0	-7.2
Education	85.1[c]	64.1	-24.6	-5.5
Health	85.1[c]	82.0	-3.6	-0.7
Share of wages in education recurrent expenditure (percent)	70.0[d]	74.0[b]	5.9	1.1
Share of wages in health recurrent expenditure (percent)	68.0[d]	73.0[b]	8.6	1.7
Primary enrollment (thousands)	509.0	662.0	30.1	5.7
Secondary and tertiary enrollment (thousands)	123.0	176.0	43.1	7.4

a. Annual average for 1983–85.
b. Annual average for 1989.
c. Annual average for 1981–83.
d. Annual average for 1981.
Source: World Bank estimates.

that have not been covered elsewhere—public administration and the private sector enabling environment.

CIVIL SERVICE REFORM. Senegal inherited a large public administration from the time when Dakar was the capital of the French West African colonies. The high cost and the increasingly poor performance of the civil service have been a major challenge to Senegal since at least the mid-1970s.[15] The government first addressed these issues in 1976, when it decided to reorganize the central ministries (*opération organigramme*) with a view toward downsizing staff, reducing wage costs, and improving efficiency. The program was abandoned because of resistance from some ministries. Since 1982 the government's adjustment program has called for maintaining a ceiling on the number of civil servants, freezing salaries, and improving civil service management. These measures have been supported by the World Bank's second, third, and fourth structural adjustment loans, and a technical assistance project, and by a series of IMF arrangements.

The most far-reaching attempts to reform the civil service have been undertaken since 1990. The government sought to restructure key ministries

Box 7.3 Civil service voluntary departure program: a policy failure after a good start

The civil service reform program, introduced by the government in January 1990, consisted of three components: (1) a major restructuring of the administration (a reduction in the number of ministries from 23 to 15, followed by an organizational audit; and the elimination of about 2,850 positions—49 percent of which by June 1990); (2) an early retirement program that could affect about 1,450 staff age 48 years and over; and (3) a privatization program of selected government services (including the Road Maintenance Department of the Ministry of Infrastructure and the Maintenance Department of the Ministry of Water Resources), which could cover about 1,300 staff. The education and health sectors were excluded from the reform program to avoid worsening the personnel shortage in these two sectors.

Because the government had always opposed a unilateral firing of civil servants, it decided to grant generous compensation packages (up to 48 months of salary, except for the two lowest grades, which would receive 60 months of salary) to entice the staff to leave the administration. The program was externally financed by France, the African Development Bank, and counterpart funds from SAL IV disbursements.

The government's voluntary departure program, which started later than originally expected, was well received by civil servants, and, as a result, 4,140 staff applied to leave the service under this program by June 1990 (box table 7.3). Of this number, only 2,030 could leave by August 1990 because some of the financing for the separation packages (provided by donors) was diverted to fill the unexpected budgetary financing gap in 1989–90. Another round of voluntary departures of 1,715 staff occurred toward the end of the 1990–91 fiscal year. Thus, as of August 1991 a total of 3,745 staff, representing about 90 percent of both the total number (by reducing staff through a voluntary departure program), institute measures to control the wage bill, and improve personnel management. The development management project sponsored several studies to facilitate the design and implementation of reform. Had they been implemented, these measures would have reduced the number of civil servants by 7.2 percent by June 1992, and brought their ratio to the population from 9 per thousand to 7.7—a ratio comparable to those of other African countries with better resource endowments. The nominal wage bill would have been reduced by 8.7 percent, from CFAF 125 billion in fiscal 1988 to CFAF 115 billion in fiscal 1991. Neither target was achieved, and the actual outcome was a move in the opposite direction.

The success of civil service reform has been mixed. The administration was restructured in March 1990, reducing the number of ministries from 23 to 15 with the elimination or merging of some departments. Key departments, such as the tax and customs departments, were strengthened. The voluntary departure program was introduced successfully and led to the departure of 3,745 staff from the payroll (box 7.3). Yet the government was unable to control recruitment or the wage bill. As of June 1992 the number of civil

of applicants and the original program, had left the civil service, at a total cost of CFAF 15.7 billion. The average cost per departee is calculated at about CFAF 4.2 million, representing nearly 3.2 years of salary, which is in line with the programmed cost. Most of these departures have come from the lower levels of the service, with the two lowest levels (of five) representing about 46 percent of the total. This is more than twice the share of these two categories in the total number of civil servants (20 percent.) Early retirees have accounted for about 43 percent of the total number of departures.

Box table 7.3 Civil service voluntary departure program, 1991

Category	SAL IV program (number)	Application (number)	Actual (as of October 1991) Number of departures	Share of total (percent)	Average cost (CFAF millions)
Nature of departure					
Voluntary departure	2,850	2,458	2,155	57.5	4.8
Early retirement	1,450	1,682	1,590	42.5	3.3
Privatization	1,309	—	—	—	—
Total	5,609	4,140	3,745	100.0	4.2
Departure by grade					
A (highest)	—	492	434	11.6	5.9
B	—	1,088	925	24.7	5.9
C	—	744	674	18.0	4.1
D	—	1,417	1,339	35.8	3.1
E (lowest)	—	399	373	10.0	2.2
Total	—	4,140	3,745	100.0	4.2

— Not applicable.
Source: Government of Senegal; World Bank staff estimates.

service personnel stood at about 64,000, or 4 percent higher than programmed, and the wage bill for the year reached CFAF 130 billion, or 13 percent higher than projected. In addition, the amount of "rappel" in arrears continued to increase, contrary to the spirit of the adjustment program. The management information system, providing data on staff and payroll, has not yet been installed.

Program implementation was not without problems. Rather than carrying out a well-designed organizational audit for which resources were made available by the donors, as originally planned, the government resorted to ad hoc procedures. It paralyzed the administration for some time. No serious follow-up took place on what became of the staff who left the administration. The most serious setback of the voluntary departure program was the inability of the government to control recruitment. After the first round of departures in June 1990, the government recruited as many as had left. This is a clear indication of the lack of coordination among ministries and the lack of a reliable management information system, two key elements of the civil service reform program and the development management project. Having adequate institutional capacity to implement the reforms is crucial to the success of the program.

REGULATORY ENVIRONMENT. The regulatory environment has improved somewhat under the adjustment program, but more must be done. The fundamental issue is attitude—civil servants "mistrust" the private sector. Administrative regulations are cumbersome and lack efficiency. The main achievements in Senegal were with the incentive systems. The investment code was revised twice, most recently in 1987, with a view toward eliminating the bias against labor-intensive investment, introducing automaticity in benefits, eliminating the special regime, and streamlining the administrative procedures for investment approval with the creation of a one-stop window (*guichet unique*). The formalities involved in setting up an enterprise have been streamlined and simplified (including the commercial code) to allow for quicker and more efficient evaluation of private sector investment applications. A March 1991 law allows the automatic approval of all such requests if not acted upon within thirty days.

In 1980 a series of export promotion measures were adopted, consisting of a duty drawback scheme and export subsidies, and both the export promotion agency (CICES) and the export insurance agency (ASACE) were strengthened. Subsidies have been extended, and the rate has increased from 10 percent of export value to 25 percent of value added. However, since 1990 budgetary difficulties have forced the government to stop honoring payments for export subsidies. In 1990 export promotion centered on resuscitating activity in the industrial free zone. Firms in this zone are now allowed to sell up to 40 percent of their output on the domestic market. The government has also set up "free points," granting all the tax advantages of firms in the zone to selected export-oriented enterprises located outside the zone.

Special agreements between the government and firms (*conventions spéciales*) provided long-term concessions to firms as an incentive to invest in large projects. These concessions, made essentially ad hoc, introduced distortions in the incentive system and led to substantial forgone revenue for the government. In 1986 about 21 companies, 15 in the industrial sector, benefited from specific protection regimes. Between 1979 and 1986 agreements for the four most important firms cumulatively cost the government some CFAF 115 billion in forgone revenue. In 1987 the government decided to phase out these agreements by simply letting them expire, and for three major companies (sugar, petroleum, and cement) specific actions were taken to reduce government concessions. Of the 15 industrial firms covered by these agreements, agreements for 4 firms had expired by 1991, 5 more will expire by 1995, and the remainder will expire by the year 2000.

Outcomes of the adjustment program

Macroeconomic outcomes

Eight key variables indicate the macroeconomic impact of adjustment: three intermediate indicators (the ratio of the budget deficit to GDP, the ratio of the current account deficit to GDP, and the real effective exchange rate index) and five outcome, or "response," indicators (economic growth rate, investment-to-GDP ratio, savings-to-GDP ratio, export growth, and the inflation rate). Figure 7.3 shows these indicators for the period 1980–91. Table 7.8 presents comparisons of these indicators for the crisis period (1979–81), stabilization period (1982–85), and partial adjustment period (1986–91).

Some observers, including the Operations Evaluation Department of the World Bank, have criticized the government's macroeconomic performance targets as too ambitious. In response, the analysis here compares the policy framework paper's projections of the selected indicators with actual outcomes for the period 1986–91.[16] While the policy framework paper projected steady economic growth of around 4 percent annually, actual rates have been within an acceptable margin of error in four of six years. The two years for which actual growth rates diverged significantly from projections are 1989 and 1991—years when rainfall was poor. Projections of savings and investment ratios to GDP have been optimistic, with actual values lower by 42 percent and 12 percent on average, respectively. Inflation has been kept remarkably low, within the projected target, because of the tight monetary and credit policy.

The fiscal-deficit-to-GDP ratio fluctuated the most widely. While the policy framework paper projected an improved fiscal position of around one percentage point of GDP annually, the actual outcome displayed wide fluctuations. Yet the overprojection does not reflect a deliberate optimism in the policy framework papers, but rather the poor implementation of fiscal reform combined with external shocks (box 7.4). The current account deficit has been less favorable than projected, due largely to poor export performance. Imports as a share of GDP have declined to a point considered harm-

Figure 7.3 Key macroeconomic indicators for Senegal, 1980–91

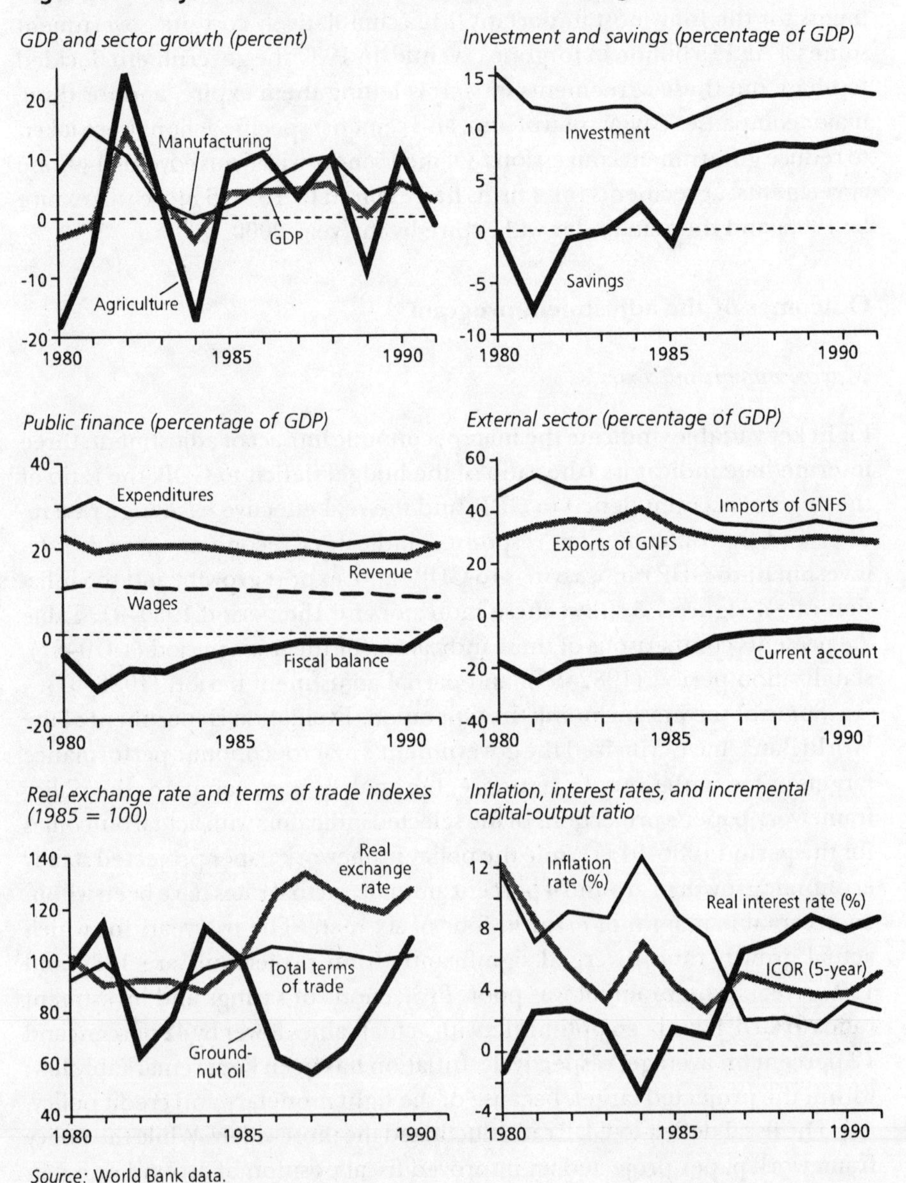

Source: World Bank data.

ful to longer-term growth. The actual export growth rate has been lower than projected by a large margin. In particular, traditional exports (groundnuts, cotton, fish, and, to some extent, phosphate) have been projected at higher rates than warranted by either world market prospects (for groundnuts) or the country's potential (for fish). The poor export performance reflects the substantial appreciation in the real exchange rate. In sum, aside from achieving a low rate of inflation, the adjustment program, as envisaged in five consecutive policy framework papers, has fallen short of even the modest projections, due in part to poor program design and implementation, in part to external shocks, and in part to optimistic assumptions.

Yet overall, Senegal drastically reduced its macroeconomic imbalances during the 1980s, particularly since 1983, although other macroeconomic indicators point to mixed success. The budget deficit was reduced from 8.8 percent of GDP in 1983 to 4.3 percent in 1990 and was completely eliminated in 1991. If interest payments were excluded, the budget position would register greater improvement—from a deficit of 5.6 percent of GDP to a surplus of 2.6 percent over the same period. The current account deficit (ex-

Table 7.8 Macroeconomic indicators, 1970–91

(annual averages; percent)

Indicator	Precrisis 1970–78	Crisis 1979–81	Stabilization 1982–85	Partial adjustment 1986–91
Final results				
GDP growth	2.3	1.8	4.3	3.2
GDP per capita growth	-0.5	-1.0	1.4	0.3
Primary sector growth[a]	0.9	1.0	5.0	3.3
Gross domestic investment/GDP	17.7	13.9	11.9	12.8
Gross domestic savings/GDP	10.5	-1.2	0.6	7.6
Growth in exports (GNFS)	6.0	-0.7	5.5	3.3
Inflation rate (GDP deflator)	7.4	9.1	10.0	2.7
Intermediate results				
Fiscal deficit/GDP[b]	-0.6	-7.1	-6.8	-2.9
Primary fiscal deficit/GDP[b]	..	..	-3.2	-0.0
Real interest (discount) rate	0.3[c]	0.5	1.0	7.3
Real effective exchange rate (1985 = 100)[d]	101.8	100.1	93.7	122.6
Producer prices/world prices of groundnuts	..	0.3	0.5	0.8
Producer prices/world prices of cotton	0.4	0.4	0.4	0.7
Current account deficit/GDP[e]	-10.4	-19.3	-18.2	-10.0
Excluding interest payments	..	-17.3	-16.3	-7.5
Scheduled debt service/GDP	2.6	7.1	9.2	9.6

a. The sector includes agriculture, livestock, fishing, and forestry subsectors. For the agriculture subsector, the first period covers 1981–85.
b. On a commitment basis and excluding grants.
c. For the period 1975–78.
d. An increase indicates appreciation.
e. Excluding official transfers.
Source: World Bank data and staff estimates.

Box 7.4 Senegal's fiscal performance: a stop-and-go approach

Senegal appears to have performed well on the fiscal front in 1984 (a year during which Senegal resumed the adjustment dialogue with the World Bank and the IMF) and in 1988 (a year prior to the drought). Indeed, the fiscal deficit (on a commitment basis and excluding external grants) had declined by more than three percentage points of GDP, reaching 2.6 percent in 1988 (box table 7.4). This adjustment, however, was unsustainable and was done in a way contrary to improving Senegal's competitiveness and to promoting long-term growth. The adjustment was made possible largely by cutting expenditures (in particular, investment and operations and maintenance expenditures) and by relying heavily on revenue windfalls, essentially from petroleum (to the tune of two percentage points of GDP, starting in 1986) and rice imports. The revenue windfalls from petroleum reflected the government's policy of maintaining the domestic prices of petroleum products when world prices declined sharply. Currently, domestic prices are two to three times world prices. The heavy dependence on petroleum revenue has two serious implications: it increases the cost of production, and it makes the revenue structure subject to the volatility of world petroleum prices.

While the substantial revenue windfalls were used "wisely" to reduce the budget deficit (contrary to the mid-1970s, when revenue windfalls from groundnuts were used to increase expenditures and borrow against future improvements in the terms of trade), they were not accompanied by an improved fiscal revenue position, despite several discretionary measures introduced under the adjustment program. The share of tax revenue in GDP dropped from 18.1 percent in 1984 to 14.3 percent in 1988, due primarily to an internal adjustment strategy, stagnation in the economy, and poor tax administration performance, particularly in the customs department.

The substantial reduction in the fiscal deficit over this period is somewhat overstated. Indeed, the official statistics should be adjusted to reflect the huge nonperforming loans of the banking system, since the government is ultimately responsible for honoring them. At the end of 1988, nonperforming loans accounted for about one-third of the net domestic assets of the banking system. Some CFAF 253 billion, equivalent to 16 percent of GDP and 93 percent of government revenue in 1988, were needed to restructure the banking system.

The financial position of the government deteriorated seriously in 1989. The budget deficit as a share of GDP widened to 4.1 percent in 1989 and 4.3 percent in 1990. While drought and border disturbances in 1989 and civil service reorganization in March 1990 played a part in this deterioration, the real problem was one of structural rigidities and laxity in expenditure controls. There was little, if any, control of the treasury special accounts; the budgetary transfers and subsidies to the parastatals continued to be relatively high; and, although the wage bill registered a decline in real terms, it remained the major expenditure item.

Economic stagnation due to the internal adjustment strategy, as well as poor tax administration and collection, continued to be part of the fiscal problem. Tax revenue remained almost constant in nominal terms despite efforts to reverse the downward trend of its share in GDP through several discretionary tax measures.

There were three main reasons for this poor performance. First, the tax base continued to erode as the reintroduction of high tariffs and the complexity of administrative regulations contributed significantly to the shrinking of the formal sector. Second, underinvoicing and smuggling continued to be a major cause of revenue loss. And third, the tax base was weakened by the numerous exemptions that, despite efforts to reduce them as part of the reform program, continued to exist. Nearly a third of total imports were exempt from the payment of customs duties in 1990. Duties thus forgone represented 80 percent of customs revenue and a third of total tax revenue.

The fiscal situation improved significantly in fiscal 1991, with the fiscal stance turning positive (0.2 percent of GDP) for the first time. However, this was achieved largely through an across-the-board cut in nonwage recurrent expenditures without an overall framework to prioritize spending. Low operations and maintenance expenditures affected every sector but particularly education, where nonwage recurrent expenditures are about 10 percent of the wage cost. Also, key expenditure items such as export subsidies were not paid for, and arrears vis-à-vis the public enterprise sector reemerged.

Box table 7.4 Government finances, selected years, fiscal 1982–92

	Share of GDP (percent)							Percent point change	
Item	*1982*	*1984*	*1987*	*1988*	*1989*	*1991*	*1992*	*1982 to 1987*	*1987 to 1992*
Revenue	20.1	19.3	18.7	17.5	16.8	18.9	18.6	-1.4	0.2
Tax revenue	18.5	18.1	14.6	14.3	13.4	15.2	15.4	-3.9	0.6
Nontax revenue	1.6	1.2	4.1	3.2	3.4	3.7	3.2	2.5	-0.4
Expenditure	28.1	25.1	21.3	20.1	20.9	18.7	19.6	-6.8	-2.6
Wages	11.0	10.3	9.0	8.5	8.6	8.1	8.5	-2.0	-0.9
Interest due	2.4	3.8	3.0	3.2	3.3	2.4	2.2	0.6	-0.6
Other current expenditure	10.7	6.2	6.5	5.5	6.2	5.4	4.1	-4.2	-1.1
Capital expenditure	4.0	4.1	2.8	2.9	2.8	2.8	4.8	-1.2	0.0
Fiscal deficit	-8.0	-5.8	-2.6	-2.6	-4.1	0.2	-1.0	5.4	2.8
Primary deficit	-5.6	-2.0	0.4	0.6	-0.8	2.6	1.2	6.0	2.2

Source: World Bank data.

cluding official transfers) experienced a similar trend—from 18.6 percent to 7.9 percent of GDP during the same period. On average, the internal and external imbalances were reduced by half during the period. Yet stabilization, particularly in the fiscal area, remains fragile, and unless additional structural reforms are now made to accelerate and sustain growth, imbalances will return.

Financial performance. The manner in which Senegal stabilized its fiscal situation during the 1980s raises serious concerns about the sustainability of its achievements and the negative impact on competitiveness and long-term economic growth. As discussed in box 7.4, fiscal improvement has not been steady, nor has it been based on real structural reforms, a clear indication of the government's stop-and-go adjustment policy and lack of commitment to fiscal reform. A review of the fiscal policy in Senegal highlights several critical issues. The first is the lack of sustainable fiscal reform. Senegal's poor revenue mobilization—for example, the tax elasticity declined from 0.8 to 0.6 during the 1980s—has forced the adjustment program to work toward reducing public expenditures, often priority expenditures.[17] This situation has become increasingly difficult to sustain, as evidenced by the recurring fiscal crises. Nominally lower fiscal deficits in recent years have been achieved through arbitrary cuts in public spending (including operations and maintenance expenditures and direct export subsidies) and ad hoc revenue measures in the absence of a balanced structure between tax and nontax revenue. If the current situation continues, the tax burden will fall increasingly on a smaller number of taxpayers, thereby encouraging attempts to "informalize" their economic activities.

Another issue is the continuing conflict between efforts to mobilize revenue and efforts to promote growth. To finance its current expenditures, Senegal continues to rely heavily on windfall revenues from petroleum (constituting 22 percent of total tax revenue) and rice imports. Relying so heavily on petroleum revenue erodes Senegal's competitiveness (domestic petroleum prices are two to three times world prices) and undermines the stability of the revenue structure given the potential volatility of world oil prices. Thus, tax administration efforts must be improved and exemptions and fraud reduced: at less than 14 percent of GDP, the current tax revenue in Senegal compares poorly with that in countries at Senegal's income level (the average for Sub-Saharan Africa is about 16 percent, and for lower-middle-income countries it is about 17 percent).

Finally, little progress in civil service reform means that the wage bill continues to be a heavy burden on the country's limited resources.[18] Given the government's budgetary constraint, the wage bill must be reduced significantly, because resource savings must be generated to reduce the over-reliance on petroleum revenue and to increase expenditures on both basic social services and the country's infrastructure, which is rapidly deteriorating. To enhance its long-term growth potential, Senegal must increase the share of investment in GDP. The second review of the World Bank's own experience with structural adjustment shows that growth in the private sector is somewhat linked to increases in public investment. For nonwage, noninterest expenditures, efficiency and sectoral reallocation can certainly be improved, but in the aggregate, the level of investment achieved prior to the austerity year (1990–91) cannot be compressed further without adversely affecting the economy.

External sector. Allowing for debt relief—a major source of foreign exchange financing—the balance of payments has registered surpluses in four of five years from 1986 to 1990 due to an improved trade account. The trade deficit, which had deteriorated up to 1985, has since improved—particularly in 1986, when prices for the country's major imports (petroleum products and rice) fell sharply. Yet, with the exception of phosphates, exports have been stagnant or falling. Between 1982 and 1990, Senegal's two key exports, fish and groundnuts, increased by only half a percentage point annually in volume terms—a dismal performance.[19] Senegal's trade balance improved because import compression was pursued, a policy that is no longer viable without adversely affecting long-term growth. The diversified export base seemingly achieved during the partial adjustment period is due more to the fact that key traditional export items lost their momentum in recent years than to a vigorous increase in nontraditional exports.

External financing assistance. Because significant structural progress has not been made on the fiscal front, Senegal continues to rely heavily on external budgetary financing (box 7.5). Senegal has received generous external financial support from the donor community, with little interruption since Independence. The amount of external support increased rapidly during the 1980s, especially during the second half, and the terms also became increasingly favorable. It is difficult to assess the contribution of external financing to the overall performance of the economy during the 1980s. One thing is clear, however: the increase in external assistance during the partial adjustment period (1986–91) was associated with a slightly positive growth in per capita income, an almost constant ratio of investment to GDP (despite the fact that public investment is donor-driven), and high public consumption, particularly the wage bill. Had it not been for "soft" external budgetary support—that is, the absence of conditionalities—Senegal would have had to cut its public wage spending drastically in order to reduce its budget deficit while dampening inflationary pressures.

Some government officials in Senegal view external budgetary assistance as an "entitlement" that can be counted on for years to come or as a line item in the budget similar to tax revenue. In the past, the high level of aid impeded adjustment unintentionally. Large sustained flows of foreign aid, with soft conditions, reduced political incentives to implement hard reforms. For example, Senegal postponed real changes in income and labor policy in the agricultural rice sector and in petroleum taxation policy, and yet continued to receive quick disbursements from the donor community. This assessment is also supported by the findings of the Berg (1990) study, which found that large external inflows "reduced Senegalese political will to make changes necessary for adjustment and slowed Senegalese political maturation by allowing the postponement of hard economic and social choices."

Box 7.5 External assistance.

Senegal has been a favored country for the donors since Independence, largely for political reasons. For a long time it has been one of the few democracies in Africa. During the 1980s, disbursement of official development assistance to Senegal more than doubled, reaching $641 million in 1991 (box table 7.5), or about 12 percent of GDP. Not only did Senegal receive a much larger share in per capita terms than before, but the gap between Senegal and other Sub-Saharan African countries widened over time. Between 1980 and 1991, per capita official development assistance (net of principal) went from $59 to $84 ($111 in 1990) for Senegal and from $20 to $37 for Sub-Saharan Africa. Senegal currently receives external financial support from 27 donors, with France, the EEC, the IDA, Japan, and the United States accounting for the bulk. Of the official development assistance disbursement during the period under review, grants represented about 50 percent, multilateral assistance 27 percent, and technical assistance 21 percent.

Senegal's debt has stabilized in recent years after a rapid increase between 1979 and 1983 and 1985 and 1987. The stock of outstanding public and publicly guaranteed debt reached $4.0 billion in 1987; after debt cancellation, it fell to $3.5 billion at the end of 1991, equivalent to 64 percent of GDP. After debt forgiveness, debt to bilateral and multilateral sources is now roughly equal. The structure and terms of Senegal's debt have also become more favorable. Medium- and long-term debt now accounts for 90 percent of the total debt stock, and concessional loans account for 55 percent. The average interest rate on all new commitments fell from 5.9 percent in 1980 to 3.7 percent in 1991, while the average maturity grew from twenty years to twenty-nine years. The average grace period rose from six years to seven years during the same period.

Between 1981 and 1991, 80 percent of external financing was channeled through the central government budget either for investment (21 percent) or for general budgetary support (60 percent). The latter became increasingly critical to adjustment during the second half of the 1980s. Debt relief, which is accounted for here as budgetary support, averaged about $91 million annually, or 26 percent of total

The study added that "Senegal is not only aid addicted, but needs continuing high levels of support to ease the structural changes that were postponed in the 1980s." The present study recommends that further adjustment support for Senegal be selective and conditional on the implementation of upfront key policy measures. Over time, external assistance should shift back to investment.

From the standpoint of balance of payments, the increase in external resources can be justified in principle on several grounds—to compensate for the real cost of adjustment, to offset the deteriorating terms of trade, and to improve the level of reserves (that is, the operations account position). The main objective is to maintain badly needed imports to sustain economic development. However, Senegal cannot really justify this policy stance, since

budgetary financing. Senegal has benefited from several rounds of rescheduling by bilateral creditors (nine Paris Club reschedulings) and commercial banks (four London Club reschedulings). Total debt rescheduling obtained by Senegal increased substantially during the Special Program of Assistance period and, cumulatively, amounted to $910 million during the 1980s.

Box table 7.5 Official development assistance flows and budgetary support, 1980–91

(US$ millions)

	Official flows			*Budget financing*			*Terms of trade*	*GDP growth*
Year	*Gross*	*Net*	*TA*	*Tied*[a]	*Untied*[b]	*Total*	*(1980=100)*	*(percent)*
1980	384	366	22	..	..	..	100	-3.3
1981	459	416	118	87	247	335	107	-1.2
1982	497	472	103	95	195	289	93	15.3
1983	434	408	99	80	194	274	91	2.1
1984	482	444	115	57	166	223	104	-4.2
1985	352	331	92	62	148	210	106	4.0
1986	690	624	122	87	283	370	112	4.6
1987	760	672	131	100	357	457	110	4.0
1988	641	601	131	101	427	528	107	5.1
1989	751	710	132	100	368	468	113	-0.4
1990	1,034	821	180	119	220	339	113	4.5
1991	720	641	172	162	253	414	109	1.2
Annual average								
1980–85	435	406	108	76	190	266	100	2.1
1986–91	776	678	145	111	318	429	111	3.2
Percentage change: Ratio of 1986–91 to 1980–85	76	67	34	46	67	61	11	50

.. Not available.

a. Project financing.

b. Including debt relief and financing for banking restructuring and civil service voluntary departure program.

Source: World Bank data; OECD (1991).

both the terms of trade and the value of merchandise exports improved after the pre-adjustment period.

The competitiveness of the economy. The competitiveness of the Senegalese economy has not improved during the adjustment period. The real exchange rate has appreciated significantly, and the cost of production has remained high. After declining from 1980 to 1985, real wages and salaries recovered somewhat during the partial adjustment period and remained uncompetitive compared with other countries. In the industrial sector, Berg and associates (1990) observe, "there has been a modest fall in real wages during recent years. But . . . this tendency has not been strong enough to convert Senegalese industry from a high-wage to a low-wage sector."

Data on factor costs in Senegal are scarce, making it difficult to draw appropriate comparisons with other countries. Nevertheless, the findings of recent studies indicate a substantial lack of competitiveness in Senegal. This lack of competitive advantage in Senegal is illustrated by the following examples:

- The average labor cost in the Senegalese modern sector is roughly equivalent to the average civil service salary. But it is 56 percent higher than in Morocco, 60 percent higher than in Malaysia, 70 percent higher than in Tunisia, and 370 percent higher than in Indonesia. Public sector wages in Senegal appear to be even further out of line when compared with per capita GDP. Average public sector wages in Senegal are almost 12 times per capita GDP (1987 data), higher than in Côte d'Ivoire (9.1 times), Cameroon (5.9 times), Morocco (4.8 times), Tunisia (3.5 times), and Ghana, Malaysia, and Mauritius (2 times). Civil service salaries in Senegal are 13 percent higher than the average in eight CFA countries (Benin, Burkina Faso, Chad, Côte d'Ivoire, Mali, Niger, Senegal, and Togo) and 430 percent higher than in six non-CFA countries (the Gambia, Ghana, Guinea, Mauritania, Morocco, and Zaire; Berg and associates 1990).
- Case studies indicate that labor costs are significantly higher in Senegal than in higher-income countries. For example, labor cost in the tuna-canning industry (an important manufacturing activity in Senegal) is 100 percent higher than in Thailand, and labor cost in the cement industry is 40 percent higher than in France (Barbier 1989). Senegal's share in the world market of canned tuna exports declined from 12 percent to 2 percent between 1976 and 1990 in favor of Thailand, which was a newcomer in the world market and which, unlike Senegal, was taxed 24 percent to enter the European market.
- In the tourism industry, which is second to the fishing industry in foreign exchange earnings, the hotel occupancy rate dropped from 45

percent in 1984 to 38 percent in 1989—below the break-even point. The cost of tourism in Senegal compares unfavorably with that in Senegal's competitors, such as Egypt, the Gambia, Morocco, Seychelles, and Tunisia. Finally, the cost of fuel and electricity necessary to produce a ton of cement in Senegal is three times the level in France. This disproportionate cost is due in part to high domestic energy costs, as discussed earlier.

The frequent changes in import policy and subsequent distortions send the wrong signals to an already weakened and uncompetitive industrial sector. Moreover, export subsidies, which are critical for offsetting the distortions in the economy from high production costs and an overvalued exchange rate, have not been paid in recent years due to the fiscal crisis. Yet some industries did adjust to a more open economy by restructuring and improving their efficiency. Some firms have increased their labor productivity and changed the composition of their output. Through improved productivity, the reforms have also led to a decline in prices.

The supply response. The cornerstone of the stabilization program in Senegal has been the compression of demand, primarily through private consumption and investment. This contraction was more pronounced in the second half of the 1980s than in the first half. Gross domestic investment in Senegal averaged 12 percent of GDP in 1982–85 and 12.8 percent in 1986–91, a ratio that is not conducive to growth and which does not compare favorably either with the average for Sub-Saharan Africa (15.5 percent of GDP) or with what is required to prevent the stock of capital from deteriorating (13 percent of GDP). Low private investment can be attributed to the stringent credit policies of the government and to economic stagnation. Despite the significant improvement in the fiscal position, the government continued to experience negative budgetary savings (tax revenue minus current expenditures), necessitating large budgetary support from external donors, a situation that is clearly not viable in the long run. Foreign savings (measured by the current account) were required to finance not only gross domestic investment but also a large proportion of domestic consumption during the 1980s. Sluggish growth in private consumption led to higher domestic savings, which became positive in 1986 and now represent 8.8 percent of GDP. One of the most likely determinants of the increase in the savings ratio is the positive real interest rates throughout most of the 1980s.

Notwithstanding the poor quality of national accounts, the average annual economic growth rate in the second half of the 1980s (3.2 percent) was 1.1 percentage points higher than in the first half of the decade. The 3.2 percent growth rate compares well with the long-term historical trend of 2.1 percent (1960–80), but is only slightly higher than the population growth rate of 2.9 percent.[20] Senegal's performance during the first half of the decade was analyzed extensively in a 1987 World Bank country economic memorandum. GDP growth was adversely affected by the severe drought of 1983–84. Yet, despite its relatively small share of GDP, agriculture continued to have a major impact on overall growth through its multiplier effect on the rest of the economy. The performance of the real sectors of the economy—agriculture and manufacturing—is discussed in detail in the next section.

Is the Senegalese economy now more efficient and diversified than before the start of partial adjustment? External factors and the time lag make the question of efficiency difficult to address. Two indicators shed light on this question: the incremental capital-output ratio and the export growth of the manufacturing sector. The stagnation in the ratio of investment to GDP from 1986 to 1991 was not accompanied by declining economic growth and thus led to a steady improvement in the incremental capital-output ratio. The five-year-lag incremental capital-output ratio went from an annual average of 7.9 during the pre-adjustment period to 3.9 during the partial adjustment period. This favorable trend could be explained by favorable weather conditions, excess capacity in many industries, and better selectivity in public investment projects. Yet it is unlikely that it can be sustained without major replacements of old equipment and machinery. For manufacturing exports, no hard evidence exists that they increased in a meaningful way between 1986 and 1991, due largely to the overvalued real exchange rate and the unreliability of the export subsidy scheme. The elasticity of nontraditional exports with respect to GDP is estimated to be lower during the partial adjustment period than during the first half of the 1980s.

The structure of the economy has diversified little during the 1980s. The share of the primary sector in GDP stayed the same, with the decline in the share of agriculture and forestry offset by the increase in the share of livestock and fishing during the second half of the decade. The share of the secondary sector increased by less than a full percentage point of GDP at the expense of the tertiary sector during the same period. The increase in the share of the informal sector in both manufacturing and services is, to a certain extent, a good indication of the large number of constraints still facing the formal sector.

Sectoral outcomes

Between 1986 and 1991, *agricultural sector* production (including forestry, livestock, and fishing) registered a modest increase of 2.3 percent annually, due largely to favorable weather conditions and despite a decline in cultivated land. The production of foodcrops increased at a faster pace than did the production of cash crops, due largely to the expansion of subsistence agriculture, internal trade liberalization, and favorable price differentials. Prospects for the agricultural sector still depend on the real exchange rate policy, the terms of trade for cash crops, and climatic conditions.

Production in the *manufacturing sector* increased in real terms more rapidly in the latter half of the 1980s, due to a vibrant informal sector. Trade liberalization, combined with the absence of progress toward real exchange rate depreciation, energy cost reductions, and labor and wage liberalization, has shifted the supply response from the formal to the informal sector. Rigidities in a more liberalized policy environment have led to serious difficulties for large-scale firms that had previously benefited from protection against imports and local competition. Overall, the manufacturing sector has been partially restructured, with medium- and large-scale industries still operating under protection. Due partly to trade liberalization reversal and partly to dynamism of small-scale enterprises, Senegal has not experienced a major deindustrialization as defined by the rapid shrinking of its industrial base. And the shift from the formal to the informal sector does not provide a satisfactory base for Senegal's long-term growth and employment.

The *public enterprise sector* has shrunk, and it can reasonably be assumed that its performance improved at least as a result of the liquidation of nonperforming public enterprises. But more detailed information on individual enterprises is necessary to provide a definite answer to the question of efficiency. While the public enterprise reform program has been moving forward, much must still be done to achieve the government's objectives.

Despite stagnant and declining real per capita public expenditures on education and health during the 1980s, the *primary education and basic health status* in Senegal has improved slightly and regional differences have narrowed. In education, the government increased the number of teachers through redeployment and introduced major innovations in primary education, such as mixed-grade classes and double shifts, allowing classrooms and teachers to be used more efficiently. In health, resources have been reallocated toward primary health care, private and donor financing has increased, and the effectiveness of preventive health services has been enhanced. Yet these achievements in social indicators are not only poor in comparison with countries at Senegal's level of income but, more important, are merely short-term gains that cannot be sustained given the current pattern and level of resource allocations to the social sectors.

The impact of adjustment policies on various *social groups* has been mixed. Overall, the rural-urban terms of trade have improved slightly in favor of the rural sector—but the improvement is due more to the decline in urban income than to increases in rural income. The real income of public wage earners declined during the 1980s, but less so among unskilled labor than among skilled labor. Thus, the wage income distribution has become less skewed. The scarcity of data makes assessing the impact of adjustment on employment difficult. It is estimated that about 8 percent of total employment in the modern sector could have been lost since 1986, largely in the modern manufacturing sector and the civil service. Most job losses in manufacturing came from the liquidation of a few companies that would ultimately have been closed with or without reforms. There is evidence that the loss of employment in the modern sector was offset by job creation in the informal sector and to a lesser extent by social safety net programs. In sum, while poverty may have become worse in Senegal in the 1980s, there is no evidence that the cost of adjustment has fallen disproportionately on the poor.

Agriculture sector. In contrast to most African countries, in Senegal the agriculture sector (including forestry, livestock, and fishing) accounts for a modest share of GDP (20 percent). However, agriculture employs about 60 percent of the labor force and provides a living for over two-thirds of the population. It also accounts for a large portion of foreign exchange earnings, with groundnut export earnings ($110 million in 1991) ranking third to fish exports and tourism earnings. Although declining in relative importance, groundnuts account for about 60 percent of farm cash income.

In the second half of the 1980s, agricultural production registered a modest increase of 2.9 percent annually. In volume terms, foodcrop and cash crop production increased by 2.9 percent and 1.4 percent annually, due largely to adequate rainfall. Acreage under foodcrop production has essentially stayed the same, whereas acreage under export crop production has declined sharply (table 7.9). Increased production and a decline in acreage have generated high yields—an annual increase per hectare of 3.0 percent for foodcrops and 3.7 percent for export crops. The extent to which the increase is due to improved inputs and technology is not known. There is evidence that these factors could not have played an important role. For example, fertilizer use, a key input, dropped from 75,000 tons in 1980 to 25,000 tons in 1990.

Given the strong land population pressure, the total foodcrop area declined significantly on a per capita basis during the 1980s, implying deteriorating labor productivity in the absence of technological improvement. In per capita terms, cereal consumption declined from 242 kilograms before adjustment to 222 kilograms during partial adjustment. While cereal production and cereal aid remained unchanged, cereal imports declined significantly. The decline in cereal imports (rice and wheat) seems to be consistent with the emphasis placed by the government (through relative prices) on the production of domestic cereals (millet, sorghum, and maize). It also reflects a good harvest, as well as continued controls on rice imports. The decline in cereal consumption does not, however, mean a decline in per capita food consumption, as Senegal is believed to have increased its fish and vegetable consumption quite considerably in recent years. Fish production increased on average by about 6 percent a year during the 1980s. Data on vegetable production are not available, but there has been a significant effort on the part of the government, farmers, and nongovernmental organizations to increase the number of wells in rural areas.

Table 7.9 Key agricultural indicators, 1980–91

Indicator	Annual average 1980–85	Annual average 1986–91	Percentage change Total	Percentage change Annual
Primary sector value added (constant 1987 prices, CFAF billions)[a]				
Total sector	259.8	308.9	18.9	2.9
Agriculture subsector	150.8	163.8	8.6	1.4
Agricultural production (thousands of tons)				
Foodcrops[b]	813.2	965.4	18.7	2.9
Export crops[c]	773.8	838.8	8.4	1.4
Total cropped area (thousands of hectares)				
Foodcrops[b]	1,227.5	1,211.9	-1.3	-0.2
Export crops[c]	1,010.0	882.6	-12.6	-2.2
Real producer prices (1980=100)				
Foodcrops[b]	105.4	106.7	1.2	0.2
Export crops[c]	102.8	100.7	-2.0	-0.4
Food imports[d]				
Value (US$ millions)	227.0	257.0	13.2	2.5
Volume (thousands of tons)	476.0	420.0	-11.8	-2.5
Food aid (thousands of tons)[e]	133.9	157.8	17.8	3.3
Export crops[c]				
Value (US$ millions)	114.0	127.0	11.4	2.2
Volume (thousands of tons)	241.0	316.0	31.1	5.6
Internal terms of trade (1987=100)[f]	94.3	97.0	2.9	0.6
Cereal per capita (kilograms)	241.8	221.8	-8.3	-1.7
Production	138.1	138.7	0.4	0.1
Imports	80.9	60.4	-25.3	-5.7
Aid	22.7	22.7	-0.3	-0.1

	Nominal protection coefficient[g]	*Domestic resource costs*[h]
Millet (lower fleuve)	1.3	0.9
Maize (casamance)	1.6	1.0
Rice (upper fleuve)	2.0	1.0
Cotton (eastern Senegal)	1.1	0.9
Groundnuts (groundnut basin)	1.8	1.3

a. The sector includes agriculture, livestock, fishing, and forestry subsectors. For the agriculture subsector, the first period covers 1981–85.
b. USAID data for millet, sorghum, maize, and rice paddy. These data differ from FAO data, which indicate higher production for millet and sorghum. According to FAO data, food production averages 855,400 tons for 1980–85 and 963,200 for 1986–90. This represents a total change of 12.6 percent, or 2.4 percent a year.
c. Oil groundnuts, confectionery groundnuts, and cotton.
d. Rice, wheat, and other foodstuffs. Volume relates only to rice and wheat.
e. FAO data covering cereals and rice paddy.
f. GDP deflators of the primary sector over the secondary sector. The primary sector includes agriculture, livestock, fishing, and forestry. The secondary sector includes groundnut oil, mining, construction, energy, and other.
g. Coefficients calculated for Dakar using 1986–87 world prices and semi-intensive technology.
h. Ratios calculated for Dakar using 1988–89 world prices and semi-intensive technology.
Source: Jones and Holleman (1991).

The shift toward foodcrops (primarily millet and maize) and away from export crops (primarily groundnuts) was more pronounced in the second half of the 1980s. The shift can be explained by the favorable price differential between foodcrops and export crops due to policy measures undertaken in the 1980s. While producer prices for foodcrops increased by 6.7 percent in real terms in 1986–90, producer prices for export crops increased by only 0.7 percent (table 7.9). This insignificant increase in producer prices for export crops reflects the government's decision in 1988 to reduce the producer price of groundnuts from CFAF 90 to CFAF 70 per kilogram due to unfavorable world prices. Within the food sector, the ratio of millet to rice prices moved only slightly in favor of millet.

Indicators of production incentives and efficiency—nominal protection coefficients and domestic resource costs—have been calculated by Jones and Holleman (1991) for five major crops (millet, maize, rice, cotton, and groundnuts) for 1987 to 1989.[21] The study concludes that, among the cereals, millet and maize have a considerably higher comparative advantage in many producing areas than does rice, which receives more protection than necessary to sustain the present level of production. Yet, given the overvalued real exchange rate, millet and maize have barely adequate protection to sustain production for local consumption in many producing areas. Of the cash crops, cotton has a higher comparative advantage than groundnuts, but receive barely enough protection to maintain production, whereas groundnuts receive quite substantial protection. The most important finding is that far too many resources have been devoted to irrigated rice production, a sector that still has to be reformed significantly despite several attempts.

Industrial sector. The industrial sector value added (comprising manufacturing, construction, mining, and energy) was 24 percent higher in 1986–90 than in 1980–85, and its share in GDP rose from 17.0 percent to 18.2 percent (table 7.10). The manufacturing subsector, which currently accounts for more than two-thirds of the sector's value added, has experienced decelerating growth since Independence: 6.1 percent annually in 1960–70, 5.3 percent during 1970–80, and only 1.2 percent in 1980–85. The subsector's growth can be attributed primarily to import substitution, which reached its limit by the mid-1980s. Employment in the manufacturing sector more than doubled between 1960 and 1985 (3 percent annually), but most of the increase occurred between 1960 and 1975. Thus, by the mid-1980s, the manufacturing sector had lost its momentum for growth and employment, for several reasons.

Sectoral constraints were well identified prior to adjustment reforms: an inefficient import-substitution strategy in a noncompetitive environment that was characterized by a cumbersome regulatory framework, a distorted incentive system, a small internal market, and high factor cost, particularly for labor and energy. These constraints were exacerbated by Senegal's inability to resort to an exchange rate adjustment policy, which proved to be crucial, particularly in more recent years when the real exchange rate appreciated substantially. In 1986 Senegal embarked on a new industrial policy (known by its French acronym, NPI), whose primary objective was to introduce a more competitive industrial structure and give the private sector a greater role in growth and employment. To improve the competitiveness of Senegalese firms, the government chose an internal liberalization strategy that sought to reduce the costs of key inputs, including petroleum and electricity.

Several factors make it difficult to assess the impact of the adjustment reforms on the performance of the industrial sector: the reform program has been implemented only partially, the adjustment period has been too short, and external conditions have been characterized by a substantial depreciation in the currencies of countries competing with Senegal.

Overall, manufacturing production was around 5 percent a year higher in 1986–91 than in 1980–85. This increase is due solely to the vibrancy of the informal sector, as supply shifted from the formal to the informal sector. Production in the modern sector declined by an average of five percentage

Table 7.10 Key industrial indicators, 1980–91

Indicator	Annual average		Percentage change	
	1980–85	*1986–91*	*Total*	*Annual*
Industrial sector				
Value added (CFAF billions, in constant 1987 prices)	204.1	260.0	27.8	4.2
Value added as a percentage of GDP	17.0	18.2	6.9	1.1
Employment	40,447.0[a]	34,886.0[b]	-13.7	-3.6
Manufacturing sector[c]				
Production index	100.0[a]	95.1	-4.9	-1.0
Value added (CFAF billions, in constant 1987 prices)	144.3	193.4	34.0	5.0
Value added as a percentage of GDP	12.0	13.5	12.5	1.9
Employment (permanent)	35,681.0[a]	30,059.0[b]	-15.8	-4.2
Export subsidy (CFAF billions)	8.1[d]	5.4[e]	-33.3	-7.9
Wages as a share of cost of production (percent)	8.2[d]	10.1[f]	23.2	4.3
Medium- and long-term credits (CFAF billions)	24.7[d]	19.2[b]	-22.3	-4.9
Effective protection rate (percent)	165.0[d]	98.0[g]	-40.6	-9.9

a. 1982–85.
b. 1986–89.
c. Defined as oil milling plus the category "other."
d. 1985.
e. 1987–89.
f. 1988.
g. 1990.
Source: World Bank data.

points between 1982–85 and 1986–89, with production of the 30 major industrial products declining by 34 percent. The industries that did well were mining, chemicals, and energy—industries that were not affected directly by reforms. Yet the performance of the sector is more positive in terms of turnover. While 14 of 19 industries surveyed in 1990 showed negative turnover in the pre-adjustment period, only 7 industries showed negative turnover in the partial adjustment period.

From 1986 to 1990 there was a loss of about 5,600 jobs, or 16 percent of the modern sector's total employment. It can be argued that most of the losses were due to the liquidation of a few companies that were bound to be closed with or without adjustment reforms. Too, other evidence suggests that the loss of employment in the modern sector was offset by job creation in the informal sector. While there was an overall decline in investment levels—10 of 16 industries reduced their investment and improved their capacity utilization—7 of 16 industries had a capacity utilization above 60 percent, the level achieved in 1985.

The reform program established new firms and closed nonperforming ones. Although hard data are not available, the significant number of private projects approved by the government's regulatory agency[22] would indicate that many firms were created during the partial adjustment period, primarily small-scale export-oriented agroindustries. Yet, between 1986 and 1989, 53 firms were closed, some of which reopened later on. An examination of the six largest ones reveal that over half of their assets were bought by similar companies.[23] Thus, some restructuring of the industrial sector occurred under the reform program.

A 1990 World Bank survey (Parker and Steel 1992) of 63 enterprises (representing at least 17 percent of the firms in the sector[24]) suggested that small-scale enterprises are more dynamic than both micro and medium- and large-scale enterprises.[25] Rigidities in a more liberalized policy environment have led to serious difficulties, particularly for large-scale firms that had at one time benefited from protection against imports and local competition. The survey showed that small-scale enterprises may have in fact compensated for the decline of large firms despite the weak demand growth in Senegal since 1986. A substantial share of small firms have managed to increase output and profits. In addition, a high proportion of small-scale enterprises were postreform creations, suggesting a relatively high rate of new investment at this level.

To analyze the firms' adjustment responses more effectively, Parker and Steel divided the sample into three categories: firms that increased production, those that remained the same, and those that reduced output. For each of these categories, the sample is broken down further into firms adopting the following measures of response (or flexibility factors): an increase in imported input, a change in product mix, the purchase of new equipment, and the adoption of an export-oriented strategy (table 7.11). The table shows that manufacturing firms that expanded successfully after 1986 were relatively flexible. The study also shows that small-scale enterprises did prove to be more flexible than others. Thus, while only 34 percent of the firms in the sample increased their production in 1990, 50 percent of the small-scale enterprises did. While 52 percent of the firms in the sample diversified their production, 57 percent of the small-scale enterprises did; and while 52 percent of the sample bought new equipment, 60 percent of the small-scale enterprises did.

According to the same industrial survey, the main factor constraints against production were low import prices (for 41 percent of firms in the sample), excess imports (36 percent), and high domestic competition (26 percent). Investment was constrained by high interest rates (89 percent), limited access to credit (73 percent), and the high cost of inputs (54 percent). Moreover, the government's negative attitude toward the private sector remains a major obstacle to industrial development (36 percent).

With respect to the labor factor, the survey found that only 5 percent of all firms interviewed (10 percent for firms with 50 or more employees) believe that salaries for qualified workers are too high, and that 10 percent of all firms (19 percent for firms with 50 or more employees) believe that the labor force constrains their operations (Parker and Steel 1992, annex tables 4.11–12). These findings are not surprising, since labor regulations do not seem to be enforced except for well-established firms. Yet this argument should not diminish the importance of deregulating the labor market, since regulation is still a major deterrent factor for potential investors and constrains movement from the informal to the formal sector.

Although the reform of the financial sector has created a more solid banking system and has restored confidence in it, Senegal's banks have become much more risk-averse and show a marked preference for short-term trade-related lending at the expense of long-term investment lending. Short-term credit now accounts for 70 percent of total lending—two-thirds for trade

Table 7.11 Distribution of flexibility factors by production trend
(industry sample, percentage of respondents)

Production response	*All*	*Increased imported raw materials share*	*Changed product mix*	*Bought new equipment*	*Are exporters*
Increased output	34	67	42	39	45
Maintained output	24	13	24	19	14
Decreased output	42	20	33	42	41
Total	100	100	100	100	100
Number of respondents	63	15	33	31	23

Source: Parker and Steel (1992), annex 4.7.

financing. Lending to industrial activities declined from 22 percent of total credit in 1985 to less than 15 percent in 1990. The upshot of this trend is that Senegalese-owned firms, especially small and medium-size ones, are finding it much more difficult to get access to credit to finance long-term investments.

In the formal manufacturing sector, domestic producers have been unable to adapt quickly to the new competitive environment in which prices are deregulated and trade is liberalized. The overvalued real exchange rate, labor market rigidities, and high energy costs prevent them from doing so. For instance, labor costs rose from 8.2 percent of the total cost of industrial production in 1985 to 10.1 percent in 1988. While trade liberalization forced some industrial firms to close between 1987 and 1989, several others took advantage of the improved incentive system to increase their productivity and diversify their production.[26] In sum, there is no hard evidence to show that trade liberalization has led to major deindustrialization in Senegal. Yet supply has shifted from the formal to the informal sector—weakening the base for Senegal's long-term growth.

Public enterprises. Is the public enterprise sector now smaller, and is it more efficient? The answer to the first question is yes. But while the reform program has been moving forward, much must still be done. Answering the second question requires more detailed information on individual enterprises. The few indicators available for selected companies indicate that, while the internal management of public enterprises has improved, productivity generally has not.[27] Since 1988 the implementation of key reforms has led to qualitative improvement in the financial and management performance of some key enterprises in the sector—for example, the power company (Sénélec), the port authority (PAD), and the railway authority (SNCS).

In the early 1980s Sénélec became a *société nationale,* responsible for operating and developing the power sector. Its managing board members and managing director were appointed by the government, and its development projects and tariff modifications required government approval. In 1987 a set of corrective measures was embodied in a contract plan between the government and Sénélec. These measures sought to improve the financial performance and management of Sénélec. Some positive results were achieved and Sénélec's financial position improved. In particular, the contract plan helped identify performance goals that can be measured and monitored. Nonetheless, the contract plan has been disappointing: the payment by the government of electricity bills is still a problem and has led to setting up cross-debt compensation operations between Sénélec and the administration; power system facilities and customer management are still very weak; and recent audits indicate daily management problems and the absence of transparency in several financial transactions. These problems are the managing director's responsibility, and their persistence shows that the managing board has not assumed its role fully. Overall, the Sénélec contract plan has been slightly positive from the financial standpoint, but has shown little improvement in managerial efficiency.

Contract plans have been signed between the government and PAD and SNCS, clarifying responsibilities between the government and the two companies. Both PAD and SNCS have been transformed from *établissements publics à caractère industriel et commercial* and *régie*, into *sociétés nationales*. The new structure has given management greater autonomy and has improved fiscal and economic performance. The companies now have more freedom to adjust tariff rates to meet their financial objectives. Yet the government has not lived up to its commitment to stop interfering in daily management (for example, personnel and procurement) and to siphon off the excess cash earmarked for heavy maintenance operations. One positive outcome of the contract plans is improved transparency. Audits of contract plans examine the companies' and the government's compliance and make interference and mismanagement public.

Social sectors and income distribution. Despite stagnant and declining real per capita public expenditures on education and health during the 1980s, most of the education and health indicators in Senegal have improved, although the quality of education and health care has declined (Berg and associates 1990). In education overall enrollment increased by one-third between the first and second half of the 1980s; secondary and tertiary school enrollment increased slightly more rapidly than primary school enrollment, and female enrollment grew more rapidly than male enrollment.[28] Regional differences have also narrowed markedly. The increase in students has been matched by a parallel increase in the number of teachers, thus preserving the student-teacher ratio. Yet most student performance indicators (dropout and repetition rates) are at or near the levels found in 1980. In the health sector standard indicators of health status indicate a marked improvement in the 1980s. Life expectancy increased from forty-five years in 1980 to forty-nine in 1991, while infant mortality declined from 147 (per thousand live births) to 81 during the same period. There has also been a sharp decline in the morbidity rates for major diseases in the 1980s, attributed largely to a successful series of vaccination campaigns. The share of children immunized rose from 17 percent to 70 percent during the period.

How can these positive achievements be reconciled with the decline in social spending? In education teachers' salaries were restrained during most of the 1980s, thus allowing more teachers to be hired. Teachers in administrative positions (estimated at 1,262 between 1985 and 1988, and somewhat less than that in 1990 after the civil service was restructured) were redeployed to teaching positions. Major innovations were introduced in primary education, such as mixed-grade classes and double shifts, allowing classrooms and teachers to be used more efficiently. In the health sector the reallocation of resources toward primary health care sharply increased the number of posts and health "huts" in the 1980s. Private and donor financing also increased. User fees became more common during the 1980s, spurred largely by budgetary cuts. According to the 1993 public expenditure review, "the structure of health sector financing has shifted away from government sources to non-governmental sources with an increased contribution from external financing." In 1989, 33.4 percent of sector funding was channeled through the budget, 11.4 percent came from local funds (primarily modern enterprises), 17.3 percent from external financing, and 37.9 percent from private sources. Finally, increased effectiveness of preventive health services—the antimalaria program, maternal and child health care programs, and the expansion program of vaccinations—has improved health status. However, these achievements in social indicators are not only poor in comparison with countries at Senegal's level of income but, more important, represent short-term gains that cannot be sustained given the current pattern and level of resource allocations.

Has Senegal reduced poverty and protected the most vulnerable groups of society during the reform process in the 1980s? The absence of household income and expenditure surveys (which are currently being generated) makes answering this question difficult. However, it can be argued that the extent of poverty in Senegal has, at best, stayed the same, for two reasons. First, there is no evidence of a substantial increase in per capita income, and thus employment generation may have been limited. Second, the adjustment program did not seek explicitly to reduce poverty, nor until quite recently was it targeted specifically at the poor. It is worth mentioning that per capita public resources to the social sectors have declined during the 1980s.

Who won and who lost as a result of the reform program? Overall, rural-urban terms of trade have improved in favor of the rural sector, but basically because urban income has dropped. Raising real prices to agricultural producers was achieved only partially. Real producer prices for millet, sorghum, and rice were 7 to 19 percent higher in 1989 than in 1980, but producer prices for cotton and groundnuts, the main source of farm cash income, were 5 to 10 percent lower. Thus, the weighted real producer price for major crops did not improve. Yet real consumer prices were 20 to 50 percent lower for millet, rice (broken), and wheat, benefiting urban consumers during the 1980s. The real income of public wage earners fell, with the income of unskilled labor (those paid at or near the legal minimum wage) declining less than the income of skilled labor. Thus, the wage income distribution became less skewed during the 1980s.

The impact of adjustment on employment is difficult to assess given the scarcity of data. It is estimated that 11,000 jobs have been lost since 1986: some 700 from bank restructuring (or 41 percent of the sector), 800 from the liquidation of some public enterprises (about 3.5 percent of the sector), 3,800 as a result of civil service reforms (about 6 percent of the number of civil servants just prior to the adjustment), and 5,600 as a result of the new industrial policy (16 percent of the modern sector employment). For the banking and civil service sectors, support in the form of project financing helped mitigate the impact on those losing their jobs—CFAF 5 million (the equivalent of thirty-two months of salary) for bank job losers and CFAF 4.2 million (thirty-eight months of salary) for civil service job losers. While hard data are unavailable, most of the separation pay was believed to be used for consumption or debt repayment. Only a small number of those who lost their job managed to reintegrate into other productive economic activities.

In sum, poverty may have become worse in Senegal in the 1980s due to stagnating per capita economic growth. The current poverty status reflects the internal adjustment strategy that Senegal chose to follow. Had Senegal implemented its adjustment program fully—particularly a substantial depreciation of the real exchange rate—per capita income would most likely have increased, and poverty would have been reduced. But the cost of stabilization and partial adjustment has also seemingly not fallen disproportionately on the poor. As Berg and associates (1990) note, "The Senegalese experience . . . does not support the argument that the 'social costs' of adjustment fall most harshly on the poorest, either in its income distribution results or in its predictions that social sector spending suffers disproportionately, with long-term negative consequences for the poor."

Notes

The author is indebted to Brian Ngo, a World Bank staff member currently with the Economic Development Institute, who contributed to the sections on fiscal policy, monetary policy, and the banking sector.

1. For more discussion of the lobbies for and against adjustment see Ka and van de Walle, pp. 47–59: "The government chose to avoid a frontal attack on these groups in the early years of the PAML (medium-term financial program). Although it is true that the public sector was hurt by the general deflationary trend, reforms of the civil service, education and the Labor Code were not addressed in a sustained manner until 1987. The government seemed to have adopted the strategy of delaying the most difficult reforms and front-loading the easy reforms."

2. Competitiveness is measured by the movement of relative prices. But the experience of newly industrialized economies shows that no simple definition of competitiveness would suffice. The competitiveness of an economy is a function not just of its wages and prices (relative to other countries), but also of nonprice factors in a changing and increasingly integrated world. These factors include the ability to absorb, use,

and develop technology to reduce production costs, improve product quality, and develop new products; and marketing strategy and arrangements covering such diverse factors as packaging, sales networks, and after-sales service.

3. The government was an active partner in tripartite annual bargaining whereby basic wage levels were determined for 27 industry groups (agriculture and domestics were excluded). The government was both an arbiter between the unions and employers and an enforcer of the wage agreements published by decree and applicable to all employers, regardless of whether they participated in negotiations. Industry wage scales were set according to the minimum wage, which the government revises on an infrequent basis.

4. While bonuses and incentive payments were negotiated freely, the "convention collective," agreed to by the unions and the employers in March 1981, established the rights of workers to a wide range of additional benefits, whose calculation was defined fairly rigidly by various factors, including the basic wage and length of employment.

5. According to a 1986 survey cited by Svejnar and Terrell (1988), average wages for unskilled workers were about 20 percent higher than the minimum wage, with the nonwage element of remuneration approaching 30 percent of total compensation. In 1985 the average annual wage and benefits in the civil service were about CFAF 2.86 million—CFAF 0.725 million of which (25 percent) were benefits.

6. Nine measures were introduced in the past three years: (1) a 5 percent increase in customs duty tax (August 1989); (2) the introduction of minimum assessed taxes on imports (September 1989) and their extension to a much larger group of commodities (July 1990); (3) an increase in a number of stamp duties (by between 50 and 100 percent) and an increased excise tax on cigarettes, alcoholic beverages, tobacco products, soft drinks, coffee, and tea (August 1990); (4) the introduction of an ad valorem customs fee of 3 percent (August 1990); (5) a reduction in deferred customs payments (1990–91); (6) a 5 percent increase in personal income tax rates (October 1990), which was later rescinded in the face of strong political resistance; (7) an increase in the rates and coverage of stamp taxes and fees (August 1990); (8) the introduction of a tax on sugar (March 1991); and (9) the institution of a transaction fee of 5 percent on sales of used motor vehicles and of 2 percent for new vehicles (March 1991).

7. In view of its significance to determining monetary and credit policy, the development of Senegal's net external position warrants a brief description. The external assets position began to stabilize in 1989 after suffering wide fluctuations in 1983–88 due to a marked deterioration in the external current account between 1983 and 1985, followed by significant private capital outflows in 1987 and 1988. Consequently, Senegal's negative position in the operations account reached a peak of CFAF 97.2 billion in June 1986. The deterioration of Senegal's external accounts through 1985 stemmed from high imports, a direct reflection of the high level of overall demand. A significant improvement in the external accounts began in 1986.

Most of this improvement can be attributed to the pursuit of strict monetary policy. The fiscal situation, which improved significantly from 1982 through 1987, deteriorated between 1987 and 1990. BCEAO's net claims on the government declined sharply in 1987. These developments reflect the availability of larger external budgetary assistance to support the country's structural adjustment program. There was also evidence of efforts to reduce net lending to the government, regardless of the statutory ceiling in BCEAO rules and regulations that limits total advances to the government to 20 percent of fiscal revenue collected in the previous year. This development was even more notable if one considers the series of measures designed to curtail government borrowing via guarantees for borrowing by public enterprises from the banking sector.

8. These rates do not capture the impact of quantitative restrictions and assume that value added averages were 20 percent of the value of final outputs—they were also based on prevailing nominal tariff rates for final goods and intermediate materials. If one assumes a larger value added ratio (say, 30 percent), then the average effective protection rates would be substantially higher: 235 percent in 1985, 123 percent in 1988, and 132 percent in 1990.

9. In the 1980s groundnut prices were raised three times and reduced twice, cotton raised three times, and rice raised three times and partially reduced twice. At the same time, the world prices of these three commodities fell.

10. Among the development banks, the Banque Nationale du Développement du Senegal (or BNDS) was the country's largest bank in terms of total assets. The three largest banks in terms of nongovernment deposits are associated with foreign banks, primarily French banks; they are SGBS, BIAOS, and CICIS. The Union Sénégalaise de Banque (USB), in which the state has a majority shareholding, is associated with French Crédit Lyonnais, which exercises managerial control. The remaining banks are small; most were created as specialized banks, for housing (BHS), industry and tourism (SOFISEDIT), and agriculture (CNCAS).

11. These studies addressed such major policy issues as indirect subsidy levels, cross-debt, and special conventions or concessions.

12. A public enterprise sector review in 1977 led to a series of reforms supported by the first parapublic sector technical assistance project (PPTA1). At its completion in 1983, a second project (PPTA2) was initiated.

13. In addition to these two policy decisions, the government also agreed to return to the private sector small and medium-size units in the productive sector and to close units that were found to be nonviable.

14. The process of cross-debt settlement entails identifying and verifying the debt, negotiating a settlement agreement between the concerned parties, and reflecting the terms of the agreement in the books of the concerned parties. At the end of December 1989, total debts owed by 60 nonfinancial public enterprises to government amounted to CFAF 57.4 billion, and debts owed by government amounted to CFAF 48.9 billion. After the mutual cancellation of debts and write-offs, and after enterprises were liquidated and privatized, total debts owed by public enterprises to government dropped to CFAF 5.6 billion (or 9.8 percent of the original amount) and debts owed by government to public enterprises dropped to CFAF 1.2 billion (or 2.5 percent of the original amount). These remaining debts are being settled over a period of three years, with only a few exceptions. About 80 cross-debt agreements among the public enterprises themselves had been signed as of October 1991, and about CFAF 8 billion (representing 60 percent of total debt) had been settled.

15. Dakar emerged from being the capital of French West Africa with the best trained civil servants in the region and the highest paid, as Senegal kept complete wage parity between African and French employees. In the early 1960s, the civil servants had seven times the average income of peasant households and twice the wage of skilled industrial workers (see Ka and van de Walle forthcoming).

16. See Rashid Faruqee (1993).

17. Tax elasticity is defined as the percentage variation in tax revenue expressed in terms of changes in GDP, but excluding the impact of discretionary measures. Several factors accounted for the decline in tax elasticity—but particularly the narrowing of the tax base, reflecting a weak economy, and the "informalization" of the economy, as the informal economy expanded rapidly away from the stagnating formal sector. The reasons for tax variation include high turnover, declining salaries in the formal

sector, low business profits, and a decline in imports, adversely affecting tax collection.

18. Even in the absence of budgetary constraints, the civil service must be downsized to improve its efficiency, given that Senegal inherited a large administration from when Dakar was the capital of the French West African colonies.

19. Among the main determinants of the poor performance of these two export items are the resource depletion and the aging fishing fleet in the fishery subsector and the keen vegetable oil substitution in the groundnut oil subsector.

20. This is an average rate for the period between the last two population censuses held in 1976 and 1988. For more recent years, the population growth rate is estimated at 3.2 percent.

21. If the domestic price is higher than the border price due to tariffs or import controls—that is, if the nominal price coefficient is greater than one—then domestic producers benefit from protectionist policy. If the opposite is true, then the domestic price is lower than the border price due to import subsidies or price controls—thus implying the taxation of domestic producers. If the domestic resource cost is less than one, the crop activity is using domestic resources effectively to generate or save a unit of foreign exchange. This situation creates a comparative advantage, since the country earns or saves foreign exchange through production.

22. In 1988 the government approved 59 projects totaling CFAF 8 billion, which created 175 jobs for about $150,000 per job.

23. These are BATA (shoes), STS (textiles), SAPAL (tuna), SARDINAFRIC (seafood), MANUTENTION AFRICAINE (vehicles), and TREFILERIE DE DAKAR (engineering).

24. This figure is based on the assumption that the number of modern industries remained at its 1986 level of 367.

25. Scale is defined according to employment: microenterprises (1–9), small-scale enterprises (10–49), and medium- and large-scale enterprises (50 and more).

26. A 1990 sample survey of 31 manufacturing firms showed that half had increased their labor productivity and changed the composition of their output. Eighteen nonprofitable firms were closed between 1987 and 1989, but several of them have reopened under new ownership. The impact on employment has generally been negative, reflecting the stagnation of the sector and the high cost of labor. Through improved productivity, the reforms have also led to price declines in about 75 percent of the subsectors examined.

27. For instance, Berg and associates (1990) show that productivity measures fell in five key enterprises from 1980 to 1988. They are OPCE (post), SENELEC (electricity), SNCS (railways), SOTRAC (urban transport), and SONES (water).

28. University enrollment has increased significantly in the recent past, reflecting in part the increased length of time that students take to complete a degree. Due to the difficulty of finding employment after graduation, students prolong their university schooling as long as possible. The University of Dakar is currently overcrowded, with a 1989 enrollment of about 16,500 students, twice its capacity.

References

Barbier, Jean-Paul. 1989. "Réflexions sur la compétitivité, comparaisons Afrique-Asie." CCCE.

Berg, Elliot, and associates. 1990. "Adjustment Postponed: Economic Policy Reform in Senegal in the 1980s." Prepared for the U.S. Agency for International Development, Dakar.

Faruqee, Rashid. 1993. "How Macroeconomic Projections in Policy Framework Papers for the Africa Region Compare with Outcomes." Policy Research Working Paper 1168. World Bank, Africa Region, Washington, D.C.

Jones, David, and Cindy Holleman. 1991. "Senegal's Structure of Protection and Comparative Advantage in Cereal and Export Crop Production." World Bank, Agriculture Division, Sahel Department, Washington, D.C.

Ka, Samba, and Nicholas van de Walle. Forthcoming. "The Political Economy of Adjustment in Senegal, 1980–91." In Stephen Haggard and Steven B. Webb, eds., *What Do We Know about the Political Economy of Economic Policy Reform?* New York: Oxford University Press.

Nellis, John. 1986. *Public Enterprises in Sub-Saharan Africa.* World Bank Discussion Paper 1. Washington, D.C.

———. 1989. "Public Enterprise Reform in Adjustment Lending." Policy Research Working Paper 233. World Bank, Country Economics Department, Washington, D.C.

OECD. 1991. *Geographical Distribution of Financial Flows to Developing Countries.* Paris.

Parker, Ron, and William F. Steel. 1992. "Small Enterprises under Adjustment in Senegal." Policy Research Working Paper 55. World Bank, Industry and Energy Department, Washington, D.C.

Svejnar, Jan, and Katherine Terrell. 1988. "Industrial Labor, Enterprise Ownership, and Government Policies in Senegal." University of Pittsburgh, Department of Economics, Pittsburgh, Pa.

World Bank. 1992. *World Development Report.* New York: Oxford University Press.

8

Tanzania: resolute action

Darius Mans

At Independence in 1961, Tanzania was one of the poorest countries in the world, with a population of some 20 million people and the eighth largest land area in Sub-Saharan Africa. Dependent largely on subsistence agriculture, the country had a small industrial base, and its base of educated and trained personnel was limited. Yet in the first six years after Independence, its economic growth surpassed 6 percent annually, favored by good weather and the absence of major external shocks. In addition, its economic policies, while moving gradually toward greater government control, were based largely on market forces. The policy regime for trade and capital movement was largely nonrestrictive, and foreign investment was encouraged as a major instrument for development.

In 1967 the government sought to increase the economic participation of indigenous Africans by enacting the Arusha Declaration, calling explicitly for a socialist society. The government extended its control throughout the economy by nationalizing all firms occupying the "commanding heights" of the economy—all the major commercial and financial institutions and some private agricultural estates. It also initiated a concerted program of collectivizing peasant farming and gave traditional agricultural cooperatives exclusive marketing rights, replacing private (mostly Asian) traders. The government also made significant strides toward improving social services, particularly access to education and safe water. In the short term, the government's strategy paid off: donor assistance to Tanzania increased rapidly during this period, real GDP grew at just under 5 percent annually during 1967–73, and gross investment rose to more than 20 percent of GDP. Yet lurking behind these gains were several structural weaknesses—declines in the productivity of public investment and in exports, dwindling domestic savings, an erosion in private sector confidence, an increase in foreign exchange controls, and a significant black market in which the premium for foreign exchange rose to over 100 percent. Then in the 1970s, Tanzania was buffeted by a series of external shocks—quadrupling oil prices, a severe drought in 1973–74, the break-up of the East African Community in 1977, and the Kagera War with Uganda.

By the early 1980s, economic decline and macroeconomic imbalances were severe. Real GDP contracted each year from 1981 to 1983. The growth in agricultural output was an anemic 2 percent—with that gain due to a weather-induced expansion in food crop production that offset the continued fall in the output of export crops—industrial output fell by 15 percent per year, and capacity utilization fell to less than 25 percent. The country's transport system and other public services deteriorated tremendously because they could not be maintained properly. The balance of payments continued to worsen with the poor performance in agricultural and manufacturing exports. Scheduled debt service on medium- and long-term debt as a ratio of exports rose more than 50 percent, and external payment arrears were substantial. Inflation rose significantly and continued unabated above 30 percent in the early 1980s.

Cautious of the government's inability to implement projects and skeptical about its willingness to address the heart of Tanzania's economic problems, foreign donors reduced their aid sharply after 1981. Consequently, imports declined to the point at which they could no longer support the economy, and widespread shortages of goods emerged. The severe imbalances in the country and the restrictive exchange and trade system led to the emergence of large parallel markets for both goods and foreign exchange. In 1983 the government launched a crackdown on black market activities, undermining and demoralizing the private sector, particularly Asian businessmen. According to several writers, the crackdown also sought to counter what was perceived to be a threat to state legitimacy (Maliyamkono and Bagachwa 1990). Yet despite the large number of arrests and convictions, no evidence was uncovered to show any organized resistance to the government. Extreme shortages of goods in the shops continued.

Despite some tentative steps toward reform with the structural adjustment program of 1982 to 1985, government reform measures had a limited impact on severe internal and external imbalances and did not elicit the external assistance needed from the donor community, primarily because of inappropriate exchange-rate policies. With discontent growing, President Nyerere decided not to continue as president, and at the end of 1985, Ali Hassan Mwinyi was elected as his successor, with free rein to embark on economic reform. What emerged was the economic recovery program, adopted in mid-1986.

The economic recovery program was based on an internal review of the weaknesses and shortcomings of the structural adjustment program, particularly its failure to stimulate a significant supply response or to generate much financial support from the donor community. During the early 1980s there was increasing debate within the government, and more broadly, about the failures of previous adjustment measures and the deepening economic crisis. Even though President Nyerere had steadfastly refused to even consider exchange rate devaluation, university-based economists took the lead in helping to organize public debates involving a wide spectrum of society on the need for more structural reform, particularly on the issue of whether the country should turn to the International Monetary Fund for help to restore economic growth. Such discussions helped to build a consensus on devaluation, on the introduction of the own-funds scheme whereby importers could import goods using their own foreign exchange on a no-questions-asked basis, and on the need to acknowledge and legitimize what was taking place in large gray markets.

Since the initial phase of the reform program succeeded in helping to jump start the stagnant economy, the role of more reform-minded technocrats increased significantly by the late 1980s. This facilitated a shift of emphasis in the reform program toward the key issue of macroeconomic instability. While some progress had been made in reducing the budget deficit, it had become apparent that the reform agenda had to address the systemic causes of the continuing instability, particularly through reforms at the microeconomic level that had important macroeconomic linkages.

At the outset of the economic recovery program, economic decision-making was dominated by a political party that remained firmly wedded to its socialist principles and was primarily concerned with economic recovery. There was no consensus on the need to move to a more liberal, market-based economy. The background, orientation, hardened attitudes, and ingrained habits of those entrusted with implementing the reforms clearly meant that the reform process would, at least initially, be difficult and slow. For example, while the World Bank and other donors pushed for quicker liberalization of agricultural export marketing, such change was impossible to implement because of resistance from the politically powerful leadership of the cooperatives, which until recently were part of the ruling political party. The debate involved a wide cross-section of interest groups, including politicians, businessmen, and labor union officials, and was accompanied by IMF and World Bank efforts to help the government formulate the economic recovery program.

The initial economic recovery program document, which was presented to donors at the 1986 consultative group meeting in Paris, provided a broad outline of policies—but focused on committing to an exchange rate policy that would completely remove the overvaluation of the shilling, and on making efforts to dramatically improve producer prices for the main export crops, including a willingness to reexamine agricultural marketing arrangements. These new directions received broad donor support at the consultative group meeting.

The first specific details of policy under the economic recovery program were announced in the budget speech of 1986 and formed the basis of a standby arrangement with the IMF in August 1986. In December, the World Bank followed with a structural adjustment program to support the economic recovery program. Many other donors also substantially increased their assistance to Tanzania. In 1987 the government entered into a first structural adjustment facility program with the IMF, followed by a second in 1988 and a third in 1990. The World Bank provided sectoral adjustment credits for industry, agriculture, and financial sector reforms, whose implementation began in 1988, 1990, and 1991, respectively. In 1989 the government embarked on the second phase of the economic recovery program (called economic recovery program II, or the economic and social action program), which was largely a continuation of the macroeconomic and structural reforms begun under the first economic recovery program but also sought to address problems in the social sectors. At the end of the third structural adjustment facility program with the IMF in 1991, the government entered into a three-year enhanced structural adjustment facility arrangement with the IMF to support the second phase of the economic recovery program. Both phases of the economic recovery program have received substantial support from the entire donor community.

The economic recovery program has dramatically turned around economic performance in Tanzania. Economic growth has been restored (figure 8.1). Exports and the level of investment have increased. In addition, the

Figure 8.1 Real gross domestic product, 1979–91

Billions of 1976 Tanzanian shillings

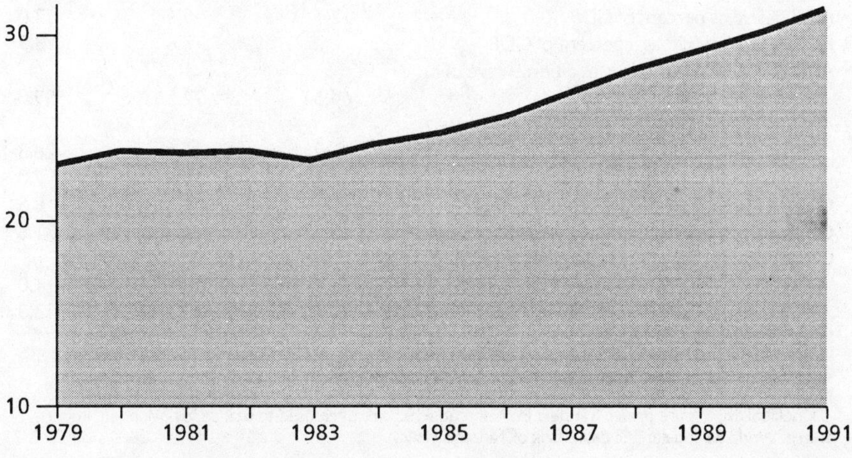

Source: Bureau of Statistics, National Accounts of Tanzania, 1976–91.

fiscal deficit has fallen substantially, and the rate of inflation has been reduced somewhat (table 8.1). Substantial progress has been made in addressing some of the major distortions in the economy—the legacy of nearly 20 years of socialist experimentation. Considering Tanzania's starting point, significant progress has been made in moving toward a more liberal, market-based economy.

Structural adjustment: lessons learned

The Tanzanian economy is better off now than it was before the reform program began. Yet Tanzania has not fully recovered from its economic crisis of the mid-1970s through the mid-1980s. At the start of the reform program the economy was plagued by an array of policy distortions and structural problems, a deep and prolonged economic crisis, and a heavy ideological bias against reform. In these circumstances, there is a temptation to argue that policy measures to relieve capacity constraints can be implemented quickly, while institutionally intensive structural reforms can only proceed slowly given the time needed to develop, achieve consensus on, and implement them. In retrospect, this thinking proved to be incorrect. Three important lessons emerge from this review of Tanzania's experience with adjustment. First, even

Table 8.1 Selected indicators of economic recovery program achievements
(percent)

Indicator	*Precrisis period 1970–80*	*Crisis years 1981–85*	*Economic recovery period 1986–91*
Average annual GDP growth in real terms	4.6	0.1	4.0
Average annual export growth in real terms	0.1	-10.4	5.6
Investment as a percent of GDP	20.1	14.3	31.6
Average annual inflation rate	14.0	31.0	25.7
Fiscal deficit[a] as percent of GDP	12.1	9.4	7.0
Primary fiscal deficit[b] as a percent of GDP	..	8.6	3.9
Agricultural producer prices as a percentage of international prices	64.5	72.5	59.0
Average annual appreciation of the real exchange rate	.2	16.1	-24.3
Central government deficit as a percent of GDP	12.1	9.4	7.0
Current account deficit as a percent of GDP	10.1	5.8	8.5
Gross domestic investment as a percent of GDP	20.1	14.3	31.6
Gross domestic savings as a percentage of GDP			
Official	..	10.4	1.0
Including unofficial exports[c]	..	10.7	13.3

.. Not available.
a. Central government deficit on a checks issued, before grants basis, including interest.
b. Central government deficit on a checks issued, before grants basis, excluding interest.
c. Unofficial exports are private transfers from abroad which are often used to finance "own-funded" imports.
Source: World Bank data; IMF data; Bank of Tanzania (1990).

among the capacity-relieving, more policy-intensive measures that were implemented, the pace of reform should have been faster. The analysis of some of these shortcomings suggests key measures that now need to be taken. Second, given the importance of some of the more capacity-intensive structural reforms to the success of the overall reform effort, they probably should have been addressed sooner. Since they were not, these reforms need to be expeditiously implemented. Third, in the sequencing of reforms, there is one critical area that has not yet received adequate attention: private sector development. While this area has been partially addressed during the economic recovery program, it should have been given greater priority.

Among the policy-intensive reforms, one of the most important was trade liberalization. In this area a number of lessons are clear from Tanzania's experience. Export promotion should have been implemented more vigorously, but it clearly was overshadowed by a program to intensify import liberalization. Import support programs financed by donors, particularly commodity import support, created distortions to the extent that they were not predicated on ensuring full collection of counterpart funds. Moreover, without sufficient action to move toward a market-determined and unified exchange rate, Tanzania effectively had an inefficient multiple exchange rate regime.

Within the open general license program, several mistakes were made in the sequencing of reform. First, an effective management and accounting system for the open general license should have been put in place when the scheme was introduced, rather than six years after it began operating. This delay only served to shake the confidence of both donors and importers in the scheme. The second mistake deals with the negative list—a list of goods that cannot be imported under the open general license. The government reduced the size of the negative list without addressing the problems associated with exchange rate overvaluation and the ineffectiveness of the customs department in minimizing import tax evasion. This led to a run on open general license resources that undermined the program's credibility as a market mechanism for getting access to foreign exchange, put local industry at a competitive disadvantage compared with imports, and favored trading over direct production activities, including exporting. Commercialization or privatization of customs and quick exchange rate unification probably would have been more effective than creating an open general license.

Among the structural measures, reform of the agricultural export market and the elimination of single-channel marketing needed to be implemented more quickly. These measures are absolutely essential (but not sufficient by themselves) to increase exports and improve macroeconomic stability, since excessive credit was granted to cooperatives and state marketing institutions to cover their large inefficiencies. Faster liberalization of agricultural export marketing and reduction of implicit taxation of agricultural exports would also have boosted growth and helped to further alleviate poverty. Since the banks have begun restricting credit to the cooperatives, there is a risk that the tight restrictions could result in farmers not being paid for all their export crop production. This would leave them with real disincentives to increase or even maintain the production of major export crops. While the legislative framework for liberalization of export crop marketing is expected to be in place by the beginning of fiscal 1994, new entrants in this field require access to processing facilities which today are exclusively in the hands of the cooperatives and take time to establish. One of the shortcomings of the adjustment process was the failure to open agricultural marketing earlier and to let the cooperatives sink or swim according to their ability to compete.

The losses of the parastatal sector were another important source of macroeconomic instability that should have been addressed earlier in the reform program. Reform should have hardened the budget constraint for parastatals, encouraged free entry and exit in areas that have been dominated by parastatals, and facilitated orderly restructuring and privatization. Delays in addressing parastatal reform have resulted in mounting financial and economic losses and declining asset values in the parastatal sector. Successful rehabilitation of a significant number of the parastatals would lead to improved productivity and overall economic performance. In addition, value added would improve immediately if the parastatals that depend on substantial subsidies to survive were closed.

Both parastatal and agriculture market reform are also essential to the emergence of good banking clients, and therefore to the future health of the banking system. By hardening the budget constraint, the financial sector reforms have played a crucial role in encouraging real side reform. However, delays in reform of the agriculture market and the parastatal sector impose real side costs and ultimately threaten the success of the financial sector reform program. Reform programs in these areas need to be implemented immediately.

Another source contributing to macroeconomic instability relates to the priority given to private sector development. The government's attitude toward the private sector has evolved considerably from the late 1960s, when the private sector was actively discouraged. Since 1990 the government has provided various incentives to private investors, recognizing that limited budgetary resources prevent the public sector from maintaining a dominant role in the productive sectors of the economy. However the indigenous private sector has been slow to develop, and there are growing concerns over a perceived "Asianization" of the economy. This has become a major political issue, slowed progress toward privatization of commercial parastatals, and delayed the liberalization of the marketing of the major export crops. It also has increased uncertainty on the part of the Asian business community, dampening their interest in making long-term investments in the country. Greater attention should have been given earlier in the reform program to strengthening indigenous entrepreneurship in particular, and the private sector in general.

Structural adjustment policies: the external environment

In addition to the internal factors described above, the external environment has also affected the progress and outcomes of the adjustment programs. Reasonably good weather has helped the adjustment program, and external aid has been vital.[1] The high level of external assistance in the form of disbursements of balance of payments support, project grants, and debt relief helped reverse the severe import compression of the prereform period. Donor financing has also helped the government sharply reduce bank borrowing to finance the deficit. While there is some concern that donor financing has been excessive and has forestalled adjustment, donors have often leveraged their assistance to accelerate the government's action on several important reforms. Yet the deterioration in Tanzania's terms of trade—which persisted from the mid-1970s throughout the adjustment program because of a substantial decline in world coffee prices, and weak world prices for other Tanzanian agricultural exports—reduced export earnings and widened the current account deficit.

Two important institutional dimensions have affected the progress of reform. First, limited managerial and technical capacities within the government have often slowed the design and implementation of reform. Second, the consensus building approach to reform—although essential for building a sense of government ownership—has occasionally delayed progress. The legal framework has also been an impediment at times. For example, laws had to be repealed before reform could proceed in the financial sector and with foreign exchange controls. Much effort during the economic recovery program was directed at reducing legal constraints by repealing and amending current legislation.[2] The absence of an official land market and lack of clarity on rights to, and transfers of, property have also affected the ability of firms to respond to reforms and to invest.[3]

Despite the ebb and flow of reform implied by these various factors, action has been resolute (see appendix 8A). The most apparent success has been that the adjustment program and external support of that program have arrested the protracted economic decline of the prereform period. The economic recovery program has dramatically improved economic performance in all major sectors. For example, the agricultural sector, which accounts for nearly half of GDP, has grown rapidly during the economic recovery program, after a growth rate of less than the rate of growth of the population during the prereform period. Too, the average annual 5 percent growth rate in agricultural GDP during the economic recovery program is more than twice the rate of growth achieved in Sub-Saharan Africa during the 1980s. The protracted decline of the industrial sector has been stemmed. Average annual growth of industry from 1986 to 1991 was nearly 5 percent, compared to a decline of the same magnitude from 1979 to 1985 (see appendix 8B for discussion of limitations of national accounts data for industry). Capacity utilization has also increased, industrial efficiency has improved, the industrial sector is diversifying into more efficient activities, and manufactured exports have increased substantially.

Prior to reforms, per capita consumption levels plummeted, and there were widespread shortages of goods in the country. During the economic recovery program, per capita consumption has increased each year. The rate of investment has increased, and Tanzania's balance of payments position has improved because its export volume has improved significantly. Despite some slippages, the government has improved its macroeconomic management by sharply reducing exchange rate overvaluation and by ending its use of the domestic banking system to finance its budget deficit. Inflation has declined somewhat, though it remains well above the average level of its trading partners. In addition, the groundwork for a solvent, competitive financial system is being laid.

Data on the distributional impact of adjustment are notoriously scarce. However, the major beneficiaries of adjustment are probably private traders, who have been able to capitalize on trading opportunities provided by import liberalization, as well as on opportunities to evade taxes.[4] Since the exchange rate overvaluation has been largely corrected, exporters who operate through official markets, particularly producers of export crops, have benefited from adjustment—so too have the private industrial firms that have been able to manage their debt exposure in foreign exchange, make their domestic manufacturing more efficient, and increase their exports. It is precisely these firms that are expanding most rapidly. It is also apparent that the increase in per capita consumption levels and greater spending power among consumers have rapidly expanded opportunities for entrepreneurs in the services sector. There also is some evidence that rural and urban poverty has diminished somewhat with the restoration of economic growth and lower real food prices. Finally, economic liberalization has undoubtedly benefited government agencies whose activities had been limited by the need to attend to the demands placed on them by the earlier regime of administrative controls—most notably the central bank.

Macroeconomic reform

Fiscal policy and management

Prior to the earlier structural adjustment program, public finances were severely strained. Poor economic performance had reduced revenue as a share of GDP during the late 1970s and early 1980s, particularly revenue from sales taxes on local manufacturing, where capacity utilization had fallen to less than 25 percent. Nevertheless, total expenditures continued to rise. By fiscal 1979 the fiscal deficit reached almost 20 percent of GDP, and domestic bank borrowing to finance the deficit rose to nearly 9 percent of GDP (figure 8.2).

On the fiscal front, the most important measures under the structural adjustment program of 1982–85 were a modest shift in the development budget toward agriculture and some increase in allocations for maintenance, increased tax collection efforts and higher taxes on beer and cigarettes, and general cutbacks in budgetary expenditures to reduce the overall deficit (figure 8.3). In addition, some 13,000 civil servants, representing less than 5 percent of the civil service, were retrenched in 1985 but many of those whose jobs were cut later found their way back into the civil service. The structural adjustment program also sought to improve expenditure monitoring and control.

By the end of the structural adjustment program in 1985, current revenue had declined by 17 percent in real terms, due primarily to a decline in income taxes accompanying the collapse of real income. Current expendi-

Figure 8.2 Budget deficit and bank borrowing, 1979–91

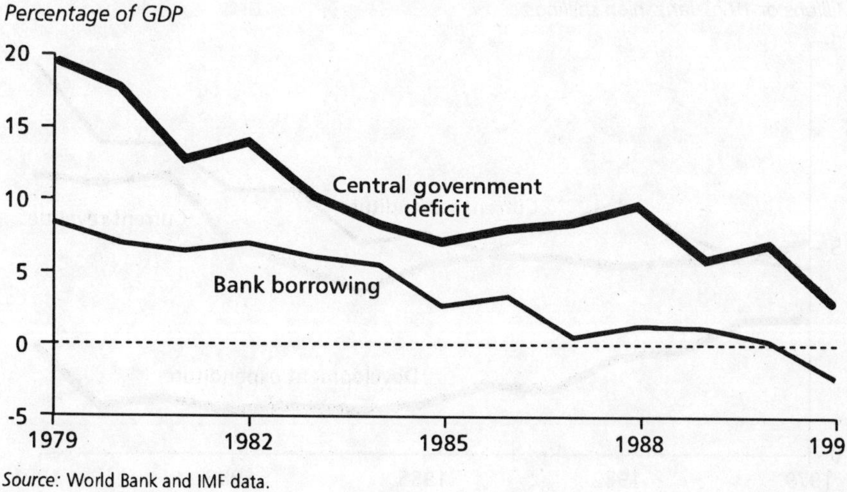

Percentage of GDP

Source: World Bank and IMF data.

tures had fallen only slightly, while developmental expenditures, which accounted for about 25 percent of total expenditures, fell by 21 percent, due largely to a decline in donor financing. It was also apparent that expenditure control was inadequate, many projects were chronically underfunded, and the bulk of donor funds were not accounted for in the budget. By fiscal 1985, the deficit had fallen to 7.3 percent of GDP, yet deficit financing by the domestic banks was still significant.

With the economic recovery program, the government adopted measures to increase revenue and reduce the growth of both current and developmental expenditures. A major medium-term objective was to eliminate domestic bank financing of the budget deficit. Government revenue was to be increased by improving the efficiency of tax collection, expanding the tax base by raising the general level of economic activity, reducing overvaluation of the exchange rate, and taxing the self-employed using presumptive income estimation methods.

The economic recovery program included several reform measures to these ends. Among the most important was a switch in the focus of public investment from new investments to rehabilitation, particularly rehabilitation of the deteriorating economic and social infrastructure. In addition, the system of indirect taxation was streamlined—customs duties and sales tax rates were reduced, particularly on imports but also on domestically produced goods. To improve revenue collection, the economic recovery program introduced preshipment inspection of imports by foreign firms for the purposes of customs valuation. Income tax rates were also reduced; corporate

Figure 8.3 Government revenue and expenditure, 1979–91

Millions of 1976 Tanzanian shillings

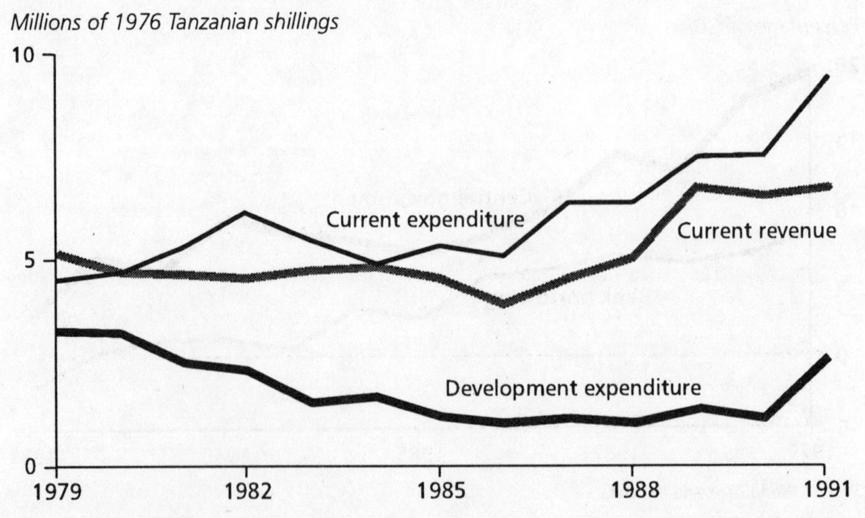

Source: World Bank data.

tax rates declined from 45 percent to 35 percent in fiscal 1993. Explicit parastatal subsidies were reduced from an estimated 2 percent of GDP in fiscal 1985 to less than 1 percent in 1991, limited primarily to subsidies for fertilizer and to specific major parastatals undergoing restructuring. A hiring freeze was imposed on new recruitment in the civil service, with certain specified categories such as teachers and medical personnel exempt.

These measures improved fiscal management. The deficit as a percentage of GDP declined substantially (figure 8.2). And deficit financing by the domestic banks showed a sustained decline. Too, the ratio of tax revenues to GDP rose to an estimated 23.5 percent of GDP by fiscal 1992, and budgetary planning and management improved.[5] In fiscal 1993 the proportion of donor funding actually captured in the budget was substantially increased.[6] In addition, a three-year rolling plan framework is in the design stage, seeking to put the budgeting and planning process in a multiyear context consistent with the overall macroeconomic program starting in fiscal 1994.

Despite these improvements, several structural weaknesses in public finances remain. While some effort has been made to generate additional revenue and improve the quality of public expenditures and mechanisms for monitoring and controlling the budget, the budget still relies heavily on donor financing.[7] Shortfalls in donor disbursements due to concerns about the pace of implementation and the accountability of donor resources have in several years compromised the government's financial program. While the introduction of economic criteria for project selection and an emphasis on completing ongoing projects rather than initiating new ones has improved public investment programming, the development budget still contains too many projects (more than 2,000). Many of these programs are severely underfunded—inconsistent with the objectives of the economic recovery program—and probably not sustainable. The tax base continues to be extremely narrow. Tanzania depends heavily on indirect taxes—particularly on domestic goods—for most of its revenue. Tax administration and enforcement are weak, as is tax compliance. While the tax revenue to GDP ratio is high in relation to other African countries, GDP is underestimated by at least 30 percent, and collections could be enhanced if the widespread import and income tax evasion could be reduced and a system of property taxation introduced. Moreover, quasi-fiscal or off-budget losses of the public sector have also increased—even with the improvement in central government finances—due to poor cost recovery among utilities and parastatals and mounting losses among the commercial parastatals, which by fiscal 1989 had reached 8 percent of GDP.

Fiscal reform has been constrained by weak administrative capacity and inadequate pay incentives in the public sector generally—particularly the civil service responsible for revenue collection. Examples of Tanzania's weak administrative capacity are numerous. The country has limited capacity to monitor budgetary developments throughout the year and to take corrective action when necessary. Too, because the recurrent and development budgets are prepared by two government ministries (the treasury and planning commission), budget coordination has been weak. The development budget is also essentially donor driven and determined. Fiscal policies cannot be executed properly because the key agencies lack effective management systems and tools. While donors have occasionally helped the government build capacity in some parts of the treasury and the planning commission, much must still be done to improve organization, management, and effectiveness in these areas.

But commitment to fiscal reform is clear—particularly since 1990—as evidenced by a sustained decline in reliance on domestic banks to finance the debt. Although some slippage occurred in fiscal 1993, domestic bank financing of the deficit had been eliminated by 1992, and the government has begun repaying the banking system for previous borrowing. The government has also demonstrated its commitment to fiscal reform by forming the high-powered Presidential Commission of Inquiry into Public Revenues, Taxation, and Expenditure. The commission has recently recommended sweeping reforms in several areas. Some of these reforms were adopted immediately in the fiscal 1993 budget—for example, reducing direct and indirect tax rates in the expectation that improved tax administration and compliance would increase revenue yields. Yet, as noted earlier, the expected benefits did not materialize, and many of the tax reductions that were made were rescinded in the middle of the year.

Monetary policy

In the late 1970s and early 1980s domestic credit expansion was driven by the public sector's demand for credit. Reflecting deficits in the financial operations of the sector, overall domestic credit increased by 31 percent annually from 1977 to 1982, compared with only 14 percent from 1975 to 1977. Bank credit to the private sector rose at only modest rates, due in part to the decline in economic activity and because credit to the public sector crowded out private sector lending.

The major objective of the earlier structural adjustment program monetary policy was to limit money growth and overall credit expansion to 15 to 20 percent annually. It also sought to gradually make real interest rates positive. Although the government did not achieve these objectives, they became a critical part of the economic recovery program, particularly in the economic programs supported by the IMF. Although deficit financing by domestic banks declined during the economic recovery program, the credit being extended to public sector financing meant that IMF targets on net domestic credit were consistently exceeded by fairly large margins (table 8.2).

Domestic credit increased by 43 percent annually from 1987 to 1989, compared with program targets of 32 percent during structural adjustment facilities I and II. The bulk of this growth stemmed from the expansion of credit to finance the deficit and from excessive credit to individual crop marketing boards, particularly the National Milling Corporation, which had enjoyed a monopoly in marketing a variety of crops. Moreover, the commercial banks continued to accrue interest on most of their public sector nonperforming loans, and were relying on their almost unlimited access to credit from the Bank of Tanzania for liquidity. The central bank could not curb the rapid expansion of credit because it lacked supporting fiscal policies—but also because the banking system was highly monopolized, effective prudential regulations were absent, and bank supervisory capacity at the Bank of Tanzania was weak (see section below on financial sector policies). The central bank could not use one of the few tools at its disposal, reserve requirements, because the banks often did not hold any deposits at the Bank of Tanzania, but still ran large overdrafts.

In addition to excessive credit creation, the banking system was facing a severe crisis by the late 1980s. All commercial banks were highly inefficient and insolvent. Consequently, a Presidential Commission of Inquiry into the Monetary and Banking System was formed. Based on its report, and agreements reached with the IMF in the context of the enhanced structural adjustment facility and the World Bank's financial sector adjustment credit, the

Table 8.2 Selected credit and monetary annual growth rates, June 1986–June 1992

(percentage increase)

Item	*1986*	*1987*	*1988*	*1989*	*1990*	*1991*	*1992*
Domestic assets (net)	23.2	25.3	46.8	47.6	28.7	6.3	22.8
Domestic credit	22.9	27.5	52.3	34.6	21.5	14.6	1.5
Claims on government (net)[a]	19.3	5.1	53.3	10.4	4.9	-19.2	3.0
Claims on other public entities and private sector	30.2	69.1	51.1	62.9	34.6	35.5	1.0
Industrial and commercial parastatals	..	..	..	..	53.3	40.7	-7.8
Selected marketing boards	3.4	53.4	-3.7	68.7	27.9	0.4	-83.7
Private sector	..	..	..	..	22.6	53.6	11.3
Cooperative unions	..	149.3	78.9	43.7	37.4	43.0	29.3
Money and quasi-money	17.7	20.2	34.8	37.5	45.1	26.8	40.5

.. Not available.

a. From June 1988 onwards includes TSh13,643 million of overdrafts by the marketing boards taken over by the government, TSh19,022 million in overdrafts of the National Milling Corporation with the National Bank of Commerce which were assured by the government in 1991/92, and TSh18,887 million in transfers to the loans and advances realization trust made in June 1992.

Source: Bank of Tanzania and IMF staff estimates.

government embarked early in 1991 on a far-reaching financial sector reform program that has had significant implications for monetary policy. The balance sheets of the banks have been cleaned up, and the Bank of Tanzania's overdraft facility was closed. A discount policy was then introduced to allow the commercial banks access to Bank of Tanzania's refinancing, but the bank discourages commercial banks from relying on borrowing from it. The commercial banks have now begun to extend credit on more prudent terms, particularly to parastatals and cooperative unions.

Current monetary and financial sector reform represents an important commitment to reform that was absent in the past. Concrete action has recently been taken to stem the essentially automatic access to central bank credit for the commercial banks. In addition, fiscal management has improved to the extent that, until the slippage of 1992–93, past pressures on the banking system to finance the deficit have been removed. The economic recovery program has enabled the central bank to exercise more independence and carry out its role appropriately. The central bank has curbed rapid monetary expansion much more effectively, but it is still constrained by losses due to delays in collecting open general license counterpart funds from local banks (box 8.1), as well as losses from gold purchases and the money creation inherent in the debt conversion program.[8]

Box 8.1 Funding of the open general license

Funding for the open general license expanded rapidly after its introduction in 1987. While it was initially financed solely by the World Bank, the African Development Bank and bilateral donors have since joined. Many bilaterals have been shifting their balance of payments support away from traditional commodity import support to the open general license because of the poor record of counterpart fund recovery by the treasury under traditional commodity import support programs—an average cash cover collection rate of only 40 percent of the amounts due, compared to the open general license design that requires all counterpart funds to be paid to the treasury. (In practice, however, there have been some problems with the flow of counterpart funds in the open general license.) In addition, the government has been channeling increasing amounts of its own scarce foreign exchange earnings, after meeting its oil and debt service payment obligations, into the open general license instead of allocating them administratively. By 1991–92 the shares of total open general license financing provided by of the World Bank, bilateral donors, the government, and the African Development Bank were 56, 28, 11, and 5 percent, respectively.

During 1991 and 1992 joint donor evaluation missions to Tanzania uncovered major problems with the accounting systems being used under the open general license, in addition to importer concerns about the transparency of access

Financial sector policies

Financial sector reform was initiated relatively late in the economic recovery program, despite the early recognition that weaknesses with the banking system had been a major constraint to growth. Prior to the reform program, the banking system was extremely monopolistic, consisting almost entirely of government-owned financial institutions. The total assets of the state-owned National Bank of Commerce, formed from the nationalization of twelve private banks in 1967, are 13 times larger than those of the Cooperative Rural Development Bank, which is the only other commercial bank on the mainland.[9] Competition in the financial sector was precluded by sectoral specialization within the commercial banks (for example, retail banking at the National Bank of Commerce and rural banking at the Cooperative Rural Development Bank), geographic specialization (in the case of the People's Bank of Zanzibar), a series of sector-specific financial institutions (the housing bank, savings bank, and development banks), and government prohibitions on the entry of new financial institutions.

Banking supervision by the Bank of Tanzania was completely inadequate and failed to halt the deteriorating financial conditions of the banks. Interest rates, which were kept largely negative in real terms until 1990, constrained

to open general license funds. When the program was introduced, insufficient attention was paid to developing accounting systems that would meet donor requirements, particularly accounting for the counterpart funds generated by open general license disbursements. Fiscal 1992 audits demonstrated that while the treasury received from the Bank of Tanzania the full counterpart value of foreign exchange disbursed through the open general license, about TSh 17 billion in counterpart funds was owed by the commercial banks to the Bank of Tanzania. The rapid expansion of the open general license also outstripped the capacity of the Bank of Tanzania to adequately manage it. While it was designed to make foreign exchange available on a first-come first-served basis, there was no mechanism for ensuring that, or for verifying that this principle was being strictly adhered to. Moreover, the perception of a lack of transparency in the allocation of resources was exacerbated by periodic shortages of open general license funding, in part due to rapid expansion of demand and to the lumpy nature of disbursements of donor money into the open general license. Due to concerns about the transparency and automaticity of the allocation of open general license resources and accountability of the system, in 1992/93 donor financing of the open general license dried up, pending improvements in the management of the open general license in these areas.

the mobilization of deposits. The structure of interest rates was strictly controlled according to the sector and the size and maturity of enterprises and thus had little to do with how credit was allocated. Financial institutions granted credit largely without accounting for the repayment capacity of borrowers. For example, about two-thirds of all bank lending outstanding at the end of 1987 went to cover the operating deficits of the crop marketing parastatals. Moreover, weak credit systems and internal controls, slow court procedures, and political influence limited the commercial banks from recovering loans or selling collateral. At the same time, the commercial banks had almost unlimited access to Bank of Tanzania refinancing, stifling their incentive to mobilize deposits and improve loan recoveries.

Thus Tanzania's financial system performed very poorly. Nearly all of the financial institutions were insolvent, and most of their loans were nonperforming. Given the extremely low capital base of most institutions in the sector and inadequate provisioning for bad debts, virtually all institutions have a substantial negative net worth. Recognizing these problems, the government established a Presidential Commission of Inquiry into the Monetary and Banking System in 1988. After two years the Commission recommended measures for enhancing the overall performance of the financial sector. The Commission presented its recommendations in 1990, calling for a radical restructuring of the financial institutions and their parastatal clients, and the elimination of single channel marketing of agricultural exports.

Building on the findings of the commission, the government has begun implementing wide-ranging financial sector reform—liberalizing interest rates, strengthening prudential banking regulations and central bank supervision, allowing the entry of private banks, and restructuring existing banks. These reforms are being supported by a World Bank financial sector adjustment credit and the IMF enhanced structural adjustment facility arrangements. The balance sheets of the existing banks are being cleaned up: nonperforming loans are being taken off the books of the commercial banks, and remaining loan losses are being fully provisioned against. Government bonds have been issued to cover the provisioning requirements and to partially meet the costs of recapitalizing the banks. This process is to be completed by October 1993, to enable the banks to meet the tough new prudential guidelines on capital adequacy adopted from the Basel standards. In addition, the National Bank of Commerce has begun to reorganize itself, including initial steps at downsizing and automating its operations. Interest rates also have been liberalized substantially, so that the central bank can now stipulate only a minimum deposit rate and a maximum lending rate. Moreover, banking supervision is being strengthened, and overdraft facilities for the commercial banks have been closed. Finally, at least one internationally known bank that operated in Tanzania before 1967 is returning to do major retail banking and trade and investment financing. And although the reforms were introduced only recently, preliminary indications are that banks are making better banking decisions, are under less pressure to lend, are extending less credit to parastatals and cooperatives, and are making more credit available to the private sector (table 8.2). Yet as discussed in the section on macroeconomic outcomes, much more is still to be done.

Exchange rate management

Until recently, exchange rate management has been a contentious issue between the government and the Bretton Woods institutions. Even in the face of the severe balance of payments crisis of the late 1970s and early 1980s, the government totally resisted devaluing the exchange rate. Consequently, the real exchange rate appreciated significantly. By 1984 a large parallel market for foreign exchange emerged, with a prevailing exchange rate that was reportedly eight times higher than the official rate. The 1984–85 budget provided the first indication of a new pragmatism in the government's approach to economic management, a devaluation of the exchange rate by one-third. This initial adjustment of the exchange rate represented a major shift in policy. The adjustment fell short, however, and the premium of the black market rate over the official exchange rate continued to rise.

One of the cornerstones of policy reform under the economic recovery program has been significant adjustment of the exchange rate. At the start of the economic recovery program the government adjusted the nominal exchange rate from TSh 17 per U.S. dollar in April 1986 to TSh 40 in June, and then gradually depreciated the real exchange rate until 1988. By the end of June 1988, the exchange rate stood at TSh 97 per U.S. dollar, more than 30 percent below the end-June 1987 level in real effective terms. While the exchange rate slipped somewhat in 1988 when the rate of nominal depreciation fell significantly below the rate of inflation, the government soon got back on track with IMF-Bank-supported programs to achieve a more realistic exchange rate.[10] Adjustment continued, leading to a cumulative depreciation of the real effective exchange rate of more than 80 percent from 1986 to 1991, and the premium in the parallel market was reduced substantially from its peak of 800 percent in 1985 to about 50 percent in 1991 (figure 8.4). Continued exchange rate overvaluation was due to the lack of overall financial discipline and supporting macroeconomic policies.

After a major exchange rate study was completed by the Bank of Tanzania, a new Foreign Exchange Act was adopted in early 1992. It provided the legislative basis for the foreign exchange bureaus that were introduced in April 1992 and was the regulatory framework within which the Bank of Tanzania would operate. While the volume of transactions passing through the bureaus was fairly limited initially, it increased substantially during the year as the open general license dried up (box 8.1).[11] The government will soon adopt such measures as an increase in export retention rates and an increase in the volume of bureau trading. In addition, the exchange rate prevailing in the bureaus is being used to set the official exchange rate, with the objective of unifying the official and prevailing exchange rates by fiscal 1994.[12] Bureaus are playing a key role in the process of unifying the exchange rate, which depoliticizes the process of setting the official exchange rate, which in the past had led to acrimonious negotiations with the IMF and the World Bank.

Government policy on exchange rate issues has come a long way. The government had always made exchange rate adjustments very reluctantly. Policymakers are now recognizing that the exchange rate should be market determined, and that adjustments are not substitutes for the more prudent management of monetary and fiscal policies.

External trade liberalization

The government responded to the balance of payments crises of the late 1970s and the early 1980s by intensifying trade controls in order to reduce imports. For example, with the collapse of exports, a decline in aid financing, and virtually no access to international credit in the early 1980s, imports fell by 40 percent in nominal terms by 1984. The government resorted extensively

Figure 8.4 Nominal and real effective exchange rates, 1980–92

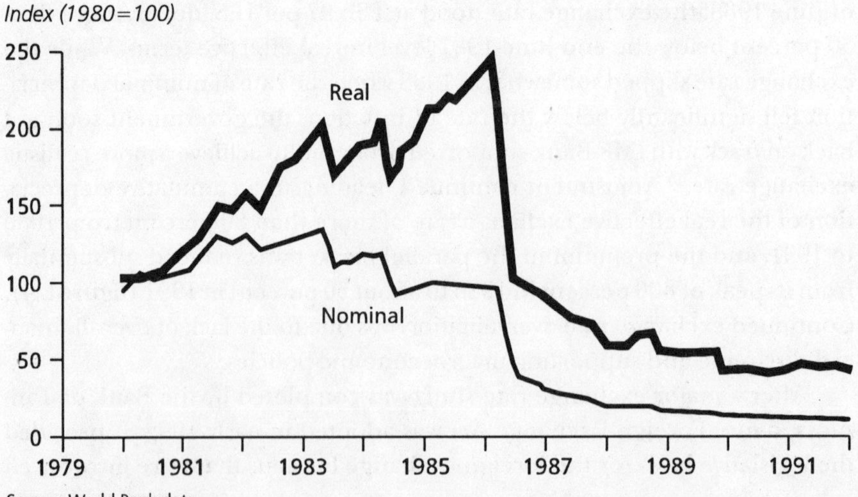

Source: World Bank data.

to quantitative restrictions. Tariff levels were also prohibitive. In the late 1970s and early 1980s, the tariff structure was relatively complex, although the bulk of imports were subject to tariff rates of zero, 20, 25, and 60 percent. However 15 other rates also applied, ranging between 15 and 200 percent. The lower rates applied primarily to intermediate and capital goods, while the higher rates applied primarily to consumer goods. Imports were also subjected to sales taxes, with over 20 different rates ranging from zero to 300 percent. These policies led to an extremely high (nearly 500 percent) average level of effective protection on domestic manufacturing and wide variation in effective protection across industries. Moreover, the degree of protection enjoyed by an industrial firm was inversely related to its economic efficiency. Several highly protected firms were economically inefficient as measured by their domestic resource costs, and some important agricultural activities had negative rates of effective protection.

Tanzania's adjustment program has liberalized international trade, particularly imports. Tariffs have been reduced significantly, as have quantitative restrictions on imports. In 1984 the government introduced an "own-funds" import scheme to deal with the severe shortages of goods in the country. This action was independent of World Bank and IMF advice. The "own-fund" scheme allowed individuals to import a specified range of consumer, intermediate, and capital goods into the country using unofficial sources of foreign exchange. As agreed with the World Bank in the context of its first structural adjustment credit, this list was subsequently expanded and today includes almost all goods (with the exception of, for example, firearms and explosives). After its introduction, own-funded imports quickly grew to account for 40 percent of total imports.

The own-funds window helped arrest the decline of several sectors, including peasant agriculture, transport, and manufacturing, because it increased the availability of imports. At the same time, the own-funds window helped dismantle the elaborate system of quantitative restrictions. Own-funded imports exposed the industrial sector virtually overnight to a trade regime in which levels of protection fell dramatically. Average levels of effective protection for industry declined from an estimated 500 percent in early 1984 to about 150 percent in 1985, and some firms effectively became disprotected due to the exchange rate undervaluation and the evasion of customs duties and sales taxes on own-fund imports.[13]

The introduction of the own-funds scheme was followed in 1987 by the introduction of the open general license facility with initial funding by the Bank. The open general license represented an important advance in foreign exchange management by giving importers access on a first-come first-served basis to foreign exchange for a few agriculture and transport sector imports specified on a positive list. The open general license played an important role early in the reform program by encouraging some official practices that were market-based rather than administrative. Based on agreements with the World Bank, the list of eligible goods under the open general license was gradually expanded over the next few years to encompass most intermediate goods for agriculture, transport, and industry, in addition to a wide range of capital goods. In January 1991 the Bank pressured the government into shifting to a negative list of goods that could not be imported under the open general license and further increasing the number of goods that could be imported. This negative list was again reduced in April 1992 in consultation with the World Bank and the IMF. The current list covers about 20 percent of nonoil imports.

The open general license has been used increasingly since its introduction (table 8.3). It accounted for less than 1 percent of total import licenses issued in its first year of operation. By 1991 it accounted for 27 percent because of the expanded range of goods eligible for importation under the facility and increased funding (box 8.1).

In addition, the rising demand for open general license resources was due to differences in the effective cost of imports across the various import windows. For example, despite exchange rate overvaluation, open general license imports were cheaper than own-fund imports because customs duties and sales taxes on own-fund imports could be evaded. Until fiscal 1992 own-funded imports were not subjected to preshipment inspection. While the government has recently moved substantially toward unifying exchange rates, the large premium on the parallel foreign exchange market has prompted importers at times to favor the open general license over own-funded imports. Although additional costs are associated with importing through the open general license (for example, the cost of opening letters of credit through an inefficient banking system and the interest costs incurred

Table 8.3 Import licenses issued under all financing windows, 1986–91

Source of funds	*1986*	*1987*	*1988*	*1989*	*1990*	*1991*
Open general license	—	—	49.70	167.50	309.97	465.39
Normal/free allocation	333.84	483.36	340.20	533.41	383.25	349.16
Import support	184.90	122.59	167.73	203.63	156.85	63.30
Loans, grants, and credits	199.28	287.82	542.73	391.79	405.59	314.43
Supplier's credit	153.88	64.34	68.18	30.00	12.98	8.39
Barter trade	11.39	13.63	10.06	5.42	2.90	4.83
Export retention	0.70	2.88	8.12	19.29	19.25	5.60
Owns exchange	475.56	514.68	638.59	484.31	448.46	493.58
Total	1,359.55	1,489.30	1,825.31	1,835.35	1,739.25	1,704.67

— Not applicable.
Source: Import Data and Analysis Department, Bank of Tanzania.

while waiting for letters of credit to be confirmed), the open general license often was a cheaper source of foreign exchange for imports than own-funds.

Aside from introducing own-funds in 1984 and a small open general license operation in 1987 on its own initiative, the government undertook most of the subsequent stages of import liberalization reluctantly—primarily reducing the size of the negative list on imports through the open general license. The successive liberalizations were undertaken in response to pressure from the World Bank and the IMF. The government intends to complete the process of import liberalization by restructuring the negative list to include only goods that it wishes to control for health and security reasons and a limited list of luxury goods. That same list would then be applied to all import windows, including own-fund imports. This process would be accompanied by a program to unify the exchange rate in fiscal 1994.

In retrospect the open general license was an important, intermediate step toward exchange rate unification. However, reducing the negative list in the face of exchange rate overvaluation may not have liberalized trade substantially, since nearly all goods could be imported under the own-funds scheme anyway. In fact it may have been counterproductive to the extent that exchange rate overvaluation would merely insure greater demand for cheaper open general license resources, leading to their exhaustion, thereby inhibiting the program from improving access to officially available foreign exchange. Moreover, the implicit subsidy to open general license users also effectively hindered the development of foreign exchange bureaus, as importers waited in the open general license queue for large import transactions rather than going to the bureaus.[14] Greater progress toward unification should have accompanied reductions in the size of the open general license negative list. In addition, rather than relying solely on preshipment inspection for improving the collection of import taxes, the government should have implemented (and still should) a program for improving the efficiency of the customs department.

It should also be noted that trade liberalization has included a substantial reduction in tariffs. In the context of the World Bank's industrial restructuring and trade adjustment credit, the tariff and sales tax structure began to be simplified gradually in 1988. By the 1992–93 budget, the maximum tariff had been reduced to 40 percent and duties on most spare parts and intermediate and raw material imports were lifted (although, again, this decision was rescinded at mid-year because revenue collections fell short of expectations). Sales taxes have also been significantly reduced and now range from 0 to 30 percent. In addition, to make tariffs binding and to improve revenue collection, the government reduced most duty exemptions and began using preshipment inspection companies for assessing customs duties payable to treasury. Nevertheless, tariff evasion is still substantial, particularly for own-funded imports.[15]

In comparison with imports, the liberalization of exports has been promoted less vigorously. The own-funds scheme introduced in 1984 obviously encouraged exports (and perhaps even some capital inflows), albeit unofficial exports. One of the more explicit measures to encourage official exports was the export retention scheme. In 1986 a few exporters were allowed to retain some of their export earnings in order to import basic inputs required to sustain their operations. Retention rates initially varied considerably among exporters. In 1988 the government began to consolidate rates, whereby a 50 percent retention rate was applied to a large number of nontraditional exports and 10 percent to traditional exports (except for a few firms that negotiated better retention rates with the Bank of Tanzania or had their projects approved by the Investment Promotion Center).[16] With the creation of foreign exchange bureaus, retention rates are again being reviewed with an eye toward abolishing surrender requirements on all nontraditional exports in 1993. In 1988 a duty drawback scheme was introduced, but administrative difficulties, including chronic underfunding in the government budget, limited its effectiveness. Finally, some progress has been made toward reducing the bureaucratic red tape and costs involved in exporting, but cumbersome export licensing and registration requirements prior to the shipment of goods make exporting expensive, particularly from border areas in Tanzania to neighboring countries. Export financing has been in extremely short supply, and the liberalization of agricultural export marketing has been delayed. Exchange rate overvaluation has penalized exporters.

In summary, trade liberalization has been a cornerstone of the economic recovery program. Acting on its own, the government implemented the own-funds scheme, conceived largely to bring in complementary imports that were urgently required to cover the widespread shortages of goods. Successive measures to liberalize imports and increase import competition were largely donor driven, particularly reducing the size of the negative list. The same was true of tariff reform until the past few years, when the government began reducing tariff rates based on relatively little analysis of their impact on revenue and levels of protection. Overall, the import regime has been very liberal and market-oriented. This is true, despite exchange rate overvaluation and the existence of quantitative restrictions from the negative list on the open general license, because importers have taken advantage of the arbitrage opportunities that exist across the various import windows. On the import side, the effective exchange rate has been much closer to a market rate of exchange, although the import regime continues to be highly segmented. Conversely, exports have been highly discriminated against.

Sectoral reform

Price and market deregulation

In the agricultural sector, Tanzania's marketing system has been essentially a compulsory single channel system since the mid-1960s, when primary village societies were established as the only buyers of crops, and a single government body was the sole exporter or distributor of goods for local consumption. In fiscal 1974, this system was modified when the government created marketing authorities for each crop as monopoly exporters. It also set producer prices for agricultural crops.

In the early 1980s, the government began to liberalize the marketing of foodcrops, which, along with processing, transportation, distribution, and storage, had previously been monopolized by the National Milling Corporation. In order to ensure better and more reliable supplies of foodgrains to consumers at lower costs, the government allowed cooperatives and individuals to market foodgrains and removed all restrictions on their transport. These changes signalled a more positive government attitude toward private farming and private markets. In 1987 the economic recovery program allowed regional cooperative unions and primary societies to sell foodgrains directly to private traders, although market outlets for farmers were still confined to the primary societies. In the following marketing season, grain trade was fully liberalized. The private sector now accounts for more than 90 percent of the trade. In addition, food self-sufficiency has improved dramatically because foodgrain production has increased substantially, and the real price of foodgrains has declined. Input distribution was also formally deregulated.

Less progress has been made toward liberalizing the marketing of agricultural export crops. The single channel monopoly remained virtually untouched except for the minor export crops, which were liberalized in 1987. Until recently, the internal marketing of six traditional crops (tea, coffee, cotton, cashew nuts, tobacco, and pyrethrum) was confined largely to the cooperative societies. Export marketing was handled largely through parastatal marketing boards, with the exception that private estates were allowed to export tea and sisal directly. In July 1990 the roles of the marketing boards for the main export crops changed. They began to act only as auctioneers or tender administrators, as agencies responsible for quality control and market intelligence (for a fee), and as handling and forwarding agents for the cooperatives.[17] In fiscal 1992 cashew marketing was fully liberalized; the private sector was allowed to buy directly from the farmers in competition with the marketing board and the cooperative unions. While cotton ginning capacity is exclusively in the hands of the cooperatives, negotiations between private companies and cooperative unions have recently been concluded for two joint venture ginneries—and Cargill, the largest private cooperation in the world, has been given the go-ahead to build a ginnery in one of the major cotton growing areas. These ginneries have been allowed to buy seed cotton and sell lint on their own account. Coffee exports are auctioned by the government-owned Coffee Marketing Board. Since fiscal 1992, all coffee has been subject to international auction by the marketing board. Until 1991 the arrangement to secure financing for oil imports required the direct sale of 40 percent of the export crop to predetermined foreign buyers.

Price liberalization in the agricultural sector has been mixed. Accompanying the liberalization of the grain trade was a change in official pricing policy. When limited competition in foodgrain marketing was allowed in 1987, official prices became the minimum prices to be paid to producers by the cooperatives, and the official consumer price was eliminated. In fiscal 1991, the minimum producer price system was replaced with a system of indicative prices that guided farmers in negotiating sales. Actual foodgrain prices paid to farmers are now determined by market conditions.

Export crop pricing has been liberalized more slowly. Until just recently, the government set producer prices without due regard for international price trends, and kept producer prices low relative to export prices, given the inefficiencies in the marketing system, thus creating a heavy implicit tax on traditional agricultural exports. Since the economic recovery program, producer prices have been kept below 60 percent of export prices, which is lower than during the crisis period of 1981 to 1985, as well as below the average from 1970 to 1980 (table 8.1).[18]

Until 1991 the government fixed producer prices for export crops; thereafter, the government switched to a system of indicative prices—again, serving merely as a guideline for negotiating prices with farmers. However, in many cases these indicative prices were actually fixed prices to be paid to farmers. Even when they were indicative, they often bore little relationship to international prices. For example, the indicative price for cotton in February 1992 far exceeded the world price under the prevailing exchange rate. Recognizing that this policy was unsustainable, the government subsequently announced a much lower price to be given to farmers as a first payment, with a second payment to be made after farmers realized export proceeds.[19] Previous pricing policies, exchange rate overvaluation, and little or no foreign exchange retention for traditional exports taxed traditional agriculture heavily. The consequent financial losses of the cooperative unions as the commercial banks were being restructured imposed major fiscal losses on the central bank, which could not collect the funds it had advanced for agriculture and had to provision against losses in the commercial banks' loan portfolios.

Recognizing the high cost of previous approaches to pricing policy, the government has begun to allow more flexible pricing in some cases. For example, in coffee, the government has ceased to announce the advance payment to be made by the cooperative unions to farmers. Each union can now decide how much advance and total payments should be made to farmers. A recent review of these advance payments shows a range of prices. Change in the pricing policy was inevitable, because government-announced advanced payments to farmers were too high in relation to the world price and to existing marketing margins, causing serious financial difficulties for many cooperative unions.

In the industrial sector, the government has undertaken a major program to deregulate prices and markets. The structural adjustment program had reduced price controls to only fifty locally manufactured product groups and six imported product categories by fiscal 1984, and the economic recovery program accelerated this program of price decontrol. By fiscal 1989 price-controlled items constituted less than 15 percent of the consumer price index weights, and many of the controlled prices were set according to international prices. Moreover, the large inflow of own-funded imports increased pressure on domestic prices to reflect international prices. Consequently, the government has nearly abolished all price controls.

Today only three prices are subject to price control: sugar, fertilizer, and petroleum products. In 1989 the government embarked on a program to reduce the subsidy for fertilizer progressively over five years to not more than 20 percent—to improve input efficiency and encourage the development of alternative distribution channels. Today the subsidy stands at 40 percent, down from 80 percent in fiscal 1991. For petroleum, domestic prices are adjusted to reflect movements in international prices and currency fluctuations. Currently, domestic prices cover the cost of imports and distribution. For sugar, prices are controlled in the absence of international standards, but the government only regulates sales of domestically produced sugar to the Sugar Development Corporation—a parastatal that then sells locally produced sugar and sugar imported by the government to local state-run distributors, which in turn sell to consumers at artificially low prices.[20] However, because more than 50 percent of market demand is supplied by sugar that is imported privately through the own-funds scheme or is produced domestically and sold to the Sugar Development Corporation at free market rates rather than at the controlled price, retail prices for sugar are market determined, effectively subsidizing traders who buy at wholesale prices. For the 1991–92 budget, the government announced its intention to decontrol the sugar price, but was forced to rescind that policy because of opposition in parliament.

Along with liberalizing imports and prices, the government deregulated domestic trade and the marketing of all imported and domestically produced industrial goods. In the early 1980s, the wholesale trade of more than fifty goods was restricted to parastatal companies. By 1991 only sixteen goods remained legally confined to state trading companies. However, in practice, no goods are confined to the state trading companies because they cannot meet the demand, and legal restrictions are not enforced.

In summary, price and marketing liberalization has proceeded much more slowly in agriculture than in industry. In industry the own-funds window and the emergence of unofficial markets have in practice ended price controls and the government's monopoly on the distribution of industrial products. In the agriculture sector the transition from a government-controlled single-channel system has been slow, starting with the relative monopoly in grain marketing. Export crop marketing is more complicated, since new facilities require considerable investment; the lead time between crop purchase and final receipt of export proceeds is long and thus requires considerable working capital to finance the cooperative unions or marketing boards that control processing. While the government acknowledges that the current export market system for agriculture has become increasingly inefficient and that it dampens prices, delays payment to producers, delivers inputs inefficiently, and generates poor quality exports, it probably acted prematurely in allowing the cooperatives to become independent before their assets could be privatized and their large arrears to the commercial banks cleared. It may take some time before the entry of new firms generates significant competition.

Labor and wage policy reform

Labor and wage policy reform during the adjustment program has been limited essentially to adjustments in the minimum wage and initial efforts to address civil service overstaffing. The government sets the minimum wage for wage employment. By 1986 the minimum wage was worth less than a third of its level in 1970. In addition to wages, civil servants also receive monetary allowances of more than 50 percent of wage remuneration. It has been estimated that the average civil servant's package of wages and monetary allowances covers only about 40 percent of the expenses of a typical household.[21] The economic recovery program made some adjustments in the minimum wage, but they were substantially below rises in the cost of living. The entire structure of wages for civil servants is fixed unilaterally by government.[22] The government also controls the wages of parastatal employees, although the electric power authority recently introduced a performance-based pay scheme; with the recent elimination of government controls on compensation as part of the parastatal reform program, other profitable parastatals are proposing to increase wages substantially. Civil service salaries are now substantially below those in both the parastatal sector and the private sector. In the public sector, real wages declined as the government attempted to maintain high employment levels in the face of a shrinking fiscal base. These wage policies have encouraged public sector workers to seek outside sources of income, prompted government managers to tolerate below-average efforts by employees, and led to deteriorating service levels in the public sector.

With the economic recovery program, the donor community has focused heavily on the overstaffing and poor performance of the civil service. In 1985 the government retrenched 12,760 employees, or about 5 percent of total employment in the civil service. Nevertheless, because of inadequate controls on hiring and the government's policy of absorbing graduates from various training institutions automatically into the civil service, about 14,000 employees were hired, including many who had previously been laid off. The civil service continues to be significantly overstaffed.

Low salaries and poor personnel management are two of the key reasons for the poor performance of the civil service. In sharp contrast with the early 1970s—when public sector workers earned much more than employees in the private sector—many street-trading and informal-sector activities now generate average earnings above those in many parts of the civil service, and salaries in the private sector are substantially higher. Thus the public sector has steadily lost some of its most qualified people, with civil service management and performance standards declining significantly. Civil servants' performance is not evaluated regularly, and a system for dismissing poor performers or rewarding good ones is absent. Training and career development opportunities in the civil service remain extremely limited. All these factors have lowered morale in the civil service and have adversely affected implementation capacity throughout government, particularly the pace of reform in the social sectors.

Previous reform efforts were half-hearted. Donors have pressured the government into putting together a comprehensive strategy for civil service reform in which an estimated 50,000 excess workers from the civil service will be retrenched (from more than 350,000 in 1991), the mandatory retirement age of 55 will be enforced, personnel controls and personnel management systems will be improved, pay scales will be reformed, and the civil service will be made more efficient, including a clearly defined, much less ambitious role for government. Much of the required technical work has been done, supported by donor assistance. In fact, the mandatory retirement age is already being enforced, and almost 3,000 civil servants have been retrenched. Despite the fact that retrenchment is only the first phase of the reform program, the other large demands on the budget, including the costs of financial sector and parastatal reform, are already constraining these reform efforts. Budgetary constraints may also delay payment reform, which is an important complement to the other reform measures needed to improve the effectiveness of government.

Public enterprise reform

Tanzania has developed a very large parastatal sector. In 1966 there were about 43 parastatals, primarily in the electricity and mining sectors. By 1988 there were 410 parastatals as a result of the nationalizations of the late 1960s and early 1970s and the basic industrial strategy which established many industrial parastatals. Today the government has a controlling interest (typically 100 percent) in some 344 commercial parastatals, distributed across all sectors of the economy.

About 275 of these are commercial parastatals that play a dominant, often monopolistic, role in many key sectors. Manufacturing parastatals account for about 60 percent of total value added in the sector and they have monopolies in several major segments of the industrial sector—beer, cigarettes, steel, and electric cables. The same is true in the services sector, including the banking industry and the hotel sector, where the state enjoys a dominant position. (Although significant new investment is now being made by the private sector.) Today, the parastatal sector accounts for an estimated 25 percent of total wage employment and about 20 percent of GDP.

The financial performance of the parastatals is poor. According to the Tanzania Audit Corporation, the government auditor of parastatal accounts, net losses after taxes but before interest payments for commercial parastatals was about 8 percent of GDP in fiscal 1989.[23] This was a substantial increase over the net profit of 3.6 percent of GDP in fiscal 1984. Many parastatals can barely cover salaries and are in large arrears—to the commercial banks and the treasury—on loans they received for working capital and fixed investment. Recent studies show that more than 50 percent of parastatals are inviable and require subsidies to continue operating. In 1991 only 43 out of 220 commercial parastatals surveyed were able to generate adequate revenue to service their debts fully.[24] The chronic lossmakers survive by running accounts receivables primarily with other parastatals—particularly the utilities. They also avoid paying the counterpart fund share of the commodity import support funds they receive, as well as their pension fund contributions and taxes. The combined value of these implicit subsidies to commercial parastatals equalled about 5 percent of GDP in 1991.

For the past ten years, the government has periodically expressed concern about the poor performance of the parastatal sector. In 1983 a government commission identified gross inefficiencies in the sector, yet little action was taken to implement the recommended remedies. In 1987 another high-level commission reported on the persistently poor performance of the parastatal sector and the need for reform. However, with the exception of a substantial reduction in direct treasury subsidies, little was done. In the past year, the financial sector reform has hardened the budget constraint for parastatals. The commercial banks have considerably tightened their lending to parastatals. Additionally, in 1992, 104 loan accounts of nonviable parastatals (including 27 accounts of commercial parastatals) were transferred to the loans and advances realization trust for recovery through liquidation. From 1986 to 1992, about 20 parastatal divestitures took place, largely in agriculture and primarily on an ad hoc basis. About 25 additional privatization deals have been in various stages of protracted negotiations due to the absence of consensus on privatization, an institutional framework for privatization, and policy guidelines on handling such difficult technical issues as valuation and parastatal debts.[25]

In 1992 the government announced a threefold plan: public service organizations that had previously been classified as parastatals would be declassified and incorporated into government departments; public utilities would remain as parastatals, but would be subject to performance contracts, and the entry of new service providers would be permitted in selected areas; and all commercial parastatals would be eligible for divestment, at least in principle. The Presidential Parastatal Sector Reform Commission was created to oversee the policy. Action on public service organizations has begun. Under the public utility reform, performance contracts for the Tanzania Railways Corporation and the Tanzania Posts and Telecommunications Corporation have recently been prepared. Privatization of commercial parastatals has accelerated, as the commission has begun to expedite final decisions and push ongoing negotiations forward. In addition, many parastatal managers have begun to sell assets and find ways to cut costs as they face hardened budget constraints. Yet parastatal managers are still uncertain about what the new rules of the game mean for them. Given the centralized approach to parastatal reform, and the fact that it will take some time for the commission to build its internal capacity and implement its master plan for privatization, there is the risk that parastatal managers and employees will quietly engage in asset stripping—de facto privatization—rather than actively explore restructuring options from the shop floor.

Despite the obvious and serious nature of the problems of the parastatal sector, it took at least ten years before a consensus and an action plan for meaningful reform emerged. The reform program is too new to evaluate. However, several factors may impede the pace of privatization: the government is still reluctant to sell the few profitable parastatals, and in the absence of a social safety net for workers who would be released, the government is reluctant to undertake the more extensive liquidations that may be inevitable.

Social sector policies

In the years after Independence, Tanzania made several impressive achievements in the social sectors. By the end of the 1970s, Tanzania's basic needs strategy had achieved many of its major goals, and most social indicators showed improvement (table 8.4). These achievements have also helped build a level of national unity that is rare in Africa. However, this massive expansion in the social sectors has proved to be financially and administratively unsustainable. Even when quantitative targets were being met, qualitative weaknesses and imbalances emerged. For example, though many children in rural areas were in school, the standard of instruction was very low because teacher training was poor and teaching materials were scarce. And although Tanzania had developed an extensive network of health care facilities, the quality of health care deteriorated because of chronic underfunding, poorly trained and unmotivated health workers, supply shortages, and overcrowded facilities.

Table 8.4 Selected social sector indicators: Tanzania and other low-income countries, 1965, 1980, and 1987

	Tanzania			*China and India*			*Other low-income countries*		
Indicator	*1965*	*1980*	*1987*	*1965*	*1980*	*1987*	*1965*	*1980*	*1987*
Daily caloric supply	1,832	2,051	2,192[a]	2,001	2,270	2,463[a]	1,976	2,050	2,226[a]
Primary education enrollment (in percent)[b]	32	104	66	83	100	117	49	70	76
Secondary education enrollment (in percent)	2	4	4	25	32	41	9	19	26
Life expectancy at birth	43	52	53	51	..	63	44	50	54
Infant mortality rate (per thousand live births)	138	101	104	114	92	..	149	..	98
Population per nurse	2,100	2,980	8,130[c]	4,420	3,322	1,710[c]	10,170	8,953	3,250[c]
Population per physician	21,700	17,560	26,200	2,930	2,626	1,640	28,080	15,486	13,910

Note: According to World Development Report classification, low-income countries comprise a total of 48 countries with an income of $545 or less in 1988.

.. Not available.

a. For 1986.

b. As a percentage of population in its age group. The total fertility rate represents the number of children who would be born to a woman if she were to live to the end of her childbearing years.

c. For 1984.

Source: World Bank data.

In 1983 district and urban councils were reestablished in order to increase community participation in service provision and reduce budgetary costs. The government also began to introduce very low user charges for some social services, despite the fact that collections fall far short of any serious cost recovery. Some encouragement has also been given to nongovernmental organizations (NGOs) to support the social sectors. For example, 220 of the 334 secondary schools are now run by NGOs.[26] NGO involvement in the health sector is also expanding. With donor assistance, several special programs in the social sectors were introduced in the early 1980s, including the essential-drugs program and the expanded program of immunization.

With the initiation of the economic and social action program in 1989, the government acknowledged that the economic recovery program had to incorporate social concerns, given the severe deterioration of the social sector. Some of the economic recovery program measures included efforts to improve budgetary expenditures for the social sectors. After allowing a precipitous decline in social services spending during the second half of the 1970s and the early 1980s, the government was able to stabilize and, more recently, slightly increase real per capita expenditures on social services, although they remain woefully inadequate. In fiscal 1992 the government also adopted a population planning policy including family planning and maternal and child health services. It also recently approved a new primary health care strategy to improve the framework for service delivery, as well as a master plan for drug procurement, and implementation guidelines for improved district health planning. These policies, though approved, have not yet been implemented. Moreover, low economic growth per capita has generated only limited employment and labor mobility. And Tanzania's social sectors are coming under even greater pressure due to the rise in incidence of AIDS and other infectious diseases. Action is clearly necessary, but the responsible line ministries are weak, and clear strategies for addressing the problems of the social sectors have not been developed.

Outcomes of the adjustment program

Macroeconomic data for Tanzania are poor. More reliable and consistent data series must be developed to give policymakers and analysts a better understanding of economic developments in Tanzania. Nevertheless, the available data confirm that the economic recovery program has made progress in addressing many of the severe distortions that prevailed in the prereform period. Exchange rate overvaluation has been reduced sharply, and the exchange rate is becoming more market determined. The central government's fiscal deficit has declined, and is now financed without recourse to local bank financing (although it still relies heavily on foreign aid). The inflation rate has declined from an average of 30 percent prior to the economic recovery program to 20 percent, but because credit is not controlled, interest rates have become positive, and the banking system is being restructured. Further progress is difficult. The current account deficit has widened because imports have been liberalized, but the deficit has been financed fully by foreign aid for the economic recovery program.

Progress is also evident, though mixed, for several key indicators. On the positive side, real GDP growth has averaged 4 percent after years of stagnation and now exceeds the rate of population growth. Per capita consumption has increased, and investment levels have recovered. After making some adjustments, savings performance also appears to have improved. While the import share of GDP has increased, growth in import volume has been relatively limited.

Progress in several areas has been insufficient. Inflation is still unacceptably high. And while the level of investment has recovered and is now relatively high, it has yet to yield higher growth, due in part to investment inefficiency. Foreign aid must also be used more efficiently. Though exports grew significantly in real terms in the first few years of the economic recovery program—particularly the export of nontraditional products—they have stagnated in the past two years. Adjusted domestic savings have improved, but they are far from adequate to support sustained, rapid growth in Tanzania. Savings must be increased by forcing public enterprises to stem their losses, by reducing taxation on financial savings, by reforming the tax system, and by discouraging private consumption of luxuries.

Macroeconomic stability continues to be elusive. Even if the current policy framework permits a sustainable growth rate of 4 percent per year, it would not allow Tanzania to reach the much higher levels of growth necessary to reduce poverty. The next stage of reforms identified in the government's policy framework paper must be decisive. The major priorities have been identified:

- Unifying the exchange rate and tariffs, bringing unofficial exports into official channels, and aggressively promoting exports.
- Getting credit growth under control.
- Implementing an action program to reduce the economic burden of the parastatal sector.
- Completing the program to reform the banking system, and thus restoring confidence in the system to help attract unrecorded private savings and allocate and mobilize financial resources efficiently.
- Improving the mobilization of domestic resources for budgetary purposes.

These actions will facilitate the macroeconomic adjustments required to sustain rapid growth.

So far, commitment to reform of the financial sector has been strong. After the commission's report was approved by the president, the government moved very quickly with initial implementation of comprehensive banking reform program. However, there are four major issues that will have to be addressed if the reforms are to succeed.

First, the proposals that have been developed with the help of consultants for restructuring the Cooperative and Rural Development Bank and the Tanzania Investment Bank did not go far enough to ensure that those institutions will become competitive. There is a risk that the government may recapitalize these institutions without adequate assurances that the kind of radical restructuring required in those institutions will take place. Privatization of the institutions will be an essential condition for turning those institutions around. Should it become impossible to find competent private partners who can participate and help guide the turnaround, liquidation of the institutions may be preferable to putting in more government funds.

Second, the capacity to implement financial sector reform also needs to be strengthened. In the Bank of Tanzania, banking supervision is still weak and must be upgraded. There also are concerns about the institutional capacity within the treasury to implement its responsibilities in the reform program, particularly the reform and restructuring of government banks. Treasury has to ensure that the bail out of the banks is accompanied by a real turnaround in their performance.

The third major challenge is to restructure the clients of the banking system. This will be essential to the growth of good banking clients in the future. Otherwise, pressures for directed credit will build again. The success achieved in the liberalization of foodgrain marketing made it possible to stem the excessive borrowing of the National Milling Corporation. However, the liberalization of agricultural export marketing—including restructuring of the cooperative unions and primary societies—is needed to guarantee the success of financial sector reform. Similarly, while the banks have begun to get much tougher on commercial parastatals and starve them of credit (a welcome change in bank behavior), this is not sustainable or desirable. A more explicit restructuring and liquidation of parastatals is required. As discussed below, programs to address these issues are just being developed, and implementation will not be easy because of the very organized and influential vested interests involved. Ideally, these real-side reforms should have preceded, or at least more quickly accompanied, financial sector reform.

Finally, the commission recommendation that the National Bank of Commerce be split to inject healthy competition into the banking system must be revisited.

Macroeconomic reform

Intermediate results. Among the most important indicators of the change in the government's macroeconomic policy stance during the economic recovery program is the real exchange rate, which has depreciated significantly (see table 8.1). Prior to the economic recovery program, the authorities were reluctant to move the exchange rate. Left alone, it increased by more than 100 percent between 1981 and 1985. As noted earlier, exchange rate reform has been the cornerstone of the economic recovery program. A more active exchange rate policy reduced the real exchange rate by about 90 percent between 1986 and 1989, and starting in 1990 the authorities adopted a policy of maintaining a constant real exchange rate.[27]

Box 8.2 Inflation

Official measures of inflation show that consumer price inflation has come down from more than 30 percent in the immediate economic recovery program period to about 20 percent since 1990. Since then, it has stayed at that level. However, the official statistics probably do not accurately reflect actual inflation because the consumer price index is seriously out of date. It is based on expenditure weights obtained from the 1976/77 household budget survey; the population weights are based on the 1978 census; and the quality of the price information collected for the consumer price index survey has declined considerably as resources for the collection of statistics decreased. Consequently, the official inflation statistics may understate the actual rate of inflation, given the rapid increase in money creation.

During the economic recovery program the proximate cause of inflation shifted from financing of the government deficit by the banking system to financing of parastatals and the inefficient agricultural marketing system. Following recent actions to strictly limit commercial bank access to central bank credit and to grant greater autonomy to the commercial banks, there is some evidence that the commercial banks have tightened up their lending to cooperatives and parastatals. However, inefficiencies in agricultural marketing may lead to further financial losses for the cooperatives and affect their ability to fully repay the reduced credits that were extended to them this year. Moreover, in fiscal 1993 the government resorted to bank borrowing to finance the fiscal deficit, due to a shortfall in expected revenues. Central bank losses have also led to an expansion in the money supply.

To reduce inflation, financial sector reforms must be complemented by measures to address the underlying causes of inflation: rapid opening of the marketing of all agricultural exports to the private sector, prudent fiscal policies and the elimination of central bank losses due to gold purchases, and debt conversion. Otherwise, persistently high levels of inflation will continue to feed expectations of exchange rate depreciation and lead to continued economic uncertainty in the private sector.

The fiscal situation in Tanzania has also improved during the reform years (see table 8.1).[28] The central government budget deficit as a percentage of GDP declined from an average of 12.1 percent in the prereform period to 7 percent between 1986 and 1991, compared with 4.1 percent in Uganda and 4.5 percent in Senegal—two other African nations undergoing adjustment.[29] By fiscal 1991, the deficit had fallen to 3.1 percent of GDP. While Tanzania's deficit was a bit higher than Uganda's and Senegal's, the initial situation in Tanzania was substantially worse and required greater adjustment. In addition to reducing the size of the deficit, the government relied far less on bank borrowing to finance the deficit.

The inflation rate had declined somewhat during the economic recovery program—from 31 percent in 1981–85 to 25.7 percent in 1986–91 (see table 8.1). By the end of fiscal 1992, the rate of consumer price inflation had fallen to 19 percent. However, as with many other countries in Africa undergoing adjustment, Tanzania has had limited success in reducing the rate of inflation from double-digit levels. This has been due to the inability of the government to enforce strict monetary control (box 8.2).

The decline in the rate of inflation during the economic recovery program has also affected real interest rates—but not the demand for credit. Interest rates rose significantly during the recovery program, despite the fact that the government did not adjust nominal interest rates significantly between 1988 and 1991. Beginning in fiscal 1989, all deposit and interest rates became positive in real terms. However the high real-interest rates did not significantly reduce the demand for credit because most bank credit went to marketing institutions, despite their poor creditworthiness. The extension of this credit has also limited credit availability to the private sector. Interest rate reform has had only a limited effect on mobilizing fresh deposits into the banking system, given the lack of confidence in the still inefficient banking system and the availability of better hedges against inflation, including real estate and, until recently, foreign exchange (Lipumba and Osoro 1991).

Prior to the economic recovery program, Tanzania's current account deficit was large and—as with many other countries undergoing adjustment programs that have received balance of payment assistance from donors—it widened during the economic recovery program (see table 8.1).

Longer-term results. The full impact of the program must be judged by its impact on GDP growth, investment, savings, imports, and exports. GDP growth in Tanzania has increased substantially during the reform program. Official statistics indicate that GDP grew from 0.01 percent annually in 1981–85 to 4 percent during the reform period.[30] The protracted decline in per capita income from the mid-1970s to 1984 was stemmed during the economic recovery program. As discussed in detail later, the agricultural sector has led the economic recovery, supported by the industrial sector. The structure of Tanzania's final demand also has changed significantly. The share of consumption has increased substantially, with per capita consumption almost catching up to the level that was lost during the prolonged period of economic stagnation. The official figures show that the share of consumption is very large, and that the share of savings is correspondingly low (table 8.5). Since consumption is measured as a residual in the national accounts, it also includes some private transfers—for example, illegal exports which are estimated to be even larger than official exports. Thus, the official figures for consumption overstate the increase in actual consumption and understate savings.

Investment has risen substantially during the economic recovery program, averaging nearly 28 percent of GDP. The share of investment in GDP is very high in comparison with the GDP of other countries. But the efficiency of investment is very low. One measure of that efficiency—an approximation of the gross rate of return on investment—shows that although it improved during the economic recovery program, it is still abysmally low (figure 8.5). It is considerably lower than that of many other countries undergoing adjustment. Incremental capital-output ratios for Tanzania are also very high, because the productivity of public investment is constrained by project delays and poor product design, and because of inefficient investment by the parastatals in particular, where reform has only just begun. In addition, real spending on machinery and equipment accounts for less than 20 percent of total investment.

Private investment has risen substantially. By 1991 it had reached 26 percent of GDP, compared with only 9 percent in 1984 (table 8.5). The large increase in private investment is remarkable, since the commercial banks have been forced to accommodate the credit demands of the public sector marketing boards, uncreditworthy cooperative unions and parastatals, and until

Table 8.5 Structure of aggregate demand, selected years
(Shares of GDP)

Item	*1976*	*1984*	*1991*
Consumption	79	93	89
Government	16	16	13
Private	63	77	76
Investment	23	15	38
Government	13	6	12
Private	10	9	26
Exports	22	7	17
Imports	24	15	46
National savings	21	7	11
Foreign savings	2	8	29

Source: Tanzania (1992b).

Figure 8.5 GDP growth as a percentage of GDI/GDP, 1981–90

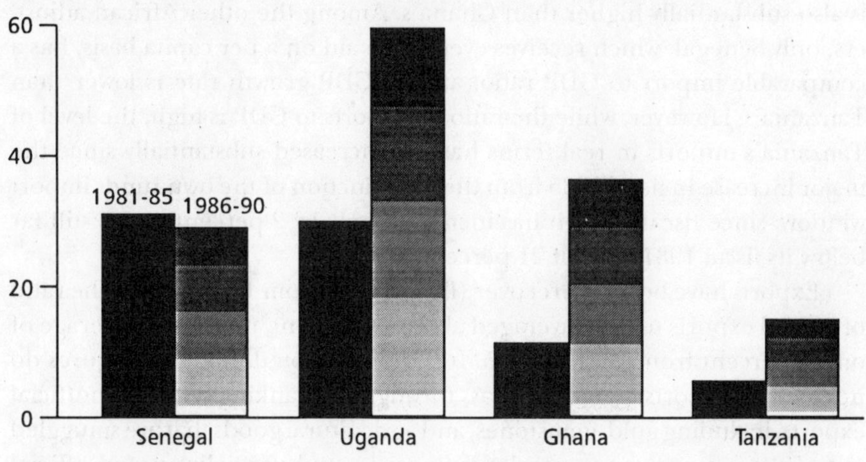

Source: World Bank data.

recently, the central government's borrowing requirements. Loans from the banking system to the private sector averaged less than 2 percent of GDP, thus contributing little to the significant increase in private investment. Conversely, recorded private savings were only about 14 percent of GDP in 1992. Obviously a large unofficial financial market is financing the private sector.

National accounts data suggest that much of investment is financed by foreign savings (table 8.5). Official statistics indicate that the domestic savings rate is now extremely low. This low rate reflects significant dissavings in the consolidated public sector, as well as low (and in some years negative) official private savings. However, as just noted, substantial sources of domestic savings are clearly not being captured in the official statistics. While Tanzania's savings rate was among the highest during the crisis years, it is now one of the lowest.

Table 8.1 also shows a second set of savings rates for Tanzania—calculated as domestic savings that include an estimate of unofficial exports (private transfers from abroad which help finance own-funds imports). While the unadjusted figures suggest that foreign aid has almost entirely substituted for domestic savings during the adjustment program, the adjusted savings rate shows that domestic savings have in fact increased from the prereform period and continue to compare favorably with rates in the other countries in the sample.

The ratio of imports to GDP increased substantially during the economic recovery program (figure 8.6). The ratio for Tanzania is also very high in comparison with the ratio of other countries that have generated higher rates of growth. The Tanzania ratio is nearly three times that of Uganda, which has registered GDP growth rates that are more than 50 percent higher, and is also substantially higher than Ghana's. Among the other African adjusters, only Senegal, which receives even more aid on a per capita basis, has a comparable import to GDP ratio, and its GDP growth rate is lower than Tanzania's. However, while the ratio of imports to GDP is high, the level of Tanzania's imports in real terms has not increased substantially since the major increase in fiscal 1985 from the introduction of the own-funds import window: since fiscal 1985, it has increased only by 2 percent and is still far below its fiscal 1981 level of 21 percent.

Exports have begun to recover (figure 8.7). From 1986 to 1990 the ratio of official exports to GDP averaged about 14 percent, up from an average of only 9 percent from 1981 to 1985. It should be noted that these figures do not include exports that do not pass through the banking system. Unofficial exports, including gold, gemstones, and agricultural goods that are smuggled out of the country are generally estimated to substantially exceed official exports, although firm estimates of their magnitude are unavailable. They remain outside the banking system because of persistent exchange rate devaluations, the high administrative cost of exporting legally due to export licensing and other bureaucratic requirements, price controls, and in some cases export bans in Tanzania. While export prices increased slightly (2 percent), the volume of official exports in 1991 was 22 percent higher than in 1986. The recovery of exports began during the initial years of the economic recovery program, due to a significant increase in nontraditional agricultural and manufactured products. As discussed later, the exports of these prod-

Figure 8.6 Ratio of imports to GDP, and growth in GDP, 1985–90

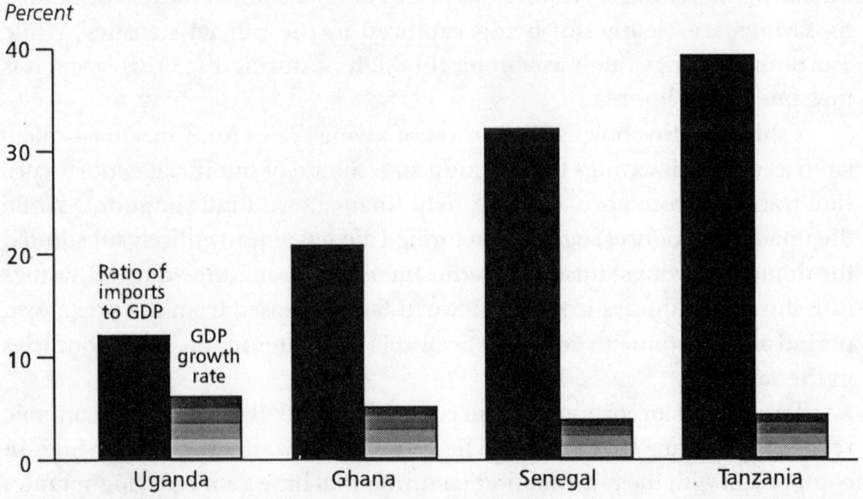

Percent
40
30
20
10
0
Ratio of imports to GDP
GDP growth rate
Uganda
Ghana
Senegal
Tanzania

Source: World Bank data.

Figure 8.7 Ratio of exports to GDP, 1981–85 and 1986–90

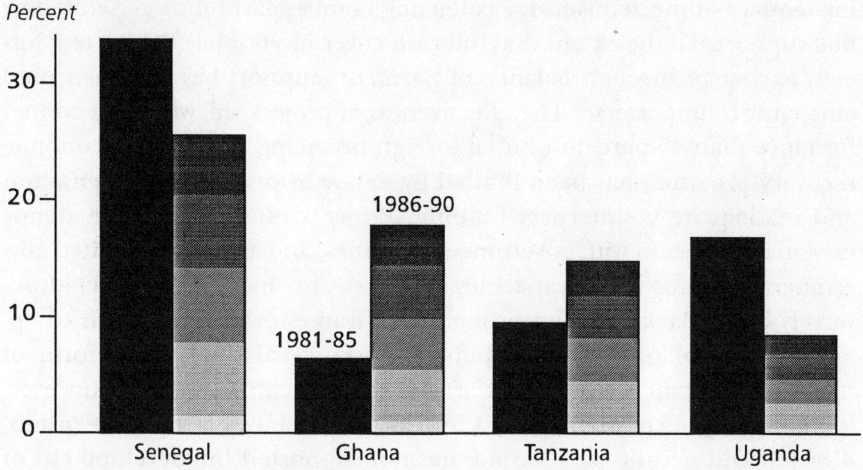

Percent

Senegal Ghana Tanzania Uganda

1981-85 1986-90

Source: IMF, *International Financial Statistics.*

ucts nearly doubled, increasing from $86 million in 1986 to $154 million in 1991. However, in real terms, total official exports have stagnated since 1990, and Tanzania's capacity to import based on official export earnings has fallen because exports have not increased enough to offset the substantial decline in Tanzania's terms of trade.

Dependence on foreign aid. Tanzania has long received a substantial amount of foreign aid. During the economic recovery program, Tanzania received nearly $6 billion of net foreign assistance in support of its adjustment program.[31] In nominal terms, this figure represents an increase of nearly 60 percent over net official development assistance received during the crisis years. However, the real contribution of official development assistance to growth is best understood when it is adjusted by changes in the terms of trade, thus capturing the net free foreign exchange made available by donors to finance imports.[32] When official development assistance is adjusted as such, average net real assistance to Tanzania during the economic recovery program was only 9 percent above the average net transfers to Tanzania during the crisis years. In fact, net real official development assistance per capita fell during the economic recovery program.

While external assistance has been critical to supporting the economic recovery program, particularly the balance of payment support that donors made available to Tanzania for liberalizing trade and financing the government budget, both donors and the government have expressed a desire to improve the effectiveness of aid. For balance of payments support, which accounted for about half of total foreign financing during the first years of the economic recovery program, concern has been expressed about the inadequacy of mechanisms for collecting counterpart funds generated by that support. To the extent that full cash cover has not been collected, foreign exchange through balance of payments support has not been used efficiently by importers.[33] The effectiveness of project aid, which accounted for more than 45 percent of total foreign financing during the economic recovery program, has been limited by delays in project implementation and inadequate counterpart funding. Projects often tend to be donor driven, inconsistent with government priorities, and a strain on limited government administrative capacities. Projects also have been affected adversely by the lack of a supporting policy framework within which to operate. Much of official development assistance also takes the form of technical assistance, the impact of which is difficult to assess.[34] However, it is generally acknowledged that technical assistance has often been misdirected and occasionally wasted, has not supported the development of the government's own internal capacity, and has not always been available or timely enough to meet the government's need for detailed technical advice to implement policies.

There has also been some concern that external aid gives the government too much scope for delaying difficult but important reform. Nevertheless, donors have withheld or delayed financing on several occasions due to the lack of progress on the policy front. For example, the consultative group meeting of 1989 was delayed substantially because the government failed to adopt a more realistic exchange rate. The second tranches of each of the World Bank's sector adjustment credits were withheld because policy conditions had not been met. In 1992 donors withheld funding for the open general license pending improvements in fund accountability, particularly the payment of counterpart funds from the commercial banks to the central bank (box 8.1). There has also been some concern that Tanzania's extreme dependence on aid could undermine the country's economic agenda and self-reliance. Two major concerns: donors finance projects that are inconsistent with government priorities, and the government looks to donors to solve problems it must face on its own.

Sectoral reform

Industrial sector. After a rapid deindustrialization in the early 1980s due to severe import compression, inappropriate economic policies, and protracted economic decline, a process of industrial recovery has begun. Manufactured exports have increased and become a major feature of industrial sector adjustment. The policy environment has also encouraged the entry of industrial firms and the expansion of efficient firms and has discouraged inefficient producers. In response to the improved incentive framework for industry, investment in industrial sector activities has risen significantly since the start of the economic recovery program. Yet decisive action must be taken on several fronts to enable the industrial sector to realize its full potential—reversing the poor performance of the parastatal enterprises (which includes privatizing profitable companies and liquidating chronic lossmakers), promoting the development of the private sector (including both indigenous entrepreneurs and Asian businesses), promoting industrial exports, and reducing unfair competition from imports due to tax evasion.

In the immediate prereform period, the manufacturing sector had nearly collapsed—this after a major import-substitution drive led by state investment in the parastatal sector had generated significant growth in the 1970s. Between 1979 and 1986, manufacturing GDP fell in real terms each year except for 1984. By 1986 manufacturing GDP was only 30 percent of its 1979 level. While other sectors also contracted, the decline in the industrial sector was even more pronounced by 1986, when the contribution of the manufacturing sector to GDP fell below 8 percent, compared with 12 percent in the mid-1970s. Capacity utilization, which had risen to 75 percent by 1975, fell drastically to only 25 percent by 1985.

Manufacturing GDP has begun to recover from the collapse of the early 1980s. Manufacturing GDP has risen significantly (23 percent from 1986 to 1991), although it has not fully recovered from the collapse of the early 1980s (figure 8.8). With the exceptions of the initial year of the economic recovery program and 1990, growth in real manufacturing has been positive each year, and real manufacturing output often grew faster than total GDP. However,

Figure 8.8 Annual growth of GDP and real manufacturing GDP, 1983–91

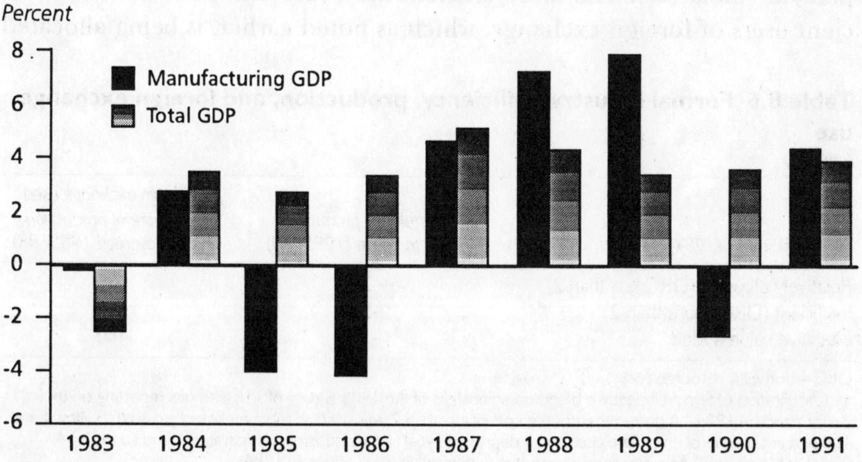

Source: Tanzania Bureau of Statistics.

from 1986 to 1991, manufacturing GDP grew by just more than 4 percent annually, on par with the growth of total GDP. Consequently, according to national accounts data, manufacturing GDP continues to account only for about 8 percent of total GDP.[35]

Nevertheless, industrial sector recovery and adjustment began in earnest during the economic recovery program. For example, capacity utilization has improved. By 1991 virtually all of the key industries covered in official industrial statistics had increased their capacity utilization to more than 50 percent, compared with only 25 percent in 1985. Such key industries as textiles, cement, and tires have increased their capacity utilization to more than 70 percent.[36]

There also is evidence that the efficiency of the industrial sector has improved. A World Bank review of the industrial sector in Tanzania provided a benchmark assessment of the level of competitive efficiency in the sector in 1985. It estimated that 37 percent of the 118 industrial activities surveyed generated negative value added at world market prices. These inefficient firms survived—and in many cases even expanded their activities—because of protection from competitive imports, price controls, and preferential and subsidized access to credit and foreign exchange. Firms with short-run domestic resource costs of greater than one (65 percent of the surveyed firms) produced more than half of gross output and used 74 percent of the total foreign exchange that was allocated to the surveyed firms.

A followup survey of the same firms in 1990 showed that firms that had been operating relatively efficiently in 1984 increased output by 28 percent from 1985 to 1990. Conversely, the production of inefficient firms contracted by 22 percent over the period. The production of the most inefficient firms—those with negative value added in 1984—contracted by 28 percent (table 8.6). The more efficient firms also tended to be more efficient users of foreign exchange, which as noted earlier, is being allocated

Table 8.6 Formal industry: efficiency, production, and foreign exchange use
(percent)

Firms' efficiency[a] (1984)	*Cumulative production value increase (1985–90)*	*Foreign exchange used as share of production value (average 1985–88)*
Relatively efficient[a] (DRC less than 2)	+ 28	22
Inefficient (DRC more than 2)	-22	69
Negative value added	-28	103

DRC—domestic resource cost

a. Classification of firms' efficiency is based on an analysis of the 1985 survey of 118 activities reporting on their performance in 1984. A domestic resource cost of less than 2 was used as relative efficiency cut-off to allow for a 100 percent margin of error (the choice of a depression year, infant industry considerations, and so forth.) An "absolutely inefficient" firm is defined as one that had negative value added in 1984.

Source: World Bank data.

Table 8.7 Exports, 1984–91
(millions of dollars)

Export	*1984*	*1985*	*1986*	*1987*	*1988*	*1989*	*1990*	*1991*
Traditional exports[a]	268	196	262	201	224	213	221	198
Minerals	34	22	13	22	16	20	32	42
Petroleum products	23	13	5	7	12	17	16	7
Manufactured goods	33	33	39	63	73	105	99	63
Other	31	21	29	54	48	60	73	42
Nontraditional exports	120	90	86	146	149	201	219	154
Total exports	388	286	348	347	373	415	441	352

a. Traditional exports include coffee, cotton, sisal, tea, tobacco, and cashew nuts.
Source: Bank of Tanzania Operations Report and Economic Survey (various issues).

on a more market-determined basis with the emergence of the open general license system.

The export performance of the manufacturing sector has also improved. Prior to the economic recovery program, manufactured exports performed very poorly. In 1984 manufactured exports amounted only to about $33 million, compared with total export earnings of $388 million (table 8.7). By 1990 manufactured exports had tripled to $99 million, although in 1991 they fell to $63 million. Nevertheless, the share of manufactured goods in total exports in 1991 was 18 percent, compared with 9 percent in 1984. Export diversification has been a significant feature of Tanzania's economic recovery, and manufactured exports have played a major role in this process.

Exporting has become much more important for manufacturers in the new economic environment. From 1981 to 1985, the ratio of exports to gross output contracted across all sectors. Since 1986, these ratios have recovered in nearly all industrial subsectors, and many are now higher than ever (table 8.8). The recovery reflects a significant decline in the antiexport bias of economic policies in Tanzania during the adjustment program, and thus an improvement in the profitability of exports. Consequently, several firms have based their expansion plans on increasing exports.[37] Semboja and Ndullu (1992) show that the recent export drive has been led by manufacturers who are already well established in the domestic market and whose costs are low by world standards. In addition, among the sample of firms they surveyed, output growth has been much faster for exporters than for nonexporters.

The ownership structure of the industrial sector has also changed significantly. Private industrial firms have expanded, while public sector firms have contracted. A 1990 World Bank survey showed that more than two-thirds of private firms increased production. Only half of the public enterprises managed to do so, and the remainder experienced a decline. Thus, it appears that the crucial determinants of firms' supply response to policy reform have been economic efficiency, ownership, and export orientation.

A significant number of new firms have entered the industrial sector during the economic recovery program. Three times as many new small-scale firms have been established in Dar es Salaam than were established throughout the country between 1967 and 1985. In mid-1991, the World Bank surveyed 131 industrial firms to ascertain how they have responded to the reforms; the survey revealed the economic significance of the substantial entry of new firms in industry. More than 80 percent of the firms established after 1986 increased their production, principally in response to what they perceived as stronger domestic demand (table 8.9). By comparison, less than half the firms established before 1980 were able to increase their production. About 6 percent of firms established after 1986 reduced their production, compared with nearly 40 percent for firms established prior to 1980. The reason for the difference is that recent entrants tend to be much more export oriented and more natural resource based. The more established producers contracted production because imports, domestic competition, and input costs, including the price of foreign exchange, rose significantly during the economic recovery program.

Another important indicator of the future direction of change in the industrial sector is the investment pattern. Several studies of the growth in total factor productivity at an aggregate level showed negligible levels during the late 1970s through the early 1980s (Shaaeldin 1988; Ndullu 1986). At that time, levels of capacity utilization were low and falling. The technologi-

Table 8.8 Export orientation by sector: exports as a percentage of gross output, 1980 and 1981–90

Sector	*1980*	*1985*	*1986*	*1987*	*1988*	*1989*	*1990*
Food manufacturing	8.0	4.0	4.4	2.7	8.8	22.8	13.4
Tobacco manufacturing	51.0	44.0	43.2	54.6	38.1	45.4	49.7
Textile and garments	14.9	5.5	7.1	13.1	17.4	21.5	29.9
Wood and wood products	1.9	0.9	2.3	3.0	4.7	23.5	17.2
Paper and paper products	0.6	1.9	10.7	54.3	49.2	23.8	38.1
Industrial chemicals and petroleum products	45.8	27.0	8.0	14.4	21.2	33.7	25.9
Pottery, china, glass, non-metallic products	14.2	38.7	17.0	13.1	38.1	37.4	42.4
Iron, steel, nonferrous metals, and fabricated metal products	3.6	1.4	2.1	3.4	4.7	2.2	4.7
Machinery, including electrical and supplies	5.8	8.3	7.1	15.1	17.1	32.0	29.8
Transport and equipment	0.2	0.2	0.07	1.0	2.2	4.1	9.6
Total	18.2	10.5	8.1	11.9	18.0	23.5	25.9

Source: Government of Tanzania, Bureau of Statistics.

Table 8.9 Quantity adjustment of industrial firms by size and age

Quantity adjustment with reasons	*Firms by size*			*Firms by age*		
	All firms	*Small firms*	*Large firms*	*Post-1986*	*1980–85*	*Pre-1980*
Increase in production	60.9	66	58.1	81.2	68.1	49.9
Stronger domestic demand	39.8	52.3	32.1	71.9	36.4	27
Foreign exchange inputs more available	5.5	0	8.7	0	0	9.5
Changes in policies	2.3	2.3	2.5	0	0	4.1
Stronger exports	2.3	0	3.7	3.1	4.5	1.3
Local raw materials more available	1.6	2.3	1.2	3.1	4.5	0
Devaluation of exchange rate	1.6	0	2.5	0	4.5	1.3
Labor more available	0.8	2.3	0	3.1	0	0
Other reasons	7	6.8	7.4	0	18.2	6.7
Decrease in production	28.1	29.4	28.3	6.2	22.7	39.3
More import competition	7.8	4.5	9.9	0	9.1	10.8
More domestic competition	5.5	6.8	4.9	0	0	9.5
More expensive imported inputs	4.7	4.5	4.9	3.1	9.1	4.1
More expensive local inputs	3.9	4.5	3.7	3.1	0	5.4
Weaker domestic demand	2.3	4.5	1.2	0	4.5	2.7
Devaluation of exchange rate	1.6	0	2.5	0	0	2.7
Other reasons	2.3	4.6	1.2	0	0	4.1
No significant change	11	4.6	13.6	12.6	9.2	10.8

Source: Dutz and Frischtak (1992).

cal capability of industrial firms was limited, and investment in industry was declining (net real investment in the manufacturing sector was falling at an average annual rate of 6.7 percent from 1981 to 1985). Unfortunately, a comparable data series on industrial investment for the period since the economic recovery program is unavailable. But there are signs of a recovery. The results of a World Bank survey of investment behavior and plans of industrial firms show that firms that have invested heavily in the past few years tend to be export oriented and economically efficient. Nearly all of the private firms sampled plan to increase investment by more than 25 percent in the next three to five years. In addition, according to the investment promotion center, a total of nearly $200 million in investments in industrial projects—the leading sector for investment approvals—have been approved since 1990 (table 8.10).

While industrial sector adjustment has shown several positive outcomes, change has not taken place as quickly as necessary in other areas of the sector. First, the reform of industrial parastatals has been delayed. Since the losses of the parastatal sector are substantial, the delay poses a serious cost to the entire economy. Moreover, indecisive action sends a signal to the private sector that the playing field is not yet level, and in the meantime, the value of parastatal assets erodes as managers become much more risk averse in this

Table 8.10 A summary of projects approved by the Investment Promotion Center between July 1990 and September 1992

	Total investment (US$)	*Total employment generated*	*Total number of local projects*	*Total number of foreign projects*	*Total number of joint venture projects*	*Total number of projects*
Industry	80,655,332	13,479	93	12	28	133
Tourism	36,374,790	5,747	19	13	17	49
Agriculture and livestock	16,506,809	13,489	14	8	18	40
Natural resources	11,909,204	4,935	11	4	17	32
Transport	26,013,592	1,760	12	3	12	27
Mining	6,023,592	1,887	2	3	3	8
Construction	4,626,492	314	2	1	4	7
Technology	36,325	9	1	0	1	2
Services	441,167	171	0	2	0	2
Total	182,587,30	41,791	154	46	100	300

Source: Investment Promotion Center.

period of uncertainty, and in some cases quietly strip assets. Labor relations continue to deteriorate, with a rising number of lockouts by the managers of disgruntled employees of parastatals in financial distress.

Second, while some effort has been made to encourage the private sector, it has not been aggressive.[38] In fact, the business environment continues to stymie the private sector. Several policies and practices have perpetuated uncertainty and discouraged the private sector—the continued tolerance and subsidization of parastatal losses, antiquated land-transfer policies and limited access to industrial sites, extensive regulatory and licensing obstacles to the entry and exit of firms, a system of tax assessment and collection that involves side payments and entrepreneurial harassment, inadequate court procedures for commercial matters, an inefficient banking system, and limited and expensive credit to the private sector. These constraints have penalized the development of indigenous entrepreneurship in particular. The government must take a more active role in identifying and addressing the constraints facing the private sector—foremost, to establish an effective dialogue. Otherwise the business potential of indigenous entrepreneurs will remain untapped.

Third, the industrial sector reform has gotten exports moving again, but Tanzania's export potential in manufactured goods is not being achieved. While export documentation procedures have been streamlined and initial steps have been taken to unify the exchange rate, they must be fully implemented as quickly as possible. More focused and selective programs must be established to improve information on export market opportunities, the trade infrastructure, and export financing. In addition, import tax evasion must be addressed so that trading is not relatively more profitable than manufacturing (for export markets in particular). This year some attempt is being made to reduce duty evasion by having preshipment inspection companies assess import tax liabilities to the treasury. However, complementary measures must be made to improve revenue collection by the customs department, thereby improving the terms on which domestic industry competes with imports.

The agricultural sector. During the economic recovery program, agricultural performance improved substantially due to good weather and improved economic policies. Foodgrain production doubled, food security improved dramatically, and real food prices declined, all of which helped consumers. The volume of traditional agricultural exports has returned to precrisis levels, and cotton has increased to record levels. The growth of nontraditional agricultural exports has been particularly impressive. Tanzania requires several measures to realize its enormous agricultural potential: unifying the exchange rate, liberalizing export marketing, reforming the cooperatives, promoting private-sector entry into export marketing, and liberalizing input distribution more effectively.

In the seven years prior to the economic recovery program, agricultural performance had slipped badly after a decade of rapid expansion. An increasingly overvalued exchange rate, deteriorating terms of trade for Tanzania's agricultural exports, and growing scarcities of goods in rural areas dramatically altered the incentive structure of farmers. Moreover, an increasingly inefficient government-controlled marketing system, disruptions in production patterns from the villagization program, and the crumbling physical infrastructure all contributed to the deteriorating environment of agriculture.[39] Agriculture growth averaged only 2 percent annually between 1978 and 1985. Export crop production was particularly hard hit—the total volume of exports fell by nearly 30 percent between 1976 and 1985, and agricultural export revenue fell from a peak of $426 million in 1977 to $184 million in 1985.

The economic recovery program has arrested the deterioration in agricultural performance, and a significant recovery of output is under way. Agricultural GDP increased by 4.9 percent annually between 1986 and 1991, more than double the growth rate in the preceding period. Growth in the marketed output of food grains and export crops has been impressive. The volume of food sales increased by about 100 percent between 1983, when marketing reforms began, and 1988.[40] Increased food availability essentially restored Tanzania's ability to feed itself and by 1990 virtually eliminated the need for food imports, which had peaked at 402,000 tons in 1985. Sales of traditional export crops (tea, coffee, cotton, cashews, pyrethrum, and tobacco) increased by 68 percent between 1985 and 1991, with cotton sales reaching record levels, and coffee, tea, tobacco, and cashew sales being restored to levels last recorded in the early 1980s (table 8.11). However, sisal and cashew nut sales still did not achieve the levels of the 1970s, and coffee and cotton sales are still far below their potential.

Another indicator of the impact of the economic recovery program on agriculture production is the impressive turnaround in nontraditional agricultural exports. Because these crops were never included in the official monopsonistic marketing channels, much of the turnaround can be attributed to reforms in foreign exchange management (exchange rate devaluation and retention schemes). Overall, the value of nontraditional agricultural exports increased fivefold since 1985, with strong growth recorded for each of the nontraditional crop groups (figure 8.9).

Improved output of food crops is due in part to good weather in the early years of the economic recovery program, but the renewed flow of consumer goods to rural areas from the trade reform also provided a powerful stimulus. Moreover, the gradual liberalization of food crop marketing since 1983 has improved the marketing efficiency and incentive structure of producers. Farmers are now served by a multichannel marketing system dominated by numerous small and medium-scale (both indigenous and Asian) traders who assemble, transport, and market staple grains in most urban centers. The grain marketing parastatal, National Milling Corporation, which had accounted for nearly 90 percent of grain marketing, now accounts only for 2 percent of marketed supply. A recent study of this largely private system suggests the emergence of an increasingly integrated marketing system that links major supply and consumer markets throughout the year. Private trade

Table 8.11 Official purchases of traditional export crops, 1980–91
(thousand metric tons)

Year	Coffee	Cotton	Pyrethrum	Tea	Tobacco	Cashews
1980	66.6	175.0	2.0	77.7	16.8	56.6
1981	55.0	133.0	1.9	74.9	16.1	44.3
1982	53.5	128.0	1.6	84.5	13.6	33.0
1983	49.1	140.7	1.4	73.0	11.0	48.3
1984	49.0	155.1	1.5	80.2	13.4	32.1
1985	52.8	108.2	1.4	74.4	12.6	19.0
1986	41.5	216.9	1.2	67.7	16.5	16.5
1987	45.7	253.7	1.4	63.8	12.9	24.4
1988	57.3	191.7	1.3	76.8	11.6	19.3
1989	53.2	113.5	1.6	79.5	11.1	17.0
1990	55.9	147.0	1.7	72.4	11.8	33.0
1991	58.0	261.9	2.2	78.0	17.0	36.0

Source: World Bank; Tanzania (1992a).

Figure 8.9 Value of nontraditional agricultural exports, 1980–90

Billions of 1990 TShs (deflated by CPI)

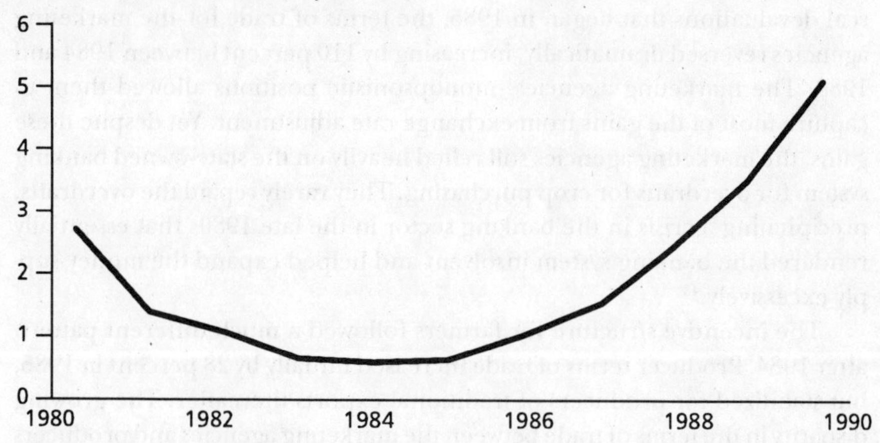

Source: Tanzania Bureau of Statistics.

has improved food availability in almost all areas, lowered consumer prices, and reduced overall maize marketing costs. An integrated maize trading network now exists, linking the major supply and consumer markets throughout the year.[41]

The increase in marketed output for food crops reversed a protracted rise in the real price of food in the prereform period and generated a dramatic decline in real prices between 1984 and 1989. Poor weather conditions in the 1990 and 1991 crop years increased prices again, but price levels are still well below the levels of early 1980s (table 8.12). Given the large share of consumer budgets that goes to food purchases, this decline in real prices has substantially benefited consumers.

The series of devaluations under the economic recovery program sought to improve the terms of trade and incentive structure for export producers. It did so for nontraditional exports, dramatically increasing the export of these crops, even if from a small base. For nontraditional exports, exporters could retain up to 50 percent of the foreign exchange and arrange exports through private marketing channels. But the situation for the producers of traditional export crops was not nearly as favorable because the economic recovery program reformed the marketing of traditional export crops only marginally. Producers were still required to market their crops through monopsonistic marketing channels dominated by inefficient cooperative unions at the farm level and government marketing boards at the point of export.[42] These institutions that absorbed the bulk of the gains in the terms of trade, leaving the incentive structure facing farmers little changed.

The terms of trade for both producers and the marketing agencies declined by about 50 percent between 1976 and 1984 (figure 8.10). With the real devaluations that began in 1985, the terms of trade for the marketing agencies reversed dramatically, increasing by 110 percent between 1984 and 1988. The marketing agencies' monopsonistic positions allowed them to capture most of the gains from exchange rate adjustment. Yet despite these gains, the marketing agencies still relied heavily on the state-owned banking system for overdrafts for crop purchasing. They rarely repaid the overdrafts, precipitating a crisis in the banking sector in the late 1980s that essentially rendered the banking system insolvent and helped expand the money supply excessively.[43]

The incentive structure for farmers followed a much different pattern after 1984. Producer terms of trade increased initially by 28 percent in 1985, but stabilized for producers of traditional exports thereafter. The growing disparity in the terms of trade between the marketing agencies and producers led to a steady deterioration in the share of declining world market prices going to farmers—by 1990 the producers' share for traditional exports was only about 40 percent.

It is clear that the largest improvements in marketing efficiency and increases in marketed output occurred for crops whose private marketing channels were most developed, such as maize, rice, and the nontraditional exports. Moreover, the marketing of these crops was expanded without excessive reliance on formal credit. For example, the trade in grains is almost entirely self-financed by private trade; previously the National Milling Corporation required up to TSh 6 billion a year in bank credit to finance crop purchases.

Table 8.12 Open market consumer prices and real price indexes, 1980–91

	Current prices (TShs per kg)			*Indexes of real open market prices (1981 = 100)*[a]		
Year	*Maize*	*Rice*	*Beans*	*Maize*	*Rice*	*Beans*
1980	3.36	7.26	6.10	87	76	101
1981	4.86	12.0	7.60	100	100	100
1982	5.54	15.43	13.91	88	100	142
1983	10.42	26.25	19.62	131	133	157
1984	13.54	35.76	31.45	125	134	186
1985	12.04	36.45	32.15	77	102	142
1986	12.04	35.83	32.17	63	76	108
1987	16.62	44.30	43.03	67	72	111
1988	21.13	61.38	63.78	65	76	125
1989	23.34	70.33	76.01	57	69	118
1990	41.68	95.96	96.46	85	79	126
1991	55.04	124.02	112.80	92	84	120

a. Deflated by consumer price index.
Source: Van den Brink (1992).

Figure 8.10 Export crop terms of trade for marketing boards and producers, 1976–88

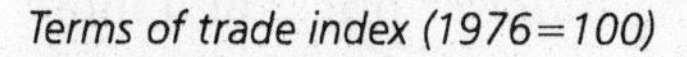

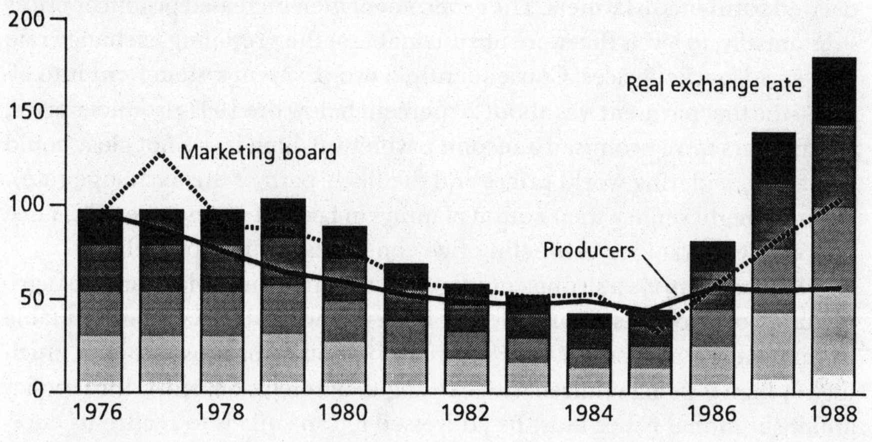

Source: Government of Tanzania.

For the traditional export crops still subject to government control, marketed output increased at a more modest pace, with production levels far below potential. The incentive structure for farmers of export crops was still poor, because they had to market through inefficient monopsonists and were burdened by poor marketing services, delayed payments, and erratic input supplies. The government has occasionally sought to increase official prices for traditional exports so as to stimulate production—and these efforts, coupled with an expansion of imports, explains the increases in the marketed volumes of traditional exports. But without market reform to address inefficiencies in the single-channel marketing system, these attempts merely exacerbated the financial situation for marketing agencies and intensified the crisis in the banking system.

Cotton is illustrative. In 1985 the official price of cotton was raised by nearly 20 percent in real terms, and the supply response over the next three years was substantial: production more than doubled to about 220,000 tons a year. However, this surge in production overwhelmed the marketing system, choked the processing and transport capacities of the cooperative unions, and delayed payments to farmers. The delays in processing and transport also left the unions and marketing boards with large unpaid overdrafts. In response the government allowed real producer prices to deteriorate, so that by 1989 all of the previous increase had eroded. Farmers responded to the falling prices by shifting out of cotton and into rice, so that by 1989 production had slipped back to 1985 levels.

The government again increased producer prices in 1991, and farmers responded with a record crop of 262,000 tons. But overdrafts to the cooperatives went unpaid. And as the financial sector was being reformed, the banks introduced stringent requirements for new overdrafts and extended less credit to the unions for the 1992 season, thus leading to lower prices and more delayed payments to farmers. The government then increased producer prices substantially, to levels that were unsustainable at the prevailing exchange rate and world market prices. Consequently, a two-payment system went into effect—the first payment was about 20 percent below the 1991 producer price, and farmers were promised a second payment (which it was not clear could be paid considering world prices and the likely path of the exchange rate). Farmers might reduce their cotton planting in favor of rice next season, since the private market for competing rice continues to function well.

Tanzania enjoys a strong comparative advantage in a wide range of agricultural commodities (table 8.13). It is blessed with abundant land suitable for expanding cultivation, and the yield potential for most crops is much higher than is being realized with existing technology. Several critical policy and institutional issues must be addressed if Tanzania is to realize its enormous potential in agriculture. These include managing the exchange rate, liberalizing the export markets of traditional agricultural products, reforming cooperatives, making inputs more accessible, improving the agricultural

Table 8.13 Ranking of agricultural exports, based on domestic resource cost ratios

	Financial analysis		*Economic analysis*	
Product	*Domestic resource cost ratio*	*Ranking*	*Domestic resource cost ratio*	*Ranking*
Traditional				
Coffee (Arabica)	1.15	14	0.66	13
Coffee (Robusta)	1.51	17	0.84	17
Cotton	1.28	16	0.68	15
Tea (outgrower)	1.20	15	0.67	14
Tea (estate)	0.53	3	0.35	4
Cashewnut (P)	0.58	5	0.30	3
Cashewnut (R)	0.5	2	0.27	2
Pyrethrum (C)	0.81	11	0.41	8
Pyrethrum (R)	0.60	7	0.31	4
Sisal (T)	1.15	14	0.76	16
Sisal (F)	0.56	4	0.36	5
Tobacco (flue)	0.69	8	0.40	7
Tobacco (fire)	0.78	10	0.44	9
Nontraditional				
Maize (MIT)	0.95	13	0.60	11
Paddy (rice)	0.77	9	0.45	10
Beans	0.59	6	0.37	6
Simsim	0.42	1	0.23	1
Cocoa	0.91	12	0.65	12

Source: World Bank-Government of Tanzania (1992).

infrastructure and extension services, and increasing the funding for agricultural services.

First, despite aggressive exchange rate management during the economic recovery program, the official exchange rate is still overvalued by 30 percent, which is a direct tax on producers of traditional crops. The government must move as quickly as possible to remove this tax by unifying the exchange rate. Provided steps are also taken to improve the competitiveness of export marketing, most of the gains from further devaluations would translate into improved prices to producers.

Second, more progress must be made toward liberalizing the export marketing of traditional agricultural products. Allowing private traders to buy from the farmers and allowing prices to be market determined are essential for dismantling the monopsony of the cooperative unions and improving the profitability of export agriculture. The government has recently decided to allow private traders to compete with the cooperative unions in export marketing. However, implementing the new policy will require that all export crop legislation be reviewed and revised to ensure its consistency with the new policy; that the government's monitoring, regulatory, and facilitating functions be redefined; that marketing boards be limited to providing auction or tender services, quality control, market information, and representation in international bodies; and that these new rules of the game be disseminated effectively to all market participants. Such transparency is important: if private traders do not understand the terms under which they will operate, their entry into the market may be delayed.

Third, cooperatives must be reformed to ensure more efficient export marketing. The recently revised cooperative legislation is expected to help foster that reform. The current cooperatives were mandated by the government, were essentially part of the official marketing system, and, until recent declarations to the contrary, were under control of the party.[44] As such the unions typically did not represent their members' interests, nor were they accountable to their members. The new legislation seeks to give control back to the members of the union and to reorganize primary societies into viable units controlled by members. The primary societies would then be free to associate with secondary unions in a way that best serves their interests. Primary societies may choose to associate with existing unions, market crops on their own, or form new associations with new unions.

Financial sector reform is also creating pressure for reform of the cooperative unions. The debts of eight heavily indebted unions that have been deemed inviable and not indispensable by the government have been taken over for liquidation by the loans and advances realization trust. However, the capacity of the banking system to restructure the other unions is limited because the collateral for most past loans to the cooperatives was seasonal stocks, not productive assets. For new loans, the banks have tightened their lending to cooperatives and insist on greater guarantees of repayment. Thus, in addition to measures to encourage the reform of cooperatives and greater financial discipline, private sector entry into agricultural processing and marketing must be promoted more aggressively. While the government has decided in principle to allow multichannel marketing, it has reservations about the capacity of the private sector to respond—a reflection of old ideological beliefs and the legacy of policies which discouraged private initiative. The government's positive experience with grain trade liberalization and the emergence of private trade in cashews despite the difficult circumstances indicate the capacity and interest of the private sector in foodgrain trade.

But export crop marketing is more complicated because the processing facilities for both cotton and coffee are currently owned by the unions or the marketing boards. New private facilities would require substantial investment capital.[45] The lead time between crop purchases and final export proceeds is long, requiring a large amount of working capital or financing to sustain purchases. To generate domestic competition quickly, the government should have used its influence over the unions to allow access for all market participants to ginning and other processing facilities owned by the unions. However, because the unions have now been declared private, the government has less influence to affect that access. In retrospect, it was probably premature for the government to have ceded control of the unions before they were restructured. Now the main avenue for effecting competition is likely to be new entries, which will take time.

Fourth, access to inputs must be made more timely. The input market is largely monopolistic, inefficient, and unresponsive to the needs of farmers. Though nominally liberalized, the system continues to be dominated by parastatal marketing boards, cooperatives, and in some instances, direct government involvement in retail distribution. The private sector has been slow to enter this business, due partly to the limited demand for inputs, particularly by growers of traditional crops, whose prices are depressed by the marketing system and the unreliability of crop sales payments. Fertilizer is the most important input, with an annual consumption of about 150,000 metric tons. Some progress has been made toward liberalizing retail trade, with private firms handling about 50 percent of the volume. But to complete the liberalization of trade at the wholesale level, the government must eliminate the remaining subsidy on fertilizer, and while the subsidy is being phased out, give private importers greater access to the subsidy to improve wholesale efficiency. Some progress was made on this front in 1992, when the Tanzania Farmers Association and a private importer were encouraged to import about 40,000 tons of fertilizer.

Fifth, the transportation infrastructure for agriculture and agricultural extension must be improved. The rural road network has suffered the most: by 1989 only 10 percent of the rural feeder roads were in good condition. The poor state of the roads and the inadequate rail network have been major bottlenecks to moving agricultural produce from the fields to the market. Both the road and the rail networks are being rehabilitated with heavy support from the donor community. For the road network, the government has received support from the World Bank and other donors in developing a comprehensive strategy and plan of action to deal with the major organizational, management, and policy issues in the subsector. Plans call for prioritizing needs in the subsector, giving the private sector a greater role, defining the respective roles of the government and the private sector, and implementing key measures to ensure the sustainability of any major investment that would be made in the network.

Finally, the funding of agricultural services must be improved. While agricultural research and extension have received substantial support by donors, government counterpart funding to complement donor projects has been inadequate. Remuneration of research workers has not been sufficient to retain well-qualified staff, and the capacity of extension workers has been limited because low and declining government funding for the recurrent costs of fuel, repair, and maintenance have hampered transport. Current expenditures to support agricultural extension, excluding salaries, fell by almost 30 percent in real terms between fiscal 1986 and 1992.

Poverty. Prior to the economic recovery program, Tanzania was one of the poorest countries in the world. Thus it is not surprising that, even after six years of adjustment, poverty continues to be widespread—about half of the population is still below the poverty line.[46] Even though comprehensive time series data on changes in the extent of poverty are not available, there is evidence that rural and urban poverty has diminished somewhat due to the restoration of economic growth. In the rural areas, adjustment policies, particularly those pertaining to the exchange rate and agricultural marketing, have increased income and consumption. However, rural services including infrastructure, social, and other support services (such as agricultural extension) have not improved significantly in relation to the preadjustment period. In fact some services—primary health care and education—have deteriorated despite significant increases in government expenditures because demand for those services has increased, resources have been misallocated, financial management has been poor, and strategies and institutional arrangements for delivering social services have been ineffective. In the urban centers, economic growth and the explosion of informal sector business activities have improved income and consumption. However, while poverty is significantly lower in urban areas than in rural areas, the standard of living among many of the urban nonpoor is low. Alleviating poverty will depend on two factors: the capacity of the economy to increase employment opportunities for Tanzania's large and rapidly growing labor force, and the creation and successful implementation of integrated sectoral strategies and action plans in the social sectors.

Poverty is pervasive in rural areas: 59 percent of village households are poor, and 90 percent of Tanzania's hardcore poverty is in rural areas. Within the rural areas, poverty is greatest in regions with low and intermittent rainfall, poor infrastructure, and poor access to markets—specifically in Kigoma, Singida, Lindi, Dodoma, Rukwa, and Ruvuma. Despite continuing widespread rural poverty, there are good reasons to believe that the adjustment program has helped reduce it. Prior to the economic recovery program, rural income had fallen significantly—by about one-half between 1978 and 1983 (Bevan, Collier, and Gunning 1989). The economic recovery program has arrested the decline, and rural living standards have risen significantly. The income of farmers who sell traditional export crops has improved because their production has increased, despite the decline in the share of export prices they receive. For nontraditional crops, export prices have improved considerably, as has total production. Real income from the sale of maize and rice, whose markets have been substantially liberalized, has increased during the economic recovery program, despite initially declining real prices for foodgrains (see table 8.12). Lower prices have also increased rural consumption, bolstered by the greater availability of consumer items, which largely dried up with the severe compression of imports in the late 1970s and early 1980s.

Yet agricultural services and infrastructure for poor farmers have not improved. As noted earlier, agricultural extension has been affected adversely by the general erosion of civil service salaries and shortages of government financing, trained personnel, and transport facilities. These problems were rampant well before the economic recovery program, but have not improved under the program and in some cases have deteriorated further. Rural roads continue to be deplorable. Transport networks for agricultural produce are inadequate and distributed unevenly throughout the country. Consequently, transport costs are very high, which together with the unreliability of rural transport, discourages regional specialization in agricultural production within Tanzania and the development of export trade with neighboring countries.

Average income in the urban areas is nearly four times greater than in the rural areas. Despite declining minimum wages, average income in the urban areas has increased because informal sector activities supplement income from formal employment.[47] Urban consumption levels have also increased, due to lower foodgrain prices. However, by international standards, urban households spend a much higher proportion of their income on food, suggesting that the standard of living is low even for households classified as nonpoor (table 8.14). Excluding the capital city of Dar es Salaam, 39 percent of urban households fall below the poverty line; in the capital, only 9 percent are below the poverty line.

Social sector. The second phase of the economic recovery program focused on improving social services, particularly for the poor. In education, real government expenditures during the economic recovery program increased by 13 percent annually. Nevertheless educational services and indicators of school achievement continue to deteriorate, particularly at the primary school level. For example, while primary school enrollment rates have risen, so have dropout rates—and the rate at which Tanzanian students make the transition to secondary school is still one of the lowest in the world.[48] With the rapid expansion of enrollment, the ratio of students to teachers has risen significantly. Teacher training institutes have not been able to keep up with the expansion. The quality of primary education also continues to be low. Many graduates of primary school are illiterate and cannot pass basic language and arithmetic examinations—due primarily to poor quality instruction, large class sizes, and a shortage of textbooks and other educational materials. In some areas parents are disillusioned, and are questioning the utility of primary schooling; some parents have even begun to withdraw their children from primary school (Cooksey 1992). The government continues to control educational curricula and teachers.

Much has been done to expand secondary school enrollment. From 1986 to 1991, local communities constructed 68 public secondary schools, which are now being managed by the government. With government encouragement, 220 of the 334 secondary schools are now being run by NGOs. Nevertheless the percentage of secondary school enrollment among eligible students is among the smallest in the world, and at 3 percent is far below the Sub-Saharan Africa average of 20 percent. The quality of the average second-

Table 8.14 Patterns of household expenditure
(percentage shares)

Item	All-Tanzania	Nonpoor	Sub-Saharan Africa
Food	73.1	70.8	62.0
Clothing	5.1	4.2	12.0
Rent and utilities	2.8	4.1	8.0
Education	0.7	0.7	5.0
Health	2.6	2.8	1.0
Other	15.7	17.4	12.0

Source: Ferreira (1992); World Bank data.

ary school education is also low and continues to decline, as measured by examination scores.

The increase in government expenditures on education has yet to be felt, because of the growing demand for educational services, particularly at the secondary level. In addition, resources appear to be misallocated within the educational pyramid, with secondary schools' receiving a small share of expenditures. During the economic recovery program, primary, adult, and higher education received more than 70 percent of current expenditures allocated to education. Most of the remaining 30 percent went to support large administrative overheads; only 10 percent of the educational budget was for secondary education. An excessive share of primary school spending goes to the Ministry of Education in Dar es Salaam, rather than for primary teachers at the local level. But even within local governments there is very limited managerial capacity, accountability, and control over expenditures. In some cases central government funds are abused. In addition, local governments have not developed the revenue base to complement federal-level resources to improve access to and the quality of primary education. Finally, while expenditures have risen, they come from a very small base and are still inadequate to meet the needs of the educational sector.

User charges have also been introduced in education, but slowly and below the levels required to recover costs. For primary schools, the charge of TSh 200 per pupil is too low to improve school finances.[49] Fees are collected at only a third of the rate that they should be. Given the poor state of primary schools, it has been difficult for the government to justify increasing fees. To encourage parents to pay the fees necessary to help support the recurrent costs of schools, the government must improve the quality of education and revenue allocation. At the secondary school level, revenue from fees has improved because collection is more stringent, and fees are rising—a fee of TSh 16,000 was recently approved by parliament. This should help improve cost recovery. The university does not impose a fee; students tend to be subsidized heavily, despite the fact that a university education is a luxury. Recent efforts to introduce cost recovery for university education met strong political resistance from students. The university was closed temporarily, and a decision was made to delay imposing user charges. In fact, student stipends, which are financed through the budget, have since been increased.

Data on trends in the health subsector are very limited. The scarce data available indicate that the major health problems in Tanzania—malnutrition, malaria, and infectious diseases, including acute respiratory infections—continue to be severe and are on the rise. In addition, adult mortality and morbidity caused by the AIDS epidemic have increased at alarming rates throughout Tanzania. AIDS has started to show a range of impacts, including a rising dependency ratio and greater pressures on the health care system.[50]

Real government expenditures on health have begun to recover, growing at an annual rate of more than 15 percent. However, real per capita expenditures remain below the levels of the 1970s and are inadequate in the face of the large and growing demand for services. Moreover, funds are misallocated within the sector. Only 24 percent of the total health budget is allocated to primary health care, which is provided at the local level. Consequently, the number of health dispensaries has not kept up with the population growth during the economic recovery program. As in the education sector, local governments are poorly equipped to carry out the greater responsibilities that have been entrusted to them. They lack the managerial capacity, accountability, and local revenue to provide primary health care effectively.

Government spending on health care has been complemented by the growth of nongovernmental and private health services during the economic recovery program. Today as much as 35 percent of health services in Tanzania are provided by NGOs, primarily churches, which provide mostly curative services. There are also a few commercial health facilities, but their charges are high, and they serve primarily the high-income population. Health care provided by the parastatals and the private sector account for an estimated 5 percent of health services. Services provided by the private sector are likely to increase with the recent decision to allow private practice by government physicians after hours.[51]

All government health services are free, with the exception of special wards in government hospitals. Recognizing that government resources are insufficient to allow the budgetary financing of health care needs, the government will introduce cost-sharing in fiscal 1994. The government also began to address the recurring drug shortage in 1991; a national drug policy was adopted whereby government central medical stores will be restructured under a management contract, and government procurement will shift to a demand driven system.

Several of the major health problems confronting Tanzania—malaria, diarrheal diseases, and respiratory infections—are closely associated with water, hygiene, and sanitation problems. Adequate water supply is also critical to freeing women's energy for child care, family production, and income-earning activities. Water supply and sanitation services have not received sufficient support. Prior to the economic recovery program, about half of the rural population had access to an adequate water supply. However, operational and maintenance inefficiencies and a decline in donor funding for the subsector, which was not compensated for by higher government spending during the economic recovery program, have reduced that number to 25 percent. Moreover, an estimated 40 percent of all households must spend more than 15 minutes to get water. While government attention has recently turned to water management, the government has been slow to introduce cost recovery measures, promote community participation by providing training and tools, improve the supply of spare parts, and make appropriate technologies available—for example, hand pumps fitted onto hand-dug or hand-drilled wells.[52]

Lessons: looking to the future

Tanzania's adjustment program focused initially on economic recovery, rather than adjustment. Priority went to improving access to foreign exchange in order to restore capacity utilization and to improve pricing signals for producers, including the extreme exchange rate overvaluation of the prereform economy. Later, liberalization was also a vehicle for increasing import competition. However in retrospect, it is clear that import liberalization has had two main shortcomings: giving inadequate attention to promoting exports to finance additional imports, thus forcing Tanzania to continue to rely on aid, and not ensuring that counterpart funds and import taxes could be collected, thus creating distortions. The consequent multiplicity of effective exchange rates undermined domestic competition. Imports were not used efficiently, and in some cases, domestic industry effectively became disprotected, favoring trading and discouraging the private sector from productive activities, including exporting.

The design of the reform program was also influenced by how it could be implemented institutionally. Exchange rate, tariff, and price reforms were among the first measures adopted. While all of these measures obviously have major economic and distributional effects, they are not difficult to implement bureaucratically. They require only that consensus be reached among a few key officials—the ministers of finance and of industry and commerce, and the governor of the central bank, in consultation with the president. After agreement was reached at that level, implementation followed quickly by administrative fiat.

The next stage of reform in Tanzania requires significant structural change, including a major restructuring of public institutions, such as the civil service and parastatals. Civil service reform is essential for downsizing the government and enabling it to carry out essential functions more effectively and to enable the private sector to respond to market opportunities and play a greater role in economic growth. The elimination of single-channel marketing needs to be implemented quickly because it is absolutely essential, although not sufficient by itself, for increasing exports and improving macroeconomic stability. Faster liberalization of agricultural export marketing and reduction of implicit taxation of agricultural exports would have boosted growth and helped to alleviate poverty. To the extent that this was politically impossible, it would have been better to restructure the cooperatives to improve their efficiency and accountability before declaring them private, and hence untouchable, by the government.

Financial sector reform must be complemented by accelerated structural reform. Tanzania's experience calls into question whether structural reform should have been carried out prior to financial sector reform. Since financial sector reform is just under way, the jury is still out on this issue. However, the evidence thus far suggests that early financial sector reform may play a critical role in the adjustment process by providing significant pressure for real restructuring. Consequently, all actors are increasingly recognizing that a political decision must be made about whether structural reform should proceed quickly, or whether financial sector reforms should be halted by pressuring the banks to lend amounts beyond levels they deem prudent.

Another important sequencing issue pertains to private sector development. While some steps have recently been taken to encourage local and foreign private investment, greater attention should have been given earlier to strengthening the private sector, particularly indigenous entrepreneurship, including allowing entry to all areas of economic activity, improving access to credit, lowering real interest rates and inflation, streamlining the investment approval process, and improving the transparency of tax assessments and collections.

Finally, the reform program should have focused more strongly on social issues. The social sectors are in crisis. Demand for social services has increased, while effective government strategies, institutional arrangements, and donor coordination for improving the delivery of water, sanitation, health, and educational services have been absent. Improved social services will be essential to reducing widespread poverty in Tanzania. The absence of a social safety net has also delayed the restructuring of the civil service and parastatal sector.

Tanzania's experience shows the limits of macroeconomic policy reforms aimed at stabilization and price reforms if the necessary microeconomic foundations are not in place. Reform of the parastatals and inefficient agricultural marketing institutions and systems, and deregulation of the economy to facilitate private sector entry and expansion and the orderly exit of unviable firms would have improved macroeconomic stability and helped to generate the higher levels of growth that are needed to reduce the nation's extensive poverty.

Appendix 8A. Summary of Tanzania's policy reforms

Fiscal policy and management

Initial situation. Persistently high fiscal deficits were financed by substantial domestic bank borrowing. There was inadequate control of expenditures, chronic underfunding, and too many projects in the public investment program; the planning system did not ensure efficient allocation of budgetary resources; and the bulk of donor funds were not accounted for in the budget.

Policy reforms implemented. Central government finances improved from a deficit of 4 percent of GDP in fiscal 1988 to a surplus of 1.5 percent in 1992 and substantially reduced reliance on domestic financing of the deficit. Monitoring of revenue and expenditure has improved slightly; preparation of a three-year rolling plan to take into account the availability of resources and intersectoral priorities has begun; and there is increased coverage of donor funding of the budget.

Assessment of progress of reforms. Until the recent slippage, overall progress in improving fiscal policy was good. However the budget is still heavily reliant on donor financing, the revenue base is extremely narrow, tax administration and enforcement are weak, and tax compliance is low. While central government finances have improved, quasi-fiscal losses have risen due to poor cost recovery and inefficiencies among utility parastatals and the mounting losses of commercial parastatals.

Monetary policy

Initial situation. The Bank of Tanzania had little control over monetary expansion, and commercial banks enjoyed almost unlimited access to Bank of Tanzania refinancing. Credit growth was excessive and fueled inflation rates of over 30 percent from 1981 to 1985.

Policy reforms implemented. In July 1992 the Bank of Tanzania closed the overdraft facilities enjoyed by the commercial banks. A penalty rate, set above their maximum lending rate, has been established to discourage commercial bank borrowing from the central bank.

Assessment of progress of reforms. The Bank of Tanzania's ability to curb rapid monetary expansion remains constrained by the absence of supporting fiscal policies; by central bank losses due to delays in collecting counterpart funds from the open general license, gold purchases, and the debt conversion program; and until the financial sector reform program that began in fiscal 1992, by excessive lending to parastatals and cooperative unions.

Financial sector reforms

Initial situation. The banking system was dominated by state banks—highly monopolized, inefficient, and largely insolvent. Much bank credit was directed by the government to the public sector and cooperative unions despite their credit problems. A multiplicity of interest rates was set by the government.

Policy reforms implemented. New private banks are being encouraged to operate. The balance sheets of the state-run banks are being restructured, including removal of the worst-performing loans to a recovery trust. Banks have received increased managerial autonomy and the right to set their own interest rates, subject to a minimum deposit rate set above the rate of inflation and a maximum lending rate.

Assessment of progress of reforms. Although reforms were introduced only in 1991, preliminary indications are that the banks are making better banking decisions, are under less pressure to lend, and are making more credit available to the private sector. In addition, new private banks, including some major international banks, expect to begin operations in Tanzania soon. While entry of new banks should continue to be aggressively promoted, much remains to be done to restructure the existing banks to ensure that they will be able to compete and that the financial sector will not continue to be dominated by one large state bank. Long overdue real-side restructuring (of parastatals and agricultural export marketing) will be essential to the development of good banking clients and the sustainability of financial sector reform.

Exchange rate management

Initial situation. The black market premium for dollars reached 800 percent in 1985. In the late 1970s export retention was allowed on a very selective basis and under very restrictive conditions. The holding of foreign exchange was illegal. All foreign exchange was allocated administratively.

Policy reforms implemented. The official exchange rate was depreciated by over 75 percent in real effective terms from 1987 to 1992, reducing the premium to 20 percent at the beginning of 1993. An increased share of export earnings was allowed to be retained and used more flexibly. Tanzanians were allowed to hold foreign currency accounts. The degree of administrative allocation of foreign exchange was reduced with the introduction of the open general license and the foreign exchange bureaus.

Assessment of progress of reforms. Previously, this had been perhaps the most politically sensitive and contentious issue between the government and the IMF and World Bank. Today, the principle of moving toward market-based systems for the allocation of foreign exchange and the determination of exchange rates has been accepted by the government, and a plan for speedy unification has been agreed upon.

Liberalization of international trade

Initial situation. Foreign exchange for imports was allocated administratively. Imports were subject to extensive quantitative restrictions and heavy effective protection: import duty rates ranged from 0 to 200 percent with additional sales taxes of up to 300 percent.

Policy reforms implemented. In 1984 the own-funds import scheme was established, which permitted individuals to import most goods using unofficial sources of foreign exchange. Import licensing became more nearly automatic with the introduction of the open general license in 1987. Importers also have access to a wide range of goods through the foreign exchange bureaus. In several steps beginning in 1987–88, the maximum tariff was reduced to 40 percent and the number of tariff categories to four. Sales tax rates on imports were also reduced to 0 to 30 percent.

Assessment of progress of reforms. Significant trade liberalization has taken place because of reforms in trade policies. The import regime has become more liberal and market oriented, although it is segmented into numerous windows. Exchange rate overvaluation and, in the case of balance of payments support funds, a poor record of payment of local currency cover has effectively subsidized some windows over others. More attention should have been given earlier to systems for ensuring the accountability and transparency of the open general license. Import liberalization should have been accompanied by reform of the customs department and faster movement to unify exchange rates. Measures to promote exports should have been implemented as vigorously and as early as reforms to liberalize imports. Exporters of traditional agricultural exports have been discriminated against by the exchange rate regime and by other means:

- Export retention was allowed on a very selective basis and under very restrictive conditions.
- Nontraditional exporters were allowed to retain an increased share of their foreign exchange earnings.
- Export registration and licensing requirements were lengthy and subject to substantial delays.
- Export documentation requirements were reduced. A duty-drawback scheme was introduced in 1988 but has been limited in effectiveness, owing to lack of funds and administrative difficulties.
- There were single channel marketing arrangements for the export of nearly all of the traditional export crops.
- Cashew nut marketing was liberalized in 1992.

Liberalization of prices and domestic trade

Initial situation. In the industrial sector 400 goods were subject to price controls in the early 1980s, and wholesale trade in over 50 major commodities was restricted to parastatals. In the agricultural sector, producer prices for traditional crops were fixed by the government and were only about 65 percent of world prices on average. Marketing of agricultural produce was done through a single government channel.

Policy reforms implemented. During the economic recovery program price controls were gradually eliminated on all products except sugar, petroleum, and fertilizer. Subsidies on the latter two are gradually being phased out. Almost all goods for sale in the domestic market have been decontrolled.

Assessment of progress of reforms. Domestic deregulation was introduced in tandem with successive measures to further liberalize imports and was often simply a formal recognition of the de facto liberalization of domestic trade that was already taking place. Price controls on sugar have proven politically difficult to remove. The successful early liberalization of foodgrain marketing was essential to demonstrate that private markets could work and to provide quick and visible benefits from reform. Despite the high cost of past export pricing and marketing policies, the marketing of traditional agricultural exports has yet to be fully liberalized, partly because of the political nature of the cooperative unions. For export crops, in the last two years the government has taken initial steps toward allowing markets to set prices and toward opening export marketing to competition.

Labor and wage policy reform

Initial situation. By 1986 the real minimum wage was less than a third of its 1970 level. Despite several attempts at retrenchment, the civil service was significantly overstaffed.

Policy reforms implemented. The minimum wage was increased, but the adjustments were substantially below rises in the cost of living. Employment guarantees to university graduates were abolished in 1991. In 1992–93 the government introduced a hiring freeze in the civil service and announced a program of retrenchment of 50,000 civil servants.

Assessment of progress of reforms. Despite earlier half-hearted efforts at civil service reform, the government has recently formulated an action plan aimed at improving the performance and morale of the civil service and the overall efficiency of the government, with retrenchment as only a first phase of the plan. Clearly it is long overdue for the government to address these issues. However, the budgetary costs of pay reform and retrenchment, and concerns about the social and political costs of retrenchment, could slow implementation of civil service reform.

Public enterprise reforms

Initial situation. There were over 300 commercial parastatals—accounting for an estimated 25 percent of total wage employment and about 20 percent of GDP—that played a dominant role in many sectors of the economy. Net losses of the sector were equivalent to about 8 percent of GDP in 1990–91. Many industrial parastatals operated at negative value added with average capacity utilization below 25 percent.

Policy reforms implemented. A number of studies were carried out over the years but little action taken until the creation of the Presidential Parastatal Sector Reform Commission in 1992, which developed an ambitious master plan for privatization that was later approved by the cabinet. A handful of ad hoc privatizations have been carried out over the last few years, involving primarily management contracts and joint venture arrangements for some of the smaller parastatals. Some of the major parastatal utilities have also entered into performance contracts.

Assessment of progress of reforms. Despite the obvious and serious nature of the problems of the parastatal sector, it took at least ten years before a consensus and an action plan for meaningful reform emerged. The reform program is too new to evaluate. Nevertheless, there are a number of issues that may slow the process of privatization, including the degradation of many parastatal assets after many years of poor maintenance, the technological obsolescence and poor location of many public sector enterprises, and a lack of interest in many of them by the private sector. There is also some reluctance to sell the few profitable parastatals. In the meantime, losses in the parastatal sector mount.

Social sector policies

Initial situation. The significant progress made during the 1970s in extending access to water, sanitation, and health and education services had eroded due to rapid population growth, chronic underfunding by the government, lack of training and poor motivation of health workers, and shortages of supplies. Private medical practice was prohibited.

Policy reforms implemented. Expanded education and health services were provided through local self-help efforts assisted by the government and NGOs. Restrictions on private practice by government physicians were removed. The government adopted a policy statement on population growth.

Assessment of progress of reforms. Public expenditures on the social sectors increased on a per capita basis during the second phase of the economic reform program, but remain woefully inadequate. The government has yet to fully integrate the social sectors into the adjustment program through effective strategies, institutional arrangements, and action plans that improve the delivery of social services. Lack of progress in the social sectors has been a major issue during the adjustment period.

Appendix 8B. Limitations of national accounts data on the industrial sector

National accounts data on industrial GDP do not properly reflect industrial growth trends for two major reasons. First, the national accounts constant price estimates of the growth of formal sector activities in the industrial sector and the spotty series on capacity utilization are based on the output of selected commodities by a number of traditional manufacturers. The commodities are spirits (Konyagi), beer, cigarettes, textiles, fertilizers, refined petroleum products, cement, rolled steel, corrugated iron sheets, dry cell batteries, radios, sisal rope, aluminum sheets, and chemicals. With the exception of textiles, chemicals, and batteries, these are all products produced by parastatals. In the case of textiles, even though the private sector accounts for 40 percent of total output of the subsector, the private sector accounts for only 10 percent of total textile production in the output series used for the national accounts estimates. Capacity utilization figures are also biased downwards because capacity utilization tends to be much higher among private firms. The same kind of pattern exists for chemicals, batteries, and other product groups covered in the official statistics.

Consequently, official measures of formal sector output and capacity utilization exclude a significant amount of activity in the private sector and do not reflect the diversification of the industrial sector that has taken place since the government embarked on the basic industrial strategy that established import substituting industries in the state sector. Official data do not include output of smaller, more dynamic private sector firms. In addition, the output of firms engaged in manufactured export activities is not captured.

Second, informal sector activities are poorly captured. The national accounts estimates of their contribution to manufacturing output is mechanically estimated to be one-third of the total value added of all manufacturing establishments. Consequently, the estimates assume that the output of the informal sector declined with that in the formal sector between 1979 and 1986. However, the informal sector rapidly expanded during the period in the face of the high rate of urbanization, the persistent economic crisis, high rates of inflation, and declining formal sector employment opportunities. Consequently, national accounts estimates for industrial production are probably grossly understated.

Notes

1. While the delay and shortfall in rain in 1992 affected the availability of power from hydro resources throughout Southern Africa, in Tanzania they have not had as large a negative impact as in other countries undergoing adjustment in Southern Africa.

2. A major effort is now underway to review all laws and revise legislation to remove the remaining impediments to reform in the business environment.

3. The recent report of the Presidential Commission on Land Reform is expected to lead to decisions to introduce land markets and clarify property rights and the process of transferring ownership.

4. To the extent that recent measures to increase tax compliance are successful, the profitability of trading should decline and make production more attractive, which will also help sustain economic growth.

5. However, in 1992–93 the fiscal deficit is projected to increase substantially due primarily to a shortfall of revenue—this because of over optimism about the revenue yield from the substantial cut in indirect taxes that was announced in the 1992–93 budget (and rescinded six months later) and because of lower than expected inflows of balance of payments support that adversely affected imports.

6. A high proportion of donor financing provided to Tanzania through the government is not captured in the budget because much large donor financing bypasses the budget—for example, technical assistance funds and direct project financing.

7. In the 1991–92 budget for example, 39 percent of total recurrent expenditures and more than 90 percent of the development budget were provided by counterpart funds generated by balance of payments support.

8. It is estimated that central bank losses in the first six months of 1992–93 accounted for 27 percent of the increase in broad money.

9. The People's Bank of Zanzibar, which is owned by the government of Zanzibar, operates exclusively in Zanzibar.

10. The slippage during 1988, plus slow progress in agricultural marketing reform, led to a delay in the preparation of the third structural adjustment facility program and a consultative group meeting for Tanzania.

11. Based on the first six months of operations, the volume of foreign exchange sold through the bureaus is likely to be equivalent to about 20 percent of total imports of goods and services in 1992–93.

12. By April 1993 the average dollar exchange rate in the bureaus was about 30 percent higher than the official rate: the parallel market rate was less than 5 percent above the bureau rate.

13. Beginning in June 1992, the government extended the contracts of its preshipment inspection agencies to include customs valuation and plans to involve the commercial banks in the collection of trade taxes.

14. Conversely, the bureaus probably were able to develop more quickly because of the unavailability of open general license resources during 1992–93, when many donors withheld open general license funds pending improvements in accounting and management.

15. Initially, preshipment inspection was required for goods valued at more than $5,000 and only for goods financed through official sources of foreign exchange. In 1991–92 preshipment inspection was extended to all goods valued at more than $5,000, regardless of the source of financing. In 1993 the threshold was reduced further to only $3,000, one of the lowest in Africa, because the $5,000 limit meant that only about 16 percent of the total value of imports was subject to inspection.

16. In practice, many traditional exporters—for example, coffee farmers—do not yet have the right to retain any of the export earnings in foreign exchange.

17. While this major change in policy drastically reduced the credit requirements of the crop authorities, the source of excess credit to cover large financial losses, because of poor pricing policies and marketing inefficiencies, merely shifted from the marketing boards to the cooperatives.

18. By 1990 the average had fallen to only 40 percent.

19. Yet farmers may not receive any second payment if, as is anticipated, world market conditions and prices for cotton do not improve.

20. In September 1992 the government announced that selected private traders would also be allowed to enter this field.

21. The upper echelon of the civil service also enjoys several in-kind benefits (for example, free housing, utilities, telephone, and transport). If all these are included, the ratio of the highest level of compensation in the civil service to the minimum wage is estimated to be nearly 50 to 1.

22. Until 1992 the national labor union was an appendage of the political party and had a limited role in wage determination. The formal link to the party was severed that year as a prelude to multiparty politics.

23. Despite periodic admonishments from the parliamentary accounts committee and the president, audits of many parastatal accounts are substantially behind schedule. As of June 1992, the accounts of 126 of the Tanzanian Audit Corporation's 281 clients were in arrears for one year or more—due in part to excess demand on the Tanzanian Audit Corporation's capacity to carry out the audits. Yet the more important source of the problem is that compliance with government requirements for the timely submission of accounts for audit continues to be quite unsatisfactory because of weak sanctions.

24. The indebtedness of parastatals, largely to the treasury, amounts to almost TSh 1 trillion.

25. For these reasons, little progress was made toward implementing the restructuring plans for three industrial subsectors (leather, textiles, and edible oils) that were developed by 1989–90 in the context of an adjustment credit for industry that was approved by the World Bank. With the reforms that began in 1992, these plans have been implemented much more quickly.

26. Although only 5 percent of the school-aged population goes to secondary school, the inability of the government to meet even these limited demands required that state control be relaxed.

27. Since 1992 the authorities have been moving the official rate so as to reduce the premium over the exchange rate in the foreign exchange bureau. The government is committed to unifying exchange rates by 1994.

28. As noted earlier, however, the budget deficit for 1992–93 could be more than 7 percent of GDP.

29. The decline in Tanzania's primary deficit (excluding interest payments) was even more pronounced, falling from an average of 8.6 percent to 3.9 percent between 1986 and 1991.

30. Official measures of GDP significantly understate total economic activity in Tanzania. In response to the economic decline of the late 1970s and early 1980s and to distorted economic policies and excessive regulations, a large unofficial, or "second," economy has emerged. By 1990 Maliyamkono and Bagachwa (1990) estimate that unofficial GDP had reached 30 percent of official GDP. The absence of time series data makes it impossible to tell whether the large unofficial economy leads to under-

statement of both the growth rate and the level of economic activity.

31. Tanzania has also received about $1 billion in debt relief since the economic recovery program.

32. As shown in Bacha (1992), net real transfers are crucial to determining the sustainability of growth and debt accumulation.

33. Cash cover repayment on traditional commodity import support programs has been as low as 40 percent. But in the case of the open general license, a 1992 joint donor mission found that, while importers typically pay full cash cover to the commercial banks, the commercial banks have not turned all those funds over to the Bank of Tanzania. This practice poses an additional problem in that it is inherently inflationary and undermines the government's program to control credit and achieve macroeconomic stability.

34. Estimates of the total amount of technical assistance given to Tanzania are difficult to obtain. It is widely conjectured that it is on the order of $300 million, but that may exaggerate slightly the actual amount received.

35. However, as noted in appendix 8B, national accounts data significantly understate the real contribution of the industrial sector, due to the rapid growth of informal industrial sector activities during the economic recovery program, and their limited coverage of formal sector activities.

36. In 1992 many of those industries may have experienced significantly lower growth and capacity utilization because of severe power rationing throughout the country. However, donor funding has been organized to address the emergency situation in the power sector and to bring on line sufficient new generation capacity in the next few years to meet the requirements of accelerated industrial growth.

37. About half of all private firms surveyed in 1990 planned to raise the export share of their total sales and significantly increase investment in their manufacturing facilities.

38. The most important steps taken to encourage private sector development generally include the measures to liberalize foodgrain marketing in 1987 and cashew nut marketing in 1991, the adoption of a National Investment Promotion Policy in 1991, the initial (but painfully slow) steps to encourage private participation in industrial parastatals, and a decision in 1992 to allow private banks to be established again.

39. Villagization, which began in the early 1970s, sought to move the rural population into centrally located villages where essential services (health, education, and water) could be provided more easily. However, farmers had little incentive to improve their productivity, were often moved long distances from their customary plots, and were required to cultivate village plots on a continuous basis, contributing to declining yields.

40. The first grain marketing reforms were undertaken in 1984, when restrictions were removed on the movement of grains by individuals across regional boundaries in lots of 500 kg or less. By 1987 all weight restrictions on interregional grain movements had been eliminated, and traders began to compete with the National Milling Corporation to supply urban centers. In 1989 the government announced that the final obstacles to farmers' selling directly to private traders were being eliminated, essentially liberalizing the entire grain trading system.

41. However, as noted in the World Bank-Government of Tanzania Agricultural Sector Review (1992), there is virtually no private storage for seasonal arbitrage, and the dependence of traders on existing transport capacities has left some food-deficit areas virtually unserved by the market.

42. Government reform of traditional export crops was essentially limited to changing the role of the marketing boards. Prior to reforms, the marketing boards were the sole buyer of crops for exports from the unions, and they required bank financing to finance these purchases. Reforms sought to transform the boards into agents acting on behalf of the unions in arranging exports of their crops on a fee basis. The purpose of this change was to eliminate the need for double financing of the crop by the banks. Cashew marketing was the one traditional crop for which reform went further; private trade in competition with the unions was allowed as of the 1991 season.

43. Accumulated arrears on crop marketing overdrafts totaled over TSh 66 billion by the end of 1991, about 45 percent of which was more than two years old.

44. The party's link with the cooperatives was severed formally in conjunction with parliamentary approval of the Cooperative Act of 1991, which seeks to create grassroot, democratic, and economically viable cooperatives.

45. As noted earlier, a few joint ventures for new processing facilities have recently been approved by the government.

46. The poverty and hard core poverty lines have recently been estimated at TSh 46,173 and TSh 31,000 respectively. These figures, and much of the data on poverty that are quoted in this section, were taken from Ferreira (1993).

47. Ferreira (1993) shows that income from informal sector business and agricultural activities contributed 44 and 34 percent of total income of urban households, respectively. In Dar es Salaam, the respective figures were 83 and 1 percent. This shows that many urban households, including those in Dar es Salaam, generate additional income from farming plots they maintain.

48. Primary school enrollment rates are still very low, particularly in rural areas where more than 88 percent of the school age population does not attend primary school. Secondary school enrollment in the rural areas is also very low—only 3.5 percent of children younger than 14 have a secondary education.

49. However, with the addition of all other school expenses, including uniforms and exercise books, primary schools can cost parents from TSh 4,000 to TSh 7,000 a year, more than 10 percent of the annual income of a minimum wage earner. By comparison, the central government's contribution to primary education is about TSh 4,000.

50. A 1991 World Bank report projects that the epidemic could reduce the GDP growth rate by 14 to 24 percent by the year 2010.

51. Despite being declared illegal in 1977, private medicine thrived in the face of the health care crisis.

52. However, household surveys have shown that people would be willing to pay for water (Whittington 1988).

References

Ahmed, Z. 1992. "A Flow of Funds Consistency Framework for Tanzania." World Bank, Southern Africa Department, Washington, D.C.

———. 1993. "Tanzania: Real Net Official Development Assistance Flows." World Bank, Eastern Africa Department, Country Operations, Washington, D.C.

Aksoy, A. 1992. "Foreign Exchange Markets and Export Incentives." World Bank, Southern Africa Department, Country Operations, Washington, D.C.

Bacha, E. 1992. "External Debt, Net Transfers and Growth in Developing Countries." *World Development* 20:1183–1192.

Bagachwa, M. S. D., A.V.Y. Mbelle, and B. Van Arkadie. 1991. "Market Reforms and Parastatal Restructuring in Tanzania." University of Dar es Salaam, Economics Department, Dar es Salaam.

Bank of Tanzania. 1990. "Tanzania: Exchange Rate Study." Bank of Tanzania, Dar es Salaam.

———. Various years. *Economic and Operations Reports.* Dar es Salaam: Tanzania Printers, Limited.

Bank of Tanzania and University of Dar es Salaam. 1992. "Structural Adjustment in Tanzania: An Evaluation of the Consequences of the Adjustment Policies During 1985–1990." Bank of Tanzania, and University of Dar es Salaam, Department of Economics, Dar es Salaam.

Bevan, D., P. Collier, and J.W. Gunning. 1989. *Peasants and Governments.* Oxford: Oxford University Press.

Booth, D. 1990. "Timing and Sequencing in Agricultural Policy Reform: Tanzania." Overseas Development Institute, London.

Cooksey, B. 1992. "Parents' Attitudes and Strategies Towards Education in Rural Tanzania." Tanzania Development Research Group (TADREG), Dar es Salaam.

Collier, P., and J.W. Gunning. 1992. "Aid and Exchange Rate Adjustment in African Trade Liberalizations." *The Economic Journal of the Royal Economic Society* 102:925–39.

Doriye, J., and M. Wuyts. 1992. "Adjustment and Sustainable Recovery—The Case of Tanzania." Institute of Social Studies, Population and Development Program, The Hague, The Netherlands.

Dutz, Mark, and Leila Frischtak. 1992. "Industrial Adjustment and Restructuring: Reflections from Tanzania." World Bank, Private Sector Development, Washington, D.C.

Economic Research Bureau. Various years. *Tanzania Economic Trends: A Quarterly Review of the Economy.* Dar es Salaam: University of Dar es Salaam.

Eriksson, G. 1991. "Macroeconomic Studies: Tanzania's Economic Recovery Program." Stockholm School of Economics, Department of International Economics and Geography, Stockholm, Sweden.

Food Studies Group. 1992. "Tanzania: Agriculture Diversification and Intensification Study." Oxford University, Oxford.

Ferreira, M. 1993. "Tanzania: A Poverty Profile." World Bank, Southern Africa Region, Washington, D.C.

Hyuha, M., and J.B. Ndulu. 1990. "Inflation and Economic Recovery in Tanzania: Further Theoretical and Empirical Analyses." University of Dar es Salaam, Department of Economics, Dar es Salaam.

Kilindo, A. L. 1991. "Inflationary Finance and the Dynamics of Inflation in Tanzania." Ph.D. dissertation, University of Dar es Salaam, Department of Economics, Dar es Salaam.

Lavy, V. 1988. "Aid and Growth in Sub-Saharan Africa: The Recent Experience." *European Economic Review* 32:1777–95.

Lenga, B. 1989. "Tanzania Struggle with the International Monetary Fund." *New African* 260:35

Lindahl, C., and W. Lyakurwa. 1987. "Proposal for an Export Development Strategy." University of Dar es Salaam, Department of Economics, Dar es Salaam.

Lipumba, N., and N.E. Osoro. 1991. "Saving Mobilization and Financial Sector Reforms." *The Tanzanian Bankers Journal.* June 1991.

Lister, S., and E. Muggeridge. 1992. "Tanzania: Public Expenditure Data." World Bank, Southern Africa Department, Washington, D.C.

Loxley, J. 1989. "The Devaluation Debate in Tanzania." In Bonnie K. Campbell and John Loxley, eds., *Structural Adjustment in Africa.* New York: St. Martin's Press.

Maliyamkono, T. L., and Mboya S. D. Bagachwa. 1990. *The Second Economy in Tanzania.* London: J. Currey.

Maxwell Stamp Associates. 1988a. "Export Promotion in Tanzania." Dar es Salaam.

———. 1988b. "The Structure and Recommendations for Reform of Nominal Tariffs in Tanzania." Dar es Salaam.

Ndulu, B. 1986. "Investment, Output Growth, and Capacity Utilization in an African Economy: The Case of the Manufacturing Sector in Tanzania." *East Africa Economic Review.* (Kenya) 2:4–30.

———. 1990a."Growth and Adjustment in Sub-Saharan Africa." African Economic Research Consortium, Nairobi.

———. 1990b. "Medium-Term Growth in Tanzania." African Economic Research Consortium, Nairobi.

Nguyuru, Lipumba. 1983. "Policy Reforms for Economic Development in Tanzania." University of Dar es Salaam, Department of Economics, Dar es Salaam.

Pritchett, Lant. 1991. "Import Allocation, Exchange Rates, and Price Controls in Tanzania." World Bank, Office of the Vice President, Development Economics and Chief Economist, Washington, D.C.

Rattso, J. 1991. "Structural Adjustment in Tanzania." Study prepared for the Ministry of Foreign Affairs, Government of Norway, Oslo.

Semboja, J., and B. Ndullu. 1992. "Trade and Industrialization." University of Dar es Salaam, Department of Economics, Dar es Salaam.

———. 1992. "The Development of Manufacturing for Export in Tanzania." University of Dar es Salaam, Department of Economics, Dar es Salaam.

Sepehri, A. 1992. "Balance of Payments, Output, and Prices in Tanzania." University of Manitoba, Department of Economics, Winnipeg.

Shaaeldin, E. 1988. "Sources of Industrial Growth in Kenya, Tanzania, Zambia, and Zimbabwe." *African Development Bank Economic Research Papers* 8:1–30.

Tanzania. 1982. "Implementation Schedule for the Structural Adjustment Program." Government Printer, Dar es Salaam.

———. 1989. "Economic Recovery Program II." Economic and Social Action Programme, Planning Commission, Dar es Salaam.

———. 1990. "Priority Social Action Program" (A summary). Planning Commission, Dar es Salaam.

———. 1991. "Review of Critical Issues: The Primary and Secondary Education Subsectors." The Planning Commission, and the President's Office, Dar es Salaam.

———. 1992a. "A Preliminary Study on the Wholesale Trade in Grains and Beans in Tanzania." Ministry of Agriculture, Marketing Development Bureau, Dar es Salaam.

———. 1992b. *National Accounts of Tanzania 1976 – 1991.* Bureau of Statistics, Dar es Salaam.

———. Various years. *The Economic Survey.* The Planning Commission, The Government Printer, Dar es Salaam.

Taylor, L. 1990. "Foreign Transfers and Import Support in Tanzania." Prepared for SIDA, Dar es Salaam.

Thomas W. Allen Associates Limited. 1991. "A Study of Various Aspects of Export Promotion and Facilitation and of Internal Trade in Tanzania." Prepared for the World Bank, Southern Africa Department, Washington, D.C.

Van Arkadie, B. 1983. "The International Monetary Fund Prescription for Structural

Adjustment in Tanzania: A Comment." University of Dar es Salaam, Department of Economics, Dar es Salaam.

Van den Brink, R. 1992. "Tanzania: Agricultural Sector Statistics." Cornell University, Ithaca, NY.

Van Wijnbergen, S. 1986. "Macroeconomic Aspects of the Effectiveness of Foreign Aid: On the Two-Gap Model, Home Goods Disequilibrium, and Real Exchange Rate Misalignment." *Journal of International Economics.* (Netherlands) 21:123–36.

———. 1990. "Aid, Export Promotion and the Real Exchange Rate: An African Dilemma." Centre for Economic Policy Research, London.

White, H. 1992. "What Do We Know about Aid's Macroeconomic Impact? An Overview of the Aid Effectiveness Debate." *Journal of International Development* 4:121–37.

Whittington, D. 1988. "Willingness to Pay for Water in Newala District, Tanzania." United States Agency for International Development, Washington, D.C. and United Nations Children's Fund, New York, NY.

———. 1992. "Policies to Encourage Foreign Direct Investment in Tanzania—with Special Attention to Exchange Controls and Debt Equity Swaps." Foreign Investment Advisory Services, Multilateral Investment Guarantee Agency, Washington, D.C.

World Bank-Government of Tanzania. 1992. "Joint Government of Tanzania and World Bank Agriculture Sector Review." World Bank, Eastern Africa, Agriculture Department, Washington, D.C., and Government of Tanzania, Ministry of Agriculture, Dar es Salaam.

9

Conclusions

Rashid Faruqee and Ishrat Husain

A common theme that emerges from the record of adjustment programs in the seven case studies is that African governments are not yet much better at managing market economies than they were at managing economies through heavy intervention. The thrust of reforms was to change the role of government to that of facilitator and catalyst in the mobilization and allocation of resources, guide and helping hand in the production and distribution of goods and services, referee in ensuring a level playing field for all economic actors, and active and direct participant in redirecting public spending to spur growth, reduce poverty, and protect the environment. The evidence of the case studies suggests that the adjustment programs in Africa have not yet succeeded in reaching those objectives, notwithstanding significant progress in that direction.

There are, of course, differences in the extent of state control and involvement in these countries stemming from their historical legacies, the orientation of their postindependence regimes, and the evolution of thinking and practices in the countries over time. But the striking finding of the seven case studies is that the global wind of change that is redefining the role of the state has not yet swept these countries, at least by contemporary standards.

The need to build capacity

There is a basic dilemma in Africa. Economic reform curtails the powers of the state through privatization, deregulation, the elimination of central planning, and a reduction in the public work force. The ensuing uncertainty, lower real wages, and lack of job security adversely affect the motives of civil servants, in some cases leading them out of public service. But the remaining tasks of government—the design, implementation, and operation of the structural adjustment program, the maintenance and operation of a framework of macroeconomic policies that provide incentives to the private sector, the resolution of infrastructural problems, and the mediation of conflicts in the civil society—all demand scarce technical and administrative skills. If civil servants lack motivation, and there is a corresponding lack of technical and administrative skills, economic reform faces enormous obstacles. This dilemma—and the frequent absence of strong development-oriented, visionary leadership fully committed to economic reforms—greatly compound the problems of implementation.

The administrative decay in Africa is rooted in the pervasive clientele politics. It could be said of many public officials that they "treat their administrative work for their ruler as a personal service based on their duty of obedience and respect" (Bendix 1962), not as a service to their country and fellow citizens. Unless there is a fundamental restructuring and professionalization of the civil service in these countries, the prospects for building implementation capacity will remain bleak—whatever the pressures from outside.

The need to convert rents to resources

Another basic problem in much of Africa is that, although the writ of the state runs large and the role of the state is all-pervasive and interventionist, there is at the same time a paralysis or breakdown of government authority. Large informal sectors have emerged in almost all the countries, bypassing and ignoring government regulations and rules. Smuggled goods are freely available at prices cheaper than domestic substitutes. Scarce government services are allocated by functionaries on the basis of political and family connections, and bribes.

A major factor inhibiting the growth of business is the generous inflow of smuggled goods allowed by customs officials, who collect rents for themselves rather than import duties for the government. Domestic industries have to pay all kinds of taxes—for example, import duties on inputs and raw materials, and taxes on sales profits and dividends. They also have to bear the higher costs of inefficient public utilities. And they face harassment and pressure from local and state government officials. No wonder their costs—despite devaluations and the greater availability of imported inputs—are less competitive than those of smuggled imported goods, whose only duties and taxes are the rents to customs officials. Re-export of illicit imported goods has become a thriving business among Ghana, Nigeria, and neighboring CFA zone countries (box 9.1).

The growth of a large private sector has been stunted in most African countries by the direct interventions of—and displacements by—the African state. But the visible buoyancy of agriculture and the urban informal sector in almost all adjusting countries provides ample testimony to the entrepreneurial skills and capacities of private economic actors. In several countries—

such as Côte d'Ivoire, Kenya, and Nigeria—private actors are in the formal sector, too. The state should nurture the growth and expansion of a broadly based private sector. But a distinction needs to be made between an unproductive rent-seeking private sector in which certain individuals or companies earn profits due to the favors and patronage of the government, and a productive private sector in which individuals or companies compete on a level playing field without special favors or concessions.

The need to broaden the support for reforms

The case studies document that the adjustment programs in these countries, except Nigeria, were conceived and formulated by a narrow group of technocrats and politicians without broad consultations with and inputs from

Box 9.1 The political economy of wheat import bans in Nigeria

In 1986 Nigeria devalued the naira from N 1 to the dollar to N 4 and imposed a ban on wheat imports. Despite the ban on imports of wheat, bread continued to be available in big cities in Nigeria, though at a much higher price to the consumer. Imports were rerouted through neighboring countries, whose imports shot up, exceeding domestic consumption.

The Nigerian consumer was paying this higher price, not as a direct result of devaluation, but because of additional transport costs (through the port of Cotonou rather than through Lagos), the margins of importers in Benin, risk premiums and returns to smugglers who moved the wheat across the borders, bribes collected by border and customs officials, and payments by the flour mills to local enforcement agencies (for keeping out of trouble). The results: cost inefficiencies, a net welfare loss to Nigeria, and substantial transfers to a small group of Nigerians at the expense of bread consumers.

The urban middle class—particularly groups on fixed incomes (the main consumers of wheat bread), whose real wages and salaries declined—attributed the sharp jump in the price of bread directly to the devaluation of the naira. But in fact, the market price of bread—before the devaluation—had already risen to reflect the parallel exchange rate that drove all transactions in Nigeria. The official devaluation announced in 1986 simply recognized this reality and unified the official and parallel market exchange rates without any significant pass-through effects on consumer prices. This can be seen from the fact that inflation rates in the two years after the 1986 devaluation were lower than those for the preceding two years (import shortages had given rise to higher inflation). But as the ban on wheat imports diverted the source of supplies from Lagos to Cotonou, and generated the chain of additional costs described above, the consumer price of bread rose substantially. True, there were unintended benefits to the economy, such as a decline in the demand for wheat, substitution by other, cheaper food items, and increased domestic production of maize and other local foods, but the consumers resented the price rise and perceived this to be the direct result of devaluation.

others. There is clear evidence that open discussion, debate, and communication and interaction involving diverse groups are the only feasible ways to effect acceptance and internalization of the programs. Trade union leaders, in particular, have often made the point that if they are consulted about the justification for various policy measures and informed about the likely consequences and objectives, they are in a better position to make a constructive contribution to both the diagnosis of problems and the prescription of solutions. Ownership of the reform program should thus be broadly based, rather than the province of a few—for example, ownership by the government in power or by an economic team comprising the finance minister, the central bank governor, the adviser to the president, and their staffs.

To be effective, the reform program should also be carried out with a shared sense of the direction in which the economy should move. Without clear goals and objectives, the achievement of reform goals—with the concomitant need to mobilize support from disparate socioeconomic forces in the country, such as private businesses, professionals, political parties, nongovernmental organizations, and students and labor unions—would prove difficult. The assumption that external approval from donors or international financial institutions will generate commitment to economic reform is not likely to prove true. It is also possible that ownership and commitment could be confined to select elements of the adjustment programs, while other elements that are not perceived to have popular support are neglected. Implementation may vary under those circumstances, with the noncontroversial elements of the package moving forward rapidly while other elements are held up.

Diverse interests and subgroups within the government itself react differently to various reforms. Public enterprise managers oppose reform if it involves closing down or retrenchment. Ministries charged with revenue collection and fiscal balances respond favorably if a reform package adds significantly to available budget resources. Civil servants respond negatively to pay scale reform and cutbacks in employment levels; they might be deterred from opposing reform, however, if it lessened or removed the legal restrictions on their private economic activities. The perception of fairness plays a role, too, in acceptance of reform measures: in Nigeria in the early years of adjustment, the military government imposed pay cuts on the military, establishing a measure of fairness and credibility for the overall program.[1]

Private constituencies often also respond differently to reform. The more competitive industrial concerns, crippled by import restrictions and shortages of foreign exchange, might support trade reform. Export-oriented farmers might be direct beneficiaries of devaluation, while producers of domestic foodcrops might respond favorably to pricing and marketing reforms. The private sector operators dependent on the government's discretion to allocate foreign exchange, licenses, and the like would oppose the program.

Farmers in general benefit from the shifting of resources from urban consumers to rural producers. Other, poorer urban groups, hit hard by budget cutbacks, might be supportive if targeted programs provided them assistance.

The politics of reform implementation, as illustrated by the experience of the seven case study countries, confirm the need for ex ante impact analysis and measures for neutralizing antiadjustment forces. In Nigeria the faltering commitment to adjustment and intermittent lapses in policy implementation were the result of stiff opposition from the urban middle classes—especially professionals, soldiers, and civil servants—who had been hit hard by the loss of implicit and explicit consumer subsidies for food, transport, and imported goods. Their opposition became a main stumbling block to further reforms.

The experiences of the seven countries spotlight the importance of appropriately handling the potential losers from reforms—including vocal middle-class groups of professionals, soldiers, civil servants, and journalists, students, the labor unions, industrialists, and universities—who are likely to be hurt by the liberalization and ensuing competition. It is a mistake to ignore them—or to repress them. They can contribute much to the development process, and they can have tremendous influence in organizing and mobilizing public opinion.

Lessons about strategy, sequence, and pace

A vigorous debate continues on the appropriate pace and sequencing of economic reforms.[2] While specific country circumstances determine what is appropriate, some general lessons can be gleaned. This section addresses the issue, in light of our country study experiences.

In formulating a strategy for implementing policy reforms, four related sets of considerations need to be taken into account: the initial conditions at the start of the adjustment process, the sequencing of economic reforms, the political economy of the reform process, and the administrative capacity to implement reforms.

Of the initial conditions, the most important is the state of the economy. How serious are the macroeconomic imbalances? Is inflation out of control, and has the official exchange rate become grossly overvalued? Has the formal sector collapsed completely (Ghana in the early 1980s), or is it still functioning, even if imperfectly (Côte d'Ivoire, Nigeria, and Senegal today)? The source of the macroeconomic crisis must be considered: adjusting to external shocks may require different measures from those to correct domestic policy errors (although many crises are due to a combination of both factors). A third consideration is the initial degree of policy distortions and underlying structural problems. The more distorted policies are initially and the more serious the underlying structural problems, the more decisive the actions required.

On the sequencing of economic reforms, some reforms must be preceded (or accompanied) by others if they are to yield economic benefits immediately. There is likely to be little near-term economic benefit from reforms implemented in the wrong order, and some reforms may be reversed or have to be repeated if they are not accompanied by others (for example, trade reform without real exchange rate realignment, financial sector restructuring without restoring macroeconomic balance).

The political economy of the reform process usually dictates whether the adjustment should be rapid or gradual. Some countries may have the political base to sustain reforms over a long period and may find a gradual improvement in performance satisfactory. Other governments, particularly new ones (Ghana in the early 1980s), may need to frontload the political pain of adjustment by making rapid reforms to take advantage of an initial wave of support and generate economic benefits that will help consolidate their political support in the longer term. In economic terms, however, more rapid reforms (assuming that they are within the implementation capacity of the government and politically sustainable) are likely to be preferable to slower ones because the benefits of adjustment will tend to be realized faster.

On the administrative capacity to implement reforms, some types of reforms are capacity-saving (that is, they reduce the demands on government's limited administrative capacity); others are capacity-using and thus complicate economic management. This distinction applies both to different categories of reforms and to alternative designs of specific reforms. Across reforms, abolishing price controls and foreign exchange allocation systems are capacity-saving, whereas privatization and civil service reform are initially capacity-using. Within reforms, replacing nontariff barriers and a highly dispersed tariff structure with a simple, single-rate uniform tariff is capacity-saving, relative to introducing a new multirate tariff structure and gradually phasing out excessive protection through declining import surtaxes. And abolishing marketing boards is capacity-saving compared with trying to restructure and run the boards better.

Each reform and the entire reform program must be within the implementation capacity of the government. Radical reforms (abolishing marketing boards, adopting a uniform tariff) may often be easier to implement administratively than gradual reforms, but it might be tougher politically to get them adopted. Capacity-saving and capacity-using reforms affect both core ministries and the specific line ministries concerned. Although administrative capacity saved in the core ministries may be fungible, it may or may not be possible to use administrative capacity saved in one line ministry to help implement reforms in other areas.

One way to think about sequencing is to consider three interrelated, overlapping groups of reforms that need to be implemented in a logical sequence (or simultaneously) if they are to produce intended benefits in good time. The first group of reforms comprises measures to realign relative prices and improve the functioning of product and factor markets. The second covers policies to restore financial balance and restructure the financial system. And the third concerns reforms to create an enabling environment for private sector expansion.

Realigning relative prices and improving the functioning of markets

Measures to liberalize and improve the functioning of domestic product and factor (particularly labor) markets should precede the liberalization of external trade—both to facilitate a supply response when external trade is liberalized and to limit the inflationary impact of exchange rate realignment.[3] Realigning the real exchange rate is the key measure for stimulating a supply response through promoting both export expansion and import substitution. It is essential to realign export expansion and import substitution, and it is essential to do this before (or simultaneously with) reforms in trade policy. Otherwise, the removal of nontariff barriers and the implementation of tariff reform will be difficult, if not impossible. Second-best trade policies (where export subsidies and high tariffs substitute for exchange rate realignment) by and large have not worked, for fiscal and administrative reasons.

Eliminating nontariff barriers (and replacing them with tariffs where necessary) should proceed before (or simultaneously with) tariff reform, but this has often received too little priority. To facilitate exports, countries should eliminate export taxes, institute duty drawbacks, and simplify administrative procedures, keeping in mind that the exchange rate and duty drawbacks should be the primary price incentives for promoting exports. Reducing the dispersion of tariff rates—while maintaining (or increasing) the average effective rate to avoid revenue losses—requires as much emphasis on eliminating exemptions and raising low rates as on cutting peak rates. The real exchange rate should be adjusted as necessary to offset the average loss of protection from tariff reductions.

Correcting financial imbalances and restructuring the financial system

The goal here is to reduce or eliminate the fiscal deficit and impose a comprehensive hard budget constraint on public enterprises. Government-sponsored credit programs and lending by government banks also need to be brought under control at the same time. All these steps need to precede (or be implemented simultaneously with) a disciplined monetary policy. Otherwise, the combination of fiscal laxity and tight monetary policy will squeeze out the private sector and threaten the solvency of the financial system. The liquidation of nonviable enterprises and the redeployment of obviously excessive (and redundant) numbers of government employees (through across-the-board reductions in force or through abolishing entire agencies) should also ideally start at this point.

Monetary discipline and positive real interest rates need to be imposed to bring aggregate demand and supply into balance, reduce inflation, and reduce the incentive for capital flight. Simultaneously, the most egregious distortions in financial sector policies—sectoral credit allocations, preferential interest rates for selected activities, lending margins that do not reflect costs, direct government and central bank intervention on behalf of lending to favored clients—need to be eliminated.

The realignment of the real exchange rate needs to precede the restructuring of the financial system to discourage new capital flight when liquidity is restored and to expose problems in bank loan portfolios that will result from restructuring the real sector. In restructuring the financial system, the first priorities are to restore a functioning payments system and to assure availability of the minimum credit needed to support a supply response as the financial system is reliquified. Strengthened bank supervision, capital adequacy, and bank restructuring; further liberalization of interest rate regulations; improved instruments of monetary management; and elimination of controls on external capital flows—all these need to be put in place over time as the economy and financial system recover.

Creating an enabling environment for private sector expansion

The first steps here are to realign key relative prices—by depreciating the real exchange rates, aligning prices of major commodities with international prices, introducing positive real interest rates, allowing real wages in the formal sector to fall as required—and to restore macroeconomic balance. Next is to restore a functioning payments system and assure availability of the minimum credit needed to support a supply response. Then begins the long-term restructuring of the financial system.

On the expenditure side of fiscal restructuring, there is need early on to provide for adequate public investment and other development expenditures—and to reduce or constrain public sector real wage rates and the real wage bill if appropriate. It is also important early on to revive a reasonable level of public investment—to precede the recovery in private investment—and to initiate long-term civil service reform. On the revenue side, excessive tax rates have to be reduced, the tax base broadened, and the tax structure rationalized in order to raise revenues while also minimizing distortions and disincentives to private sector expansion. Measures must be initiated to improve the legal and regulatory framework and to signal a commitment to pursuing reforms on a sustained basis over the long term, including reforms of the investment code, labor law, business law, competition policy, and the judicial system. Finally, privatization of viable public enterprises must be started, but for this to succeed, there must be an economic environment in which private enterprises can expand.

Within each of the above interrelated reform agendas, individual measures may be undertaken simultaneously or in sequence depending on the economic situation in the adjusting country and the reform strategy. Actions on the three overlapping reform agendas also need to be coordinated with each other. For example, exchange rate realignment is the second step in realigning relative prices, the fifth step in correcting financial imbalances, and the first step in creating an enabling environment. Fiscal restructuring appears as the first step for correcting financial imbalances and the first and third steps for supporting private sector expansion. Note, too, that many of the politically difficult actions required to generate a timely private sector supply response need to come early in the adjustment process and that limits on implementation capacity will need to be taken into account in designing the various reforms.

Summary

Sound macroeconomic policies and stability are the cornerstones of sustainable economic development, and African countries need to pursue these policies to respond and adjust to domestic and external shocks promptly—and to send credible signals to the private sector. The adjustment programs need not be the extremes of either shock therapy or the gradualist approach. A hybrid or mixed approach is most desirable, with some key reforms done simultaneously, in one shot—and others following in an integrated, overlapping way. But the programs should usually follow two phases from the viewpoint of implementation capacity. At first, the reforms should be capacity-saving; only with progress in these reforms should adjustment proceed to capacity-using reforms. Because programs are more sustainable when positive results are quickly evident, the first phases of the program should focus on areas where results are quick. This also helps in enlisting support for the total program. Also to be acknowledged is that three difficult areas of reform—public enterprise reform, civil service reform, financial sector reform—require more time to tackle. Given the close relationships between import liberalization, public enterprise reform, government finance, and financial sector reform, this whole set of reforms should be attempted simultaneously and consistently. Import liberalization, if done too rapidly, will reduce the profitability of domestic firms competing with imports and thus affect their ability to service debt owed to the financial institutions. Public enterprises, unless restructured and faced with a hard budget constraint, will continue to create portfolio problems for their creditor institutions. The government deficit, if not reduced sufficiently, will crowd out the private sector from engaging in activities that have become viable under the new incentive structure. Fixing only one of these distortions at a time is likely to be of little value.

In the end, it must be emphasized that these general lessons about the sequencing and pace of reforms can help in the design of the broad outlines of an optimal policy package. But they cannot substitute for country-specific analysis. For the optimal package must be tailored to the specific circumstances of each country.

Notes

1. The discussion is drawn from Gulhati (1988).
2. Lawrence Hinkle provided draft inputs to this section.
3. In cases of unregulated domestic monopolies, external trade in the specific products concerned may also need to be liberalized initially to provide some competition for the monopoly.

References

Bendix, R. 1962. *Max Weber: An Intellectual Portrait.* Garden City: Doubleday.

Gulhati, R. 1988. *The Political Economy of Reform in Sub-Saharan Africa.* EDI Policy Seminar Report 8. Washington, D.C.: World Bank.